UNIX: ®

An Open Systems Dictionary

The authoritative source
of jargon-free definitions
for more than 6,000 common and
uncommon open systems terms

William H. Holt
and
Rockie J. Morgan

Resolution Business Press, Inc.

Published by:
Resolution Business Press, Inc.
11101 N.E. 8th St., Suite 208
Bellevue, WA 98004
Phone: 206-455-4611
Fax: 206-455-9143
Internet address: rbpress@halcyon.com

Manufactured in Canada
First Printed in August 1994

Library of Congress Cataloging in Publication Data
Main entry under title:

Holt, William H.
UNIX: An Open Systems Dictionary

ISBN 0-945264-14-3

Acquisitions Editor: John Spilker
Project Editor: Karen Strudwick
Technical Editor: Charles Hand

Dedication

This dictionary is dedicated to the people of the European and Assured Distribution System Program Offices (1981-1989). Especially the administrative assistants - "Little" Kim, Vanessa and "Big" Kim, who had to put up with all the strange terms thrown at them. Ron and Clif, who were the best bosses, teachers and friends anyone could ask for. Jim, with whom many hours of midnight oil were burnt to help sell the concept of making UNIX an operational reality. And, to the rest who, in 1982, were answering the question "Why UNIX?" The answer they provided helped make UNIX a "household" word: first, in the Air Force logistics community, and then throughout the Air Force. Yours was a true pioneering effort. You made a difference.

- 640! -

To my wife and children, for their love, support and disbelief.

-RJM-

Contents

About the Authors

William H. (Bill) Holt is the manager of Production Open Systems Administration for US WEST NewVector Group, Inc., based in Bellevue, Washington. NewVector manages the cellular communications for US WEST. Bill has been involved with UNIX since 1982. He was both the program manager and program director for the first attempt of an operational implementation of UNIX in the U.S. Air Force. The program was designed to provide expanded logistics support to U.S. Air Forces in Europe. Bill has been in his current position since 1989 when he retired from his first career as an Air Force supply officer. He is responsible for the operation of the production UNIX computer systems and data network for NewVector. Bill is currently president of the national Sequent users group and has twice served as its vice president. He also is a founding member of the Massive Open Systems Environment Standards group (MOSES). In addition, Bill serves as a member of the Readers Advisory Council of Network Computing magazine. He has a Bachelor of Science degree in Retail Marketing from California State University, Fresno, and a Master of Science degree in Management from Troy State University, Alabama.

Rockie J. Morgan is director of engineering for Excell Data Corp., a Microsoft Solutions provider in Bellevue, Washington. He currently manages software development applications for Windows NT platforms. He previously managed a software development group for Pyramid Technology Corp., where he worked on a high-performance massively scaleable computer system for Pyramid. Rockie has worked on various UNIX systems for more than a decade, most of that time for Pyramid Technology. He previously was the UNIX product manager for DECwest Engineering, working on the predecessors for DEC's Alpha microprocessor and Microsoft's NT operating system. He also worked for Siemens-Nixdorf in Munich, Germany, and for various hospital data processing departments in California.

Contributors

The authors would like to recognize the individuals who contributed to the collection and creation of the terms listed in *UNIX: An Open Systems Dictionary*. The following provided some of the terms and definitions, motivation and inspiration, or graciously agreed to wade though and review the original drafts:

Ron Chalecki, GM-15, United States Air Force
Ron Christian, UNIX Consultant
Clif Collier, Lt Colonel, United States Air Force (retired)
David Bertman, Sequent Computer Systems, Inc.
Jim Daup, Lt Colonel, United States Air Force
Roger Day, US WEST NewVector Group, Inc.
Fernando Diaz, Graduate Student, University of Washington
Dennis Dooley, NCR Corporation
Robert Frank, Colonel, U.S. Air Force (retired), Lawrence Livermore National Laboratories
Katherine Johnson, Lt Colonel, United States Air Force
Doug Keller, GM-13, United States Air Force
Keith Ker, Lawrence Livermore National Laboratories
Jack Remick, Author
Steve Schribner, Computer Sciences Corp.
Kevin Smallwood, Purdue University
Dan Volkman, US WEST NewVector Group, Inc.

Foreword

John Black
Senior Vice President
Telecommunications Operations
Oracle Corp.

The wonderful thing about UNIX is that there are 14 ways to do everything. This flexibility gives UNIX a richness and adaptability that we all treasure. It also creates thousands of solutions and implementations that need names so that they can be discussed. The result is a rich new dialect. This is the first book that explains the UNIX dialect.

Bill Holt and Rockie Morgan have defined over 6,000 terms, abbreviations and names. They have defined the UNIX dialect. They have given us the basic tool that we need to communicate. Their definitions are crisp, clear and consistent. There is extensive cross-referencing. Synonyms are listed, but referenced to the preferred term. This tool allows people to use the UNIX dialect in a consistent way for the first time.

UNIX: An Open Systems Dictionary could not be better timed. Computing is getting more complex very rapidly. Hardware and software power and complexity is accelerating. Networks are getting more complex. New initiatives such as the Information Highway, are being launched weekly. The terminology is becoming a major barrier to communication.

Communications, especially technical communications, are increasingly filled with "Alphabet Soup" an confusing technical terms. Now we can decipher the "Alphabet Soup." Technical terms are often used inconsistently. Now we have an authority on the right way to use technical terms. Is the correct usage "machine language" or "machine code"? Holt & Morgan say it is machine language. This book makes it possible to regularize our usage of terminology and to communicate more effectively.

In this increasingly complex environment, people are usually the major brake on change. The biggest time-sink in implementing any system is communicating to everyone what is going on. This book helps people to communicate. It promotes understandability through consistent use of terminology. It allows people who do not understand a term to look it up. Managers may actually be able to understand what technical people are saying. Technical people may actually start using words the same way. As people communicate more effectively, the number of misunderstandings and misimpressions may be reduced. Conflict may be eliminated, or at least be more focused and fact-based. That will lead to quicker understanding and resolution. This book gives us humans another chance to keep up with the rate of change in the UNIX environment.

The authors deserve strong recognition for their highly professional efforts in assembling this dictionary. The UNIX dialect didn't just happen. It has deep historical roots in VMS, MVS, VM, DOS and other computing environments. The authors have decades of experience with UNIX and its predecessors. This lengthy experience shows in the thoughtful definitions that not only clarify the meaning, but also tell the derivation of the term (see "bug" for an example). Their perspective is broader than just UNIX, so you get an industry-wide view when a UNIX term is clarified (see "DOS-to-UNIX command comparison").

The highest tribute I can pay the dictionary is that it is really useful. The draft copy I have is a bit dog-eared. Somehow it has never moved from the surface of my desk to the adjoining bookcase. I just keep using it. It has corrected announcements for my employer. It has made letters from standards bodies understandable. It has helped me draft papers. It is a tool I've needed.

Holt & Morgan will be a classic reference work, like Kernighan & Ritchie.

Introduction

English is a difficult language to learn. Many, if not most, words have multiple meanings and subtle nuances that confuse virtually everyone who learns the language. Computerese, a true dialect of English, has a richness and wealth of multiple meanings and subtle nuances all its own. Then, computerese adds layers to the confusion by creating its own subdialects. There is the MVS language spoken by the IBM shops. For those who work with DEC, there is VMS. The home or office personal computer users speak DOS with all of its variations: MS-DOS, PC-DOS, Novell DOS and CP/M. Finally, there is the UNIX tongue.

UNIX has to be among the worst when it comes to varying definitions and terms. The UNIX subdialect has its own subdialects including X/Open's UNIX System V and its predecessors; University of California at Berkeley's 4.4 BSD and its predecessors; Microsoft Corporation's XENIX (for personal computers); Carnegie-Mellon University's Mach; Chorus/Mix from Chorus Systemes, SA; and other UNIX look-alikes.

In addition, major corporations and standards organizations claim to have the last word in defining UNIX and all of its terms. AT&T, Novell/USL and others champion System V, Release 4. The Open Software Foundation and its sponsors champion a UNIX that is everything except AT&T's. X/Open, International Organization for Standards and American National Standards Institute champion standards for database, communications, computer languages and applications development. To further muddy the waters, the Institute of Electrical and Electronic Engineers entered the fray with the Portable Operating System Interface for Computer Environments (POSIX).

Furthermore, in 1993 the University of California, Berkeley, departed from the UNIX operating system business with its final release, 4.4BSD. AT&T sold the UNIX Systems Laboratories and rights to the UNIX trademarks to Novell, Inc. Finally, in late 1993, Novell, Inc. transferred the rights to UNIX trademarks to X/Open Company, Ltd.

Confused? You are not alone. However, through a combination of training, hands-on experience, reading some of the books listed in the references and use of this dictionary, the haze can be lifted.

The UNIX User

What is a UNIX user? Below are some *less than serious* definitions of UNIX users. There are several other versions available within the industry. Which are you?

beginner **1.** Has no idea what a terminal is and even less knowledge of computers. **2.** Asks, "What's a vee-eye?" **3.** Thinks UNIX is someone with a sex problem.

novice **1.** Has heard about the editor and is trying to find out who he or she is to get some free help reviewing documents. **2.** Used rm for the first time but with an "*".

basic user **1.** Finally figured out where the computer is. **2.** Uses some of the attributes of vi without blowing away files, most of the time. **3.** Heard about dbx and wonders why a stereo component is part of a computer system.

user **1.** No longer afraid to create nroff documents using vi and is seriously looking for the documentation on tbl. **2.** Uses rm and the "*" again, but not together. **3.** No longer wears a puzzled look when people talk about POSIX, X/Open, AIX, BSD, etc., not because the terms are understood, just that they have been heard before. **4.** Looks in the company parking lot, without success, for the police cars whenever they the system administrators are overheard discussing what has been discovered by COPS.

expert **1.** Has attended a UNIX users conference. **2.** Is approached by other users with questions and requests for help, giving the right answer more than 50 percent of the time. **3.** Has sent for Open Systems Today but has not received the first copy.

guru **1.** Makes changes to the kernel, without source code. **2.** Knows the answers to all the questions, generally before they are asked. **3.** Takes phone calls from Ken, Dennis or Bill when they are stumped. But, not collect.

system administrator Seen by users (who don't know better) as being a closed-minded, opinionated individual who tells users "no", without knowing why or having a good reason.

wizard **1.** Has a large personal library of UNIX books, most of which look like they have been opened. **2.** Knows of the existence of the Bourne shell, C shell and Korn shell. **3.** Member of a users group which, in some cases, may even be a UNIX users group.

How the Information is Presented

There are two major operating environments, or universes, in UNIX: (1) Novell and X/Open Co. Ltd., more commonly known as AT&T (ATT), and (2) University of California, Berkeley Software Distribution (BSD). Unless specified, the commands identified in the dictionary run in either universe. When a universe is identified, it merely indicates that the command ran in that universe at the time this edition was written. Fortunately, the vast majority of UNIX commands can be moved (ported) from one universe to the other. And, with each new release or update to System V or the final release of BSD, the number of commands limited to a specific universe grows smaller.

In addition, some commands and terms originate from or are related to other environments than ATT and BSD. These are identified as XENIX *(XEN)*; POSIX *(POS)*; published commands that are fairly well accepted *(OTH)*; or Internet *(INET)*.

Full definitions are provided under the most commonly accepted term. Related terms and synonyms direct you to the defined term. For example, the commonly understood term visual editor is defined. Associated terms display editor, full face editor, full screen editor and screen editor reference the visual editor. If the authors had used full definitions throughout, *UNIX: An Open Systems Dictionary* would be much longer and considerably more expensive.

If at all possible non-technical definitions are given. The authors did find a few terms that could not be put into non-technical language, an unfortunate shortcoming of computerese.

All entries have been alphabetized letter by letter. Terms that begin with a symbol or punctuation mark, such as ".profile" or "/dev", are found in the correct alphabetic sequence with the . or / ignored. Similarly, blank spaces have been ignored, so that the entry for "access date" precedes that for "accessibility". An entry beginning with lower-case letters, such as "ac", comes before a similar entry that starts with upper-case letters, such as "AC".

Finally, UNIX gurus have not agreed on the proper spelling of many of the terms that have been created over the past 20 years. Among these are file system and filesystem; data base and database; path name and pathname; LISP, Lisp, and lisp; and, multi user, multiuser and multi-user. The authors use the most widely accepted spelling of such terms and define the terms under that particular spelling.

Key

Symbol	Meaning
⏎	Carriage return or Enter key
(ATT)	AT&T-related command or term
(BSD)	Berkeley Software Distribution-related command or term
CLP	Command line prompt
(INET)	Internet-related command or term
(OTH)	Other - Third party additions
(POS)	POSIX-related command or term
(XEN)	XENIX-related command or term

Future Editions

Every effort has been made to ensure the accuracy and completeness of this dictionary. If you have any comments or suggestions regarding the accuracy or completeness of a definition or about a missing entry, please write to us: Resolution Business Press, 11101 N.E. 8th St., Suite 208, Bellevue, WA 98004; or by e-mail: rbpress@halcyon.com.

Trademarks

4.2BSD is a trademark of the University of California, Berkeley
4.3BSD is a trademark of the University of California, Berkeley
4.4BSD is a trademark of the University of California, Berkeley
88open is a trademark of 88open Consortium Ltd.
Accell is a trademark of Unify Corporation
ACT/88 is a trademark of 88open Consortium Ltd.
AIX is a registered trademark of International Business Machines Corporation
ARCnet is a registered trademark of Data Point Corporation
AT is a registered trademark of International Business Machines Corporation
AT&T is a trademark of American Telephone and Telegraph Company.
AT&T Mail Service is a trademark of American Telephone and Telegraph Company
A/UX is a trademark of Apple Computer, Inc.
AVS/88 is a trademark of 88open Consortium Ltd.
BBN is a trademark of Bolt, Beranek and Newman
BSD is a trademark of the University of California, Berkeley
CGA is a trademark of International Business Machines Corporation
Chorus/Mix is a trademark of Chorus Systemes, SA.
CP/M is a trademark of Digital Research Inc.
DC/OSx is a trademark of Pyramid Technology, Inc.
DEC is a registered trademark of Digital Equipment Corporation
DECnet is a trademark of Digital Equipment Corporation
DG/UX is a trademark of Data General Corp.
Documenter's Workbench is a trademark of UNIX System Laboratories, Inc.
DR DOS is a registered trademark of Novell, Inc.
DYNIX is a registered trademark of Sequent Computer Systems, Inc.
DYNIX/ptx is a registered trademark of Sequent Computer Systems, Inc.
EGA is a trademark of International Business Machines Corporation
EMACS is a trademark of UniPress Software, Inc.
Ethernet is a registered trademark of Xerox Corporation
EUNICE is a trademark of the Wollongong Group
Fresco is a trademark of The X Consortium.
Hewlett-Packard is a registered trademark of Hewlett-Packard Company
HP is a registered trademark of Hewlett-Packard Company
HP-UX is a registered trademark of Hewlett-Packard Company
IBM is a registered trademark of International Business Machines Corporation
INFORMIX is a registered trademark of Informix Software, Inc.
Intel is a trademark of Intel Corporation
ITS/88 is a trademark of 88open Consortium Ltd.
Lotus is a registered trademark of Lotus Development Corporation
Mach is a trademark of Carnegie-Mellon University
Macintosh is a registered trademark of Apple Computer, Inc.
Micro Channel is a registered trademark of International Business Machines Corporation.
Microsoft is a registered Trademark of Microsoft Corporation.
MLisp is a trademark of UniPress Software, Inc.
MKS Toolkit is a trademark of Mortice Kern Systems, Inc.
MNP is a registered trademark of Microcom Systems, Inc.
MS-DOS is a registered trademark of Microsoft Corporation.
MULTIBUS is a registered trademark of Intel Corporation.
MVS is a trademark of International Business Machines Corporation.
NCR is a registered trademark of the NCR Corporation.
NeWS is a registered trademark of Sun Microsystems Inc.
NeXT is a trademark of NeXT, Inc.
NFS is a registered trademark of Sun Microsystems Inc.
NonStop-UX is a trademark of Tandem Computer Inc.
Novell is a registered trademark of Novell, Inc.

Olivetti is a registered trademark of Ing. C. Olivetti.
OPEN LOOK is a registered trademark of X/Open Company, Ltd.
Open Software Foundation is a trademark of Open Software Foundation, Inc.
Operating System/2 is a registered trademark of International Business Machines Corporation.
OS/2 is a registered trademark of International Business Machines Corporation.
OSF is a trademark of Open Software Foundation, Inc.
OSF/MOTIF is a trademark of Open Software Foundation, Inc.
OSx is a trademark of Pyramid Technology, Inc.
PAL is a trademark of International Business Machines Corporation.
PC/AT is a trademark of International Business Machines Corporation.
PC-DOS is a trademark of International Business Machines Corporation.
PDP-11 is a registered trademark of Digital Equipment Corporation.
Pentium is a trademark of Intel Corp.
PostScript is a registered trademark of Adobe Systems, Inc.
POSIX is a trademark of Institute of Electronic and Electrical Engineers.
PowerPC is a trademark of International Business Machines Corporation.
ProComm is a registered trademark of Datastorm Technologies, Inc.
PROCOMM PLUS is a trademark of Datastorm Technologies, Inc.
PROFS is a registered trademark of International Business Machines Corporation.
QNX is a registered trademark of Quantum Software Systems Ltd.
SAA is a registered trademark of International Business Machines Corporation.
SNA is a trademark of International Business Machines Corporation
Solaris is a registered trademark of Sun Microsystems, Inc.
SPARC is a trademark of SPARC International, Inc.
Sun is a registered trademark of Sun Microsystems, Inc.
Sun Microsystems is a trademark of Sun Microsystems, Inc.
SunOS is a trademark of Sun Microsystems, Inc.
System/370 is a trademark of International Business Machines Corporation
Tandem is a trademark of Tandem Computer Inc.
TPC Benchmark is a trademark of the Transaction Processing Performance Council
TUXEDO is a registered trademark of X/Open Company, Ltd.
UI-ATLAS is a trademark of the UNIX System Laboratories, Inc.
UNIX is a registered trademark of X/Open Company, Ltd.
UnixWare is a trademark of UNIX Systems Group.
UniForum is a trademark of UniForum
Unisys is a trademark of Unisys Corporation
Univel is a trademark of Univel, Inc.
UTS is a trademark of Amdahl Corporation
VAX is a registered trademark of Digital Equipment Corporation
VGA is a trademark of International Business Machines Corporation
VMS is a registered trademark of Digital Equipment Corporation
VP/ix is a trademark of INTERACTIVE Systems Corporation and Phoenix Technologies Ltd.
VUE is a trademark of Hewlett-Packard Company
Windows is a trademark of Microsoft Corporation
Windows NT is a trademark of Microsoft Corporation
WordPerfect is a registered trademark of WordPerfect Corporation
Writer's Workbench is a trademark of X/Open Company, Ltd.
X is a trademark of The X Consortium
X 11 is a trademark of The X Consortium
X Window System is a trademark of The X Consortium
X11/NeWS is a trademark of Sun Microsystems, Inc.
XDOS is a trademark of Hunter Systems, Inc.
XENIX is a registered trademark of Microsoft Corporation
Xerox is a registered trademark of Xerox Corporation
XGA is a trademark of International Business Machines Corporation
XNS is a trademark of Xerox Corporation
X/Open is a registered trademark of X/Open Company, Ltd.
XWIN is a trademark of the UNIX System Laboratories, Inc.

All brands or product names mentioned herein are trademarks or registered trademarks of their respective companies.

The UNIX Family Tree

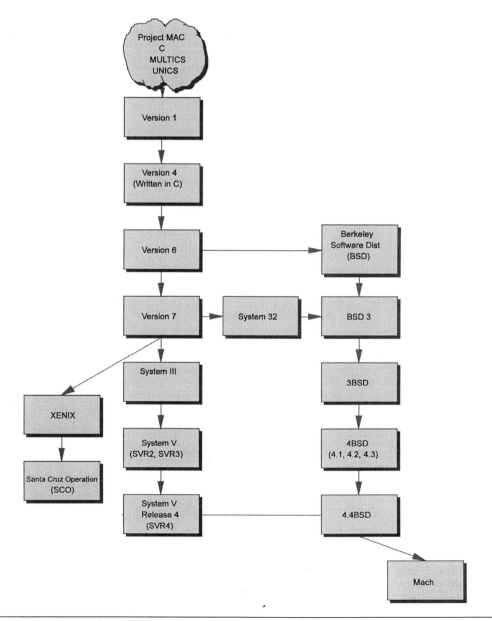

Symbols and Numbers

!   Jargon for exclamation point. **1.** Often called BANG, a jargon term originating with the *Batman* television series and comics, in which a bang from a crashing sound or gun shot was emphasized with an exclamation point. **2.** When used with square brackets, modifies the meaning of the input, e.g. if used with numbers *[!3], the command will perform on all files except those ending in the number 3. **3.** In the C shell, can be used to repeat commands when a user has a command history (that is, a log of commands which have been run) operating, e.g. !! means repeat the last command and !5 means repeat command number 5. *See* history. **4.** Hostname delimiter in UNIX-to-UNIX CoPy addresses, e.g. yourhost!myhost!myname. *See* UUCP, Internet and network.

Symbol for pound sign. **1.** Metacharacter or special character which is the default system erase character for AT&T Co.'s UNIX. *See* metacharacter and erase character. **2.** Comment sign in programs recognized by all three major shells (Bourne shell, C shell and Korn shell). A line preceded by a pound sign is recognized as explanatory text, not a command, and does not affect the operation of the shell program. *See* shell.

$ Symbol for dollar sign. **1.** Default command or system prompt displayed when a user is running the Bourne shell. *See* system prompt and Bourne shell. **2.** Metacharacter used in regular expressions of the ed, ex, vi, sed, grep, egrep and awk programs. Used to match specified characters at the end of a line. *See* metacharacter and regular expression.

%   Symbol for percent sign. Default command or system prompt for users running the C shell. *See* system prompt and C shell.

&   Symbol for ampersand. **1.** Symbol used to initiate a process which the user wants to run in the background. For example:

CLP> nroff -mm file name1 file name2 & ⏎

See background process and nroff. **2.** Metacharacter used in a regular expression of the ex or sed programs to repeat a regular expression. *See* metacharacter and regular expression.

'   Symbol for backquote. Character used in shell scripts to identify a command that is to be executed. The command's output is interpreted as parameters to the original command.

()   Symbol for parentheses. Metacharacter used in regular expressions in the egrep and awk programs. Used to create a subexpression to match strings in conjunction with other metacharacters, such as *, ? or +. For example, *(myil)* would match strings like kajmyilb or tnfmyilb. *See* metacharacter and regular expression.

* Symbol for asterisk. Metacharacter used in regular expressions that is called the file name expansion or wild card. Can be used anywhere in a string as a substitute for any unknown number of characters, including one or more blank spaces. For example, a user can view or manipulate files containing the number 1 in their names, e.g. book1, chapter1, chapt1, by entering the command followed by *1. Only those files ending in 1, regardless of the preceding characters, will be acted on. Likewise, if the command was followed by only an asterisk, all files in the directory would be acted on. Used as a metacharacter within regular expressions for the ed, ex, vi, sed, grep, egrep and awk programs. *See* metacharacter and regular expression.

+ Symbol for plus. Metacharacter used in regular expressions to match one or more characters identified before the plus, e.g. ka+j would match kaj and kaaj but not kj since the letter a has to be in the string. Used only with the egrep and awk programs. *See* metacharacter and regular expression.

. Symbol for dot. **1.** Character used to indicate the current location in a file, path, etc. **2.** Bourne and Korn shell command used to read a file and execute the lines of the file as if they were input on a command line. *See* source and command line. **3.** When a user lists the contents of a directory, indicates the current working directory along with the permissions, ownership and last date it was updated. *See* current directory. **4.** Abbreviation for current working directory when used as part of a command.

CLP> cp ~pbethel/tstdata . ⏎

This command will copy the file tstdata from user account pbethel to the current working directory of the user who input the command. This assumes pbethel has established the appropriate permissions for the user to read the file. *See* current working directory. **5.** Regular expression metacharacter used in the ex, ed, vi, sed, grep, egrep and awk programs to match

any single character, e.g. a string search in a file for k.j matches any string of characters which starts with a k, is followed by any character and ends with j, such as kaj. **6.** Electronic-mail variable. *See* e-mail and .mailrc variables (Appendices F and G).

/ Symbol for slash. Also called solidus. File separator. Used to distinguish individual directories and files, e.g. /usr/SHE/collier/myfile indicates that myfile is an individual file or directory of collier, which is an individual file or directory of SHE. *See* path.

; Symbol for semicolon. **1.** Punctuation mark used as a command separator in shell scripts and C language programs. *See* shell script and C language. **2.** Special character used on the command line to separate multiple commands. *See* command line.

< Symbol for less than. Used in the command line when a user wants to modify the standard input to include an existing file. For example:

CLP> mail < file name user-name ⏎

will create an electronic-mail message to the user named in the line. The e-mail will contain a file which has been redirected into that message. *See* standard input, command line and greater than symbol.

> Symbol for greater than. Used as part of the command line when a user is changing the standard output. Tells the system the name of a file or device to which the user wants the command output sent. By using two greater than symbols, the user can indicate that the output is to be added to an existing file. *See* redirect and less than symbol.

? Symbol for question mark. Metacharacter used within regular expressions as a wild card for a single character, e.g. a command followed by ?1 will act only on files with file names that are two characters long and end in the number 1. Used in the egrep and awk programs. *See* metacharacter and regular expression.

@ Symbol for at sign. **1.** Metacharacter used as the line kill character on standard UNIX systems. *See* metacharacter and kill character. **2.** Character used in the vi editor program to indicate a line has been deleted. *See* vi. **3.** *(INET)* Character used in an Internet electronic-mail address. Precedes the name of the computer to which the message is being sent. For example:

ker@tis.llnl.gov

indicates the mail message is being sent to user "ker" at the "tis.llnl.gov" host. *See* Internet, SNMP, e-mail, domain and bang path.

[] Symbol for brackets. Metacharacter used within regular expressions to match any character contained in the brackets. For example:

CLP> cat chapt[1,3,5,7] chapt.odd ⏎

combines files called chapt1, chapt3, chapt5 and chapt7 into a new file called chapt.odd. A hyphen can be used to separate the characters in the brackets and indicate a range. For example:

CLP> cat chapt[1-7] book ⏎

combines any file named chapt1, chapt2, chapt3, chapt4, chapt5, chapt6 or chapt7 into a new file named book. Used as a metacharacter within regular expressions for the ed, ex, vi, sed, grep, egrep and awk programs. *See* metacharacter and regular expression.

[ ] Symbol for square brackets. Metacharacters used in wild card matching in file searches, file manipulations, etc. In a search, a computer looks for only those characters enclosed in square brackets, e.g. a command followed by [xyz]4 will act only on files which start with an x, y or z followed by the number 4. *See* metacharacter, character-class and regular expression.

**** Symbol for backslash. For personal computer users, in UNIX, this is not a file separator. Rather, it is a metacharacter used in regular expressions in the ed, ex, vi, sed, grep, egrep and awk programs to turn off the special meaning of the metacharacters. *See* regular expression, slash and metacharacter.

^ Symbol for caret. **1.** Technically, a circumflex. A metacharacter that has many uses and meanings in UNIX. **2.** Representation of a control character, e.g. Ctrl d can be written as ^d. **3.** Metacharacter used in regular expressions in the ed, ex, vi, sed, grep, egrep and awk programs. Used to match character strings at the beginning of a line. **4.** C shell indicator which shows that a substitution has been made in a command line input. For example:

CLP> ^string1^string2 ⏎

means substitute string1 with the new string2 for string 1 in the previous command, and then execute the new command. *See* metacharacter.

' Symbol for single quote. **1.** Special character that tells the shell to ignore the normal meaning of characters placed between single quotes. Can be used to override the meaning of metacharacters, e.g. the asterisk (*), used as a wild card, is only an asterisk when enclosed by single quotes. *See* metacharacter. **2.** Special character used to make a single argument. Everything input between an opening and closing single quote becomes a single argument. *See* metacharacter and argument.

| Symbol for vertical bar. Metacharacter used in regular expressions of egrep and awk. Separates two regular expression to match either or both strings in a line, e.g. tnf | kaj would identify each incident of the string tnf and/kaj in a line. *See* metacharacter and regular expression.

{} Symbol for braces. Also referred to as the grouping command. Braces are used to mark the beginning and ending of program blocks executed by a process. For example, if a user wants the process to perform two separate functions, e.g. change directory (cd command) and then list (ls command) the contents of the directory and redirect the output to a new file, the commands along with the desired file paths would be enclosed in braces. **2.** Used when performing file expansion when normal wild card matching is not available. For example, if a user wants to copy or move files kay, ily and tnf located in the same directory to a new location, he would input the copy command, identifying the full directory path of the three files with the three files enclosed in braces and then followed by the path to where the user wants to move the files.

~ Symbol for tilde. Control character used as a shortcut. Can reduce the number of key strokes when moving from one working directory to another. When used alone, takes a user to that person's home directory. Used with a login ID, places a user in that user's account. Used with a plus sign, gives a user the absolute path of the current working directory. *See* metacharacter and regular expression.

½ inch tape Commonly called VHS. *See* VHS tape storage.

1Base5 Institute of Electrical and Electronic Engineers' standard for the physical layer of an Ethernet network developed by the AT&T Co., known as *StarLAN*. Uses existing phone lines and transmits data at 1 megabit per second over a distance of 500 meters. *See* IEEE, Ethernet, 10Base2, 10Base5 and 10Base-T.

1K VGA 1000 video graphics array. A video graphics array monitor with a resolution of 1024 x 768 pixels. *See* VGA and pixel.

2B + D Commonly called BRI (Basic Rate Interface). *See* BRI.

2-D array Commonly called 2-D data. *See* 2-D data.

2-D data Two-dimensional **data**. Graphical display of data, using x and y coordinates on the screen to represent an object's length and width, as in drafting. *See* 3-D data.

2-D graphics Commonly called 2-D data. *See* 2-D data.

2MSL time Amount of Transmission Control Protocol time used to turn off the connection between two hosts when the transmission of data has been completed. *See* TCP.

2PC Abbreviation for but more commonly called two-phase commit. *See* two-phase commit.

3B Journal Quarterly journal published by Owens-Laing Publications Ltd. for users of AT&T Co.'s 3B computers.

3B Net AT&T Co.'s Ethernet-compatible network for interconnecting AT&T's 3B computers.

3BSD Third **B**erkeley **S**oftware **D**istribution. A University of California, Berkeley, UNIX operating system based on 32V and released in 1980. A forerunner of 4.X Berkeley Software Distribution. The first operating system to provide demand paging. *See* 32V, BSD and paging.

3-D array Commonly called 3-D data. *See* 3-D data.

3-D data Three-dimensional **data**. Data used to form three-dimensional graphics displays, showing length, width and height. *See* 2-D data.

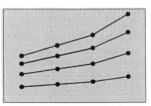

Data shown on a two dimensional chart

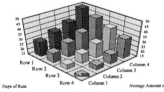

Data shown in a three dimensional form

3-D graphics Commonly called 3-D data. *See* 3-D data.

3GL Third-generation language. Procedural computer programming language, e.g. C, COBOL, Pascal or FORTRAN. To use it, a programmer must have explicit knowledge of how data is stored or maintained. In contrast, a 4GL or database query language, e.g. SQL, simply presents an interface to the data, so a programmer need not have such detailed working knowledge.

4.1BSD Fourth Berkeley Software Distribution, First Release. University of California, Berkeley, version of the UNIX operating system released in 1981 to replace the 32V operating system. Included significant improvements over 3BSD, e.g. it was the first operating system to incorporate the vi editor, C shell and sockets. *See* BSD, 3BSD, vi, C shell and sockets.

4.2BSD Fourth Berkeley Software Distribution, Second Release. University of California, Berkeley, version of the UNIX operating system released in 1984. Included significant improvements over 4.1BSD, e.g. the Transmission Control Protocol/Internet Protocol and Ethernet protocol for communication. *See* 4.1BSD, TCP/IP and Ethernet.

4.3BSD Fourth Berkeley Software Distribution, Third Release. University of California, Berkeley, version of the UNIX operating system that was released in 1986. Became a faster and more reliable operating system with the addition of such features as the Fast File System and Xerox Network System. *See* Fast File System and XNS.

4.4BSD Fourth Berkeley Software Distribution, Fourth Release (hence four point four). Two versions of 4.4BSD were released: 4.4BSD-Encumbered, released in late 1992; and a modified version of 4.4BSD called 4.4BSD-Lite, released in 1994. 4.4BSD was the last version of the Berkeley Software Distribution that was released. *See* 4.4BSD-Encumbered, 4.4BSD-Lite, BSD and CSRG.

4.4BSD-Encumbered Fourth Berkeley Software Distribution, Fourth Release (hence four point four) **Encumbered**. One of the two final versions of the Berkeley Software Distribution operating system released by the Berkeley Computer Systems Research Group. Improvements include support for International Organization for Standardization/Open Systems Interconnection networking, an enhanced virtual memory system, better security, new C language utilities, and compliance with Portable Operating System Interface for Computer Environments P1003.1 and P1003.2 standards. 4.4BSD-Encumbered is only released to computer sites that run UNIX/32V, UNIX System III or UNIX System V, and possess a source license from the AT&T Co. or UNIX Systems Laboratories. *See* 4.4BSD-Lite, BSD, CSRG, ISO/OSI and POSIX.

4.4BSD-Lite Fourth Berkeley Software Distribution, Fourth Release (hence four point four) **Lite**. One of the two final versions of the Berkeley Software Distribution operating system released by the Berkeley Computer Systems Research Group. 4.4BSD-Lite was released in early 1994 following the settlement of a lawsuit between the University of California and the UNIX Systems Laboratories. Distribution of 4.4BSD-Lite is not limited and users are not required to have any previous licenses from the University of California, AT&T Co. and/or UNIX Systems Laboratories. *See* 4.4BSD-Encumbered, BSD and CSRG.

4GL Fourth-generation language. Programming language in which coding is expressed as data objects (usually contained in a database) instead of algorithms, e.g. Access by Unify Corp. and INFORMIX by Informix Software Inc. This approach makes programming easier and the programmer requires less technical knowledge.

4T + Specification developed by the Faster Ethernet Alliance and released in December 1993. Designed to run Ethernet on four pair unshielded twisted pair cable (common telephone wire) at a transmission rate of 100 megabits per second. The alliance, composed of 3Com Corp., Sun Microsystems Inc., SMC, SynOptics Communications Inc. and Grand Junction Networks, was formed to create and implement a fast Ethernet protocol based upon Carrier Sense Multiple Access/Collision Detection. *See* fast Ethernet, Fast Ethernet Association, CSMA/CD, Ethernet, 100Base-VG, 100VG-AnyLAN and 100Base-X.

5.4 Jargon for UNIX System V, Release 4. Normally pronounced *FIVE DOT FOUR*. *See* SVR4.x.

/5bin Bin directory in the Berkeley Software Distribution operating system that contains commands like those in AT&T Co.'s System V. *See* System V and BSD.

5 x 8 Pronounced and spelled *five by eight*. Jargon for a computer system and/or application that is operational and requires support, 5 days a week and 8 hours a day.

007 Benchmark designed to simulate computer-aided design functions to test the effectiveness of object-oriented databases. Developed at the University of Wisconsin and released in mid-1993, it consists of 157 tests used to evaluate numerous ODBMS operations, e.g. various queries and database modifications, as well as the scalability and complexity of the ODBMS. *See* ODBMS.

7 x 24 Pronounced *SEVEN BY TWENTY-FOUR*. Also spelled 7 by 24. Jargon for a computer system and/or application that is operational and requires support seven days a week, 24 hours a day.

8-bit computer Computer that uses 8-bit data paths, in which 8 bits form a byte. Transfers information between memory (or other storage) and the processor 8 bits at a time. *See* bit and byte.

8MM tape Magnetic tape format that uses 8-millimeter video cartridges for electronic storage media. *See* 9-track and DAT.

9.6 Pronounced *9 DOT 6*. Jargon for 9600 baud, a standard data communication speed. *See* baud.

9 dot 6 Pronunciation of 9.6, a jargon for 9600 baud. *See* 9.6.

9-layer ISO stack Nine-layer International **O**rganization for **S**tandardization **stack**. Tongue-in-check term that modifies the existing Open Systems Interconnection Reference Model (OSIRM). The current 7 protocol layers are the applications layer, presentation layer, session layer, transport layer, network layer, data link layer and physical layer. The 9-layer ISO stack adds politics (layer eight) and religion (layer nine) in an attempt to create standards which address the range of discussions, disagreements and differences of opinion on the functionality of OSIRM and changes that may be needed. *See* OSIRM.

9-track **1.** Jargon for half-inch magnetic tape as contrasted with cartridge tape, 8-millimeter video and 4-millimeter Digital Audio Tape systems. Data is read or written 8 bits at a time on a 9-track tape system, with 1 bit read or written onto each track or parallel stripe running the length of the tape. The ninth track records a parity bit for validating the correctness of the 8 data bits. *See* DAT and parity. **2.** De facto computer data interchange format. Most computers have the ability or option to read or write 9-track tapes. Commonly written either at 1600 bytes per inch (bpi) phase encoded, or at 6250 bpi. Typically available in 600- to 2400-foot reels. Can contain up to 150 megabytes of information on a 2400-foot reel at 6250 bpi. *See* bpi and MB.

9-track tape unit used in large systems

10Base2 Ten (signal speed of 10 megahertz) base (baseband network) two (approximate distance in meters between repeaters). Formal name for thinnet or cheapnet. Institute of Electrical and Electronic Engineers 802.3 committee's standard for the physical layer of an Ethernet network that uses more inexpensive coaxial cable. Transmits data at a rate of 10 megabits per second over a maximum distance of 185 meters. Limited to no more than 30 devices connected, but not repeated, in a segment. Such networks are cheaper to install, but are smaller in size and less reliable because they do not use thick shielded cable. *See* IEEE, Ethernet, thinnet, baseband, broadband, 1Base5, 10Base5 and 10Base-T.

10Base5 Ten (signal speed of 10 megahertz) base (baseband network) five (approximate distance in meters between repeaters). Formal name for thicknet. Institute of Electrical and Electronic Engineers standard for the physical layer of an Ethernet network that uses thick, expensive coaxial cable laid in conduit. Transmits data at a rate of 10 megabits per second over a maximum distance of 500 meters. Limited to no more than 100 devices connected, but not repeated, in a segment. Such networks are more expensive to install, but enable transmission over greater distances (1000 meters versus 300 meters for thinnet) and offer more reliability due to the shielded cable used. *See* IEEE, Ethernet, baseband, broadband, 10Base2, 1Base5 and 10Base-T.

10Base-F Ten (signal speed of 10 megahertz) base (baseband network) F (Fiber). Institute of Electrical and Electronic Engineers 802.3 Ethernet committee's standard for Ethernet over fiber-optic cable network. Transmits data at a rate of 10 megabits per second over a fiber network. Does not limit the number of devices that can be connected, but not repeated, in a segment. *See* IEEE, baseband, broadband and Ethernet.

10Base-FB Ten (signal speed of 10 megahertz) base (baseband network) FB (Fiber Backbone). Institute of Electrical and Electronic Engineers 802.3 Ethernet committee's standard for a fiber-optic backbone network. Transmits data at a rate of 10 megabits per second over a fiber backbone. Does not limit the number of de-

vices that can be connected, but not repeated, in a segment. Provides unlimited repeaters to connect Ethernet lines between distribution hubs and remote locations on a network. *See* IEEE, baseband, broadband and Ethernet.

10Base-FL Ten (signal speed of 10 megahertz) base (baseband network) FL (Fiber Link). Institute of Electrical and Electronic Engineers 802.3 Ethernet committee's standard for fiber link on a fiber-optic network. Transmits data at a rate of 10 megabits per second over a fiber link. Does not limit the number of devices that can be connected, but not repeated, on a segment. Increases the maximum distance between a workstation and the host on a 10Base-T network to 2000 meters compared to 200 meters on a 10Base2 network. *See* IEEE, Ethernet, baseband, broadband and 10Base-T.

10Base-T Ten (signal speed of 10 megahertz) **base** (baseband network) **T** (twisted pair). Developed by SynOptics Communications Inc. as a high-speed, 10 megabits-per-second transmission method over unshielded twisted-pair wiring. Accepted by the Institute of Electrical and Electronic Engineers 802.3 Ethernet committee as the standard for Ethernet transmission over UTP in September 1990. Provides for Ethernet transmissions over a distance of up to 100 meters. Does not limit the number of devices that can be connected, but not repeated, on a segment. *See* Ethernet, UTP, DIW-24, baseband and broadband.

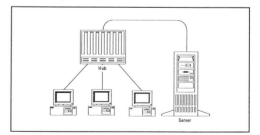

10Base-T offers one of the simplest and most inexpensive LAN designs. High quality twisted-pair telephone cable connects the Ethernet adapters to a hub. Unlike conventional Ethernet setups, a 10Base-T network will not fail if one adapter card malfunctions.

16-bit computer Computer that uses a 16-bit data path, in which 16 bits form a word. Transfers information between memory (or another storage device) and the processor 16 bits at a time. *See* bit and word.

18-USC 1030 Formal designation for the Federal Computer Fraud and Abuse Act of 1986. Commonly called the hacker law. *See* hacker law.

19.2 Pronounced *NINETEEN DOT TWO* or *NINETEEN TWO*. Jargon for a standard communication speed of 19,200 baud. *See* baud.

19MM tape Commonly referred to as VHS-tape storage. *See* VHS tape storage.

23B + D Commonly called PRI (Primary Rate Interface). *See* PRI.

32-bit computer Computer that uses a 32-bit data path, in which 32 bits form a long word. Information is transferred between memory (or another storage device) and the processor 32 bits at a time. *See* bit and long word.

32V Pronounced *THIRTY-TWO V*. Variant of AT&T Co.'s UNIX Version 7, developed in 1978 for Digital Equipment Corp.'s VAX 32-bit processors. *See* Version 7.

56-Kbps Commonly called DDS (Digital Data Service). *See* DDS.

64-bit computer Computer that uses a 64-bit data path, in which 64 bits are used to form a long word. Information is transferred between memory (or another storage device) and the processor 64 bits at a time. *See* bit and long word.

100Base-TP One hundred (signal speed of 100 megahertz) base (baseband network) twisted pair (cable). Original name for the 100Base-X fast Ethernet protocol. *See* 100Base-X.

100Base-VG One hundred (signal speed of 100 megahertz) base (baseband network) voice grade (over twisted pair cable). Fast Ethernet protocol jointly created by AT&T Microelectronics and the Hewlett-Packard Co. Capable of transmitting up to 100 megabits of data per second. *See* fast Ethernet, 100VG-AnyLAN and 100Base-X.

100Base-X One hundred (signal speed of 100 megahertz) base (baseband network). Also called 100BaseX. Originally called 100Base-TP. Alternative fast Ethernet protocol developed by the Fast Ethernet Alliance formed by 3Com Corp., Sun Microsystems Inc., SMC, SynOptics Communications Inc. and Grand Junction Networks to compete with the 100Base-VG and 100Base-AnyLAN protocols. Released in October 1993 and based on the Ethernet 10Base-T protocol that uses Carrier Sense Multiple Access/Collision Detection for transmission over twisted pair cable. Also operates on fiber-optic cable. *See* fast Ethernet, CSMA/CD, 100Base-VG, Fast Ethernet Association, 100VG-AnyLAN and 4T +.

100VG-AnyLAN One hundred (signal speed of 100 megahertz) voice-grade AnyLAN (operates on any type of local area network architecture). Commonly called the Fast Token Ring protocol. Capable of transmitting data at up to 100 megabits per second. Designed to run as either Token Ring or Ethernet, but does not have an interface between Token Ring and Ethernet network topologies. Jointly created by IBM Corp. and the Hewlett-Packard Co., based upon the Hewlett-Packard and AT&T Microelectronics' 100Base-VG protocol for fast Ethernet. Provides improved bandwidth required for multimedia applications. *See* fast Ethernet and multimedia.

186 Jargon term for the microprocessor designed by Intel Corp. Formally called the Intel 80186. A forerunner to the 286. Had limited use in Tandy 1000 and a few other computers. *See* 286.

286 Jargon term for the microprocessor designed by Intel Corp. Formally called the Intel 80286. A 16-bit processor found in IBM Corp.'s PC/AT and compatible systems. Released in 1982 as the successor to the Intel 8086 and 8088 microprocessors. Runs at speeds from 6 to 16 megahertz. *See* microprocessor, 16-bit computer and PC.

300 *(ATT)* One of the tplot graphic filters that handles the special plotting functions of the DASI 300, GSI 300 and DTC 300 terminals. *See* tplot and filter.

300S *(ATT)* Pronounced *THREE HUNDRED S.* One of the tplot graphic filters that handles the special plotting functions of the DASI 300s terminal. *See* tplot and filter.

386 Jargon term for the Intel 80386 microprocessor and successor to the Intel 80286. A 32-bit processor released by Intel Corp. in 1985 that has a clock speed of up to 40 megahertz. *See* microprocessor, clock speed, 32-bit computer, 386DX, 386SX and PC.

386DX Jargon term and new name for the original Intel 80386 microprocessor, which has a 32-bit internal architecture and a 32-bit external data path. *See* microprocessor, 32-bit computer, 386, 386SX and PC.

386SX Jargon term for a version of the original Intel 80386SX microprocessor, released by Intel Corp. in 1988. A less expensive version of the 386DX that has a 16-bit data path. *See* microprocessor, 16-bit computer, 386DX and PC.

414 Gang Group of computer crackers named for the Milwaukee, Wisconsin, telephone area code (414). One of the first organizations dedicated to breaking into computer systems. The 414 Gang operated in the early 1980s, breaking into systems in the United States and Canada. *See* hacker.

450 *(ATT)* One of the tplot graphic filters that handles the special plotting functions of the DASI 450 terminal. *See* tplot and filter.

486 Jargon term for the Intel 80486 microprocessor and design successor to the 80386. The 486 has a clock speed of up to 66 megahertz. *See* PC, clock speed and microprocessor.

586 Jargon term for the Intel 80586 microprocessor and design successor to the 80486, released by Intel Corp. in 1993. Marketed under the name Pentium, and also called P5. The 586 has a clock speed of up to 100 megahertz. *See* clock speed and microprocessor.

630 *(ATT)* One of the tplot graphic filters that handles the special plotting functions of the DASI 630 terminal. *See* tplot and filter.

733 *(INET)* Original name for the 822 electronic-mail message format. Named for the Internet Request for Comment 733 which defines electronic mail format. *See* 822.

822 *(INET)* Electronic-mail message standard format. Named for the Internet Request for Comment 822 which defines electronic mail format. *See* Internet and RFC.

1170 Commonly called Spec 1170. *See* Spec 1170.

1170 specification Commonly called Spec 1170. *See* Spec 1170.

1822 *(INET)* Forerunner of the X.25 protocol. Advanced Research Projects Agency Network packet switch protocol named for the technical report originally describing the protocol. *See* X.25, ARPANET and packet switch network.

4014 **1.** *(ATT)* One of the tplot graphic filters that handles Tektronix 4014 terminal plotting features one page at a time. *See* tplot and filter. **2.** Graphics display device manufactured by Tektronix Corp. **3.** Describes hardware or software compatible with the Tektronix 4014.

8086 Jargon term for the Intel 8086 chip. Released by Intel Corp. in 1978 and used in the original IBM Corp. PS/2 Model 25 and Model 30 personal computers. The 8086 operates on 16 bits of data at a time and has a 20-bit data path (that is, it can read or write to memory and data devices

20 bits at a time). Typical 8086 chips processed data at rates of 4.77 megahertz, 8 megahertz and 10 megahertz. *See* microprocessor, 8088 and PC.

8088 Jargon term for the Intel 8088 chip. Released in 1979 and used in several of IBM Corp.'s personal computers, e.g. the PC, PC/XT and PCjr. Like the 8086, the 8088 processes 16 bits of data at a time. Unlike the 8086, the 8088 has an 8-bit data path. The 8088 has clock speeds of 4.77 megahertz and 8 megahertz. *See* 8086, 16-bit computer, microprocessor and PC.

8514/A IBM Corp. proprietary graphics chip and protocol. Provides a resolution of 1,024 x 768 pixels. *See* CGA, EGA, Super VGA, VGA and XGA.

29000 Reduced Instruction Set Computing microprocessor developed by Advanced Micro Devices. *See* RISC.

68000 Motorola Inc.'s 16-bit microprocessor developed in the late 1970s and found in numerous embedded systems. The 68000 was the first of the family with a 24-bit address and 16-bit data bus. *See* 16-bit computer.

68010 Successor to Motorola Inc.'s 68000 microprocessor. A 16-bit microprocessor developed in the early 1980s. *See* 16-bit computer.

68020 Successor to Motorola Inc.'s 68000 and 68010 microprocessors. A 32-bit microprocessor developed in the mid-1980s. Has a 32-bit address and 32-bit data bus with clock speeds of 16, 20, 25 and 33 megahertz. *See* 32-bit computer.

68030 Successor to Motorola Inc.'s 68000 and 68020 microprocessors. A 32-bit microprocessor developed in the late 1980s with memory management for paging built into the chip. Has clock speeds of 16, 20, 33, 40 and 50 megahertz. *See* 32-bit computer.

68040 Motorola Inc.'s 32-bit microprocessor, successor to the 68030 microprocessor. Has a clock speed of 25 megahertz. Includes separate internal floating-point and memory management units.

80286 Commonly abbreviated and called 286. *See* 286.

80386 Commonly abbreviated and called 386. *See* 386.

80486 Commonly abbreviated and called 486. *See* 486.

80586 Commonly abbreviated and called 586. *See* 586.

88000 Reduced Instruction Set Computing microprocessor developed by Motorola Inc. *See* RISC.

A

a   Abbreviation for **atto**. *See* atto.

A   Address. Data file required to operate Domain Name Service. Contains the address of a host. A separate file is maintained for each host address, e.g. a host address and gateway address consisting of the host's or gateway's name and its Internet Protocol address. *See* DNS and IP.

ABEND   Abnormal **end**ing. Termination of the operation of a program caused by an error.

ABI   Application Binary Interface. Specification that defines how application interfaces should run on various hardware architectures when using UNIX System V, Release 4. Aims to ensure binary compatibility among applications running in the same family of central processing units. Software developed using ABI can be used on different manufacturers' hardware without being recompiled. System calls needed for specific hardware are maintained in libraries. Jointly developed by AT&T Co. and Sun Microsystems Inc. Supported by UNIX International as the standard for application interfaces. *See* SVR4.x, CPU, ANDF and UI.

ABI Verification Suite   Commonly abbreviated and called AVS/88. *See* AVS/88.

ABI Verification Suite/88   Commonly abbreviated and called AVS/88. *See* AVS/88.

abort   **1.** To end or stop a program, function, script, process or procedure before it is completed. **2.** Library routine used to generate a stop that ends a program before it normally would be completed. *See* library routines.

absolute address   Commonly called machine address. *See* machine address.

absolute path   Also called fully qualified path. The full address of, or path to, a file starting at root or /, e.g. /upc/staff/whholt1/myfile. Fully defines the relationship or path of a file in the UNIX hierarchical file structure. *See* pathname, relative pathname and hierarchical file system.

absolute pathname   Commonly called absolute path. *See* absolute path.

Abstract Syntax Notation 1   Commonly abbreviated and called ASN.1. *See* ASN.1.

ac   **Ac**counting tool used to provide a daily summary of each system user's activity.

AC   Alternating current. Standard 120-volt electrical current that changes polarity (plus and minus) 60 times a second. *See* DC.

acceleration   Speed with which a cursor on a video display screen responds to the movement of a mouse.

acceleration rate   Measurement of how fast keystrokes are repeated on a keyboard. Used to describe the functionality of a keyboard.

acceleration responsiveness
Measurement of the time a key is depressed before that keystroke is repeated. Used to describe the functionality of a keyboard.

---

accelerator key Commonly called command key. *See* command key.

accept *(ATT/XEN)* Line printer system command. Used to turn on a line printer so it will accept print jobs. *See* lp.

Accept *(ATT)* UNIX System V, Release 4 restricted electronic-mail command. Used to identify users with permission to use specific electronic-mail services. *See* e-mail, SVR4.x, rmail and Deny.

acceptance testing Process of ensuring that a newly installed computer system or software package meets the buyer's specified requirements before the buyer pays for it. An acceptance test should be developed using the requirement specifications described in the contract between vendor and customer. Once the vendor has installed and turned over ownership of the system or software, the customer should test the system or software to ensure it meets the requirements and terms of the contract.

access 1. Communication with or input to an operating system, data base manager, utility or program. The level of access, or permissions, granted by system security to a user or program that wants to communicate, execute programs and receive a result. The most basic level of access is through an account, or directory, with a password, which allows an authorized user to log on a system. 2. Routine used by the system, first to determine if a user or process has permissions to access a file, and if so, to determine the level of permission. *See* access permissions, FIO, file attributes and permissions.

access control Combination of hardware, software utilities and prudent system administration to monitor, record and control access to the system. *See* security.

access control list 1. X Window System term for a list of remote hosts that can access the X server. *See* X Window System and server. 2. UNIX enhancement that provides the ability to limit access to files and directories to specified users. Com-

monly abbreviated and called ACL. *See* ACL.

access date Date a file was last accessed and only read by the user. *See* creation date and modification date.

accessibility Network's ability to be accessed by a user who has the necessary permissions. Allows the user to operate a device or application programs from any location on the network.

access method 1. Way in which users gain access to a computer system and the corresponding software used to manage input and output of data. 2. Networking term for the means to control how and when stations on a network can transmit data.

access mode Bit pattern that describes a file or directory's level of protection, or permissions. *See* umask, bit pattern and permissions.

access period Specified period of time during which access to a computer resource is granted.

access permissions Commonly called permissions. *See* permissions.

access rights Commonly called access. *See* access.

access speed 1. Average length of time taken by disk drive heads to move into position to read or write information from or to a disk drive. 2. Average length of time between the moment information is passed to system memory and when it is returned.

access time Commonly called access speed. *See* access speed.

access unit Element of the X.400 standard. Describes the interface between X.400 systems and non-X.400 systems, e.g. faxes. Developed by the International Telecommunication Union Telecommunication Standardization Sector, formerly called the Consultative Committee on International Telegraphy and Telephony.

See ITU-T, e-mail, X.400, UA, MTA and message store.

account Also called user account. Directory established to allow access, or entry, to a computer system operating under UNIX by an authorized user, person or program. Created and administered by the system administrator(s).

accountability Computer system's ability to monitor and trace activity so that individual users can be held accountable for their actions.

accounting Function of the UNIX operating system. Mechanism for tracking user and system activity on the computer. Data is collected on user connect time, command usage, frequency of command use, disk utilization and communication line usage. System accounting information can be used to determine improper use of the system, the need for upgrades and/or billing for usage.

accounting management Process used for cost management of a network or computer system whereby usage costs are charged to a specific user or user group. *See* charge back.

acct 1. Accounting. All System V accounting programs. *See* acctcms, acctcom, acctcon1, acctcon2, acctdisk, acctdusg, acctmerg, accton, acctprc1, acctprc2 and acctwtmp. 2. Command used to turn on and off system accounting.

acctcms *(ATT)* Accounting command summary. Command used to prepare system accounting summaries of commands executed. A summary of all processes started by the runacct accounting system shell script is prepared by reviewing records, summing up the number of times a command has been run and printing a report of command usage. A useful tool in determining which commands are most heavily used or hog the system. *See* runacct, acct and hog factor.

acctcom *(ATT/XEN)* Accounting command. Command used to search for and print a history of the commands that have

been executed. Offers many options to restrict or alter the data reported, and is a useful tool for determining who was doing what when. Information provided can include the name of the command, who used it, when it was started, when it was ended, amount of time (in seconds) that the central processing unit was used and size.

acctcon *(ATT)* Accounting connect-time. Set of accounting commands used to collect and report data related to the amount of time a user or host is connected to a network or computer system. *See* connect time, acctcon1 and acctcon2.

acctcon1 *(ATT)* Accounting connect-time 1. Accounting system program started by the runacct accounting system shell script that calculates the amount of time a user or host is connected to a network or computer system from login and logout records in the System V accounting files. Generally used as part of a system accounting script. *See* acctcon2, connect time and runacct.

acctcon2 *(ATT)* Accounting connect-time 2. Accounting system program started by the runacct accounting system shell script that summarizes the amount of time each user is connected to a network or computer system, recorded by the acctcon1 program. *See* runacct, acctcon1 and connect time.

acctdisk *(ATT)* Accounting disk. Accounting system program started by the dodisk accounting system shell script that summarizes and reports disk space usage by user identification. *See* dodisk.

acctdusg *(ATT)* Accounting disk usage. Accounting system program started by the dodisk accounting system shell script that collects disk usage information by login ID. This information is then summarized and reported by acctdisk. *See* acctdisk and dodisk.

acctmerg *(ATT)* Accounting merge. Accounting system program started by the runacct accounting system shell script. Combines and totals the accounting information from other System V accounting programs, such as acctdisk and acctcon2, before that information is summarized by other programs. *See* runacct.

accton *(ATT/XEN)* **Ac**counting **on**. Accounting system program used to turn on and off process accounting. *See* kernel.

acctprc *(ATT)* **Ac**counting **pr**ocess. Set of programs used to maintain accounting data on processes that are run on the system. *See* acctprc1 and acctprc2.

acctprc1 *(ATT)* **Ac**counting **pr**ocess. 1. Accounting system program started by the runacct accounting system shell script that adds user names to the accounting information. Normally, process accounting records only the user identification number. *See* runacct, acctprc2 and UID.

acctprc2 *(ATT)* **Ac**counting **pr**ocess. 2. Accounting system program started by the runacct accounting system shell script that summarizes accounting information. This data is then formatted by the acctprc1 program, by user name and user identifier. *See* runacct, acctprc1 and UID.

acctsh *(ATT)* **Ac**counting **sh**ell. Accounting system program used to collect and process data on shell processes.

acctwtmp *(ATT)* **Ac**counting **wtmp**. Accounting system program used to write comments to the /etc/wtmp file. Records a history of significant events, e.g. system startup, reboots or shutdown, to the wtmp file. *See* /etc/wtmp.

ACE **A**dvanced **C**omputing **E**nvironment. A group whose membership grew to almost 100 companies in the United States, Great Britain, Denmark, Germany, Sweden, India and Korea before it was disbanded in 1992. Formed in April 1991 to support a new computer hardware architecture based upon Reduced Instruction Set Computing using MIPS Computer Systems Inc.'s computer chips and one of four operating systems: Microsoft Corp.'s Windows NT, IBM Corp.'s OS/2 3.0, The Santa Cruz Operation's XENIX and AT&T Co.'s System V, Re-

lease 4 modified for ACE. Members included Microsoft, MIPS Computer Systems, Digital Equipment Corp., Banyan Systems, Inc. and UNIX Systems Laboratories. *See* RISC, ARC and MIPS.

ACE initiative Commonly called ACE. *See* ACE.

ACK **Ac**knowledgment. Communications signal returned to the sending source, indicating a message has been received successfully. *See* NACK.

acknowledgment Commonly abbreviated and called ACK. *See* ACK.

ACL **A**ccess **C**ontrol **L**ist. Provides the ability to limit access to files and directories to specified users. Originated in the MULTICS operating system, and has been included as an enhancement in UNIX System V, Release 4 Extended Security and System V, Release 4 Extended Security and Multiprocessing. *See* MULTICS, SVR4 ES and SVR4 ES/MP.

acoustic coupled modem Also called an acoustic coupler. Modem with a coupling device that can be attached to a telephone handset for sending and receiving data. *See* modem.

Acoustic coupled modem

acoustic coupler 1. Jargon for an acoustic coupled modem. *See* acoustic coupled modem. 2. Device used to transmit data over telephone lines by converting digital signals into audio signals. Has a special coupler into which a telephone handset can be placed to allow data to be transferred between a computer and telephone system. *See* modem.

acousto-optics Technology used to apply compact disk optical data storage to tape media. *See* CD-ROM, WORM, DOTS and optical tape.

ACSE Association Control Service Element. Set of Open Systems Interconnection services used to establish communication links between applications. *See* OSI.

ACT/88 Application Compatibility Test/88. Certification suite developed by the 88open Consortium Ltd. for binary compatibility of applications offered by independent software vendors. Checks to see if the application software correctly interfaces with the kernel and library. Also tests development tools to see if they output the correct formats. *See* 88open Consortium, AVS/88, ITS/88 and shrink-wrapped.

Action-Team for the Integration of Management Systems Commonly called AIMS (Association for the Integration of Network Management Systems). *See* AIMS.

active file system Any mounted, or active, file system that can be accessed by users. *See* file system.

active open Action taken by a client to establish a Transmission Control Protocol connection with a server. *See* client, server and TCP.

active open socket Socket used to establish a connection with a remote host to transfer data over a network using the Transmission Control Protocol. *See* TCP, socket and passive open socket.

active tool UNIX security-related programs that interacts with the operating system to make the necessary changes, when need, to the configuration of the operating system. Active tools can change file permissions that do not match system standards; monitor incoming network traffic, rejecting connections that do not meet site criteria; and watch for possible break-ins by unauthorized persons. *See* passive tool.

Active Users Protocol Commonly abbreviated and called USERS. *See* USERS.

active window Terminal window where input is taking place. *See* window.

actor Commonly called task. *See* task.

ACU Auto call unit. Modem that performs automatic dialing under the control of a program.

acuset *(ATT)* Auto call unit set. Command used to make a connection between an auto-dial modem and the communication lines. *See* ACU and modem.

Ada High-level programming language named for the first woman programmer, Ada Byron, Countess of Lovelace. Developed in the 1970s for the Department of Defense as the standard language for embedded computers installed on weapon systems such as aircraft, tanks and ships.

ADAPSO Association of Data Processing Service Organization. Former name of the Information Technology Association of America. *See* ITAA.

adapter Any piece of hardware that is attached to a computer and used to connect the system with other hardware devices.

adb A debugger or absolute debugger. Oldest of the UNIX debuggers. Gives programmers the ability to interactively debug software. Commonly used to look at cores to determine causes of system outages. *See* debugger.

ADCCP Advanced Data Communication Control Procedure. American National Standards Institute implementation of IBM Corp.'s synchronous data link control protocol. *See* SDLC.

addbib *(BSD)* Add bibliography. One of the refer utility commands. Creates or modifies a bibliographic database. *See* refer, indxbib, lookbib, roffbib and sortbib.

addgrp *(ATT)* Add group. Command used by the system administrator to add a user to a group. *See* group and delgrp.

add host *(ATT)* Remote File Sharing sysadm menu command used to add hosts to the password file. *See* RFS and sysadm.

ADDMD **A**dministrative **D**irectory **M**anagement **D**omain. An X.500 directory management hierarchy. *See* X.500.

add nameserver *(ATT)* **Add name server.** Remote File Sharing sysadm menu command used to add a new name server host to the domain. *See* RFS, sysadm, domain and name server.

address **1.** Specific integer number that identifies the computer memory location where data can be found. **2.** Name or number that identifies a computer, printer or other output device on a network. **3.** Number that uniquely identifies a host on a network.

Address Commonly abbreviated A. *See* A.

addressable cursor Function of a terminal. Allows an application program being run by a user to control the movement of the cursor on a terminal screen.

address family Common or related addresses used in domain communication. *See* domain.

address format Common set of rules that describes the way in which an address is composed to ensure that data will flow from one location to another. The UNIX-to-UNIX CoPy address format for sending an electronic-mail message to a user on a remote host is hostname!userid, e.g.:

wp-eds!daup

In contrast, the Simple Mail Transfer Protocol of an Internet address is userid@hostname, e.g.:

keller@wp-eds.mil

See UUCP, SMTP, Internet and e-mail.

address mask Commonly called network mask. *See* network mask.

address range Lines in a file on which an operation is to be applied in an ed or other text editing program. *See* editor.

address resolution **1.** Process of relating, or identifying, an address to a physical device. *See* ARP. **2.** *(INET)* Changing the numerics of an Internet address into a physical address to determine the location of the receiver of a message.

Address Resolution Protocol *(INET)* Commonly abbreviated and called ARP. *See* ARP.

address space **1.** Section of memory address (either physical or virtual) allocated to a process. *See* process, fork, vfork, physical memory and virtual memory. **2.** Location where user data is stored on a disk.

adduser *(OTH)* Shell script or program used to add a new user to the system. Adds user identification to the /etc/passwd and /etc/group root files, creates the new user directory, and establishes electronic-mail accounts and initial password, among other things. *See* shell script and rmuser.

adjtime **A**djust **time**. System call used in conjunction with the timed daemon or Network Time Protocol to make gradual corrections in time errors on a network's slave systems. *See* system call, timed and NTP.

adjust **1.** *(OTH)* Shell script used to correct permission settings in files identified by the holes shell script. *See* shell script, permissions and holes. **2.** *See* justify.

adm **Adm**inistration. System administration software program similar to sysadm. *See* sysadm.

ADMD **A**dministrative **M**anagement **D**omain. Also called Administration Management Domain. Term used in the X.400 mail handling system, developed by the International Telecommunication Union Telecommunication Standardization Sector, formerly called the Consultative Committee on International Telegraphy and Telephony. Software responsible for the external (gateway-to-gateway) management of electronic-mail messages. *See* ITU-T, X.400, electronic mail, gateway and PRMD.

admin **1.** *(ATT/XEN)* Program for creating and administering a file indicating default actions to be taken during the installation of new software programs. **2.** Abbreviation for administration or system administration. **3.** Jargon for anything related to the maintenance and operation of a UNIX system. *See* system administration. **4.** *(ATT/XEN)* **Admi**nistration. One of the 13 commands within the Source Code Control System (SCCS) used to create and administer files created with SCCS. *See* SCCS, cdc, comb, delta, get, help, prs, rmdel, sact, sccsdiff, unget, val, vc and what.

administration Commonly called system administration. *See* system administration.

Administration Management Domain Commonly abbreviated and called ADMD. *See* ADMD.

administrative database Files and/or directories used to maintain information on user and group accounts.

Administrative Directory Management Domain Commonly abbreviated and called ADDMD. *See* ADDMD.

Administrative Least Privilege Security feature which divides the privileges and power of a superuser into functions that are performed by others. *See* feature and security.

Administrative Management Domain Commonly abbreviated and called ADMD. *See* ADMD.

administrative security System of establishing and enforcing policies and procedures on use and access to a computer.

administrative state Also called state. Condition in which all multi-user processes are functional but only the console has access to the system. Used when necessary to prevent users from accessing the system and updating or adding data, e.g. when the operating system is being updated, the system is being rebooted or backed up, and analysis is being performed following unscheduled outages.

ADP **A**utomatic **D**ata **P**rocessing. Commonly called DP (data processing). *See* DP.

AdUUG **A**delaide **U**NIX **U**sers **G**roup. UNIX users group founded in 1986 at the University of Adelaide, Australia.

adv *(ATT)* **Adv**ertise. Remote File Sharing command used to make resources on a computer available to users on a network. *See* RFS, DA, share, shareall and unadv.

Advanced Computing Environment Commonly abbreviated and called ACE. *See* ACE.

Advanced Data Communication Control Procedure Commonly abbreviated and called ADCCP. *See* ADCCP.

Advanced Interactive Executive Commonly abbreviated and called AIX. *See* AIX.

Advanced Peer-to-Peer Networking Commonly abbreviated and called APPN. *See* APPN.

Advanced Programming-to-Programming Communications Commonly abbreviated and called APPC. *See* APPC.

Advanced Research Projects Agency (INET) Commonly abbreviated and called ARPA. *See* ARPA.

Advanced Research Projects Agency Network (INET) Commonly abbreviated and called ARPANET. *See* ARPANET.

Advanced RISC Computer Commonly abbreviated and called ARC. *See* ARC.

Advance Program-to-Program Communications Commonly abbreviated and called APPC. *See* APPC.

adventure Early dungeon game on UNIX systems. *See* rogue.

advertising Notifying that When a resource is available to the domain name server on a system using the Remote File Sharing program. *See* RFS, domain name server, adv and unadv.

advisory lock Security measure that is implemented only when specifically requested by a process. *See* lock.

AEP Application environment profile. Definition of the components needed to support and operate an application in a specified environment, e.g. real-time systems.

AES Application Environment Specification. Open Software Foundation Inc.'s term for the standards developed to run an application environment that can be used on different hardware platforms. Provides specification for application interface, syntax and protocol. *See* OSF.

AET Application Entity Title. Open Systems Interconnection term for a network application. *See* OSI.

AFIPS American Federation of Information Processing Societies. U.S. association of organizations related to or having an interest in the computer industry.

AFP AppleTalk File Protocol. Transaction processing protocol for Apple computers.

AFS Andrew File System. Protocol developed at Carnegie-Mellon University and used to manage files on a distributed computing environment on a Transmission Control Protocol/Internet Protocol network. Named for the Andrew Project, which took its name from the university's two founders, Andrew Carnegie and Andrew Mellon. *See* distributed computing and TCP/IP.

AFUU Association Francaise Des Utilisateurs D'UNIX. French UNIX users group formed in 1982.

age buffer list List of buffers maintained in the file system buffer cache, the contents of which have not yet proven to be of any value. *See* buffer and file system.

agent Simple Network Management Protocol architecture term for either programs or a combination of hardware and software used to maintain information about devices or applications on a network. Responds to requests from the management station to provide data for use by the network manager. *See* SNMP, Internet, NMS and MIB.

aging Using the length of time an item has been in place as the key to an action. *See* password aging.

ai Autoindent. Toggled option in the vi editing program that, when set, starts each line of text in the same column, automatically creating whitespace beside the text. *See* vi, toggle, whitespace and noai.

AI Artificial intelligence. **1.** Programmed instructions that enable a computer to mimic certain human or biological characteristics and functions, e.g. reasoning, vision, learning and understanding natural (human) language. **2.** Pseudo-science related to astrology that deals with knowledge representation, image recognition, speech recognition, natural language analysis and just about anything else outside the mainstream of computer science that needs government funding. Modern research in artificial intelligence traces its beginnings to 1968 when the HAL 9000 computer in the film 2001: A Space Odyssey ran amuck, stole the story and generally warped the minds of an entire generation of future computer geeks. *See* computer nerd.

AIMS Association for the Integration of Network Management Systems. Also called Action-Team for the Integration of Management Systems. Group formed in 1992 by Network Managers Inc., IBM Corp., Comdisco Systems Inc. and Cray Communications Ltd. Its purpose is to develop network management applications capable of running on networks offered by various vendors and application programming interfaces that allow computers to share data among themselves over various networks. Headquartered in London, and is a part of the Network Management Forum. *See* NMF.

AIX Advanced Interactive Executive. IBM Corp. version of UNIX that is based on the Open Software Foundation Inc.'s

OSF/1 operating system. *See* OSF and OSF/1.

ALAP AppleTalk Link Access Protocol. Apple Computer Inc.'s proprietary networking standard used by Macintosh computers and peripherals to access a network.

alarm **1.** Threshold set for acceptable behavior of either hardware or software applications that, when exceeded, signals a problem or impending problem. Can be sent in the form of an electronic-mail message, terminal beep, printed message or screen message. **2.** *(ATT)* System call used to schedule an alarm signal. Sends the signal SIGALRM to an active process after a specified number of seconds have elapsed. *See* signal values (Appendices I and J).

alert Error message sent to a predesignated location. *See* alarm.

Alex *(INET)* Daemon developed by Vincent Cate of Carnegie-Mellon University. Allows users to mount Internet as a Network File System file tree to locate and access data more easily. *See* Internet and NFS.

algorithm Formula or set of mathematical rules used in program development to perform a task that follows a logical path in a set number of processes.

alias **1.** Alternative term for command. Used to reset the format of a standard UNIX command to a format defined by a user. Also can show and export the new format. *See* unalias. **2.** Shortcut, generally used to reduce the number of key strokes, as when a user redefines or renames a UNIX command, with or without arguments, or combines several other commands into a new, user-defined command. Aliases are normally created by a user in a .aliases file or in .cshrc or .login. For example, in the .alias file a user would create: alias "pa -aux" = pa. This would provide a new command, allowing the user to input only pa to run a ps-aux command. *See* .aliases, .cshrc, .login and unalias. **3.** Shortened format for an elec-

tronic-mail address for either a single user or a combination of several users:

Name	Alias
rockie	rmorgan@netcom.com
davidf	feldman_david@tandem.com
slick	kleven@sequent.com

An alias of sysadmin would be used to send mail to:

cedgman@fred
dv@wilma
msjacob@fred
sstarck@fred
bjohns@uswnvg
vbredeh@fred
ftollef@nv5
whholt@uswnvg

See e- mail

aliasing Also called jaggies. Effect that resembles a series of steps, and is seen in curved and diagonal lines in low-resolution computer-generated pictures. The pixels, or dots, which are used to create the picture are arranged in rectangular patterns. If the resolution is too low, the spaces within these pixel patterns show up, creating a jagged effect. Also causes flickering of objects on the screen. *See* anti-aliasing, IG, raster and pixel.

Example of aliasing

align **1.** To position read and write heads of a disk or tape drive so they can correctly place or retrieve information from the storage medium. **2.** To correctly place the pattern of an integrated circuit chip on the silicon wafer. *See* IC, mask and wafer. **3.** To place characters on a sheet of paper or screen in a predesigned location, e.g. left, where the first character of each line is placed in the same column on the left side of the screen or page; or right, where the last character of each line is placed in the same column on the right side of the screen or page; or centered, where the mid-point of a line of characters is located in the middle of the screen or page; or decimal, where a decimal point is used to align whole and decimal numbers in a column.

alive Jargon for a computer system that is active and running properly.

All-hazards Situation Assessment Prototype Commonly abbreviated and called ASAP. *See* ASAP.

Allman, Eric Author of sendmail, which he wrote while studying at the University of California, Berkeley. Also wrote the me macros for use with the troff text formatting program. *See* sendmail, me macros and troff.

alloc *(ATT)* Program used to **alloc**ate available free blocks of disk space in a specific file system.

allocated inode list List of the inodes in use that is maintained by the operating system. *See* inode.

allowmeas *(OTH)* Commonly called sudo. *See* sudo.

alpha Prefix indicating that only alphabetical characters can be or have been used, e.g. as in a field or variable in a database. In contrast, only numbers may be used in a numeric field or variable while a combination of letters and numbers may be used in an alphanumeric one. *See* alphanumeric and numeric.

Alpha Digital Equipment Corp. computer line/microprocessor project that resulted in a new product line. Alpha computer architecture is based upon a 64-bit Reduced Instruction Set Computing microprocessor chip with a clock speed of 150 megahertz. It can perform 300 million instructions per second and 150 million floating point operations per second. Alpha computers range from desktop models to large, mainframe-like

systems. *See* RISC, clock speed, MIPS and megaflops.

alphanumeric Prefix indicating that a combination of alphabetic characters and numbers can be or have been used, e.g. as in a field or variable in a database. In contrast, only alphabetic characters may be used in an alpha field or variable while only numbers can be used in a numeric one. *See* alpha and numeric.

alpha test Initial testing performed on products intended for commercial use. Performed by people not related with the product's development to determine its compliance with design specifications and requirements. *See* system test and beta test.

AlphaWindow Terminal technology developed by the Display Industry Association. Provides X Window System-like support for character-based American Standard Code for Information Interchange-based applications and terminals. Also provides such options as the ability to run multiple applications simultaneously and to transfer data among windows and applications. *See* X Window System, ASCII and DIA.

alternate file Term in the vi and ex editing programs for the previous file edited and its associated buffers. *See* vi, ex and current file.

alternating current Commonly abbreviated and called AC. *See* AC.

Alternet Commercial provider of connectivity to the Internet. Located in Falls Church, Virginia. *See* Internet.

ALU Arithmetic/Logic Unit. Portion of the central processing unit that manages all the arithmetic and logic operations. *See* CPU.

Amdahl's Law Facetious proposition that says the execution time of a program is determined by the slowest portion of the program. Named for Eugene "Gene" Amdahl, architect of the IBM Corp. System 360, who left IBM and founded Amdahl Corp.

American Federation of Information Processing Societies Commonly abbreviated and called AFIPS. *See* AFIPS.

American National Standards Institute Commonly abbreviated and called ANSI. *See* ANSI.

American Standard Code for Information Interchange Commonly abbreviated and called ASCII. *See* ASCII.

AMIX Hebrew acronym for the Israeli UNIX Users' Group formed in 1985.

Amoeaba Operating system developed at the Free University and Center for Mathematics and Computer Science, Amsterdam. An early object-based distributed operating system characterized by a microkernel-based client/server architecture. *See* microkernel.

amp ampere. Basic unit of measurement for electrical current. Also abbreviated a or A. Equal to watts divided by volts, 6.26 x 10^{18} electrons or the basic electrical charge transferred in a second by a constant current. *See* volt and watt.

ampere Commonly abbreviated and called amp. *See* amp.

ampersand (&) **1.** Symbol used to initiate a process which the user wants to run in the background. For example:

    CLP> nroff -mm file name1 file name2 & ⏎

See background process and nroff. **2.** Metacharacter used in a regular expression of the ex or sed programs to repeat a regular expression. *See* metacharacter and regular expression.

analog Measurement of data using a physical model, e.g. a continuous variation in voltages. In comparison, in digital measurements, data is represented by binary numbers (0 or 1). *See* digital.

analog computer Type of computer that is normally used for either industrial or scientific computation of continuous physical variables, e.g. pressure, temperature or voltage. *See* digital computer.

analog display Continuous physical display of analog or physical variables, e.g. voltage or miles per hour, using numbers and a pointer like an odometer or voltage meter in a car.

analog signal Signal transmitted in a continuous form by electrical waves. The signal is transmitted in its original format, e.g. the sound of a person's voice or other noise is converted into electrical vibrations and carried from point A to point B. In contrast, a digital signal is used to send information in discrete or discontinuous operations using the binary numbers 0 and 1. *See* digital signal.

analysis paralysis When work on a product or project is delayed or not started because the people involved are being overly cautious. Every aspect is analyzed, re-analyzed and analyzed again. When the initial analysis is finished, the "what if?" questions begin and each question is analyzed, re-analyzed and analyzed again. Much time is consumed and many documents are prepared, but no usable product or project results.

ANDF Architecture Neutral Distribution Format. Technology that allows application software to be used on dissimilar computer systems. Supported by the Open Software Foundation Inc. to promote a vendor-independent, or open systems, approach to software development. *See* OSF and ABI.

Andrew File System Commonly abbreviated and called AFS. *See* AFS.

A news Alternative name for the first version of netnews, a set of programs used to exchange and read articles on the USENET, an international UNIX bulletin board. *See* netnews and USENET.

anonymous ftp *(INET)* File Transfer Protocol login with little or no security. Allows a user to access a system by using "anonymous" as the login name and "guest" as the password. Generally used on Internet systems that provide publicly accessible files. *See* FTP.

AN-SEE Pronunciation of ANSI, the abbreviation for American National Standards Institute. *See* ANSI.

ANSI American National Standards Institute. Pronounced *AN-SEE*. Formerly known as the American Standards Association. The coordinating and approval body for national data processing (including communications) standards within the United States. Does not develop standards, only approves those submitted by standards development groups or professional association, e.g. Institute of Electrical and Electronic Engineers. Submits U.S. standards to the International Organization for Standardization for adoption as international standards. Composed of more than 1,000 professional organizations, trade associations and companies. *See* IEEE and ISO.

ANSI C C language standard approved by the American National Standards Institute and specifically developed for UNIX System V, Release 4. Defines language semantics and syntax, execution environment and composition of the library and header files. *See* ANSI, ANSI X3J11, SVR4.x and C language.

ANSI character set 256 American National Standards Institute standard 8-bit characters. *See* ANSI.

ANSI C Transition Guide UNIX System V, Release 4 documentation on writing new C language programs or upgrading old C language programs to conform with ANSI C standard. *See* SVR4.x, C language and ANSI C.

ANSI X12 American National Standards Institute standard working group for Electronic Data Interchange standards. Started in 1979; the first version of the standard was available in 1983. *See* ANSI and EDI.

ANSI X3.129-1986 American National Standards Institute standard, used with ANSI X.3.130 to define the Intelligent Peripheral Interface standard. *See* ANSI and IPI.

ANSI X3.130-1986 American National Standards Institute standard, used with ANSI X.3.129 to define the Intelligent Peripheral Interface standard. *See* ANSI and IPI.

ANSI X3.131-1986 American National Standards Institute standard that defines the Small Computer System Interface standard. *See* ANSI and SCSI.

ANSI X3.159-1989 American National Standards Institute standard that defines the specification for C language. *See* ANSI and C language.

ANSI X353.3 American National Standards Institute specification for the End System to Intermediate System protocol. *See* ANSI and ES-IS.

ANSI X3B11.1 American National Standards Institute standard working group that sets disk format standards for write-once-read-many technology. *See* ANSI and WORM.

ANSI X3H3.6 American National Standards Institute standard for X Window System. *See* ANSI and X Window System.

ANSI X3J3 American National Standards Institute standard for FORTRAN compiler. *See* ANSI and FORTRAN.

ANSI X3J11 American National Standards Institute standard which a vendor is required to meet to implement C language. Defines language semantics and syntax, execution environment and composition of the library and header files. *See* ANSI, SVR4.x and C language.

ANSI X3J16 American National Standards Institute standard which a vendor is required to meet to implement C++. Defines language semantics and syntax, execution environment and composition of the library and header files. *See* ANSI and C++ language.

ANSI X3S3.3 American National Standards Institute standard working group that sets network and transportation layer protocol standards. *See* ANSI and transportation layer.

ANSI X3T5.4 American National Standards Institute standards working group that sets network and directory standards. *See* ANSI and X.500.

ANSI X3T9.2 American National Standards Institute specification for the second generation of the Small Computer System Interface. *See* ANSI and SCSI-2.

ANSI X3T9.3 American National Standards Institute specification for intelligent peripheral interfaces. *See* ANSI.

ANSI X3T9.5 American National Standards Institute standards working group for Fiber Distribution Data Interface. *See* ANSI and FDDI.

anti-aliasing Process of smoothing the edges of a computer-generated picture. *See* aliasing, IG, pixel and raster.

a.out Default file name assigned to the output from the ld, as and cc commands of the UNIX C language compiler, assembler and/or loader. *See* as, cc and ld.

AOW Asia and Oceania Workshop. Organization originally formed to promote Open Systems Interconnection standards and development of open systems products for computer networking in Asia. Now focuses on other open operating systems and interfaces as well. *See* OSI, EWOS and OIW.

ap Autoprint. Toggled variable in the ex and vi editors. When set, it displays the current line when a user performs a delete, copy, join, substitute, undo or shift command. *See* ex, vi and toggle.

Apache Group Original name for the Mips ABI Group, renamed the Mips SVR4 Special Interest Group in 1992 and again renamed the Mips ABI Group in 1993. *See* Mips ABI Group.

API Application Program Interface. Set of specifications used to define the programming language, functions and program calls that provide the high-level connection between an application and operating system or services, such as windows,

toolkits, etc. Provides a standard way to write applications. *See* TLI.

APIA Commonly called XAPIA. *See* XAPIA.

APP Application Portability Profile. Standard developed by National Institute of Standards and Technology that describes requirements for operation in a specific environment. *See* NIST.

APPC Advanced Programming-to-Programming Communications. Element of IBM Corp.'s System Network Architecture (SNA) protocol used to establish the environment needed for programs to communicate over a network. Provides the ability for processes to communicate with another process on a computer in an SNA network. *See* SNA.

append 1. Electronic-mail program variable. *See* .mailrc variables (Appendices F and G). 2. To make an addition to the end of a word, line or file in an editor or word processor. 3. To combine the text of two files by adding the text of the first file to the end of the second file. *See* greater than symbol.

append mode Condition in which an editor or word processing program is set to add text to the end of a word, line or file.

Apple Macintosh UNIX Commonly abbreviated and called A/UX. *See* A/UX.

AppleShare Apple Computer Inc.'s network solution based upon AppleTalk and the AppleTalk Filing Protocol. *See* AppleTalk and AFP.

AppleTalk Local area network protocol based upon the Open Systems Interconnection model and developed by Apple Computer Inc. for Macintosh computers. *See* LAN, OSI, OSIRM, AppleShare and MAC.

AppleTalk Filing Protocol Commonly abbreviated and called AFP. *See* AFP.

AppleTalk IP Internet Protocol implementation developed by Apple Computer Inc. for Macintosh computers. *See* IP.

AppleTalk Link Access Protocol
Commonly abbreviated and called ALAP. *See* ALAP.

application 1. Job, work or function that is performed or accomplished with software, e.g. using a spreadsheet to do mathematical computations or a word processor to create and format letters. 2. Collection of programs that work together to generate a specified output or result. *See* application program.

Application Binary Interface
Commonly abbreviated and called ABI. *See* ABI.

Application Entity Title Commonly abbreviated and called AET. *See* AET.

application environment profile
Commonly abbreviated and called AEP. *See* AEP.

Application Environment Specification
Commonly abbreviated and called AES. *See* AES.

application gateway Hardware and software that allows the transfer of data between networks using different protocols.

application layer Set of related functions that provide application services between hosts, e.g. TELNET and File Transfer Protocol in Internet Transmission Control Protocol and Internet Protocol (TCP/IP). In International Organization for Standardization/Open Systems Interconnection, the application layer is the seventh layer. In the TCP/IP, the application layer is the fourth layer. *See* layer, TCP/IP architecture, Internet, TCP, IP, ISO/OSI, OSIRM and FTAM.

application package Commonly called application program. *See* application program.

application portability Ability to move an application program without modify-

ing it from one type of computer hardware to another.

Application Portability Profile
Commonly abbreviated and called APP. *See* APP.

application program Software specifically designed to perform one or more functions or tasks, e.g. accounting and inventory control. Application programs can either be purchased off-the-shelf to meet broad requirements of many people or organizations, or specifically developed to meet the needs of one individual or company.

application protocol Specific set of rules and standards that provide network services, e.g. login and mail. *See* services.

application server Computer that is dedicated to running a specific application on a network, e.g. an electronic-mail server.

application software Commonly called application program. *See* application program.

application-specific integrated circuits
Commonly abbreviated and called ASIC. *See* ASIC.

Applications Program Interface
Commonly abbreviated and called API. *See* API.

apply *(BSD)* Command that allows a user to run more than one command with the same arguments.

APPN Advanced Peer-to-Peer Networking. IBM Corp. proprietary protocol announced in early 1991. Used to interconnect dissimilar IBM computers (workstations, minicomputers and mainframes) running a variety of operating systems. Can be used to dynamically send applications to computer systems and maintain a network topology. Thus, changes in a network can be recorded and other nodes on the network can be updated as modifications are made.

appropriate privileges S p e c i f i e d method of defining a process with function calls and options to identify the types and levels of permissions needed to access it. *See* process, function call and permissions.

apropos *(BSD)* Command used to identify any standard command on a UNIX system with a keyword lookup. Allows users to search on-line manual pages by inputting key words or strings which, if found, will provide information on the associated command.

ar *(ATT/XEN)* **Ar**chive. Command used to create and maintain archive libraries. *See* archive.

ARC **A**dvanced **R**ISC **C**omputing. Technical advisory group to the Advanced Computing Environment responsible for developing specifications for software to run on Reduced Instructions Set Computing-based computer systems. Composed of Compaq Computer Corp., Digital Equipment Corp., MIPS, Microsoft Corp. and The Santa Cruz Operation Inc. *See* ACE and RISC.

archie **1.** Commonly spelled Archie. *See* Archie. **2.** Command used to initiate access to the Archie database.

Archie *(INET)* Also spelled archie. Database developed at McGill University in Montreal, Quebec, to provide a list of locations, e.g. nodes on the Internet, at which users can find free software on the Internet. The Archie database is located on various computer systems throughout the United States, Canada, Europe and Australia. Name derived from the word archive. *See* Gopher, WAIS and Internet.

Architecture Neutral Distribution Format Commonly abbreviated and called ANDF. *See* ANDF.

archive To move data from active on-line or near-line storage to inactive or off-line storage, e.g. moving data from a disk drive to a tape. To reduce storage space, data is usually compressed during archiving.

archiver Category of system backup utilities, e.g. cpio and tar. Used to make full or partial backups of the file system. In addition, permits selected files to be recovered. *See* file system, cpio and tar.

ARCnet **A**ttached **R**esource **C**omputer **Net**work. Local area network interface board developed by Data Point Corp. A LAN protocol that competes with Ethernet, Token Ring and Fiber Data Distributed Interface. Runs at 2.5 million bits per second. *See* LAN, Ethernet, Token Ring and FDDI.

ARCnet Plus **A**ttached **R**esource **Com**puter **Net**work **Plus**. Enhanced version of Data Point Corp.'s ARCnet that increases the transmission rate, packet size and number of nodes that can be supported. *See* ARCnet.

arcv *(ATT/XEN)* Command used to convert archive files from the Digital Equipment Corp.'s DEC PDP-11 operating system to UNIX System V. Provided for backward compatibility with UNIX Version 6 and is nearly obsolete.

argc Argument count. First parameter in a C language program that contains the number of arguments which can be passed to the program. *See* argument and argv.

argument Modifier or variable added to a UNIX command to indicate which data is to be acted on, e.g. an option or name of a file that modifies a command to perform a specific function. *See* option, mandatory argument and optional argument.

argument count Number of arguments or variables in a program.

argument list Collection of file names that can be accessed with either the vi or ex editor. *See* vi and ex.

argument zero Command to be initiated by the shell. Any additional options or arguments are sequentially numbered following the command:

```
CLP> cat <argument zero> file name1 <argument1>
file name2 <argument 2>
```

argv **Arg**ument **v**alue. Also called argument vector. Second parameter in a C language program that contains the value of the arguments passed to a program. *See* argc, argument and array.

arithmetic Command used to start a game to test knowledge of arithmetic facts.

Arithmetic/Logic Unit Commonly abbreviated and called ALU. *See* ALU.

ARM *(INET)* **A**RPANET **R**eference **M**odel. Also referred to as the TCP/IP protocol suite. Document that contains the definition of the ARPANET layered set of protocol suites which make up the Defense Advanced Research Projects Agency's Internet program. *See* ARPANET, Internet, applications layer, transport layer, internet layer, network layer and physical layer.

arp *(ATT)* Command used to start the **A**ddress **R**esolution **P**rotocol program. Can be used to display or modify tables that translate Internet Protocol addresses to Ethernet addresses. *See* ARP, Ethernet and Internet.

ARP *(INET)* **A**ddress **R**esolution **P**rotocol. Set of programs that is part of the Internet Protocol Suite developed by the Defense Advanced Research Projects Agency which translates an Internet Protocol address into an Ethernet address. *See* Internet, DARPA and Ethernet.

ARPA *(INET)* **A**dvanced **R**esearch **P**rojects **A**gency. Department of Defense agency started in 1973 by Dr. Robert Kahn. Original name for the government research organization responsible for creating and implementing the Internet. The name was changed to the Defense Research Projects Agency (DARPA) due to the military emphasis and funding by the Department of Defense. Changed from DARPA back to ARPA in the early 1990s

to reflect the organization's change in emphasis from military operations. *See* ARPANET, Internet and DARPA.

ARPANET *(INET)* **A**dvanced **R**esearch **P**rojects **A**gency **NET**work. Forerunner of the long haul packet switch networks and the Internet. Established in 1969 and funded by the Defense Advanced Research Projects Agency, when that organization was known as the Advanced Research Projects Agency. The original test sites included the University of California, Los Angles; University of California, Santa Barbara; University of Utah; and Stanford Research Institute International. Grew to more than 20,000 hosts before it was shut down and replaced by the Defense Research Internet in 1991 as the backbone to the Internet. *See* DARPA, Internet, SRI International and DRI.

ARPANET host access protocol *(INET)* Specific set of rules and standards used in ARPANET for communications between a host and an ARPANET node. *See* ARPANET and node.

ARPANET Reference Model *(INET)* Commonly abbreviated and called ARM. *See* ARM.

array **1.** Sequential arrangement of one or more objects that are similar, e.g. disk drives. **2.** One or more data items arranged sequentially in a computer's memory, a concept supported by most computer languages. Individual array elements are accessed using the array name and a subscript. In the C programming language, any data type may be declared as an array, with the first data item referred to as the zero element. Thus, an array of 50 integers can be declared and named using:

```
int myarray[50];
```

The first and last elements of "myarray." are:

```
myarray[0];
myarray[49];
```

Programming languages such as FORTRAN use 1 as the subscript to the first element in an array, which can confuse novice programmers and those translating a program from one language to another. Other languages, such as Pascal, allow the array to be declared using any integer value, in the belief that this makes the program more robust.

arrow keys Keys located on the right-hand side of most keyboards. Depending upon the terminal emulator used, can be used to move the cursor up or down one line at a time or left or right one character at a time. *See* terminal emulation.

article USENET News messages. *See* USENET.

artificial intelligence Commonly abbreviated and called AI. *See* AI.

artificial reality Term first introduced in the mid-1970s by Myron Krueger to describe computer-generated responsive environments. A computer-based display system that captures actions of the human body in graphic representations. These are used to generate images on projection systems capable of producing illusions of actions that take place in real life. *See* cave and virtual reality.

as Assembler. The assembler program that is used on most UNIX systems. *See* assembler.

asa *(ATT)* Command used to interpret American Standards Association carriage control characters. An ASA carriage control character is the first character in each line of a file that is printed. These are not printed. They are interpreted as:

Character	Meaning
	(Blank) single new line before printing
0	Double new line before printing
1	New page before printing
+	Overprint previous line.

Generally, FORTRAN programs use ASA carriage control characters to control pa-

per movement in printers. This convention dates to when printers were huge electromechanical devices that used paper ribbons (and later stored programs) to determine where the top of a page was. *See* ASA.

ASA American Standards Association. Original name of the American National Standards Institute. *See* ANSI.

ASAP All-hazards Situation Assessment Prototype. Geographic information system software developed by the Federal Emergency Agency following Hurricane Andrew in 1992. First used in coordinating disaster relief during the flood of 1993 in the Midwest. Composed of commercial and custom software used for modeling, data management and reporting to predict they type, location and severity of damage to an area. Data for ASAP is provided by Air Force U-2 reconnaissance aircraft and satellites. *See* GIS.

ASCII 1. American Standard Code for Information Interchange. Pronounced *ASS-KEY*. A national standard for American computer code that has a standard 7-bit code with a parity code used for the interchange of data between software and hardware. The current ASCII standard consists of 128 characters, composed of the English letters A to Z (upper case) and a to z (lower case), digits, symbols, punctuation marks and control characters. 2. Standard for encoding data. 3. Common standard set used on most UNIX systems.

ASCII characters Set of 128 characters (binary values of 0 to 127) created with a standard 7-bit code with a parity code that represent letters, numbers, symbols, etc. Used for the interchange of data between software and hardware. The standard character set does not include symbols, letters and punctuation marks for foreign languages and graphic symbols. An 8-bit version with an additional 128 characters exists to provide these missing symbols.

ASCII terminal American Standard Code for Information Interchange **terminal**. Any computer terminal or printer capable of interpreting ASCII data. *See* AS-CII.

American Standards Association Commonly abbreviated and called ASA. *See* ASA.

ASCII text Data file containing words, program sources, shell scripts and/or other text that conforms to the 7-bit American Standard Code for Information Interchange standard. Most UNIX systems use ASCII text for recording character data. *See* ASCII.

Asia and Oceania Workshop Commonly abbreviated and called AOW. *See* AOW.

ASIC Application-specific integrated circuit. Integrated chips designed and manufactured to perform a specific function, e.g. video or input/output. *See* IC.

A-SINK Pronunciation of async, the slang term and abbreviation for asynchronous. *See* async.

asktime *(XEN)* **Ask time.** Command used to determine the time of day.

ASN.1 Abstract Syntax Notation 1. International set of rules and symbols developed by Open Systems Interconnection. Used to establish and define information, protocols and programming languages. *See* OSI.

aspect ratio Measurement used in graphics to show the relationship between the height and width of an image.

assembler Program that makes software usable by a computer. Converts symbolic terms into machine instructions that a computer is capable of understanding and executing. *See* assembly language, as and machine language.

assembler language Commonly called assembly language. *See* assembly language.

assembly language Command language that includes symbolic terms and statements which correspond to computer instructions. Each assembly language

instruction corresponds directly to a machine language instruction. *See* machine language and mnemonic.

asset errors Errors resulting from a UNIX-to-UNIX CoPy transmission. Normally indicates problems with the system that should be investigated immediately. *See* UUCP.

ASS-KEY Pronunciation of ASCII, the acronym for American Standard Code for Information Interchange. *See* ASCII.

Association Control Service Element Commonly abbreviated as ACSE. *See* ACSE.

Association for the Integration of Network Management Systems Commonly abbreviated as AIMS. *See* AIMS.

ast **A**synchronous **s**ystem **t**rap. Signal, or message, that originated with VAX systems to start an interrupt in a program. Incorporated by the Fourth Berkeley Software Distribution, Third Release as a means of handling the rescheduling of processes.

asterisk (*) Metacharacter used in regular expressions that is called the file name expansion or wild card. Can be used anywhere in a string as a substitute for any unknown number of characters, including one or more blank spaces. For example, a user can view or manipulate files containing the number 1 in their names, e.g. book1, chapter1, chapt1, by entering the command followed by *1. Only those files ending in 1, regardless of the preceding characters, will be acted on. Likewise, if the command was followed by only an asterisk, all files in the directory would be acted on. Used as a metacharacter within regular expressions for the ed, ex, vi, sed, grep, egrep and awk programs. *See* metacharacter and regular expression.

asymmetric multiprocessing Type of minicomputer multiprocessor architecture in which the processors have a master and slave relationship, in contrast to the co-equal relationship found in symmetric multiprocessing. The master central processing unit (CPU) totally controls all the other CPUs in the computer and there is dedicated memory assigned to each CPU. The CPUs are assigned to a single specific task, e.g. managing disk input/output or network traffic flow. In addition, since only one copy of the operating system kernel is used by all the CPUs, the master CPU must provide instructions to the slave CPUs one at a time, serially. *See* CPU and SMP.

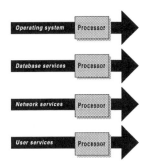

An asymmetrical system assigns a particular task to each processor

async Pronounced *A-SINK*. Jargon term and abbreviation for asynchronous.

asynchronous communications
Method of communication between computers and/or devices that allows information to be sent and received without pre-arranged synchronization. One wire sends and a second wire receives, and all data being transmitted or received one bit at a time. *See* handshake.

asynchronous computing Sequential approach to the interaction between a computer and other devices, e.g. a modem or printer. A computer operation takes place either when the device needed for the function is available or when the computer receives a signal (indication) that one step in the process is finished and it can move to the next one.

asynchronous event notification *(POS)* POSIX.4 real-time operating system term. Form of interprocess communication used to notify a process of an asynchro-

nous action, e.g. input/output activity or message transmission. *See* POSIX.4 and RTOS.

asynchronous interface 1. Communications interface. Transmission of data includes start and stop signals which indicate when a previous task, e.g. computer instruction or data transmission, has been completed and the next can start. *See* serial and bit. 2. Ability of a computer to perform both data transmission and data computations at the same time. 3. Transmission of data where each character has a start and stop element that independently controls the data stream.

asynchronous I/O *(POS)* POSIX.4 (real-time operating system) term. Form of interprocess communication that enables a process to initiate multiple, simultaneous input/output requests to devices, e.g. disks. *See* POSIX.4 and RTOS.

asynchronous terminal Terminal designed to send and receive data asynchronously. Start and stop bits are used to indicate if the terminal is going to send or is ready to receive data.

Asynchronous Transfer Mode
Commonly abbreviated and called ATM. *See* ATM.

Asynchronous Transfer Mode Forum
Commonly abbreviated and called ATM Forum. *See* ATM Forum.

at Command that allows several commands to be run later and allows the user

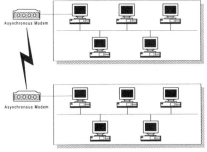

Asynchronous modems often are used to link workgroups.

to specify the time those commands are to be executed. *See* batch, atq, atrm, atrun and cron.

ATF Automatic Track Following. Signals used in Digital Audio Tape technology to center the tape head on the data track. *See* DAT and DDS.

Athena Toolkit Original X Window System toolkit or X library released by the Massachusetts Institute of Technology's Project Athena. *See* X toolkit.

Athena widget set Set of X Window System software widget development tools, e.g. buttons and scrollbars, originally provided with the X software package released by the Massachusetts Institute of Technology's Project Athena. *See* widget.

Atlanta 17 Forerunner of the Houston 30 which became the User Alliance for Open Systems. *See* User Alliance for Open Systems.

Atlas Also called UI-ATLAS. UNIX International Inc. architecture for computer and network management similar to the Open Systems Interconnection networking model. Contains five layers: an operating system, communication protocols, system performance tools, user interface to applications and programming tools. Introduced in 1991. *See* UI and OSI.

ATM 1. Asynchronous Transfer Mode. Also called cell relay. A digital switching standard developed by the International Telecommunication Union Telecommunication Standardization Sector, formerly called the Consultative Committee on International Telegraphy and Telephony. Applies to a synchronous network that can simultaneously transmit data, voice and full-motion video signals for multimedia use over local and wide area networks on fiber-optic cable. Packet technology that uses small fixed-sized packets (53 bytes) which permit data, graphics, still and motion video, and voice signals to be transmitted. The packets use 5 bytes for control, e.g. header information, and 48 bytes for data. An ATM network can transmit information at 25 megabits per second between desktop terminals up to 2.4 gigabits per second between nodes on a network. In the event of a sudden large, rapid increase in traffic, an ATM network can dynamically allocate additional capacity to handle the load. When the traffic increase ends, that capacity can be re-allocated. Developed in the early 1980s and based upon metropolitan area network standard. *See* ITU-T, LAN, WAN, MAN, STM, SONET, multimedia technology and fiber-optic. **2.** Automated Teller Machine. Computerized system used in banking. Introduced in the 1970s for withdrawing and depositing money without the personal assistance of a teller.

ATM Forum **A**synchronous **T**ransfer **M**ode **Forum**. Consortium of companies formed to establish specifications for interoperability of Asynchronous Transfer Mode products. Among its more than 250 company members are AT&T Co., IBM Corp. and Motorola Inc. Headquartered in Mountain View, California. *See* ATM.

atomicity Relational database term for an all-or-nothing guarantee of the completion of a transaction.

atq *(ATT)* **at** **q**ueue. Command used to provide a list of the *at* jobs that are waiting to be run. *See* at.

atrm *(ATT)* **at** **r**e**m**ove. Command used to remove either the *at* or batch jobs that have been queued to be run later. *See* at and batch.

atrun **At** **run**. System program responsible for running the *at* programs. Activated by the cron daemon on a regular basis. Checks the *at* directory for programs that are to be run. *See* at, cron and batch.

at sign (@) **1.** Metacharacter. Used as the line kill character on standard UNIX systems. *See* metacharacter and kill character. **2.** Character used in the vi editor to indicate a line has been deleted. *See* vi. **3.** *(INET)* Character used to an Internet electronic-mail address. Precedes the name of the computer to which the message is being sent. For example:

ker@tis.llnl.gov

indicates the mail message is being sent to user "ker" at the "tis.llnl.gov" host. *See* Internet, SNMP, e-mail, domain and bang path.

Attached Resource Computer NETwork ARCnet Commonly abbreviated and called ARCnet. *See* ARCnet.

Attached Resource Computer NETwork ARCnet Plus Commonly abbreviated and called ARCnet Plus. *See* ARCnet.

attachment Commonly called enclosure. *See* enclosure.

attach routine Program used during startup or autoconfiguration to establish the software necessary for the computer to communicate with and control external devices, e.g. printers, modems and terminals. *See* autoconfiguration.

AT&T Co. Parent company of Bell Laboratories, at which the initial UNIX operating system, C language and utilities such as Writer's Workbench were developed by Brian Kernighan, Dennis Ritchie and Ken Thompson. Sold the rights to UNIX to UNIX System Laboratories Inc. in 1993. *See* UNIX, USL, C language, WWB, Kernighan, Brian W. and Ritchie, Dennis M.

atto Prefix for 10 (1/1,000,000,000,000,000,000) or one-quintillionth. Commonly abbreviated a.

attributes 1. Characteristics of a file, program, variable, etc. *See* file attributes. 2. Characteristics of a hardware device, peripheral, application program, etc., that is attached to a computer or communications network.

AT&T Windowing Utilities Set of programs included in UNIX System V, Release 4 for developing window environments. *See* SVR4.x and window.

audit Review of the operating system for problems or security violations.

auditing Process of reviewing data regarding the use of the system that has been collected by the computer operating system, e.g. to determine possible security violations or configuration requirements.

auditing programs Programs that examine, or audit, functions on the system and identify potential problems, e.g. configuration requirements, or security violations. *See* find and secure.

AURORA One of the gigabit test-bed networks developed by the U.S. government, industry and university representatives. Tests technologies and applications which are used in implementing networks and supercomputers capable of transmitting gigabits of data per second. Designed to test Asynchronous Transfer Mode, an IBM Corp. high-speed protocol, multimedia applications, host interface devices and switches. Participating in AURORA are Bell Atlantic, BellCore, IBM Corp., Massachusetts Institute of Technology, MCI, NYNEX and the University of Pennsylvania. *See* HPCC, NREN, ATM, BLANCA, CASA, MAGIC, NECTAR and VISTANet.

authentication Process of verifying a user, computer, program or other's identity and level of authorized access to a network, computer, program or other part of a system.

authentication service Facility used on computers which are part of a network to determine a user's right and level of access to the network. *See* authentication and Kerberos.

auto-answer modem Modem set to automatically answer data communications (telephone calls) and connect remote callers to the host computer. *See* modem and ACU.

auto-boot Parameter set on a computer system by the system administrator. When it is on, if there is a crash the computer will automatically try to come back up to the level set by the system administrator, e.g. single user or multiple user. If it is off, the system will stay down until

---

the system administrator manually brings the computer back up.

Auto Call Unit Commonly abbreviated and called ACU. *See* ACU.

autoconfiguration Process during booting, or bootstrapping, in which a computer identifies the external hardware attached to the system and then loads the software required to operate that hardware. *See* attach routine and boot.

autoexec Ability of an operating system to start automatically when turned on. *See* boot.

autoindent Commonly abbreviated and called ai. *See* ai.

automated penetration Use of a program to penetrate computer security.

automatic line feed Command set in either software or hardware to advance the paper by a line when a printer receives a carriage return command. *See* linefeed and carriage return.

automatic mount list List of remote resources that are automatically made available when the Remote File Sharing system is started. *See* share, automatic share table, share table and RFS.

automatic reboot Ability of a computer system to restart itself after an error has caused the system to fail.

automatic share table List of resources that are automatically made available to remote users when the Remote File Sharing system is started. *See* share, share table, automatic mount list and RFS.

Automatic Track Following Commonly abbreviated and called ATF. *See* ATF.

automount Daemon used to automatically mount the Network File System. Used with the master map to activate remote resources. Also maintains a record of actual or attempted use of all NFS-related directories. *See* daemon, NFS, automounter, direct map and master map.

automounter Feature in the Network File System that permits remote resources to be activated as they are required. When a user no longer needs the resource, it is unmounted. This is done without any special effort by the system administrator. *See* NFS, automount, direct map and master map.

auto-nice Feature that allows the scheduling priority of a long-running process to be automatically adjusted downward, allowing processing of other jobs. *See* nice.

autoprint Variable in the ex and vi editors. *See* ap, ex and vi.

autowrite Commonly abbreviated and called aw. *See* aw.

AUUG Australian UNIX System Users' Group formed in 1975.

A/UX Apple Macintosh UNIX. A variation of the UNIX operating system developed by Apple Computer Inc. to run on the Macintosh computer. Based on System V with Berkeley Software Distribution extensions.

auxiliary swapper Commonly abbreviated and called xsched. *See* xsched.

availability Continued operation of a computer, providing continuity of access and functionality to users.

avatar Also called the root user account on some computer systems. *See* root.

AVS/88 ABI Verification Suite/88. Application Binary Interface certification test developed by the 88open Consortium Ltd. Used to determine if a vendor's computer and operating system complies with the 88open standards. *See* 88open Consortium, ACT/88, ITS/88 and ABI.

aw Autowrite. Toggled vi option that, when set, automatically writes changes to a buffer before running vi editing program commands. *See* vi, toggle and noaw.

awk Command and programs named after developers Alfred **A**ho, Peter **W**einberger and Brian **K**ernighan. Used for simple database management functions. The awk command allows users to search for specific strings or relationships and then, depending on the output of the search, perform a function. The following awk example calculates the average of a list of numbers read from standard input (stdin):

```
awk 'BEGIN {total = 0} \
    {total +=$1}
    END {print total/NR}'
```

See nawk, Perl, string, CPU and DBMS.

awm Window manager in the X 11, Release 3 version of the X Window System. *See* twm.

B

b 1. Abbreviation for bit. *See* bit. 2. Abbreviation for baud. *See* baud. 3. Abbreviation for binary. *See* binary.

B Abbreviation for **byte**. *See* byte.

babble 1. Cross-talk between two or more communications channels. 2. Also called computerese. *See* computerese.

Baby Bells Jargon for the Regional Bell Operating Companies. *See* RBOC.

back Backgammon. Command used to start a backgammon game.

backbone Network that provides primary connectivity between hosts or hosts and nodes on a network. *See* node.

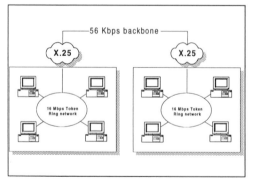

In the above example, an X.25 network transmits information between two networks.

back clipping plane Distance beyond which graphic objects are not displayed on a screen.

back door Software or hardware hole in a computer system that allows system security to be bypassed.

back end Jargon for a database application program running on a server that responds to client computer requests. Functions include data protection, storage and manipulation. *See* front end and client/server.

background Processing environment in which shells or programs operate at a low priority, independently of the input media, and do not tie up system resources. This allows a user to run additional shells or programs at the same time. When the background operation is finished, a notice is sent to the screen. Shells or programs operating in the foreground receive higher processing priority because they tie up terminals and other output devices until their operations are completed. *See* background process and ampersand.

background job Commonly called background process. *See* background process.

background process Command, program and/or process that has a low processing priority and does not tie up system resources. Initiated either by a user or program and operates independently of an input device. When a user starts a background process, the terminal is freed and other commands may be entered. Also referred to as background program. *See* ampersand and job control.

background program Commonly called background process. *See* background process.

backing storage Secondary storage area used to hold a process temporarily moved from main memory as a result of paging or swapping. *See* process, secondary storage, paging and swapping.

backplane Circuitry needed to connect the various boards and elements required for a computer system to operate.

backquote (') Symbol for backquote. Character used in shell scripts to identify a command that is to be executed. The command's output is interpreted as parameters to the original command.

backslash (\) For personal computer users, in UNIX, this is not a file separator. Rather, it is a metacharacter used in regular expressions in the ed, ex, vi, sed, grep, egrep and awk programs to turn off the special meaning of the metacharacters. *See* regular expression, slash and metacharacter.

backspace To move the cursor to the left one or more spaces or columns. Deletes the characters in those spaces. *See* cursor and backspace key.

backspace key Key found on most keyboards that is used to move the cursor to the left one space or column at a time. Alternatively, Ctrl h or the left arrow key can be used to move the cursor to the left one space at a time. In the vi editor, either of the above alternatives can be used in the edit mode, or "h" or "number h" can be used to backspace one or a number of spaces. *See* arrow keys and vi.

backup 1. *(ATT/XEN)* Program used to perform incremental file backups. Provides the ability to run file backups in an interactive mode. 2. Also spelled back-up and back up. To make a copy of files to an alternative storage medium that is kept in the event the primary storage medium fails and the data is damaged or lost. A process that should be done regularly whether using a mainframe, mini, micro or personal computer. For mainframe, mini or microcomputer systems, backups are normally done to tape. On personal computers using diskettes, backups are recorded on an alternative set of diskettes. Personal computers with hard disks are backed up either to diskettes or streaming

tape. Failures can be caused either by human error where a file, directory or the entire disk or diskette is erased. Failures also can be caused by the mechanical failure of a disk that erases data or destroys the disk. *See* full backup, partial backup and incremental backup.

backup table *(ATT)* Table which contains information related to backups, e.g. instructions, timing, criteria, list of files to be backed up and storage medium to be used. *See* bkreg.

bacteria Commonly called logic bomb. *See* logic bomb.

BAD **B**roken **a**s **d**esigned. Jargon for a program that does not work well or at all due to poor design.

bad144 *(BSD)* Command that marks bad blocks on a disk drive and reallocates new blocks that are to be substituted. Can be used only on systems that follow the DEC Standard 144 for disk formatting. *See* block, DEC Standard 144., badsect and badblk.

badblk *(ATT)* **Bad bl**ock. Command used to repair bad blocks of disk space on a system. *See* block and bad block.

bad block Any area of a mass storage device, e.g. a disk, that is unable to properly store data.

badsect *(BSD)* **Bad sect**or. Command used to repair bad blocks of disk space on systems that are unable to use the bad144 command. *See* bad144.

bad sector Area of a mass storage device, e.g. a disk, that cannot be used due to incorrect formatting or a physical defect. *See* sector.

bad sector forwarding Ability of a computer to automatically redirect information addressed to a bad sector to a good sector of a mass storage device. *See* sector.

bad sector table Table maintained by the computer of good sectors that are available on a mass storage device. When the computer finds information addressed to a bad sector, it checks the bad sector table to find available good sectors in which to store the data. *See* bad sector forwarding.

bandwidth Measurement of the range of frequencies available for transmitting signals. For example, the bandwidth of a communications network is determined by subtracting the lowest frequency from the highest frequency in the combinations band, measured in bits per second. The bandwidth of a display monitor measures the frequency range to which the monitor can respond, measured in megahertz.

bandwidth on demand Ability of a communications network to automatically expand the bandwidth committed to a user and/or transmission when needed, e.g. to support an increase in voice, video conferencing or multimedia transmissions. *See* ATM.

BANG Jargon for exclamation point. *See* exclamation point.

bang path Address syntax used by UNIX-to-UNIX CoPy (UUCP). In the bang path the host name(s) is followed by the user name, and the two are separated by an exclamation point, e.g. lrc-eds!twallen is the bang path to send an electronic-mail message to a host named lrc-eds and a user called twallen. If the host does not have a direct link with lrc-eds and the message has to be routed to a host, wp-eds, that does have such a link, the bang path becomes wp-eds!lrc-eds!twallen. *See* UUCP, exclamation point and e-mail.

bang syntax UNIX-to-UNIX CoPy format for routing that uses an exclamation point as a separator between elements of the address. For example:

wp-eds!kjohnson

indicates a host named wp-eds and a user named kjohnson. *See* bang path.

banner *(ATT)* Command to create a banner of characters. The limit is 10 characters per 80-column line. Standard output is to the input terminal but can be redirected to a file or alternative device. *See* standard output, redirect and device.

bar Derived from foobar. *See* foobar.

bar code Code that appears in bars of different widths mainly on consumer product labels. The width of each bar has a specific meaning or value, e.g. the price of an item. The code can be electrically or optically read with a scanner and converted to data.

barf Jargon for a software program that stops. *See* ABEND.

barrelling Distortion on a video monitor resulting in a bulge in the top, sides and/or bottom of an image. *See* blooming, bowing, convergence, flicker, keystone, persistence and pincushioning.

bas *(ATT)* **Bas**ic. Interactive command language similar to BASIC. *See* BASIC.

base Also called a radix. Basis for a system of numbers, e.g. base 2 for binary, base 8 for octal, base 10 for decimal and base 16 for hexadecimal. *See* binary, octal, decimal and hexadecimal.

baseband Communication term for a network that uses a single unmodulated signal. All nodes on the network must be involved in every transmission. *See* node and broadband.

Base Brand X/Open Co. Ltd.'s branding program for a basic operating environment standard. *See* X/Open and brand program.

basename *(ATT/XEN)* General-purpose library routine that provides a file name by removing the path extensions, leaving only the file name. *See* library routines and dirname.

base priority First priority assigned to a process.

BASE Profile Minimum set of software components that make up X/Open Co. Ltd.'s Common Applications Environment, the set of standards defined in the X/Open Portability Guides. Includes definitions for system calls and libraries, commands and utilities, C language, and internationalization. *See* X/Open, CAE,

XPG, PLUS Profile and OPTIONAL Components.

base standard Document defining a limited subject, e.g. a graphical user interface or communication protocol. *See* standard and profile.

bash Bourne Again Shell. Free Software Foundation's shell or command interpreter that provides Bourne shell syntax, command line editing, job control and C shell command history. *See* shell, C shell, rbash and FSF.

BASIC Beginner's All-Purpose Symbolic Instruction Code. Basic programming language used for personal computers. Developed at Dartmouth University in the 1960s specifically for academic computing use, but now widely used because it is relatively easy to learn and to use in developing applications.

Basic Combination Programming Language Commonly abbreviated and called BCPL. *See* BCPL.

basic commands Commands that are most used by UNIX users. *See* cat, cd, echo, exit, man, more and who.

Basic Encoding Rules Commonly abbreviated and called BER. *See* BER.

basic input/output system Commonly abbreviated and called BIOS. *See* BIOS.

Basic Network Utilities Commonly abbreviated and called BNU. *See* BNU.

basic rate interface Commonly abbreviated and called BRI. *See* BRI.

batch *(ATT)* Command that provides the user a method of running several commands later. Executes the commands when resources are available, not at a specified time.

batch processing 1. Running several data processing jobs in a group, sequentially. **2.** Running only one process at a time. One process has to be completed before the next can start.

Batch Simple Mail Transfer Protocol Commonly abbreviated and called BSMTP. *See* BSMTP.

baud Measurement of the number of bits per second that can be transmitted in a system. Named for Emile Baudot (1845-1903), who developed the Baudot Code originally used to measure the speed of telegraph transmissions.

baud rate Data transmission speed measured in approximately 1 bit per second, e.g. 2400 baud equals 240 8-bit characters per second with start and stop characters.

BB Bulletin Board. The named server or address manager of the Tuxedo System/T or core transaction monitor that allows multiple users to access and send transactions to a server at the same time element of Tuxedo. Also maintains statistics on address usage to provide load balancing. *See* Tuxedo System/T and Tuxedo.

BBS Bulletin board system. Information exchange system provided by vendors, computer organizations or commercially, through subscription. A user can gain access to a BBS by computer using a phone/modem or, if the BBS is part of an existing network, through the communications network itself. Once logged in, the user can search for specific information, public domain software or personal messages, or deposit information for others to use. Note: Software taken from a BBS has been known to contain viruses. Users should check such software and use it with caution.

bc *(ATT/BSD/XEN)* Basic calculator. Interactive desk calculator that is a preprocessor for a dc, an interactive desk calculator program. Has a high-level syntax similar to C language and is capable of basic mathematical computations. Co-authored by Lorinda Cherry and Robert Morris. *See* dc.

BCD 1. Binary coded decimal. Data coding process that uses a set of four binary 0s and 1s to represent data. Predecessor to the Extended Binary Coded Decimal Interchange Code used to encode data on punch (Hollerith) cards. *See* binary and EBCDIC. **2.** *(BSD)* Command used to convert text into a punch card image.

bcheck *(ATT)* Boot **check**. Older program used to run file system checks. Replaced by the more comprehensive fsck command. *See* fsck, file consistency check and file system.

bcheckrc *(ATT)* Boot **check** run control. Shell script for initializing the system. Run by the init daemon before starting the run level of the system. *See* shell script, init and /etc/rc?.d.

/bck *(ATT)* Backup. UNIX System V, Release 4 root file system directory used to hold (mount) the file system needed to recover files. *See* SVR4.x and file system.

BCPL **B**asic **C**ombination **P**rogramming **L**anguage. Forerunner of MULTICS, UNIX, B language, C language and C++ language. Developed at Cambridge University in the late 1960s by Martin Richards. *See* MULTICS, B language, C language, UNIX and C++ language.

BCS **1.** **B**inary **C**ompatibility **S**pecification. Temporary set of standards outlining the requirements of System V binary compatibility. Incorporated into and replaced by Application Binary Interface. *See* binary and ABI. **2.** **B**inary Compatibility Standard. Set of standards developed by the 88open Consortium Ltd. Used to develop applications that can be run on various versions of the UNIX operating system which are installed on computers using the 88000 microprocessor from Motorola Inc. *See* BCS1 and BCS2. **3.** **B**inary Compatible **S**oftware. Software that is developed to a binary standard. Allows software to be freely transferred between computers of the same type, e.g. Lotus Development Corp.'s software, developed using BCS for the Intel 386 microprocessor, can run on either a DOS or UNIX 386 computer. *See* shrink-wrapped.

BCS1 **B**inary **C**ompatibility **S**tandard 1. First set of standards for developing applications to run on the XENIX operating system. *See* BCS, b and XENIX.

BCS2 **B**inary **C**ompatibility **S**tandard 2. Second set of standards for developing applications to run with UNIX System V, Release 4.3. *See* SVR4.x and BCS.

BCUUG **B**ritish **C**olumbia **U**NIX **U**sers **G**roup. UNIX users group formed in 1984.

bdevsw **B**lock **dev**ice **sw**itch table. Table containing the kernel data structure used to map into a device driver address each number that specifically identifies what type of device and device driver is required for a block device. *See* block device, cdevsw, mapping, major device number and device driver.

BDF **B**itmap **D**isplay **F**ont. Also called **B**itmap **D**istribution **F**ormat. X Window System font format based upon the American Standard Code for Information Interchange (ASCII) bitmap. As a result of being ASCII format, BDF is slower than other fonts since the ASCII format has to be converted to a bitmap before being displayed. *See* X Window System, ASCII, PCF and SNF.

bdiff *(ATT/XEN)* **B**ig **diff** or difference. Variation of the diff command used to compare extremely large files. *See* diff.

beautify Variable in the ex and vi editors. Commonly abbreviated bf. *See* bf.

Because It's Time Network Commonly abbreviated and called BITNET. *See* BITNET.

beep Audible sound that emanates from a terminal normally because an error has been made in an input. Result of receiving a Ctrl g signal from the computer.

Beginner's All-Purpose Symbolic Instruction Code Commonly abbreviated and called BASIC. *See* BASIC.

BEE-ROUTER Pronunciation of brouter. *See* brouter.

Beginning of Tape Commonly abbreviated and called BOT. *See* BOT.

behavior Object Management Group term for computations that produce a final product or generate another request. *See* OMG and request.

Beijing Computer virus found in European and Canadian computers to commemorate the June 4, 1989 incident at China's Tienanmen Square. *See* virus.

bell Commonly called beep. *See* beep.

BellCore Bell Communications **Research**. Formed following the 1984 AT&T Co. divestiture. Performs a research and development function for the Bell Operating Companies and Regional Bell Operating Companies.

Bell Laboratories Developer of UNIX and the C language. Division of AT&T Co. responsible for research and development of computer systems and communications.

bells and whistles Jargon for added functionality or features provided in either a hardware or software product that makes it more attractive to buyers.

benchmark Specified standard to which numeric values can be assigned and against which performance can be measured. *See* user-level benchmark and kernel-level benchmark.

benchmark suite Collection of benchmarks, or standards, that measure the ability of computer hardware, application software or an operating system to perform functions, e.g. the time taken to perform one or more processes, and throughput and input/output speed. *See* benchmark.

BER 1. Bit error rate. Measurement of the cleanliness of a transmission line in the number of errors for a set of bits, e.g. 1 per 10^5 BER. 2. Basic Encoding Rules. Data encoding rules for Open Systems Interconnect language. *See* OSI.

Berkeley Computer Systems Research Group Commonly abbreviated and called CSRG. *See* CSRG.

Berkeley enhancement Program originally developed for the University of California, Berkeley, version of UNIX and then incorporated into a standard UNIX release by either a vendor or user, e.g. the more command. *See* more.

Berkeley Internet Name Domain Commonly abbreviated and called BIND. *See* BIND.

Berkeley Quality Software Commonly abbreviated and called BQS. *See* BQS.

Berkeley services Group of UNIX network commands developed by the University of California, Berkeley. *See* rcp, rlogin, rsh, rwho, ruptime and sendmail.

Berkeley Software Distribution Commonly abbreviated and called BSD. *See* BSD.

beta test Pre-production test of a new software or hardware product. Conducted at an end-user's site in a standard production environment. Used to identify and fix any problems that arise in a production environment before general release of the product. *See* system test and alpha test.

bf Beautify. Option in the ex and vi editors that, when set, prevents the user from entering most control characters into a text file. Exceptions include tab, new line and form feed. *See* ex and vi.

BFD Big f@#$&*% deal. Jargon used to express indignation over policy decisions that have an impact on computer operations.

bfs 1. *(ATT/XEN)* Big file scanner. Command used to scan very large files that cannot be accessed using standard UNIX editors. In this mode, the files cannot be changed by the user, but most of the ed commands and functionality can be used. *See* ed. 2. Boot file system. Special type of file system in UNIX System V that contains the standalone programs needed to start the operating system.

bg Background. Command used to restart in the background a process that has been suspended. *See* background, foreground, fg, resume and stop.

---

biased scheduling Enhanced UNIX scheduling process that enables system administrators to set upper and lower limits on the amount of central processing unit time used by a specific process. *See* scheduling and CPU.

BiCMOS Bipolar Complementary Metal Oxide Semiconductor. Integrated chip technology used in designing high-density, high-performance integrated circuits.

bidirectional 1. Flow of data either to or from a point, using the same communications link, e.g. from a central processing unit through a bus to peripheral devices. 2. Type of printer on which the print head moves from left to right and then from right to left, without making a carriage return.

bidirectional printing Method of printing in which the print head moves from left to right and then from right to left, without making a carriage return. Used to increase the printer's speed.

biff 1. *(BSD)* **B**ark **if** from **f**ound. Command used to notify the system that users are to be informed when new electronic mail arrives. *See* e-mail. 2. Jargon term for notifying a user that a new electronic-mail message has arrived.

Big Blue Jargon for IBM Corp., referring to the traditional blue color of the older System/360 and System/370 computer systems.

big I *(INET)* Jargon for the Internet, when spelled with a capital I. *See* Internet.

big iron Jargon for large mainframe computers with high-powered central processing units, fast throughput and numerous disks encased in large metal cabinets. Capable of handling large numbers of instructions, users, transactions and data. *See* mainframe and dinosaur.

bigot Anyone who is totally prejudiced toward a particular operating system, computer vendor, etc.

billion instructions per second Commonly abbreviated and called BIPS. *See* BIPS.

billisecond Commonly called nanosecond. *See* NS.

bin Abbreviation for **bin**ary. *See* binary.

/bin UNIX root directory that contains the executable commands. Also can be established by a user to locate either non-system or user-unique executable files. Named for binary.

binaries Jargon for binary software. *See* binary software.

binary Numbering system that has only two numbers, 0 (off) and 1 (on), which are used for the storage of computer information. Numbers between 0 and 255 can be stated with an eight-digit binary number. Binary digits are called bits.

binary code Commonly called binary software. *See* binary software.

binary coded decimal Commonly abbreviated and called BCD. *See* BCD.

Binary Compatibility Specification Commonly abbreviated and called BCS. *See* BCS.

binary compatibility standard Commonly called shrink-wrapped. *See* shrink-wrapped.

binary digit Commonly abbreviated and called bit. *See* bit.

binary distribution Compiled release of an operating system. *See* binary software and source code.

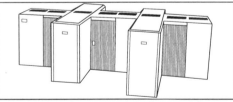

Big iron is the term used for large mainframe computers

binary file File containing data in binary words, which is in machine readable form. *See* binary.

binary large object. Commonly abbreviated and called BLOB. *See* BLOB.

binary license License that allows the user to run a software program, but not to modify it. With a binary license, the user receives a compiled version of the kernel without any source files.

binary number Commonly called binary. *See* binary.

binary semaphores *(POS)* POSIX.4 (real-time operating system) term. Used to synchronize several processes that are working on one function. *See* POSIX.4 and RTOS.

binary software Software compiled into computer readable form. Also called binary code, or binary distribution when referring to a release of an operating system which does not contain source code.

binary synchronous communications Commonly abbreviated and called bisync. *See* bisync.

bind Communications term for disabling a receiving device, e.g. a gateway, router or bridge, so it will not receive specific types of data.

BIND *(INET)* **B**erkeley **I**nternet **N**ame **D**omain server. 4.3 Berkeley Software Distribution program that manages the host and Internet Protocol address relationship. Matches the hostname, e.g. smeds, with the Internet Protocol numeric address, e.g. 26.21.0.4. *See* Internet, IP Address and Internet Protocol Suite.

binding 1. Object Management Group term for combining programs and the data related to a request in response to that request. *See* OMG, request, static binding and dynamic binding. **2.** Term related to the Network File System to describe both a client's search for a server that has required information and the process of establishing communications with the server. **3.** *(POS)* Programming

and operating system term for interface between an application, database, operating system, etc. For example, the Institute of Electrical and Electronic Engineers Project 1003.1c working group has developed the Portable Operating System Interface for Computer Environments specification for the bindings or interface between the kernel and C language. *See* POSIX and C language. **4.** Program compiler process of changing a symbolic name or address to machine language.

bin-mail Commonly written /bin/mail. *See* /bin/mail and mail.

/bin/mail Also spelled bin-mail. Original electronic-mail system used to deliver local mail. *See* mail.

biod 1. Block **i**nput/**o**utput **d**aemon. Background program used to start and manage input and output of block data for the Network File System. Automatically started when NFS become available to users. *See* daemon, block and NFS. **2.** Network administration command used to start the block input/output daemon.

BIOS Basic **I**nput/**O**utput **S**ystem. MS-DOS term for a layer of software built into the hardware that provides a standard interface to disks, keyboard, monitor and some communications hardware. Provides an interface between the central processing unit and peripheral devices, as well as a method of control for the central processing unit over those devices. *See* CPU and peripheral.

biosensor Specialized input device, e.g. glasses or bracelets, used to measure muscle movement through electrodes that monitor the electrical activity of muscles. *See* virtual reality.

Bipolar Complementary Metal Oxide Semiconductor Commonly abbreviated and called BiCMOS. *See* BiCMOS.

BIPS Billion **i**nstructions **p**er second. *See* MIPS.

birds-of-a-feather Commonly abbreviated and called BOF. *See* BOF.

BISDN Broadband Integrated Services Digital Network. Based upon the Integrated Services Digital Network, BISDN is a set of specifications for an end-to-end integrated voice, video, digital data and packet switch data network operating at between 150 and 600 megabits per second. The backbone transport mechanism is provided by Asynchronous Transfer Mode, a digital switching standard for a synchronous network capable of simultaneously transmitting data, voice and full-motion video for multimedia use over local and wide area networks on fiber-optic cable. *See* ISDN and ATM.

BISON 1. Bull, ICL, Siemens, Olivetti and Nixdorf. Jargon term for the five European computer companies that formed X/Open Co. Ltd. Note: Siemens and Nixdorf is now Siemens-Nixdorf. *See* X/Open. **2.** Version of yacc, the UNIX parsing utility. Found in the GNU is Not UNIX operating system. *See* FSF, GNU, yacc and parse.

bisync Binary Synchronous Communications. Old protocol that used special characters to identify the beginning and end of each unit of data transmitted. Developed by IBM Corp. for synchronous transmission of data.

bisynchronous communication
Commonly abbreviated and called bisync. *See* bisync.

bit Binary digit. Smallest unit of data understood by a computer. *See* binary and byte.

bit block transfer Commonly abbreviated and called bitblt. *See* bitblt.

bitblt Bit block transfer. Method of clearing, setting or moving a graphics image by moving individual pixels (bits). Simultaneously manipulates data in blocks of bits rather than a single bit of data at a time. *See* bit and pixel.

bit bucket Imaginary bucket into which all characters, files, directories and other information is sent when lost because either the user presses the wrong key, or

the output is redirected to the UNIX bit bucket (/dev/null), or the computer crashes and is not capable of saving the document the user has been working on.

bit error rate Commonly abbreviated and called BER. *See* BER.

bitmap 1. Sequential bits used to graphically represent images. Commonly called raster graphics. *See* raster graphics. **2.** Jargon for the graphic presentation produced by manipulating bits to form a picture on a monitor.

bit map Commonly spelled bitmap. *See* bitmap.

Bitmap Display Font Commonly abbreviated and called BDF. *See* BDF.

Bitmap Distribution Format
Commonly abbreviated and called BDF. *See* BDF.

bit-mapped graphics M o n o c h r o m e, grayscale and color terminal technology that enables each pixel on a screen to be controlled by a specified bit (location) in memory. Accurate control of each pixel makes graphics displays sharper. *See* pixel, grayscale, 2-D data and 3-D data.

BITNET Because It's Time Network. Academic computer network, started at City University of New York, that in combination with the Computer+Science Network has become the Corporation for Research and Educational Networking. *See* CSNET and CREN.

bit pattern Data stored and displayed in a pattern that has specific meaning to a computer or application program.

bit plane Graphics term indicating the number (or depth) of bits that represent a single pixel. Most monochrome monitors have a single bit plane while grayscale and color monitors have several (usually in powers of 2). *See* pixel.

bits per second Commonly abbreviated and called bps. *See* bps.

bitwise 1. Manipulating data as a string or series of bits. *See* bit. **2.** Instructions in

C language that include the bitwise AND (&), inclusive OR (|), exclusive OR (^), shift left (<), shift right (>) and one's complement (~).

bj Blackjack. Command used to start a blackjack game.

bkreg *(ATT)* Backup **reg**ister. Command used to establish and maintain a backup table. *See* backup table.

blackout Total loss of electrical power (zero volts) for more than one cycle.

BLANCA One of the gigabit test-bed networks developed by the U.S. government, industry and university representatives. Tests technologies and applications used in implementing networks and super-computers which can transmit gigabits of data per second. Designed to test various aspects of Asynchronous Transfer Mode (ATM), e.g. hardware, distributed applications and operation of Internet protocols over ATM. Participating in BLANCA are AT&T Co., Lawrence Berkeley Laboratories, National Center for Supercomputing Applications at the University of Illinois, University of California, Berkeley, and University of Wisconsin. *See* HPCC, NREN, ATM, Internet, AURORA, CASA, MAGIC, NECTAR and VISTANet.

B language Forerunner of the C language. An early machine-transportable programming language derived from the Basic Combined Programming Language. Developed in the late 1960s by Ken Thompson and further modified by Dennis Ritchie, both of AT&T Co.'s Bell Laboratories. The new language was named C language and used to write the UNIX operating system. *See* C language, Project Mac, Space Travel, Thompson, Ken, Ritchie, Dennis M., Project MAC, Space Travel and Bell Laboratories.

blank character Empty space considered to be a character and generated by depressing the space bar on a keyboard.

blank line Line containing no characters, generated by either depressing the enter or return key on a keyboard, or entering a carriage return and line feed command from a program.

bleeding edge Sarcastic variation of the term leading edge. Implies that the latest technology being implemented is failing painfully or is takes a lot of hard work to keep operating. *See* leading edge.

BLOB **B**inary **l**arge **ob**ject. Files in object-oriented or relational database management systems that are used to store large, undetermined types of data. Data cannot be edited in these files. *See* OO and RDBMS.

block 1. *(ATT)* Shell layer command used to stop the display of output from one shell layer while the user is working in another shell layer. *See* shl, resume and unblock. 2. Measurement of the amount of data maintained as a unit in input or output devices; or the capacity of a storage device, file system, file or directory; or how that space is allocated. AT&T UNIX systems (prior to System V, Release 4) use 512-byte blocks; XENIX systems use 512-byte blocks; Berkeley Software Distribution systems (other than the fast file system) use 1,014-byte blocks and the fast file system uses 8,192-byte blocks. *See* byte, data block, file system, boot block, super block, inode and storage block.

block address Location of a block on a disk. *See* block.

block device Storage device, e.g. a disk drive, that supports the input and output of data in blocks of fixed size, either 512 bytes or 1,024 bytes. *See* character device and block I/O.

block device files Commonly called block special file. *See* block special file.

block device interface 1. Software interface developed specifically to address block devices, e.g. disk drives, tape drives and controllers, within the UNIX kernel. *See* block device table. 2. Device that incorporates some kind of data buffering. *See* raw device.

block device table List maintained in the computer of all pieces of hardware capable of transmitting blocks of data, including all standard hardware which the computer manufacturer thinks may be connected to the computer. Non-standard devices can be added to the list.

blocking factor Block size (number of bytes) of data to be transferred from one storage medium, e.g. a disk, to another, e.g. a tape. *See* block.

block I/O 1. Block input/output. Device used for passing blocks of data. **2.** Method of passing data in a group rather than a character at a time, thereby reducing the input/output time.

block number Commonly called block address. *See* block address.

block size 1. Predetermined size of a block of data maintained in a file system. Can vary among systems. *See* file system. **2.** Smallest unit of data that a block device can handle.

block special file Files that contain interface definitions for block devices, e.g. disk drives, tape drives and controllers. Provide the ability to establish block communication between the operating system and an input/output device, most commonly a disk drive. Mask the hardware characteristics of the device. *See* block device, block device interface and special file.

block started by symbol seqment
Commonly abbreviated and called bss segment. *See* bss segment.

block striping Disk and data management technique for writing alternating blocks of data across multiple disks. Blocks of data are alternately transferred to the disks in parallel. Provides for faster transfer of data by splitting the information in multiple paths that are written simultaneously. *See* striping, byte striping and RAID.

Block Transfer Commonly abbreviated and called BLT. *See* BLT.

blooming Distortion on a video monitor resulting in an image loosing focus when it becomes brighter. *See* barrelling, bowing, convergence, flicker, keystone, persistence and pincushioning.

blow away Jargon term for deliberately removing a file or directory.

BLT Block **T**ransfer. Data transfer method developed as part of the VMEbus to allow large, contiguous blocks of data to be moved.

Blue Book 1. Also called the Network Independent File Transfer Protocol. Specification for the file transfer protocol of the British national research and development network. *See* JANET. **2.** The 1988 communications standards developed by the International Telecommunication Union Telecommunication Standardization Sector, formerly called the Consultative Committee for International Telegraphy and Telephony. **3.** The 1985 reference guide on page-layout and graphics-control language for Adobe System Inc.'s PostScript printers.

B news Set of programs used by USENET, a worldwide UNIX bulletin board, to exchange messages. A rewritten version of A news, the first set of programs used for message exchange. Developed at the University of California, Berkeley. *See* USENET.

BNU Basic **N**etwork **U**tilities. Official AT&T Co. name for HoneyDanBer UNIX-to-UNIX CoPy. *See* HoneyDanBer UUCP.

board Jargon for a printed circuit board. *See* printed circuit board.

BOF Birds-of-a-feather. Informal meeting, at conferences, of people with a common interest in a subject, e.g. a specific operating system, the Internet or one of the Internet protocols, or electronic mail.

boilerplate Standardized formats and/or sections of text repetitively used in various documents. Originally a journalism term picked up in word processing.

bold Character attribute whereby strokes in the character are thicker than normal, making the character appear darker on a display screen or on a printed page.

boldface Commonly abbreviated and called bold. *See* bold.

bomb Program in a computer that starts an adverse action, e.g. a Trojan horse. Cannot spread or reproduce itself, unlike a virus or worm. Until started, remains inactive. *See* Trojan horse, virus and worm.

Boolean Pertaining to any data operation that assumes logical truth values, e.g. TRUE or FALSE, on or off, go or no-go.

Boolean operations 1. Instructions that operate on Boolean data types. Originate from Boolean algebra, named for George Boole, which works with logical rather than numerical relationships. *See* Boolean. 2. Logical programming operations (AND, OR, XOR and NOT).

boom Three-dimensional (3-D) display device used to replace head-mounted display units, e.g. 3-D glasses. A boom is suspended so it can swivel freely. The position of the boom communicates the user's location in relation to the image being projected to the computer. *See* 3-D graphics.

boot 1. Program used to start the UNIX operating system. 2. Bootstrapping. Used interchangeably with reboot. To make the system operational by starting the internal operation of the computer, loading the necessary software from secondary storage (tape or disk) to main memory and starting the programs. Generally, starting a program or computer. After a crash, a reboot is required to bring the system back to life. *See* bootstrapping.

/boot UNIX System V, Release 4 root file system directory that contains files used to configure a new operating system. *See* SVR4.x, UNIX and root file system.

boot block Area of a disk set aside for the programs needed to start the computer.

The first block on the first disk of a disk controller. *See* block.

bootdevice register List that contains the name of the device from which the system should be booted.

boothowto register List that controls the level, or state, to which the system should automatically be brought, e.g. single-user or multi-user.

BOOTP Bootstrap Protocol. Protocol for loading X Window System servers from the network. *See* X Window System.

bootparamd *(ATT)* **Boot parameter** daemon. Background program used to provide and manage the information required by a diskless workstation to start a client/server process. *See* daemon, diskless, client/server and boot.

boot program Small program used to bootstrap, or load and start, the UNIX kernel or other main program into a computer's main memory. *See* boot.

bootstrapping Formal name for the process of starting a computer. *See* boot, warm boot and cold boot.

bootstrap program Program that contains the instructions needed to start a computer. *See* boot.

Bootstrap Protocol Commonly abbreviated and called BOOTP. *See* BOOTP.

BOOT SUM Pronunciation of btsoom, the abbreviation for Beats the s@!t out of me. *See* btsoom.

BOT Beginning of tape. Jargon for the electrical mark used to indicate the beginning of data recorded on a magnetic tape.

bottom half Programs in the operating system that are started as a result of an interrupt signal. *See* top half.

bounce Jargon for taking the computer from multi-user state to single-user state, then back to multi-user state. Normally, a system administrator will bounce a computer when all other efforts have failed to correct a situation, e.g. to kill a process or clear a hung process. *See* state and hung.

Bourne Again Shell Commonly abbreviated and called bash. *See* bash.

Bourne shell Command language interpreter for UNIX System V and the Berkeley Software Distribution written by Steven R. Bourne. Available on most UNIX systems but lacks the user-interactive capabilities found in the C shell and K shell. Predominantly used for writing scripts. Uses the dollar sign ($) as the default prompt. *See* C shell and Korn shell.

bowing Distortion on a video monitor resulting in a curve, in the same direction, on opposite sides of an image. *See* barrelling, blooming, convergence, flicker, keystone, persistence and pincushioning.

box Jargon for computer hardware.

bpi Bits per inch. Measurement of the amount of data placed on a tape, per inch.

B protocol B news program rewritten to conform to the Defense Advanced Research Projects Agency protocols. *See* USENET, B news and DARPA.

bps Bits per second. Measurement of the speed at which data is transferred over a modem. To determine the number of characters a modem is capable of transferring per second, divide the bps rating by 10, e.g. a 4800 bps modem is capable of transferring 480 characters per second.

BQS Berkeley Quality Software. Jargon for software developed by a programmer of questionable expertise, with little or no testing and documentation.

braces {} **1.** Also referred to as the grouping command. Braces are used to mark the beginning and ending of program blocks executed by a process. For example, if a user wants the process to perform two separate functions, e.g. change directory (cd command) and then list (ls command) the contents of the directory and redirect the output to a new file, the commands along with the desired file paths would be enclosed in braces. **2.** Used when perform-

ing file expansion when normal wild card matching is not available. For example, if a user wants to copy or move files kay, ily and tnf located in the same directory to a new location, he would input the copy command, identifying the full directory path of the three files with the three files enclosed in braces and then followed by the path to where the user wants to move the files.

brackets [] Metacharacter used within regular expressions to match any character contained in the brackets. For example:

CLP> cat chapt[1,3,5,7] chapt.odd ⏎

combines files called chapt1, chapt3, chapt5 and chapt7 into a new file called chapt.odd. A hyphen can be used to separate the characters in the brackets and indicate a range. For example:

CLP> cat chapt[1-7] book ⏎

combines any file named chapt1, chapt2, chapt3, chapt4, chapt5, chapt6 or chapt7 into a new file named book. Used as a metacharacter within regular expressions for the ed, ex, vi, sed, grep, egrep and awk programs. *See* metacharacter and regular expression.

brain-damaged Jargon for a fundamental problem with application software or an operating system. There are two basic types of problems that can occur. First, the developers have left out elements of the software so it does not perform properly. Second, the software has become corrupted and no longer performs properly. *See* brain dead.

brain-dead Jargon for software that is not functioning. *See* brain-damaged.

branch Level of a hierarchical database or file system connected to the root or uppermost level of the hierarchy. *See* root and leaf.

branded subassembly Hardware component that is well-known and recognized within the industry, e.g. Intel Corp. and Motorola Inc. chips, NEC Corp. and Seagate Technology Inc. disk drives.

brand program X/Open Co. Ltd.'s program establishing standards to certify brands. Indicates a vendor's software has been tested and certified by X/Open and meets (and will continue to meet) X/Open open systems standards, based upon the specifications of the third edition of the X/Open Portability Guide (XPG). Once certified, the vendor can use the X/Open logo on the product. *See* X/Open, XPG, BASE Profile, PLUS Profile, Source Code Brand and Base Brand.

brc *(ATT)* Shell script for initializing the system before running /etc/rc?.d while taking the system from single-user to multi-user mode. *See* shell script, /etc/rc?.d and mode.

bread *(ATT)* **Block read.** UNIX kernel algorithm that provides buffered blocked input/output. The underlying kernel mechanism supporting block devices.

breada *(ATT)* **Block read a**head. UNIX kernel algorithm that provides blocked input/output with read-ahead capability. Implemented on the assumption that the most likely data block to be read next will be that immediately following the one just read.

break 1. Shell command that stops, or exits, a loop generated by a for, while, select or until command. *See* for, while, select, until and continue. 2. Interrupt signal sent to a process, program or communication message transmission. Stops the process, program or transmission.

breakpoint Mechanism to stop or suspend execution of a program at a specific address or location. In debugging, execution of a program is stopped when a breakpoint (an address, line number, function name or subroutine name) is reached.

breakpoint fault System trap, or signal, used to establish and manage breakpoints set by a system debugger. *See* breakpoint and debugger.

breaksw Break switch. Command used in C shell programming to indicate the end of switching commands, which are to be executed in a case string search. *See* case, C shell, endsw and swtch.

brelse *(ATT)* **Block release.** Kernel function used to scan for and release unused block data buffers.

BRI Basic Rate Interface. One of two types of Integrated Services Digital Networks. Uses a twisted pair cable divided into two 64 kilobit-per-second channels to carry data and voice traffic. Also called 2B + D for two bearer channels for voice and data and one signal channel for network management. *See* ISDN and PRI.

bridge Hardware device used to connect multiple networks by passing packets. Can pass all data between networks or be set to selectively pass traffic by filtering certain packets. Users on separate networks connected by a bridge appear to be on a single network. A bridge works at the data link layer (layer 2) in the Open Systems Interconnection. *See* OSI, OSIRM, data link layer, router, repeater, gateway and brouter.

British Standards Institute Commonly abbreviated and called BSI. *See* BSI.

brk *(ATT)* **Break.** System call used to increase the amount of memory allocated by a process. *See* system call and process.

broadband Local area network technology used to operate multiple communication networks on a single cable. Through broadband, messages are sent as radiofrequencies over single inbound and outbound cables, which are divided allowing different networks to operate through a separate frequency on the one cable. *See* LAN and baseband.

Broadband Integrated Services Digital Network Commonly abbreviated and called BISDN. *See* BISDN.

broadcast 1. Also called multicast. Information that is sent to either all or a large number of users of a system at the same time. *See* IP multicasting. 2. Request made by a host on an Ethernet network for information, e.g. the address of another host. *See* ARP and bootp.

broadcast message Similar to broadcast, except it generally refers to an immediate message that is sent only to those currently logged on to the system at the same time. *See* broadcast and wall.

broadcast storm Any message sent on a network which results in simultaneous responses from all nodes on the network. Each response then generates a simultaneous response from each of the other nodes. The generation and response of messages continues until the network goes down or steps are taken to break the cycle. Has many causes, from a malfunctioning system that sends spurious packets to an improper setting in which requests for input are sent in hundreds or thousands per second instead of one or two per second. *See* node.

broken as designed Commonly abbreviated and called BAD. *See* BAD.

broken pipe Signal sent to the writer of a pipe when its reader has exited. Notifies the writer that no further data is being read. *See* signal and pipes.

brouter Pronounced *BEE ROUTER*. Combination of a bridge and router. A brouter can determine the path of a packet and connect two networks with different protocols. *See* bridge, router and packet.

brownout Planned reduction in voltage.

browse To search through files for information.

bs *(ATT)* Interpretive language resembling a cross between BASIC and C language. *See* BASIC and C language.

BSD **1.** Berkeley Software Distribution. University of California, Berkeley, version of the UNIX operating system. Starting in 1974, the university began working with AT&T Co.'s UNIX Version 4. BSD actually was developed in 1975 by Ken Thompson and was based upon UNIX Version 6. BSD incorporated the vi text editor and more sophisticated network-

ing facilities for Ethernet and Transmission Control Protocol/Internet Protocol interfaces. The final release is the Fourth Berkeley Software Distribution, Fourth Release. In abbreviations, e.g. 4.4BSD, the first number (4) indicates the particular version and the final number (.4) stands for which release of that version. *See* Thompson, Ken. **2.** Abbreviation for BSD/XENIX Compatibility Guide, Part 1. UNIX System V, Release 4 documentation on Berkeley Software Distribution and XENIX commands which are not included in UNIX System V, Release 4 but are in the compatibility package. *See* SVR4.x, XENIX and XNX.

BSD/XENIX Compatibility Guide, Part 1 Commonly abbreviated and called BSD. *See* BSD.

BSD/XENIX Compatibility Guide, Part 2 Commonly abbreviated and called XNX. *See* XNX.

BSI British Standards Institute. British counterpart to the American National Standards Institute. *See* ANSI.

BSMTP *(INET)* Batch Simple Mail Transfer Protocol. Protocol developed to connect non-Internet hosts running UNIX-to-UNIX CoPy to Internet hosts. Looks and operates like the Simple Mail Transfer Protocol. *See* Internet, UUCP and SMTP.

bss segment Block started by symbol segment. Measurement of the amount of memory the kernel should allocate for the unstarted data segment of a program. *See* data segment and text segment.

btsoom Beats the s@!t out of me. Pronounced *BOOT SUM*. Used as a response either to a question that exceeds a user's computer knowledge or ability, or when a user does not know what is happening or why.

bubble memory Process of storing data as magnetic dots, called bubbles, on a semiconductor device. Provides faster throughput and lowers power consumption since the read/write process is totally electronic. Data remains in memory until it is physically removed, even if there is a power failure.

bucket Jargon for bit bucket. *See* bit bucket.

buffer 1. Storage area or memory in a printer or other hardware device that allows data sent from a computer to be temporarily stored (queued) for future action. Computers are capable of transmitting data at much higher rates than printers or other devices can process the data. A buffer frees the computer to perform other actions while the slower printer completes the print job. It prevents loss of data due to differences in speed. 2. Temporary storage area used to collect small groups of data into larger blocks which can be more efficiently processed by a computer, terminal or printer. 3. Storage area in the computer where data is temporarily placed during processing, e.g. the vi text editor establishes temporary buffers for text processing. *See* vi, named buffer and unnamed buffer.

buffer cache Also called a buffer pool. Storage area in high-speed memory where frequently used data from disks is temporarily stored. Data in memory can be accessed much more quickly than from disk.

buffered Process or method of using a buffer to manage data processing. *See* buffer.

buffer pool Commonly called buffer cache. *See* buffer cache.

bug Problem in either hardware or software that prevents the system from operating either at full capacity or at all. Term attributed to the late Rear Admiral Grace Hopper, USN. Originated during the search for the cause of a computer failure, in which a fried moth was found in the wiring of a Harvard Mark II that caused a short and brought down the system.

build To create or make, e.g. a file, document or directory.

built-in command Any command built into a program or process that is started and run by the program.

built in editor Editor provided by a program, e.g. most electronic-mail systems provide the user a choice of editors to create the text of an electronic-mail message. *See* e-mail.

bulk eraser Commonly called degausser. *See* degausser.

bulletin board Commonly abbreviated and called BB. *See* BB.

bulletin board system Commonly abbreviated and called BBS. *See* BBS.

Bull, ICL, Siemens, Olivetti and Nixdorf Abbreviated and commonly known as BISON. *See* BISON

Bunch, the Burroughs, Univac, NCR, Control Data Corp. and Honeywell. An older slang term for established, conservative mainframe systems manufacturers, e.g. "IBM and the BUNCH." Burroughs and Sperry Univac are now Unisys Corp., NCR Corp. is a subsidiary of AT&T Co. and Honeywell is owned by Groupe Bull.

bundling Practice of selling hardware and software or multiple software products as a single package, generally for less than the total cost of all the component products if they were purchased separately.

burn-in One of the quality tests performed on electrical circuits in computer equipment during the manufacturing process. During the burn-in process, the temperature may be varied from below freezing to above 100 degrees Fahrenheit to test the circuits in a computer or its components while they are operating. In some tests, the input voltage may be varied.

Burroughs, Univac, NCR, Control Data Corp. and Honeywell Abbreviated and known as the Bunch. *See* Bunch, the.

---

burst 1. Transmission of a continuous data stream at a high rate of speed. 2. Process of separating continuous form paper into separate sheets.

bursty Jargon for the intermittent, on-demand transfer of data at high speed over a local area network. Data flow is variable, ranging from zero to the possible peak rate of the network, with user access and use being random. *See* burst, LAN and stream-oriented.

bus Electrical or mechanical connection and communication between the various components of a computer. Can mean either the design of the electrical interface, or the board or device used for the physical connection. Typical buses include VME, MULTIBUS and small computer system interface. *See* VMEbus, MULTIBUS and SCSI.

bus adapter Hardware item that can be attached to the bus interface of a computer to allow communication with a different type of bus protocol.

bus arbitration Process of determining which computer resource is allowed to use a bus.

bus master Process that takes control of an expansion bus, access memory or other peripheral device independent of the central processing unit. *See* bus and process.

button 1. Input mechanism on a mouse. The user moves the mouse to position the pointer on the screen and then depresses a button to initiate an input action to the computer. *See* mouse and click. 2. Screen image resembling a button that is used to start a specific task by the computer. The task is activated by placing the cursor on the button and clicking the mouse.

BUUG Belgium UNIX User Group. UNIX users group formed in 1985.

bwrite *(ATT)* **B**lock **write**. Kernel function used to flush, or write, dirty (modified) data blocks from computer memory to disk.

byte Single computer character that equates to a letter or number, consisting of 8 bits. A computer with random access memory (RAM) rated at 640 kilobytes can handle 66,536 computer characters at one time. A disk rated at 40 megabytes can store 41,963,040 computer characters, while one rated at 1 gigabyte can store 1,073,741,824 characters. Bytes are arranged to represent letters, numbers or symbols. The exact representation depends on the programs in which they are used. *See* bit, RAM, KB, MB and GB.

BYTE Magazine published by McGraw-Hill. Originally written for personal computer users with articles on personal computers, CP/M, MS-DOS, OS/2 and the Macintosh Operating System. Over the past few years, the number of articles on UNIX has increased.

byte striping Technique for spreading alternating bytes of data across two or more devices. *See* striping, block striping and RAID.

C

c Abbreviation for **centi**. *See* centi.

C Abbreviation for C language. *See* C language.

cache memory Area of memory in the computer set aside for temporary storage of the data that has most recently been taken from main memory. The computer anticipates what data the programs in operation will need and pulls this into the cache memory. This results in faster access and transfer of data than would be possible if the information had to be retrieved from main memory.

How cache memory works

A caching system allows the computer to search for data in memory before searching for the information stored on slower disk drives.

cache/memory management unit Commonly abbreviated and called CMMU. *See* CMMU.

caching Making copies of data in local, high-speed storage. *See* cache memory.

caching-only server Go-between host. Confirms which hosts on any Domain Name Service network are authorized to receive authoritative data, and then holds the data until it can be passed on. Not authorized to possess authoritative data on any DNS network. *See* DNS.

caching server Any host on a Domain Name Service network that is authorized to receive data.

CAD Computer-aided design. Use of hardware, software and peripherals for computerized design of products.

CAE 1. Common Applications Environment. Standards developed by X/Open Co. Ltd. for implementation of application software. Includes standards for the operating system, compilers, tools, data management, networking interfaces and graphical user interface. The three levels in CAE are: BASE Profile, which contains the minimum software components needed; PLUS Profile, which contains the BASE Profile and definitions for the implementation of COBOL, FORTRAN, Pascal and other programming languages; and OPTIONAL Components, which contains the BASE Profile, PLUS Profile and definitions for Ada, interprocess communication and source code transfer. *See* X/Open, XPG, BASE Profile, PLUS Profile, OPTIONAL Components and GUI. **2.** Computer-aided engineering. Computerized analysis of an engineering design for functionality, manufacturing requirements, performance capabilities, etc.

CAI Computer-assisted instruction. Commonly called CBT (computer-based training). *See* CBT.

cal *(ATT/BSD/XEN)* Calendar. Personal daytimer of dates and meetings. Command used to display a calendar. The output format varies depending on the arguments input by the user. Displays a specified year or a month of a year between 1 and 9999 A.D.

CAL Computer-augmented learning. Commonly called CBT (computer-based training). *See* CBT.

calendar 1. *(ATT/XEN)* Command used to set up an electronic reminder service that provides a user a personal calendar of business and social activities. 2. Also called calendaring or scheduling. Groupware or collection of programs used to maintain personal and/or group calendars or schedules.

calendaring Also called scheduling. Commonly called calendar. *See* calendar.

call Commonly called execute. *See* execute.

CALLBACK Variable for UNIX-to-UNIX CoPy (UUCP) that, when set to "yes," requires the host system to call the remote system before allowing a UUCP connection to take place. *See* UUCP.

call-back Field in the file USERFILE used for security purposes in calling back to the remote system to complete a UNIX-to-UNIX CoPy transfer. *See* USERFILE and UUCP.

call-back modem Type of modem used to provide an additional layer of physical security for systems that can be accessed by phone. Contains the user account names and remote phone numbers of authorized users. A user calls the system, identifies himself and then hangs up. The call-back modem dials the preprogrammed phone number for that user and, when a connection is made, allows the user to follows the normal log on process.

caller Network File System term for one process that makes another process initiate a procedure call. *See* NFS.

Caller Field in the L-devices and L.sys files used to indicate the type of connection made by the modem, e.g. autodial modem, X.25 PAD or Transmission Control Protocol/Internet Protocol. *See* L-devices and L.sys.

Call unit Optional field in the L-devices file that holds the pathname for a device file of the modem used to dial remote hosts. *See* L-devices.

CAM Committee Common Access Method **Committee**. Committee of 35 UNIX companies formed to choose a standard interface for SCSI-3 from existing vendor standards. *See* SCSI-3 and CAM.

CAMI Computer Aided Manufacturing International. Standards body for computer-aided manufacturing. Composed of 70 companies.

campus LAN Commonly called MAN (metropolitan area network). *See* MAN.

cancel 1. *(ATT)* Line printer (lp) system command. Stops specific print jobs or all the jobs for a printer that were created with the lp command. Included in the file system operation command menu of the UNIX System V, Release 4 Framed Access Command Environment. *See* lp, lpstat, SVR4.x, FACE and file system. 2. To delete or erase a command line before executing it. 3. To stop or abort a command or program that is running.

cancel key Commonly called Del key. *See* Del key.

canned Also called canned software or canned package. Jargon for software developed by a computer vendor or a third party that can be used immediately, with no modification.

canned package Commonly called canned. *See* canned.

canned software Commonly called canned. *See* canned.

canonical I/O Commonly called cooked mode. *See* cooked mode.

Canonical Name Commonly abbreviated and called CNAME. *See* CNAME.

capacity Amount of data that can be stored or processed by a tape, disk drive, memory, etc.

capacity planning Process of anticipating the demand for hardware or network resources to meet the needs of users. To ensure sufficient hardware or network bandwidth is available, a variety of factors are considered, including volume of traffic on a network; number of users for each computer; number of computers on a network; need for on-line and off-line storage space; quantity of input and/or output. In addition, environmental requirements, e.g. floor space, electricity and uninterruptible power supplies, are evaluated to support operational needs.

CAP-MAIL Pronunciation of Mail. *See* Mail.

caps lock key Key on a standard keyboard that locks all alphabetic keys so that letters appear in upper case. Numeric and special characters generally remain in lower case. Capitalizes all characters on only a limited number of terminals.

captoinfo *(ATT)* Command used to convert termcap information into terminfo information. *See* termcap and terminfo.

capture Word processing and graphics term for making a copy.

carbonless paper Paper manufactured with a chemical coating that produces an original and one or more copies without placing carbon paper between the sheets.

card 1. Jargon for a printed circuit board. *See* printed circuit board. 2. Abbreviation for computer cards or IBM cards. *See* computer cards.

card cage Jargon for the frame or chassis designed to hold printed circuit boards within a computer.

caret (^) 1. Technically, a circumflex. A metacharacter that has many uses and meanings in UNIX. 2. Representation of a control character, e.g. Ctrl d can be written as ^d. 3. Metacharacter used in regular expressions in the ed, ex, vi, sed, grep,

egrep and awk programs. Used to match character strings at the beginning of a line. 4. C shell indicator which shows that a substitution has been made in a command line input. For example:

```
CLP> ^string1^string2 ⏎
```

means substitute string1 with the new string2 for string 1 in the previous command, and then execute the new command. *See* metacharacter.

carriage return Key found on a typewriter keyboard which has been replaced by the Enter key on a computer keyboard. Moves the page ahead, or down, a line in the text. A term still common among computer users. Abbreviated CR or <CR>. *See* Enter key.

carrier protocol Any communication protocol used to transport the encapsulated messages of another communication protocol, called the payload protocol, between two networks. *See* encapsulation and payload protocol.

Carrier Sense Multiple Access Commonly abbreviated and called CSMA. *See* CSMA.

Carrier Sense Multiple Access/Collision Detection Commonly abbreviated and called CSMA/CD. *See* CSMA/CD.

cartridge tape Self-contained magnetic tape storage medium. A spool of tape is contained in a plastic case. Standard cartridge tapes vary in capacity from 200 megabytes to 25 gigabytes.

Cartridge Tape Controller Utilities Set of programs included in UNIX System V, Release 4 for storing and retrieving data on magnetic tape. *See* SVR4.x.

CASA One of the gigabit test-bed networks developed by the U.S. government, industry and university representatives. Tests technologies and applications used in implementing networks and supercomputers which can transmit gigabits of data per second. Designed to test network-based application development for supercomputers. Participating in CASA are the Jet Propulsion Laboratory, Los Alamos Laboratory, MCI, Pacific Bell, Supercomputing Center of California Technical Institute and US WEST. *See* HPCC, NREN, AURORA, BLANCA, MAGIC, NECTAR and VISTANet.

case **1.** Signifies whether letters are capitalized or not. *See* lower case and upper case. **2.** Shell command used to make comparisons between values of data.

CASE **C**omputer-**a**ided **s**oftware **e**ngineering. Pertaining to software development programs that use established computer capabilities, e.g. graphs, in developing software applications, from initial planning to program and user documentation.

case operator Commonly called case. *See* case.

case sensitive Indicates whether a system, command, etc. requires input to be made in either upper-case or lower-case letters.

cat **C**oncatenate. Command used to combine multiple files into a new file:

CLP> cat <options(s)> file name1 file name2 ..file nameN >newfile ⏎

2. Command used to create a file:

CLP> cat <options(s)> file name ⏎

3. Command used to display the contents of a file to the standard output, normally the user's screen:

CLP> cat options(s) > file name ⏎

The first generally accepted method of displaying the contents of a file, e.g. "I'll cat /etc/passwd to find his/her userid." Many new commands, e.g. pcat and zcat, retain the term cat to indicate a display operation. *See* pcat, standard output and zcat.

CAT **C**omputer-**a**ssisted **t**raining. Commonly called CBT (computer-based training). *See* CBT.

catching a signal A process that is receiving a signal handler. *See* signal handler and signal.

catclose *(ATT)* **Cat**alogue **close**. C language programming library routine used to close a message catalog. *See* catgets and catopen.

catenate Jargon for concatenate. *See* concatenate.

catenet Network of dissimilar hosts or dissimilar networks connected by gateways that are capable of performing protocol conversion via hardware and/or software.

catgets *(ATT)* C language program library function used to retrieve a specific string from a catalog of messages. Used to implement software in which the program is independent of the native language of the computer in which its messages are printed. *See* catopen and catclose.

cathode ray tube Commonly abbreviated and called CRT. *See* CRT.

catman **Cat** **man**ual. Command used to format manual pages that describe UNIX commands. *See* man and makecats.

catopen *(ATT)* **Cat**alogue **open**. C language programming library routine used to open a catalog of program messages to be read by the catgets function. *See* catgets and catclose.

caught signal Signal or software interrupt that is sent and successfully stops a process. *See* signal.

cave Virtual reality display method that uses multiple devices to project images on the walls and ceiling, providing an illusion of being part of the images being displayed. *See* virtual reality and artificial reality.

cb **C** **b**eautify. Program used to format the text of C language source code, making it look neat, pretty and more readable.

CBF **C**omputer-**b**ased **f**ax. System that allows a computer to generate and receive facsimile communications. Can include optical character recognition technology, scanners and facsimile boards to capture, convert and manipulate text and graphics. *See* fax and OCR.

CBL Computer-based learning. Commonly called CBT (computer-based training). *See* CBT.

C-block Data buffer that contains the information (C-list) for the transmission of data to and from a terminal. *See* I/O and C-list.

cbreak mode Mode or means of processing inputs in which commands are entered directly from the terminal with no system controls, buffer or inputs.

CBT Computer-based training. Also called computer-assisted instruction (CAI), computer-augmented learning (CAL), computer-based learning (CBL) and computer-assisted training (CAT). Educational programs run on a computer that can be designed to provide supplemental information to conventional training programs for one or more people.

cc 1. C compiler. Used on most UNIX systems to compile C language programs. Converts high-level code into machine-readable language by invoking other programs, e.g. a preprocessor, linguistic analyzer, compiler, assembler and link editing loader. *See* compiler, as, cpp and ld. 2. Carbon copy. Header in electronic-mail messages in which the user can indicate which individual(s) are to receive a copy of the message. *See* e-mail.

ccat *(ATT)* Compact cat. Command used to view text files on the input screen that have been compacted, or compressed. *See* cat and compact.

CCITT Consultative Committee on International Telegraphy and Telephony. Also was called the International Telegraph and Telephone Consultative Committee and the Comité Consultatif Internationale de Télégraphie et Téléphonie. Renamed International Telecommunication Union Telecommunication Standardization Sector in 1993. *See* ITU-T and V standards.

CCR Commitment, Concurrency and Recovery. An Open Systems Interconnection term for a distributed processing service that allows continuous operations.

CCS 1. Common Command Set. Set of common commands agreed to by vendors of Small Computer System Interface disks. Includes four levels of commands: mandatory, which are prescribed by the standard; extended, which support high-level devices; operational, which provide functionality but are not mandatory; and vendor-unique, which are defined by the manufacturer. Started in 1985 and formalized in 1990 with the release of SCSI-2. *See* SCSI and SCSI-2. 2. Common Communications Support. Part of IBM Corp.'s networking architecture that defines protocols and communication architectures which interface with the System Application Architecture. One of the increasing number of IBM terms entering the UNIX language with the growth of large UNIX production systems. *See* SAA.

CCTA Central Computer and Telecommunications Agency. British counterpart to the National Institute of Standards and Technology. *See* NIST.

cd Change directory. Command that allows a user to change from one working directory to another.

```
CLP> cd directory-name⏎
```

changes directory to directory in current directory path.

```
CLP> cd ../ ⏎
```

changes directory to the directory immediately above the current working directory.

```
CLP> cd ../../ ⏎
```

changes directory to two directories above the current working directory. Add a ../ for each level of directory you want to go up.

CLP> cd /directory/directory/directory (absolute path) ⏎

changes to the specified directory at the end of the path.

CLP> cd /usr/SHE/northup ⏎

changes to user account "northup".

CLP> cd /usr/SHE/northup/kim ⏎

changes directory to the directory "kim" in user account "northup". Or, the short cut on changing directories to other user accounts is

CLP> cd ~northup/kim ⏎

All of these assume the user has permissions to access the user accounts and/or directories. *See* current working directory, relative pathname and tilde.

CD Collision detection. Process of determining when data transmission has failed because a sending and a receiving device have transmitted data simultaneously. The sending location will detect the data collision as a result of the presence of corrupted data in the transmission. When a collision is detected, transmission will be stopped and then restarted at random time intervals. *See* CSMA/CD. **2.** Committee draft. Working documents for proposed standards being developed by the International Organization for Standardization and International Electrontechnical Commission Joint Technical Committee 1. *See* JTC1.

cdb C debugger. Source program debugger for C language programs. *See* debugger, C language, dbx and xdb.

cdc *(ATT/XEN)* Change delta comments. One of the 13 commands within the Source Code Control System (SCCS) used to change the words used to explain a change to a SCCS file created with the delta command. *See* SCCS, DELTA, admin, comb, delta, get, help, prs, rmdel, sact, sccsdiff, unget, val, vc and what.

CDDI Copper Distributed Data Interface. Implementation of the Fiber Distribution Data Interface protocol, capable of transmitting data at up to 100 megabits per second, using less expensive twisted pair wire instead of fiber-optic cable. *See* FDDI.

CDE Common Desktop Environment. Specification developed by the Common Open Software Environment (COSE) group for an application programming interface for a common UNIX graphical user interface that permits development of applications which can run across multiple computer platforms. Addresses interoperability of desktop computing, graphics, multimedia, network operations, object-oriented technology and system management. *See* COSE, API and GUI.

cdevsw Character device switch table. Table containing the kernel data structure used to map character device major numbers into device driver addresses. *See* character device, mapping, major device number and device driver.

cdpath C shell version of the CDPATH environmental variable. Used to specify paths to be checked when the cd command is used. Not set by the system; users must define the variable. *See* cd and CDPATH.

CDPATH Environmental variable in the Bourne and Korn shells. Used to specify paths to be checked when the cd command is used. Not set by the system; users have to define the variable. *See* cd, Bourne shell and Korn shell.

CD-RDx Compact disk read-only memory database standard developed by the

CD-ROM

Central Intelligence Agency. *See* CD-ROM and High Sierra specification.

CD-ROM Compact disk read-only memory. Also called compact disk read-only media. Read-only mass storage device based on audio compact disk technology. Can provide between 540 and 666 megabytes of data storage. Best-suited to storing fairly static data that is used on a regular basis.

CDS Cell Directory Service. Component of the Open Software Foundation's Distributed Computing Environment Distributed Naming Service. Manages local users and their addresses. *See* OSF, DCE, DNS, GDA, GDS, XDS and Directory Service.

CD Write-Once Ad Hoc Advisory Committee Commonly called the Frankfurt Group. *See* Frankfurt Group.

cell 1. Basic unit of administration within the Distributed Computing Environment. Used in applications that share administrative and security services. *See* DCE. 2. Addressable storage unit within memory used to store a bit of information in an electrical charge. 3. Intersection of a row and column in a spreadsheet used to contain data. Each cell has an address based upon the row and column that intersects, e.g. d5 would indicate the fourth column and fifth row. 4. Fixed length block of data consisting of a field of information and a header formed for transmission over a network. *See* ATM.

Cell Directory Service Commonly abbreviated and called CDS. *See* CDS.

cell relay Also called Asynchronous Transfer Mode. Communications transmission technology that requires data to be transmitted in fixed-length cells of 53 bytes. This speeds up the rate of transmission because resources do not have to be used to compute the size of the data cells during either transmission or receipt of communications. Provides the ability to transmit data, voice and video information. *See* ATM and SMDS.

CEM Command Execution Module. Set of commands used to manage devices using the Small Computer System Interface protocol. *See* SCSI.

centi Prefix for 10^{-2} (1/100) or one-hundredth. Commonly abbreviated c.

centisecond One-hundredth of a second.

Central Computer and Telecommunications Agency Commonly abbreviated and called CCTA. *See* CCTA.

central console Commonly called management station. *See* management station.

centralized computing Computer system in which one central computer does all the processing control, etc. Opposite of decentralized processing. *See* decentralized computing.

central processing unit Commonly abbreviated and called CPU. *See* CPU.

CERFnet *(INET)* California Education and Research Federation **NET**work. Located in San Diego, California. *See* Internet.

CERT Computer Emergency Response Team. Organization funded by the federal government and located at Carnegie-Mellon University. Monitors the Internet, informs users of potential hacker activity, repairs damage and tracks down hackers. Can be reached via electronic mail through the Internet at cert@sei.cmu.edu. *See* Internet.

CF Common facilities. Object Management Group term for functions or utilities that can be used by different applications. *See* OMG and utility.

cflow *(ATT)* C flowgraph. Command used to build a graph of external references for C language, yacc, lex and assembler program files. *See* C language, yacc, lex and assembly language.

CGA Color graphic adapter. First color video system for personal computers to provide either a resolution of 320 x 200 pixels with four colors or 640 x 200 pixels with two colors. CGA monitors support

---

limited graphics applications. Developed by IBM Corp. in 1981. *See* 8514/A, EGA, super VGA, VGA, XGA and pixel.

CGM Computer Graphics Metafile. National Institutes of Standards and Technology test suite based upon an American National Standards Institute standard that permits graphics packages to be used on different types of hardware. *See* NIST and ANSI.

chaining When a running program calls another program.

Challenge-Handshake Authentication Protocol Commonly abbreviated and called CHAP. *See* CHAP.

change management Process of controlling system changes by a predefined method or process.

Chaos Computer Club European forerunner of the Legion of Doom. Formed by a group of hackers to cause problems for the government-controlled networks in Germany. After discovering a major security hole in DEC's VMS version 4.5, group members broke into and set themselves up as system administrators on computers throughout Europe and the United States. *See* Legion of Doom.

CHAP Challenge-Handshake Authentication Protocol. Security protocol used in the Point-to-Point Protocol (PPP) to continually verify the identity of peer computers during a PPP connection. Challenge messages are sent by the authenticator computer to which the peer, or connecting, computer must correctly respond; if the peer computer does not, the authenticator will terminate the connection. *See* PPP and PAP.

CHAR Programmer's Guide: **Char**acter User Interface (FMLI and ETI). UNIX System V, Release 4 documentation for programmers to develop interfaces between applications and terminals that have no graphical capabilities. *See* SVR4.x, FMLI and ETI.

character 1. Any piece of data that is represented by a control character or a single printable letter, number or symbol. Characters are normally 8, 16 or 32 bits long. *See* bits. **2.** Specified sequence of bits that represents an individual graphic symbol.

character-based user interface Commonly abbreviated and called CUI. *See* CUI.

character buffer list Commonly abbreviated and called C-list. *See* C-list.

character-class Set of characters that are enclosed in square brackets [ ]. Used in a search to indicate that a match is to be sought for any character within the brackets, e.g.:

CLP> ls -l kaj [tnf] ⏎

would produce a list of all files starting with kaj and followed by a t, n or f.

character code Unique code for each character that a computer can recognize. *See* ASCII.

character device Any device that handles, processes or passes information using any number of characters at a time, from a single character to large blocks of characters, e.g. terminals, printers and modems. *See* block.

character device files Commonly called character special files. *See* character special files.

character device interface 1. Kernel device driver used to communicate with a character device, e.g. a terminal or modem. **2.** At times, a raw or unbuffered disk device. *See* raw device.

character device switch table Commonly abbreviated and called cdevsw. *See* cdevsw.

character device table List maintained in the kernel that contains the device driver routines for character-oriented devices. *See* kernel and device driver.

Character Generator Protocol
Commonly abbreviated and called CHARGEN. *See* CHARGEN.

character I/O Communication with a peripheral device or remote system one character or byte at a time, with no buffering.

character pitch Commonly called pitch. *See* pitch.

character position Location of a character displayed on a video screen.

character set Group of characters related by specific, predetermined criteria.

character special files Files that contain the character device interface definitions for character devices, e.g. terminals, printers and modems. *See* character device, character device interface and special file.

character string Commonly called string. *See* string.

characters per inch Abbreviated and commonly referred to as cpi. *See* cpi.

characters per second Commonly abbreviated and called cps. *See* cps.

character user interface Commonly abbreviated and called CUI. *See* CUI.

charge back System of billing users for using computer system resources. Can be based on a combination of factors, e.g. central processing unit use, number and duration of connections to the system, amount of disk space used and use of special devices or service.

chargefee *(ATT)* Accounting system shell script used to set up charge back fees to users for use of system resources. *See* charge back and shell script.

CHARGEN *(INET)* **Char**acter **Gen**erator Protocol. Defense Advanced Research Projects Agency Internet protocol. Sends the originator American Standard Code for Information Interchange data, and is used by programmers and other users for debugging. *See* DARPA, Internet and AS-CII.

chat Jargon for an electronic conversation between users. *See* talk and write.

Chat Field in L-devices responsible for performing the login function to a remote host for a UNIX-to-UNIX CoPy session. *See* L-devices and UUCP.

chat script Commonly called Login script. *See* Login script.

chdir **Ch**ange **dir**ectory. System call that changes the current working directory. *See* system call and cd.

cheapernet Also called cheapnet. Commonly called thinnet. Cheaper net rhymes with Ethernet, a type of Ethernet network wiring that uses thin, unshielded coaxial cable which is cheaper to install than other types of thick coaxial cable. *See* thinnet.

cheapnet Also called cheapernet. Commonly called thinnet. *See* thinnet.

check *(ATT)* UNIX System V, Release 4 command in the software installation and information management menu. Performs the same function as the pkgchk command, and is used to confirm that new software has been installed and is functioning properly. *See* pkgchk.

checkall *(ATT)* Fast file system checking procedure used to validate the soundness of a file system. *See* fsck, file consistency check and file system.

checkcw *(ATT)* **Check** constant **w**idth. Command in the Documenter's Workbench set of text formatting programs. Used to confirm the width established in a text, created with the cw command. *See* DWB and cw.

check disk Commonly called parity disk. *See* parity disk.

checkdoc **Check doc**ument. Command used to check for errors in a document prepared with mm macros' dot commands. Outputs a list of errors. *See* mm macros.

checkeq *(ATT)* **Check eq**n or equation. Command in the Documenter's Workbench set of text formatting programs.

Used to validate the eqn typeset mathematics commands. *See* DWB and eqn.

checkers *(ATT)* Command used to start a checkers game.

checkmm *(ATT)* **Check** **m**emorandum **ma**cro. Command in the Documenter's Workbench set of text formatting programs. Used to validate the format of documents created to run with the nroff mm macros. *See* DWB, nroff and mm macros.

checknews *(OTH)* **Check news**. Command used with the USENET bulletin board to determine if there are any new articles to be read. *See* USENET.

checknr *(BSD)* **Check nr**off. Command used to validate the format of documents created with ms inputs to run with the nroff and troff formatting programs. *See* ms macros, ditroff, nroff and troff.

checkpointing Process of maintaining checkpoints during a file transfer. If a connection fails, the file transfer restarts at the last checkpoint, precluding the need to retransmit the entire file.

check status *(ATT)* Command in the Network File System sysadm menu (the Network File System Control) that is used to check the status of NFS operations. *See* NFS and sysadm.

checksum Also spelled check sum. Simple error detection method. A value derived by using the output of a mathematical computation performed on a block of data to determine if any of the data has been corrupted. Normally found in the header of a data message. *See* CRC, ECC and header.

check sum Commonly spelled checksum. *See* checksum.

chess *(ATT)* Command used to start a chess game.

chfn *(BSD)* **Ch**ange **f**i**n**ger. Command used to change the data in the /etc/passwd file that is read by the finger command. *See* finger.

chgrp **Ch**ange **gr**ou**p**. Command used to change the group of a file or directory. Can be run on a file or directory only by the owner or root.

chief information officer Commonly abbreviated and called CIO. *See* CIO.

child Jargon for child process. *See* child process.

child directory Commonly called subdirectory. *See* subdirectory.

child process New process which is started by and is part of another process. The other process is then called the parent process. *See* parent process.

ching Command used to start the Ching game.

chip Jargon for integrated circuit. Silicon wafer with embedded circuitry that allowed the hardware industry to miniaturize central processing units, enhance speed and increase memory capacity. Contains the logic, or processing, functions of a computer.

chkey *(ATT)* **Ch**ange **key**. Command used to change the password used for encryption keys. *See* DES, NFS, public-key cryptography, encryption key and newkey.

chmod 1. **Ch**ange **mod**e. Command that changes permissions on a file or directory. Can be run on a file or directory only by the owner or root. A number or combination of numbers added to the command sets the permissions for a file, e.g. 0, no permissions; 1, execute permission; 2, write permissions; 3, write and execute permissions; 4, read permission; 5, read and execute permissions, 6, read and write permissions; 7, read, write and execute permissions.

CLP> chmod 666 (file or directory name) 🗎

sets the permission to read and write for all users. Use of numbers to set permissions assumes the user understands all the possible mathematical combinations to set permissions. If the mathematical combinations are not known,

CLP> chmod u+r file name ⏎

says to + (add) read permissions for the user to whatever permissions currently exist for the specified file. Any combination of user, group, other, read, write or execute along with + (add) or - (subtract) can be used to set permissions on a file or directory. **2.** System call used to change access permissions for a file. *See* system call.

Chorus Fourth-generation UNIX operating system look-alike based upon modular microkernel operating system design. Developed by Chorus Systemes SA of France. *See* microkernel and Chorus/Mix.

Chorus/Mix UNIX operating system look-alike developed by Chorus Systemes SA of France. A multiuser and multiprocessing operating system that integrates the Chorus microkernel and portions of UNIX System V. A modular microkernel operating system capable of supporting fault tolerant, multiprocessing and parallel processing systems. The microkernel was developed by Chorus Systemes through a program sponsored by the National Institute for Research in Computers and Automation, the French equivalent of the Massachusetts Institute of Technology. *See* microkernel and MP UNIX.

chown 1. System call used to change the owner of a file. *See* system call. **2. Change owner.** Command used to change the owner of a file or directory. Can be run on a file or directory only by the owner or root.

chroot 1. System call used to change the **root** directory, restricting the user environment. *See* system call. **2.** *(ATT)* **Change root.** Command available only to the system administrator that is used to change the root directory of a command or process. *See* process.

chsh *(BSD)* **Change shell.** Command used to change the default shell identified in the /etc/passwd file for the user. Can be

executed either by the user or root. *See* shell.

churning Commonly called thrashing. *See* thrashing.

ci *(BSD)* Check in. Command used to check for, and move into the correct file, revisions of files managed by Revision Control System. *See* RCS.

CIA++ C Information Abstractor Plus Plus. Set of tools used to perform software analysis. Used to build a database of information drawn from C++ programs and analyze the data that has been collected. *See* C++ language and design recovery.

CICS Customer Information Control System. One of the many IBM Corp. terms that have made their way into the UNIX language with the growth of large UNIX production data centers. A transaction monitor used for large end-to-end transaction processing in a client/server environment. Can reset and restart a transaction if it fails. *See* transaction processing, client/server and TPM. *See* transaction processing, client/server and TP.

CIDR *(INET)* Classless Interdomain Routing. Attempt by the Internet Engineering Task Force to overcome the shortage of Internet Protocol (IP) addresses. Eliminates the three-level, Class A, B and C host IP addresses. *See* Internet, IP, IP address, PIP and SIP-P.

CIM 1. Computer-integrated manufacturing. Computerized manufacturing concept for automating factories. In CIM, parts are precision-cut by machinery using instructions that are encoded by a computer. A fully integrated system includes manufacturing, inventory control, shipping and billing. *See* MRP and MRP-II. **2. Corporate Information Management.** Department of Defense program to minimize duplication of computer systems in each of the military services. The program is designed to enhance effectiveness and reduce costs by cutting the number of unique computers through standardization and consolidation, and by re-doing processes of the military serv-

---

ices. **3.** Computer input microfilm. Use of microfilm or microfiche as a computer input source.

CIMP Common Information Management Protocol. Commonly abbreviated and called CMIP (Common Management Information Protocol). *See* CMIP.

C Information Abstractor ++
Abbreviated and commonly referred to as CIA++. *See* CIA++

CIO Chief information officer. Individual in a corporation, normally a vice president, who has ultimate responsibility for the computing and network operations.

cip *(ATT)* Program developed for use with AT&T Co.'s TELETYPE 630 terminal. Used for interaction with pic and troff programs to generate pictures. Not a standard UNIX program but is provided separately by AT&T for the TELETYPE 630 terminal. *See* pic and troff.

ciphertext Gibberish that results from encrypting text. *See* encrypt and plaintext.

CIR Committed information rate. Measurement used with frame-relay technology to indicate the bandwidth which a switch is capable of handling. *See* frame-relay.

circuit Direct or switched connection between one point and another.

circumflex (^) Commonly called caret. *See* caret.

CISC Complex Instruction Set Computing. Central processing unit architecture used in most computers. CISC CPUs are designed so that the majority of the processor's instructions are combined and contained in microcode on a read only chip. This speeds up access to outside devices to obtain processing instructions. *See* CPU, RISC and WISC.

CJK China, Japan and Korea. Group of representatives from the United States, China, Japan, Korea, Taiwan and Hong Kong, formed to develop common com-

puter character sets for Asian languages. *See* i18n and l10n.

ckbupscd *(ATT)* Command used to run a check on the file system backup schedule. *See* file system.

ckpacct *(ATT)* Check process accounting log. Accounting system shell script that checks the size of the /usr/adm/pacct process accounting file to ensure it does not become too large. *See* /usr/adm/pacct.

CLAN Cordless local area network. Uses radio frequencies instead of cable to transmit data. *See* LAN.

C language Programming language developed by Brian Kernighan and Dennis Ritchie of AT&T Co.'s Bell Laboratories in 1972. A general-purpose programming language that is the basis of UNIX and is most noted for its hardware independence and availability on many different platforms. Named the C language because it was developed and patterned after the B language created in the late 1960s by Ken Thompson. *See* Thompson, Ken, Ritchie, Dennis M., B language and Bell Laboratories.

C++ language C Plus Plus language. Originally called C with classes. An extension of the C language. The primary UNIX object-oriented programming language, developed at AT&T Co.'s Bell Laboratories by Bjarne Stroustrup in the early 1980s. *See* OOP, Bell Laboratories and Smalltalk.

class 1. Any group of printers having similar characteristics. All printers in a class should be able to adequately fulfill a user's requirements, e.g. laser printers on the third floor, high-speed line printers in a computer room or a dot matrix printer located in an office. *See* LP, classes and destination. **2.** Object-oriented programming term for program code for a group of similar or associated items used in developing a program, e.g. functions or services. *See* OOP and encapsulation.

Class Field in the L-devices and L.sys files used to identify the physical characteristics of the connection, e.g. modem speed, direct connect line speed or port number. *See* L-devices and L.sys.

class-based scheduler Process scheduling system in which processes are divided into separate prioritized classes that identify the importance of a process to the central processing unit. *See* time-sharing class, real-time class, system class and CPU.

classes *(ATT)* UNIX System V, Release 4 line printer services menu command similar to the lpadmin command. Used to place printers into groups. *See* SVR4.x, lpadmin and class.

Classless Interdomain Routing
Commonly abbreviated as CIDR. *See* CIDR.

cleanup *(ATT)* UNIX System V, Release 4 Framed Access Command Environment file system operations menu command. Performs routine system housekeeping, e.g. deleting core files and truncating logs. *See* SVR4.x, FACE and file system.

clear *(BSD)* Command used to erase all the characters from a screen, so that only the user prompt is visible on the screen. *See* prompt.

cleartext Commonly called plaintext. *See* plaintext.

clear-to-send Commonly abbreviated and called CTS. *See* CTS.

clerk Term used in the Open Software Foundation Inc.'s Distributed Computing Environment distributed time service. Any network host that synchronizes its time from the time server host on the network. *See* OSF, DCE, DTS and time server.

CLI Command line interface. One of the functions of a shell. Defines a user-input command into terms the operating system can understand. *See* shell and operating system.

C library Programmer's library of shortcuts for writing C programs. The C library

consists of pre-written and tested application routines that can be used for common operations to avoid writing new code.

click Process of depressing and then releasing a button on a mouse. *See* mouse and button.

click to activate One of the three methods used to activate a window. The user places the pointer in the window and clicks the mouse once to activate the window. *See* mouse, click, window, real estate and double click.

client 1. Computer that can operate by itself to perform many functions, e.g. the manipulation of subelements of a database. May not have sufficient random access memory or disk capacity to manipulate the entire database and may have to rely on another computer or server for storage of the complete database. *See* server and RAM. 2. Software program that performs specified functions independent of the primary applications or operating system, or simply requests a server to perform the specified action and return the results to the client, e.g. a terminal emulator within a communications package or the window management programs of the X Window System. *See* server and X Window System. 3. Network Time Protocol term for a computer at a lower level than, or further away from, a host with a master clock. *See* NTP, stratum, peer and server.

client caching In a Remote File Sharing network, the ability of a local host to temporarily store data from a remote host instead of constantly moving data across a network. *See* RFS.

client list Remote File Sharing system file created by a system administrator with the share command. Contains the names of hosts with permissions to access local resources. *See* share and RFS.

client permissions Permissions granted to remote hosts to access local resources. Set by the system administrator using the share command. *See* share, permissions and RFS.

client process In a system that has client/server relationships, sequential operations that initiate another process on the server or host system. *See* client, server and process.

client/server **1.** Relationship in network and distributed systems in which one computer (client) requests data or support from another computer (server). *See* client, server, DDM and DPM. **2.** In the X Window System, a client is specifically the application software and the server is the X Window System terminal. *See* X Window System.

How Client/Server works

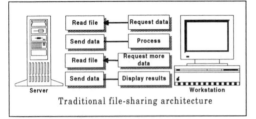

Traditional file-sharing architecture

In the traditional file-sharing architecture, used by most PC LANs, the workstation processes all data provided by the server. This architecture results in heavier network traffic.

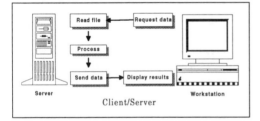

Client/Server

In client/server architecture, the two computers work together to accomplish a task. The client, sometimes referred to as a "front-end", is a standalone computer which requests the server to perform a task. After the server processes the request, it returns the results to the client. Unlike the more traditional file-sharing architecture, the client/server minimizes network traffic.

client/server processing Commonly called distributed processing. *See* distributed processing.

C-list Character buffer **list**. Mechanism in the UNIX kernel to manage the allocation of resources needed to support and buffer data to and from character devices, e.g. printers, terminals and plotters, one character at a time.

CLNP Connectionless Network Protocol. Government Open System Interconnection Profile protocol that allows information to be sent from one site to another without a session being established in advance. Data packets can be sent between sites in any order and then reassembled properly at their final destination. Uses datagrams, or packets, that include addressing information in each packet. Like the Internet Protocol, provides the protocol for interhost connection over a communications network. *See* OSI, GOSIP, UDP/IP, datagram and packet switch network.

CLNS Connectionless Network Service. Commonly called CLNP (Connectionless Network Protocol). *See* CLNP.

clobber Jargon for overwriting or deleting a file. Frequently done unintentionally.

clock **1.** *(ATT)* C language routine used to obtain the elapsed central processing unit time in microseconds used by a process. **2.** Signal used within a computer to set and run timing sequences (processes) within the computer. Keeps track of time so processes do not collide.

clock cycle Single-cycle   (off/on/off) pulse of a central processing unit's clock. *See* clock speed.

clock hand Process of managing page replacement in memory. Runs like a clock in an endless loop, with a pointer that moves through the pages like clock hands, looking for those to be moved out of memory. *See* paging.

clock per instruction Commonly abbreviated and called CPI. *See* CPI.

clock rate Also called machine cycle. Measurement of the speed at which a central processing unit runs program instructions. *See* CPU.

clock speed Measurement of the operating speed of a computer or integrated circuit. The number of times per second the clock synchronizes the computer operations. Normally measured in megahertz (n millions of cycles per second). Also can be measured in hertz (n cycles per second) or kilohertz (n thousands of cycles per second). Clock speed is most noticeable to the user in the time it takes the computer to perform a mathematical function or write characters to a screen. *See* clock and MHz.

clone Generally refers to computer hardware or software that closely resembles an original, and offers most of or all the same functionality at a lower cost. Normally fully interchangeable with the original.

close *(ATT)* System call used to close an open file. *See* system call and open.

closedir *(BSD)* **Close dir**ectory. Command used to close a directory file opened with the opendir library function. *See* opendir.

closef Close file. Routine used to de-allocate an i-number to the inode table. *See* FIO and inode table.

clri *(ATT/XEN)* **Clr** **i**node. Older program used to perform file system checks. Replaced by the fsck command. *See* fsck, file consistency check and inode.

CLTP Connectionless Transport Protocol. Open Systems Interconnection protocol that provides for packet transmission. Sends packets, called datagrams, from an application program on a host to an application program on a remote host(s). Does not guarantee data delivery.

cluster 1. Pages of memory that are physically located next to one another and are grouped together. 2. When a number of computers function as a single computer. They are connected by a high-speed network and work as a large computer with many central processing units. *See* CPU.

cmask Creation mask. System wide default that sets the access permissions on system and user files and directories when they are created. *See* umask and permissions.

CMC Common Message Call. An application programming interface to aid developers in developing electronic-mail and mail-related applications when they do not understand the supporting mail system. *See* e-mail.

CMIP *(INET)* Common Management Information Protocol. Also called Communications Management Information Protocol. An international hierarchical and secure network management and monitoring protocol originally developed by IBM Corp. and 3Com Corp., and endorsed by Open Systems Interconnection. Used to facilitate data exchange with Transmission Control Protocol/Internet Protocol networks. CMIP is transport protocol-independent and is used on other protocols, e.g. IBM's Systems Network Architecture. *See* Internet, OSI, TCP/IP, CMIS, SNMP and SNA.

CMIP Over Logical Link Control
Commonly abbreviated and called CMOL. *See* CMOL.

CMIP Over TCP/IP Commonly abbreviated and called CMOT. *See* CMOT.

CMIS *(INET)* Common Management Information Services. Also called Communications Management Information Services. Open Systems Interconnection definitions of services for Transmission Control Protocol/Internet Protocol networks. *See* Internet, OSI, TCP/IP, CMIP and SNMP.

CMMU Cache/Memory Management Unit. Integrated circuit or component that performs memory management, address translation and data caching. *See* cache memory.

CMOL Common Management Information Protocol **O**ver **L**ogical **L**ink Control. Network management protocol developed by IBM Corp. and 3Com Corp. in 1990. Uses the second layer (data link layer) of the Open Systems Interconnection protocol stack to reduce the amount of memory needed to support either the Common Management Information Protocol or Simple Network Management Protocol. *See* CMIP, OSI, data link layer and SNMP.

CMOS Complementary **metal** **o**xide semiconductor. Integrated chip technology used for random access memory that requires very low power for operation. With less heat being emanated, there is less danger of damage to the hardware. *See* RAM.

CMOT *(INET)* Common **M**anagement Information Protocol **O**ver **T**CP/IP. Set of communications standards developed to move networks from the Internet Transmission Control Protocol/Internet Protocol to the Open Systems Interconnection protocols. *See* TCP/IP, Internet, OSI and CMIP.

cmp *(ATT/BSD/XEN)* **C**om**p**are. Command used to compare the contents of two files, either text or non-text, and display the first instance of a difference between them. If run without an option, provides the character and line number of the first difference only.

CNAME Canonical **Name**. Data file required for the operation of Domain Name Service that contains aliases, or nicknames, for a host. *See* DNS.

C News Set of programs and files used to manage user access to and use of USENET news. *See* USENET and news.

Cntl **C**o**nt**ro**l** key. Also abbreviated Ctrl. *See* Ctrl key.

Cntrl **C**o**ntr**o**l** key. Also abbreviated Ctrl. *See* Ctrl key.

co *(BSD)* **C**heck **o**ut. Command used to validate or create a text file from the Revision Control System revisions history file. *See* RCS.

coax Jargon for coaxial cable. *See* coaxial cable.

coaxial cable Thick twisted pair cable with an outer shield to protect communications signals from electromagnetic interference.

cobble Jargon for patching together unconventional, unexpected or workaround solutions to keep a computer system or application running, e.g. dumping data to tape and personally carrying the tapes to another system, in the same date center, instead of establishing a communications network.

COBOL **C**ommon **B**usiness **O**riented **L**anguage. Developed as part of a Department of Defense project by a team that included the late Admiral Grace Hopper. Released in 1960. Provided the first programming language with English-like commands, commonly used in non-UNIX business applications. *See* Hopper, Grace Murray.

code **1.** Commands and instructions understood by a computer, written either in a form that is easily understood by people, e.g. C language, or in a machine language. **2.** Jargon for a program.

code review Process of using independent reviewers to assess reviewing software code written by other individuals.

coding Process of writing programs, or code, for computer systems. *See* code.

coff *(ATT)* Command used to change Common Object Format File files into a.out format. *See* COFF and a.out.

COFF **C**ommon **O**bject **F**ormat **F**ile. Revised format of C language executable and object files providing support for dynamically linked object libraries. Used to create shrink-wrapped software programs that are easily transportable between computers which use the same architecture, e.g. UNIX programs for 386-based systems. Replaced by Executable and Link Format in UNIX System V, Release 4. *See* executable, object file, library, OMF, XCOFF, SVR4.x, C language and ELF.

col **1.** *(ATT/XEN)* Command used with files that contain embedded characters which may not be compatible with video terminals. Removes those characters so the contents of the file can be displayed and read on a terminal. **2.** Filter that remove reverse line feeds from nroff output files to produce columns. *See* linefeed and nroff.

colcrt *(BSD)* Command that acts as a filter and allows the user to direct the output of an nroff file, in finished format, to a screen for review. *See* nroff.

cold boot Also called boot or reboot. To start a system after the power has been turned off and then back on. *See* boot and warm boot.

cold start Commonly called cold boot. *See* cold boot.

collision Condition on a network in which two devices transmit data packets simultaneously. Since data can be transmitted by only one device at a time, the packets collide and are not delivered to the intended location.

collision detection Commonly abbreviated and called CD. *See* CD.

color graphic adapter Commonly abbreviated and called CGA. *See* CGA.

color mode Number of bits stored for each pixel on a color monitor. Each color mode, e.g. minimum color or true color, equals the maximum number of distinct colors that can be displayed. *See* pixel, minimum color, pseudo color, high color and true color.

color monitor Also called RGB monitor. Video monitor that uses separate signals to display mixtures of the three primary colors (red, green and blue) to form varying shades.

color palettes Encoding of the colors to a graphics card to be recognized by color graphics hardware.

Coloured Book Collection of protocol specifications of the British national research and development network. Each specification is identified by a Coloured Book of a different color. Coloured Book protocols are also used in Australia and New Zealand. *See* JANET.

colrm *(BSD)* **Col**umn **rem**ove. Command used to remove columns from a file and write the result to standard output, normally the user's terminal screen. *See* standard output.

column Vertical element of an array, e.g. vertical component of a spreadsheet. *See* row.

column mode Word processing term for the ability to edit text in columnar format.

COLUMNS Environmental variable in the Korn shell that defines the width of edit windows.

comb *(ATT/XEN)* **Comb**ine. One of the 13 commands in the Source Code Control System used to combine several delta files or changed files into a single file. *See* SCCS, admin, cdc, delta, get, help, prs, rmdel, scat, sccsdiff, unget, val, vc and what.

Combus Communication bus. Institute of Electrical and Electronic Engineers standard for a high-speed communication bus that integrates data, voice and image transport and processing.

Comité Consultatif Internationale de Télégraphie et Téléphonie Commonly abbreviated CCITT. Name changed to International Telecommunication Union Telecommunication Standardization Sector in 1993. *See* ITU-T.

comm *(ATT/XEN)* **Comm**on. Command used to compare two files in order to identify common lines. Can only be used with text files.

command **1.** Abbreviation for command line. *See* command line. **2.** Input instruction to an operating system or application software. Has a specific format that initiates an established process, resulting in a known output format in which only the data will vary depending on the information available within the system. Commands may have varying arguments or qualifiers that can modify either the output format or the data to be processed, or both. *See* command line. **3.** Synonym for a program. User request for the system to perform a specified task or function. **4.** Tool that can be used by itself or in combination with other commands. *See* tool.

command directories Collection of UNIX root directories that contain commands, including /bin, /usr/bin, /etc and /usr/lib.

Command Execution Module
Commonly abbreviated and called CEM. *See* CEM.

command file File that contains executable commands. *See* shell script.

command interpreter Program that reads keyboard and/or user inputs and changes them into instructions that the computer understands. The UNIX command interpreter is the shell. *See* shell.

command key Character or key that is assigned a specific function by a software package, e.g. when the vi editor is in the command mode, the letter o becomes the command key to open text editing on succeeding lines. *See* vi commands (Appendix T).

command language Instructions that are entered directly by a user, and not selected from a menu, to control a computer's operations.

command language interpreter
Commonly called shell. *See* shell.

command line In the simplest terms, all the characters that make up a command, including the arguments. Begins with the first character on the line and ends at the point on the line where the user depresses the enter key. *See* command and argument.

command line argument Commonly called option. *See* option.

command line interface Commonly abbreviated and called CLI. *See* CLI.

command mode Term in the vi editor that indicates a user is entering and executing commands and not inputting text. In command mode, the user is able to move around in the document, e.g. to perform cut-and-paste functions. *See* vi, insert mode and cut and paste.

command name First word entered on a command line to initiate a computer process. All words or characters following the command name are arguments. *See* command line and argument.

COMMANDS Variable for UNIX-to-UNIX CoPy (UUCP) that is used to define the commands which a remote system is allowed to run during a UUCP connection. *See* UUCP.

command substitution Ability in C shell to modify and re-input a previously run command. By substituting a string in an argument or option in a previously executed command, a user can obtain different data or results, e.g. if a user inputs:

CLP> vi ~whholt/kaj/meilb ⏎

when they intended to input:

CLP> vi ~whholt/kaj/myilb ⏎

they could, after exiting the new file, perform a command substitution as follows:

CLP> ^meilb^myilb^ ⏎

See string.

comment Portion of a program that contains information or comments related to its operation. Each line of a comment is preceded by a pound sign (#) to indicate to shell language not to execute the line. In C language source code, comments are preceded by the string "/*" and followed by the string "*/". *See* pound sign.

comment out To turn off the function performed by a line of code by placing a pound sign (#) at the beginning of the line. *See* pound sign.

comments Statement preceded by a delimiter in a program or script that explains what the program will do. *See* delimiter and script.

comment sign Commonly called pound sign. *See* pound sign.

Commitment, Concurrency and Recovery Commonly abbreviated and called CCR. *See* CCR.

Committed Information Rate
Commonly abbreviated and called CIR. *See* CIR.

Common Access Method Committee
Commonly called CAM Committee. *See* CAM Committee.

Common Applications Environment
Commonly abbreviated and called CAE. *See* CAE.

Common Business Oriented Language
Commonly abbreviated and called COBOL. *See* COBOL.

Common command set Commonly abbreviated and called CCS. *See* CCS.

Common Communications Support
Commonly abbreviated and called CCS. *See* CCS.

Common Desktop Environment
Commonly abbreviated and called CDE. *See* CDE.

Common Facilities Commonly abbreviated and called CF. *See* CF.

Common Information Management Protocol Commonly abbreviated and called CIMP. *See* CIMP.

common-key Term related to the Data Encryption Standard and secure Remote Procedure Call for the method used by both a client and server to encrypt and decrypt the conversion key. Generated by the Keyserver using the client's secret key and the server's public key. *See* DES, RPC, client, server, encrypt, decrypt, conversation-key, public-key, private-key, keylogin, Keyserver, timestamp, credential, verifier and window.

Common Management Information Protocol *(INET)* Commonly abbreviated and called CMIP. *See* CMIP.

Common Management Information Protocol Over Logical Link Control
Abbreviated and commonly referred to as CMOL. *See* CMOL.

Common Management Information Protocol over the Transmission Control Protocol/Internet Protocol *(INET)* Commonly abbreviated and called CMOT. *See* CMOT.

Common Management Information Services Commonly abbreviated and called CMIS. *See* CMIS.

Common Message Call Commonly abbreviated and called CMC. *See* CMC.

Common Object File Format
Commonly abbreviated and called COFF. *See* COFF.

Common Object Request Broker Architecture Commonly abbreviated and called CORBA. *See* CORBA.

Common Object Services Specification
Commonly abbreviated and called COSS. *See* COSS.

Common Open Software Environment
Commonly abbreviated and called COSE. *See* COSE.

COMMS Customer-Oriented Manufacturing Management Systems. Computer-automated manufacturing management systems used to manage production schedules based upon the customer's delivery schedule.

communication Function of the UNIX operating system. Enables one computer to "talk" to another, passing programs or data. *See* UUCP.

communication domain Commonly called domain. *See* domain.

communication protocol Common set of rules, formats or standards used for communication either within a system, or between a computer and external devices, or between computers.

communications commands U N I X commands that facilitate communications between users or computer systems. *See* e-mail, RFS, NFS, FTP, SMTP and UUCP.

Communications Management Information Protocol Commonly abbreviated and called CMIP. *See* CMIP.

communications segment A d j a c e n t grouping of sequence numbers and the data associated with the sequence numbers. *See* sequence number.

communications utility Software program that starts and then monitors communications between the computer system on which it is running and other computers with other computers.

CommUNIXcations Monthly magazine provided to UniForum members that publishes the latest news and related to UNIX hardware, software and applications. *See* UniForum.

compact *(ATT)* Command used to reduce the size of a text file. Compresses a file for storage on a disk or for transmission over a data network, Used to conserve storage area or decrease network overhead. A compacted file is normally 25 to 40 percent the size of the original file. *See* compress, uncompress, compression, compression algorithm, pack, pcat and unpack.

compact disk read-only media
Commonly abbreviated and called CD-ROM. *See* CD-ROM.

compact disk read-only memory
Commonly abbreviated and called CD-ROM. *See* CD-ROM.

companion PC Commonly called subnotebook computer. *See* subnotebook computer.

compatibility 1. Ability of existing software applications to run when the operating system is upgraded. 2. Ability of

application programs to operate on a variety of computers offered by different vendors.

compatible Capacity of hardware and/or software to function together.

compatible package Software package that allows programs written for other UNIX operating systems to run on UNIX System V, Release 4. *See* SVR4.x.

Compatible Time Sharing System
Commonly abbreviated and called CTSS. *See* CTSS.

compile Process of converting high-level programming language into machine-readable instructions. *See* high-level programming language.

compiler Program used to convert programs written in high-level programming language into machine-readable instructions which a computer can understand and act on. *See* source code, assembly language and machine language.

compiler virus Illegal program or virus put into a compiler that adds a Trojan horse or other form of virus when programs containing specific commands are compiled. *See* compiler, virus and Trojan horse.

complementary metal oxide semiconductor Commonly abbreviated and called CMOS. *See* CMOS.

complete pathname Commonly called absolute pathname. *See* absolute pathname.

Complex Instruction Set Computing
Commonly abbreviated and called CISC. *See* CISC.

compound command Group of commands, combined to do complex jobs.

compound mail Commonly abbreviated and called multimedia mail. *See* multimedia mail.

compress Command used to reduce the size of files by approximately 50 percent using the Lempel-Ziv algorithm. *See* compressdir, uncompress, compression, compression algorithm, LZ, pack, pcat and unpack.

compressdir *(BSD)* Shell script for reducing the size of all files contained in a directory. Uses the compress command. *See* compress.

Compressed Serial Line Internet Protocol *(INET)* Commonly abbreviated and called C-SLIP. *See* C-SLIP.

compression Any technique used to decrease data storage or transfer requirements by reducing the size of files, e.g. by removing gaps or empty fields. *See* compact, compress, pack and pcat.

compression algorithm Set of specific mathematical rules or formulas used to reduce the size of data files. Common compression algorithms include simple schemes in which repeated characters or strings of characters are replaced by a symbol and the number of repetitions, e.g. the Huffman used by pack, and the Lempel-Ziv used by compress, in which common substrings are replaced by a 9- to 16-bit token representing the substring. *See* algorithm.

computer Machine capable of accepting information and processing it according to specified instructions. Can make computations, perform logic operations and otherwise process information at extremely high speeds. Composed of hardware (e.g. central processing unit, memory, communications interface and internal storage media) and software (e.g. operating system and application programs). Accessed by using display terminals, keyboards, external storage media, etc.

computer-aided design Commonly abbreviated and called CAD. *See* CAD.

Computer-Aided Manufacturing International Commonly abbreviated and called CAMI. *See* CAMI.

computer-aided software engineering Commonly abbreviated and called CASE. *See* CASE.

computer-assisted instruction Commonly called CBT (computer-based training). *See* CBT.

computer-assisted training Commonly called CBT (computer-based training). *See* CBT.

computer-augmented learning Commonly called CBT (computer-based training). *See* CBT.

computer-based fax Commonly abbreviated and called CBF. *See* CBF.

computer-based learning Commonly abbreviated and called CBL. *See* CBL.

computer-based training Commonly abbreviated and called CBT. *See* CBT.

computer bomb Commonly called bomb. *See* bomb.

computer cards Also called Hollerith cards, IBM cards, punch cards or cards. Input and output media developed by Dr. Herman Hollerith for the 1890 census. In 1928 an 80-column computer card was developed by IBM Corp. to input, store and transmit computer data. A series of rectangular holes were punched in them to represent a specific set of characters. In many cases, hundreds of thousands of cards were required to represent a single program.

Computer Emergency Response Team Commonly abbreviated and called CERT. *See* CERT.

computerese Technical dialect spoken only by computers and computer nerds. *See* computer nerd.

computer geek Commonly called computer nerd. *See* computer nerd.

computer integrated manufacturing Commonly abbreviated and called CIM. *See* CIM.

Computer Graphics Metafile
Commonly abbreviated and called CGM.
See CGM.

computerize To convert an operation that
is done manually into one that can be
performed on a computer, usually so that
it can provide more efficient, precise and
error-free results.

computer nerd Also called computer
geek. Stereotype of a person who lives
and breathes computers, and appears to
have no life outside of his or her keyboard,
monitor and/or computer programs.
Seen and described by those without as
much dedication to the workings of computer systems or software as someone
who walks around with a dazed or fara-
way look, generally has no social life, talks
only to himself and/or terminals, and
speaks or understands only computerese.
Also is known to start counting at 0 instead of 1. *See* computerese and super
computer nerd.

Computer Oracle and Password System
Commonly abbreviated and called COPS.
See COPS.

**Computer Professionals for Social Re-
sponsibility** Commonly abbreviated and
called CPSR. *See* CPSR.

computer room environment
Commonly called controlled environment. *See* controlled environment.

Computer Science Network Commonly
abbreviated and called CSNET. *See*
CSNET.

Computer Users of Europe Commonly
abbreviated and called CUE. *See* CUE.

computer virus Commonly called virus.
See virus.

**Computing Systems: The Journal of the
USENIX Association** Quarterly journal,
free to USENIX Association members,
that publishes articles on UNIX and related systems. *See* USENIX Association,
The and ;login:.

comstat *(INET)* Internet mail daemon
used to inform the user when new electronic mail has arrived. *See* Internet,
daemon and e-mail.

concatenate To combine two or more files
into a single file. *See* cat.

conceptware Jargon for software in the
initial stages of development when the
idea for the software is being discussed.

concurrency Process of providing multiple users simultaneous access and the
ability to update the same data.

Concurrent C/C++ language Extension
of the C and C++ languages, offering parallel programming. *See* C language, C++
language and parallel programming.

concurrent license Commonly called dynamic license. *See* dynamic license.

concurrent processing Process of running more than one process at a time on a
computer. *See* multiprocessing and parallel processing.

Concurrent Version System
Commonly abbreviated and called CVS.
See CVS.

condition Operational state of a computer or software. *See* mode and state.

conditional execution When the start of
one program is dependent on the successful completion of another program.

conditional statement Element of a program that tests for predefined conditions
to determine which part of the program is
to be started next.

conductor Material with the property to
easily conduct electricity, e.g. copper,
gold, silver and other metals. *See* semiconductor and non-conductor.

conferencing Facility on computer systems that allows users at different geographic locations to exchange
information or participate in electronic
meetings, e.g. through bulletin board systems such as USENET News and pro-

grams such as write and talk. *See* USENET, talk and write.

confidentiality Security method that makes the computer system, user accounts and files inaccessible to unauthorized persons.

/config *(ATT)* UNIX System V, Release 4 root file system directory that holds the files used to create a new operating system. *See* SVR4.x and root file system.

config 1. *(ATT)* Configuration. Program executed to identify, initialize and name hardware devices on a system.) 2. Key word used in creating the kernel by identifying the size and location of the root directory and swap and paging areas. 3. *(BSD)* Command used to create the contents of the directories in /usr/sys which contain the configuration of the kernel, e.g. type of central processing unit, maximum number of users, timezone and limit on user disk space.

Config File used in UNIX System V, Release 4 Basic Network Utilities that permits the system administrator to manually override selected parameters used for protocols supported by UNIX-to-UNIX CoPy. *See* SVR4.x, BNU and UUCP.

config file Jargon term or abbreviation for configuration file. *See* configuration files.

configuration Components of a computer system. The total configuration consists of: the capability of the computer, e.g. the amount of random access memory available, and the number and size of the disk drives; the software, including the version of the operating system and any additional applications software; the type and number of peripheral devices, e.g. terminals and printers; and performance tuning and communications parameters.

configuration directory List of files with the information needed to configure the UNIX operating system. The primary system configuration directory is /etc for AT&T Co.'s UNIX operating systems and /SYS for the Berkeley Software Distribu-

tion operating system. *See* configuration and configuration files.

configuration files Files located in /etc for the AT&T UNIX operating systems and /sys for the Berkeley Software Distribution *(BSD)* operating system. Configuration files in the AT&T operating system include /etc/passwd, which contains a database of users on the system, and /etc/checklist, which contains a list of file systems to be checked by the fsck command. Examples of BSD configuration files are found in directories such as /sys/conf, which contains a file with the configuration for the system kernel, and /sys/net, which contains the kernel files for hardware used to connect to networks.

configuration management Process in which all physical and logical aspects of a computer system or communications network are identified, tracked and managed. Assets maintained in configuration management include, but are not limited to, make and model of a computer, type and version of an operating system, types and versions of application programs, and numbers and versions of peripherals.

configuration procedure Process followed by a system administrator to match the files, device drivers, etc., within the kernel to the hardware and applications used with the computer. *See* device driver and kernel.

configuration value Parameter or datum used to specify an option that can be configured.

conforming POSIX applications with extensions *(POS)* UNIX applications which, along with Portable Operating System Interface for Computer Environments (POSIX) functions, use functions that comply with POSIX standards but are not developed as part of POSIX. *See* POSIX.

conforming POSIX shell application *(POS)* UNIX shell that uses extensions along with Portable Operating System Interface for Computer Environments (POSIX) functions. These functions comply with International Organization for Standardization or national standards, and are fully documented. *See* extension, ISO, shell and POSIX.

connection 1. Communications path between a sender and receiver. Starts with the communication software or protocol of the sender and ends with the communication software or protocol of the receiver. 2. Physical or logical link either between nodes on a network or between a computer and its peripherals.

connectionless mode Commonly called connectionless service. *See* connectionless service.

Connectionless Network Protocol Commonly abbreviated and called CLNP. *See* CLNP.

Connectionless Network Service Commonly abbreviated and called CLNS. *See* CLNS.

connectionless service Packet switch communications networks in which there are neither pre-established paths between the sending and receiving nodes for the data to follow nor dedicated communication lines between hosts on the network. There is no pre-established connection between the sender and receiver before data transmission. Each packet contains the data along with the address of the receiver. This allows each packet to act independently, traveling from node to node on a network as traffic load and availability of nodes permit. When all packets arrive at the receiving location, they are reassembled into their original condition. *See* datagram, node and CLNP.

connectionless transport Use of datagrams or packets to send messages that include the addressing information. A connection between the sender and receiver is not established before sending data. *See* UDP.

Connectionless Transport Protocol Commonly abbreviated and called CLTP. *See* CLTP.

connection-oriented network service Commonly abbreviated and called CONS. *See* CONS.

connection-oriented service Communication where data is transferred, in order, over virtual circuits. Communication is made in three distinct steps: connection between sender and receiver; data transfer; and termination of the connection.

connect request Berkeley Software Distribution term for a system-to-system request initiated by a user for access to a remote host. *See* BSD.

connect time Amount of time a user or host is connected to a network or computer system.

CONS Connection-oriented network service. Government Open System Interconnection Profile feature used in a subnetwork that bypasses use of the Connectionless Network Protocol and uses virtual circuits. *See* GOSIP and CLNP.

consistency check Process used to ensure data matches established criteria. *See* fsck.

console 1. Also called console monitor or system console. Terminal that is specifically attached to a port which has been reserved for system administration. There is direct communication between the console and central processing unit. The console remains active when the system is taken to single-user mode and all other ports have been turned off. *See* single-user state. 2. Terminal or workstation used by network administrators to manage and control the network and devices connected to it. More commonly called management station. *See* management station.

console logging Recording system messages, e.g. alarms or errors on the console. *See* console.

console monitor Commonly called console. *See* console.

console processor Separate processor or computer that only interacts with the primary central processing unit. Used to start up and shut down the system, to monitor the system and to perform hardware or software diagnostics.

consortium Association formed as a partnership among users, vendors and others with common objectives. Cannot develop formal standards but can prepare informal standards or influence the contents of formal standards. *See* de facto, de jure and MOSES.

Consultative Committee on International Telegraphy and Telephony Commonly abbreviated and called CCITT. Name changed to International Telecommunication Union Telecommunication Standardization Sector in 1993. *See* ITU-T.

context search While in the text editor, examination of a text document for a specific pattern or string. *See* string and editor.

context switching In multi-tasking, process of switching, as required, data needed to run a process (the context) on a central processing unit with data used to run another process. Can be used instead of allocating set blocks of CPU time to each process.

contiguous file Any file stored in an adjacent area of a disk. *See* fragmentation and defragmentation.

contingency planning Commonly called disaster planning. *See* disaster planning.

continue Shell command used to cause the next incident of a do, for or while command.

continue signal Commonly called sigcont. *See* sigcont.

continuous feed paper Paper that comes in fanfolds or rolls with perforations between each sheet and small holes down both sides. These allow it to be attached to the sprockets of a printer and automat-ically fed through the printer. Comes in a variety of sizes and finishes; can be supplied in bulk (by the box); and is available in blank sheets or as preprinted business forms, e.g. invoices.

control character American Standard Code for Information Interchange character that performs special functions most often related to initiating specific functions within a computer system. Users initiate control characters by simultaneously depressing the control key and another key, or keys. For example, certain characters can start or stop a printer; a Ctrl g can initiate a bell or buzzing sound on terminals capable of audible sound; and a Ctrl h can cause the cursor to move one space backward. A control character is represented by a caret (^). *See* ASCII and control key.

control code Commonly called control character. *See* control character.

control key Commonly abbreviated Ctrl key. *See* Ctrl key.

controlled environment Physical conditions of a computer room consisting of the power, temperature and humidity. Each variable has an acceptable tolerance range established by the computer vendor for proper operation of the hardware. The variables are constantly monitored to ensure they remain within these ranges. In addition, electrical power is provided on a separate circuit with an uninterrupted power supply. This protects against power surges and brown outs, and provides battery backup.

controller Key word used in building the kernel to identify the controller for the disk and tape drives along with the type of bus interface. *See* kernel.

Control Program for Microcomputers Commonly abbreviated and called CP/M. *See* CP/M.

control terminal Commonly called terminal device file. *See* terminal device file.

conv *(ATT)* **Convert.** Command used to call macros used to convert text to uppercase, lowercase or standard 7-bit ASCII characters.

convergence Ability of a video monitor to properly align colors on the monitor, preventing the bleeding of colors between images and characters. *See* barrelling, blooming, bowing, flicker, keystone, persistence and pincushioning.

conversation-key Term related to the Data Encryption Standard and secure Remote Procedure Call. The conversation-key is generated by the Keyserver to encrypt and decrypt the timestamp. *See* DES, RPC, client, server, encrypt, decrypt, common-key, public-key, private-key, keylogin, Keyserver, timestamp, credential, verifier and window.

conversion Process of changing data from one format to another.

convert *(ATT)* **Convert**. Command used to change archived UNIX System V, Release 1 or XENIX files into UNIX System V, Release 2 archive files. Can be used with the -5 option to convert pre-System V files into files that can be read by System V.

cooked Jargon for a file that is a finished product. A cooked file is generated by running the original file through either the nroff or troff text processing program to create a formatted, finished product. *See* nroff, troff and raw.

cooked mode **1.** Also called line mode. State of terminal input operation. Indicates there is input from a terminal and that the computer will take no action until the carriage return or enter key has been depressed. *See* cbreak mode and raw mode. **2.** Mode of operation in which input uses the UNIX input/output system for character interpretation. Supports basic editing and flow control, specifically the delete or backspace, ^S or ^Q, the interrupt (^C or DEL), etc. Slower than the raw mode but is device-independent, providing portability.

Cooperation for Open Systems in Europe Commonly abbreviated and called COSINE. *See* COSINE.

cooperative processing Commonly called distributed processing. *See* distributed processing.

copen *(ATT)* Routine used for managing user input/output to create new files.

Copper Distributed Data Interface Commonly abbreviated and called CDDI. *See* CDDI.

coprocessor Alternative processor(s) designed to perform a specific function, e.g. mathematical computation, thereby relieving the central processing unit and enabling it to operate faster. *See* CPU.

COPS Computer Oracle and Password System. Also called Computer Oracle Password and Security system. Software program, composed of shell files and C programs, used by system administrators to identify and close security holes in a system, e.g. permission settings and easy-to-decipher passwords. Developed by Dan Farmer in 1989 while working on an independent study project at Purdue University.

copy **1.** *(ATT)* UNIX System V, Release 4 Framed Access Command Environment command used to make a copy of a file. *See* SVR4.x, FACE and cp. **2.** Category of system backup utilities. Copiers duplicate everything on the system; they do not allow a single file or file system to be recovered, e.g. the AT&T Co. volcopy. *See* file system and volcopy. **3.** To make a duplicate of a file or move all or part of text, graphics, etc., from one file to another or from one part of a file to another. **4.** *(XEN)* Command used to copy several files at the same time.

copycat Polite term for companies that circumvent patents or copyrights on products to avoid paying fees to the owners.

copyleft Policy of the Free Software Foundation, which stipulates any software developed using free software from FSF must be provided free to other users. *See* FSF.

copy-on-write Memory management method. Data or text pages are copied only when a process writes them to a disk. When a program attempts to write to a shared page or block of memory, the data is copied so the program has its own copy. Other programs sharing the data continue to see the original, unchanged version.

CORBA Common Object Request Broker Architecture. Object Management Group (OMG) specification for the Object Request Broker. Standard jointly developed in 1991 by the OMG and X/Open Co. Ltd. that outlines a messaging specification for communication between software applications based upon objects. CORBA is used in combination with the Common Object Services Specification to form the architecture of the OMG's object oriented applications programming. *See* OMG, COSS, object and ORB.

cordless LAN Commonly abbreviated and called CLAN. *See* CLAN.

core **1.** Record written to file of the data in a computer's memory, either when a system crashes or when a running program tries to do something illegal. **2.** File in which a record is saved of the data in a computer's memory when a system crashes. *See* crash and panic. **3.** Also called internal memory, internal storage, main storage and primary storage. Term for main memory. Originated when memory in a computer was magnetic material known an inductor coreSee main memory.

core dump **1.** Process of saving a copy of the data in memory when a memory error occurs, e.g. as a result of a memory segmentation fault or system crash. **2.** Synonym for core, or the file created as a result of a crash. *See* crash.

corefile *(ATT)* Program used to evaluate or edit an aborted object file or core.

core file Commonly called core. *See* core.

core image Commonly called core dump. *See* core dump.

coremap Commonly spelled core map. *See* core map.

core map Data structure of the kernel used to manage main memory.

Corporate Facilitators of Object-Oriented Technology Group formed to promote the need for a standard interface with object-oriented databases to the standards organizations. *See* OO, OOP and OMG.

Corporation for Open Systems International Commonly abbreviated and called COS. *See* COS.

Corporation for Research and Education Networking Commonly abbreviated and called CREN. *See* CREN.

correlative database Set of guidelines and rules maintained in a primary dictionary that eliminates the need for users to know the exact structure of a database.

corrupted State of any system or file that has been accessed or changed without authorization.

COS Corporation for Open Systems International. Organization similar to UNIX International, founded in 1986. Formed by user companies to promote connectivity and interoperability of computer and communications hardware by using Open Systems Interconnection protocols and standards. Membership consists of 30 companies, including ARCO, DHL Systems and McDonald's. Located in McLean, Virginia. *See* OSI, UI and SPAG.

COSE Common Open Software Environment. Pronounced COZY. Group announced at the UniForum conference in March 1993, organized to provide a standard graphical user interface for desktop UNIX, known as the Common Desktop Environment. The standard does not address portability of an application between vendor hardware, but does provide a common look and feel to reduce training costs if hardware is changed. Has more than 70 vendor members but was originally formed by the Hewlett-Packard Co., IBM Corp., The Santa Cruz Operation Inc., SunSoft Inc., Univel Inc. and UNIX System Laboratories Inc. Univel and UNIX Systems Laboratories are now the UNIX Systems Group. The effort was seen by many as a means to end the UNIX Wars and fend off potential in-roads by Microsoft Corp.'s Windows New Technology by providing a single standard specification. *See* GUI, CDE, Spec 1170, UNIX Wars and NT.

COSINE Cooperation for Open Systems in Europe. Program sponsored by the European Commission to connect European research and development networks using Open Systems Interconnection.

COS Mark Corporation for Open Systems International term indicating a product has been certified for its compliance to Open Systems Interconnection standards. *See* COS and OSI.

COSS Common Object Services Specification. Set of specifications developed by the Object Management Group (OMG) and used to define the object service, e.g. object naming, event modification and life cycle. Used with the Common Object Request Broker Architecture to form the architecture of OMG's object-oriented applications programming. *See* OMG, CORBA and object.

count 1. Term in the vi editor program for the number placed in front of a vi command, e.g. 3dd, deletes the line the cursor is currently on and the following two lines, so that if the cursor was on line 256, lines 256, 257 and 258 would be deleted. *See* vi and vi commands (Appendix T). **2.** Pointer used by the kernel to track the location of the next free block in the superblock's free list. *See* kernel, superblock and free list.

coupler Jargon for an acoustic coupled modem. *See* acoustic coupled modem.

courier Term used in the Open Software Foundation Inc.'s Distributed Computing Environment distributed time service. A local server that connects with a global server to synchronize time. *See* OSF, DCE, DTS, time server, global server and local server.

COZY Pronunciation of COSE, the acronym for the Common Open Software Environment. *See* COSE.

cp *(ATT/BSD/XEN)* Copy. Command used to make a copy of a file. Leaves the source file in its original state and creates a mirror image of it with a new file name.

cpi Characters per inch. Measurement of the number, and therefore the size, of letters (characters) that can be printed horizontally. The higher the number, the smaller the size of the character. Most printers generally output at 10 or 12 cpi. *See* pitch, elite and pica.

CPI Clocks per instruction. Number of clock cycles needed to complete a single processor instruction. *See* clock cycle.

cpio *(ATT/XEN)* Copy input/output. Probably the most commonly used program for running system backups. Developed to replace tar, the cpio command that copies files from or between storage media. *See* tar and backup.

CP/M Control Program for Microcomputers. Operating system for personal computers developed in 1976 by Digital Research Inc. *See* DOS.

cpp C preprocessor. Command used to preprocess C language macros, similar to m4. Called by the cc program, which manipulates data before the data is sent to another process for actual processing. *See* C language, cc and m4.

cprs *(ATT)* Command used to compress object files. *See* object.

cps Characters per second. Measurement of the output, or transmission, of characters over communications lines, data buses and other transmission media.

cpset *(ATT)* Command used to install object files in bin directories. *See* object and /bin.

CPSR Computer Professionals for Social Responsibility. Organization of computer professionals that works to foster understanding of legal and social issues related to computer use.

cpu Key word used in building the kernel to identify the type of central processing unit on which the kernel is to run. *See* CPU.

CPU Central processing unit. The brain of a computer, where all computations are done and programs are executed or run. In older systems there was a single CPU but in more modern computers there are multiple CPUs that work together. *See* chart below.

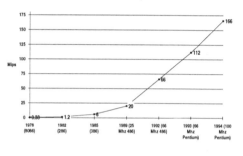

Faster is better

Using Intel microprocessors as an example, the speed of microprocessors has skyrocketed in a few short years. In 1978, the 8086 was capable of 330,000 instructions per second while in 1994 a Pentium processor could operate at 166 mips.

CPU time Central processing unit time. Time needed by a CPU to run program instructions. *See* CPU.

crack Jargon for an attempt by an unauthorized individual to gain access to a system, obtain user or system passwords, access user files, etc. *See* cracker and hacker.

cracker Technically, the correct term for what has become the current definition of a hacker. One who exceeds or attempts to exceed his level of access to a computer system. *See* dark-side hacker and hacker.

craps *(ATT)* Command used to start a craps game.

crash **1.** *(ATT)* Command used to determine the cause of a system failure. Displays outputs of the operating system and examines core dumps. *See* core and panic. **2.** Any time the system stops its normal functions without systematically stopping user or system processes. Usually indicates an unplanned system failure, but can be induced when trying to isolate a problem with the system. Many times caused by an OH S*!T!! or OOPS!! command. *See* OH S*!T!! command and OOPS!! command.

crash dump Image of the computer system's memory at the time of a system crash. *See* core.

crashme *(OTH)* Program used to determine the various ways in which failure of an operating system can be caused. Used by system administrators to find weaknesses in an operating system and the conditions which should be avoided to prevent system outages.

crash recovery Ability of a computer to restart operations following a crash.

CRC Cyclic redundancy check. Mathematical technique used in testing and eliminating errors introduced in data transmission, or used in security to determine if a file has been modified. The receiver of the transmission performs exact calculations on each block of data transmitted. The block is repeatedly transmitted until either the data received is correct or the number of retransmissions allowed is exceeded. As a security check, CRC is used to compare the current size of a file to the original file size, maintained in a database.

CRC algorithm Commonly abbreviated and called CRC. *See* CRC.

creat *(ATT)* System call used to create a file. *See* system call.

create **1.** *(ATT)* Shell layer command used to start a new shell layer with an optional name. *See* shl, delete and kill. **2.** UNIX System V, Release 4 Framed Access Command Environment file system operations command menu. Used to start an editor to create a new file. *See* SVR4.x, FACE, file system and editor. **3.** To make a new file.

creation date   Date a file was first created. *See* access date and modification date.

creation mask   Commonly abbreviated and called cmask. *See* cmask.

credential   Term related to the system security for the Remote Procedure Call. A credential is sent by the client for all RPC transactions to identify the user making a request. *See* RPC, client and verifier.

cref   *(ATT)*   **C**ross-**ref**erence. Command used to create a cross-reference list of C language or assembler programs. *See* C language and assembler.

CREN   Corporation for Research and Educational Networking. Academic research and development network formed by combining the Because It's Time NETwork and Computer+Science Network. *See* BITNET and CSNET.

C++ Reseller Alliance   Collection of vendors teamed with UNIX System Laboratories Inc. to enhance and sell products based on C++. Members include Apple Computer Inc., NCR Corp., The Santa Cruz Operation Inc., Sequent Computer Systems Inc. and Sun Microsystems Inc. *See* C++ language.

crippleware   Jargon for software from which critical elements have been deliberately removed by the manufacturer. This is a strategy aimed at enticing buyers to purchase upgrades containing the missing elements.

Cutaway of monitor with cathode ray tube in the foreground.

crlf   Abbreviation for **c**arriage **r**eturn and **l**ine **f**eed.

cron   Also called the system alarm clock or time keeper. Daemon that starts other programs identified in the computer system's crontab at a pre-established time. Location of the crontab varies among the types and versions of the UNIX operating system. *See* crontab.

cron.allow   File containing a list of users authorized to use the cron daemon. *See* cron.

cronlog   Commonly written as /usr/adm/cronlog. *See* /usr/adm/cronlog.

crontab   **1.** *(ATT)* Command that generates or displays files containing the commands to be executed by the cron daemon. **2.** Before System V, Release 2 and early versions of the Berkeley Software Distribution *(BSD)*, a file in /usr/lib, and after System V, Release 2, a file in /usr/spool/cron. Contains the files listing all the programs to be run by the cron daemon. In 4.3BSD, a new file /usr/lib/crontab.local was added that lists all the programs run by cron. *See* cron.

crontab.local   Commonly written as /usr/lib/crontab.local. *See* /usr/lib/crontab.local.

cross compiler   Compiler that can convert programs into machine instructions for more than one type of computer. *See* compiler.

crosstalk   **1.** Communications term used to describe the overlapping of signals in adjoining frequencies. **2.** Digital Audio Tape term for the overlapping of signals between tracks. *See* DAT.

CRT   **1.** Cathode ray tube. Screen portion of a video display terminal. Consists of a large electronic vacuum tube with an electron gun and screen. Characters are created on the screen by electronic transmissions that charge or uncharge spots. This causes the phosphor coating on the inside of the vacuum tube to glow, generating the characters. *See* electron gun. **2.** Video display terminal. *See* terminal.

crunch Jargon for the arithmetic functions performed by a computer.

crypt 1. C language library routine that generates an encrypted password by taking the user's input and adding information. *See* library routines, salt and encrypt. **2.** *(ATT/BSD/XEN)* Specialized library routine used to encrypt and decrypt a file. Files are run through an encryption algorithm with a key word or password assigned to the file owner. If someone other than the owner accesses the file, without decrypting it, all that person will see is gibberish. *See* library routines and encrypt. **3.** Command used to encrypt passwords, based on the Data Encryption Standard encryption algorithm. *See* DES algorithm.

cryptography Commonly called encryption. *See* encryption.

csh 1. C shell. Command used to start the C shell. **2.** UNIX abbreviation for a user who is running the C shell. *See* C shell.

C shell Command language interpreter for the Berkeley Software Distribution and used in UNIX System V written at the University of California, Berkeley, by Bill Joy. Not as widely distributed as the Bourne shell but is considered to be more interactive and user-friendly. Uses the percent sign (%) as the default prompt.

.cshrc C shell run command. System file established in the Berkeley Software Distribution and UNIX System V, Release 4 user account. Normally used to establish variables defined by the user. Read during the login sequence for user-defined aliases, paths to be read for commands, user-modified umask, prompt, etc. *See* BSD and SVR4.x.

CSLIP *(INET)* Compressed Serial Line Internet Protocol. Commonly spelled C-SLIP. *See* C-SLIP.

C-SLIP *(INET)* Compressed Serial Line Internet Protocol. Also spelled CSLIP. Im-

proved version of SLIP developed in 1989 by Van Jacobson of Lawrence Berkeley Laboratories. Reduces the number of bytes of data transmitted without affecting transmission quality. *See* SLIP, PPP, Internet Protocol Suite and Internet.

CSMA Carrier Sense Multiple Access. Communications technique that allows multiple users access to the same channel for connection to a computer. The communications network has sufficient ability to recognize when the channel is in use and to delay transmission by other users until the channel is free.

CSMA/CD Carrier Sense Multiple Access/Collision Detection. Sometimes referred to as CSMA-CD. Carrier Sense Multiple Access network system which also can determine when two nodes are trying to transmit data at the same time and delay transmission of one until the channel is free. The common method of channel management used for Ethernet local area networks. *See* CSMA and Ethernet.

CSNET Computer+Science Network. Academic research and development network used to maintain and transfer data for universities, research laboratories and other organizations. With BITNET, formed the Corporation for Research and Education Networking. *See* CREN and BITNET.

csplit *(ATT/XEN)* Context **split**. Command used to divide large files into small files based on arguments specified by the user. *See* split.

CSRG Computer Systems Research Group. Also called the Berkeley Computer Systems Research Group. University of California, Berkeley, group responsible for developing the Berkeley Software Distribution. Formed in the early 1980s when the Defense Advanced Research Projects Agency funded a project to develop a single operating system to be used for government research. CSRG did little development. It attempted to obtain software from other agencies and/or companies and incorporate it into the Berkeley Software Distribution *(BSD)*. Closed in late 1992 with the final release of Berkeley UNIX, 4.4BSD. *See* BSD and DARPA.

ct *(ATT/XEN)* **C**all **t**erminal. Command used to dial through an attached modem and phone line from a host computer to a remote computer. Once a connection is made, a getty is generated to start the login process. *See* modem and getty.

ctags **C**reate **tags**. Command used to create a tags file containing function and data definitions of objects in C language, Pascal, FORTRAN and Lisp source code. *See* tags file and source code.

ctcfmt *(ATT)* **C**artridge **t**ape **f**or**m**a**t**. Command used to format a cartridge tape.

ctrace *(ATT)* **C** language **trace**. C language debugger used to trace source code statements.

Ctrl c Standard UNIX interrupt instruction that can be changed by the user. Input when a user wants to stop a program or has created a lock situation. Under normal circumstances, this will free the lock. *See* lock.

Ctrl d UNIX end-of-file character. Used to force an end-of-file and terminate access to a file. Also can be used to log off from or exit the system.

Ctrl key **1. Control key**. Found on the lower left-hand corner of most keyboards. Used with alphabetic or special keys to transmit a specific sequence of instructions to either the software or hardware, e.g. Ctrl c to interrupt a process; Ctrl z to suspend operations; and Ctrl \ to quit. **2.** Key used in combination with other keys to modify the operation of a computer by stopping or starting a function.

CTS **C**lear-**t**o-**s**end. Communications signal indicating a data terminal is ready to receive data.

CTSS **C**ompatible **T**ime **S**haring **S**ystem. Forerunner of MULTICS and eventually UNIX, developed by the Massachusetts

Institute of Technology in 1964. *See* MULTICS, UNICS and UNIX.

cu **C**all **U**NIX or call up. Command used to connect with another UNIX system or most computers with asynchronous American Standard Code for Information Interchange communications. Provides for a virtual connect, allowing either systems or users to make a connection, log on and perform normal UNIX commands and functions as if they had a direct connection to the system. *See* asynchronous communications and ASCII.

cubic *(ATT)* Command used to start a 4-by-4-by-4 tic-tac-toe game.

cuckoo's egg Program placed in a system by a hacker that substitutes for a standard program and allows the hacker to gain unauthorized access to data. Term introduced by Clifford Stoll in his book The Cuckoo's Egg. *See* hacker and Trojan horse.

CUE **C**omputer **U**sers of **E**urope. Organization formed in 1992 and composed of more than 400 European information services managers. Lobbies the governing bodies of the European Community and individual countries on laws and regulations affecting the use of computers and software.

CUI **C**haracter-based **u**ser **i**nterface. Computer input made a character at a time through a keyboard.

cumulative trauma disorder Commonly called RSI (repetitive strain injury). *See* RSI.

cunix *(ATT)* **C**onfigure **UNIX**. System administration command used to set up a new UNIX operating system.

current directory Commonly called current working directory. *See* current working directory.

current file Editor term referring to the file currently being edited.

current line **1.** Line on which the cursor is located in text during text processing. **2.**

Line in the edit buffer on which modifications are being made.

current name server Primary or secondary name server that is currently acting as the domain name server, which monitors and maintains the file-sharing environment for the network. *See* DNS, primary name server and secondary name server.

current working directory Directory in which the user is currently working and which gives him direct and immediate access to the files it contains.

curses *(ATT)* Screen handling library of routines written by Mark Horton. Allows users to control the location of the cursor on the screen. Interacts with either the AT&T Co. termcap or the Berkeley Software Distribution terminfo files to provide the ability to design software that will fully function through any terminal. Allows windows to be created on American Standard Code for Information Interchange terminals. *See* termcap, terminfo, cursor, ASCII terminal and dumb terminal.

cursor Symbol on the terminal screen that indicates where the next character will be input or appear. May be a small blinking line or constant reverse video block. Its appearance can generally be selected by a user from the set-up options on his terminal, personal computer or personal computer communications package.

cuserid *(ATT)* Character **user id**entifier. Standard input/output library routine used to obtain a login name of a user associated with a specific process. *See* library routines.

customer friendly Derivation of the term user friendly. Describes the ease of use of a software program, computer, peripheral device, etc. *See* user friendly.

Customer Information Control System Commonly abbreviated and called CICS. *See* CICS.

Customer Oriented Manufacturing Management Systems Commonly abbreviated and called COMMS. *See* COMMS.

cut *(ATT/XEN)* Command that allows the user to extract only specific fields or columns from a file or standard output. The extracted data appears on the screen, and can be redirected to a file or printer. *See* paste and standard output.

cut and paste To transfer text within and between documents. Word processing term derived from the old method of cutting up paper documents and pasting the pieces together in a rearranged order to form a new document.

cut sheet feeder Attachment for printers that enables a user to automatically feed in single sheets of paper instead of using fanfold or continuous feed paper. Normally offered as an option at additional cost. *See* fanfold paper and continuous feed paper.

CVS Concurrent Version System. Based upon the Revision Control System and used to manage program source code and text libraries. Provides the ability for multiple users to each make configuration changes to the same source files at the same time without affecting one another's work. *See* RCS.

cw *(ATT)* Constant width. Command in the Documenter's Workbench set of text formatting programs. Used to establish a constant width font for text developed with the troff text formatting program. *See* DWB and troff.

cwd *(BSD)* Current working directory. C shell environmental variable used to maintain a record of the current working directory. *See* current working directory.

CWD Shell environment variable that can be turned on or off. When turned on, a record of the current working directory is maintained.

C with classes Original name for C++. *See* C++ language.

cxref Cross-reference. Command used to generate a cross-reference of C language programs by evaluating the files within the programs.

cyberspace Term introduced by William Gibson in the book Neuromancer to define the shared virtual universe operating within all the world's computer networks.

cycle **1.** Any combination of tasks, commands or duties performed on a periodic basis. **2.** A clock cycle, or a single tick of a system clock, e.g. a system with a 10 megahertz clock ticks 10 million times per second. **3.** Operations performed in a single tick of a system clock, e.g. moving data from a processor into storage.

cyclical redundancy check Commonly abbreviated and called CRC. *See* CRC.

cylinder Disk tracks that can be reached from one position of the disk head assembly.

cylinder group Collection of adjacent cylinders which the file system uses to store common data. Part of the Berkeley Software Distribution hardware and software method of speeding disk access. *See* cylinder, Fast File System and file system.

D

d Abbreviation for **deci**. *See* deci.

D12 *(POS)* First voting ballot on the draft standards for POSIX.1. *See* POSIX.1 and D13.

D13 *(POS)* Approved POSIX.1 standard. *See* POSIX.1 and D12.

da Abbreviation for **deca**. *See* deca.

DA Domain administrator. Individual using the primary master server of a domain. Responsible for registering the domain with the Network Information Center, assigning names to hosts within the domain and ensuring hosts comply with the requirements of the NIC and Domain Name Service. *See* NIC, primary master server, domain and DNS.

DAC 1. Discretionary access controls. Permissions set by users establishing the level of access to a file by the owner and others. Incorporated by the Portable Operating System Interface for Computer Environments (POSIX) 1003.6 security working group for optional security controls and implemented in UNIX System V, Release 4 ES. *See* ACL, POSIX and SVR4 ES. **2.** Digital-to-Analog Converter. Technology used to convert digital information to analog in various forms, e.g. changing voltage.

DAD Distributed application development. Method developed by the Message-Oriented Middleware Consortium that permits applications to communicate between distributed computers. *See* MOM and middleware.

daemon Pronounced *DAY-MON*. Program that waits for a certain occurrence, then goes into operation to automatically manage other programs or processes. A continuous or long-running process that performs system functions, e.g. init and cron. Runs in the background, independent of users. The term was first used with computers by Mick Bailey while he was working on a predecessor to UNIX at the Massachusetts Institute of Technology. *See* init and cron.

daisy chain Interface that allows data to pass from one device to another in a series. Most commonly, disk and tape drives are daisy chained.

daisy wheel Print mechanism for letter-quality impact printers. Name is derived from the device's wheel shape, which has raised print characters along the edge. *See* daisy-wheel printer.

daisy-wheel printer Type of impact printer that uses a daisy wheel to produce type on paper. The wheel spins to the desired character, which is struck by a hammer and makes an imprint through an ink ribbon onto the paper. Produces letter-quality type, or type equivalent to that produced by an electric typewriter. Multiple print styles are available through removable print wheels. *See* daisy wheel.

DAP Directory Access Protocol. Protocol used in Open Systems Interconnection X.500 directory services to run inquiries against a Directory System agent and obtain information about users on the network. *See* OSI, X.500, DSA, DUA, DSP, DIT, DN and DISP.

daps *(ATT)* Device-independent troff postprocessor for the Autologic APS-5 phototypesetter. *See* ditroff.

dark operation Commonly called lights-out operation. *See* lights-out operation.

dark-side hacker Preferred term among computer professionals for a cracker, rather than the commonly used "hacker." *See* cracker and hacker.

DARPA *(INET)* **D**efense **A**dvanced **Re**search **P**rojects **A**gency. Department of Defense agency started in 1973 by Dr. Robert Kahn. Original sponsor of the Internet. Responsible for managing research projects related to national defense. Originally known as ARPA, the agency's name was changed to DARPA due to its predominantly military emphasis and funding by the Department of Defense. With the change of emphasis and reduction in military funding, the name was changed back to ARPA in the early 1990s. *See* ARPA, ARPANET and Internet.

DARPA Internet *(INET)* Commonly called Internet. *See* Internet.

DASD **D**irect-**a**ccess **s**torage **d**evice. Pronounced *DAZZ-DEE. See* disk.

DASD farm **D**irect-**a**ccess **s**torage **d**evice farm. Jargon term for an exceptionally large number of disk drives on a computer. *See* DASD.

DAT 1. **D**igital **A**udio **T**ape. Type of magnetic tape that transfers and records data digitally, rather than analogically. DAT tapes are based on helical scan technology, which was originally developed for videocassette recording on 4- and 8-millimeter tape. This technology provides high-density recording and large data storage capacity on small, low-cost tape. DAT tapes are capable of storing up to 3 gigabytes of uncompressed data. *See* helical scan. 2. **D**ynamic **a**ddress **t**ranslation. Conversion of a relative address of a memory location to an absolute address; done as needed to support the operation of an application when loaded into memory.

data 1. Plural of datum. Information, e.g. files, letters and numbers, that can be communicated, stored in a computer for modification, display, printing or other uses, and finally used or processed by humans. *See* datum. 2. Basic information that a computer is capable of manipulating.

data base Commonly spelled database. *See* database.

database Collection of common or similar items, e.g. a company's inventory or mailing list of customers. Composed of records (data) and fields (location) of data in a record, combined with a set of operations to add, delete, search and manipulate the data. *See* hierarchical database, RDBMS, flat file, record and field.

Data Base Administrator Commonly abbreviated and called DBA. *See* DBA.

database locking Process of granting or guaranteeing exclusive access by a process to read or write information in a database, one or more records in the database or one or more files in the database. Other processes are queued. *See* read consistency and versioning.

Database Management System Commonly abbreviated and called DBMS. *See* DBMS.

database server Computer platform devoted to the storage and operation of a database and database management system. Users normally operate, access and manipulate data from a client computer. *See* client/server and DBMS.

data bits Number of bits in a byte, as used in communications software, terminal emulators and modems to define characters for transmission. Each character is represented by either 5, 6, 7 or 8 distinctive bits. Common in both UNIX and PC data transmission software is either 7- or 8-bit characters. Both parties in the communication must use the same number of bits to communicate. The original ASCII character set specifications used 7 bits to create 128 characters. Older communications equipment thus used 7 bits to represent its character set. Communications standards evolved to incorporate 8-bit character sets as these became standard. In addition, a bit precedes and follows each transmission to identify the start and stop of a data communication. Some data transmission schemes include a parity bit, which is used to ensure accurate transmission by matching the number of bits (odd or even) being used in the system.

data block Element of a file system, along with the boot block, superblock and i-nodes. Used to store all the information contained within directories or files of a file system on a computer. *See* block and free blocks.

data collection system Real-time computer system that collects and processes data to immediately update files. *See* RTOS.

data communications Movement of data between locations by telephone line, packet switch networks, microwaves, etc.

Data Communications Equipment Commonly abbreviated and called DCE. *See* DCE.

Data/DAT One of the two competing data formats used for data access and retrieval in Digital Audio Tape technology. Data/DAT was developed by Hitachi and GigaTrend, the other, Digital Data Storage, was developed by Sony and the Hewlett-Packard Co. There are two formats used with Data/DAT. The first is sequential, which has a data transfer rate of 177 kilobytes per second and holds 1.27 gigabytes of data. The second is random, which has a data transfer rate of 136 kilobytes per second and holds 1 gigabyte of data. *See* DAT and DDS.

data dictionary One of the components of a database management system which contains a list of the description and location of the files, fields, variables, etc. used in the database. *See* DBMS.

data dipper Front-end application on a client computer responsible for starting database queries and processing the data received from the server. *See* client/server.

data encryption Systematic method of scrambling data for storage and/or transmission to protect it from unauthorized access.

Data Encryption Standard Commonly abbreviated and called DES. *See* DES.

data export Process of reading information from a database so it can be read or used by another application or database. *See* data import.

data field Column or consecutive columns required to store a single piece of information, e.g. an address or phone number.

data-flow diagram Commonly abbreviated and called DFD. *See* DFD.

data glove Glove used as an input device to capture gestures within a computer system. It is wired with sensors and connected to a computer to transmit movements to the computer. *See* 3-D data and data suit.

data-grade UTP Commonly called DTP (data grade twisted pair). *See* DTP.

datagram Communications packet that contains both data and complete address information for the user who is to receive the data. *See* packet and UDP.

data highway Commonly called the electronic highway. *See* electronic highway.

data import Process of reading information into a database from another application or database. *See* data export.

data integrity Quality and completeness of data contained in a database. Can be defined for any data on a computer system. Describes data that is in a format which conforms with the predefined state, e.g. data structure, rows, columns, table size and location, allowing the data to be processed by the computer system without error.

data link Single connection between two points on a network.

data link layer Second layer of the International Organization for Standardization/Open Systems Interconnection model network. Corrects errors, controls transmission of data between contiguous nodes on a network, and delivers messages within a single network. *See* ISO/OSI, OSIRM, HDLC, SDLC and node.

Data Link Provider Interface Commonly abbreviated and called DLPI. *See* DLPI.

data management Function of the UNIX operating system that logically organizes user data into groupings called files, making it easier to access, update and management the information.

data model Method used by an application or database designer to describe the layout of the application's data structure and the functions of each file in that structure. Allows the files to be accessed, updated, modified, etc.

Data Presentation Management Commonly abbreviated and called DPM. *See* DPM.

data processing Commonly abbreviated and called DP. *See* DP.

data rate Measurement in bits per second of the speed at which data is transferred from one medium to another. *See* baud.

data record Collection of related data fields that pertain to the same subject. *See* data field.

data region Commonly called data segment. *See* data segment.

data segment Initialized data portion of an executable file from a C language program in a.out format. The other segments are block started by symbol segment and text segment. *See* a.out, bss segment and text segment.

data sharing Ability of multiple users or processes to access and use the same data at the same time.

data-space Visual representation of complex information.

data staging Moving data, based upon predefined storage policies and plans, from main storage, e.g. from disk drives to a secondary storage medium, such as disc platters or tape.

data stream Serial data resulting from an input or output operation. *See* STREAMS.

data structure Design of the files and information within the files in a database.

data suit Input device that covers the entire body and is used to capture gestures within a computer system. It is wired with sensors and connected to a computer to transmit movements to the computer. *See* 3-D data and data glove.

data superhighway Commonly called NREN (National Research and Education Network). *See* NREN.

Data Terminal Equipment Commonly abbreviated and called DTE. *See* DTE.

data terminal ready Commonly abbreviated and called DTR. *See* DTR.

data warehouse Also called information warehouse. Term originally coined by William Inmon. Repository for enterprise data, regardless of either the operating system used by that data, e.g. UNIX or a proprietary system, or the purpose for which the data is used, e.g. for inventory control, manufacturing or customer billing. Users may directly access the information in a data warehouse but not corporate production data, and is in a format that can be understood and used by non-technical personnel.

date *(ATT/XEN)* UNIX command used to indicate or set the date and time currently recorded in the system. If input by a user or by the system administrator without an argument, the date and time recorded on the computer is displayed. When input by the system administrator with an argument, the date and/or time on the computer system is changed. Only the system administrator has permissions to change the date and time. Date and time are indicated as MMDDHHMMYY (month 11 - day 30 - hour 23 - minute 00 - year 88). The time is displayed in 24-hour clock or military time. (Hint for those not used to 24 hour clock time: If the number is greater than 12, subtract 12, e.g. 2300 - 12 = 11:00 p.m. Therefore, to set the date and time as Nov. 30, 1988, 11:00 p.m., enter: 1130230088).

datetime *(ATT)* UNIX System V, Release 4 system setup menu command similar to the date command. Used to display, set or reset the date and time on a computer. *See* date.

datum Singular form of data. *See* data.

Davenport Group Group of UNIX system vendors, software vendors and publishers formed to develop a standard interchange format for document exchange between developers and publishers. Located in Sebastopol, California.

DAY-MON Pronunciation of daemon. *See* Daemon.

DAYTIME *(INET)* Defense Advanced Research Projects Agency Internet protocol. Sends the day and time in an American Standard Code for Information Interchange character string. *See* DARPA, Internet and ASCII.

Daytime Protocol *(INET)* Commonly called DAYTIME. *See* DAYTIME.

DAZZ-DEE Pronunciation of DASD, the abbreviation for direct access storage device. *See* DASD.

DBA Data Base Administrator. Individual who is responsible for the administration (creation, updating and control) of a database.

DBMS **D**ata**b**ase **m**anagement **s**ystem. Software program that provides an interface between the user and data to access, query, create, store, manipulate and output information. Uses either a relational or hierarchical structure to store and manage data. In a relational database, data is stored based upon the relationship of the data, with the relationship used as the basis for storage and retrieval of data. In a hierarchical database, data is stored in a hierarchy structure. A DBMS consists of an interface with users, data management and a file system.

dbx Source program debugger introduced in the Fourth Berkeley Software Distribution, Second Release. A debugger capable of displaying source code common to AT&T Co.'s System V-compatible UNIX systems. *See* BSD and debugger.

.dbxint System file established in each user account for users to establish aliases for debugger commands. *See* dbx.

dc *(ATT/XEN)* Desk calculator. Interactive program that acts like a programmable desk calculator. Co-authored by Lorinda Cherry and Robert Morris. *See* bc.

DCA Defense Communications Agency. Known as a purple suit agency because it is staffed by personnel from branches of the military. Responsible for operation of the Defense Data Network. *See* DDN.

DCE 1. **D**ata **C**ommunications **E**quipment. Any communications device used in the transmission of data, e.g. a modem or terminal server. 2. Cabling configuration used to connect peripheral devices, e.g. modems, to a computer. 3. **D**istributed **C**omputing **E**nvironment. Open Software Foundation Inc.'s (OSF) architecture for developing application software to be used on heterogeneous networks. Contains tools for developers like remote procedure calls; system services such as a network directory service, security and time synchronization; and, data sharing services for diskless workstations and a distributed file system. Enables a process scheduled for a system that is backlogged to be moved to another system with available processing power. The exchange can be made with other UNIX computers or proprietary systems, as long as DCE is running on the receiving computer. Originally designed to be separated from but work with OSF's Distributed Management Environment (DME), used to manage software, peripherals and computer systems within a heterogeneous network. In November 1993, OSF announced DME was to be included in DCE as a single standard. *See* OSF, DME, ONC, WOSA, Threads library, RPC, Security Service, Directory Service, DTS, Diskless Support Service and DFS.

DCE Directory Service C o m m o n l y called Directory Service. *See* Directory Service.

DCE Threads Commonly called Threads library. *See* Threads library.

dcheck *(ATT)* Directory check. Older program used to perform file system checks on directories. Replaced by the more comprehensive fsck. *See* fsck and file system check.

dcopy *(ATT)* Data copy. Data copying utility used to reorganize the stored data while copying is taking place. Disk files are moved to better utilize space and speed access to data, and information is compressed to free space.

DC/OSx Pyramid Technology Inc.'s UNIX System V, Release 4 operating system. *See* SVR4.x.

dd Command used to convert and/or copy files. Can be used to copy files from device to device, from device to file or from file to device; make an image copy of data being copied; convert files from American Standard Code for Information Interchange to Extended Binary Coded Decimal Interchange Code, and vice versa; and convert data on tapes from or into formats common to IBM Corp. or Digital Equipment Corp.'s VAX computers. *See* image copy, restore, ASCII and EBCDIC.

DDCMP Digital Data Communications Message Protocol. Digital Equipment Corp.'s synchronous protocol.

DDI Device Driver Interface. Introduced in AT&T Co.'s System V, Release 4. Defines the device driver and hardware interface to improve compatibility between a device, e.g. disk or tape drive, and computer hardware. *See* SVR4.x, device driver and DKI.

DDM Distributed Data Management. Client/server database management architecture in which applications that are to be executed are loaded on the client. *See* client/server, DPM and DTP.

DDN *(INET)* Defense Data Network. Department of Defense Internet network connecting military locations, research agencies and contractors.

DDRM Device Driver Interface/Driver-Kernel Interface Reference Manual. UNIX System V, Release 4 system documentation for creating and maintaining device drivers. *See* SVR4.x and device driver.

DDS 1. Digital Data Storage. Data storage format developed by Sony Corp. and the Hewlett-Packard Co. that has become one of the two format standards for Digital Audio Tape. The first products were released in 1989. DDS is audio Digital Audio Tape that has data organization along with error correction. It has a data transfer rate of 183 kilobytes per second and a tape can hold up to 1.3 gigabytes of data. *See* DAT and Data/DAT. 2. Digital Data Service. Also called 56-Kbps. Standard data communication service available since the early 1970s. DDS is point-to-point leased lines with a maximum bandwidth of 56 kilobits per second.

DDT Archaic term for a program used to debug software that originated for DEC Debugging Tape. *See* debugger.

dead Jargon term for a computer that has ceased operation or shut down.

deadlock When two processes are waiting for resources controlled by the other. Term more popularly used in the United States while the preferred term in Europe is deadly embrace. *See* hung.

deadly embrace Term more popularly used in Europe. The preferred term in the United States is deadlock. *See* deadlock.

dead on arrival Commonly abbreviated and called DOA. *See* DOA.

dead space Write-once/read-many term for a file that has been stored, retrieved and modified. When the modified file is written to the disk, a new file is created and the original file remains on the disk as dead space.

debug Process of searching for and correcting logic and/or structural errors in programs.

debugger Program used to locate and correct errors in another program. *See* debug, adb, dbx and sdb.

deca Prefix for 10^1 (10) or ten. Abbreviated da.

decapsulation Process in network communication in which the receiving location looks at the header of an incoming message to determine if the message contains data and, if it does, removes the header. *See* encapsulation.

decentralized computing Movement of computer processing functions from a single or central machine to multiple computers spread across a network. *See* centralized computing.

deci Prefix for 10^{-1} (1/10) or one-tenth. Commonly abbreviated d.

decimal 1. Describes a number system using base 10. The decimal system uses numbers 0 through 9. 2. Any circumstance where there are 10 possible selections.

decision support systems Commonly abbreviated and called DSS. *See* DSS.

DECnet Proprietary networking protocol developed by Digital Equipment Corp.

decode Process of converting encoded data into an understandable form.

decrypt *(OTH)* Command used for both encryption and decryption of a file, which prompts the user to create the encryption key. *See* encryption, decryption and encryption key.

decryption Process of converting data that has been encrypted back into an understandable form. *See* encryption.

DEC Standard 144. Digital Equipment Corp.'s standard disk bad block format used on VAX and PDP-11 systems.

dedicated server network Standard LAN network architecture with a computer dedicated as a server that runs network operating system software. Client computers send requests to the server for processing. *See* LAN, network, server, client and peer-to-peer network.

dedicated terminal 1. Any terminal assigned to a single specific purpose or task. 2. Term sometimes used interchangeably with hardwired to describe a terminal that is connected to a computer with a dedicated communications cable. *See* hardwired.

DEE-RAM Pronunciation of DRAM, the acronym for dynamic random access memory. *See* DRAM.

de facto Also called public specification. Informal standard not officially recognized by a formal national or international organization that approves standards. *See* de jure.

default 1. Automatic action taken by a command, program, etc. unless a change is specified with an argument or option. *See* command, argument and option. 2. Current setting or definition of a function or layout, e.g. number of characters per line or number of lines per page, that are automatically set when the system is turned on or activated. Default settings can be changed either for a current (one-time) use or permanently (until they need to be changed again) by saving the new settings.

default creation mask   C o m m o n l y called cmask (creation mask). *See* cmask.

default rule   Definition of a default setting. *See* default.

defaults   *(ATT)* UNIX System V, Release 4 command in the software installation and information management menu. Used to establish default actions to be taken when a new software package is being installed. The default actions are steps to be taken when a problem occurs while a program is being loaded. *See* admin.

default value   Assumption made by a program about a specific action, if no specific instruction is provided by the user.

Defense Advanced Research Projects Agency   *(INET)* Commonly abbreviated and called DARPA. *See* DARPA.

Defense Communications Agency   Commonly abbreviated and called DCA. *See* DCA.

Defense Data Network   Commonly abbreviated and called DDN. *See* DDN.

Defense Message System   C o m m o n l y abbreviated and called DMS. *See* DMS.

Defense Research Internet   *(INET)* Commonly abbreviated and called DRI. *See* DRI.

defragmentation   Process to merge fragmented files into a whole, improving disk access and response time. *See* contiguous file and fragmentation.

defunct process   Commonly called zombie. *See* zombie.

defunct state   Zombie process created when a child process cannot end correctly because it is no longer recognized by its parent process. When a defunct state exists, either the init daemon, which controls all processes, will take over and kill the process, or the system administrator

will kill the process. *See* zombie, init, child process and parent process.

degauss   Magnetic process used to erase data from magnetic tapes or diskettes.

degausser   Device used to generate a magnetic field to erase magnetic tapes or diskettes. Also can be used to aid the display of colors on a video monitor by demagnetizing the coil of the electron gun used to activate the phosphor on the vacuum tube.

de jure   Formal or legal standard specified by a recognized national or international organization that approves standards, e.g. Portable Operating System Interface for Computer Environments (POSIX). *See* de facto, POSIX, ISO, OSI, ANSI and ITU-T.

del   Commonly called kill. *See* kill.

delete   **1.** *(ATT)* Shell layer command used to stop a shell layer. Added to the UNIX System V, Release 4 Face Access Command Environment file system operations command menu. *See* shl, create, SVR4.x, FACE and file system. **2.** To remove from the system, e.g. to delete a file or characters of a file.

Delete key   Commonly abbreviated Del key. *See* Del key.

delgrp   *(ATT)* **Del**ete **grp**oup. Command used by the system administrator to delete a user from a group. *See* group and addgrp.

delimiter   **1.** Marker, or special character, e.g. a colon (:), that identifies the end of a field or record in a database file. **2.** Character used to separate words, arguments, options, etc., on a command line. Normally a space in UNIX.

delivery   Term for the movement of electronic mail from a message transfer agent to the recipient's user agent in the X.400 standard. Developed by the International Telecommunication Union Telecommunication Standardization Sector, formerly called the Consultative Committee on International

Telegraphy and Telephony. *See* ITU-T, X.400, MTA, UA, submission and relay.

Del key **Del**ete **key**. Used as an interrupt to abort a process. *See* abort and process.

delta **1.** *(ATT/XEN)* One of the 13 Source Code Control System (SCCS) programs used to install changes to a SCCS file. *See* SCCS, admin, cdc, comb, get, help, prs, rmdel, sact, sccsdiff, unget, val, vc and what. **2.** A change.

DELTA Term for the changes made to a source code file using the Source Code Control System. *See* SCCS.

demand paged virtual memory
Commonly called demand paging. *See* demand paging.

demand paging Process in which only those parts of a program that are being actively used are kept in memory. *See* paging and swapping.

demigration Moving a file from a file server to a desktop client on a network. *See* file migration.

demodulation Process of converting previously modulated or wavelike analog data into its original form, e.g. converting a signal from the analog form in which it was transmitted over a telephone line back to its original digital form for processing by a computer. *See* modulation and modem.

demon Commonly spelled daemon. *See* daemon.

DEMOS **D**ialogin **P**ortable **O**perating **S**ystem. Developed by the Soviet I.V. Kurchatov Institute of Atomic Energy, Advanced Training Institute of the Ministry of the Automobile Industry of the USSR and Scientific Production Union Tsentroprogrammsystem. A UNIX Version 7 look-alike developed in the early 1980s. DEMOS/32 and DEMOS 2.1/V, later versions developed in the mid-1980s, were based upon the Berkeley Software Distribution. *See* Version 7, BSD, INMOS and MNOS.

Deny *(ATT)* UNIX System V, Release 4 restricted electronic-mail command. Used to restrict electronic-mail access to users. *See* SVR4.x, rmail, e-mail and Accept.

Department of Defense Commonly abbreviated and called DOD. *See* DOD.

depth cueing Use of visual characteristics, e.g. shading, texture, color and interposition, to provide a cue for the z-coordinates or distance of an object.

deroff *(ATT)* **De**lete **roff**. Command used to remove nroff, troff, tbl and eqn format commands from a file. *See* nroff, troff, tbl and eqn.

DES **D**ata **E**ncryption **S**tandard. Encryption standard for unclassified federal computer and network systems. Originally developed at IBM Corp. and codenamed the Lucifer cipher. After it was released to the public by IBM, DES was adopted by the National Bureau of Standards as the national cryptographic standard in 1977. *See* DES algorithm, RPC, client, server, encrypt, decrypt, commonkey, public-key, private-key, keylogin, Keyserver, timestamp and window.

DES algorithm **D**ata **E**ncryption **S**tandard **algorithm**. Standard set of formulas or mathematical rules developed by the National Institute of Standards and Technology to encrypt clear text documents. Uses a 56-bit key to encrypt documents. *See* NIST and DES.

descriptive language Human-readable output, e.g. graphs, tables and text, produced in finished documents by using embedded formatting commands in the nroff and troff programs. *See* text formatting, nroff, troff and procedural language.

descriptor table List established for every process executed by a program that identifies the input/output functions that were started.

descrypt *(OTH)* Command used with Data Encryption Standard algorithm to encrypt and decrypt a file. *See* DES, encrypt and decrypt.

design recovery Process used to reconstruct software design from the source code. *See* source code.

desktop computing Using personal computers that share data, in an office environment. The data can be distributed among the personal computers, maintained on a personal computer which is used as a server or host, or maintained on mini- through mainframe computer systems at a remote location with the personal computers interconnected on a communications/data network.

desktop database Class of database management systems that can operate independently of other programs and run on a personal computer. Enable a single user to develop and analyze information databases and generate reports.

Desktop Management Task Force Commonly abbreviated and called DMTF. *See* DMTF.

desktop manager Element of a graphical user interface (GUI) that acts as the interface, or connection, between the user and the GUI. The desktop manager contains the library of icons available to users for controlling data, operating the computer and applications, and developing graphical applications. *See* GUI and icon.

desktop publishing Process of using a personal computer, high-quality printer and specialized software to produce documents and publications, e.g. reports and newsletters, that include graphics, multiple columns, multiple typefaces and other embellishments. Some personal computer desktop publishing software, e.g. WordPerfect, have been ported to UNIX.

destination 1. Commonly called destination host. *See* destination host. 2. Name given to a printer, indicating where a print job is to take place.

destination file File which is created or to which data is to be sent as a result of the execution of a program or a command, e.g. copy.

destination host Host or computer on a network that is the ultimate destination of a data transmission.

Destiny Code name for the UNIX Systems Laboratories desktop UNIX System V, Release 4 product. Called SVR4.2 when it was released as a product. *See* SVR4.x, desktop computing and UnixWare.

detached process Commonly called background process. *See* background process.

/dev Root directory that contains the files necessary to manage the hardware drivers for terminals, printers and other hardware used on the system. *See* device driver.

/dev/error System directory that contains a list of hardware or software system errors and panic conditions. *See* panic.

/dev/fd System directory that contains a list of files with open file descriptors. *See* file descriptor.

/dev/kmem Pseudo-device through which authorized programs can read or modify the operating system's kernel memory. *See* pseudo-device and kernel.

/dev/mem Pseudo-device through which authorized programs can read or modify the computer system's virtual memory. *See* pseudo-device and virtual memory.

/dev/null Special files called the destination file in UNIX. Also called the UNIX bit bucket. Can be selected as the standard output, or default destination, when no output is wanted, and as the standard input when there is nothing to be input. Frequently used in application testing when the developer wants to test a function that will result in an output but the contents of the output are meaningless to the test. The contents are redirected to /dev/null, where they are effectively deleted upon arrival. *See* bit bucket.

/dev/tty **1.** Files in the system directory used to manage the generic terminal connections. **2.** Pseudo-device that is synonymous with the input terminal, e.g. /dev/tty10 for the tenth port on a computer. The characters and/or numbers following /dev/tty are dependent on the particular UNIX implementation. *See* pseudo-device.

Devconfig Device **conf**iguration. File in UNIX System V, Release 4 Basic Network Utilities used only when STREAMS based communication is used. Contains the definition of STREAMS modules required for operating the output devices. *See* SVR4.x, BNU and STREAMS.

development Activities required to deliver a complete and tested software application or change.

development language C o m m o n l y called programming language. *See* programming language.

development utilities Set of programs designed to help program developers write and compile programs, e.g. ar, as, install, make and yacc. *See* compile, ar, as, install, make and yacc.

devfree *(ATT)* Command used to remove a device and process from a table that reserves the device for that process. *See* devreserv.

device **1.** Hardware element connected to the central processing unit, e.g. an external device such as a printer or terminal, or an internal device such as a disk drive or tape drive. **2.** Key word used in creating the kernel to identify the terminal, network, graphic and other devices not managed with a controller. *See* kernel. **3.** Any data object that appears to an application as a device. *See* CPU.

Device Field in L-devices used to specify the name of the device, e.g. the port number /dev/tty10, to which direct connect lines are attached. *See* L-devices.

deviceck *(OTH)* **Device** check. Shell script used for modified permissions on

system device files or the addition of new and unauthorized device files. *See* shell script and device files.

Device Drive Interface/Driver-Kernel Interface Reference Manual. Commonly abbreviated and called DDRM. *See* DDRM.

device driver Program that provides the interface between the operating system and a peripheral device. Software within a computer that translates commands into terms understood and acted upon by a piece of peripheral hardware, e.g. tape drive, controller or disk drive.

Device Driver Interface Commonly abbreviated and called DDI. *See* DDI.

device driver standard calls The following are standard calls within device drivers:

Call	Description
close	Indicates the end and terminates connection to the device
ioctl	Used to establish
open	Indicates need to use the device and to be ready for other commands
read	Request to get data from a device
write	Transmission of data or control characters to a device

device files Files resident in the /dev directory containing the numbers that uniquely identify a device to the kernel. Used to identify the type and location of a specific device so that output can be sent to and input received from that device. *See* major device number, minor device number, kernel and special file.

device flags Data used by device drivers that specifically identifies each type of device and the information and format needed for it to operate. *See* device driver.

device-independent Describes a program which to function does not need to know the specifications of the devices being used. The device or special files are responsible for maintaining the information needed to communicate with each device attached to the computer. *See* device files.

device interrupt Signal sent by the device driver to a bus to indicate an action to be taken. *See* device driver and bus.

Device-Kernel Interface Commonly abbreviated and called DKI. *See* DKI.

devicename File name in the /dev directory that identifies a peripheral device. *See* file system.

device number Address or path to which information flows to reach a device. If a printer is connected via a port, the port number is referred to as the device number. Vendors use unique naming schemes to identify the locations of devices. *See* major device number and minor device number.

Device/phone number Field in L.sys that ties a connection type identified in the Caller field to a specific phone number. *See* L.sys and Caller.

Devices File on systems using Honey-DanBer UNIX-to-UNIX CoPy or UNIX System V, Release 4 Basic Networking Utilities (/etc/uucp/Devices) that specifies the name of the device through which connection is made, type of device and transmission speed. *See* HoneyDanBer UUCP, UUCP, SVR4.x, baud, BNU and L-devices.

device server Hardware device needed and yet to be put on the market. An upgraded terminal server which would provide an interface between any asynchronous device and an Ethernet local area network. *See* terminal server, asynchronous communications, Ethernet and LAN.

device special files Commonly called special files. *See* special file.

devinfo *(ATT)* **Dev**ice **info**rmation. Command used to obtain information about a device, e.g. device name and number.

devnm *(ATT/XEN)* **Dev**ice **n**umber. Command used to display the device number associated with a file.

devreserv *(ATT)* **Dev**ice **reserv**e. Command used to add to a table the name of a specified device and the process for using the device. *See* devfree.

df Disk free. Command used to determine the amount of file space already used and the amount available for use on a disk. *See* file system.

DFD Data-flow diagram. Tool used in the development of new software. Depicts the current automated or non-automated system, additions or modifications to the process created by the new software and the requirements. *See* ERD.

dfmounts Distributed File System, Network File System or Remote File Sharing command used to display resources on the local host that are available for use and the remote hosts that are using them. *See* DFS, NFS, RFS, dfshares, mount, share, shareall, unshare and unshareall.

dfs Commonly written as /etc/dfs. *See* /etc/dfs.

DFS Distributed File System. Element of the Open Software Foundation Inc.'s Distributed Computing Environment and part of UNIX System V, Release 4. A common set of commands for the Network File System and the Remote File Sharing. Provides a set of tools used to manage a distributed network environment. Aims to create a true distributed network, providing users transparent access to any file they have permission to use. File systems on all hosts in a network are referred to by a common name that is known by each host on the network. *See* OSF, DCE, SVR4.x, NFS and RFS.

dfshares Distributed File System, Network File System or Remote File Sharing command used to display remote resources available to the local host and local resources available to remote hosts. *See* DFS, NFS, RFS, dfmounts, mount, share, shareall, unshare and unshareall.

dfspace Disk free **space**. Command used to compute the percentage of available free disk space for each file system. *See* file system.

dfstab Commonly written as /etc/dfs/dfstab. *See* /etc/dfs/dfstab.

DGbyte Disk **gigabyte**. Measurement of disk capacity as exactly 1 billion bytes compared to the standard definition of a gigabyte as or 1,073,741,824 (or 2^{30}) bytes.

dgmon **1.** *(ATT)* Diagnostic **mon**itor program. Set of tests provided in UNIX System V with AT&T Co.'s 3B2 computers to identify and correct hardware problems. **2.** Command used to start the diagnostic monitor program. *See* /dgn.

/dgn *(ATT)* UNIX System V, Release 4 root file system directory that holds all the programs used to perform system diagnostics. *See* SVR4.x, dgmon and root file system.

DG/UX UNIX operating system developed for Data General Corp.'s computer systems.

Dhrystones Public domain benchmark program used to measure the performance, in millions of instructions per second, of a computer's central processing unit. Its measurements are based on common C language, Ada or Turbo Pascal operations, including integer arithmetic, string manipulation and function calls. They specifically exclude floating point arithmetic, which is measured using the Whetstone benchmark. *See* CPU, mips and Whetstone.

DIA **D**isplay **I**ndustry **A**ssociation. Group of hardware, software and communications companies, formed in early 1991 to develop and promote standards for X Window System-like functionality on American Standard Code for Information Interchange display terminals. Among its 30 members are AT&T Co., Digital Equipment Corp., The Santa Cruz Operation, Siemens-Nixdorf Information Systems, Inc., Wyse Technology Inc., Applied Digital Data Systems and Televideo

Systems, Inc. Located in Palo Alto, California. *See* X Window System, ASCII terminal and AlphaWindow.

diag Pronounced *DYE-AG*. Jargon term for diagnostic test. *See* diagnostic test.

diagnostic message Commonly called error message. *See* error message.

diagnostic monitor program
Commonly abbreviated and called dgmon. *See* dgmon.

diagnostic output Commonly called core dump. *See* core dump.

diagnostics Jargon term for diagnostic test. *See* diagnostic test.

diagnostic test Single program or set of programs within computers; sub-elements of computers, e.g. memory boards; or peripherals, that determine if there is a problem or malfunction within any of the elements. Normally, diagnostics are run only when initiated by the system administrator or maintenance personnel. More sophisticated systems always run diagnostics in the background; these can send either a message to the system console or electronic mail, alerting the system administrator to a current or pending failure. *See* self-test.

dial back modem Commonly called call back modem. *See* call-back modem.

Dialcodes File on systems running HoneyDanBer UNIX-to-UNIX CoPy (UUCP) or UNIX System V, Release 4 Basic Networking Utilities. Contains the phone number abbreviations for UUCP. *See* HoneyDanBer UUCP, UUCP, SVR4.x, BNU and L-dialcodes.

dialer Commonly called modem. *See* modem.

Dialer Field in L-devices that contains the make and model of the modems being used. *See* L-devices.

Dialers File in /usr/lib/uucp on systems running HoneyDanBer UNIX-to-UNIX CoPy or UNIX System V, Release 4 Basic

Networking Utilities (/etc/uucp/Dialers). Contains the description of codes needed to make dialers and modems work. *See* HoneyDanBer UUCP and modem.

dialog Programs capable of communication and action. A specific string is sent by one program to another with an expected response. When a correct response is received, a predetermined action is taken. If an incorrect response is received, the dialog program may take any of several actions, including recording an error in log, sending the error message to a screen or taking corrective action to elicit the expected response.

dialog box Screen display that contains a list of options presented as text, icons or other graphical displays, from which the user selects simple or complex instructions to be passed to the computer. *See* GUI.

diction Feature of the Writer's Workbench text processing tools. Used to locate and recommend changes in wordy sentence structure. *See* WWB.

die Single piece or wafer of silicon upon which the pattern of an integrated circuit is etched. *See* IC, wafer and reticle.

diff Difference. Command used to compare two files. Identifies and displays the differences on text files. On binary files, indicates if the files are identical or different, but does not display the differences.

diff3 *(ATT/XEN)* Difference 3. Command used to compare three files. Can only be used on text files.

diffmk *(ATT/XEN)* **Difference mark.** Command used to compare two versions of a document formatted with the troff or nroff program. It creates a third file with the differences marked that produce change bars in the final, printed output. *See* nroff and troff.

dig *(INET)* **Domain information groper.** Program that looks up Internet addresses of users and hosts. *See* Internet, nslookup and whois.

digest Electronic-mail message containing user mail messages that have been sent between mail transfer agents. *See* MTA.

digital Measurement of physical conditions, data transmission or storage of age data with binary numbers (0 or 1). In comparison, in analog measurements, data is represented using electrical or other physical relations, e.g. a continuous variation in voltages. *See* binary and analog.

Digital Audio Tape Commonly abbreviated and called DAT. *See* DAT.

digital computer Electronic computational device that processes information in discrete or discontinuous operations using the binary numbers 0 and 1, indicating on or off. Electronic fluctuations, or combination of 0s and 1s, are used to represent characters or symbols, which can be combined to provide instructions to the computer to perform a process and output information. In comparison, an analog computer processes a continuous flow of physical data. *See* digital, binary and analog computer.

Digital Data Communications Message Protocol Abbreviated and commonly known as DDCMP. *See* DDCMP.

Digital Data Service Commonly abbreviated and called DDS. *See* DDS.

Digital Data Storage Commonly abbreviated and called DDS. *See* DDS.

digital display Presentation of data that is represented by binary numbers (0 or 1) in the form of a numeric electronic display. *See* digital, binary and analog display.

Digital Network Architecture Commonly abbreviated and called DECNET. *See* DECNET.

Digital Optical Tape System Commonly abbreviated and called DOTS. *See* DOTS.

digital signal Communication signal used to send information in discrete or discontinuous operations using the binary numbers 0 and 1, indicating on or off. e.g. transmission within or between computers. In comparison, an analog signal processes a continuous flow of physical data. *See* analog signal.

digital signature Method by which receivers of a message are assured it was originated by the individual identified as the sender, e.g. through use of public and private-keys to encrypt and decrypt a message. *See* public-key and private-key.

Digital Signature Standard Commonly abbreviated and called DSS. *See* DSS.

Digital-to-Analog Converter Commonly abbreviated and called DAC. *See* DAC.

dinosaur 1. Jargon term for any computer, operating system, etc., that has been outstripped by technology yet remains in use. 2. Originally, term used by mini- and microcomputer enthusiasts to describe large mainframes. *See* big iron, minicomputer, microcomputer and mainframe.

DIP Dual In-line Package. Housing used to enclose and attach integrated circuits to a circuit board. A rectangular ceramic or plastic case, approximately .33 inch wide and 1.5 inches long, that has a row of metal connector pins on both sides of the case. Provides protection and speeds manufacturing by making it easier to attach the IC to a circuit board. *See* IC.

DIP switches Dual In-line Package switches. Small switches on a printer, personal computer or other computer equipment that allow the user to modify settings, functions or characteristics, e.g. baud rate for a printer.

dirck *(OTH)* Directory check. Shell script used to check system directories for unauthorized write permissions. *See* shell script and write permission.

dircmp *(ATT/XEN)* Directory compare. Command used to compare the contents of two directories and display the differences.

direct-access storage device Commonly abbreviated and called DASD. *See* DASD.

directed broadcast Broadcast message sent to a remote network to which the author is not directly connected.

direct map Collection of information needed for the Network File System automounter to activate a remote resource. *See* NFS, master map and automount.

direct memory access Commonly abbreviated and called DMA. *See* DMA.

directory 1. One of the eight types of UNIX files. In simple terms, a file of files. A directory may contain no information, files or additional directories. 2. Table of file names.

directory access mode Commonly called access mode. *See* access mode.

Directory Access Protocol Commonly abbreviated and called DAP. *See* DAP.

Directory and File Management Utilities Set of programs included in UNIX System V, Release 4 to manipulate and manage files and directories. *See* SVR4.x.

directory commands Group of UNIX commands that act on or modify directories. *See* cd, chgrp, chmod, chown, cpio, dircmp, dirname, du, find, ls, mkdir, mv, pwd, rm, rmdir and tar.

directory hierarchy Commonly called hierarchical directory. *See* hierarchical directory.

Directory Information Shadow Protocol Commonly abbreviated and called DISP. *See* DISP.

Directory Information Tree Commonly abbreviated and called DIT. *See* DIT.

Directory Schema Open Systems Interconnection X.500 term for the set of specifications for the information categories contained in a directory. *See* OSI, X.500, DUA, DSA, DAP, DSP, DIT, DN and DISP.

directory service Network service used to identify a user name to an electronic-mail address on a network. *See* X.500.

Directory Service Also called DCE Directory Service. Based upon the X.500 standard for directory services, developed by the International Telecommunication Union Telecommunication Standardization Sector, formerly called the Consultative Committee on International Telegraphy and Telephony. Element of the Open Software Foundation Inc.'s Distributed Computing Environment. Provides the means to control names of resources on the network used to manage both local and global users of DCE by enabling the movement of data between users and devices on the network. *See* OSF, DCE, CDS, DNS, ITU-T, X.500 and GDS.

directory services Set of services, e.g. files, printers and application software, that allow various tasks to be performed on a network.

Directory System Agent Commonly abbreviated and called DSA. *See* DSA.

Directory System Protocol Commonly abbreviated and called DSP. *See* DSP.

directory tree Commonly called hierarchical directory. *See* hierarchical directory.

Directory User Agent Commonly abbreviated and called DUA. *See* DUA.

dirname *(ATT/XEN)* **Directory name.** General-purpose library routine used to extract portions of pathnames, generally for writing shell scripts. *See* library routines, shell script and basename.

dirty **1.** Any executable program that has been changed. **2.** Memory that has been recently used but not yet reallocated.

dirty page Commonly called dirty. *See* dirty.

dis *(ATT)* **Dis**assemble. Command used to take apart executable or object files. *See* executable file and object file.

DIS **1.** Document Image Subset. Addition to the Massachusetts Institute of Technology X Window System, Release 6 that allows limited manipulation, e.g. allows documents to be scanned in and faxes to be rotated and scaled on the screen. *See* X Window System, X11R6 and fax. **2.** Draft International Standard. Draft document of an International Organization for Standardization standard. *See* ISO.

disable **1.** *(ATT)* Line printer system command. Used by the system administrator to turn off print jobs being sent to line printers. *See* lp and enable. **2.** *(XEN)* Command used to disable a terminal. **3.** To turn off or prevent normal operation.

disassembler Program used to convert machine language code into the assembler language code from which it was originally produced. *See* assembly language and machine language.

disaster planning Also called contingency planning. Preparing for adverse incidents, which may or may not happen, including loss of computing facilities, hardware crashes, software crashes, database corruption, network outages and unplanned loss of key personnel. *See* disaster recovery.

disaster recovery Planned process of restoring computer operations following the loss of a computer system or computer operations due to a natural or manmade catastrophe. *See* disaster planning.

disc Flat, round, non-magnetic platter used to read, write and store data for optical-based storage devices. Used in the same manner as a disk or floppy disk but spelled with a "c" when used with optical storage devices. *See* CD-ROM and disk.

discretionary access controls
Abbreviated and referred to as DAC. *See* DAC.

disk 1. Platter within a disk drive used for information storage. Spelled "disc" when referring to a storage platter used with optical storage media. *See* disc and platter. 2. Jargon term for disk drive. *See* disk drive. 3. Key word used in building the kernel to identify the tape drives managed by a controller. *See* kernel.

diskadd *(ATT)* Command used to partition a disk. *See* partition.

disk array Method of providing fault resistance, high availability, high capacity and high performance for disks. Composed of several disks arranged to spread data across several devices that either provides higher capacity or redundancy. *See* disk mirroring.

disk caching Moving selected text, data or other information from a disk drive and temporarily storing the information in memory to speed up the search and retrieval time while an application is running. The increase in speed is due to the electromechanical nature of a disk as compared to the electrical nature of memory.

disk commands Group of UNIX commands that act on or modify disks. *See* dd, df, du, fsck, mount and umount.

disk controller Interface card that connects a disk drive to a computer system.

disk crash Failure of a disk drive that normally results in loss of data. *See* head crash.

disk drive Also called hard drive. Mass-storage device containing rigid magnetic surfaces, or disks, that rotate at extremely high speed, and are enclosed in a sealed container. Capable of storing large quantities of data, ranging from 10 or more megabytes on a personal computer to 2 or more gigabytes on large UNIX systems. Used to look for, read and write data. Data is moved from the disk drive to the computer's memory to be acted upon. When it is no longer required, the data is either returned to the disk drive or deleted.

Disk Drive Post-HDA Testing Consortium Thirty-member group of manufacturers, vendors and maintenance companies that aims to establish standard disk-drive testing procedures.

diskette Flexible plastic surface with an oxide coating, encased in a plastic jacket, used to magnetically write, store and read data on various types of computers, from personal computers to large minicomputers. used for magnetically writing, storing and reading data on various types of computers, from personal computers to large minicomputers. Originally called a floppy disk, 8 inches in diameter. Currently, diskettes are 5.25 (mini-floppy) or 3.5 inches (microfloppy) in diameter. Depending on the format, a standard 5.25-inch diskette can hold up to 1,213,952 bytes while a 3.5-inch diskette can store up to 1,457,664 bytes. There are 3.5-inch super-floppy diskettes capable of holding between 10 and 50 megabytes of data. In addition, diskettes come in 1-, 1.5-, 2- and 2.25-inch sizes.

3.5 inch floppy diskette

diskette drive Commonly called floppy drive. *See* floppy drive.

disk duplexing Creating a complete duplicate copy of a disk inpout/output system, e.g. including disk drives, controllers, cables and power supplies. Data is written through both input/output channels to provide complete redundancy should a component fail

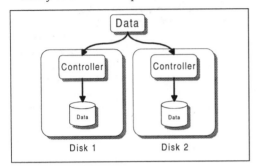

Disk duplexing writes data to separate disk systems to guard against the possible failure of one system.

disk farm Jargon term for a large collection of disks.

diskformat *(ATT)* **Disk format**. Program used to format disk drives.

disk gigabyte Commonly abbreviated and called DGbyte. *See* DGbyte.

disk grooming Removing files from a disk after they have been archived to another storage medium, e.g. from disk drives to disc platters or tape. *See* archive.

disk head Portion of a disk drive that reads, writes and/or erases data on a storage device.

disk head sorting Routine that sets up queues or lines or requests for disk access. An algorithm runs the requests in a sequence that most effectively accesses the disks, thereby reducing the amount of time it takes for searches and for reading and/or writing data.

disk label Volume identifier created by the labelit command and written on a disk. Contains the file system name and volume name. *See* labelit, file system and volume name.

diskless Pertaining to a type of workstation that provides all the functionality of a workstation or personal computer but lacks mass storage media. Diskless workstations are totally dependent on the host or server for all file storage. *See* workstation and PC.

Diskless Support Service Function of the Open Software Foundation Inc.'s Distributed Computing Environment that provides support for diskless workstations on a network. *See* OSF, DCE and diskless.

disk megabyte Commonly abbreviated and called DMbyte. *See* DMbyte.

disk mirroring Facility to simultaneously write data to two or more disks. Provides redundancy to protect against head crashes or other disk failures. If one disk drive fails, the data is available on another drive.

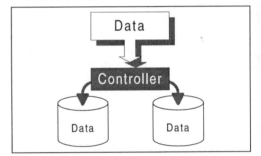

Disk mirroring writes data to separate disks to guard against the possible failure of one disk drive.

Disk Operating System Commonly abbreviated and called DOS. *See* DOS.

disk pack Large, moveable storage medium designed to perform a role similar to tape backup with the high speed of disk drives. Normally a group of five or twelve disk platters that can hold from 50 to 300 megabytes of data.

disk partition Contiguous sections of a disk or disks used to store common groups of information or data, e.g. a file system or swap area has a specified disk partition. *See* file system and swap.

disk priority Level of importance assigned to a process for obtaining disk access. Can be changed manually. *See* nice.

disk spanning Use of more than one physical disk to create a large virtual disk. *See* virtual disk.

disk striping Commonly called striping. *See* striping.

diskusg *(ATT)* **Disk us**age. Accounting system program used to report the amount of disk usage by user account. *See* acctdusg and userid.

DISP **D**irectory **I**nformation **S**hadow **P**rotocol. Used in the Open Systems Interconnection X.500 to move and replicate information between Directory System Agents on a network. *See* OSI, X.500, DSA, DAP, DSP, DIT, DN and DUA.

dispadmin *(ATT)* Command used to modify or display information on the process scheduler that determines the priority of a process. *See* real-time class, system class and time-sharing class.

display 1. *(ATT)* Remote File Sharing sysadm menu command used to display a list of the networks available to a local host, when in the Supporting Networks Management menu. *See* RFS and sysadm. 2. *(ATT)* Remote File Sharing sysadm menu command used to display the current permissions for users and groups, when in the User and Group ID Mapping Management menu. *See* RFS, sysadm, set uid mappings, set gid mappings and permissions. 3. Process of providing data to users in a visual form, e.g. displaying data in printed form through a printer or video terminal. 4. Alternative term for a terminal with a cathode ray tube. *See* CRT. 5. Text formatting term used to describe text which the user wants printed exactly as it was input. *See* floating display and static display.

display cycle Commonly called refresh rate. *See* refresh rate.

display device Any device capable of visually displaying data, e.g. a printer or terminal.

display domain *(ATT)* Remote File Sharing sysadm menu command used to display the local host's domain. *See* RFS, sysadm and domain.

display editor Commonly called visual editor. *See* visual editor.

Display Industry Association Commonly abbreviated and called DIA. *See* DIA.

display management X Window System term for starting or stopping a user session. *See* X Window System.

display resolution Commonly called pixel rating. *See* pixel rating.

display unit Device used by an individual to access the computer and display data stored in it, e.g. a dumb terminal, personal computer, X Window System terminal or workstation. *See* X Window System.

distant host Commonly called remote host. *See* remote host.

distfile **Dist**ribution **file**. File used with the rdist command to establish the rules which must be followed in determining if a file on a remote host is to be updated. *See* rdist and primitive.

Distinguished Name Commonly abbreviated and called DN. *See* DN.

distributed application Application software that is divided into segments, located and executed on several computers in a network. *See* distributed computing.

distributed application development Commonly abbreviated and called DAD. *See* DAD.

distributed computing Decentralizing data processing using distributed databases, distributed applications, networks, computer centers and personal computers. Can be limited to either multiple computers at the same location which share data, or to multiple computers at different locations around the world which use a high-speed network to transmit data between the computer systems and users. *See* distributed database and distributed application.

Distributed Computing Environment
Commonly abbreviated and called DCE. *See* DCE.

distributed database Single, logical database with the physical storage of the data distributed over multiple computer systems. Database records can be accessed or updated as if they were local files via a network from any of the computer systems. *See* NFS and RFS.

Distributed Data Management
Commonly abbreviated and called DDM. *See* DDM.

Distributed Directory Service
Commonly called Directory Service. *See* Directory Service.

distributed file system File system in which user files and programs are located on more than one computer system. The user has access to all the data and program files, regardless of which computer they are stored on and as if they were on a single local system. *See* NFS and RFS.

Distributed File System Commonly abbreviated and called DFS. *See* DFS.

Distributed Management Environment
Commonly abbreviated and called DME. *See* DME.

distributed memory multiprocessor
Computer with multiple central processing units, each with memory. *See* CPU, MP, loosely coupled processor architecture and shared memory multiprocessor.

Distributed Naming Service
Commonly abbreviated and called DNS. *See* DNS.

distributed processing Computer network architecture in which users, application programs, data, etc., are located on several different computers. Data can be processed on any or many of the computers, although to the user the operation will appear to be accomplished on a single computer.

Distributed Security Service
Commonly abbreviated and called DSS. *See* DSS.

Distributed Time Service Commonly abbreviated and called DTS. *See* DTS.

Distributed Transaction Processing
Commonly abbreviated and called DTP. *See* DTP.

distribution medium Type of data storage device or medium on which original software or updates are provided, e.g. a tape or diskette. An initial release of an operating system, however, can be distributed on the hard disk of a computer system and updates can be shipped on a communications network.

DIT Directory Information Tree. Open Systems Interconnection X.500 global directory. Hierarchical structure of all the data available on a network that allows users access to data from remote locations. *See* OSI, X.500, DUA, DSA, DAP, DSP and DN.

dither Computer graphics term for the intermingling of various colored dots to form new colors.

ditroff Device-independent **troff**. The original troff formatting program was designed to run on a specific typesetter. ditroff is a modified version of troff, designed by Brian Kernighan to run on typesetters, terminals and printers. Most troff programs running on current systems are in reality ditroff. *See* troff and Kernighan, Brian W.

divvy *(XEN)* **Divvy**, or divide up. Command used to divide a disk into partitions.

DIW-24 D-type Inside Wiring, 24 gauge. Telephone wire. *See* UTP.

DIX Digital Equipment Corp., Intel Corp. and Xerox Corp. Consortium formed in

1979 by the three companies to advance the development and use of Ethernet local area networks. *See* Ethernet.

DKI Driver Kernel Interface. Introduced in AT&T Co.'s System V, Release 4. Provides the first standard for the interface between the kernel and device drivers. *See* SVR4.x, kernel, device driver and DDI.

DKUUG Dansk UNIX-system Bruger Gruppe. The Danish UNIX user group formed in 1983.

D language Language used to model the operational behavior of graphical tools used for X Window System application programs. Includes a compiler, debugger and interpreter to enable programmers to design, write and test the tools with the application programs. *See* X Window System, X toolkit, widget, xlib and UIMS.

DLL Dynamic link library. Application library used to store components of an application software, e.g. a specific object or task, that can be shared by multiple applications.

DLPI Data Link Provider Interface. STREAMS protocol used for interface with the device driver under UNIX System V, Release 4. *See* SVR4.x, STREAMS and device driver.

DMA 1. Direct memory access. Computer circuits that that allow the direct transfer of large blocks of data between main memory and peripheral devices without using the central processing unit. *See* CPU. 2. When system memory is accessed directly from a device instead of being queued or preprocessed by a software program.

DMbyte Disk megabyte. Measurement of disk capacity at exactly 1 million bytes compared to the standard definition of a megabyte as 1,048,576 (2^{20})bytes.

DME Distributed Management Environment. Programs in the Open Software Foundation Inc.'s OSF/1 operating system that provide a set of standard software products, e.g. application programming interfaces and management applications. Used to manage software, peripherals and computer systems within a heterogeneous network. Supports features such as the Simple Network Management Protocol and Common Management Interface Protocol. Originally designed to be separate from but work with OSF's Distributed Computing Environment (DCE), used to develop application software to be used on heterogeneous networks. In November 1993, OSF announced DME was to be included in DCE as a single standard. *See* OSF, OSF/1, SNMP, CMIP and DCE.

dmesg *(XEN)* Display messages. Command used to turn on and off the writing of messages to the console.

DMS Defense Message System. Department of Defense worldwide communication system. Based upon military-modified versions of the X.400 standard for a message handling system for electronic mail, which was developed by the International Telecommunication Union Telecommunication (ITU-T) Standardization Sector, formerly called the Consultative Committee on International Telegraphy and Telephony; and an X.500 standard for a network services system, which was developed by the International Organization for Standardization/Open Systems Interconnection and ITU-T. The military specification adds four more precedence levels for routing messages and greater security. *See* X.400, X.500, ITU-T and ISO/OSI.

DMTF Desktop Management Task Force. Group formed in 1992 to write application programming interfaces that can be run by a network management station. Among the members are Intel Corp., IBM Corp., Microsoft Corp. and Novell Inc.

DN Distinguished name. Open Systems Interconnection X.500 term for an entry in a network directory. Each DN has a distinct name. *See* OSI, X.500, DUA, DSA, DAP, DSP, DIT and DISP.

DNA Digital Network Architecture. Proprietary protocol developed to run on Digital Equipment Corp.'s product line, commonly referred to as DECNET.

dname *(ATT)* Domain **name**. Remote File Sharing command used to display the name of the domain which the host is in, establish the name of the host's domain or identify the type of network being used. *See* RFS, domain and rfstart.

DNS 1. *(INET)* Domain Name Service. Protocol implemented by Internet to identify domain names to an Internet Protocol address. Used to route mail to remote hosts. Also used to get information about other hosts and users of a host on a network, either within or across domains, e.g. a list of available resources and addresses for the host that has resources available. Included in the application layer of UNIX System V, Release 4 Transmission Control Protocol/Internet Protocol. *See* Internet, SVR4.x, TCP/IP and domain. 2. Distributed Naming Service. Facility within the Distributed Computing Environment that permits network resources to be found by users who do not know where these are on the network. *See* DCE, CDS, GDA, GDS and XDS.

DNS domains *(INET)* High-level domains, or common groupings, within the Internet are:

Domain	Type
ARPA	Initial ARPA domains
COM	Commercial/business
EDU	Colleges and universities
GOV	Government organizations
INT	International organizations.
MIL	Military
ORG	Miscellaneous groups
NET	Network administration host
Country Code	Two digit alpha indicating the country

See DNS and Internet.

do Programming function used to mark the beginning of a block of commands to be executed by the Bourne shell or Korn shell following a for or while loop. *See* Bourne shell, Korn shell, for and while.

DOA Dead on arrival. Jargon term for a newly purchased computer system that arrives broken and will not work the first time it is used. *See* infant mortality.

document 1. Something which is created or edited, and contains words and/or numbers, and generally some thought. 2. A collection of words, numbers, symbols, letters, etc. stored on a disk, diskette, tape, etc. that can be displayed, modified, printed, etc. 3. To create and maintain data in order to establish a record of events.

documentation Instructions provided by a software developer or hardware manufacturer on how to use the item. Can be either on-line or printed.

Documenter's Workbench Commonly abbreviated and called DWB. *See* DWB.

Document Image Subset Commonly abbreviated and called DIS. *See* DIS.

document instance One of two components of a document created with the Standard Generalized Markup Language. Refers to the data, or text, of the document. The other element, called the Document Type Definition, defines the structure of the data, including the re-usable data objects. *See* SGML and DTD.

Document Type Definition
Commonly abbreviated and called DTD. *See* DTD.

DOD *(INET)* Department of Defense. Also abbreviated DoD. Major supporter of UNIX and packet switch protocols (X.25 and 1822) in their infancy and the original sponsor of the Internet through the Defense Advanced Research Projects Agency. *See* X.25, 1822, DDN, DARPA, Internet and ARPANET.

DOD Internet *(INET)* Commonly abbreviated and called DDN. *See* DDN.

DOD IP *(INET)* Commonly abbreviated and called IP. *See* IP.

dodisk *(ATT)* Accounting system shell script that is run before the runacct program to collect and process statistics on file and disk usage for system accounting. *See* runacct.

dollar sign ($) **1.** Default command or system prompt displayed when a user is running the Bourne shell. *See* system prompt and Bourne shell. **2.** Metacharacter used in regular expressions of the ed, ex, vi, sed, grep, egrep and awk programs. Used to match specified characters at the end of a line. *See* metacharacter and regular expression.

domain 1. Territory or range of control or commonality. In networking, for example, a naming convention used to identify the hierarchical relationships between computers or hosts and networks; the relationships are considered like a family of like protocols and addresses. A second example is a Remote File Sharing network where a domain is considered a logical grouping of computers. *See* domain address and RFS. **2.** Indication of legal ownership, including the right of disposal, of a computer product. Public domain software can be used freely by anyone, and government domain software can be freely used by government agencies but must be licensed for use by non-government agencies.

domain address Unique name that identifies a computer within a network hierarchical relationship between computers or hosts and networks, e.g.:

tnf.my.ilb

The computer or host, named tnf, is located in the subdomain of my, which is part of the domain ilb. All of which means that the host tnf is on a network named my that is controlled by or is part of a larger network named ilb. The domain address could be extended to show other subdomain relationships, e.g.:

tnf.kaj.my.ilb

Domain Administrator Commonly abbreviated and called DA. *See* DA.

domain information Commonly called rfmaster. *See* rfmaster.

domain information groper Commonly abbreviated and called dig. *See* dig.

Domain/IX UNIX look-alike developed by Apollo Computer before Apollo was purchased by the Hewlett-Packard Co.

domain member list File maintained by the primary name server in a Remote File Sharing system. Contains a list of all hosts in the domain and their passwords. *See* RFS, primary name server, domain and rfadmin.

domainname *(BSD)* Command used to set or display the name of the current domain. *See* domain, Internet and hostname.

Domain Name Pointer Commonly abbreviated and called PTR. *See* PTR.

domain name server Host in a Remote File Sharing system that acts as the central point or primary name server on a network. Monitors and maintains the file-sharing environment for the network. *See* RFS, DNS, primary name server and secondary name server.

Domain Name Service Commonly abbreviated and called DNS. *See* DNS.

done Korn shell command statement that indicates the end of a do, while and until statement. *See* do, while and until.

dos *(ATT)* Command found in the XENIX Compatibility Package of System V, Release 4. Used to link MS-DOS to the UNIX operating system as well as to run MS-DOS under UNIX. *See* SVR4.x.

DOS **D**isk **O**perating **S**ystem. Generic term for the operating system used on personal computers. Controls the running of application programs and manages the interface among applications, users and the PC, e.g. input and output, program scheduling, data management, external devices and mass storage devices (tape or disk). DOS is only capable of single-user operation, and allows the user to run only one task at a time. There is no generic system or program called DOS. Several major companies have developed versions of DOS, e.g. MS-DOS, PC-DOS, Novell DOS and CP/M. *See* MS-DOS, PC-DOS, Novell DOS and CP/M.

dos2unix *(ATT)* **DOS to UNIX**. Command used to convert DOS formatted files to UNIX format. Specifically, deletes the return, leaving only the linefeed at the end of each line in a file. *See* unix2dos.

dosadmin *(ATT)* **DOS admin**istration. Menu-driven interface found in the XENIX Compatibility Package of System V, Release 4, that is used to set up and administer MS-DOS commands running under the UNIX environment. *See* SVR4.x.

doscat *(ATT/XEN)* **DOS** concatenate. Command that originated in XENIX and now is included in the XENIX Compatibility Package of System V, Release 4. Used to either combine images of DOS files into a single file or redirect them to standard output. *See* SVR4.x and cat.

doscp *(ATT/XEN)* **DOS copy**. Command that originated in XENIX and now is included in the XENIX Compatibility Package of System V, Release 4. Used to copy an image of a file between UNIX- and DOS-based computers. *See* SVR4.x and copy.

dosdir *(ATT/XEN)* **DOS dir**ectory. Command that originated in XENIX and now is included in the XENIX Compatibility Package of System V, Release 4. Provides an output of the contents of a directory in DOS format. *See* SVR4.x.

dosformat *(ATT)* **DOS format**. Command found in the XENIX Compatibility Package of System V, Release 4. Used to format an DOS disk. *See* SVR4.x and format.

dosinstall *(ATT)* **DOS install**. Command found in the XENIX Compatibility Package of System V, Release 4. Used to install DOS on a UNIX system. *See* SVR4.x.

dosls *(ATT/XEN)* **DOS list**. Command that originated in XENIX and now is included in the XENIX Compatibility Package of System V, Release 4. Provides an output of the contents of a DOS directory in UNIX format. *See* SVR4.x and ls.

dosmkdir *(ATT/XEN)* **DOS make dir**ectory. Command that originated in XENIX and now is included in the XENIX Compatibility Package of System V, Release 4. Used to create an DOS directory. *See* SVR4.x.

dosopt *(ATT)* **DOS opt**ions. Command found in the XENIX Compatibility Package of System V, Release 4. Used to link options to DOS commands which are to be started from the UNIX prompt. *See* SVR4.x.

DOS Protected Mode Interface
Commonly abbreviated and called DPMI. *See* DPMI.

dosrm *(ATT/XEN)* **DOS remove**. Command that originated in XENIX and now is included in the XENIX Compatibility Package of System V, Release 4. Used to delete an DOS file. *See* SVR4.x.

dosrmdir *(ATT/XEN)* **DOS remove dir**ectory. Command that originated in XENIX and now is included in the XENIX Compatibility Package of System V, Release 4. Used to remove a DOS directory. *See* SVR4.x.

DOS-to-UNIX command comparison

Following are examples of basic DOS and UNIX comparable commands:

DOS	UNIX	Command Function
CD	pwd	Display the full pathname of the current working directory
COMP or FC	diff	cmp or comm
COPY	cp	Copy one file to a new file
DATE	date	Display or change the current date recorded in the computer
DIR or TREE	ls	Display the files in the current directory
ERASE or DEL	rm	Delete a file
MD or MKDIR	mkdir	Make a new directory
MORE	more	pg or less
PRINT	lp or lpr	Direct the contents of a file to a printer
RENAME	mv	Relocate or rename a file
RD or RMDIR	rmdir or rm -r	Delete a directory
SIZE	df or du	Display disk usage
TIME	date	Display or change the current time recorded in the computer
TYPE	cat	Display a file

dot *(.)* **1.** Character used to indicate the current location in a file, path, etc. **2.** Bourne and Korn shell command used to read a file and execute the lines of the file as if they were input on a command line. *See* source and command line. **3.** When a user lists the contents of a directory, indicates the current working directory along with the permissions, ownership and last date it was updated. *See* current directory.

4. Abbreviation for current working directory when used as part of a command.

CLP> cp ~pbethel/tstdata . ⏎

This command will copy the file tstdata from user account pbethel to the current working directory of the user who input the command. This assumes pbethel has established the appropriate permissions for the user to read the file. *See* current working directory. **5.** Regular expression metacharacter used in the ex, ed, vi, sed, grep, egrep and awk programs to match any single character, e.g. a string search in a file for k.j matches any string of characters which starts with a k, is followed by any character and ends with j, such as kaj. **6.** Electronic-mail variable. *See* e-mail and .mailrc variables (Appendices F and G).

Dot 0 *(POS)* Jargon term for the Institute of Electrical and Electronic Engineers' Portable Operating System Interface for Computer Environments (POSIX) P1003.0 working group responsible for creating and maintaining *The POSIX Guide. See* IEEE, POSIX and IEEE P1003.0 working group.

Dot 1 *(POS)* Jargon term for the Institute of Electrical and Electronic Engineers' P1003.1 working group originally responsible for defining the Portable Operating System Interface for Computer Environments (POSIX) interfaces between application programs and the operating system. *See* IEEE, POSIX and IEEE P1003.1 working group.

Dot 2 *(POS)* Jargon term for the Institute of Electrical and Electronic Engineers' Portable Operating System Interface for Computer Environments (POSIX) P1003.2 working group responsible for developing a standard for shell, commands and utilities. *See* IEEE, POSIX and IEEE P1003.2 working group.

Dot 2 Classic *(POS)* Jargon term for the first portion of the Institute of Electrical and Electronic Engineers' Portable Operating System Interface for Computer Environments (POSIX) P1003.2 working group project responsible for developing a standard for the command line and functional interfaces to P1003.2 utilities. *See* IEEE, POSIX and IEEE P1003.2b project.

Dot 3 *(POS)* Jargon term for the Institute of Electrical and Electronic Engineers' Portable Operating System Interface for Computer Environments (POSIX) P1003.3 working group responsible for developing a standard for test and verification test suites for POSIX compliance. *See* IEEE, POSIX and IEEE P1003.3 working group.

Dot 4 *(POS)* Jargon term for the Institute of Electrical and Electronic Engineers' Portable Operating System Interface for Computer Environments (POSIX) P1003.4 working group originally responsible for developing a standard for a real-time version of UNIX. *See* IEEE, POSIX and IEEE P1003.4 working group.

Dot 5 *(POS)* Jargon term for the Institute of Electrical and Electronic Engineers' Portable Operating System Interface for Computer Environments (POSIX) P1003.5 working group responsible for developing a standard for Ada language interface. *See* IEEE, POSIX and IEEE P1003.5 working group.

Dot 6 *(POS)* Jargon term for the Institute of Electrical and Electronic Engineers' developing Portable Operating System Interface for Computer Environments (POSIX) P1003.6 working group responsible for POSIX system security standards. *See* IEEE, POSIX and IEEE P1003.6 working group.

Dot 7 *(POS)* Jargon term for the Institute of Electrical and Electronic Engineers' Portable Operating System Interface for Computer Environments (POSIX) P1003.7 working group originally responsible for developing POSIX system administration standards for utilities and interfaces in a distributed environment. *See* IEEE, POSIX and IEEE P1003.7 working group.

Dot 8 *(POS)* Jargon term for the Institute of Electrical and Electronic Engineers' Portable Operating System Interface for Computer Environments (POSIX) P1003.8 working group originally responsible developing standards for networking of POSIX systems. *See* IEEE, POSIX and IEEE P1003.8 working group.

Dot 9 *(POS)* Jargon term for the Institute of Electrical and Electronic Engineers' Portable Operating System Interface for Computer Environments (POSIX) P1003.9 working group responsible for developing for the FORTRAN-77 language interface. *See* IEEE, POSIX and IEEE P1003.9 working group.

Dot 10 *(POS)* Jargon term for the Institute of Electrical and Electronic Engineers' Portable Operating System Interface for Computer Environments (POSIX) P1003.10 working group originally responsible for developing a standard for an application environment profile for supercomputers. *See* IEEE, POSIX and IEEE P1003.10 working group.

Dot 11 *(POS)* Jargon term for the Institute of Electrical and Electronic Engineers' Portable Operating System Interface for Computer Environments (POSIX) P1003.11 working group responsible for developing a standard for an application environment profile for on line transaction processing. *See* IEEE, POSIX and IEEE P1003.11 working group.

Dot 12 *(POS)* Jargon term for the Institute of Electrical and Electronic Engineers' Portable Operating System Interface for Computer Environments (POSIX) P1003.12 working group originally responsible for developing standards for network applications programming interface. *See* IEEE, POSIX and IEEE P1003.12 working group.

Dot 13 *(POS)* Jargon term for the Institute of Electrical and Electronic Engineers' Portable Operating System Interface for Computer Environments (POSIX) P1003.13 working group responsible for developing standards for application environment profiles for real-time system support. *See* IEEE, POSIX and IEEE P1003.13 working group.

Dot 14 *(POS)* Jargon term for the Institute of Electrical and Electronic Engineers' Portable Operating System Interface for Computer Environments (POSIX) P1003.14 working group responsible for developing standards for multi-processing computer environment. *See* IEEE, POSIX and IEEE P1003.14 working group.

Dot 15 *(POS)* Jargon term for the Institute of Electrical and Electronic Engineers' Portable Operating System Interface for Computer Environments (POSIX) P1003.15 working group originally responsible for developing standards for traditional interactive multi-user system, e.g. batch queuing. *See* IEEE, POSIX and IEEE P1003.15 working group.

Dot 16 *(POS)* Jargon term for the Institute of Electrical and Electronic Engineers' Portable Operating System Interface for Computer Environments (POSIX) P1003.16 working group responsible for developing standards for C language interfaces to system services. *See* IEEE, POSIX and IEEE P1003.16 working group.

Dot 17 *(POS)* Jargon term for the Institute of Electrical and Electronic Engineers' Portable Operating System Interface for Computer Environments (POSIX) P1003.17 working group originally responsible for developing standards for Name Space/Directory Services. *See* IEEE, POSIX and IEEE P1003.17 working group.

Dot 18 *(POS)* Jargon term for the Institute of Electrical and Electronic Engineers' Portable Operating System Interface for Computer Environments (POSIX) P1003.18 working group originally responsible for developing a standard for Platform Environment Profile, a description of the standard UNIX multi-user computer. *See* IEEE, POSIX and IEEE P1003.18 working group.

Dot 19 *(POS)* Jargon term for the Institute of Electrical and Electronic Engineers' Portable Operating System Interface for Computer Environments (POSIX) P1003.19 working group originally responsible for developing a standard for FORTRAN-90 Language interface. *See* IEEE, POSIX and IEEE P1003.19 working group.

Dot 20 *(POS)* Jargon term for the Institute of Electrical and Electronic Engineers' Portable Operating System Interface for Computer Environments (POSIX) P1003.20 working group responsible for developing a standard for the Ada language interface for real-time extensions. *See* IEEE, POSIX and IEEE P1003.20 working group.

Dot 21 *(POS)* Jargon term for the Institute of Electrical and Electronic Engineers' Portable Operating System Interface for Computer Environments (POSIX) P1003.21 working group responsible for developing a standard for real-time distributed computing systems. *See* IEEE, POSIX and IEEE P1003.21 working group.

Dot 22 *(POS)* Jargon term for the Institute of Electrical and Electronic Engineers' Portable Operating System Interface for Computer Environments (POSIX) P1003.22 working group responsible for developing the Open Systems Environment Security Framework Guide. *See* IEEE, POSIX and IEEE P1003.22 working group.

dot command 1. In the command mode of the vi editor, the dot command (given by depressing the period) repeats the last command. *See* command mode and vi. 2. Commonly called dot request. *See* dot requests. 3. Command in the Bourne and Korn shells that is started with a dot (.) and followed by a file name. Tells the shell to read and execute what is in the file.

dot dot (..) Symbolic abbreviation for the parent directory of the current working directory. When a user lists the contents of a directory, the name of the parent directory is not provided, only the permissions, ownership and last date of update. *See* dot, current working directory and parent directory.

dot files Also called hidden files. Jargon term for files whose file names are preceded by a dot (.). These files are hidden for convenience only, and are only displayed when the -a argument is used with the ls command. *See* ls.

dot groups *(POS)* Jargon term for the various Institute of Electrical and Electronic Engineers Portable Operating System Interface for Computer Environments (POSIX) standards groups. *See* POSIX and IEEE.

dot matrix Electronic pattern of dots that identifies the shape and size of characters or images being output on a printer or video device.

dot matrix printer Printer which forms print characters on paper using a combination of dots created through an electronic matrix. The print head of a dot matrix printer contains a box with 9 or 24 pins. The printer uses an electronic matrix to identify how each character should be formed and then control the printer pins that strike the printer ribbon to form the character on paper. A dot matrix printer that has a graphics card installed is capable of printing pictures, graphs and other graphics.

dot pitch Distance, in millimeters, between adjacent dots of the same color on a monitor, e.g. measurement of the distance between the red dot in one group composed of a red, green and blue dot, and the red dot in the closest set of three dots. *See* dot pitch and triad.

dot requests Formatting commands in the nroff program. Each command begins with a dot (.) that instructs the program to format the document in a certain way at that point, e.g. .bp (break page) results in a new page. *See* nroff.

DOTS Digital Optical Tape System. Data storage system that combines optical compact disk storage technology with tape storage media. Combines the high data storage and transfer rates of compact disks with the rewriting ability and low cost of tapes. *See* CD-ROM, WORM, acousto-optics and optical tape.

dots per inch Commonly abbreviated and called dpi. *See* dpi.

Dot Zero Commonly written Dot 0. *See* Dot 0.

double Part of the Writer's Workbench text processing tools. Command used to locate words that are repeated in a text file, e.g. "words words." *See* WWB.

double click To depress a button on a mouse twice. Allows the user to either choose and execute an option or activate a window. *See* mouse, click, click to activate and real estate.

double strike Commonly called bold. *See* bold.

down When the computer system is not working.

download Moving data or software packages from one computer to another or from one storage medium to another, e.g. creating a text file on a UNIX computer and then moving it either to a diskette or hard disk of a personal computer where it can be edited with a word processor or desktop publishing program. Movement can be in either direction, but generally means from a host computer to a client. *See* upload.

downsizing Moving applications from large computers to smaller computers, e.g. from mainframes to minicomputers or personal computers, or from minicomputers to personal computers, so the computers used match the user's business needs.

downtime Period of time in which the computer system is inoperative. *See* uptime.

DP Data processing. Electronic processing of data. Includes storage, manipulation, reporting and/or providing information to users.

dpi 1. Dots per inch. Measurement of the number of dots per linear inch on a display screen. The greater the dpi, the better the screen resolution (clarity). *See* pixel. 2. Measurement of the number of dots per inch made by a dot matrix printer. *See* dot matrix.

DPM Distributed Presentation Management. Client/server database architecture in which the full application runs on the server and applications used only for presentations run on the client. Reduces the size, or hardware requirements, of the computer being used as the client. *See* client/server, DDM and DTP.

DPMI DOS Protected Mode Interface. Quasi standard for extended memory (greater than 640 kilobytes) for personal computers. Developed by a committee of 11 companies.

dpost *(ATT)* Command used to convert output from the troff text formatting program into PostScript page description language. *See* troff and PostScript.

draft quality Quality of printed output, inferior to letter quality. Fewer dots and less pressure are used to imprint the characters, thus increasing the speed of printing. Documents produced this way are normally used as working copies only. *See* letter quality.

drag To depress the button on a mouse to move the cursor across the screen and complete a specific operation. *See* mouse.

drag-and-drop Application programming interface started in Motif and implemented in the Common Open Software Environment group's Common Desktop Environment specification. With drag-and-drop, a mouse is used to move an object from one location to another. An object represented by an icon, such as a spreadsheet file, can be moved from a file manager and dropped on the spreadsheet application to be manipulated by the application. *See* drag, icon, COSE and CDE.

DRAM Dynamic random access memory. Pronounced *DEE-RAM*. Extension of read-only memory. Uses main memory, which can be read or written to by the central processing unit or other computer hardware devices. Has to be updated (recharged) regularly to prevent data in memory being lost when capacitors supporting the DRAM lose their charge. In addition, all information stored in a DRAM is lost when the computer is turned off. *See* CPU.

DR DOS Digital Research Disk Operating System. Original name for Novell DOS. The name was changed in early 1993. *See* Novell DOS.

DRI *(INET)* Defense Research Internet. Defense Advanced Research Projects Agency's replacement communications network for the ARPANET backbone of the Internet. Offers communications speed of 1.5 megabits per second, 25 times faster than the ARPANET.

dribbleware Slow, calculated release of information about a product long before its actual release. Or partial releases of a product over time. Term attributed to Rachel Parker, executive editor of news for *InfoWorld* magazine.

drill down Ability of a database application program to provide additional information on a subject by highlighting the subject with the cursor. Once the subject has been highlighted and the call for more information initiated, e.g. by clicking a mouse or depressing the enter key, a new window normally is created to display the additional information.

driveability Ease of moving applications between graphical user interfaces. *See* GUI.

driver Jargon term for device driver. *See* device driver.

Driver Kernel Interface Commonly abbreviated and called DKI. *See* DKI.

DSA Directory System Agent. Term related to the Open Systems Interconnection X.500 directory services for the software and computers that contain a portion of the directory. A DSA is normally responsible for the information related to a single organization or subset of an organization, and is maintained on a separate computer. *See* OSI, X.500, DUA, DAP, DSP, DIT, DN and DISP.

DSP Directory System Protocol. Open Systems Interconnection X.500 directory services protocol used to send inquiries between Directory System Agents to obtain information about users on the network. *See* OSI, X.500, DSA, DAP, DUA, DIT, DN and DISP.

DSS 1. Decision support systems. Originated in the IBM Corp. environment in the 1960s. Designed to provide planners and decision model developers faster methods to analyze corporate data and make projections. 2. Distributed Security Service. Open Software Foundation Inc.'s security mechanism for the Distributed Communication Environment. A multilevel security system that uses Kerberos authentication and an authorization system. *See* OSF, DCE and Kerberos. 3. Digital Signature Standard. National Institute of Standards and Technology standard for encrypting digital signatures for electronic document exchange. Used to authenticate the sender of a document and confirm that the document has not been altered. *See* NIST and EDI.

DTD Document Type Definition. One of two components of a document created with the Standard Generalized Markup Language. Defines the structure of the text, which further defines the usable data objects and their relationship with other data objects in the document. The other element, called the document instance, is the data, or text, of the document. *See* SGML and document instance.

DTE 1. Data terminal equipment. Generic term for the source equipment (terminal) used for data communications transmission. 2. Cabling configuration used to connect peripheral devices, e.g. terminals, to a computer.

dtoc *(ATT)* Directory table of contents. One of the table of contents (toc) graphical table of contents routines. Creates a table of contents for directories and subdirectories. *See* toc.

DTP 1. Distributed Transaction Processing. Also called DXP. X/Open Co. Ltd.'s standard for managing a transaction that may be originated on one computer, use databases or resources on another and update a database on still another. Implements protocols to ensure the transaction is completed, or to back out of any changes it may have made should it fail. *See* X/Open, DDM, DPM and client/server. 2. Desktop publishing. Process of using a personal computer system and printer for creating documents, such as catalogs, brochures and newsletters. An industry created by the Apple Macintosh computer and the laser printer. 3. Data grade twisted pair. High grade unshielded twisted pair cable used for 10Base-T local area networks. *See* DIW-24, Ethernet, LAN, 10Base-T and UTP.

DTR Data terminal ready. RS-232-C standard that indicates a terminal or computer is ready to transmit data over a communications line.

DTS Distributed Time Service. Function within the Open Software Foundation Inc.'s Distributed Computing Environment. Manages clock synchronization of computers on a network. *See* OSF, DCE, time server and clerk.

du Disk usage. Command used to determine the amount of space used by specified files or directories or in the current working directory. *See* current working directory.

DUA Directory User Agent. Term related to the Open Systems Interconnection X.500 directory services for the client software that represents or performs actions for a user. X.500 services are accessed through the DUA by users. *See* OSI, X.500, DSA, DAP, DSP and DISP.

Dual In-line Package Commonly abbreviated and called DIP. *See* DIP.

Dual Intermediate System-to-Intermediate System Commonly abbreviated and called Dual IS-IS. *See* Dual IS-IS.

Dual IS-IS **Dual** Intermediate System-to-Intermediate System protocol. Open Systems Interconnection expansion to the Intermediate System-to-Intermediate System for router-to-router communications. *See* OSI and router.

dual-ported random access memory Commonly called VRAM (video random access memory). *See* VRAM.

dual universe Computer systems that are capable of running both the System V and the Berkeley Software Distribution UNIX operating systems, e.g. Pyramid Technology Inc.'s OSx and Sequent Computer Systems Inc.'s DYNIX operating systems. *See* universe.

Duke UUCP Duke University UNIX-to-UNIX CoPy. UUCP program no longer used. Developed at Duke University and released in early versions of the Berkeley Software Distribution, Sun Microsystems Inc.'s SunOS operating system and Digital Equipment Corp.'s Ultrix operating system. *See* UUCP.

dumb Jargon term for a dumb terminal. *See* dumb terminal.

Dumb luck prevails over skill and cunning once again One of the more common ways computer and/or UNIX problems are resolved.

dumb terminal Jargon term for any terminal used for data communication that is incapable of independent processing. Either a video display or hard-copy ASCII asynchronous terminal that uses only simple control codes for data communication, normally a character at a time.

dumb tube Commonly called dumb terminal. *See* dumb terminal.

dumdum *(OTH)* Shell script designed to perform incremental backups. *See* incremental backup.

dummy parameter Commonly called positional variable. *See* positional variable.

dump 1. *(BSD)* Backup program which provides for incremental backup of file systems. *See* image copy, incremental backup, Towers of Hanoi and restore. 2. *(ATT)* Command used to output specified sections of object files or archives of object files. 3. *(ATT)* File in the /etc/default directory which indicates there is data from a system dump in the swap device. As a system is being brought up, the system administrator is notified of the data and is given the opportunity to save the data before it is removed from the swap device.

dumpdev Kernel parameter used to set the major and minor device numbers for the dump device. *See* dump device, major device number and minor device number.

dump device Storage device used to write the output of a core dump when a system encounters an unrecoverable problem. *See* core and panic.

dump parameter Part of the kernel description file. Identifies the location where a core dump is to be placed if there is a system crash. *See* kernel description file, core dump and crash.

dup *(ATT)* Duplicate. System call that copies an open file descriptor. *See* file descriptor.

dup inode Condition in which a file is referenced twice in the superblock. Indicative of damage to the file system and normally results in a system crash. *See* superblock and crash.

duplex Ability to send communications in both directions at the same time over a single communications link. *See* full-duplex, half-duplex and simplex.

duplicate block Any block that is being accessed by two or more inodes. *See* block and inode.

dvi troff **De**vice-independent typesetter run **off**. Developed to run on several types of phototypesetters. The original version of the troff program was developed to operate a specific phototypesetter. *See* troff and phototypesetter.

DWB Documenter's Workbench. Set of text formatting programs, which is an add-on application software package. *See* nroff, troff, pic, grap, cw, eqn, man, mm macros, mv macros, neqn and tbl.

DX Directory Exchange. Interim approach to implementing X.500 directory services. Enables mail to be transferred between systems running the X.400 message-handling system for electronic mail. *See* X.400 and X.500.

DXP Alternative abbreviation for Data Transaction Processing. *See* DTP.

DYE-AG Pronunciation of diag, the Jargon term for diagnostic test. *See* diagnostic test.

dynabook Forerunner to the personal computer developed at the Xerox Palo Alto Research Center 10 years before the release of the Apple Macintosh. The dynabook was capable of using windows technology, icon displays with mouse control and pull-down windows. *See* Xerox PARC.

dynamic address transaction Commonly abbreviated and called DAT. *See* DAT.

dynamic allocation 1. Free-flow allocation or reallocation of memory or peripheral devices based on availability, not on specified use. 2. Parallel processing term for the use of processor resources. In dynamic allocation, processor resources designated for use in a program are not pre-allocated and can be used for other tasks until required by the specific process. *See* parallel processing, task and static allocation.

dynamic binding Object Management Group term for combining a program that responds to a request and data needed to satisfy the request, after the request is made. *See* OMG, request, binding and static binding.

dynamic file system Also called scalable file system. File system that can be modified while the computer is running.

dynamic kernel Kernel that is divided into segments so that only the necessary portions are loaded when needed. Can be upgraded or modified while the system is running.

dynamic license Concept in software licensing used to accommodate a network's software requirements. Software used on a network is licensed by the vendor according to the number of users who will have access to it, not to the single central processing unit that will control the software. The application software can be moved from one central processing unit to another as required. *See* CPU and site license.

dynamic linking Process of binding for C language library functions at run time instead of link (or compile) time. In theory, produces smaller executable images and enables bugs to be fixed in the libraries without recompiling or relinking all existing executable images. First introduced in UNIX with System V, Release 3. *See* C language and library.

dynamic link library Commonly abbreviated and called DLL. *See* DLL.

dynamic load balancing Ability of central processing units (CPUs) to schedule and reschedule themselves. The CPUs determine how much processing each unit is currently handling and then spread the work load to ensure all are equally busy with the current work load.

dynamic memory Memory created with electrical circuits. When power is turned off, information in the memory is lost. Called dynamic because the memory controller must periodically read (refresh) the contents of the memory to avoid losing this information.

dynamic random access memory
Commonly abbreviated and called DRAM. *See* DRAM.

DYNIX Sequent Computer Systems Inc.'s UNIX operating system based upon the Berkeley Software Distribution. *See* BSD and dual universe.

DYNIX/ptx Sequent Computer Systems Inc.'s UNIX operating system based upon AT&T Co.'s UNIX System V. *See* System V.

E

e 1. Rand Corp. editor, available in public domain. *See* editor and public domain. **2.** Programming language based upon the C language.

E Abbreviation for **exa**. *See* exa.

E2PROM Electronically Erasable Programmable Read-Only Memory. Also called EEPROM. Type of chip used for coding special computer instructions which can be electronically erased and reprogrammed. *See* PROM and EPROM.

EARN European Academic Research Network. Research and development network in Europe used to connect universities and research organizations.

eb Errorbells. Variable in the ex and vi editors that, when set, results in a ringing bell or beeping noise to alert users they are about to receive an error message. *See* ex and vi.

EBCDIC Extended Binary Coded Decimal Interchange Code. Pronounced *EB-SEE-DICK*. Standard character format on IBM Corp. systems. *See* ASCII.

EBONE European Backbone. Informal group, formed in 1991, that is composed of computer companies, European communication networks and users. Includes more than 35 groups that volunteer their resources to form an integrated European backbone network.

EB-SEE-DICK Pronunciation of EBCDIC, the abbreviation for Extended Binary Coded Decimal Interchange Code. *See* EBCDIC.

ECC Error correction code. Also called error checking and correction. Method used to record corrupted data on disks or Digital Audio Tape technology. Parity bits are added to the data, and used to detect errors and reconstruct the data if there are errors. *See* DAT, DDS, parity and byte.

ECC correction Information added to data to detect and possibly correct data transmission errors. Single bit errors, e.g. a 1 instead of a 0 or vice versa, can be corrected. Multiple bit errors can only be detected. *See* ECC.

echo Command used with an argument, normally a text message, to display the argument on the screen; or used with a path to direct the argument to the device named in the path.

CLP> echo word ⏎

displays the word on the screen. If multiple words are used, they must be enclosed in double quotes:

CLP> echo "Your statement to be displayed." ⏎

The following will send the message in quotes to the terminal device attached to port tty14 and display it on the screen or printer:

CLP>echo "Have a nice life."> /dev/tty14 ⏎

See device and path. **2.** Command used in a program to instruct the computer to send the message that follows. Or a command used under certain conditions to send an error message to standard output using echo "error message text"; or to send a specific message.

ECHO *(INET)* Defense Advanced Research Projects Agency Internet protocol. Returns a copy of any data that has been transmitted to the originator. Allows the sender to compare the original with the copy and to find out how long the transmission took. Used to debug software and isolate faults. *See* DARPA and Internet.

echoing Display of characters on a terminal screen as a result of input either from a keyboard or a computer program. *See* echo and duplex.

Echo Protocol *(INET)* Commonly abbreviated and called ECHO. *See* ECHO.

ECMA European Computer Manufacturers Association. European computer vendors group that does much the same work as the Institute of Electrical and Electronic Engineers for the American National Standards Institute. Develops and documents standards for the Open Systems Interconnection. *See* IEEE, ANSI, IFIP and OSI.

ECOMP EMACS Compiler. Precompiler used with later versions of EMACS to interpret programming code and produce macros. *See* EMACS and macro.

ed Editor. A simple command-oriented line editor program that allows the user to create or modify a text file. Developed by AT&T Co.'s Bell Laboratories. *See* ex, editor, line editor and Bell Laboratories.

EDAC Error Detection and Correction memory. Memory system that uses a parity algorithm to detect multiple bit errors and correct single bit errors.

ed commands Basic ed commands:

Command	Description
a	Append text. Allows the user to add new text following the current line.
d	Delete current line or specific line

Command	Description
h	Help. Explains to user why a command input resulted in a ? from the system.
p	Request for a prompt for the next command line
q	Quit. Leave editor without making any updates to the file.
t	Transfer. Used to copy one or more lines of text to a specified line in the text.
u	Undo. Reverse the previous editing action.
/string/	Editor string search.
s/string/string1/	Substitute. Look for string and replace it with string1.
?	Not a command. It is a response from the system when you input an illegal or incorrect command.

EDI Electronic Data Interchange. Protocol for the electronic transmission of business documents. A specialized version of electronic mail used to send invoices, purchase orders and other types of business forms. *See* e-mail, X.435 and ANSI X12.

EDIFACT Electronic Data Interchange for Administration, Commerce and Transport. United Nations standard for international exchange of information. *See* EDI.

edit 1. To add, delete, rearrange or modify information in a file. Sometimes also used to mean create, but create is not used as a synonym for edit. *See* create. 2. Very basic editor in the Berkeley Software Distribution. *See* editor and BSD.

edit buffer Temporary storage area used to retain files that are being created or edited. *See* buffer.

editing commands UNIX commands used to create, modify or format text. *See* vi, ex, ed, EMACS, nroff, troff, DWB and WWB.

Editing Macros Commonly abbreviated and called EMACS. *See* EMACS.

editing mode State or operating condition of an editing program in which text can be displayed, changed, added or deleted.

Editing Utilities Set of programs included in UNIX System V, Release 4, to create or update files. *See* SVR4.x.

editor Software program which allows the user to perform word processing functions and create or update a file. *See* UNIX editor.

EDITOR 1. Environmental variable in the Korn shell that identifies the editing program, e.g. ed, vi or EMACS, to be used for editing the history list. 2. Electronic-mail variable for identifying the editor used to create an e-mail message. *See* e-mail and .mailrc variables (Appendix F).

edit session Period of time in which someone uses a text editor.

EDIX Visual editor developed for IBM Corp. personal computers and ported to AT&T Co. computers as a third-party option.

edquota Edit quota. System administration command used to set the disk quota when a new user account is established.

EEPROM Commonly written E2PROM. *See* E2PROM.

EFF Electronic Frontier Foundation. Formed by computer industry leaders Mitch Kapor of Lotus Development Corp. and Steve Wozniak of Apple Computer Inc. in 1990, following government action against hackers during the May 8, 1990, Operation Sun Devil raids. Aims to educate and inform computer users of changes in the industry, and guard against infringement of First Amendment rights due to investigation and arrest of hackers. Headquartered in Washington,

D.C. *See* CPSR, Operation Sun Devil, hacker and Legion of Doom.

effective group identifier Commonly abbreviated and called EGID. *See* EGID.

effective user identifier Commonly abbreviated and called EUID. *See* EUID.

efl 1. Extended FORTRAN language. Block structured superset of the FORTRAN language. 2. Preprocessor used to generate FORTRAN language statements from a block structured meta language.

EGA Enhanced Graphics Adapter. IBM Corp.'s color video system with a resolution of 640 x 350 pixels. Acceptable for use with graphics packages. *See* 8514/A, CGA, super VGA, VGA, XGA and pixel.

EGID Effective group identifier. Part of the UNIX security system. Identifies the group to which the user currently belongs. Used to determine if a user has permission to access files. *See* GID and file system.

EGP *(INET)* External Gateway Protocol. Also called Exterior Gateway Protocol. A routing protocol used in ARPANET gateways to pass data between separate networks. *See* ARPANET and gateway.

egrep *(ATT)* Extended grep. Command used to search a file for a specified pattern. A variation of the grep command except it uses full regular expressions (both alphanumeric and special characters) to perform the search. Written by Alfred Aho. *See* grep, fgrep and regular expression.

EIA Electronic Industry Association. The United States electronics standards organization which specifies electronics characteristics required of interface hardware.

EIA 578 Standard for the interface which integrates a fax and modem for use in a personal computer. Uses similar command functions to Hayes modems. *See* fax and modem.

EIS Executive information systems. Originated in the IBM Corp. computing environment in the early 1980s. Designed to provide senior corporate personnel fast and accurate access to critical corporate data.

EISA Extended Industry Standard Architecture. Bus technology developed by nine companies: Compaq Computer Corp., Ing. C. Olivetti, Hewlett-Packard Co., AST Research, Inc., Seiko, Epson Corp., Tandy Corp., NEC Corp., Wyse Technology and Zenith Data Systems Corp. Released in 1988. Provides improved throughput, based upon the 16-bit Industry Standard Architecture. Transfers data 32 bits at a time. *See* Gang of Nine, ISA, bus and 32-bit computer.

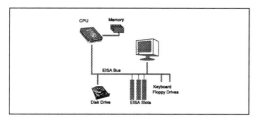

The EISA bus allows 16-bit and 32-bit devices to work together in the same system.

electrical noise Interference with electronic signals caused by external sources, e.g. power supplies or other signals which have not been properly shielded.

Electrical Numerical Integrator and Calculator Commonly abbreviated and called ENIAC. *See* ENIAC.

electromagnetic interference
Commonly abbreviated and called EMI. *See* EMI.

electron gun Internal element of a cathode ray tube. Used to transmit, or shoot, electron beams that charge or uncharge dots. This creates a glow in the phosphor coating on the inside of the vacuum tube, generating the characters. *See* CRT.

Electronic Data Interchange
Commonly abbreviated and called EDI. *See* EDI.

electronic filing system Information or data filing system that is established, updated and maintained on and with the use of a computer.

Electronic Frontier Foundation
Commonly abbreviated and called EFF. *See* EFF.

electronic highway Known as *wired nation* in the 1970s. Formally called the National Information Infrastructure. Also called data highway, super data highway, information highway, The Information Highway or TIH. Combination of fiber-optic cable, televisions, personal computers and multimedia technology that provides users in-home services, such as video on demand, and interactive television services, such as home shopping.

electronic mail Commonly abbreviated and called e-mail. *See* e-mail.

Electronic Mail Association
Commonly abbreviated and called EMA. *See* EMA.

electronic publishing Using electronic media, e.g. diskettes and compact disks, instead of paper to distribute information.

Electronics Industry Association
Commonly abbreviated and called EIA. *See* EIA.

electronic software distribution
Commonly abbreviated and called ESD. *See* ESD.

electronic vaulting Jargon term for the electronic transmission of data to storage devices either at the primary data center or off-site, at other locations.

electron trapping optical memory
Commonly abbreviated and called ETOM. *See* ETOM.

elevator sorting algorithm Algorithm used to control and manage input and/or output for disk access. Allows access to the data on the stacked platters of a disk drive. just as an elevator services the floors of a multistory building.

elf *(ATT)* executable and linking format. Executable and linking format library routine used to assess and work Executable and Linking Format files. *See* library routines and ELF.

ELF 1. Executable and Linking Format. Object file format for C language in UNIX System V, Release 4 that replaces Common Object Format File. *See* object, C language, SVR4.x and COFF. 2. Extremely low frequency. Electromagnetic radiation, from 5 megahertz to 2 kilohertz, which forms part of the magnetic radiation from video screens and is suspected of having negative affects on users' DNA and RNA. *See* VLF.

elif else if. Shell command marking the beginning of the "else" part of an "if - then - else" conditional statement. Includes an additional comparison test. Reacts the same as if a programmer wrote "else if." If the commands following the if statement in a shell program fail, then the commands following the elif statement will be run. *See* if, then, else and fi.

elite Unit of measurement on a typewriter that describes the number of characters, or pitch of print, and equals 12 characters per linear inch. *See* pitch, cpi and pica.

ellipsis (...) Programming documentation symbol. Whenever three dots appear with a command, they indicate the command is capable of processing more than one argument:

```
CLP> vi file name . ⏎
```

means vi can work more than one file name argument at a time, as in:

```
CLP> vi file name1 file name2 ⏎.
```

elm *(OTH)* Command to access the ELM electronic-mail package. *See* ELM and e-mail.

ELM *(OTH)* Electronic mail. Public domain electronic-mail package based on the vi text editor. *See* e-mail and vi.

else Shell command marking the beginning of the "else" part of an "if - then - else" conditional statement. Statements following the else are executed when the when the results of the if expression are false. *See* if, then, elif and fi.

em 1. Jargon term for electronic mail. *See* e-mail. 2. In printing, a unit of measurement, primarily for column width. Originally based on the width of the capital M in the particular type font being used.

EMA Electronic Mail Association. Organization of electronic-mail vendors and users based in Arlington, Virginia. Formed to promote the implementation and interconnection of electronic-mail systems. *See* e-mail.

emacs Command used to start the EMACS editor. *See* EMACS.

EMACS Editing Macros. Also spelled Emacs. An alternative visual editor. First written at Carnegie-Mellon University by James Gosling. A GNU is Not UNIX version was first written by Richard Stallman of the Free Software Foundation while at the Massachusetts Institute of Technology Lincoln Laboratories. Several other versions of EMACS have been written based upon MULTICS (the forerunner to UNIX), an EMACS-like editor written at AT&T in C language and a public domain GNU EMACS version. EMACS contains many built-in programming functions, making it well-liked by programmers. Unlike the vi editor, EMACS does not have an input and command mode.

.EMACS_pro System file established in user accounts for users of EMACS to set editor options or keys. *See* EMACS.

EMACS commands *See* Appendix A.

email Commonly spelled e-mail. *See* e-mail.

e-mail Electronic **mail**. Also spelled e mail or E-mail. Also called messaging. Form of communications that enables a user to send messages, documents, etc. to other users on either the same system or remote computers. With the write and talk commands, a message must be sent while the recipient is using the system, but with e-mail the message can be sent to a file or electronic-mail box where the recipient can read it later. *See* write, talk, multimedia and enclosure.

E-mail Commonly spelled e-mail. *See* e-mail.

emanation security Combination of physical and/or electronic devices used to prevent access by finely tuned eavesdropping equipment to data that is being transmitted or to the electronic emission (through electronic waves from a monitor, cable, microwave, etc.) of data that is being stored or transmitted to other locations from a computer.

embedded command Command placed in a text file, e.g. .c3 in the nroff program to center text. *See* nroff.

EMD Ethernet Media Driver. Optional software package available with UNIX System V, Release 4, that provides the software required to support TCP/IP Ethernet. *See* Ethernet, SVR4.x, TCP/IP and NSU.

EMI Electromagnetic interference. Interference or other effects caused by magnetic fields, electrical discharge (static electricity) or high-frequency radiation.

empty directory Directory containing, at best, the dot and dot dot entries.

empty string Commonly called null string. *See* null string.

emulator Hardware and/or software which allows a terminal and/or computer to appear to be another type of device. Quite common in communications software for personal computers, enabling the user's terminal to emulate a variety of standard terminals.

en In printing, a unit of measurement half the width of the capital M in the particular font being used. Used primarily for column width.

enable 1. *(ATT/XEN)* Line printer (lp) system command used to start or allow print jobs to be sent to line printers. *See* lp and disable. 2. To turn on hardware or software. Indicates a hardware device, e.g. a printer, is switched on and capable of performing its function; or that a software function has been started and users or other software programs may have access to the program.

enabling technology Technology that can be used by other vendors to interface products without having to create new or modify existing software code.

encapsulation 1. Process used in network communication to pack data for transmission. The sending host places a header message on the transmission informing the receiving host(s) about the data. *See* decapsulation. 2. Using one communication protocol, called the carrier protocol, to carry messages of another protocol, known as the payload protocol. Normally data is encapsulated when different protocols are used on local area networks (LANs) that are interconnected by a wide area network (WAN). For example, the LANs might use Novell Inc.'s Internetwork Packet Exchange or Apple Computer Inc.'s AppleTalk protocol and the WAN might run the Transmission Control Protocol/Internet Protocol (TCP/IP). Messages from the LAN, including all the appropriate header and trailer information, would be encapsulated and carried over the TCP/IP WAN from one LAN to another. *See* LAN, WAN, IPX, AppleTalk and IPX. 3. Programming term used to describe the process of combining data and procedures to form objects capable of either independent action or interaction with other objects. *See* object, OOP, class, inheritance and polymorphism.

encapsulation bridge Communication hardware device used to encapsulate the messages of one communication protocol so that they can be carried over a communications network that uses a different type of protocol. *See* encapsulation.

enclosure Also called attachment. Electronic-mail term for a file or image (binary, text, fax, etc.) sent within an electronic-mail message. *See* e-mail.

encode To put data into computer-readable code.

encrypt 1. *(ATT)* Command used to perform encryption or decryption of a file. *See* encryption and decryption. 2. C language library routine used to encrypt or decrypt data. *See* library routines.

encryption Process of turning understandable text into gibberish so that anyone who gains access to a file will not be able to read its actual contents without using the encryption key, or password. *See* encryption key, encrypt and decrypt.

encryption key Password used to gain access to a file which has been encrypted. *See* encryption.

endgrent C language library routine used to close access to the system group file when a program is completed. *See* library routines, getgrnam, getgrid, getgrent and setgrent.

endless loop Continual repetition of a task by a program caused by an error in program logic or if the application has been corrupted. Normally, the only way to exit is by killing the program. *See* exit and loop.

end-of-file Commonly abbreviated and called EOF. *See* EOF.

end-of-file character Commonly abbreviated and called EOF indicator. *See* EOF indicator.

end-of-file indicator Commonly abbreviated and called EOF indicator. *See* EOF indicator.

end-of-line Commonly abbreviated and called EOL. *See* EOL.

end-of-line indicator Commonly abbreviated and called EOL indicator. *See* EOL indicator.

endpwent C language library routine used with the getpwent system call to close access to the system password file when a program is finished. *See* library routines, getpwent and setpwent.

endsw End switch. Command used in C shell programming to indicate the termination of the switch command to be executed in a case string search. *See* case, C shell, breaksw and switch.

end system Open Systems Interconnection term for a host with applications that enable it to communicate with any of the seven layers of the OSI protocol suite. *See* OSI and OSIRM.

End-system-to-intermediate-system Commonly abbreviated and called ES-IS. *See* ES-IS.

end-to-end encryption Process used in a network to provide data security during transmission from one location to another. Data is encrypted when it enters the network, transmitted, then decrypted by the network before being released to the receiving host.

end-user Any person who uses a computer, computer products or output.

end-user computing Putting computer power in the hands of non-technical computer users to enhance performance. Normally done by providing a user with a personal computer. But can also be accomplished by using networks of personal computers, minicomputers, microcomputers and mainframes. *See* end-user, decentralized computing and networks.

Energy Star Program implemented by the Environmental Protection Agency (EPA) to recognize personal computer (PC) manufacturers that reduce the consumption of electricity needed to operate a PC. Manufacturers whose products consume 30 watts or less when the PC is idle may use the EPA's Energy Star logo in their advertising. *See* green PC.

engine 1. Jargon term for the central processing unit. 2. Computer system minus the applications, e.g. database engine. 3. Basis, e.g. standard or protocol, used to develop software or application packages. For example, the Simple Mail Transfer Protocol, X.25, could be the engine a company would use to develop and run an electronic-mail package. *See* SMTP, X.25 and e-mail.

enhanced graphics adapter Commonly abbreviated and called EGA. *See* EGA.

enhanced print Repeated striking by the pins of a dot matrix printer to create a darker imprint of characters, numbers or symbols. Produces near-letter-quality results.

Enhanced Small Device Interface
Commonly abbreviated and called ESDI. *See* ESDI.

Enhanced Storage Module Device
Commonly abbreviated and called ESMD. *See* ESMD.

ENIAC Electrical Numerical Integrator and Calculator. Sometimes called Electrical Numerical Integrator and Computer. Pronounced *ENNY ACK*. The first large digital computer. Contract let to Eckert and Mauchly in 1944 to create a system to calculate ballistics tables. Developed at the University of Pennsylvania in 1946, it continued in use until 1955. The ENIAC was 1800 square feet in size and contained more than 18,000 vacuum tubes. While working with the ENIAC, the late Rear Admiral Grace M. Hopper is credited with coining the term "bug" to describe a computer failure that was traced to a fried moth in the wiring. *See* Hopper, Grace M.

ENNY-ACK Pronunciation of ENIAC, the acronym for the Electrical Numerical Integrator and Calculator, the first major digital computer. *See* ENIAC.

enroll *(BSD)* Command used to provide password protection for electronic mail.

enter 1. Also called return. Jargon term for Enter key. *See* return and Enter key. 2.

Process of inputting new data, text, programs, etc., to a computer system.

Enter key Also called return key. Located on the far right of the middle row of the alphabetic keys on a keyboard. On keyboards with numeric pads, there is a second Enter key in the lower right-hand corner. Enter keys located in either place will function with either alphabetic or numeric entries. Depressing the Enter key sends a signal to the computer that either the user is finished with the current line and is ready to move to the next line (thus functioning like a carriage return), or a command is to be processed.

enterprise computing Ability of computer users within an organization to access information resources regardless of where the resources are located.

enterprise net Wide area network through which enterprise computing is accomplished. *See* WAN and enterprise computing.

enterprise servers UNIX-based mainframe or supercomputer-size system. Offers corporate-wide on-line transaction processing. *See* OLTP.

enterprise solutions and standards
Commonly abbreviated and called ESS. *See* ESS.

enterprise-specific MIB Commonly called an extended MIB. *See* extended MIB.

entity Any element of a network or computer system that requires administration, e.g. terminal server or modem.

entity-relationship diagram
Commonly abbreviated and called ERD. *See* ERD.

env *(ATT/XEN)* Command used to set, display or modify user environment variables. *See* environment variables.

ENV Korn shell environmental variable used when the user logs in. Sets the path to the environment file which sets user variables, options, aliases, etc.

envelope Information (address) used by the mail transfer agent to deliver electronic mail. Contains the heading with the address and body or text of the message. A date stamp is added each time the message passes through a new message transfer agent. *See* e-mail and MTA.

environment **1.** Series of parameters that define the shell variables that are used by the shell and passed to subsequent commands and programs. *See* environment variables. **2.** Components that make up the physical conditions in which a computer operates, e.g. temperature, humidity and electricity. *See* controlled environment and office environment.

environment file File used with the Korn shell in combination with the .profile to establish and run the user's environment. *See* .profile, ENV and environment.

environment variables Variables established when a user logs in or an application program is run. Define which shell is to be used, how the terminal screen displays characters, which commands or programs a user may access and use, etc. Some environment variables can be defined by users in their .profile (Bourne shell), .cshrc (C shell) or .profile (Korn shell). The variables are maintained by the shell and passed to commands and programs. Typical environment variables identify the user; the user PATH, which identifies the commands the user can execute; TERM, or terminal type; etc. *See* .profile, Bourne shell, .cshrc, C shell, Korn Shell and shell.

EO Erasable optical. Optical storage medium that can be erased and rewritten. *See* M/O and WORM.

EOF **1.** End-of-file. Last character of a file. **2.** Signal sent to the kernel that indicates the end of the file. *See* EOF indicator.

EOF indicator Special character or symbol used to indicate the end of a file. For UNIX, it is control d.

EOL End-of-line. Last character of a line.

EOL indicator Special character or symbol used to indicate the end of a line. For UNIX, it is the dollar sign ($).

EPHOS European Procurement Handbook for Open Systems. Contracting specifications for purchasing Open Systems Interconnection products developed by the European Community. *See* OSI.

Epoch Universal date from which clock time in UNIX is measured. The original developers of UNIX arbitrarily selected 00:00 a.m., January 1, 1970, as the system's Epoch. Clock time in UNIX is measured in seconds; each day is 86,400 seconds long and a year is 31,557,807 seconds long. However, on UNIX systems in the 1970s and early 1980s, the maximum value of an integer was only 136 years worth of seconds. Time, therefore, had to be measured from a point in the fairly recent past, not from the astronomical Epoch, which started December 24, 4713 B.C. In addition, since UNIX was developed in the early 1970s, most of the interesting developments in the system's history could be expected to occur in the near future. Thus, the developers chose a convenient date in the then-recent past. They could have just as well picked Kernighan's birth date or the time and date of the Watergate break-in, but January 1, 1970, was politically neutral.

EPROM Erasable Programmable Read-Only Memory. Also called reprogrammable read-only memory or RPROM. Chip used for coding special computer instructions which can be electronically erased and reprogrammed. Can be coded with special equipment, then erased with ultraviolet light and coded again. *See* PROM and E2PROM.

e protocol Error-free **protocol**. Data protocol supported by UNIX-to-UNIX CoPy (UUCP) available in UNIX System V to pass data between networks. Assumes data is being transferred error-free and performs neither error checking nor flow control functions. It is an updated version, released with HoneyDanBer UUCP, and used mainly for communication over

Transmission Control Protocol/Internet Protocol local area networks. *See* UUCP, LAN, TCP/IP, HoneyDanBer UUCP, f protocol, g protocol, G protocol, t protocol and x protocol.

eqn *(ATT)* **Eq**uatio**n**. Part of the Documenter's Workbench set of text formatting programs. A troff preprocessor that formats mathematical expressions. Developed in 1975 by Brian Kernighan and Lorinda Cherry of AT&T Co.'s Bell Laboratories. *See* DWB, troff, neqn and Bell Laboratories.

erasable optical Commonly abbreviated and called EO. *See* EO.

Erasable Programmable Read-Only Memory Commonly abbreviated and called EPROM. *See* EPROM.

erase 1. Keyboard function which allows the user to move the cursor back one or more spaces, deleting the character in each space. This can be done either through command line inputs or within editors. The erase key is normally Ctrl h, but can be defined by the user with the stty command. *See* control character and stty. 2. Signal sent to the kernel that erases the previous character. *See* erase character.

erase character American National Standards Institute character established in the terminal set up routines to backspace and delete characters. In UNIX System V, Release 4, the erase character is defined as either the backspace key or Ctrl h. *See* ANSI, SVR4.x, erase and kill.

ERD **E**ntity-**r**elationship **d**iagram. Tool used to express the relationships between two or more data objects. *See* DFD.

ergonomics Study of the interaction between people and office environments in relation to comfort and safety. In computing, it addresses the machine or system and human interface. Takes into account such variables as the brightness, clarity and refresh rate of a computer screen, the feel and layout of a computer keyboard, the tilt and swivel bases, and location of controls, all specifically intended for the safety and comfort of the users.

errdead *(ATT)* **Err**or **dead**. Utility used to extract error log information from a system that has crashed.

errdemon *(ATT)* **Err**or **demon**. Background program used to manage the recording of system error messages.

errdump *(ATT)* **Err**or **dump**. Command used by a system administrator to output the contents of an error history file.

errlog *(ATT)* **Err**or **log**. Daemon used to record kernel error messages in a file.

ERRLOG **Err**or **log**. List of the error messages received during an actual or attempted UNIX-to-UNIX CoPy (UUCP) transmission. Includes the error, UUCP command, process identifier, and date and time. *See* UUCP, PID and asset errors.

errno **Err**or **n**umber (**no.**). Collection of error messages which provides an indication of why a system program has failed.

ERRNO *(ATT)* **Err**or **n**umber (**no.**). Korn shell variable. Used mainly to debug programs. Maintains the numeric value of the last system call which failed. *See* system call.

error 1. *(BSD)* Command used to analyze compiler-generated errors. Places the message, containing these standard errors, as a comment in the area of the source code that generated the problem. *See* compiler and source code. 2. Any quantifiable variance from the expected norm.

errorbells Variable in the ex and vi editors. Commonly abbreviated eb. *See* eb.

error checking Any test for data validity.

error correction coding Commonly abbreviated and called ECC. *See* ECC.

Error Detection and Correction Memory Commonly abbreviated and called EDAC. *See* EDAC.

error handling Ability of a computer program to compensate for an error while the program is running. Error handling varies widely. Some programs have no error handling, others can send an error message and the more sophisticated programs will attempt to correct the error without sending a notification or aborting.

error logging Ability of the UNIX operating system to monitor and record errors in the hardware.

error message Message sent to a user indicating a mistake in a program or command input being run. Could emanate from either an incorrectly written program or an input mistake or corruption of a program in the operating system or application software.

error message buffer Area set aside for saving a copy of all system error messages sent to the console terminal.

errpt *(ATT)* Error report. Utility used to format and print error reports.

errstop *(ATT)* Error stop. Command used to stop the error login daemon. *See* errdemon.

esac Case, spelled backward. Signifies the end of a case statement. *See* case.

escape 1. Term related to the use and function of shell processes. The escape mechanism allows the shell to react to the literal meaning instead of the special function of a character, e.g. pound sign (#), asterisk (*) and question mark (?). 2. Mechanism that allows a user or program to suspend a shell operation, start a new shell and run commands. 3. Electronic-mail variable. *See* .mailrc variables (Appendix F).

escape character Character that tells the shell to ignore the special meaning and use the literal meaning of the character that follows. Escape characters vary with the application. The backslash (\) is the escape character for the shell, e.g. if the pound sign (#) is used as the erase character and it is to be input literally, it must

be preceded by a backslash (\#). The exclamation point (!) is the escape character for the interactive command, e.g. if a user is in an ELM electronic-mail session and wants to escape to the shell without ending the session, the user must input an exclamation point followed by a command to execute a single command or an exclamation point followed by a carriage return to establish a new shell.

escape key Commonly written Esc key. *See* Esc key.

escape sequence String of characters sent to devices, e.g. printers, to initiate specified commands or tasks.

Esc key Escape key, found on the terminal keyboard. Sometimes used like the control key, in combination with other keys, to initiate special commands or functions on a printer or terminal screen, e.g. Esc key either initiates or turns off character attributes such as double high, double wide and bold. Also used in some older communications software to suspend communications.

ESD 1. Electrostatic discharge. Commonly called static electricity. High-voltage, low-current electricity generated by rubbing two objects together, e.g. clothing and the human body. Can damage the internal parts of a computer if a person who is not grounded touches a board or the frame. 2. Electronic software distribution. Use of computers, specialized software and data network communications to distribute software to computers on a network.

ESDI Enhanced Small Device Interface. Based on Storage Module Device. Provides an interface between small computers and disk drives. *See* SMD.

ES-IS End-system-to-intermediate-system. Protocol which provides the ability for hosts (end systems) and routers (intermediate systems) to locate and communicate with each other. *See* router and IS-IS.

ESMD Enhanced Storage Module Device. Advanced version of Storage Module Device used to connect larger computers to disk drives. *See* SMD.

ESS Enterprise solutions and standards. Rules and guidelines established by a company or organization for software development, implementation and management.

Essential Utilities Set of programs included in UNIX System V, Release 4, to perform common essential tasks, e.g. to create a new directory, determine the date or find out who is logged on. *See* SVR4.x.

ESS-RAM Pronunciation of SRAM, the acronym for static random access memory. *See* SRAM.

/etc Etcetera. Root directory where the system administration and configuration files are maintained.

/etc/bkup *(ATT)* UNIX System V, Release 4 root file system directory which contains the files used to back up and restore the system. *See* SVR4.x and root file system.

/etc/checklist File containing the names of file systems that should be checked by the fsck command. *See* fsck and file system.

/etc/cron.d *(ATT)* UNIX System V, Release 4 root file system directory which contains the files used to manage the cron daemon. *See* SVR4.x, root file system, cron and crontab.

/etc/default *(ATT)* UNIX System V, Release 4 root file system directory which contains the files used to manage default system parameters, e.g. login attempts and password aging. *See* SVR4.x and root file system.

/etc/dfs *(ATT)* Distributed File System directory. UNIX System V, Release 4 root file system file for the Distributed File System. Contains the system files used for the Distributed File System. *See* /etc/dfs/dfstab, /etc/dfs/fstypes and /etc/dfs/sharetab.

/etc/dfs/dfstab *(ATT)* Distributed File System table. UNIX System V, Release 4 root file system file for the Distributed File System. Used to open resources for access by remote users or to automatically allow access to resources when the system goes into multi-user state. *See* SVR4.x, root file system, DFS and multi-user.

/etc/dfs/fstypes *(ATT)* Distributed File System file system types. File in the UNIX System V, Release 4 root file system which contains a list of all the software loaded for the Distributed File System. Records the type of file sharing system being used, e.g. the Remote File Sharing system, the Network File System or both. *See* SVR4.x, root file system, DFS, file system types, RFS and NFS.

/etc/dfs/sharetab *(ATT)* Distributed File System share table. UNIX System V, Release 4 root file system file for the Distributed File System. Created by the share command to maintain a list of all local and remote resources being used. *See* SVR4.x, root file system, DFS and share.

/etc/ethers *(ATT)* File containing a database which matches computer host names with Ethernet addresses.

/etc/ff *(ATT)* Command used to display file names and statistics for a file system. *See* file system.

/etc/fsstat *(ATT)* Command used to display file system statistics. *See* file system.

/etc/fstypes *(ATT)* Command used to display file system type. *See* file system.

/etc/fuser *(ATT)* Command used to display processes using a file or file structure. Can be used to terminate those processes.

/etc/gettydefs Get tty (getty) definitions. System file containing the definitions for a port, used by the getty program.

/etc/group Root file in which the members of a group and group identifier relationships are maintained. *See* GID.

etch Process that uses a chemical reaction to remove material in forming a specific pattern, e.g. to etch the pattern on a silicon wafer to form an integrated circuit. *See* IC.

/etc/hosts File which contains information about Internet hosts, e.g. host names, addresses, aliases and administrators. *See* Internet and DNS.

/etc/hosts.equiv File used to maintain a list of trusted hosts. Checked by the system for access authorization whenever a user attempts to log in with either the rlogin or rsh command. *See* rlogin and rsh.

/etc/inetd.conf File which contains a list of hosts automatically available when the Internet daemon is started. *See* inetd and Internet.

/etc/init.d *(ATT)* Directory in the UNIX System V, Release 4 root file system that holds files used during system state changes. *See* SVR4.x and root file system.

/etc/inittab *(ATT)* Root file containing a table of instructions for the init program. *See* init.

/etc/lp *(ATT)* Directory in the UNIX System V, Release 4 root file system which holds the configuration files used to operate printers. *See* SVR4.x and root file system.

/etc/mail *(ATT)* Directory in the UNIX System V, Release 4 root file system which contains the files used to operate the electronic-mail system. *See* SVR4.x, root file system and e-mail.

/etc/mail/cnfg *(ATT)* **Mail c**onfiguration. UNIX System V, Release 4 mail file used to manage the optional parameters which control how the electronic-mail system works. *See* SVR4.x and e-mail.

/etc/mail/lists *(ATT)* UNIX System V, Release 4 electronic-mail file which contains distribution lists, e.g. if /etc/mail/lists contains the line:

mgrs:sstarck,cedgman,nelda

then mail sent to mgrs will be automatically forwarded to sstarck, cedgman and nelda. *See* SVR4.x and e-mail.

/etc/mail/mailsurr *(ATT)* **Mail sur**rogate. UNIX System V, Release 4 electronic-mail file used to manage delivery of electronic mail to users and other systems. *See* SVR4.x and e-mail.

/etc/mail/mailx.rc *(ATT)* **Mailx r**un commands. UNIX System V, Release 4 electronic-mail file which contains the run commands for mailx commands. *See* SVR4.x, mailx and .rc file.

/etc/mail/namefiles *(ATT)* UNIX System V, Release 4 electronic-mail file which contains a list of the system electronic-mail aliases. *See* SVR4.x, e-mail and alias.

/etc/mail/names *(ATT)* UNIX System V, Release 4 electronic-mail file which contains name aliases, e.g. if /etc/mail/names contains the line.

dvolkma:dv

then mail sent to dvolkma will be automatically forwarded to dv. *See* SVR4.x, e-mail and alias.

/etc/mnttab *(ATT)* **M**ount tab**le**. File in the UNIX System V, Release 4 root file system for the Distributed File System. Created by the mount command to maintain a list of all local and remote file systems that are active. *See* SVR4.x, root file system, file system, DFS, setmnt and mount.

/etc/netmasks File which contains the addressing information for the network and subnetworks needed to implement the Internet Protocol. *See* IP.

/etc/passwd Root file in which encrypted user passwords and user identifier information are maintained. Can be read by anyone, which may leave a system open to attack. *See* UID and /etc/shadow.

/etc/profile System file that is read by the system.

/etc/rc?.d *(ATT)* Directory in the UNIX System V, Release 4 root file system in which files are located when the system state is changed. The ?. changes to match the current system state. *See* SVR4.x, root file system and state.

/etc/rfs/rmnttab *(ATT)* Table used with the Remote File Sharing system which contains a list of resources to be made available for use by remote hosts. *See* RFS and rmnttry.

/etc/saf *(ATT)* Directory in the UNIX System V, Release 4 root file system which contains the files used for local operation of Service Access Facility. *See* SVR4.x, root file system and SAF.

/etc/shadow *(ATT)* UNIX System V file used in combination with the /etc/passwd file to provide additional password security. Encrypted passwords are maintained in /etc/passwd, which can be read by any user. However, these passwords can be transferred to /etc/shadow, to which only root has access. *See* /etc/passwd and root.

/etc/shutdown Commonly called shutdown. *See* shutdown.

/etc/ttydefs *(ATT)* UNIX System V, Release 4 file that replaces /etc/gettydefs., which contains the configurations definitions of ports. *See* SVR4.x, SAF and SAC.

/etc/ttys *(BSD)* Root file containing a table of instructions for the init program. *See* init.

/etc/uucp/Devices *(ATT)* Commonly called Devices. *See* Devices.

/etc/uucp/Dialers *(ATT)* Commonly called Dialers. *See* Dialers.

/etc/uucp/Grades *(ATT)* Commonly called Grades. *See* Grades.

/etc/uucp/Sysfiles *(ATT)* Commonly called Sysfiles. *See* Sysfiles.

/etc/uucp/Systems *(ATT)* Commonly called Systems. *See* Systems.

/etc/vfstab *(ATT)* Virtual file system table. File in the UNIX System V, Release 4 root file system for the Distributed File System. Identifies the resources to automatically be shared when the system goes into multiuser state. *See* SVR4.x, root file system, DFS and multi-user.

/etc/whodo *(ATT)* Command used to find out what users are doing on the system.

/etc/wtmp Generally pronounced W-TEMP. Sometimes called who temp. Log of entries resulting from user logins and processes generated by the init daemon. Shows who did what when. The entries are accumulated until system accounting is done; then the current entries are archived and new entries are recorded. *See* init and runacct.

etherfind Ethernet find. Sun Microsystems Inc.'s tool used to locate data packets on an Ethernet local area network. *See* Ethernet.

Ethernet Local area network developed by the Xerox Palo Alto Research Center, Intel Corp. and Digital Equipment Corp. in 1973. Ethernet is a passive system connected by either thicker shielded coaxial cable or thinner non-shielded cable with a 10 megabits-per-second standard. The active portion of the network, or driver of the communications, resides on the components of the network, e.g. personal computers, minicomputers or microcomputers. Information is transmitted over a wire in packets. There have been three versions of Ethernet: the original 1980 version; a 1982 revised version; and the 1983 Institute of Electrical and Electronic Engineers 802.3

standard. *See* Xerox PARC, Mbps, IEEE and FDDI.

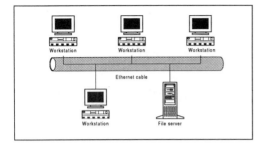

A typical Ethernet setup where all computers on the network are linked by a coaxial cable.

How Ethernet works

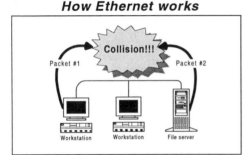

Ethernet stations normally transmit when the cable is free. But when the workstation and file server transmit at the same time, causing a collision, each station must retransmit the data after waiting a random period of time.

Ethernet Media Driver Commonly abbreviated and called EMD. *See* EMD.

Ethernet meltdown When an Ethernet network has neared or reached its full capability, and is transmitting data either extremely slowly or not at all.

ether pseudo-device Term used to describe pseudo-devices established to support Ethernet connectivity within the kernel. *See* pseudo-device, Ethernet and kernel.

ethers Jargon term for /etc/ethers. *See* /etc/ethers.

ether, the Jargon term for nothing or unknown output location. *See* bit bucket.

ETI Extended Terminal Interface. Term coined with the release of UNIX System V, Release 4 to describe the C language library used to develop the terminal enhancements for windows and character placement. *See* SVR4.x.

ETOM Electron trapping optical memory. Optical technology that uses lasers to write, read and erase data to and from memory. Provides speed in accessing, reading and writing data; offers high storage density; and extends the life of the medium by placing less physical stress on it.

EUC Extended UNIX Codes. Set of codes based upon standards developed by the International Organization for Standardization that provide the ability for applications to translate and display data in a foreign language. *See* i18n and ISO.

EUID Effective user identifier. Part of the UNIX security system, the EUID identifies the user who owns a program. The EUID of a process is checked for permission before a user can access a file system and specific files and directories within that system. *See* UID and file system.

Eunice Wollongong Group's UNIX operating system look-alike.

European Academic Research Network Commonly abbreviated and called EARN. *See* EARN.

European Backbone Commonly abbreviated and called EBONE. *See* EBONE.

European Computer Manufactures Association Commonly abbreviated and called ECMA. *See* ECMA.

European Procurement Handbook for Open Systems Commonly abbreviated and called EPHOS. *See* EPHOS.

European UNIX User Group Commonly abbreviated and called EurOpen. *See* EurOpen.

European Workshop on Open Systems Commonly abbreviated and called EWOS. *See* EWOS.

EurOpen Originally called the European UNIX User Group (EUUG). The name was changed in 1990. EurOpen was formed in 1976 by a few UNIX programmers to promote the use of UNIX in Europe. It has grown to include members from more than 20 major European countries, including the former Soviet Union. Membership is also open to companies from those countries. Headquarters are located in Herts, United Kingdom. *See* InterEUnet and World Forum of Open Systems Users.

EUUG Original name of the European UNIX User Group formed in 1976. The name was changed in 1990 to EurOpen.

EUUG-S Svenska Unixanvandares Forening. The Swedish UNIX Users' Group formed in 1983.

eval Shell command used to evaluate shell variables and then run the output as arguments of other shell variables. *See* shell variable and argument.

event 1. Anything that must take place before a process or function can run. 2. Jargon term for a very bad occurrence, e.g. "They had a security event." 3. Significant occurrence on a network or computer system, e.g. an alarm, alert or change.

event polling Approach to implementing an operating system where tasks are accomplished in a repetitive, scheduled sequence.

EWOS European Workshop on Open Systems. Organization originally formed to promote Open Systems Interconnection standards and development of open systems products for computer networking. Since its inception, has changed its charter to include other open operating systems and interfaces. *See* OSI, AOW and OIW.

ex 1. Editor that allows the user to create or modify a text file. Like the ed editor, ex is a line editor. Written at the University of California, Berkeley. *See* ed, editor and line editor. 2. awk abbreviation for arith-

metic or string expression. *See* awk and regular expression.

exa Represents 10^{18} (1,000,000,000,000,000,000) or quintillion. Abbreviated E.

Exchange Access SMDS Commonly abbreviated and called XA-SMDS. *See* XA-SMDS.

exclamation point (!) 1. Symbol for exclamation point. 1. Often called BANG, a Jargon term originating with the *Batman* television series and comics, in which a bang from a crashing sound or gun shot was emphasized with an exclamation point. 2. When used with square brackets, modifies the meaning of the input, e.g. if used with numbers *[!3], the command will perform on all files except those ending in the number 3. 3. In the C shell, can be used to repeat commands when a user has a command history (that is, a log of commands which have been run) operating, e.g. !! means repeat the last command and !5 means repeat command number 5. *See* history. 4. Hostname delimiter in UNIX-to-UNIX CoPy addresses, e.g. yourhost!myhost!myname. *See* UUCP, Internet and network.

ex commands *See* Appendix B.

exec 1. Shell command used to start or execute arguments. *See* shell and argument. 2. Jargon term for starting a program. 3. Execute. Part of the system's process control mechanism. The exec family of system calls includes execl, execv, execle, execve, execlp and execvp. Replaces the current process context with a new program image and executes or starts a program. *See* system call and process control.

executable 1. Any command, file or program which has the execute permission turned on, so instructions are loaded and run by the computer. Permission will vary by user and group; therefore, one user may be able to execute a command while others may not. *See* execute. 2. Describes software that the computer can understand and run. *See* executable code.

Executable and Linking Format
Commonly abbreviated and called ELF. *See* ELF.

executable code Machine instructions or language which can be read and run by the computer. *See* object.

executable file File with executable permissions. Any file that runs or is executed like a command or program. *See* executable.

execute 1. Process of running, or starting, a program to perform a previously defined operation, e.g. executing a program in order to obtain data or information. The data or information either is collected in a file where it can be displayed on demand or directed to a printer to produce hard copy. 2. In UNIX, part of the changeable permissions on a file or directory, "read, write and execute." A user can only run either a system or user command if the execute permission is turned on.

execute bit Permission bit established for a directory which allows users to access the directory. *See* permission bits and execute permission.

execute permission Access permission established to enable users to run a program or give them access to a directory. Execute permissions are represented by an x, e.g. when an ls -l (for long format) command is run to display a list of files/directories, the files/directories are shown first with the permissions rwxrwx--x indicating the owner has read, write and execute permission; members of the owner's group have read, write and execute permissions; and all others have only execute permission. In addition, other information is displayed, e.g. the name and size of the file. *See* permissions.

execution speed Commonly called runtime. *See* runtime.

execution time Commonly called runtime. *See* runtime.

executive information systems
Commonly abbreviated and called EIS. *See* EIS.

exit 1. *(ATT)* Command used to log off the system. Included in the UNIX System V, Release 4 Framed Access Command Environment file system operation command menu. *See* SVR4.x, FACE and file system. 2. Shell command used to perform a graceful termination when a shell process ends. 3. Function of an application software which either ends a specific task or element of the software or the entire application program. *See* exit code. 4. System call issued when a process has ended, instructing the kernel to close all related processes and files, release resources, etc. *See* system call.

exit code Signal sent by the process terminating a program used to determine level of completion.

exit status Commonly called exit code. *See* exit code.

exit value Numerical value returned by a program or command on completion. Typical UNIX commands return either a 0 (zero) if they are successfully completed or a non-zero value to indicate an error or other exceptional condition.

expand *(BSD)* Command used to expand tabs in a file to an equivalent number of blank spaces. Frequently used as a filter. *See* filter.

expandability Ability to increase a computer system's capability, usually by small increments in a predefined pattern, by adding software or hardware peripherals.

expansion slot Physical location on the chassis of a computer that can be used to hold additional boards for memory, central processing units, etc., as a computer's capabilities are expanded.

expert 1. Individual who has attended a UNIX users conference. 2. Individual who is approached by other users with questions and requests for help, and gives the right answer more than 50 percent of the time. **3.** Individual who has sent for Open Systems Today but has not received the first copy.

ExperTips Quarterly newsletter that publishes articles on system administration, programming, security and source code for C language programs and shell scripts.

/export *(ATT)* UNIX System V, Release 4 root file system directory used by the Network File System as the root of the export file system tree. *See* SVR4.x, root file system, NFS and file system.

export **1.** To outwardly exchange or modify data from its standard format to an alternative format recognized by a different operating system or application software package. *See* import. **2.** To move a variable from a parent to a child process. **3.** To extend the value of an environmental variable to all processes running under a shell. **4.** Network File System command used to list file systems available for remote mounting, or activation, by other networked computer systems. *See* NFS.

exportfs Export file system. Network File System command used to make resources on a computer available to users on a network. *See* NFS, file system, adv, share and shareall.

expr *(ATT/BSD/XEN)* Expression. Command used to evaluate its arguments as an arithmetic expression. Frequently used to do arithmetic and string functions in shell scripts. *See* argument, regular expression and shell script.

expreserve *(BSD)* Ex preserve. Command used to check the /tmp directory for files which were being edited when the system crashed. Sends an electronic-mail message to the file owner indicating the file is in /tmp and explaining how to retrieve it. *See* /tmp.

expression Commonly called regular expression. *See* regular expression.

.exrc Ex run command. System file established in user accounts. An initialization file for the ex, edit, vi and view editing programs, contained in the user's home directory. Whenever a user starts one of the editors, the editor looks for the specific execution commands the user has established in .exrc, e.g. having lines in a text file automatically wrap at a specified column.

exstr *(ATT)* Extract string. Command used to extract character strings from C language source files. *See* C language.

Extended Binary Coded Decimal Interchange Code Commonly abbreviated and called EBCDIC. *See* EBCDIC.

extended graphics array Commonly abbreviated and called XGA. *See* XGA.

Extended Graphics Array Commonly abbreviated and called XGA. *See* XGA.

Extended Industry Standard Architecture Commonly abbreviated and called EISA. *See* EISA.

extended MIB Extended management information base. Also called enterprise-specific MIB or private MIB. A vendor-specific database of management information related to the vendor's network product.

Extended Terminal Interface Commonly abbreviated and called ETI. *See* ETI.

Extended UNIX Code Commonly abbreviated and called EUC. *See* EUC.

extensible Pertaining to a software application or hardware system that allows other components to be added to meet new requirements or to take advantage of new technology.

extension Add-on. Feature added to enhance the standard functionality of an operating system, programming language or application program.

Exterior Gateway Protocol *(INET)*
Commonly abbreviated and called EGP.
See EGP.

External Data Representation
Commonly abbreviated and called XDR.
See XDR.

External Gateway Protocol Commonly
abbreviated and called EGP. *See* EGP.

external program Non-memory-resident
program. Stored and run from a device
instead of a central processing unit. *See*
stored program and CPU.

external signal Signals sent between
processes as part of interprocess communication. *See* signal and IPC.

extremely low frequency Commonly
abbreviated and called ELF. *See* ELF.

eyacc *(BSD)* Extended yet another compiler-compiler. A program that generates
a C language program that parses a grammar specified as the eyacc input. eyacc is
based on the older yacc but provides better error recovery. *See* yacc.

eyephone Head-mounted display unit
for three-dimensional graphics display
that combines visual and auditory displays. *See* 3-D graphics.

F

f   Abbreviation for **femto**. *See* **femto**.

f77   FORTRAN 77 compiler provided with UNIX systems. The lingua franca of scientific and technical computer programming. *See* ratfor.

face *(ATT)* Command used to start the Framed Access Control Environment. *See* FACE.

FACE Framed Access Control Environment. Windows- and menu-based user interface for terminals, released with UNIX System V, Release 4. Provides American Standard Code for Information Interchange terminals the capability of windows and pop-up menus. In addition, provides the ability to use menus and function keys in system administration, and file, program and printer management. *See* SVR4.x, window, ASCII terminal and pop-up menu.

facsimile Commonly abbreviated and called fax. *See* fax.

factor *(ATT/BSD/XEN)* Command used when working on mathematical computations to determine the prime factor of a number.

falloc File table **alloc**ation. Routine used to allocate an inode from the file table when a new file is created. *See* FIO and inode table.

false 1. Value other than 0 (zero), indicating a program has not been successfully completed. 2. Program that always re-

turns an unsuccessful exit status. False returns exit(1). A false.c looks like:

```
main()
{
    exit(1);
}
```

Normally used in writing shell scripts to terminate a loop.

fancier *(OTH)* Modified version of the dumb script used to transfer data from a computer to a line printer. *See* LP, dumb and simple.

fanfold paper Paper folded like a fan into a stack. Has small, regularly spaced holes along the left and right edges which allow it to be continuously and quickly fed through a printer. The sheets are perforated on either two or all four sides so they can be cleanly separated.

FARNET Federation of American Research **Net**works. Association composed of the organizations that run local, state and national networks and use the National Science Foundation Network as a backbone. *See* NSFNet.

fastboot *(BSD)* Shell script used to reboot the system without performing a file system check. *See* shell script and file consistency check.

fast Ethernet Jargon term for an Ethernet local area network capable of transmission rates of up to 100 megabits per second. *See* Ethernet, 100Base-VG, 100VG-AnyLAN, 100Base-X and 4T +.

Fast Ethernet Alliance Group composed of 3Com Corp., Cabletron Systems

Inc., David Systems Inc., Digital Equipment Corp., Sun Microsystems Inc., SMC, SynOptics Communications Inc. and Grand Junction Networks. Formed to support the implementation of the fast Ethernet protocol based upon use of Carrier Sense Multiple Access/Collision Detection used in the original Ethernet protocol. *See* fast Ethernet, Ethernet, CSMA/CD, 100Base-VG, 100VG-Any-LAN, 100Base-X and 4T +.

Fast File System Improvement in the Fourth Berkeley Software Distribution, Second Release, that enhanced file access time by writing data in larger blocks. Developed to compensate for the slow, mechanical operations of a hard disk drive. Incorporated in AT&T Co.'s System V, Release 4. *See* BSD and SVR4.x.

Fast SCSI Fast Small Computer System Interface. Protocol within the SCSI-2 standard. Allows data to be transmitted at 10 megabytes per second and provides an 8- or 10-bit data path. *See* SCSI and SCSI-2.

fast Token Ring Protocol first proposed in late 1993 by the Hewlett-Packard Co. and IBM Corp. for Token Ring networks capable of transmitting data at 100 megabits per second. *See* Token Ring and 100VG-AnyLAN.

Fast-Wide SCSI Fast-Wide Small Computer System Interface. Protocol within the SCSI-2 standard. Allows data to be transmitted at 20 megabytes per second and provides a 16-bit data path. *See* SCSI and SCSI-2.

fatal error Program failure resulting in termination of the application software by the computer. *See* nonfatal error.

fat finger Typing or input error. Normally a very dumb mistake.

fault 1. Process in which the central processing unit (CPU) tries to reference a virtual memory address that is not in the computer's main memory. When a fault occurs, the CPU then loads the missing memory page from the program image or retrieves the information from the system's swap space. 2. Hardware error preventing proper operation. Can be caused by a disk crash, power supply failure, etc.

fault rate Measurement of page faults produced by a specific process. *See* page fault.

fault tolerance Reliability of a program or computer. Ability of a computer or program to produce or continue to operate even when there has been a system error, or failure, in the software or hardware.

fault tolerant General term for computers with built-in fault tolerance. *See* fault tolerance.

fax 1. Facsimile equipment. Equipment used to transfer text and/or images over communications lines. Capabilities are identified by groups based on resolution and transmission speed. 2. Jargon term for a document sent or received by facsimile equipment. Fax use in business varies from internal distribution of documents to increasing contacts with customers and sending out press releases.

Fax machine

fax broadcasting Using facsimile transmissions to notify customers or others in an organization of an impending event. *See* fax.

fax-on-demand Commonly abbreviated and called FOD. *See* FOD.

fc *(ATT)* Fix command. Korn shell command that provides users access to their history file. Used to list the commands run, set the number of commands to be retained in the history file, and edit and re-execute commands. *See* history file and execute.

FCEDIT *(ATT)* Fix command **edit**. Environmental variable used with the Korn shell to set the editor to be used with the fc command. *See* fc.

fclose File **close**. C language library routine used to open files for reading and/or writing data. *See* library routines, fopen, fread, getc, fgetc, gets, fgets, scanf, fscanf, fwrite, putc, fputc, puts, fputs, printf and fprintf.

fcntl File **control**. System call used to manage opened files for access, update, etc., by users or programs. *See* open file and system call.

FCSI Fiber Channel Systems Initiative. Joint fiber communications project involving the Hewlett-Packard Co., IBM Corp. and Sun Microsystems Inc. Designed to transmit data at a rate of up to 1 gigabyte per second and operate over both fiber-optic and twisted pair cables.

FDDI Fiber Distribution Data Interface. Pronounced *FIDDY*. An optical fiber-based local area network, American National Standards Institute standard that was originally developed by Xerox Corp.

The maximum standard rate of FDDI data transmission is 100 megabits per second with an effective rate of 30 to 40 megabits per second up to approximately 100 kilometers. FDDI uses Token Ring technology for access control. *See* fiber-optic, LAN, Mbps ANSI and Token Ring.

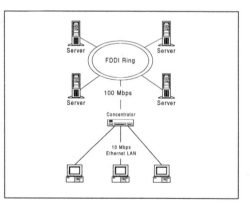

An FDDI network that provides highspeed connection between the servers.

FDDI-II Fiber Distribution Data Interface, second (**II**) version. Used to support multimedia technology. Allocates bandwidths to permit transmission of voice, video, high-resolution graphics and images and other communications, along with data. *See* FDDI, multimedia technology, HRC and Token Ring.

fdstat *(ATT)* File descriptor **stat**us. Command used to print status information about open file descriptors in the /dev/fd system directory. *See* file descriptor and /dev/fd.

FDX Abbreviation for full-duplex. *See* full-duplex.

FE Field engineer. Computer repair person who makes office calls.

feature **1.** Function the software program can perform, e.g. providing a menu from which the user can make a selection either by inputting a number or letter or placing the cursor on the choice. **2.** Term used in system security for the visible aspects developed to perform a specific security function, e.g. a password. *See* I & A, auditing, DAC, ACL, Trusted Path, Administrative Least Privilege and MAC. **3.** Dressed-up bug. *See* bug.

Federal Computer Fraud and Abuse Act of 1986 Commonly called the hacker law. *See* hacker law.

Federal Information Processing Standard Commonly abbreviated and called FIPS. *See* FIPS.

Federal Networking Council Commonly abbreviated and called FNC. *See* FNC.

Federal Open Systems User Council Organization of government agencies including the National Institute of Standards and Technology and National Aeronautics and Space Administration. Formed to promote and establish common requirements for open systems standards among federal agencies. *See* GOSIP.

Federal Research Internet Coordinating Committee *(INET)* Commonly abbreviated FRICC. Replaced by the Federal Networking Council. *See* FNC.

Federation of American Research Networks Commonly abbreviated and called FARNET. *See* FARNET.

FEDUP Federation to Evict Dumb and Useless Phraseology. Name credited to Paul Korzeniowski, editor-at-large for Communications Week, for an imaginary association. Meant to express exasperation over the tendency by the computer and communications industry to coin different terms that mean the same thing.

feep Jargon term for beep. *See* beep.

femto Prefix for 10^{-15} (1/1,000,000,000,000,000) or one-quadrillionth. Abbreviated f.

femtosecond Abbreviated fs. *See* fs.

FEP Front end processor. Intelligent peripheral device capable of performing preprocessing. Frees a computer for more important activities.

ferror Standard input/output library routine used to return the last error from a file opened with the fopen system call. *See* library routines, fopen and fclose.

fetch policy Process followed in handling faults for systems which use paging. *See* paging.

ff *(ATT)* Command used to display file names and statistics for a file system. *See* file system.

fg Foreground. Command used to move a process running in the background to the foreground. Starts a process that has been suspended. When started with fg, the process will run in the foreground. *See* background process, foreground process, bg, resume, stop and job control.

fgetc Standard input/output library routine used to read information from files opened with fopen, a C language library routine. *See* library routines, fopen, fread, getc, fclose, gets, fgets, scanf, fscanf, fwrite, putc, fputc, puts, fputs, printf and fprintf.

fgets Standard input/output library routine used to read information from files opened with fopen, a C language library routine. *See* library routines, fopen, fread, getc, fgetc, gets, fclose, scanf, fscanf, fwrite, putc, fputc, puts, fputs, printf and fprintf.

fgrep *(ATT)* Fast **grep**. Command that is similar to both grep and egrep in that it is used to search files. Differs from grep and egrep because it searches for specified character strings instead of patterns. *See* grep and egrep.

fi If, spelled backward. Shell command used to indicate the end of an if command structure. *See* if, then, elif and else.

fiber Jargon term for fiber-optic.

Fiber Channel Commonly used but incorrect spelling of the Fibre Channel protocol. *See* Fibre Channel.

Fiber Channel Systems Initiative Commonly abbreviated and called FCSI. *See* FCSI.

Fiber Distribution Data Interface Commonly abbreviated and called FDDI. *See* FDDI.

fiber-optic Describes the use of thin filaments of glass to transmit laser light to carry communications.

Fiber-Optic Inter Repeater Link Commonly abbreviated and called FOIRL. *See* FOIRL.

Fibre Channel High-speed channel or direct point-to-point communications protocol. Originally developed to provide high-speed direct connection between a computer and peripheral devices.

FIDDY Pronunciation of FDDI, the abbreviation for Fiber Distribution Data Interface. *See* FDDI.

field Predefined location that contains one piece of information, e.g. a name, address, price, unit of issue or stock number, in a database, terminal output, form, application software, etc.

field delimiter Commonly called field separator. *See* field separator.

field engineer Commonly abbreviated and called FE. *See* FE.

field separator Special character in a database which identifies the end of one field and the beginning of another. *See* delimiter and field.

field specifier Argument, preceded by a plus sign (+), used with the sort commands to indicate on which field a sort operation should be started. Conversely, the number of fields that should be excluded from the sort. *See* sort.

field upgradeable Describes a computer or peripheral device that can be upgraded without being sent back to the factory.

fifo First-in-first-out. Also called named pipe or unnamed pipe. Special temporary file used in internal communications that are created by processes to communicate with other processes. Output data from one communication file is sent to a fifo to be read by another file. Data is read on a "first-in-first-out" basis. *See* special file, named pipe, unnamed pipe and pipe.

FIFO First-in-first-out. AT&T Co. interprocess communications method in System V. Data to be sent from one process to another first goes to a fifo file where it is stored temporarily until the receiving process is ready for it. FIFO schedules all processes with the same priority on a first-come-first-served basis. *See* FILO, IPC and fifo.

FIFO special files *(POS)* Portable Operating System Interface for Computer Environments (POSIX) file used for access, writing and reading by multiple processes. A FIFO special files can be opened by more than on process at the same so information can be passed from one process to another. *See* POSIX, IPC and file.

file 1. *(ATT/XEN)* Command used to determine a file type, e.g. if the file is text and what type of text, source code and what type of source code. 2. Text, document, program or other information stored within a computer that can be written to and/or read from, and identified by a specific file name. 3. Datum treated as a separate identifiable unit. 4. In UNIX there are three types of files. *See* directory, ordinary file and special file. 5. In Portable Operating System Interface for Computer Environments (POSIX) there are five types of files. *See* POSIX, ordinary file, character special files, block special files, FIFO special file and directory.

file access mode Commonly called access mode. *See* access mode.

file access permissions Commonly called permissions. *See* permissions.

file aging Using the date when a file was created, modified or most likely last accessed to determine if the file can be deleted.

file attributes General collection of information about a file or its status, including the type of file, its inode, its size, what device the file is on, the number of links, the owner's user identifier, the group's group identifier, last time the file was read, last time the file was modified, and last status change. *See* UID.

filec C shell toggle variable. When set, enables file name completion. *See* C shell, toggle variables and file name completion.

file caching Method used with distributed file systems to increase performance and reduce network traffic by temporarily storing the contents of a file in main memory. *See* distributed file system.

file commands Group of UNIX commands which act on or modify files. The list of file commands is extremely long, but the most common include cat, dd, egrep, file, grep, ln, mv, pg, rm, touch and unpack.

file comparison commands Group of commands used to compare the contents of files. *See* bdiff, cmp, comm, dd, diff, diff3, diffmk, dircmp, sccsdiff, sdiff and uniq.

file consistency check **1.** Process of testing a file system for correctness or errors caused by a hardware error. Typical file consistency check utilities, e.g. the fsck command, test for unreferenced inodes, missing blocks, blocks marked as free and in a file, and wrong block counts. *See* fsck. **2.** Process of testing any file for consistency or correctness. *See* inode and file system.

file creation mask Set of numbers used to determine the permissions for a file when it is created. *See* umask.

file description Record maintained on how a file has been accessed by a process or group of processes. A file description differs from a file descriptor. A file descriptor refers to only one file description; several file descriptors can refer to the same file description. *See* file descriptor.

file descriptor **1.** Information required to manage the processing of a file each time it is accessed. When a file is opened, a file descriptor is established containing the file's disk address, size, creation date and time, last access date and time, date and time of last modification, link information and permissions. *See* file description. **2.** Numeric that identifies the action to be taken on the input or output of a process. As standard input (0 or stdin), the input is sent from the location or device at which the system accepts user commands, normally a terminal; as standard output (1 or stdout), the output is sent to the location to which the system sends the results of a command, e.g. the terminal on which the command was entered by a user; or as standard error (2 or stderr), the output is sent to the default location to which UNIX commands send error messages. *See* standard input, standard output and standard error.

file gap Space at the end of a file indicating the end of a file. *See* file marker.

file group class When the process accessing a file has a group identifier that is the same as the file's group identifier but not the same as the user identifier of the file. *See* GID and UID.

file handle Network File System term for a key sent by the server to a client that is used to confirm and speed future requests between the two. *See* NFS, key, client and server.

file locking Ability of an operating system to prevent access to a file by other processes while a process is updating the file.

file management system Programs of an operating system that manage the organization of the file structure, e.g. file creation, deletion, naming, access and modification.

file marker Any special data or hardware-generated signal used to delimit the beginning and end of a file on a stream-oriented device, e.g. a tape drive.

file migration Moving files from their original location, e.g. a desktop client to a file server on a network. *See* demigration.

file name Specific identifier for a file or collection of data. No two files can have the exact same name within a common directory. But, in a user account, multiple files can have the same name as long as they are in separate subdirectories belonging to the user account.

filename Commonly spelled file name. *See* file name.

file name completion Feature of the Tenex C shell and Korn shell to expand a partially typed file (path) name given the first few characters. *See* filec, TC-shell and Korn shell.

file name expansion **1.** Process followed by the shell interpreter to convert the contents of a command line, including metacharacters, into actual file names. *See* command line and metacharacter. **2.** Another name for the asterisk metacharacter. *See* asterisk.

file name extension Set of characters added to the end of a file name and separated from it by a period. Indicates the type of data contained in the file, e.g. in Microsoft Corp.'s Word for Windows and other word processing programs, *.doc* indicates a file is a document file.

file name generation Commonly called file name expansion. *See* file name expansion.

file parameter Part of the kernel description file. Establishes the maximum number of files that can remain open simultaneously. *See* kernel description file.

file path Set of directories and files that are searched to locate a file, executable command, etc.

file preallocation File and disk management process used with large or continually accessed files. Sets aside adjacent disk areas, allowing for growth of the files, to increase disk access speed.

file protocol *(BSD)* Commonly abbreviated and called f protocol. *See* f protocol.

filesave *(ATT)* Shell script used to back up a file system from one disk to another. *See* shell script and file system.

file server **1.** Smart disk drive. In a network, a file server is a personal computer or minicomputer, the primary function of which is to provide mass data storage and executable files. **2.** Program running on a local computer which provides remote computers access to files on the local computer.

file sharing Ability to share files among systems and users. *See* NFS and RFS.

file size **1.** Maximum size, in bytes, allowed for a file on a system. Limits are determined and set by the system administrator. *See* byte. **2.** Number of characters in a file.

file structure Design of the data storage methodology specifically used or recognized by the kernel of an operating system. *See* kernel.

file system Any portion of a disk that has been formatted to store UNIX information and can name files, recognize file names and control access to files.

filesystem Commonly spelled file system. *See* file system.

file system check Commonly called file consistency check. *See* file consistency check.

File System Safe Universal Character Set Transformation Format Commonly abbreviated and called UTF. *See* UTF.

file system types File system implemented to support specific file types. Normally used when implementing networks where files are to be shared between hosts on the network. *See* file system, s5, bfs and ufs.

file transfer Network function which allows users to move files from one host to another. *See* FTP and FTAM.

File Transfer, Access and Management Commonly abbreviated and called FTAM. *See* FTAM.

File Transfer, Access and Manipulation Commonly abbreviated and called FTAM. *See* FTAM.

File Transfer, Access and Method Commonly abbreviated and called FTAM. *See* FTAM.

File Transfer Protocol *(INET)* Commonly abbreviated and called FTP. *See* FTP.

file type UNIX and the Portable Operating System Interface for Computer Environments (POSIX) contain a total of eight different types of files. In UNIX there are three basic types of files: directories, ordinary files and special files. There are five types of files identified in POSIX: directories, regular files, character special files, block special files and FIFO special files. (Regular file and ordinary file are synonymous and are the same type of file.) The eighth file type is UNIX-domain sockets, found in the Berkeley Software Distribution. *See* directory, ordinary file, special file, character special files, block special files, FIFO special files, UNIX-domain sockets and BSD.

fill In word processing, to adjust text spacing on lines so all lines are of equal length.

filling Commonly called fill. *See* fill.

fill-on-demand page fault Commonly abbreviated and called page fault. *See* page fault.

fill-on-demand page table entry Commonly abbreviated and called PTE. *See* PTE.

FILO First-in-last-out. Storage and retrieval methodology in which the first data stored is the last that can be accessed. *See* FIFO.

filter Program used in between two programs. Receives and modifies input information provided by one program and sends the results to another program. *See* standard input and standard output.

filters *(ATT)* UNIX System V, Release 4 line printer services menu command similar to the lpfilter command. Used to add, delete, modify and list filter programs that perform special functions, e.g. underlining, in preprocessing files before they are printed. *See* SVR4.x and lpfilter.

final copy Complete printed output of any type of file.

finc *(ATT)* Fast incremental backup. Command used to selectively copy an entire file system to tape. *See* file system and frec.

find Command used to locate files. Searches the file path provided, one file at a time, until the given string is located or all the files are checked without locating the desired string. Along with the specific file name, find will search for creation, modification or access dates. Included in the UNIX System V, Release 4 Framed Access Command Environment file system operations command menu. *See* string, creation date, modification date, access date, SVR4.x, FACE and file system.

finger Shell script that displays user information and can be used by anyone. This information is more extensive than the data provided by the who command, e.g. full name, phone numbers, address or text describing the user. *See* who.

FINGER *(INET)* **Finger** Protocol. Defense Advanced Research Projects Agency Internet protocol. Sends information about users who are currently active to any user who requests it. *See* DARPA, Internet and finger.

fingerd Finger daemon. Responsible for starting and managing the programs needed to obtain information with the finger command about users on local or remote hosts. *See* finger and daemon.

finger entry Information in the /etc/passwd file that identifies the user, location and telephone number which is called by the finger command. *See* finger.

Finger Protocol *(INET)* Commonly called FINGER. *See* FINGER.

FIO File Input/Output. Set of routines designed to manage file tables. *See* access, closef, falloc, owner, suser and inode table.

FIPS Federal Information Processing Standard. Developed and published by the National Institute of Standards and Technology. Defines federal government standards used in the acquisition of computer hardware and software. *See* NIST.

FIPS 146 v.1 Federal Information Processing Standard **146 version1**. Also called FIPS v. 1. Commonly called GOSIP 1. *See* GOSIP 1.

FIPS 151 Federal Information Processing Standard **151**. Formally called NIST FIPS 151. *See* NIST FIPS 151.

fire up Jargon term for starting a computer, operating system, application, etc. *See* boot.

firewall Combination of hardware and software applications used to create a gateway and provide controlled access from an external network to an internal corporate or organizational network. By reviewing all traffic and selectively allowing data to pass, the firewall protects the internal network from possible hostile action.

firmware Programs loaded into read only memory to prevent them from being erased when power is turned off, e.g. system programs, processes and documentation used to start a computer system or maintain system functions. Can only be modified under program control. Normally loaded by the manufacturer of the chip to be installed during the manufacturing process. Also can be downloaded from a remote location, e.g. through a modem connection made by the computer system's supplier, who, using the right codes and/or keys, overwrites or updates the current firmware with new firmware; or changed with updates to the operating system or features of the operating system. *See* ROM.

firmware state Also called state 5. System state used to execute firmware programs and commands, e.g. system hardware diagnostics. *See* firmware.

first-in-first-out Commonly abbreviated and called FIFO. *See* FIFO.

first-in-last-out Commonly abbreviated and called FILO. *See* FILO.

first level bootstrap Process of loading the first portions of the programs that call and start the boot program from disk. *See* boot.

fish *(ATT)* Command used to start the card game Fish.

FISK Pronunciation of fsck, the abbreviation for file system check. *See* fsck.

FIVE BY EIGHT Pronunciation of 5 x 8. *See* 5 x 8.

FIVE DOT FOUR Pronunciation of 5.4, the Jargon term for UNIX System V, Release 4. *See* SVR4.

five nines Jargon term for the elusive measurement of computer or network system reliability. Indicates a system is reliable 99.999% of the year; the remainder of that time, i.e. (365 days x 24 hours x 60 minutes) x .00001 = 5.26 minutes, is equivalent to the amount of downtime.

fixdirs *(OTH)* **Fix di**rectories. Shell script used to delete write permission for users from system directories. Creates a log of the users for whom permission has been deleted. *See* shell script and write permission.

fixed disk drive Commonly called disk drive. *See* disk drive.

fixed length record Any record that contains a set, constant number of characters. *See* variable-length record.

fixed space printing System of printing in which all letters, numbers and characters are of equal width and the horizontal spacing is the same. *See* proportional printing.

fixterm *(XEN)* Command used to set permissions on a file.

flag Command line argument. *See* option.

flame Jargon. Abbreviation for inflammatory statement(s). A good flame is an equal mixture of both heat, e.g. an inflammatory comment, and light, e.g. facts, logic and/or reasoning. In electronic communication, e.g. mail or news articles, it is customary to precede a flame with the term "flame on" and to end it with "flame off," which indicates the remainder of the statement is not part of the flame.

flame off Jargon term to indicate the end of a flame, or inflammatory statement, in an electronic message. *See* flame and flame on.

flame on Jargon term to indicate the start of a flame, or inflammatory statement, in an electronic message. *See* flame and flame off.

flash Toggled option in the vi editing program which provides a visible (flashing) message on the screen instead of an auditory (bell) message when a user inputs an error. *See* vi and toggle.

flash card Commonly called flash memory. *See* flash memory.

flash memory Form of replaceable or removable memory developed for personal computers, used for nonvolatile memory in laptop or smaller computers. Introduced by Intel Corp. in late 1990. A flash memory card is normally about the size of a credit card (85.6 mm by 54 mm by 3.3 mm); has capacity of between 1 and 8 megabytes and a mean time between failure of 100,000 hours or more; and can run programs and use standard input/output.

flat file Also called flat file database. Collection of data records stored in a simple sequence. Does not use a specified structure or hierarchy to manage the relationship between the records. Frequently used to report or export data from a database to another program that is incapable of interpreting or querying the database directly. *See* database.

flat file database Commonly called flat file. *See* flat file.

flexible disk Commonly called diskette. *See* diskette.

flexible license Commonly called dynamic license. *See* dynamic license.

flicker Disruptive flashing light coming from a monitor, resulting in eye fatigue. Caused by a refresh rate that is too slow for the brightness of the screen. *See* refresh rate.

floating display Text formatting term used to describe portions of text that a user wants displayed exactly as they were entered. The relevant text is moved in total to the next page if there is insufficient room on the current page. *See* display and static display.

floating license Commonly called dynamic license. *See* dynamic license.

floating point Data type used to express real numbers as a mantissa and exponent. The range of the mantissa and exponent are hardware-dependent. *See* mantissa.

floating point accelerator Commonly abbreviated and called FPA. *See* FPA.

floppy Jargon term for floppy. *See* diskette.

floppy diskette Commonly called diskette. *See* diskette.

floppy drive Also called disk drive. Normally a mass storage medium for personal computers using diskettes. Also used on some older or smaller UNIX computers, which use diskettes as a storage medium. Used to read data from or write data to a diskette. *See* diskette.

flow control Commonly called handshake. *See* handshake.

flowgraph Graphical output used in C language programming to list or show the relations of functions within the program which are called by other functions. *See* C language and cflow.

flush 1. Word processing term meaning all lines of type are aligned with either one or both margins. *See* justify. 2. To clean out, e.g. "to flush the buffer" or to remove all data from the buffer. *See* buffer.

fmli *(ATT)* Command used to start the Forms and Menu Language Interpreter. *See* FMLI.

FMLI *(ATT)* Forms and Menu Language Interpreter. Feature in UNIX System V, Release 4 to aid programmers in writing applications with pop-up menus and windows, similar to the Framed Access Command Environment. Includes backup utilities, system diagnostics, network services, printer management and software management. *See* SVR4.x, pop-up menu, window and FACE.

fmt Format. Simple text formatting program which indents and justifies paragraphs in text files by filling in lines, joining lines, creating breaks, etc.

fmtflop *(ATT)* Format floppy disk. Command used to format a floppy diskette.

fmthard *(ATT)* Format hard drive. Command used to format a hard disk drive.

fmtmsg *(ATT)* Format message. Command used to format a message before it is sent to the standard error, or system console. *See* stderr.

FNC *(INET)* Federal Networking Council. Replaced the Federal Research Internet Coordinating Committee. A committee of federal agencies responsible for planning the needs of the Internet. *See* Internet.

FOD Fax-on-demand. Method used by companies to provide information to customers through facsimile transmission. A caller can request information by entering a series of numbers on a touch-tone phone in response to recorded voice directions. Callers can indicate what information they require and give the phone number of their fax machine. Shortly after, the information is faxed directly to the caller's fax machine. *See* fax.

FOIRL Fiber-Optic Inter Repeater Link. Institute of Electrical and Electronic Engineers 802.3 Ethernet committee's standard that was the forerunner to the 10Base-F standard for Ethernet over fiber-optic. *See* IEEE and 10Base-F.

fold Command used to display long lines on fixed width output devices, e.g. printers.

folder 1. Electronic-mail variable. *See* .mailrc variables (Appendix F). 2. Electronic-mail term for a file or directory that a user places in an incoming or outgoing electronic-mail message for storage. 3. Alternative name for a directory when using a file manager application in a graphical user interface environment. *See* GUI.

font 1. Character set which has the same style, size, etc., of typeface. Font settings enable the user to select either draft or letter-quality type on a dot matrix printer. In addition, the user can select a style, e.g. Roman or italic, and can indicate the number of characters per inch. *See* Roman and italic. 2. Graphic representation of alphanumeric characters.

font server Computer within a network which contains the font files. *See* font.

foo Derived from foobar. *See* foobar.

foobar 1. Variable name used in any type of syntax to mean whatever is being referred to at the time, or even nothing significant, e.g. foobar can be used to describe how the command "cat" is used to combine two files into a new file:

```
CLP> cat foo bar foobar ⏎
```

Often simply called foo. 2. Pronunciation and spelling of FUBAR, the acronym for f*@!#d up beyond all repair. *See* FUBAR.

footer Word processing term for text printed in the bottom margin of a page, e.g. a page number. *See* header.

footprint Physical space required for a piece of hardware.

fopen File open. C language library routine used to open files for reading and writing. *See* library routines, fclose, fread, getc, fgetc, gets, fgets, scanf, fscanf, fwrite, putc, fputc, puts, fputs, printf and fprintf.

for Shell command used to run loops or repetitive processes. The for statement executes one or more commands, substituting the control variable with one or more values in a list, e.g. the ls command may be simulated by:

```
for v in *
do
        echo $v
done
```

See do and done.

forced unmount Process in which a system administrator turns off access to local resources without methodically shutting down the system. A forced unmount kills, or terminates, any active process.

foreground process Interactive processing started by a user from an input terminal. A process that is directly tied to and controlled by an input terminal, and must be completed before a user may have control of the terminal. Has a higher priority than a background process, but only one foreground process may be run at a time. *See* background process.

foreign tape A tape whose recording was not created on the computer onto which it is being loaded.

fork Part of the systems process control capability. A system call that makes a copy of an ongoing process to create an identical new process. *See* system call, process control, parent process and child process.

formal standard Commonly called de jure standard. *See* de jure.

format 1. Command used to format floppy diskettes used on a UNIX system. *See* diskette. 2. Specified layout, number and pattern of tracks and sectors on a disk. *See* track and sector. 3. Specific structure of data used to store information on a mass storage device. 4. Appearance of a document. Includes length, width, type of character set or font, tabs and spacing used. *See* formatting.

formatting Process that sets up a diskette or hard disk so the computer can write data to or read data from the diskette or drive. Specific address information and timing marks are added to the device to identify the sectors. Diskettes or disk drives can be used by many different brands of computers. Each computer company uses a different layout for the way its computers write and read data. The diskettes and disk drives have to be formatted to the methodology chosen by the manufacturer before information can be used. *See* sector.

formatting command Form of embedded command which specifies how a document is to be laid out, e.g. in the nroff text formatting program, .ls2 means double spacing and .ll65 specifies 65 characters per line. *See* embedded command and nroff.

formatting program Text manipulation program that takes raw input along with command instructions embedded in the text to create a finished product. *See* nroff, troff and formatting command.

form feed Process or button that advances the paper on a printer to the top of the next sheet.

forms *(ATT)* UNIX System V, Release 4 line printer services menu command similar to the lpforms command. Used to create custom forms for specified print jobs. *See* SVR4.x and lpforms.

Forms and Menu Language Interpreter Commonly abbreviated and called FMLI. *See* FMLI.

FORTRAN Formula Translator. High-level programming language developed in 1957 for use in mathematics, science and engineering.

FORTRAN-77 Standard FORTRAN language used from 1978 to 1990 when the FORTRAN-90 standard was introduced by the American National Standards Institute X3J3 committee. Derived its name from 1977, the year its standards were defined. *See* FORTRAN-90 and ANSI X3J3.

FORTRAN-90 The 1990 definition of the FORTRAN language that replaced FOR-TRAN-77. In general, FORTRAN-90 is backward compatible with FORTRAN-77, unless the program uses names newly reserved by the FORTRAN-90 standard. *See* FORTRAN-77 and ANSI X3J3.

fortune Command used to obtain a randomly displayed aphorism or pithy saying. Some systems provide an -o. option with fortune for obscene sayings.

Forum Computer virus that is more irritating than damaging. Causes the keyboard to click and the system to slow down on the 18th of each month. *See* virus.

Forum, The International organization formed by UniForum and EurOpen to advance open systems worldwide. *See* UniForum and EurOpen.

forwarder Commonly called application gateway. *See* application gateway.

FPA 1. Floating point accelerator. Computer processor hardware that performs arithmetic operations on floating point data, typically much faster than the floating point emulation performed by a processor. 2. Any computer hardware that directly manipulates floating point data.

FPLA Field-programmable logic array. Commonly abbreviated and called PLA. *See* PLA.

fpr *(BSD)* FORTRAN Print. Command used to format or print a FORTRAN output file. *See* FORTRAN.

fprintf C language standard input/output library routine used to format and write information to a file opened with fopen, a C language library routine. *See* library routines, fopen, fread, getc, fgetc, gets, fgets, scanf, fscanf, fwrite, putc, fputc, puts, fputs, printf and fclose.

f protocol *(BSD)* File protocol. Data protocol supported by UNIX-to-UNIX CoPy available in Berkeley Software Distribu-

tion to pass data between networks. Used to transfer a full file, using 7-bit characters. Assumes data is being transferred error-free and performs neither error checking nor flow control functions. Used mainly for communication over X.25 networks. With error detection and correction modems, can be used for serial communication. *See* UUCP, X.25, e protocol, g protocol, G protocol, t protocol and x protocol.

FPU Floating point unit. Commonly called FPA (floating point accelerator). *See* FPA.

fputc C language standard input/output library routine used to write a single character, or byte, of information to a file opened with fopen, a C language library routine. *See* library routines, fopen, fread, getc, fgetc, gets, fgets, scanf, fscanf, fwrite, putc, fclose, puts, fputs, printf and fprintf.

fputs C language standard input/output library routine used to write a string to a file opened with fopen, a C language library routine. *See* library routines, fopen, fread, getc, fgetc, gets, fgets, scanf, fscanf, fwrite, putc, fputc, puts, fclose, printf and fprintf.

fractional T-1 T-1 communication channel that is divided into multiple 56-kilobits-per-second (Kbps) channels. A T-1 channel can be divided into as many as 24 fractional T-1 channels, each 56 Kbps. *See* T-1.

fractional T-3 Multiplexed fiber-optic network used for packet and frame-relay switching. Developed to provide levels of service between a T-1 and T-3 communication link. Provides transmission speeds of 4.6, 6.2, 7.7 and 10.8 megabits per second. *See* T-1, T-2, T-4 and frame-relay.

fragment Part (generally one-fourth) of a file system data block. Fragments are allocated to conserve disk space when a file or part of a file is smaller than a block. *See* block.

fragmentation 1. Process of dividing files into separate pieces to use available disk space. Fragmented files create more work for the computer because they increase the time needed by disk drives to perform read and write operations. *See* defragmentation and contiguous file. **2.** Term related to distributed databases. Process of breaking a database into segments and spreading the data across several host computers. This enables information in the database to be accessed faster and more effectively. **3.** *(INET)* Process in which an Internet gateway breaks a packet into smaller segments because a network cannot handle the size of the original packet. Each smaller packet is called a fragment. Fragments are reassembled at the receiving host and delivered to the user or data file. *See* Internet, gateway, reassembly and MTU.

fragment descriptor table List of free fragments, their sizes and addresses. *See* fragment.

frame 1. Rectangular element created on a screen which is used as an independent subregion to display information or make inputs to the computer, operating system and/or application software. Applicable to any windowing application software, e.g. Microsoft Windows in DOS, X Window System or the UNIX System V, Release 4 Framed Access Command Environment. *See* X Window System and FACE. **2.** Stream of bits that describes a complete packet. *See* packet.

Framed Access Control Environment
Commonly abbreviated and called FACE. *See* FACE.

frame-relay Standard for a statistically multiplexed wide area packet switch network technology based upon the X.25 protocol. Such networks provide the ability to interconnect data communications equipment from different vendors to pass data. These networks can transmit data at speeds of 2.048 megabits per second or more. Unlike other newer packet switch technology, e.g. Integrated Service Digital Network or Asynchronous Transfer Mode, frame-relay is not capable of voice transmission. *See* X.25, ISDN, ATM and WAN.

Frame Relay Implementors Forum
International organization of vendors formed in 1990 to work on national and international frame-relay standards for hardware. Among its members are AT&T Co., US Sprint and Northern Telecom. *See* frame-relay.

Frankfurt Group Also called the CD Write-Once Ad Hoc Advisory Committee. Among its members are Digital Equipment Corp., Sony Corp. and N.V. Phillips. Aims to develop specifications for write-once compact disk-read only memory (CD-ROM) and a common file format to be used with write-once CD-ROMs. *See* WORM and CD-ROM.

fread *(ATT)* File read. C language standard input/output library routine used to read information from a file opened by fopen, a C language library routine. *See* library routines, fopen, fclose, getc, fgetc, gets, fgets, scanf, fscanf, fwrite, putc, fputc, puts, fputs, printf and fprintf.

frec *(ATT)* finc recover. Command used to recover a file system saved to tape using either the finc or volcopy commands. *See* file system, finc and volcopy.

free C language library routine used to release memory previously allocated by malloc, a C language library function. *See* library routines.

free blocks Unused data blocks available for use by a file. *See* data block.

free list List of non-allocated elements of a data structure, e.g. of memory, inodes, file tables or disk quota.

Free Software Foundation Commonly abbreviated and called FSF. *See* FSF.

free space Space available for writing data on a device, e.g. a disk or tape.

free space reserve Padding in the space available for the file system. Normally, when disk space is allocated for a file system, 10 percent is held in reserve to ensure the operating system can continue to work if the disks become full. *See* file system and free space.

freeware Software written by people for their own use and then is given to others.

frequency Also called pulse. Measurement of the rate of speed at which electrical current alternates polarity. Normally measured in cycles per second (hertz), 1,000 cycles per second (kilohertz) or 1,000,000 cycles per second (megahertz). *See* AC, HZ, K and MHz.

Fresco Enhanced object-oriented graphics tool-kit for windows, added to the Massachusetts Institute of Technology X Window System, Release 6. *See* X Window System.

FRICC *(INET)* **F**ederal **R**esearch **I**nternet **C**oordinating **C**ommittee. Forerunner to the Federal Networking Council. *See* FNC.

friction feed System for feeding single sheets of paper into a printer. Uses rollers to apply pressure to the paper. *See* tractor feed.

fried Jargon term for a computer outage that is due to a power problem resulting in burned electrical circuits.

fritterware Software developed for no known use.

frm *(BSD)* **Fr**o**m**. Command used to display the names of the senders and subject of electronic-mail messages contained in a file. *See* e-mail.

from **1.** *(BSD)* Command used to display the name of the senders and subject of unread electronic-mail messages. *See* e-mail. **2.** Part of the message header of an electronic-mail message which identifies the user who sent the electronic-mail message. *See* e-mail.

front end **1.** Jargon term for a front-end processor. *See* FEP. **2.** Jargon term for an application running on a client computer that starts data queries to the server, then presents, preprocesses and manipulates

data. *See* back end and client/server. **3.** Jargon term for front money, or prepayment, for part of the cost of a new computer system.

front-end processor Commonly abbreviated and called FEP. *See* FEP.

frozen screen When a user types characters and nothing changes on the screen. However, even though nothing may appear on the screen, the computer may be reading the inputs. An irritated user who is logged in as root should avoid pounding on the keyboard since this can cause the system to crash. *See* crash, soft reset and hard reset.

frustum of vision Three-dimensional graphic display in which all objects are visible. *See* 3-D graphics.

fry **1.** Jargon term for applying excessive electrical current to a computer. *See* UPS and disaster recovery. **2.** Jargon term for the failure of computer hardware which has been left running after the air conditioning has broken down on a very hot day. *See* disaster recovery.

fs **F**emto**s**econd. One-quadrillionth of a second (1/1,000,000,000,000,000).

fscanf Standard input/output library routine used to read or scan information from a file that has been opened with fopen, a C language library routine. *See* library routines, fopen, fread, getc, fgetc, gets, fgets, scanf, fclose, fwrite, putc, fputc, puts, fputs, printf and fprintf.

fsck **F**ile **s**ystem **c**hec**k**. Pronounced *FISK*. Command used by the system administrator to check for and repair problems with data stored on disks. Examines the consistency of data on the disks. Has replaced several older commands, each of which performed different functions that had to be run separately.

fsdb *(ATT)* **F**ile **s**ystem **d**ebugger. Command used to edit file systems to correct errors or other modifications. *See* file system.

fseek C language standard input/output function to explicitly set the position of a file opened with fopen. The position of a file is the number of the next byte to be read, counting from the beginning of the file. Thus, seeking to position 0 will cause the first byte of the file to be read next. fseek permits positioning relative to the beginning of the file, the end of the file or the current position. *See* fopen, fread, getc, fgetc, gets, fgets, scanf, fscanf, fwrite, putc, fputc, puts, fclose, printf and fprintf.

FSF Free Software Foundation. Founded by Richard Stallman and located in Cambridge, Massachusetts. FSF's philosophy is that all software should be free for people to use; developers can then charge for any consulting work related to the use of the software. FSF requires software developers to send users source code for the software. Users are expected to return any modifications to the developer. *See* source code, GNU, GNU C, G++ and GNU emacs.

fsflush *(ATT)* File system flush. Manages the disk input and output by periodically running the sync system call to write buffers to disk. *See* I/O and sync.

fsplit *(ATT)* FORTRAN split. Command used to separate programs, subroutines and functions from f77 files, ratfor files, or elf multi-routine FORTRAN source program files. Breaks a FORTRAN source file into separate files for each subroutine or function. *See* f77, ratfor, elf and FORTRAN.

fsstat *(ATT)* File system statistics. Command used in conjunction with the fsck command to look for a flag in the superblock which indicates whether the file system needs to be checked. *See* superblock and file system.

FSS-UCS-TF File System Safe Universal Character Set Transformation Format. Commonly abbreviated and called UTF. *See* UTF.

fstat *(ATT)* File statistics. System call used to get status information on a file currently being accessed. *See* system call.

fstypes Commonly written as /etc/fstypes. *See* /etc/fstypes.

FSTypes File System Types. File system implemented to support specific file types, e.g. the bfs FSTypes is used to maintain the standalone programs needed to bring the operating system up. *See* file system types, /etc/dfs/fstypes, /etc/fstypes, file system, s5, bfs and ufs.

fsync *(BSD)* File system synchronize. System call used to clean up disk and file systems. Checks the contents of the buffer cache against the data on the disk. Only data that has been modified is updated from the buffer cache to the disk. *See* file system, system call, buffer cache and sync.

FTAM File Transfer, Access and Management. Also called File Transfer, Access and Manipulation or File Transfer, Access and Method. Open Systems Interconnection application layer protocol accepted as the standard in open systems architecture for file transfer between systems. Suggested as a replacement for the File Transfer Protocol for system-to-system movement of files. *See* FTAM Type 1, FTAM Type 2, FTAM Type 3, skinny FTAM, FTP, application layer and ISO/OSI.

FTAM Type 1 File Transfer, Access and Management Type 1. Optional specification for FTAM that uses unstructured or American Standard Code for Information Interchange text files. *See* FTAM and ASCII text.

FTAM Type 2 File Transfer, Access and Management Type 2. Optional specification for FTAM that uses formatted text files. *See* FTAM.

FTAM Type 3 File Transfer, Access and Management Type 3. Optional specification for FTAM that uses unstructured binary files. *See* FTAM and binary file.

ftp *(INET)* Command used to start a File Transfer Protocol session. Entering ftp without a host name on a command line opens a session on a local system without a direct connection to a remote host. Entering ftp followed by a remote host name opens a session with a direct connection to a specified remote host. *See* FTP.

FTP *(INET)* File Transfer Protocol. Defense Advanced Research Projects Agency protocol used to move or copy files, directories and directory trees between computers. Allows the user to perform additional file or directory manipulation on remote computer hosts, e.g. listing directories and files, and switching between directories. Requires a user to enter a password before the person is allowed access to a remote host.

FTP commands *(INET) See* Appendix C.

ftpd *(INET)* File Transfer Protocol daemon. File Transfer Protocol Internet server daemon which starts up and runs the File Transfer Protocol processes. *See* Internet, daemon and FTP.

ftw **1.** *(ATT)* File tree walk. Command used to search for a specific string within a directory. Similar to the find command. *See* find. **2.** *(ATT)* C programming language library routine used to search a file system tree when checking files. *See* library routines and file system.

FUBAR F*@!#d up beyond all repair. Commonly pronounced and spelled *foobar*. Also referred to as fouled up beyond all repair. Jargon term for a computer, computer operation, software application or any situation with serious problems that has no chance of being fixed. An expletive is sometimes substituted for fouled, as was the custom during World War II when the term originated in the U.S. Army.

full backup Copy of all data stored on the disks of a computer system. *See* backup, partial backup and incremental backup.

full disk backup Commonly called full backup. *See* full backup.

full dump Jargon term for full backup. *See* full backup.

full-duplex Commonly abbreviated FDX. Data communication in which simultaneous communication is taking place in both directions in a data channel. *See* duplex, half-duplex and simplex.

full-face editor Commonly called visual editor. *See* visual editor.

full-image backup Making of complete copy of all data stored on a file system . *See* full disk backup, image copy and file system.

full pathname File address or pathname stated so that the structure is fully represented, to its root, e.g. the full pathname to a file called myfile is /usr/SHE/chalecki/myfile. *See* path and pathname.

full-screen editor Commonly called visual editor. *See* visual editor.

fully qualified pathname Commonly called full pathname. *See* full pathname.

Fu Manchu Computer virus that searched computer files for the names of political leaders, e.g. Ronald Reagan and Margaret Thatcher, and inserted derogatory remarks about them. First located in Great Britain in 1989. *See* virus.

fumount *(ATT)* Forced **unmount**. Remote File Sharing command used to unmount, or turn off, a resource that was available for use by remote hosts. *See* RFS, unshare, umount and rfstop.

function Any specialized operation that is performed by a computer, e.g. a style command in the Writer's Workbench text processing tools, which performs the function of checking grammar in text. *See* routine, style and WWB.

functional standard Commonly called profile. *See* profile, definition 3.

function call Element of a program that invokes a predefined special operation. *See* function.

function keys Set of programmable keys on personal computers, workstations or smart terminals which perform user- or program-defined operations. Depending on the personal computer keyboard used, there are 10 to 12 function keys either located across the top of the keyboard or along one side.

function prototype ANSI C term. Defines arguments for a function. *See* ANSI C and function.

funware Jargon term for games resident in read-only memory. *See* firmware and ROM.

fusage *(ATT)* Remote File Sharing command used to display input/output usage for either local or remote file systems. *See* RFS, I/O and file system.

fuser *(ATT)* Find **user**. Command used to display processes using a file or file struc-ture. Similar to but slower than the ps command. Optionally kills any process using a file or file structure. *See* ps.

Futurebus+ Institute of Electrical and Electronic Engineers standard for a future generation of computer buses. *See* IEEE and bus.

FUUG Finland UNIX User Group. Finnish UNIX users group formed in 1984.

fwrite File **write**. C language command used to write information to files that have been opened with fopen, a C language library routine. *See* fopen, fread, getc, fgetc, gets, fgets, scanf, fscanf, fclose, putc, fputc, puts, fputs, printf and fprintf.

fwtmp *(ATT)* Accounting system program used to update the date in the wtmp log when the system date is changed with the date command. *See* /etc/wtmp and date.

G

G Abbreviation for **giga**. *See* giga.

G++ Version of the C++ programming language released by the Free Software Foundation. *See* FSF and C++ language.

G2 Group 2. Also spelled Group II. Standard for facsimile transmission systems that was replaced by the G3 standard. Developed by the International Telecommunication Union Telecommunication Standardization Sector, formerly called the Consultative Committee on International Telegraphy and Telephony. *See* ITU-T, fax, G3 and G4.

G3 Group 3. Also spelled Group III. Standard for facsimile transmission systems that is used for both analog and digital phone lines. Defines digital encoding, protocols, compression and digital encoding. Developed by the International Telecommunication Union Telecommunication Standardization Sector, formerly called the Consultative Committee on International Telegraphy and Telephony. *See* ITU-T, fax, G2 and G4.

G4 Group 4. Also spelled Group IV. Standard for facsimile transmission systems that is used only for digital phone lines and Integrated Services Digital Network. Features include a higher transmission rate, error correction and detection, color, and better resolution than the G3 standard. Developed by the International Telecommunication Union Telecommunication Standardization Sector, formerly called the Consultative Committee on International Telegraphy and Telephony. *See* fax, ITU-T, G2, G3 and ISDN.

gadgets Graphical objects, not directly related to a window, contained in X Window System toolkits and used to create graphical applications. *See* X Window System, GUI and widget.

Gang of 14 Jargon term for the 14 companies that formed the Micro Channel Development Association. *See* MCA and MCDA.

Gang of 21 Jargon term for the 21 companies that formed the Advanced Computing Environment. *See* ACE.

Gang of Nine Jargon term for the nine companies united in 1988 by Compaq Computer Corp. to support the Extended Industry Standard Architecture. The remaining companies were Ing. C. Olivetti, Hewlett-Packard Co., AST Research Inc., Seiko Epson Corp. Inc., Tandy Corp., NEC Corp., Wyse Technology and Zenith Data Systems Corp.. *See* EISA.

gap Unused space between files on a disk or tape.

garbage 1. Jargon term for undesired data in files or memory. 2. Jargon term for inaccurate input to or output from a computer. *See* GIGO.

garbage collection System's ability to collect or reclaim unused portions of memory for other use, without that memory specifically being released by applications.

garbage in-garbage out Commonly abbreviated and called GIGO. *See* GIGO.

gated *(BSD)* **Gate**way **d**aemon. Pronounced *GATE-DEE*. Internet background program which manages the interface and traffic between a host on a Transmission Control Protocol/Internet Protocol network and a gateway. *See* Internet, daemon, RIP, TCP/IP and gateway.

GATE-DEE Pronunciation of gated, the abbreviation for gateway daemon. *See* gated.

gateway Computer dedicated to managing the interface between two or more similar or dissimilar networks. Operates at the Application Layer (layer 7) in the Open Systems Interconnection. Passes only data or protocols if the recipient or protocol is recognized by the other side. *See* OSI, OSIRM, application layer, router, repeater, bridge and brouter.

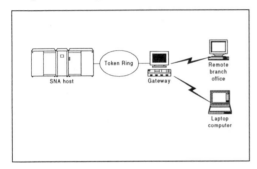

The dedicated computer provides a link or gateway between the mainframe and remote computers.

gather *(ATT)* Command used to collect the files needed to run a Remote Job Entry batch job. *See* RJE and batch.

gawk GNU **awk**. Replacement for awk written by the Free Software Foundation. *See* awk, nawk, GNU and FSF.

GB Abbreviation for **gigabyte**. *See* gigabyte.

Gbps Gigabits per second. Measurement of the rate of data transfer in units of 1,000,000,000 bits per second.

GBps Gigabytes per second. Measurement of the rate of data transfer in units of 1,000,000,000 bytes per second.

Gbyte Abbreviation for **gigabyte**. *See* gigabyte.

gcore Command used to create or save a core image of a process, or an image of the process in main memory. *See* core.

GCOS 1. General Comprehensive Operating System. Honeywell timesharing operating system. Originally developed by General Electric Corp. in the 1970s and called General Electric Comprehensive Operating System (GECOS). **2.** Field in the /etc/passwd file containing personal information about users. Name resulted from using GCOS-based computers at Bell Laboratories, where UNIX was developed. *See* Bell Laboratories.

GDA Global Directory Agents. A Distributed Naming Service facility in the Open Software Foundation Inc.'s Distributed Computing Environment. Used to look up locations in the Global Directory Service if the information is not locally available. *See* OSF, DCE, DNS, CDS, GDS, XDS and X.500.

gdev *(ATT)* Collection of graphic programs for devices including graphics terminals and plotters. *See* ged, graph, graphics, gutil, spline, stat, toc and tplot.

GDS Global Directory Service. Open Software Foundation Inc.'s implementation of the X.500 directory service for managing Distributed Computing Environment remote users and user addresses. *See* OSF, DCE, DNS, CDS, GDA, XDS and X.500.

GECOS General Electric Comprehensive Operating System. Original name of GCOS. *See* GCOS.

ged *(ATT)* Graphical editor. Program used to display and edit GPS files on Tektronix 4010 series display terminals. *See* graph, GPS, graphics, gutil, spline, stat, toc and tplot.

gencat *(ATT)* **Gen**erate **cat**alogue. Utility to create and maintain text databases for internationalizing software. *See* i18n.

gencc *(ATT)* **Gen**erate **C** **c**ompiler. Inter-active command used to make a front-end to a C compiler command by overriding default cc libraries, flags and options. *See* cc.

gender bender Attachment that can be added to cables to change the gender of a cable connection, e.g. a female/female gender bender is added to a male cable connection to turn it into a female cable connection.

gender changer Commonly called gen-der bender. *See* gender bender.

General Comprehensive Operating Sys-tem Commonly abbreviated and called GCOS. *See* GCOS.

General Framework for Access Control Commonly abbreviated and called GFAC. *See* GFAC.

Generic Window Manager Commonly abbreviated and called gwm. *See* gwn.

geocoding Process of matching data to map grids while conforming to the curva-ture of the earth. *See* GIS.

geographic information system Commonly abbreviated and called GIS. *See* GIS.

geometric correction Commonly called geocoding. *See* geocoding.

get **1.** *(ATT/XEN)* One of the 13 Source Code Control System commands used to retrieve a specific version of a SCCS file. *See* SCCS, admin, cdc, comb, delta, help, prs, rmdel, sact, sccsdiff, unget, val, vc and what. **2.** Simple Network Manage-ment Protocol system management mes-sage. Used by the network manager to obtain information about devices on the network. *See* SNMP, set and trap.

getc **Get** **c**haracter. System macro used to read information from files opened by fopen, a C language library routine. *See* macro, fopen, fread, getc, fgetc, fclose, fgets, scanf, fscanf, fwrite, putc, fputc, puts, fputs, printf and fprintf.

getcwd C language library routine used to obtain the pathname of the current working directory. *See* library routines.

getegid *(ATT)* **Get** **e**ffective **g**roup **i**denti-fier. System call used to retrieve the effec-tive group identifier of the individual who started a process. *See* system call, UID, getgid, real UID, EUID, geteuid, chmod and SUID.

getenv *(ATT)* **Get** **env**ironment. Library routine used in C language programming to obtain the environmental variables needed for an application. *See* library rou-tines and C language.

geteuid *(ATT)* **Get** **e**ffective **u**ser **i**denti-fier. System call used to display the effec-tive user identifier of the individual who started a process. *See* system call, UID, getgid, real UID, EUID, getegid and SUID.

getgid *(ATT)* **Get** **g**roup **id**entifier. Sys-tem call used to display the real group identifier of the individual who started a process. *See* system call, GID, getuid, real GID, EGID, geteuid and getegid.

getgrent *(ATT)* **Get** **g**roup **ent**ry. C lan-guage library routine used in searching for problems in the /etc/group file to ex-tract the next entry, following the pointer, from the group file. *See* library routines, getgrnam, getgrid, setgrent, endgrent and pointer.

getgrgid *(ATT)* **Get** **g**roup **g**roup **id**enti-fier. C language library routine used to search the system group file for a specific group identifier and to open a pointer if it is found. *See* library routines, GID, getgrnam, getgrent, setgrent, endgrent and pointer.

getgrnam *(ATT)* **Get** **g**roup **nam**e. C lan-guage library routine used to search the system group file for a specific group name and to open a pointer if it is found. *See* library routines, getgrgid, getgrent, setgrent, endgrent and pointer.

gethostbyaddr **Get** **h**ost **b**y **addr**ess. Sys-tem call used to query files to identify the name of a remote host by inputting the host's address. *See* system call.

gethostbyname Get host by name. System call used to query files to identify the address of a remote host by inputting the host's name. *See* system call.

gethostname *(BSD)* **Get host name.** System call used to identify the name of the computer host, which has been set by the sethostname system call. *See* system call and sethostname.

getitimer Get interval timer. C language library routine used to store the interval timer specified for a process. The computer system maintains three interval timers: real (wall-clock), virtual (time used by a process) and profiled (like virtual time, but includes the time taken by the kernel to perform functions for a process). *See* library routines and setitimer.

getlogin *(ATT)* **Get login.** C language library routine used to identify a user's login identifier, the name assigned to a user account, on a specific terminal. *See* library routines and login ID.

getopt *(ATT/XEN)* **Get option.** C language library routine used to break up and look at shell commands to determine if illegal options have been used. In UNIX System V, getopt is available but has been replaced with getopts. *See* getopts, getoptcvt, C language, library routines and parse.

getoptcvt *(ATT)* **Get option and convert.** Command used to convert shell commands read in older versions of UNIX by the getopt command into a format that can be read by the getopts command now used in UNIX System V. *See* getopt and getopts.

getopts *(ATT)* **Get options.** Command used to break up and look at shell commands to determine if illegal options have been used. Once the option arguments have been checked, the command is run. Replaced the getopt command, which should no longer be used. *See* getopt and getoptcvt.

getpass *(ATT)* **Get password.** C language library routine used to read a password and prompt. *See* library routines.

getpid *(ATT)* **Get process identifier number.** System call that displays the process identifier, a unique number assigned to each process started on a computer system, of a process. *See* system call and PID.

getpw *(ATT)* **Get password.** C language library routine used to open the system password file and search for the password entry for a specified user identifier number. *See* library routines, getpwent, UID and passwd.

getpwent *(ATT)* **Get password entry.** C language library routine used to open the system password file, set the pointer at the first entry in the file and keep the file open while program routines are run on the file. *See* library routines, setpwent, endpwent and pointer.

getpwnam *(ATT)* **Get password name.** C language library routine used to get an entry from the system password file for a specific login identifier, the name assigned to a user account. *See* library routines and login ID.

getpwuid *(ATT)* **Get password user identifier.** C language library routine used to get an entry from the system password file for a specific user identifier. *See* library routines and UID.

gets Standard input/output library routine used to read information from files opened by fopen, a C language library routine. *See* library routines, fopen, fread, getc, fgetc, fclose, fgets, scanf, fscanf, fwrite, putc, fputc, puts, fputs, printf and fprintf.

getservbyname *(ATT)* **Get service by name.** Command used to return information about a networking service kept in the /etc/services file.

getsockopt Get socket options. System call used to display the options set by the setsockopt system call for a specific socket, which is used to establish the two way communications channel between the processes needed to exchange data. *See* system call, sockets, setsockopt and IPC.

gettable *(ATT)* **Get table**. Command used to retrieve a host table formatted for use on the Internet network from a specified host. The table then can be converted by the htable command into a format that is understood by the local network library. *See* Internet and htable.

gettimeofday *(BSD)* **Get time of day**. C language library routine used to get the current system time, displayed in microseconds. *See* library routines.

gettxt *(ATT)* **Get text**. C language library routine used to retrieve text from messages in a local messages database. *See* library routines.

getty **Get a tty**. UNIX user login manager. Program that monitors terminal ports for users attempting to log in. Started by the init daemon when a user tries to log in. Begins the login process and establishes the port characteristics, e.g. speed and parity. *See* tty, init, baud rate and parity.

getuid *(ATT)* **Get user identifier**. System call that displays the real user identifier the login identifier or name assigned to the account of the user who started a process. *See* system call, UID, login ID, getgid, real UID, EUID, geteuid and getegid.

getw **Get word**. Standard input/output library routine used to read information from files opened with fopen, a C language library routine. *See* library routines, fopen, fread, getc, fclose, gets, fgets, scanf, fscanf, fwrite, putc, fputc, puts, fputs, printf and fprintf.

getwd *(BSD)* **Get working directory**. Command used to determine which directory the user is. *See* current working directory.

GFAC **General Framework for Access Control**. Document that outlines security standards for commercial computer installations. Similar to the Orange Book,

which outlines the security standards for computer systems established by the Department of Defense. *See* Orange Book.

GFLOPS **Giga floating point operations per second**. Measurement in 1 billion increments of the number of floating point operations per second. *See* giga and FPA.

Ghostscript Free Software Foundations GNU is Not UNIX version of Adobe System Inc.'s PostScript page description language. *See* FSF and GNU.

GID **Group identifier**. Part of the user and system security management system. Groups of common users are established to enable easy access and exchange of information among users within a group. Each group is identified by a 16-bit numeric indicating the permissions, or levels of access to the system, assigned to members of the group.

.gid.rules *(ATT)* **Group identifier rules**. File used in the Remote File Sharing system by the idload command to establish group access permissions in the mapping translation table. *See* RFS, idload, permissions, GID and mapping translation table. The full file path is /etc/rfs/auth.info/.gid.rules.

gif **Graphics interchange format**. Format developed by CompuServe for storing and transferring bitmaps of pictures. *See* bitmap.

gig Jargon term for **gig**abyte. *See* gigabyte.

giga Prefix for 10^9 (1,000,000,000) or one billion. Commonly abbreviated G.

Gigabit Highway Association Formed by the Technology Forums of Lino Lakes, Minnesota, to develop a standard for interface specification for high-speed local area and wide area network protocols such as Asynchronous Transfer Mode, frame-relay and High Performance Parallel Interface. *See* LAN, WAN, frame-relay, ATM and HiPPI.

gigabit test bed Joint efforts by the U.S. government, industry and universities, started in 1990, to test technologies and applications which are needed to implement networks and supercomputers capable of transmitting gigabits of data per second. *See* HPCC, NREN, AURORA, BLANCA, CASA, MAGIC, NECTAR and VISTANet.

gigabyte Measurement commonly used for 1 billion bytes but actually equal to 1,073,741,824 bytes (2^{30} bytes). Measurement of the number of bytes of information stored on disk, tape, memory or other medium, or the amount of data passed by a network or communication device, or between devices.

giga floating point operations per second Commonly abbreviated and called GFLOPS. *See* GFLOPS.

giga instructions per second. Commonly abbreviated and called gips. *See* gips.

gigaops 1 billion operations per second. Measurement of the performance of a central processing unit in billions of instructions per second. *See* CPU.

GIGO Garbage-in-garbage-out. Basic tenet of any computer system. The quality of the data that comes out of a computer system depends on what users put into that system. Similarly, the operation of a computer system depends on the computer environment provided and how it is maintained. If bad data is put in, bad data will come out.

gips Giga instructions per second. Measurement of the integer performance, or computing power, of a central processing unit (CPU), interpreted as the number of billions of instructions per second the CPU can process. *See* mips.

GIS Geographic information system. Technology born of the space and computer age. Real-time geographic data provided by satellites, terrain radar and/or aerial photography is used to develop, organize and display data. Combines 2-D images of maps, etc. with multimedia to create a graphical environment. An example of GIS is the Federal Emergency Management Agency's All-hazards Situation Assessment Prototype software used to manage disaster response needs. Data for ASAP is provided by Air Force U-2 reconnaissance aircraft and satellites. *See* 2-D data, multimedia and ASAP.

glare Reflection of light from a monitor screen.

glass house Jargon term for a controlled data center for large mainframe operations. The environment in the center is controlled; people may look through a window into the center, but access is granted to only a select few.

glitch Hardware or software problem, in some ways similar to but not considered as severe as a bug or crash. Normally minor and short-lived. Occasionally, problems are diagnosed as glitches but are really bugs. *See* bug and crash.

global Action or variable that relates to an entire document, file, program or system, e.g. in a global search, the user instructs the computer to look through the entire document for each occurrence of a specified string of characters. A global variable can be accessed by an entire program while a local variable is only accessible to one section of the program. *See* string and global flag.

global account User account that gives access to multiple computers on a network. *See* local account.

global clock algorithm Algorithm used with paging to determine which pages are moved from memory to the memory buffer or disk when the computer needs to free up memory. The term "clock" is a reference to the way in which the free list pointer follows the dirty list pointer, much like the hands of a clock following each other around the clock's face. This algorithm is now an anachronism; most modern VM systems use a SVR3 demand paging system that flushes dirty pages from memory without the aid of a daemon. *See* paging.

Global Directory Agents Commonly abbreviated and called GDA. *See* GDA.

Global Directory Service Commonly abbreviated and called GDS. *See* GDS.

global flag Editing program term related to a search for all occurrences of a string of characters in a file:

```
CLP> :g/s/string1//string2/g ⏎
```

The first g indicates the entire document is to be searched for string1. The s indicates string2 should be substituted for string1 in the text. The last g is the global flag, indicating that this substitution should be made wherever string1 occurs in the document. Without the last g, only the first occurrence of string1 on a line would be changed.

Global Network Navigator *(INET)* Commonly abbreviated and called GNN. *See* GNN.

global server Term used in the Distributed Time Service, a function within the Open Software Foundation Inc.'s Distributed Computing Environment. The network host that synchronizes the time for other hosts on an extended local area network or wide area network. *See* OSF, DCE, DTS, time server, local server, courier, LAN and WAN.

globbing Process of a shell expanding wild cards to generate a file name. For example, an asterisk (*) could be used in a string to identify files with various characters between common characters; a search for t*f would locate all files beginning with t and ending with f, such as tnf and tif.

glossary *(ATT)* Command used to display definitions contained in the UNIX Programmer's Manual, e.g. entering "help glossary" on the command line provides a menu, and entering "glossary term name" provides a definition of the term.

glove Computer interface technology in which a user wears a glove containing special sensors to transmit commands that control images on a screen.

glyph Picture of an object displayed on a terminal screen.

GNMP **Government Network Management Profile.** National Institute of Standards and Technology set of federal government standards, or profiles, for various types of networks, including Token Ring, Ethernet and Fiber Distribution Data Interface. *See* NIST.

GNN *(INET)* **Global Network Navigator.** Resources center used to look up press releases, product brochures, papers and demonstration software; establish interactive communication with a company; and for other research tasks related to the Internet. Created by O'Reilly & Associates, and announced during the August 1993 Interop conference. *See* Internet.

GNU **GNU is Not UNIX.** Free operating system, similar to UNIX, developed by the Free Software Foundation while at the Massachusetts Institute of Technology Lincoln Laboratories. Provides an EMACS editor and other UNIX look-alike utilities, including a C compiler and Korn shell. *See* FSF and Herd, The.

GNU C **GNU is Not UNIX C**-like language. Freeware version of a C language look-alike developed by Richard Stallman of the Free Software Foundation. *See* C language, FSF, GNU and G++.

gnuchess **GNU is Not UNIX chess.** Chess game provided by the Free Software Foundation. *See* FSF and GNU.

GNU emacs **GNU is Not UNIX emacs.** Freeware version of EMACS developed by Richard Stallman of the Free Software Foundation. *See* FSF, GNU and EMACS.

GOO-IE Pronunciation of GUI, the acronym for graphical user interface. *See* GUI.

Gopher *(INET)* Database developed at the University of Minnesota, known as the Golden Gophers. Provides a list of locations where users can find free software on the Internet. Has been in operation since late 1992. The Gopher database is an X.400 mail hub, supports X.500 directory services, and connects many computer systems throughout the United States. Also supports the Multipurpose Internet Mail Extensions, used to send and receive messages with audio, video, non-ASCII text, etc., and Group III facsimile standards, used to convert different protocols, e.g. PostScript and digital images, into fax. *See* Archie, MIME, fax, G3 and Internet.

go routine Software used with Digital Equipment Corp. UNIBUS architecture to start input/output when all the required resources are available for the process. UNIBUS is specifically designed for medium- to low-speed peripheral devices. *See* I/O and UNIBUS.

GOSIP **G**overnment **O**pen **S**ystem **I**nterconnection **P**rofile. Also called the Government Open Systems Interconnect Profile. Formally called NIST FIPS 146. The federal government standard requiring federal agencies to use International Organization for Standardization and Open Systems Interconnection protocols in networking operations. Started in 1979 by the Department of Commerce's National Institute of Standards and Technology. *See* GOSIP 1, GOSIP 2, GOSIP 3, NIST, FIPS, ISO and OSI.

GOSIP 1 Formally called NIST FIPS 146 v.1. Standard implemented in August 1990 that requires vendors to comply with international Open Systems Interconnection standards. These include the File Transfer, Access and Management and X.400 Message Handling System; International Telecommunication Union Telecommunication Standardization Sector, formerly called the Consultative Committee on International Telegraphy and Telephony, X.25 protocol; and the Institute of Electrical and Electronic Engineers standards for Ethernet, Token Bus and Token Ring networks. Addresses networking as it relates to file transfers and X.400 message handling. *See* GOSIP, GOSIP 2, GOSIP 3, OSI, FTAM, X.400,

ITU-T, X.25, IEEE, Ethernet, Token Bus and Token Ring.

GOSIP 2 Formally called NIST FIPS 146 v.1. Expansion of the networking abilities of the FIPS v.1 standard. Adds the Open Systems Interconnection Virtual Terminal, Integrated Service Digital Networks and End System-to-Intermediate System protocols. Implemented in October 1992. *See* GOSIP, GOSIP 1, GOSIP 3, OSI, VT, ISDN and ES-IS.

GOSIP 3 Formally called NIST FIPS 146 v.1. Expansion of the networking abilities of the FIPS v.1 standard based upon industry and Canadian and U.S. government requirements known as the *Industry/Government Systems Specification*. When implemented in 1994, it is expected to include industry protocols, e.g. Manufacturing Automation Protocol, with protocols currently mandated by the government, e.g. message handling system for electronic mail (X.400) and directory services (X.500). *See* GOSIP, GOSIP 1, GOSIP 2, MAP, X.400 and X.500.

gotcha Any unexpected occurrence that may or may not affect the operation of a computer system. May result in a system crashing, degradation in performance, a delay in installation of a new application or peripheral, etc. Caused by any of a number of problems, including an OOPS!! or OH S*!T!! command; bug in an application, operating system or hardware; new policy; security breach. *See* OOPS!! command and OH S*!T!! command.

goto **1. Go to**. Programming command used to indicate a function to be performed after a specified event. **2.** Command in the vi editor program used to locate the cursor on a specific line. *See* vi commands (Appendix T).

gouraud Process of smooth shading polygons (set of vertices) using bilinear interpolation. *See* polygons, phong shading and wire frame.

government domain Class of software that is developed for government use and paid for by the government. Can be freely used by a federal government agency. Licensing rights have to be obtained by non-government agencies before use.

Government Network Management Profile Commonly abbreviated and called GNMP. *See* GNMP.

Government Open System Interconnection Profile Commonly abbreviated and called GOSIP. *See* GOSIP.

gprof *(BSD)* Graph **prof**ile. System analysis tool first developed and released by the Berkeley Software Distribution. An improved version of the profile command. Used to call and display graph information from specified programs to determine how well an application performs. Can give programmers performance speeds measured in milliseconds. *See* profile.

g protocol Data protocol, developed by Greg Chesson and supported by UNIX-to-UNIX CoPy (UUCP). Used to pass data using 8-bit transfers over asynchronous serial lines between networks. Files are broken into packets and a checksum (error detection method) is run for errorless transmission. The g protocol is an older version supported by all UUCP versions, but is less effective than newer, faster networks. *See* UUCP, LAN, G protocol, e protocol, f protocol, t protocol and x protocol.

G protocol Enhanced version of the g protocol, released with UNIX System V, Release 4. Data protocol supported by UNIX-to-UNIX CoPy (UUCP) to transfer data 8 bits at a time over asynchronous serial lines between networks. Files are broken into packets and a checksum (error detection method) is run for errorless transmission. Supports all window and packet sizes. *See* UUCP, LAN, g protocol, e protocol, f protocol, t protocol and x protocol.

GPS *(ATT)* Graphical primitive string. Method of defining and storing graphical information as a series of lines, arcs and

text. *See* graph, graphics, gutil, spline, stat, toc and tplot.

grace period Time which a superuser gives users to log off a computer system after the shutdown program is started. *See* superuser and shutdown.

Grades Formally called /etc/uucp/Grades. File used in Honey-DanBer UNIX-to-UNIX CoPy (UUCP) rewrite and/or the UNIX System V, Release 4 Basic Network Utilities. Used to divide program priorities for UUCP data transfer. Establishes communications priorities between nodes on outbound UUCP connections. The default priorities are high, medium and low, with all high priority links being established before medium, and medium before low. *See* HoneyDanBer UUCP, UUCP, uuglist, SVR4.x and BNU.

granularity Process of dividing an application, program, process, etc. into the smallest distinguishable element so it can be easily broken into smaller segments for identification and analysis.

grap *(ATT)* **Grap**h. Part of the Documenter's Workbench text formatting programs, found in the troff preprocessor. Developed in 1984 by John Bentley and Brian Kernighan at AT&T Co.'s Bell Laboratories. Used for charts and graphs. Translates data points into drawing commands used by the pic program before the troff text processor is run. *See* DWB, troff, pic and Bell Laboratories.

graph 1. *(ATT)* Command used to draw graphs based on numerical data in specified files. Can only be used on terminals capable of graphic functions. 2. Pictorial representation of two or more variables.

graphical user interface Commonly abbreviated and called GUI. *See* GUI.

graphics 1. *(ATT)* Command used to access graphical and numerical analysis commands. 2. Ability to display or print data in graphical form, e.g. lines and bitmaps. *See* bitmap.

graphics system Commonly called imaging model. *See* imaging model.

Graphstones Private benchmark containing more than 100 separate drawing tests developed by Workstation Laboratories.

grave (') Commonly called backquote. *See* backquote.

Gray Book British version of the American Standard Code for Information Interchange electronic-mail format, similar to the format of the Simple Mail Transfer Protocol. *See* JANET, ASCII, e-mail and SMTP.

grayscale Also spelled gray scale. Alternative to color or black-and-white terminals or fax equipment. Offers up to 16 shades of black and white, or gray.

greater than symbol (>) Used as part of the command line when a user is changing the standard output. Tells the system the name of a file or device to which the user wants the command output sent. By using two greater than symbols, the user can indicate that the output is to be added to an existing file.. *See* redirect and less than symbol.

greek *(ATT)* Filter used to set up extended character sets to do elaborate printing for various graphic terminals.

Green Book 1. Specification for the remote login protocol of the British national research and development network. *See* JANET. 2. 1992 communications standards developed by the International Telecommunication Union Telecommunication Standardization, formerly the Consultative Committee for International Telegraph and Telephony. 3. 1985 reference guide on the design of the PostScript page description language. 4. X/Open Compatibility Guide that defines an environmental superset of Portable Operating System Interface for Computer Environments (POSIX) and System V Interface Definition. Includes descriptions of a standard utility toolkit, system administration, etc. *See* X/Open,

POSIX and SVID. **5.** *(POS)* IEEE P1003.1 POSIX Operating Systems Interface standard. *See* POSIX.

green machine Commonly called green PC. *See* green PC.

green PC Also called green machine. Green refers to environmental improvements in personal computer (PC) technology. PCs, including monitors and peripherals, can now be built to consume less electricity; when idle by either using 30 watts of power or less, or automatically turning off after a certain period of time has elapsed. Health hazards linked to the use of PCs are also being addressed, ranging from eye, back and wrist strain to reduction in electromagnetic emissions. The amount of consumables used in operating PCs and peripherals also has been reduced; batteries, printer cartridges, paper and disks can now be recycled. *See* Energy Star.

grep Global regular expression. Also called global regular expression print, grab regular expression and print and/or global regular expression processor. Command that allows the user to search for a particular pattern of characters in one or more files. The result of the search can be output to a file, screen or another device. *See* egrep and fgrep.

grok **1.** Jargon term for an individual who completely and intimately understands something. Originated in Robert Hienlien's *A Stranger In A Strange Land.* **2.** To completely understand something, almost by intuition. Conversely, if an individual does not grok something, that person does not understand it to the extent they wish.

group Collection of common or related user accounts. Users in the same group can share files and directories if they have the appropriate level of permissions for the file or directory. *See* /etc/group and permissions.

groupadd *(ATT)* System administration command used to add a new group and group identifier to a system. *See* group and GID.

groupdel *(ATT)* System administration command used to delete a group from a system. *See* group.

group ID Commonly abbreviated and called GID. *See* GID.

group identifier Commonly abbreviated and called GID. *See* GID.

Group II Commonly abbreviated and called G2. *See* G2 and ITU-T.

Group III Commonly abbreviated and called G3. *See* G3 and ITU-T.

Group IV Commonly abbreviated and called G4. *See* G4 and ITU-T.

grouping command Commonly known as *braces*. *See* braces.

groups Command used to show to which groups a user belongs.

groupware 1. Any hardware and/or software technology used to improve the ability of people to work together. Software classified as groupware is developed for and used by multiple users to share information, e.g. an operating system such as UNIX, electronic mail, bulletin boards and the Internet network. Groupware hardware includes peripheral devices used to support multiuser computer systems, ranging from projectors that display computer output, to telephone lines used in computer connections. Term was coined in 1977. **2.** Peripheral device, ranging from a projectors used to display computer output, to telephone lines used in computer connections.

grpck *(ATT)* **Group** check. Command used to perform a group file consistency check, verifying the correctness of entries. *See* file consistency check and pwck.

GRX Abbreviation for grayscale. *See* grayscale.

GUI Graphical User Interface. Pronounced *GOO-IE*. Graphical program or extension to an operating system that simplifies the operation of a computer. Allows a user to launch programs and perform complex operations by, for example, highlighting icons and pulling down menus and dialog boxes with a mouse or pointing device instead of typing a series of commands. Popularized by the Apple Macintosh in the early 1980s and adapted to UNIX through Motif, OPEN LOOK, VUE, etc. *See* Motif, OPEN LOOK, VUE, icon and window.

GUI builder Commonly called UIMS (user interface management system). *See* UIMS.

Guide, the *(POS)* Jargon term for POSIX.0, the *Guide to POSIX Open Systems Environment*. *See* POSIX.0.

gulf/usr/group Persian Gulf UNIX users group formed in 1989.

guru Knowledgeable UNIX system administrator or programmer.

gutil *(ATT)* Graphic **util**ities. The graphics utilities in UNIX System V. *See* SVR4.x.

GUUG Vereinigung Deutscher UNIX Benutzer (German UNIX Systems User Group). The West German UNIX Users' Group was formed in 1984.

gwm Generic Window Manager. Newer, more configurable window manager that can be made to emulate either the Motif window manager or the OPEN LOOK window manager. *See* X Window System, window manager, mwm and olwm.

H

h Abbreviation for **h**ecto. *See* hecto.

hack **1.** Originally, a reference to any work that was not done well. **2.** To make authorized or unauthorized changes to a standard program. **3.** Jargon term for gaining or attempting to gain access to a system on which the user is not authorized, regardless of intent or purpose, and usually for the challenge or thrill of accomplishment. **4.** Clumsy programming design used to get a job done quickly with no thought for aesthetics. **5.** Advanced dungeon game based upon the rogue dungeon game.

hacker **1.** Originally, reference to anyone who devoted his life to computers. *See* dark-side hacker and cracker. **2.** Jargon term for an unauthorized user who obtains or attempts to obtain access to a computer system, regardless of intent or purpose, and usually for the challenge or thrill of accomplishment. *See* 414 Gang.

hacker law Federal Computer Fraud and Abuse Act of 1986, formally called 18-USC 1030. First introduced in 1984 but modified into its current form in 1986. Prohibits unauthorized access to computers at universities, research centers, military and other installations in which the federal government has an interest. Also makes the unauthorized distribution of computer passwords a misdemeanor. Other proposed laws are being considered which would add penalties of up to 10 years in prison for initiating viruses or Trojan horses. The act has six parts: 1030a1, which addresses unauthorized access to classified computers; 1030a2, which restricts unauthorized access to computers used by financial institutions; 1030a3, which addresses unauthorized access to computers used solely or partially by the federal government; 1030a4, which covers the use of federal government computers to commit fraud; 1030a5, which addresses unauthorized access to federal government computers resulting in the alteration, loss or damage to data costing $1,000 or more; and 1030a6, restricting unauthorized access to computers used for bulletin boards. *See* virus and Trojan horse.

half-duplex Commonly abbreviated HDX. Method of data communications that allows information to be transmitted back and forth between a computer and a device but only in one direction at a time. *See* duplex and full-duplex.

half-inch tape Commonly called VHS tape storage. *See* VHS tape storage.

halt *(BSD)* Command used by the system administrator to instantly suspend central processing unit operations. *See* CPU.

haltsys *(XEN)* Command used to shut down the system.

hamming code Error-correcting code in Redundant Array of Inexpensive Disks technology. *See* RAID and ECC.

handle Term used by the Object Management Group for a specific object or software used to replicate the function of a hardware device. *See* OMG, name and object.

handler Commonly called signal handler. *See* signal handler.

handshake Exchange of communication signals and procedures between communication devices to establish and control the flow of data between them. Go, no go signals are passed between devices to regulate data flow and prevent congestion.

hang **1.** Jargon term for when a computer system stops and waits for an event which it expects to happen but does not. **2.** Jargon term for adding a peripheral device to a computer system, e.g. to hang an external disk drive off a computer.

hangman Command used to start the word game hangman.

haptic interface Input device capable of capturing tactile responses in the skin as well as measuring resistance to motion or pressure in the body's muscles and joints.

hard coded Also spelled hard-coded or hardcoded. *See* hard-coded.

hardcoded Also spelled hard-coded or hard coded. *See* hard-coded.

hard-coded Also spelled hard coded or hardcoded. Discouraged practice of coding a parameter value in such a way that an application must be rebuilt from source code to change the value.

hard copy Also spelled hard-copy or hardcopy. *See* hard-copy.

hardcopy Also spelled hard-copy or hard copy. *See* hard-copy.

hard-copy Also spelled hard-copy or hardcopy. Printed copy of a text file or other document. *See* soft copy.

hard crash **1.** Any computer system crash or panic that is not readily repaired by rebooting, or restarting, the system. **2.** Computer system crash caused by a hardware failure.

hard drive Commonly called disk drive. *See* disk drive.

Cutaway view of a typical 3.5 inch or 5 inch hard drive

hard limit Hardware or software capacity or user quota that cannot be increased or exceeded. *See* quota and soft limit.

hard link Directory entry referencing the same data as another directory entry in the same file system. Can only be made within the same file system. *See* link, file system, soft link and inode.

hard reset Jargon term for turning the power switch off and then on again to reinitialize a terminal. Originates from an earlier practice of grounding the reset pin on a microprocessor. Used when a soft reset, using software, fails and the terminal remains locked. Turning off the power to a terminal is a signal to reinitialize that the system cannot ignore. If this fails, contact your system administrator. If you are the system administrator, contact your vendor maintenance personnel. *See* soft reset.

hardware Physical or electronic components of a computer system, e.g. cabinets, wiring and circuit boards. *See* software, firmware and peripheral.

hardware-dependent Also called machine-dependent. Any operating system or application software capable of operating on only one type of computer. *See* hardware-independent.

hardware-independent Also called machine-independent. Any operating system or application software capable of operating on more than one type of computer. *See* hardware-dependent.

---

hardware interrupt Message sent to a central processing unit (CPU) from a hardware component indicating that the peripheral has completed an action or is ready for new instructions, e.g. a disk controller sends a signal to the CPU that it has completed a task. *See* software interrupt.

hardware trap Interrupt signal resulting from an internal error in the central processing unit. *See* CPU.

hardwired 1. Describes a form of connection between a peripheral device and a computer, e.g. a cable that connects a terminal device directly to the computer, thus creating a hardwired terminal. Synonym for dedicated or slave. 2. Synonym for hard-coded. *See* hard-coded.

hash Commonly called hashing. *See* hashing.

hashcheck *(ATT)* Routine used by the spell program to maintain spelling dictionaries. Used to read the compressed list of words in the dictionary and output the contents for the spelling check. *See* spell, hashmake and spellin.

hashing 1. Function within the C shell used to enhance performance. Process of building a table of commands in a user's path variable and then searching just the table, not the full file path, to execute the commands. *See* C shell, hash table and rehash. 2. Creating and using hash tables. *See* hash table.

hashing algorithm Algorithm used to locate data in a database.

hashmake *(ATT)* Routine used by the spell program to maintain spelling dictionaries. The first step in converting words that are to be used in creating or updating a spelling list. Converts the text into a code that can be used to create the compressed spelling list. *See* spell, hashcheck and spellin.

hash table Database lookup table created by an indexing procedure that allows database records to be quickly retrieved. *See* hashing and rehash.

HCI Human-computer interface. How a user interacts, makes inputs to and receives outputs from a computer.

hcreate *(ATT)* Hash table **create**. C language library routine used to allocate space for a hash table. *See* library routines, hsearch and hdestroy.

HCS Heterogeneous Computer Systems. University of Washington research program to develop a method of better integrating diverse hardware and software environments.

hd *(XEN)* Command used to output files in **hexade**cimal characters. *See* od.

HDB Abbreviation for HoneyDanBer UNIX-to-UNIX CoPy. *See* HoneyDanBer UUCP.

hdestroy *(ATT)* Hash table **destroy**. C language library routine used to destroy a hash table. *See* library routines, hcreate and hsearch.

HDF Hierarchical Data Format. Public domain standard file format developed by the National Center for Supercomputing Applications for large digital images and text.

HDLC High-Level Data Link Control. International Organization for Standardization protocol used to bundle (frame) user data into packets for transmission over a network. *See* ISO, ADCCP and SDLC.

HDTV High-definition television. Video graphics processor using enhanced scanning, higher resolution (1920 x 1035 pixels) and finer pixel shapes to improve picture quality. HDTV workstations process video and graphics in real time, providing extremely high-quality images for medical and scientific use. *See* pixel.

HDX Abbreviation for half-duplex. *See* half-duplex.

head 1. Command used to print a specific number of lines of a file or output of a program. Prints the first 10 lines of a file by default. Normally used with exceptionally large files. *See* tail. **2.** Magnetic device in a disk drive that transfers data to and from the platter. *See* platter.

head crash Failure of a disk drive that occurs when the head physically touches the platter and scrapes off the oxide coating, destroying the data. *See* head and platter.

header 1. Electronic-mail variable that allows a user to turn on or off the display of the header on electronic mail messages. *See* e-mail. **2.** Indication of the beginning of a file, message or other data element, containing information related to the data, e.g. its destination, level of priority, quantity and type of file. **3.** Address element of an electronic-mail message which contains the electronic-mail addresses of the sender and receiver, subject of the message, users to whom carbon copies have been sent, etc. *See* e-mail. **4.** Data printed in the top margin of a document.

header file File containing source code definitions of macros and variables. *See* macro.

head mounted display Commonly abbreviated and called HMD. *See* HMD.

head tracking Process of monitoring head movement to create robotic movements that simulate head motion.

heap Portion of memory reserved by a program to temporarily store data. Its size cannot be determined until the program is run. The kernel manages unallocated memory and assigns heap space as needed; it reclaims the space after it is discarded by the program. Heap memory is allocated explicitly under program control using malloc, a C language library function, to dynamically request allocation of memory for a program or process. Heap memory is not automatically freed and must be freed explicitly. *See* kernel and stack.

hecto Prefix for 10^2 (100) or 1 hundred. Abbreviated h.

helical scan Technology originally developed for high-quality recording of televi-

sion signals in 1956 and incorporated in video cassette reorders in 1974. Adopted for Digital Audio Tape and 8mm tape-drive technology. Provides high-density and -quality recording and playback because it moves both the head and tape to eliminate loss of space between data tracks. *See* DAT, 8mm tape and longitudinal recording.

help 1. (*ATT*) One of the 13 Source Code Control System commands used to display the meaning of SCCS commands or messages related to the Source Code Control System. *See* SCCS, admin, cdc, comb, delta, get, prs, rmdel, sact, sccsdiff, unget, val, vc and what. **2.** On-line assistance or documentation. Help commands are included in other commands, e.g. the shell layer command to provide users command syntax, and in the UNIX System V, Release 4 Framed Access Command Environment file system operations command menus to explain the commands in the menu. *See* SVR4.x, FACE and shl.

helpadm (*ATT*) Command used to modify the user help database.

Herd, The The Free Software Foundation's (FSF) version of its UNIX-based operating system. Most of the FSF's program names are based on GNU, e.g. GNU C and GNU emacs, but The Herd is the collection of all the GNU programs and the encompassing operating system. *See* GNU.

here document Also called here file. Document or file used as input to a shell program. *See* redirection and standard input.

hertz Commonly written Hz. *See* Hz.

Hesiod Program developed as part of Project Athena at the Massachusetts Institute of Technology. Shows the relationship of users logged into a system to the systems and files on a network that they use. *See* Project Athena.

Heterogeneous Computer Systems
Commonly abbreviated and called HCS. *See* HCS.

heterogeneous network Network of computer systems and devices of varying types, using various protocols and operating systems, and manufactured by various vendors. Normally requires a bridge, or protocol converter, to work with other networks. *See* bridge.

heuristic Solving problems through trial and error by dividing larger problems into smaller units. Also the technical term for both wild-ass guess and second wild-ass guess, nontechnical methods of finding the cause of hardware and software problems. *See* WAG and SWAG.

hex Abbreviation for **hex**adecimal. *See* hexadecimal.

hexadecimal Refers to a numeral system, the base number of which is 16. Changed from sexadecimal in the early 1960s. Along with the 0 and 1 used in the binary system, the hexadecimal system uses 2, 3, 4, 5, 6, 7, 8, 9, A, B, C, D, E and F. Decimal numbers between 0 and 255 can be stated with a two-digit hex number.

hexcalc **Hex**adecimal **calc**ulator. Calculator program that uses a mouse and was developed for the X Window System. *See* dc.

hidden character Nonprintable character used to perform a special function, e.g. backspace or erase.

hidden file Commonly called dot file. *See* dot files.

hierarchical database Database model in which data is stored using a family-tree type of relationship, with the parent controlling the child record. Each child record can have only one parent record, but a child can be a parent of another child record. *See* database.

Hierarchical Data Format Commonly abbreviated and called HDF. *See* HDF.

hierarchical directory Type of directory structure used in UNIX that organizes data into levels with a common purpose, much the same as a family tree is presented. The starting point of this structure

is called root and is represented by a slash (/). *See* hierarchical file system.

hierarchical file system File system or data management system which places files in a ranked order to aid in visualization and organization. UNIX uses a hierarchical file structure which resembles an inverted family tree, with the root (/) being the starting point. All file subsystems except root can be added to or removed from the system. The figure below displays the UNIX hierarchical file system to a typical user's account:

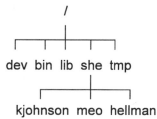

See root and file system.

hierarchical storage system Commonly abbreviated and called HSM. *See* HSM.

hierarchy Concept based on levels and dependencies. All components of an hierarchy have a ranked order and are dependent on and controlled by those in the next highest layer. The UNIX operating system is based on an hierarchy starting at the root, or kernel level, which manages the interface between the operating system and the computer. The hierarchy extends down to user files or text documents that are created, accessed and viewed by commands. *See* hierarchical file system.

high color Color mode of a computer color monitor in which 15 bits are stored for each pixel. Enables 32,768 distinct colors to be displayed. *See* color mode, pixel, minimum color, pseudo color and true color.

high-definition television Commonly abbreviated and called HDTV. *See* HDTV.

High Level Data Link Control
Commonly abbreviated and called HDLC. *See* HDLC.

high-level programming language
Forerunner to FORTRAN that was developed in 1954. Designed to allow programs to be developed in mathematical terms versus machine language. Eventually, high-level programming language became a generic term for any language which uses words rather than symbols, e.g. C language, FORTRAN and COBOL. *See* C language, FORTRAN and COBOL.

highlight Process of marking a specified item or area on a screen by changing how the characters in that area are displayed, e.g. by using reverse video, underlining or blinking.

High Performance Computer and Communications Program Commonly abbreviated and called HPCC. *See* HPCC.

High Performance Parallel Interface
Commonly abbreviated and called HiPPI. *See* HiPPI.

high res Jargon term for high resolution. Describes a display monitor with a high density of pixels and/or anti-aliasing, which provides smooth-edged, true-to-life pictures. *See* pixel, anti-aliasing and low res.

High Sierra specification International Organization for Standardization group's industrywide standards for CD-ROM data. At its meeting near Lake Tahoe, Nevada, in 1985, the group established the basis for the ISO 9660 specifications, which define the file and record structure of CD-ROM discs. *See* ISO, CD-ROM and CD-RDx.

high-speed draft Setting on a dot matrix printer that uses the minimum number of dots to form a character, thereby increasing the printing speed but decreasing the sharpness of the printed output.

high-speed printer Commonly abbreviated and called HSP. *See* HSP.

high-speed serial interface Commonly abbreviated and called HSSI. *See* HSSI.

high watermark Indicator of the largest amount of data which can be put into the data buffer before suspending an activity, e.g. input/output. Used to manage the flow of data. *See* low watermark.

HINFO Host Information. Data file required for the operation of the Domain Name Service which contains basic information on the type of hardware and operating system used by the host. *See* DNS.

HiPPI High-Performance Parallel Interface. A 32-bit bus architecture capable of transmitting data at more than 100 megabits per second. Developed to speed interprocessor memory communication. *See* IPI and SCSI.

histchars History characters. C shell environmental variable used in setting or redefining characters to start history commands.

HISTFILE History file. Environmental variable used with the Korn shell to set the name of the history file that will hold a list of previously run commands. *See* history file.

history Command used to display the contents of a history file, a list of previously run commands. The number of commands displayed depends on the quota established in the user's environment. *See* .history.

.history *(BSD)* File maintained by the system of commands executed by the user while that individual is logged on to the system. Deleted or cleared when the user logs off. *See* execute.

history file File maintained by the system of commands executed by the user while that individual is logged on to the system. Deleted or cleared when the user logs off. *See* execute.

history list Commonly called history file. *See* history file.

history substitution Taking a command from the history file and running it as if it were a newly input command. *See* history list.

HISTSIZE History size. Environmental variable used with the Korn shell to set the number of commands to be maintained in the history file. *See* history file.

HLL High-level languages. *See* high-level programming language.

HMD Head mounted display. Three-dimensional (3-D) display device, e.g. a pair of goggles or a helmet, with miniature video monitors for each eye that generate 3-D images. *See* 3-D graphics.

hog factor Amount of time used by the central processing unit to process a program, expressed in percentage points. *See* CPU and process.

hold Electronic-mail variable. *See* .mailrc variables (Appendices F and G).

hole Physical space, or gap, between data blocks in a file, usually a database. Occurs when the disk drive read/write head skips a location, or sector on the disk. Attempts to access data in a hole will simply show that the hole contains binary zeroes, i.e. that no data exists there.

holes *(OTH)* Shell script that generates a list of files that might need permission changes to enhance security. *See* shell script and permissions.

holey file File which skips 1,024 bytes or more between the writing of one byte and the writing of the next. *See* byte.

holidays *(ATT)* Accounting system text file that contains a list of holidays.

holy wars Connotation of religious furor over an issue or operating systems, e.g. discussions and disagreements among supporters of UNIX and MVS, UNIX System V and Berkeley Software Distribution, Microsoft Corp.'s Windows NT and IBM Corp.'s OS/2. In 1993 the holy war was waged between Novell Inc. and Mi-

crosoft for pre-eminence in the desktop environment.

home 1. Starting point of a cursor on a screen. Varies with the application. **2.** First column of the first line on the screen for a terminal cursor which is not interacting with a software application. **3.** First addressable location on the screen, e.g. the first cell or A1 in a standard spreadsheet application, in application software. This may be the first column of the first line on the screen. *See* home key. **4.** *(BSD)* C shell environmental variable containing the full path of the home directory. *See* HOME.

/home UNIX System V, Release 4 root file system that contains user home directories and files. *See* SVR4.x and root file system.

HOME *(ATT)* User environmental variable. Indicates the first working directory that a user accesses after logging in to a system. *See* environment variables.

home directory Specific directory with which each person in a UNIX system is associated. Identified by the same name as the user identifier. Each time a user logs in, the individual is brought by the system to that specific directory. *See* UID.

home key Used to return the cursor to the home position of the terminal or application software. The location of the key varies with the keyboard but is generally on the right-hand side. *See* home.

HoneyDanBer UUCP UNIX-to-UNIX CoPy (UUCP) program. The name is based upon the UNIX logins for Peter **Honey**man, **Da**vid A. Nowitz and **Br**ian E. Redman, who wrote the program in 1983. Replaced the original UNIX-to-UNIX CoPy in AT&T Co.'s System V, Release 2. Known in UNIX System V, Releases 3 and 4 as the *Basic Networking Utility*. Provides enhanced network and dialer support, remote system support, and improved security. *See* UUCP and BNU.

Hopper, Grace Murray Rear Admiral, USN (1906-92). The grandam of the computer industry known as *Amazing Grace*. Often overlooked for her contributions to the computer industry, among them helping to develop COBOL, the first programming language with English-like commands. Also credited with coining the term "bug" when an ENIAC computer failure was traced to a fried moth in the wiring. Was the first woman to receive the National Medal of Technology. *See* ENIAC.

horizontal application Application software that has broad use and implementation instead of specific industry use, e.g. word processors and office automation software. *See* vertical application.

horizontal scrolling Moving the cursor to the left or right along a line of text that extends off the edge of the screen to view as much of it as possible.

horizontal spacing Measurement of the number of characters per inch on a line of print. *See* fixed space printing and proportional printing.

horsepower Jargon term for the computing power or capability of a computer system or network. Computer horsepower is the computing power of the central processing unit (CPU). Normally stated in either the type of CPU or number of millions of instructions per second (mips), e.g. Intel Pentium, Motorola 68040 or 120 mips. Network horsepower is the operating throughput of the capacity, e.g. a Token Ring network maximum throughput is 16 megabits per second and a Fiber Distributed Data Interface network is 100 megabits per second. *See* CPU, mips, Token Ring and FDDI.

host 1. Also called host computer, host processor or host system. Any primary, self-sufficient computer system that uses terminal devices to provide multiple users access to applications, databases, programming languages, etc. **2.** Also called host node. Any multi-user computer system that is connected to a network and is capable of supporting user access to databases, application programs, connection to the network or other network hosts, etc.

Host computer

host computer Commonly called host. *See* host.

host group *(INET)* Set of hosts on a network identified by a single Internet Protocol address to which a single message can be broadcast. *See* Internet, IP address and IP multicasting.

host ID *(INET)* **Host id**entifier. Specific number that is part of the 32-bit Internet IP address assigned by the Network Information Center. Identifies the local or host address on a network. *See* Internet, IP address, net ID and NIC.

hostid *(BSD)* **Host id**entifier. Command used to establish or display the host identifier for a computer system on a network.

host identifier *(INET)* Commonly abbreviated and called host ID. *See* host ID.

Host Information Commonly abbreviated and called HINFO. *See* HINFO.

hostname *(BSD)* Command used to establish or print the name of a computer on a network.

host node Commonly called host. *See* host.

host processor Commonly called host. *See* host.

host record Commonly called host table. *See* host table.

hosts Commonly written as /etc/hosts. *See* /etc/hosts.

hosts.equiv Commonly written /etc/hosts.equiv. *See* /etc/hosts.equiv.

host system Commonly called host. *See* host.

host table *(INET)* Table used to determine addresses of remote hosts. Contains a list of hosts known to the computer system, their known host aliases and addresses on the Internet network. *See* Internet and Internet address.

hot backup Commonly called hot replacement. *See* hot replacement.

hot key 1. Term used with menu selections where a character is highlighted, indicating which key is to be pressed for that menu selection. 2. Special key or set of keys used to switch access between applications.

hot replacement Replacement of hardware, e.g. a disk drive, in a computer system that is capable of remaining in operation during the repairs.

hot swap Also called on-line insertion. Ability to replace component parts of a computer system, e.g. disk drives, while the computer is operational.

Houston 30 Group originally called the Atlanta 17. Renamed the User Alliance for Open Systems in September 1990. *See* User Alliance for Open Systems.

hp *(ATT)* Command used to process the special functions available on the Hewlett-Packard Co.'s HP 2621 and 2640 terminals. Emulates an HP 2621 raster-graphics terminal.

hp2621 Command used to process the special functions on the Hewlett-Packard Co.'s HP 2621 raster graphics terminal. Emulates the HP terminal.

HPCC High Performance Computing and Communications Program. National agency established in 1992 following the passage of the High Performance Computing Act of 1991. Its purpose is to manage the research and test development efforts of the gigabit test beds formed by the U.S. government, industry and universities. Research and development efforts are concentrated on technologies and applications needed to implement networks and supercomputers capable of transmitting gigabits of data per second. *See* NREN, AURORA, BLANCA, CASA, MAGIC, NECTAR and VISTANet.

hpio *(ATT)* Hewlett-Packard input/output. Backup program specifically developed for the Hewlett-Packard Co.'s HP 2645A terminal, which has its own tape drives.

HPPI High-Performance Parallel Interface. Alternative abbreviation for HiPPI. *See* HiPPI.

HP-UX Modified version of AT&T Co.'s System V, Release 3 with Berkeley Software Distribution Release 4.3 for the Hewlett-Packard Co.'s HP 9000 computer.

HRC Hybrid ring control. Fiber Distribution Data Interface protocol that includes packet switching and the addition of multiple bandwidth channels for multimedia. *See* FDDI-II and multimedia.

hsearch *(ATT)* Hash table **search**. C language library routine used to locate where an entry can be found. *See* library routines, hcreate and hdestroy.

HSM Hierarchical storage management. Combination of various types of hardware, e.g. fixed disk and removable storage, with intelligent data or filesystem management application software. Reduces the cost of storing data by enabling it to be moved from one type of storage medium to another, based on how frequently the data must be accessed. Active data, or data currently in use, is maintained on fixed disk drives for immediate access. Data that can be retrieved in a few hours, minutes or less is moved to near-line storage, e.g. an optical disk system. Information that can be made available in several hours or in a few days is moved to off-line storage, e.g. tape back-up.

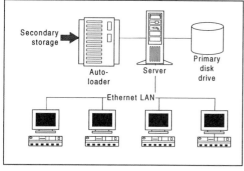

Old data is stored on a multi-tape autoloader system. The data quickly can be restored to the primary storage system if it is needed.

HSP High-speed printer. Any printer capable of printing 300 lines per minute or more.

HSSI High-speed serial interface. De facto standard interface for high-speed data transmission (45 megabits per second or greater) developed by Cisco Systems Inc.

htable *(ATT)* Host **table**. Command used to format Internet host tables available from the Internet network into the local format used by the network library routines. *See* Internet and gettable.

hub Device used to connect several other devices together, e.g. in a hub/spoke architecture, a central connection box, or hub, is used to pass messges or data from a computer to one or more other computers connected to the hub.

human-computer interface Commonly abbreviated and called HCI. *See* HCI.

human readable form Computer data that has been converted into a format, e.g. printout, that can read by humans.

hung Jargon term for either a process or system which is in a state that prevents any further activity, such as when a process or program goes into a loop or a system is waiting on a failed device or semaphore.

.hushlogin *(BSD)* User environmental variable placed in a user's home directory that turns off login messages which normally are sent to the user, e.g. the message of the day. *See* motd.

HUUG Hungarian UNIX User Group. UNIX user group formed in 1987.

hybrid ring control Commonly abbreviated and called HRC. *See* HRC.

hypertext Way of displaying expanded information in a document. By selecting certain words in the text, e.g. by highlighting them, additional information is provided on that subject or links to other documents are activated which bring a related document to the screen.

Hyper VGA **Hyper** video graphics array. Video graphics array monitor with a resolution of 1600 x 1200 pixels. *See* VGA, CGA, EGA, super VGA, XGA and pixel.

hyphen *(ATT)* Part of the Documenter's Workbench set of text formatting programs. Identifies hyphenated words in text, nroff or troff files. *See* nroff, troff and DWB.

Hz Hertz. Measurement of electrical frequency or the time it takes to alternate polarity from positive to negative. Equals 1 cycle per second; 1 megahertz (MHz) equals 1,000,000 cycles per second. *See* frequency.

I

i_list block Commonly called inode table. *See* inode table.

i2u Italian UNIX Systems User Group formed in 1984.

i14y Abbreviation for interoperability, with 14 letters removed between the i and y.

i18n **1.** Abbreviation for internationalization, with 18 letters removed between the i and n. Ability of programmers to develop and implement application programs, utilities and operating systems that are customized for local languages and customs. **2.** UniForum Technical Committee group working on internationalization, or customizing, of application programs, utilities or operating systems to local languages or customs. *See* l10n.

i286 **1.** *(ATT)* Pre-System V, Release 4 command used to test if a computer system has an Intel 286 central processing unit. If so, the command returns a 0 (TRUE) value; otherwise, it returns a non-zero (FALSE) value. *See* SVR4.x, CPU and machid. **2.** Intel 286. Commonly abbreviated and called 286. *See* 286.

i386 **1.** *(ATT)* Pre-System V, Release 4 command used to test if a computer system has an Intel 386 central processing unit. If so, the command returns a 0 (TRUE) value; otherwise, it returns a non-zero (FALSE) value. *See* SVR4.x, CPU and machid. **2.** Intel 386. Commonly abbreviated and called 386. *See* 386.

i486 Intel **486**. Commonly abbreviated and called 486. *See* 486.

I & A Identification **and** authentication. Element of the UNIX security system that is responsible for confirming a user's password when the person logs in. *See* feature.

IAB *(INET)* Internet Activities Board. Originally called the Internet Control and Configuration Board. The name was changed in 1983. An independent committee of technical researchers and professionals responsible for managing the design and engineering of the Internet. Manages the requests for comment process, and establishes and documents standards for the Internet through the Internet Engineering Task Force and the Internet Research Task Force. *See* Internet, RFC, IETF and IRTF.

ialloc *(ATT)* Inode **alloc**ation. Program used to allocate free inodes on specific disks or devices. *See* inode.

iBCS Intel Binary Compatibility Specification. Original name for the Intel Binary Compatibility Specification, Edition 1. *See* iBCS-1.

iBCS-1 Intel Binary Compatibility Specification, Edition 1. Originally called iBCS. A standard developed in 1988 to define a limited set of programming functionalities to develop shrink-wrapped applications for UNIX System V, Release 3.2. *See* shrink-wrapped and SVR3.x.

iBCS-2 Intel Binary Compatibility Specification, Edition 2. Developed in 1990 to replace iBCS-1. Provides programmers a set of standards used to develop shrink-wrapped software applications designed and ported to a specific type of central processor unit, e.g. Intel 80386 or 80486. for XENIX and UNIX System V, Release 3.2 and earlier versions, limited capabilities with UNIX System V, Release 4.3, and complete capabilities with UNIX System V, Release 4.4. *See* shrink-wrapped, SVR3.x and SVR4.x.

IBM cards Commonly called computer cards. *See* computer cards.

ic Ignorecase. Variable in the ex and vi editors that, when set, does not differentiate between uppercase and lowercase letters during a search operation. *See* ex, vi and noic.

IC Integrated circuit. Conceptualized in 1959 and developed in the early 1960s by Robert Noyce. Called a computer on a chip since hundreds or thousands of separate functions can be integrated on a single chip. Composed of a small silicon wafer with electrical circuits etched into the surface. *See* chip, silicon and wafer.

I-CASE Integrated computer-aided software engineering. Extension of CASE technology. Gives designers the ability to code software automatically from design specifications.

ICEUUG Iceland UNIX User Group formed in 1986.

icheck *(ATT)* Integrity check. Older program used for file system checks that has been replaced by the fsck command. *See* fsck and file consistency check.

ICMP *(INET)* Internet Control Message Protocol. One of the protocols of the Internet Protocol Suite developed by the Defense Advanced Research Projects Agency. Used in host-to-host communication to manage network routing and report Internet Protocol errors. *See* Internet Protocol Suite, DARPA and IP.

icon Small graphic image that represents data or a command on a graphics system, e.g. on X Window System, Macintosh and Microsoft Windows. Permits an operating system to be more user-friendly. Allows a user to point a mouse and click on an icon instead of typing a series of complex commands to start a program or load a document. Beside representing programs, icons can symbolize peripherals, e.g. disk drives and printers. *See* dynabook, windows, X Window System and workstation.

Icons used to launch programs in Microsoft Windows interface

iconv *(ATT)* ISO **conv**ersion. Utility used to convert characters from one code into those of another code, e.g. characters in American Standard Code for Information Interchange English into Spanish. *See* ASCII.

id *(ATT/XEN)* Command used to display user name, user identifier number, group name and group identifier number as well as the names of active processes. If there is a difference between the current and original user identifiers, the original one will be displayed; the same will be done with the group identifier. Normally used when tracking a problem, to see which user or process started a specific process. *See* real GID, EGID, real UID and EUID.

IDE Integrated development environment. Combination of a programming language compiler, which can translate source code to binary code that a computer can run; a linker, used to place individual pieces of code into an executable file; a debugger, used to locate problems in the code; a browser, used by the programmers to look through the file containing the programming code; and an editor, used to create and modify the code to provide a standard application programming development environment.

IDEA International Data Encryption Algorithm. Encryption algorithm developed by James Massy and Xudjia Lai. Encrypts text in 64-bit blocks and uses solely a secret key to encode and decode the information. Only those who know the key can create or read the message. *See* DES, encrypt and decrypt.

ideal Program used with the nroff or troff text processing programs to generate graphs. *See* nroff and troff.

ident **1.** *(BSD)* Command used to print the name of the kernel maintained in the Source Code Control System or Revision Control System files. *See* SCCS and RCS. **2.** Key word used in creating the kernel to identify the name of the kernel.

Identification and authentication
Commonly abbreviated and called I & A. *See* I & A.

idle Inactivity of a user who is logged into a system but is not making any input either on the keyboard or with a mouse. *See* idle time.

idle time Period of time during which a user is not making any input either on the keyboard or with a mouse to the computer. Also recorded when a user starts an active process in the background but does not make any input while the process in being executed. *See* idle and background process.

idload *(ATT)* Remote File Sharing command used to establish the mapping translation tables, a file containing user identifiers and permission used by the Remote File Sharing system to determine access by remote users; to display the current uid.rules and gid.rules, files used in the Remote File Sharing system to establish access permissions in the mapping translation tables; or to display the current mapping translations for the system. *See* RFS, mapping translation table, uid.rules, UID, gid.rules and GID.

ID mapping Establishing permissions for remote users to gain access to an entire computer system. *See* uid.rules, gid.rules and mapping translation table.

IDP Internet **D**atagram **P**rotocol. Xerox Corp.'s Network Service, similar to the Internet Protocol. *See* IP and XNS.

IEC International Electrotechnical Commission. Sister organization on international standards to the International Organization for Standardization. Responsible for electrical and electronic standards. *See* ISO and JTC1.

IEEE Institute of Electrical and Electronics Engineers. International standards organization formed in 1963 by electrical engineering organizations from the United States and other countries. Develops electrical and communications standards which, in the United States, are submitted for approval to the American National Standards Institute. *See* ANSI and ISO.

IEEE P1003.0 Guide *(POS)* Institute of Electrical and Electronic Engineers Project **1003.0 Guide**. The IEEE Portable Operating System Interface for Computer Environments (POSIX) executive overview of the POSIX working groups. *See* IEEE, Project 1003 and POSIX.

IEEE P1003.0 working group *(POS)* Institute of Electrical and Electronic Engineers Project **1003.0 working group**. The IEEE Portable Operating System Interface for Computer Environments (POSIX) working group responsible for creating and maintaining the IEEE P1003.0 Guide. *See* IEEE, POSIX, Project 1003 and IEEE P1003.0 Guide.

IEEE P1003.1 working group *(POS)* Institute of Electrical and Electronic Engineers Project **1003.1 working group**. Also called System Interface. The IEEE Portable Operating System Interface for Computer Environments (POSIX) working group originally responsible for defining the interfaces between application programs and the operating system. The working group has been divided into subgroups for system interface, language-independent specifications and C language bindings. The System Interface document, *IEEE Std 1003.1-1990*, was released in 1990. *See* IEEE, POSIX, Project 1003, IEEE P1003.1a project, IEEE P1003.1b project, IEEE P1003.1c project, IEEE P1003.1d project, IEEE P1003.1e project, IEEE P1003.1f project and IEEE P1003.1h project.

IEEE P1003.1a project *(POS)* Institute of Electrical and Electronic Engineers Project **1003.1a project**. The IEEE Portable Operating System Interface for Computer Environments (POSIX) project that was originally responsible for defining system interface requirements. After the 1003.1-1990 standard was released, the project group began working on miscellaneous additions to the standard, e.g. checkpoint/restart, interfaces for file tree walking and symbolic links. *See* IEEE, POSIX and Project 1003.

IEEE P1003.1b project *(POS)* Institute of Electrical and Electronic Engineers Project **1003.1b project**. The IEEE Portable Operating System Interface for Computer Environments (POSIX) project responsible for defining computer language-independent specifications. In 1993 the work of the IEEE P1003.4 working group on real-time operating systems requirements was transferred to the IEEE P1003.1b project. The project's work includes asynchronous input and output, binary semaphores, interprocess communication, memory mapped files and shared memory, priority scheduling, process memory locking, real-time signal extensions, synchronized input and output, and timers. *See* IEEE, POSIX, Project 1003 and RTOS.

IEEE P1003.1c project *(POS)* Institute of Electrical and Electronic Engineers Project **1003.1c project**. The IEEE Portable Operating System Interface for Computer Environments (POSIX) project responsible for developing kernel standards for C language code. In 1993 the responsibilities of the IEEE P1003.4a working group for developing a standard for threads were transferred to the IEEE P1003.1c project. *See* IEEE, POSIX, Project 1003, C language, threads and RTOS.

IEEE P1003.1d project *(POS)* Institute of Electrical and Electronic Engineers Project **1003.1d project**. The IEEE Portable Operating System Interface for Computer Environments (POSIX) project created in 1993 with the transfer of the IEEE P1003.4b project responsibilities. IEEE P1003.1d project is responsible for real-time UNIX additions requested by the X/Open Co. Ltd., UNIX International and the Open Software Foundation Inc. It also is responsible for device control, execution time monitoring, interrupt control, sporadic servers and time-outs for blocking services. *See* IEEE, POSIX, Project 1003, RTOS, X/Open, UI and OSF.

IEEE P1003.1e project *(POS)* Institute of Electrical and Electronic Engineers Project **1003.1e project**. The IEEE Portable Operating System Interface for Computer Environments (POSIX) project was created in 1993 when the responsibilities of the IEEE P1003.6 working group were split between the IEEE P1003.2c and P1003.1e projects. The IEEE P1003.1e project is responsible for POSIX system security standards for system interface requirements. *See* IEEE, POSIX, Project 1003, DAC and MAC.

IEEE P1003.1f project *(POS)* Institute of Electrical and Electronic Engineers Project **1003.1f project**. The IEEE Portable Operating System Interface for Computer Environments (POSIX) project was created in 1993 with the transfer of the IEEE P1003.8 working group's responsibilities. The IEEE P1003.1f project is responsible for standards for networking of POSIX systems. *See* IEEE, POSIX, Project 1003, network and TFA.

IEEE P1003.1g project *(POS)* Institute of Electrical and Electronic Engineers Project **1003.1g project**. The IEEE Portable Operating System Interface for Computer Environments (POSIX) project was created in 1993 with the transfer of the IEEE P1003.12 working group's responsibilities. The IEEE P1003.1g project is responsible for developing standards for application programming interfaces and protocol-independent processing. *See* IEEE, POSIX, Project 1003, API and PII.

IEEE P1003.2 working group *(POS)* Institute of Electrical and Electronic Engineers Project **1003.2 working group**. The IEEE Portable Operating System Interface for Computer Environments (POSIX) working group formed in 1986. Responsible for developing a standard for shell, commands and utilities. The initial shell and utilities standard, IEEE Std 1003.2-1992, was released in 1992. *See* IEEE, POSIX, Project 1003, shell and utilities.

IEEE P1003.2a project *(POS)* Institute of Electrical and Electronic Engineers Project **1003.2a project**. The IEEE Portable Operating System Interface for Computer Environments (POSIX) project responsible for user portability extension or supplement to the basic IEEE P1003.2 standard. The primary responsibility of the project was to provide standard commands not found in shell scripts, such as vi. The IEEE P1003.2a project was disbanded when its work was adopted in the IEEE Std 1003.2-1992 standards document. *See* IEEE, POSIX, Project 1003 and UPE.

IEEE P1003.2b project *(POS)* Institute of Electrical and Electronic Engineers Project **1003.2b project**. The IEEE Portable Operating System Interface for Computer Environments (POSIX) P1003.2 project was responsible for developing a standard for the command line and functional interfaces to P1003.2 utilities. *See* IEEE, POSIX, Project 1003 and IEEE P1003.2 working group.

IEEE P1003.2c project *(POS)* Institute of Electrical and Electronic Engineers Project **1003.2c project**. The IEEE Portable Operating System Interface for Computer Environments (POSIX) project was created in 1993 when the responsibilities of the IEEE P1003.6 working group were split between the IEEE P1003.1e and P1003.2c projects. The IEEE P1003.2c is responsible for developing standards for POSIX system security extensions for

shells and utilities. *See* IEEE, POSIX, Project 1003, DAC and MAC.

IEEE P1003.2d project *(POS)* Institute of Electrical and Electronic Engineers Project **1003.2d project**. The IEEE Portable Operating System Interface for Computer Environments (POSIX) project was created in 1993 when the responsibilities of the IEEE P1003.15 working group were transferred to the IEEE P1003.2d project. The IEEE P1003.2d project is responsible for developing standards for batch queuing. *See* IEEE, POSIX and Project 1003.

IEEE P1003.2 working group *(POS)* Institute of Electrical and Electronic Engineers Project **1003.2 working group**. The IEEE Portable Operating System Interface for Computer Environments (POSIX) working group, formed in 1986 and responsible for developing a standard for shell, commands and utilities. IEEE Std 1003.2-1992, the initial shell and utilities standard, was released in 1992. *See* IEEE, POSIX, Project 1003, shell and utility.

IEEE P1003.3 working group *(POS)* Institute of Electrical and Electronic Engineers Project **1003.3 working group**. The IEEE Portable Operating System Interface for Computer Environments (POSIX) working group was formed in 1986 and was developing a standard for test and verification test suites for POSIX compliance. The initial test methods standard, IEEE Std 1003.3-1991, was released in 1991, followed in 1992 by a more detailed test standard, IEEE Std. 1003.1-1992. *See* IEEE, POSIX, Project 1003 and PCTS.

IEEE P1003.4a project *(POS)* Institute of Electrical and Electronic Engineers Project **1003.4a project**. The IEEE Portable Operating System Interface for Computer Environments (POSIX) project originally responsible for developing standards for threads needed to control processes in a real-time operating system environment. In 1993 the work of the IEEE P1003.4a project was transferred to the IEEE P1003.1c project. *See* IEEE, POSIX, Project 1003, IEEE P1003.1c project and threads.

IEEE P1003.4b project *(POS)* Institute of Electrical and Electronic Engineers Project **1003.4b project**. The IEEE Portable Operating System Interface for Computer Environments (POSIX) project originally responsible for developing standards for real-time UNIX additions requested by X/Open Co. Ltd., UNIX International and the Open Software Foundation Inc. In 1993 the work of the IEEE P1003.4b project was transferred to the IEEE P1003.1d project. *See* IEEE, POSIX, Project 1003 and IEEE P1003.1d project.

IEEE P1003.4 working group *(POS)* Institute of Electrical and Electronic Engineers Project **1003.4 working group**. The IEEE Portable Operating System Interface for Computer Environments (POSIX) working group originally responsible for developing a standard for real-time UNIX, known as *POSIX Real-time Extensions and Profiles*. In 1993 the work of the IEEE P1003.4 working group was transferred to the IEEE P1003.1b, 1003.1c and 1003.1d projects. In addition, the work on application environment profiles for real-time systems of the IEEE P1003.13 working group was moved to the IEEE P1003.4 working group. *See* IEEE, POSIX, Project 1003, IEEE P1003.1b project, IEEE P1003.1c project and IEEE P1003.1d project.

IEEE P1003.5 working group *(POS)* Institute of Electrical and Electronic Engineers Project **1003.5 working group**. The IEEE Portable Operating System Interface for Computer Environments (POSIX) working group responsible for developing a standard for Ada language interface. In 1992 the initial Ada binding standard, IEEE Std 1003.5-1992, was released. *See* IEEE, POSIX, Project 1003 and Ada.

IEEE P1003.6 working group *(POS)* Institute of Electrical and Electronic Engineers Project **1003.6 working group**. The IEEE Portable Operating System Interface for Computer Environments (POSIX) working group responsible for developing POSIX system security standards, known as *POSIX Security Extensions*. In

1993 the work of the IEEE P1003.6 working group was transferred to the IEEE P1003.1e project. *See* IEEE, POSIX, Project 1003 and IEEE P1003.1e project.

IEEE P1003.7 working group *(POS)* Institute of Electrical and Electronic Engineers Project **1003.7 working group**. The IEEE Portable Operating System Interface for Computer Environments (POSIX) working group originally responsible for developing POSIX system administration standards for utilities and interfaces in a distributed environment. In 1993 the work on these projects was transferred to the P1387.x projects; P1003.7 became P1387.1, P1003.7.1 became P1387.4, P1003.7.2 became P1387.2 and P1003.7.3 became P1387.3. *See* IEEE, POSIX, Project 1003 and system administration.

IEEE P1003.7.1 project *(POS)* Institute of Electrical and Electronic Engineers Project **1003.7 project**. The IEEE Portable Operating System Interface for Computer Environments (POSIX) project responsible for developing standards for printer system management. Its work was transferred to the IEEE P1387.4 project in 1993. *See* IEEE, POSIX and Project 1003.

IEEE P1003.7.2 project *(POS)* Institute of Electrical and Electronic Engineers Project **1003.7 project**. The IEEE Portable Operating System Interface for Computer Environments (POSIX) project responsible for developing standards for software management. Its work was transferred to the IEEE P1387.2 project in 1993. *See* IEEE, POSIX and Project 1003.

IEEE P1003.7.3 project *(POS)* Institute of Electrical and Electronic Engineers Project **1003.7 project**. The IEEE Portable Operating System Interface for Computer Environments (POSIX) project responsible for developing standards for user and group management. Its work was transferred to the IEEE P1387.3 project in 1993. *See* IEEE, POSIX and Project 1003.

IEEE P1003.8 working group *(POS)* Institute of Electrical and Electronic Engineers Project **1003.8 working group**. The

IEEE Portable Operating System Interface for Computer Environments (POSIX) working group originally responsible for developing standards for networking of POSIX systems. Known as *POSIX Transparent File Access*. In 1993 the work of the P1003.8 working group was transferred to the P1003.1f project. *See* IEEE, POSIX, Project 1003 and IEEE P1003.1f project.

IEEE P1003.9 working group *(POS)* Institute of Electrical and Electronic Engineers Project **1003.9 working group**. The IEEE Portable Operating System Interface for Computer Environments (POSIX) working group responsible for developing for the FORTRAN-77 language interface. In 1992, the initial FORTRAN-77 standard, IEEE Std 1003.9-1992, was released. Following the standard's release, the group was disbanded. *See* IEEE, POSIX, Project 1003, IEEE P1003.19 working group and FORTRAN-77.

IEEE P1003.10 working group *(POS)* Institute of Electrical and Electronic Engineers Project **1003.10 working group**. The IEEE Portable Operating System Interface for Computer Environments (POSIX) working group originally responsible for developing a standard for an application environment profile for supercomputers. Known as *POSIX Supercomputing*. In 1993 the work of the IEEE P1003.15 working group on queuing for batch processing was transferred to the IEEE P1003.10 working group. *See* IEEE, POSIX, Project 1003 and supercomputer.

IEEE P1003.11 working group *(POS)* Institute of Electrical and Electronic Engineers Project **1003.11 working group**. The IEEE Portable Operating System Interface for Computer Environments (POSIX) working group responsible for developing a standard for an application environment profile for on-line transaction processing. *See* IEEE, POSIX, Project 1003, AEP and transaction processing.

IEEE P1003.12 working group *(POS)* Institute of Electrical and Electronic Engineers Project **1003.12 working group**. The IEEE Portable Operating System Interface for Computer Environments (POSIX) working group originally responsible for developing standards for network applications programming interface. In 1993 the work of the P1003.12 working group was transferred to the P1003.1g project. *See* IEEE, POSIX, Project 1003 and IEEE P1003.1g project.

IEEE P1003.13 working group *(POS)* Institute of Electrical and Electronic Engineers Project **1003.13 working group**. The IEEE Portable Operating System Interface for Computer Environments (POSIX) working group responsible for developing standards for application environment profiles for real-time system support. The responsibilities of the P1003.13 working group have been transferred to the P1003.4 working group. *See* IEEE, POSIX, Project 1003, AEP and RTOS.

IEEE P1003.14 working group *(POS)* Institute of Electrical and Electronic Engineers Project **1003.14 working group**. The IEEE Portable Operating System Interface for Computer Environments (POSIX) working group responsible for developing standards for multiprocessing computer environment. Responsibilities of the IEEE P1003.18 working group on Platform Environment Profile, or description of the standard UNIX multiuser computer, were transferred to the IEEE P1003.14 working group in 1993. *See* IEEE, POSIX, Project 1003, PEP and MP.

IEEE P1003.15 working group *(POS)* Institute of Electrical and Electronic Engineers Project **1003.15 working group**. The IEEE Portable Operating System Interface for Computer Environments (POSIX) working group originally responsible for developing standards for traditional interactive multiuser system, e.g. batch queuing. Known as *POSIX Batch Queuing Extensions*. Responsibilities of the P1003.15 working group were transferred to the IEEE P1003.10 working group and the P1003.2d project in 1993. *See* IEEE, POSIX, Project 1003 and IEEE P1003.2d project.

IEEE P1003.16 working group *(POS)*
Institute of Electrical and Electronic Engineers Project **1003.16 working group**. The IEEE Portable Operating System Interface for Computer Environments (POSIX) working group responsible for developing standards for C language interfaces to system services. *See* IEEE, POSIX, Project 1003 and C language.

IEEE P1003.17 working group *(POS)*
Institute of Electrical and Electronic Engineers Project **1003.17 working group**. The IEEE Portable Operating System Interface for Computer Environments (POSIX) working group originally responsible for developing standards for Name Space/Directory Services. The responsibilities of the group were transferred to the IEEE P1224 working group. *See* IEEE, POSIX, Project 1003, X.500, IEEE P1224 working group and NS/DS.

IEEE P1003.18 working group *(POS)*
Institute of Electrical and Electronic Engineers Project **1003.18 working group**. The IEEE Portable Operating System Interface for Computer Environments (POSIX) working group originally responsible for developing a standard for Platform Environment Profile, a description of the standard UNIX multiuser computer. Responsibilities of the IEEE P1003.18 working group were transferred to the IEEE P1003.14 working group. *See* IEEE, POSIX, Project 1003 and IEEE P1003.18 working group.

IEEE P1003.19 working group *(POS)*
Institute of Electrical and Electronic Engineers Project **1003.19 working group**. The IEEE Portable Operating System Interface for Computer Environments (POSIX) working group originally responsible for developing a standard for FORTRAN-90 language interface. The group's work was discontinued in 1993. *See* IEEE, POSIX, Project 1003, IEEE P1003.9 working group and FORTRAN-90.

IEEE P1003.20 working group *(POS)*
Institute of Electrical and Electronic Engineers Project **1003.20 working group**. The IEEE Portable Operating System Interface for Computer Environments (POSIX) working group responsible for developing a standard for the Ada language interface for real-time extensions. The responsibilities of the P1003.20 working group were transferred to the IEEE P1003.5 working group in 1993. *See* IEEE, POSIX, Project 1003 and IEEE P1003.5 working group.

IEEE P1003.21 working group *(POS)*
Institute of Electrical and Electronic Engineers Project **1003.21 working group**. The IEEE Portable Operating System Interface for Computer Environments (POSIX) working group originally responsible for developing a standard for real-time distributed computing systems. *See* IEEE, POSIX and Project 1003.

IEEE P1003.22 working group *(POS)*
Institute of Electrical and Electronic Engineers Project **1003.22 working group**. The IEEE Portable Operating System Interface for Computer Environments (POSIX) working group responsible for developing the Open Systems Environment Security Framework Guide. *See* IEEE, POSIX and Project 1003.

IEEE P1201 working group *(POS)* Institute of Electrical and Electronic Engineers Project **1201 working group**. The IEEE Portable Operating System Interface for Computer Environments (POSIX) working group responsible for developing standards for the X Window System library of programs. *See* IEEE, POSIX, xlib and X Window System.

IEEE P1201.1 working group *(POS)* Institute of Electrical and Electronic Engineers Project **1201.1 working group**. The IEEE Portable Operating System Interface for Computer Environments (POSIX) working group responsible for developing standards for a windowing toolkit to establish a standard graphical user interface. *See* IEEE, POSIX, GUI and LAPI.

IEEE P1201.2 working group *(POS)* Institute of Electrical and Electronic Engineers Project **1201.2 working group**. The IEEE Portable Operating System Interface for Computer Environments (POSIX) working group responsible for developing standards and recommended practices for the graphical user interface driveability guide. *See* IEEE, POSIX and GUI.

IEEE P1224 working group *(POS)* Institute of Electrical and Electronic Engineers Project **1224 working group**. The IEEE Portable Operating System Interface for Computer Environments (POSIX) working group responsible for developing standards for X.400 electronic-mail handling interface and X.500 directory services. *See* IEEE, POSIX, X.400 and X.500.

IEEE P1237 working group *(POS)* Institute of Electrical and Electronic Engineers Project **1237 working group**. The IEEE Portable Operating System Interface for Computer Environments (POSIX) working group responsible for developing standards for the remote procedure call interface. *See* IEEE, POSIX and RPC.

IEEE P1238 working group *(POS)* Institute of Electrical and Electronic Engineers Project **1238 working group**. The IEEE Portable Operating System Interface for Computer Environments (POSIX) working group responsible for developing a programming interface to the association control service element. *See* IEEE, POSIX and ACSE.

IEEE P1238.1 working group *(POS)* Institute of Electrical and Electronic Engineers Project **1238.1 working group**. The IEEE Portable Operating System Interface for Computer Environments (POSIX) working group responsible for developing standards for File Transfer Access Method application interface. *See* IEEE, POSIX and FTAM.

IEEE P1238.2 working group *(POS)* Institute of Electrical and Electronic Engineers Project **1238.2 working group**. The IEEE Portable Operating System Interface for Computer Environments (POSIX) working group responsible for developing standards for a common application interface. *See* IEEE and POSIX.

IEEE P1387.1 project *(POS)* Institute of Electrical and Electronic Engineers Project **1387.1 project**. Original work on creating standards for system administration was accomplished by the IEEE P1003.7 working group. P1003.7 projects were transferred to the P1387 working group, and P1387.1 was initiated to outline a standard for a general framework for system administration. *See* IEEE and POSIX.

IEEE P1387.2 project *(POS)* Institute of Electrical and Electronic Engineers Project **1387.2 project**. Originally called the IEEE P1003.7.2 project, and renamed in 1993. A Portable Operating System Interface for Computer Environments project responsible for developing standards for software management. *See* IEEE and POSIX.

IEEE P1387.3 project *(POS)* Institute of Electrical and Electronic Engineers Project **1387.3 project**. Originally called the IEEE P1003.7.3 project, and renamed in 1993. A Portable Operating System Interface for Computer Environments project responsible for developing standards for user and group management. *See* IEEE and POSIX.

IEEE P1387.4 project *(POS)* Institute of Electrical and Electronic Engineers Project **1387.4 project**. Originally called the IEEE P1003.7.1 project, and renamed in 1993. A Portable Operating System Interface for Computer Environments project responsible for developing standards for printer system management. *See* IEEE and POSIX.

IESG *(INET)* Internet Engineering Steering Group. Committee responsible for managing the Internet Engineering Task Force. Responsible for the daily operation of the Internet, and resolution of short- and mid-term problems with the protocol and architecture. *See* Internet, IAB and IETF.

IETF *(INET)* Internet Engineering Task Force. One of the two task forces of the Internet Activities Board. Responsible for solving short- and mid-term operational problems related to the Internet network; and recommending Internet standards, e.g. internationalization of electronic mail, and Transmission Control Protocol/Internet Protocol standards. Composed of 40 working groups managed by the Internet Engineering Steering Group. Members are selected from industry professionals and vendors with experience in research, design or operation of networks based on the architecture of the Internet. *See* Internet, IAB, IESG, RFC and IRTF.

if 1. Shell command used to perform basic program control. Executed to test the truth of a statement or condition, e.g.

> **if** *condition1* **then**
> *Statement1*
> **end**

Based on the results, it then runs other commands. *See* then, else, elif and fi. **2.** *(INET)* Command used to identify the properties of an interface with Internet protocols. *See* Internet.

ifconfig Interface **config**ure. Network administration command used to display and set network interface configurations.

IFIP International Federation for Information Processing. International research group that does similar work to that of the Institute of Electrical and Electronic Engineers for the American National Standards Institute, developing and documenting standards for the Open Systems Interconnection. *See* IEEE, ANSI, ECMA and OSI.

ifree *(ATT)* Inode **free**. Obsolete command replaced by fsck. Used to free specific inodes, each containing descriptive information about a file that is used by a system to access and manage that file, on a disk or device. *See* inode and fsck.

IFS 1. Internal field separator. Characters used by shell commands to separate words on a command line. **2.** Environmental variable used in the Bourne and Korn shells to set the value of the internal field separators, e.g. space, tab and new line characters which the shells look for to

separate words. *See* Bourne shell and Korn shell.

IG **I**mage **g**eneration. Class of computer graphics technology that generates photo-quality pictures used in computer-aided training, design, engineering and manufacturing.

iget *(ATT)* Inode **get**. Program called by the namei routine to allocate an inode number to a file. *See* namei, inode and iput.

IGMP *(INET)* Internet Group Management Protocol. Used by a host to inform other hosts on the network of its willingness to accept broadcast messages from a specific group. *See* Internet and IP multicasting.

ignore Electronic-mail variable. *See* .mailrc variables (Appendix F).

ignore action Instruction to ignore a signal. *See* signal.

ignorecase Variable in the ex and vi editors. *See* ic.

ignoreeof 1. **Ignore** **e**nd-**of**-**f**ile. Originally a C shell variable and incorporated in the Korn shell. When set, stops the user from being logged off if the end of file character (Ctrl d) is input. *See* C shell and Korn shell. **2.** Electronic-mail variable. *See* .mailrc variables (Appendix F).

IGOSS **I**ndustry and **G**overnment **O**pen **S**ystems **S**pecification. Proposed Open Systems Interconnection standards specification for protocols jointly developed by the U.S. and Canadian governments and industry, including the Manufacturing Automation Protocol and Technical Office Protocol, X.400, Point-to-Point Protocol, Fiber Distribution Data Interface and frame relay. *See* ISO/OSI, MAP, TOP, X.400, PPP, FDDI and frame-relay.

IGP *(INET)* **I**nterior **G**ateway **P**rotocol. Internet protocol used to connect routers. *See* Internet and router.

i-list Commonly called inode table. *See* inode table.

IMA Interactive Multimedia Association. Trade organization of more than 40 companies that is based in Washington. Establishes and writes standards in multimedia technology. Members include IBM Corp., Apple Computer Inc. and NCR Corp. *See* multimedia.

image copy Exact byte-for-byte copy of a file.

image generation Commonly abbreviated and called IG. *See* IG.

image processing Ability of a computer system to electronically capture any type of image, from handwritten letters to photographs.

imaging model Graphical user interface term for the method used to display graphics, fonts, etc. on a screen. *See* GUI.

imake Improved version of the make program used to compile source code to create, update and maintain application programs. Allows users to customize application programs. *See* make.

IMAP Interactive Mail Access Protocol. Used to send and receive electronic mail between personal computers and UNIX electronic-mail systems. *See* POP.

imapd Interactive Mail Access Protocol daemon. Background program used to manage connectivity and transfer electronic mail between a UNIX host and personal computer.

immersion Feeling of being there created through use of virtual reality. The user has the sensation of being surrounded by and part of the created image and capable of interacting with projected objects. *See* virtual reality.

IMP *(INET)* Interface Message Processor. Initial name for the Packet Switch Node on the ARPANET, a forerunner to the Internet. *See* ARPANET, PSN and Internet.

import To introduce data from one operating system or application program to another, or to modify data from its standard format to an alternate format recognized by a different operating system or application software package. *See* export.

imp pseudo-device Pseudo-device used to support connectivity to the ARPANET. *See* ARPANET and pseudo-device.

impulse Short-term surge of excess voltage, ranging from 100 to 500 volts.

IMS Information management system. Commonly called DBMS (database management system). *See* DBMS.

inbox File designated by an electronic-mail user for storing incoming electronic-mail messages. *See* e-mail.

incremental backup Recording copies of only new files or directories and files that have been modified since the previous backup was made to an alternative storage medium. *See* backup, partial backup and full backup.

incremental file backup Commonly called incremental backup. *See* incremental backup.

indent *(BSD)* Command used to indent and format C language source code. *See* C language.

indentation Word processing term for moving the first character on a line to the right of the left margin by a given number of spaces. *See* margin.

independent software vendor Commonly abbreviated and called ISV. *See* ISV.

index Number, word, etc. which indicates the location of information, e.g. a byte in a file or record, fields in a record, files or records on a disk.

index node Commonly abbreviated and called inode. *See* inode.

indirect block Inode data block used to extend inode block addresses by pointing to other inode blocks instead of user data. Permits files to be larger than the size normally accommodated by the data block scheme of the UNIX file system. *See* data block, inode and block address.

Industry and Government Open Systems Specification Commonly abbreviated and called IGOSS. *See* IGOSS.

Industry Standard Architecture Commonly abbreviated and called ISA. *See* ISA.

indxbib *(BSD)* Part of the refer program package, used to build inverted indices of bibliographic data. *See* refer, addbib, lookbib, roffbib and sortbib.

INed Screen editor program available on IBM Corp.'s interactive systems, including IBM UNIX releases.

inet *(INET)* Abbreviation for the family of protocols used on the Internet network. *See* ARP, ICMP, Internet, IP, TCP and UDP.

inetd *(INET)* Internet daemon. Originally released in the Fourth Berkeley Software Distribution, Third Release. Program started by the Service Access Facility which manages the protocols, addressing, etc. related to connections on the Internet network. *See* Internet, daemon, BSD, TCP/IP, FTP, TELNET and SMTP.

inetd.conf Commonly written as /etc/inetd.conf. *See* /etc/inetd.conf.

infant mortality Jargon term for a computer system that fails within the first few days after installation. *See* DOA.

infocmp *(ATT)* Terminfo compare. Command used to compare and display the contents of terminfo, the collection of files that describe a terminal and the signals used by it. *See* terminfo.

informal standard Commonly called de facto standard. *See* de facto.

information highway Commonly called the electronic highway. Also called The Information Highway and abbreviated TIH. *See* electronic highway.

Information Highway, The Commonly abbreviated TIH. Commonly called the

electronic highway. *See* electronic highway.

information sharing Collective use of data, including both local and distributed data, by users.

information superhighway Jargon term for the National Research and Education Network. *See* NREN.

information systems Commonly abbreviated and called IS. *See* IS.

information technologies Commonly abbreviated and called IT. *See* IT.

information technology Commonly abbreviated and called IT. *See* IT.

Information Technology Association of America Commonly abbreviated and called ITAA. *See* ITAA.

information warehouse Commonly called data warehouse. *See* data warehouse.

inheritance Concept in object-oriented programming that permits developers to identify various objects, e.g. functions performed, and the set of common elements and operations that are shared by these objects. Allows different program functions to use or inherit the characteristics or data of other objects, e,g. if a specific color is assigned to an object in the class, the color is automatically passed to other objects in the same class. *See* object. OOP, class, encapsulation and polymorphism.

init Initialize. Daemon that is the father of all processes in UNIX. The first process that is started when a system is activated. Creates all subsequent processes, watches all terminals and forks, or creates, an additional init process for each user who logs on. Controls the level or state in which the operating system runs. *See* daemon, process, fork, level and state.

INITCLASS *(ATT)* Parameter of the UNIX System V, Release 4 kernel configuration. Sets the system class that will be started by the init daemon when the system starts multi-user processing, e.g. TS for time share class and RT for real-time class. *See* SVR4.x, system class and init.

initdefault Part of the init process for starting the operating system. Sets the level, or state, of the operating system. *See* init, level and state.

initialize To turn on or start, e.g. initialize a computer or printer. Can be either a physical process, in which the user turns on the power switch, or a software process, in which the user enters a command on the keyboard that is sent to the system.

inittab Commonly written as /etc/inittab. *See* /etc/inittab.

ink-jet printer Nonimpact printer. Similar to a dot-matrix printer in that characters, graphs and pictures are created with a series of dots literally squirted onto the paper. Multiple fonts are available for selecting both style and size of print. Can be classified by the flow of ink (continuous or on-demand) and the type of ink (liquid or solid) that it uses. Continuous ink flows all the time, with the excess being drained away. On-demand ink flows only when needed. In contrast to liquid ink, solid ink is a wax that is melted and then squirted out.

INMOS UNIX look-alike developed in the former Soviet Union at the Institute of Control Machines in the early 1980s. Based upon the VAX PDP-11 operating system. *See* MOS, MNOS and DEMOS.

i-node Commonly spelled inode. *See* inode.

inode Index **node**. Also called information node or interior node. Contains file descriptor information (vital statistics) for a single file which the system needs to access and manage the file, e.g. the size and type of the file, where the file is stored, who owns and has access to the file, when last a user accessed the file and when last the inode was updated. All inodes are kept in an inode table. When a user enters a file name to access a file, the system uses the file name to find the inode

number. This will lead it to the file's inode in the inode table. With the information in the inode, the system can locate the file for the user. *See* file descriptor.

inode block Commonly called inode table. *See* inode table.

inode number Commonly abbreviated and called inumber. *See* inumber.

inode table List of all active inodes on the system, maintained in main memory. *See* inode.

input **1.** Data imported into and used for processing in a computer. **2.** To enter data into a computer system.

input error Error made while inputting data into a computer or converting it to a machine-readable form.

input file Source file, the contents of which are used as a command or data for further processing.

input mode Commonly called insert mode. *See* insert mode.

input/output Commonly abbreviated and called I/O. *See* I/O.

input/output device Commonly abbreviated and called I/O device. *See* I/O device.

input redirection When a user, in entering a command line, changes the standard input to include an existing file. For example, a user could send a file called "tnf" through electronic mail to another user, kjohnson, with the following single command line input:

    CLP> mail kjohnson < tnf ⏎

See standard input and command line.

insert Text editor term, meaning to add text or information to a file.

insert mode Text editor mode in which a file can be opened and modified. *See* command mode.

install **1.** *(ATT)* Command used to load binary software (commands) and manual pages to the appropriate directories. *See* binary software. **2.** *(ATT)* UNIX System V, Release V command in the software installation and information management menu. Used to install a new software package. Similar to a function of the pkgadd command. *See* pkgadd.

/install *(ATT)* UNIX System V, Release 4 root file system directory in which the utilities for installing and deleting are mounted, or activated, by the sysadm command. *See* SVR4.x, sysadm and root file system.

installation Steps necessary to activate hardware, an operating system or application software.

installpkg *(ATT)* **Install package.** Program released with UNIX System V, Release 4 for installing standard software. *See* SVR4.x.

Institute of Electrical and Electronics Engineers Commonly abbreviated and called IEEE. *See* IEEE.

Instructional WorkBench Commonly abbreviated and called IWB. *See* IWB.

instruction set Processes required by a computer to function. *See* RISC, CISC and WISC.

instructions per clock Commonly abbreviated and called IPC. *See* IPC.

insulator Commonly called non-conductor. *See* non-conductor.

int C language integer data type. All computers represent numeric data as a string of bits. The number of bits in this string is entirely hardware-dependent and depends on the size of the computer's word. Some older computers had a 16-bit word. Most current computer systems use a 32-bit word. Thus, the length of the computers word determines the length of integer data. Almost all computer systems use the uppermost bit to represent the sign of the remaining bits. If the uppermost bit is on, the remaining bits represent a negative number. If the uppermost bit is off, the remainder of the word is positive. Thus,

on 16-bit systems an int can represent a number between -32768 and 32767 and on 32-bit systems, an int can represent a number between -2147483648 and 2147483647. Since it is frequently useful to have numbers that range from 0 to some maximum value, almost all modern computers implement an "unsigned" integer data type. In unsigned integers, the uppermost bit is NOT used to represent the sign, but rather extends the precision of the data. Thus an unsigned 16-bit integer represents values from 0 through 65535, and an unsigned 32-bit integer represents values from 0 through 4294967295.

integrated CASE Commonly abbreviated and called I-CASE. *See* I-CASE.

integrated circuit Commonly abbreviated and called IC. *See* IC.

integrated development environment Commonly abbreviated and called IDE. *See* IDE.

integrated office software Commonly abbreviated and called IOS. *See* IOS.

Integrated Service Digital Network Commonly abbreviated and called ISDN. *See* ISDN.

integrated testing Process of verifying the interaction of all modules of a software program or computer system. Used to determine if subsystems, hardware, operating systems, application programs, and/or business functions work together reliably and consistently according to the specification.

integrity Protection of software and data files on a computer from unauthorized modification.

Intel 286 Commonly abbreviated and called 286. *See* 286.

Intel 386 Commonly abbreviated and called 386. *See* 386.

Intel 486 Commonly abbreviated and called 486. *See* 486.

Intel 8086 Commonly abbreviated and called 8086. *See* 8086.

Intel 8088 Commonly abbreviated and called 8088. *See* 8088.

Intel Binary Compatibility Specification Commonly abbreviated and called iBCS. *See* iBSC.

Intel Corp. Based in Santa Clara, California, Intel was founded in 1986 and manufactured the first microprocessor. The company is the leading manufacturer of microprocessors, mainly used in IBM Corp.'s personal computers. *See* chart of Intel CPUs.

intelligent gateway Inter- or intranetwork communication traffic cop. Makes message-routing decisions based on known network conditions, e.g. host availability and traffic load.

Intelligent Peripheral Interface Commonly abbreviated and called IPI. *See* IPI.

intelligent terminal Commonly called IWS (intelligent workstation). *See* IWS.

intelligent workstation Commonly abbreviated and called IWS. *See* IWS.

interact *(ATT)* UNIX System V, Release V command in the software installation and information management menu. Similar to the pkgask command. In a file, it collects the questions a software package asks about the system during installation and prepares responses to them before the package is installed. *See* pkgask.

interactive Ability of a program to allow a user to directly interact with a computer. Enables the user to receive an immediate response to an input.

Major Intel CPUs

Chip	Year Introduced	Clock Speed	MIPs	Internal Bus Width	External Bus Width	Number of Transistors
8086	June 1978	5 MHz	0.33	16 bit	16bit	29,000
		8 MHz	0.66			
		10 MHz	0.75			
8088	June 1979	8 MHz	0.33	16 bit	8bit	29,000
		8 MHz	0.66			
286	February 1982	8 MHz	1.20	16 bit	16 bit	130,000
		10 MHz	1.50			
		12 MHz	2.66			
386 DX	October 1985	16 MHz	6.00	32 bit	32 bit	275,000
	February 1987	20 MHz	7.00			
	April 1988	25 MHz	8.50			
	April 1989	33 MHz	11.40			
386 SX	June 1988	16 MHz	2.50	32 bit	16 bit	275,000
	January 1989	20 MHz	4.20			
386 SL	October 1990	20 MHz	4.21	32 bit	16 bit	855,000
	September 1991	25 MHz	5.30			
486 DX	April 1989	25 MHz	20.00	32 bit	32 bit	1,200,000
	March 1990	33 MHz	27.00			
	June 1991	50 MHz	40.70			
486 DX2	March 1992	50 Mhz	40.70	32 bit	32 bit	1,200,000
	August 1992	66 MHz	54.00			
486 SX	September 1991	16 MHz	13.00	32 bit	32 bit	1,850,000
	April 1991	20 MHz	16.50			
	September 1991	25 MHz	20.00			
Pentium	May 1993	60 MHz	100.00	64 bit	64 bit	3,100,000
	May 1993	66 MHz	112.00			
	March 1994	90 Mhz	150.00			
	March 1994	100 Mhz	166.00			

Interactive Mail Access Protocol
Commonly abbreviated and called IMAP. *See* IMAP.

interactive mail access protocol daemon Commonly abbreviated and called imapd. *See* imapd.

Interactive Multimedia Association Commonly abbreviated and called IMA. *See* IMA.

interactive program Any software program that functions by enabling a user to directly interact with a computer, e.g. a spreadsheet or word processing program. Enables the user to receive an immediate response to an input.

interblock gap Blank space on a tape that separates records or groups of records.

InterEUnet Inter Europe UNIX network. Transmission Control Protocol/Internet Protocol long-distance network developed by EurOpen (formerly EUUG), the European UNIX User Group, to connect the UNIX systems of its member countries and companies in Australia, North America and Japan. *See* EUUG.

Inter Europe UNIX network Commonly abbreviated and called InterEUnet. *See* InterEUnet.

interface 1. Relationship or connection, either hardware (physical) or software (protocol), that permits data to be sent or exchanged. May be established between computers and peripherals, e.g. printers, modems or communications systems; or between humans and computers, e.g. keyboards, mice or graphical icons. 2. To manage and control the flow of data. 3. *(ATT)* Program used with the line printing program that outputs the data to be printed. *See* LP. 4. Object Management Group term for the description of an object or an object's functions. *See* OMG and object.

Interface Message Processor *(INET)* Commonly abbreviated and called IMP. *See* IMP.

Interior Gateway Protocol *(INET)* Commonly abbreviated and called IGP. *See* IGP.

interlacing Process of scanning video images on a screen by alternating between odd and even lines, allowing low-resolution monitors to display at higher resolution. Normally use of interlacing results in flicker. *See* flicker and non-interlacing.

interleave 1. To alternate the sequence of accessing memory addresses or disk sectors to reduce access time. Requires two separate memory units or disk sectors to be implemented, one to store and access data with an even number and one for an odd number address. 2. To combine elements of two application programs in a manner that allows them to run at the same time.

interleaving Used in Digital Audio Tape technology as part of the process to reduce and check for data recording errors. Splits data and writes it to two adjacent tracks on a tape, alternating between the two. *See* DAT and ECC.

intermediate system Open Systems Interconnection term for a router, or system responsible for relaying communications between hosts on a network. *See* OSI and router.

Intermediate-system-to-intermediate-system Commonly abbreviated and called IS-IS. *See* IS-IS.

internal file separator Commonly abbreviated and called IFS. *See* IFS.

internal memory Commonly called main memory. *See* main memory.

internals Jargon term for any element considered to be the "guts", or core, of a system, application, etc.

internal signal Signal generated by the kernel in response to events.

internal storage Commonly called main memory. *See* main memory.

International Data Encryption Algorithm Commonly abbreviated and called IDEA. *See* IDEA.

International Electrotechnical Commission Commonly abbreviated and called IEC. *See* IEC.

internationalization Process of creating standard software, e.g. UNIX operating system, that takes into account variations in culture or language. *See* i18n.

International Organization for Standardization Commonly abbreviated and called ISO. *See* ISO.

International Organization for Standardization Development Environment Commonly abbreviated and called ISODE. *See* ISODE.

International Organization for Standards Commonly abbreviated and called ISO. *See* ISO.

International Public Sector Group for Information Technology Commonly abbreviated and called IPSIT. *See* IPSIT.

International Standard Commonly abbreviated and called IS. *See* IS.

International Standards Organization Commonly abbreviated and called ISO. *See* ISO.

International Telecommunication Union Telecommunication Standardization Sector Commonly abbreviated and called ITU-T. *See* ITU-T.

International Telegraph and Telephone Consultative Committee Commonly abbreviated CCITT. Name changed to International Telecommunication Union Telecommunication Standardization Sector in 1993. *See* ITU-T.

internet When spelled with a lower case "i", refers to any collection or interconnection of smaller networks with a router to form a single, large network. *See* router and Internet.

Internet When spelled with an upper case "i", refers to a single large network of smaller federal government, academic and corporate research and development networks, e.g. ARPANET. Also called big I. In 1993 there were approximately 1.8 million computers with over 20 million users connected by over 11,000 networks in 125 countries on the Internet. *See* ARPANET, Internet Protocol Suite, DARPA and internet.

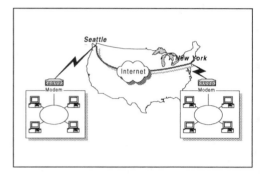

Many companies and organizations use the Internet to transmit data between various offices or networks.

Internet Activities Board *(INET)* Commonly abbreviated and called IAB. *See* IAB.

Internet address *(INET)* Commonly abbreviated and called IP address. *See* IP address.

Internet Control and Configuration Board *(INET)* Original name of the Internet Activities Board. *See* IAB.

Internet Control Message Protocol *(INET)* Commonly abbreviated and called ICMP. *See* ICMP.

Internet daemon *(INET)* Commonly abbreviated and called inetd. *See* inetd.

Internet Datagram Protocol Commonly abbreviated and called IDP. *See* IDP

Internet Engineering Steering Group *(INET)* Commonly abbreviated and called IESG. *See* IESG.

Internet Engineering Task Force
(INET) Commonly abbreviated and called IETF. *See* IETF.

Internet Group Management Protocol
(INET) Commonly abbreviated and called IGMP. *See* IGMP.

Internet host address *(INET)* Commonly abbreviated and called IP address. *See* IP address.

internet layer *(INET)* Protocol layer of the Defense Advanced Research Projects Agency's Transmission Control Protocol and Internet Protocol. Packages data packets, adds a header, determines where the packets are to be sent, and then passes the data to the correct interface for transmission. *See* DARPA, datagram, TCP/IP architecture, TCP/IP and Internet.

Internet MIB Subtree *(INET)* **Internet Management Information Base Subtree.** Hierarchical structure used to describe network devices and their attributes. Used on the Internet network. *See* Internet and MIB.

Internet network model *(INET)* Commonly called ARM (ARPANET Reference Model). See ARM.

Internet Protocol *(INET)* Commonly abbreviated and called IP. *See* IP.

Internet Protocol Suite *(INET)* Collection of standard protocols used to transmit data over the Internet network. Developed under the sponsorship of the Defense Advanced Research Projects Agency. *See* Internet, DARPA, ARM, 1822, ARP, ICMP, IP, RARP, TCP, TCP/IP, UDP and X.25.

Internet Research Task Force *(INET)* Commonly abbreviated and called IRTF. *See* IRTF.

Internet Society *(INET)* Nonprofit organization formed in 1991 to promote the growth of the Internet and to include the use of this network in international research. Responsible for training users, database maintenance and interaction with organizations related to the Internet, specifically sponsorship of the Internet Engineering Task Force and Internet Activities Board. Membership is predominantly composed of individuals; there is limited corporate involvement. Headquarters are in Reston, Virginia. *See* Internet, IAB and IETF.

internetwork Multiple local area networks linked by a router. *See* LAN and router.

Internetwork Packet Exchange
Commonly abbreviated and called IPX. *See* IPX.

Internet Worm Standalone program which shut down over 6,000 computers worldwide in November 1988 after its creator, a former Cornell University graduate student, Robert Tappan Morris Jr., released it on the Internet and ARPANET networks. It took more than two days and hundreds of people to contain and stop the Internet Worm, at an estimated cost of as much as $100 million in indirect expenses and $10 million in direct expenses. Morris was the first person tried and convicted under the Federal Computer Fraud and Abuse Act of 1986. He was sentenced to three years' probation, a fine of $10,000 and 400 hours of community service. The sentence was appealed to the Supreme Court, which upheld it in late 1991. *See* virus, Trojan Horse, ARPANET, Internet and hacker law.

interoperability 1. Originally referred to the successful exchange of data between application software. 2. Ability of a computer system to exchange and use data from another computer system. 3. Complete set of standards for interfaces, services and formats that makes it easier to move data and application software between computer and network systems.

Interoperability Test Suite/88
Commonly abbreviated and called ITS/88. *See* ITS/88.

interpersonal computing Phrase coined by Steve Jobs, co-founder of Apple Computer Inc., to describe the growth of shared or enterprise computing in the 1990s. *See* enterprise computing.

interpreter 1. Program which reads source-code statements from programming languages and translates them into programs that can be read by a computer. Normally custom-designed to work with specific languages. 2. Program which reads and executes instructions that are input by a user or file.

interprocess communication
Commonly abbreviated and called IPC. *See* IPC.

interprocess communications message passing *(POS)* UNIX System V facility used to route messages between two or more cooperating processes. Message queues are created with the msgget system call. Messages are added to the queue with the msgsnd system call and removed from the queue with the msgrcv system call. Integrated into POSIX.4 (real-time operating system) to provide assured communication between processes. *See* POSIX.4 and RTOS.

Interprocess Communications Utilities
Set of programs included in UNIX System V, Release 4 to monitor and manage interprocess communications. *See* SVR4.x and IPC.

interrupt Either a hardware- or software-generated signal that causes a temporary break in the normal flow, or context, of a running system. When an interrupt is detected, the kernel blocks off (and thus prevents) lower priority interrupts, saves the context of the process being run, and services the interrupt. After servicing the interrupt, the kernel restores the process context and resumes execution. If the interrupt detects an error condition, e.g. a divide by zero, the kernel may simply abort the process and select another for execution. *See* signal.

interrupt handler Software used to manage and process interrupt signals. *See* hardware interrupt.

interrupt key Key or combination of keys used to stop a command. Can be control c, Del or delete key, or Rub key.

interrupt latency Length of delay between when an interrupt signal is received and when the computer starts the first instruction of the program run for that interrupt.

interrupt request Commonly abbreviated and called IRQ. *See* IRQ.

interrupt vector Address for the location of the procedures that the system is to follow when it receives a known interrupt. *See* interrupt.

interrupt vector table List of all known interrupt vectors. *See* interrupt vector.

intr Interrupt character sent to the kernel that terminates a running process. *See* process.

intrinsics library X Window System object-oriented library used by the widget library to manage, create and delete widgets. *See* X Window System, widget library and widget.

intro *(ATT)* Introductory section in each of the documentation modules, e.g. commands, routines, etc., that provides an overview, e.g. intro(1) is an overview of programming commands; intro(2), system calls; and into(3), functions and libraries.

i-number Commonly spelled inumber. *See* inumber.

inumber Inode **number**. Two-byte number in a file name which gives either the disk address of a file or the position in the inode table of the inode that provides necessary information to locate that file. *See* inode and inode table.

invisible character Any character without a graphical representation, e.g. the control character for a system that represents a line feed. *See* control character.

invoke Commonly called execute. *See* execute.

I/O **1.** Input/output. Process of communicating or passing data among computers or with peripheral devices, e.g. disk or tape drives, printers or terminals. **2.** Physical device, e.g. port, through which data is communicated.

ioctl *(ATT)* Input/output control. System call used to establish, control and manage input and/or output to devices. *See* I/O, system call and device.

I/O device Any peripheral that allows input and/or output to or from a computer, e.g. a terminal or printer.

I/O redirection Changing the movement of information from the standard output, usually the terminal, to an output device or file selected by the user, e.g. a printer. *See* I/O and standard output.

IOS Integrated office software. Software package which combines a variety of applications, e.g. word processing, spreadsheet, database management and electronic mail, into a single integrated tool.

iostat Input/output statistics. Command used to extract and report on input and output statistics from the operating system kernel, specifically input and output for disk drives and terminals. *See* I/O and kernel.

I/O stream Data required by or resulting from a process, generated in a constant flow or stream.

I/O supervisor Part of an operating system which manages input/output. *See* I/O.

IP *(INET)* Internet Protocol. Provides the protocol for interhost connection over a communications network. Breaks a message into packets, and then addresses, routes and reassembles the packets. Originally developed by the Advanced Research Projects Agency for use on the Internet. Commonly called TCP/IP (Transmission Control Protocol/Internet Protocol). *See* ARPA, Internet and TCP/IP.

IP address *(INET)* Internet Protocol **address**. A 32-bit number which specifically identifies where a host can be found in any network using Transmission Control Protocol/Internet Protocol. Consists of a network address number and host address number unique to the host's network. Networks and network addresses are identified as Class A, B or C, depending upon the network size and functionality. A Class A address indicates a large network, e.g. ARPANET and MILNET; a Class B is a medium-size network, e.g. that of a company like Microsoft Corp.; and Class C is a smaller network, e.g. that of a college or university, or a single host on a network. Class D and E addresses are reserved. *See* Internet, net ID, host ID, domain address and IP multicasting.

IPC Interprocess communication. Ability of a running process to communicate, or exchange data, with other processes. Composed of semaphores, messages and shared memory. *See* process, semaphore, message and shared memory.

ipcrm *(ATT/XEN)* Interprocess communications **rem**ove. Command used to stop selected interprocess communication by removing the identifier of message queues, semaphore sets or shared memory. *See* IPC.

ipcs *(ATT/XEN)* Interprocess communications status. Command used to output status information on interprocess communications currently active on the system, e.g. the amount of shared memory being used. *See* IPC.

IP datagram *(INET)* Basic unit of information transmitted over the Internet network. Consists of a message or data being sent, address of the originator and host, data on the amount of information being passed and if it has been fragmented, etc. *See* Internet, datagram and fragmentation.

IPI Intelligent Peripheral Interface. American National Standards Institute standard for a high-speed parallel bus developed by a group of system and peripheral vendors led by IBM Corp. Defines a standard interface using a 16-bit parallel path between a disk controller and a disk drive for mini- and mainframe computers. *See* ANSI, SCSI and HiPPI.

IP Multicast Backbone *(INET)* Commonly abbreviated and called MBone. *See* MBone.

IP multicasting *(INET)* Internet Protocol **multicasting.** Experimental protocol first proposed in 1986. Used to broadcast information from one host to many other hosts. A single copy of the message is sent with an address that allows the data to be delivered to many receiving hosts. *See* Internet and host group.

IP network number *(INET)* Used to identify a specific network using the Internet Protocol. *See* Internet and IP.

IP next generation *(INET)* Internet Protocol **next generation**. Commonly abbreviated IPng. *See* IPng.

IPng *(INET)* Internet Protocol next generation. Collective term for the proposed replacements for the Internet Protocol, including the P Internet Protocol, Simple Internet Protocol, Simple Internet Protocol-P Internet Protocol, Classless Interdomain Routing and Transmission Control Protocol/User Datagram Protocol with Bigger Addresses. *See* Internet, IP, IP address, PIP, SIP, SIP-P, CIDR and TUBA.

IP router Commonly called gateway. *See* gateway.

IPSIT International Public Sector Group for Information Technology. One of the user organizations formed to defend customers against the standards organizations and the UNIX Wars. An international group of organizations responsible for government procurement specifications that is attempting to obtain a single standard for open system architecture. *See* UNIX Wars, User Alliance for Open Systems and POSC.

iput *(ATT)* Inode **put**. Program that is called when an inode number is released by a file that has been deleted. Returns the number to the free inode list. *See* inode and iget.

IPX Internetwork Packet Exchange. Novell Inc. protocol used to establish, maintain and terminate connections on a local area network. Does not guarantee delivery of data. *See* SPX.

iron Jargon term for computer hardware. *See* big iron.

IRQ Interrupt request. Communication lines reserved for hardware devices to communicate with the central processing unit (CPU) when a device needs CPU time. *See* CPU.

IRTF *(INET)* Internet Research Task Force. One of two task forces of the Internet Activities Board responsible for managing the Internet, and for long-term research and development of technology for operating this network. *See* Internet, IAB and IETF.

IS **1.** Information systems. One of the many terms used to refer to an organization's computer department. *See* DP, MIS and IT. **2.** International Standard. International Organization for Standardization standard, approved by vote by that body's members.

ISA Industry Standard Architecture. Personal computer bus architecture released by IBM Corp. in 1981. Transfers data either 8 bits (XT) or 16 bits (AT) at a time. *See* bus, EISA, local bus, 8-bit computer and 16-bit computer.

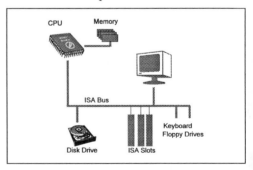

The ISA bus transfers data at a fixed rate of 8 MHz between the CPU and peripherals.

ISDN Integrated Services Digital Network. Set of specifications for end-to-end integrated voice, video, digital data and packet switch data network. Result of an international effort to establish standards spanning national boundaries and interests. Three services are available: B, D and H-channels. A B-channel is used for voice, dial-up access to remote hosts, etc. and operates at a maximum of 64 kilobits per second. A D-channel is used for low-bandwidth packet data and runs at a maximum of 16 kilobits per second. An H-channel is used for multimedia and file transfers, running between 384 kilobits and approximately 2 megabytes per second. There are two ISDN configurations: basic rate interface (BRI), which provides two B-channels and one D-channel; and primary rate interface (PRI), which offers 23 B-channels and one D-channel. ISDN was first implemented in 1986. *See* BRI, PRI and SS7.

ISDN 1 Integrated **S**ervices **D**igital **N**etwork **1**. Also called National ISDN. First national ISDN standard agreed to in 1991. Establishes standards for interoperable equipment. *See* ISDN.

IS-IS

Intermediate-**s**ystem-to-**i**ntermediate-**s**ystem. International Organization for Standardization/Open Systems Interconnection-supported protocol that defines network protocol for routing communication between intermediate systems, or routers, which then send the information to a host. *See* ISO/OSI, router, ES-IS and OSPF.

isize **I**node **size**. Total number of blocks of inodes. *See* inode.

ismpx *(ATT)* Command used with windowing to determine the type of connectivity between the terminal and the system.

ISO Derived from the Greek word ISOS, which means equal, and commonly used as the acronym for the International **Or**ganization for **S**tandardization. The organization also is incorrectly referred to as the International Standards Organization or International Organization for Standards. Approval authority that accepts and certifies international standards for telecommunications. These standards are accepted by some member countries as laws and the codes are strictly enforced. Headquartered in Geneva, Switzerland. *See* IEC and JTC1.

ISO 646 International Organization for Standardization standard for English language character set in which each character consists of 7 bits.

ISO 9000 First of the ISO 9000 Standards. A guideline for selecting quality standards. *See* ISO 9000 Standards.

ISO 9000 Standards Set of standards including both guidelines and requirements for certification of quality management systems. Stems from a British standard called BS 5750, developed in 1979. ISO 9000 Standards were first adopted by both Europe and the United States in 1987. The European version is known as EN29000, and the American as Q-90. The set is composed of five standards: ISO 9000, ISO 9001, ISO 9002, ISO 9003 and ISO 9004, which include several business functions, e.g. contracting, customer support, design, documentation and testing. *See* ISO 9000, ISO 9001, ISO 9002, ISO 9003 and ISO 9004.

ISO 9001 Second of the ISO 9000 Standards. Addresses quality requirements from design to post-installation service. *See* ISO 9000 Standards.

ISO 9002 Third of the ISO 9000 Standards. A reduced version of ISO 9001, addressing only production and installation and excluding design, development and service. *See* ISO 9000 Standards.

ISO 9003 Fourth of the ISO 9000 Standards. Provides quality requirements for only testing and final inspection. *See* ISO 9000 Standards.

ISO 9004 Fifth of the ISO 9000 Standards. A guideline for an overall quality management system. *See* ISO 9000 Standards.

ISO 9660 Commonly called High Sierra specification. International Organization for Standardization standard for compact disk read-only memory. *See* High Sierra specification and CD-ROM.

ISO 10089 International Organization for Standardization standard for magneto-optical media. *See* ISO and M/O.

isochronous Continuous, uninterrupted flow of data that provides constant delivery of audio and video frames and the gaps between frames required for use of motion pictures in multimedia technology. *See* multimedia technology and Max Headroom effect.

isochronous Ethernet Name given to the specification for an Ethernet local area network capable of transmitting data at 100 megabits per second, providing an uninterrupted, constant flow of data needed for multimedia productions. *See* multimedia technology.

ISO conforming POSIX application
(POS) Any application using the Portable Operating System Interface for Computer Environments (POSIX) standard, an approved standard of the International Organization for Standardization. *See* POSIX and ISO.

ISODE International Organization for Standardization Development Environment. Suite of development tools and applications developed in 1986 that complies with Open Systems Interconnection protocols. Makes it easier for developers to application software that can operate over Transmission Control Protocol/Internet Protocol networks. *See* ISO, OSI and TCP/IP.

ISO DP 9945-1 International Organization for Standardization international standard document for system interface. *See* ISO and IEEE P1003.1 working group.

ISO DP 9945-2 International Organization for Standardization international standard document for shells and utilities. *See* ISO, shell, utility and IEEE P1003.2 working group.

ISO DP 9945-3 International Organization for Standardization international standard document for system administration. *See* ISO and IEEE P1003.7 working group.

ISO/IEC Joint Technical Committee 1
Commonly abbreviated and called JTC1. *See* JTC1.

ISO IP International Organization for Standardization Internet Protocol. Jargon term for the ISO Connectionless Network Protocol. *See* ISO, IP, CLNS and CONS.

isolation Method of security whereby users are separated to prevent them from gaining access to one another's accounts.

ISO/OSI International Organization for Standardization/Open Systems Interconnection. Network interconnection model. Specifies protocols for open systems communication between hosts. Jointly developed by the International Organization for Standardization and International Telecommunication Union Telecommunication Standardization Sector, formerly known as the Consultative Committee on International Telegraphy and Telephony. *See* ISO, OSI and ITU-T.

ISO/OSI model Commonly called OSIRM (Open Systems Interconnection Reference Model). *See* OSIRM.

ISO/OSI protocol suite Commonly called OSIRM (Open Systems Interconnection Reference Model). *See* OSIRM.

ISO stack International Organization for Standardization **stack**. Jargon term for the seven layer Open Systems Interconnection Reference Model (OSIRM). OSIRM is a set of protocols developed by the International Organization for Standardization/Open Systems Interconnection for network functions that provide for communication between products of various vendors. *See* OSIRM and ISO/OSI.

ISO TP International Organization for Standardization **t**ransaction **p**rocessing. Also called OSI TP. Jargon term for the

ISO transaction processing standard. Set of standards for performing transaction processing on multivendor and multi-communications platforms. Provides guidelines for the operation of databases, database management and monitor programs. *See* ISO, transaction processing, TP and DBMS.

ISV Independent software vendor. Companies which develop and sell commercial software packages, independent of computer manufacturers.

IT Information technology or information technologies. One of the list of terms, e.g. DP, IS and MIS, that describe computer, communication and information management. Aims to provide all end-users the information they need to do their work.

ITAA Information Technology Association of America. Originally formed in 1961 as the Association of Data Processing Service Organization (ADAPSO). National trade association headquartered in Arlington, Virginia. Composed of more than 500 computer software and service companies. Works with Congress, other federal agencies and state legislatures and agencies on computer-related public policy issues.

italic Style of type in which the characters slant toward the right.

iterate Commonly called loop. *See* loop.

iteration One incident of a task repeated several times.

ITS/88 Interoperability Test Suite/88. Conformance test developed by the 88open Consortium Ltd. Determines if the kernel and library interfaces will work for UNIX systems running on computers using Motorola 88000 chips. *See* ACT/88, AVS/88 and 88open Consortium.

ITU-T International Telecommunication Union Telecommunication Standardization Sector, formerly called the Consultative Committee on International Telegraphy and Telephony. United Nations organization charged with developing recommendations for worldwide standards for interconnecting telephone equipment. Standards established by ITU-T are recommendations and compliance is voluntary. ITU-T recommendations begin with the letter "X", e.g. X.25, X.400 and X.500. ITU-T is also responsible for the V series of modem standards. *See* V standards.

IUUG Irish UNIX User Group formed in 1983.

IWB Instructional WorkBench. On-line UNIX training program that includes standard training modules and also enables users to develop special courses. *See* CBT and learn.

IWS Intelligent workstation. Any terminal with the ability to perform functions independent of the host computer, e.g. a personal computer.

J

jabber Any device on a network that is transmitting incorrect electrical signals over the network. Normally caused by a faulty network interface board on a computer or other node on a network.

jack Connector, either male or female, in a telephone system. *See* RJ-xx.

jaggies Jargon term for the jagged look of lines in computer-generated pictures. Caused by aliasing. *See* aliasing.

jam Signal sent by a workstation or other network device to inform other devices when a packet collision happens while the device is transmitting.

JANET Joint Academic Network. British national research and development network.

Japanese Industrial Standardization Committee Commonly abbreviated and called JIS. *See* JIS.

Jargon File Digest of hacker Jargon terms, which can be read on USENET, an international UNIX bulletin board. *See* USENET.

JCL Job Control Language. IBM batch-oriented process developed in the 1960s. Provides a link between an operating system and application software used to manage processes. *See* TSO.

Jerusalem Also called PLO virus. Computer virus first discovered in Jerusalem's Hebrew University in 1987. Strikes only on Friday the 13th and stops a computer from processing commands.

JES Job Entry Subsystems. IBM batch and print spooling system. *See* spooling.

JIS Japanese Industrial Standardization Committee. Japanese version of the American National Standards Institute, the coordinating and approval body for national standards within the United States. *See* ANSI.

JIT Just-In-Time. Originally a manufacturing buzzword for the use of computer-based estimating tools and manufacturing techniques that are used to match an organization's level of production with the quantity of orders or requirements. Now applied to activities which use multimedia technology, such as training. With a personal computer multimedia package, a worker can receive training in the specifics of any subject, from computer applications to aspects of a production line in manufacturing.

job 1. Several processes which have the same process group identifier. 2. Widely used acronym for process, a program or element of a program running in memory. *See* process. 3. Collection of related processes used to accomplish a specific task.

Job Accounting Utilities Set of programs included in UNIX System V, Release 4, to monitor and measure system usage. *See* SVR4.x and accounting.

job completion message Message sent to a user or another process indicating that the computer has completed a process.

job control Management of jobs, or processes, that are running or are to be executed in the background, e.g. the ability to start, stop or suspend, kill or move a process from foreground to background operation. *See* multi tasking.

job control command Command used to end, resume, stop or suspend, or move jobs between foreground and background operations.

job control commands Following is a list of job control commands:

Command	Description
Ctrl-z	Temporarily suspend a process.
bg	Restart a stopped process in the background.
fg	Restart a stopped process in the foreground.
jobs	Display a list of background and stopped processes.
kill	Kill or terminate a process.
stop	Stop or suspend a process.

Job Control Language Commonly abbreviated and called JCL. *See* JCL.

job control shell Specialized shell that is part of the Bourne shell, used to provide support for job control functions. Provides the tools to manage processes being run in the background, e.g. an extensive formatting program, so a user can run other processes at the same time. *See* background process, jsh and job control.

Job Entry Subsystems Commonly abbreviated and called JES. *See* JES.

job ID Number assigned to a process, or job, so that it can be tracked and managed by a job control shell. *See* PID and job control.

jobs Command used to display a list of all the jobs, or processes, currently running. *See* job.

join 1. Command used to join related lines of text into a new, single line of text. 2. Command used in database operations to create a new database file from the data in two other database files, based on key elements.

Joint Academic Network Commonly abbreviated and called JANET. *See* JANET.

jotto *(ATT)* Command used to start the word game jotto.

journal file Used to maintain the commands and changes to a text or data file. Established in /tmp, the system directory which stores temporary files, whenever a file is opened with the vi editor program. *See* /tmp and vi.

Joy, Bill Co-author, with Chuck Haley, of the first Berkeley Software Distribution, a version of the UNIX operating system developed at the University of California, Berkeley, in the mid-1970s and derived from AT&T Co.'s UNIX Version 6. Also wrote the vi editor program and the C shell. After Joy left Berkeley, he co-founded Sun Microsystems Inc. *See* BSD, vi and C shell.

Joy's Law Attributed to Bill Joy, co-founder of Sun Microsystems Inc. States that the maximum computing power for any year is the number of millions of integer operations per second being equal to the number 2 raised to the power of the current year minus 1,984. *See* Joy, Bill and MIPS.

jsh 1. *(ATT)* Job control shell. Command used to start the job control shell, a specialized shell used to manage processes, or jobs, when they are run in the background. *See* job control shell and job. 2. Abbreviation for job control shell. *See* job control shell.

JTC1 ISO/IEC Joint Technical Committee 1. Committee formed by the International Organization for Standardization and the International Electrotechnical Commission to avoid duplication of effort by the two organizations. Manages international standards related to UNIX. *See* ISO and IEC.

jterm *(ATT)* Command used to reset, or restart, a window when using a window terminal. *See* layers and window.

juice Jargon term for electricity.

jukebox Data storage device available as either a tape, a write-once/read-many optical storage medium or a magneto-optical device that contains several storage media for massive storage and retrieval of data. Name derived from the old record players which stored many records. *See* WORM and M/O.

julian date Calendar date used within computer systems, and by the military and other organizations. Composed of four numbers representing the year and day of the year. The first digit (0 through 9) indicates the year, and the remaining three digits represent the day of the year, e.g. October 5, 1987, would be represented as 7279.

JUS Japan UNIX Society. Japanese UNIX users group.

justification Alignment of the margins on one or both sides of a document. Normally, in a justified document, full lines of text are all flush, or end in the same column on the right-hand side of the page. *See* justify and margin.

Justified text on a page where both the text is flush to the margin on each side of the page.

justify Process of formatting a document. Spaces are automatically added between words so that, for example, all lines of text start in the same column on the left-hand side of a page and end in the same column on the right-hand side.

Just-in-time Commonly abbreviated and called JIT. *See* JIT.

jwin *(ATT)* Command used to determine the size of a window when multiple terminal sessions have been established using windowing software. *See* layers and window.

K

K Abbreviation for **kilo**. *See* kilo.

KA9Q *(INET)* Call sign-like name for the Transportation Control Protocol/Internet Protocol used for an amateur packet radio system. *See* TCP/IP.

Kb Abbreviation for **kilobit**. *See* kilobit.

KB Abbreviation for **kilobyte**. *See* kilobyte.

Kbit Abbreviation for **kilobit**. *See* kilobit.

kbit/s Abbreviation for **kilobits** per second. Commonly written kbps. *See* kbps.

kbps Kilobits per second. Measurement of the rate of transmission of data in 1,000 bits per second. *See* bit.

Kbyte Abbreviation for **kilobyte**. *See* kilobyte.

KDC Key Distribution Center. Computer in a Kerberos based secure network. Issues network access tickets to authenticated users for use of resources on the network. Maintained in a highly secure room to prevent tampering. *See* Kerberos.

keep Electronic-mail variable. *See* .mailrc variables (Appendix F).

keepalive packet Function within the Transmission Control Protocol which allows data to be maintained in the network for a period of time if the destination host or network is not operating. If the destination host or network is still unavailable after that time elapses, the data is returned to the sending host. *See* TCP and keepalive timer.

keepalive timer Used in conjunction with the keepalive packet to maintain information in a network for delivery to a host that is currently not available. Sets the amount of time that information is retained before it is returned to the sender.

keep it simple stupid Abbreviated and commonly known as KISS. *See* KISS.

keepsave Electronic-mail variable. *See* .mailrc variables (Appendix F).

Kerberos User-authentication method developed by the Massachusetts Institute of Technology. First released in 1986, Kerberos originated from the MIT Project Athena in the late-1980s, when it was recognized that network security and access authentication was needed for a campuswide network of workstations. Named after the Greek mythological three-headed hound, Cerberus, that guards the gates of Hades. Combines the use of a password and a private-key encryption to authenticate users, applications and computers on a Transmission Control Protocol/Internet Protocol network. Chosen by the Open Software Foundation Inc. as its network security scheme, and called the Distributed Computing Environment. *See* OSF, DCE, private-key and TCP/IP.

Kermit Data transfer protocol used on UNIX and personal computers. Developed in 1980 by Frank da Cruz at Columbia University to allow different computers to communicate with one another. Sends traffic in a standard packet of 94 bytes. Capable of sending multiple files with a single command. Also can establish a connection between different versions of Kermit by determining the lowest common level of communication protocol. Named for the Muppet character, Kermit the Frog. *See* Xmodem, Xmodem-G, Ymodem, Ymodem-G and Zmodem.

kernel Heart, or core, of the UNIX operating system. Called the traffic cop since it is responsible for managing all the elements that make up the system. Manages the interface between user programs and input/output devices, main memory, scheduling, and maintenance of the file system. Only portion of the UNIX operating system which interacts with the hardware. Therefore, the only part of UNIX which is modified for use by different computers. *See* file system.

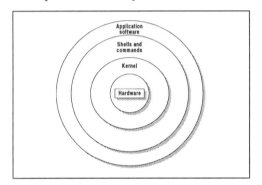

The kernel is at the heart of the operating system. It is the interface between the hardware and the rest of the system.

kernel address space Portion of memory used to store programs and data that can be addressed only by the kernel, the program which manages all elements of a UNIX system. *See* kernel and protected memory.

kernel description file Describes devices attached to the system and the different kernel settings. Each system comes with a standard kernel description file. Can be tailored by the system administrator using the sysdef command. *See* kernel, device and sysdef.

kernel hacker Anyone with the skills and knowledge, plus access permissions, who can modify the way in which the kernel, or core, of the UNIX operating system is programmed.

kernel-level benchmark Standard used to evaluate operating system capacity, throughput and hardware interface. *See* benchmark and user-level benchmark.

kernel map Functionality of the Fourth Berkeley Software Distribution, Third Release which manages page table entries for addressing of user processes. *See* BSD and PTE.

kernel mode Hardware state in which the computer grants specific access rights and privileges to a running process. Used by the operating system to prevent the user from accidentally destroying critical data structures. A process that requires system calls to run must operate in the kernel mode, which permits access to the kernel. *See* kernel and system call.

kernel process Any process created by the kernel, or core, of the UNIX operating system that runs totally within the kernel, e.g. any process that manages the operation and interface between the kernel and system hardware. *See* kernel.

kernel space Area in memory allocated to run kernel operations, e.g. system calls. *See* kernel and system call.

Kernighan, Brian W Invented the name UNIX as a play on MULTICS while he was working on the MULTICS project at the AT&T Bell Laboratories' Computer Research Center in the late 1960s. Along with Alfred Aho and Peter Weinberger, developed the awk programming utility used to manipulate text files. Wrote the C programming language with Dennis Ritchie. Also wrote ditroff, or device independent troff, by modifying the troff preprocessor to run on typesetters, terminals and printers. In 1975, along with Lorinda Cherry, developed eqn, or equation, a troff preprocessor that formats mathematical expressions. In 1981, developed pic which translates a graphics language into troff commands for drawing simple pictures.

With John Bentley, in 1984 developed grap, or graph, which translates data points into pic drawing commands that are used by pic before troff processing. Along with other team members who were involved in the development of UNIX, developed the UNIX-like operating system called Plan 9. *See* MULTICS, Bell Laboratories, Plan 9 and Ritchie, Dennis M.

key 1. Password used during encryption and decryption to gain access to readable data. 2. Lever of a keyboard that is depressed to send an electrical signal representing a specific character to the operating system of the computer.

keyboard Terminal input device which provides direct interface between the user and the system. Has typewriter-like keys, function keys that can be defined by either users or programs, and usually a numeric keypad.

The typical keyboard has 101 keys.

keyboarding Jargon term for using a terminal keyboard to enter data into a computer.

Key Distribution Center C o m m o n l y abbreviated and called DC. *See* DC.

key encryption key Commonly called master key. *See* master key.

keylogin Command used with the Remote Procedure Call of the Network File System to activate, or decrypt, the password used for Data Encryption Standard to access encrypted files. *See* RPC, NFS, DES, client, server, encrypt, decrypt, common-key, conversation-key, public-key, private-key, Keyserver, timestamp, credential, verifier and window.

keyserv Daemon used with a secure Network File Sharing system to store private keys, or passwords, that are part of the authentication process required to log in to another system. *See* NFS and private-key.

Keyserver Function of the Remote Procedure Call used to store a decrypted key for an encrypted file until the user has access to a secure host. A secure connection is made between a client and host by using the keyserv daemon to authenticate each other. *See* RPC, DES, client, server, encrypt, decrypt, common-key, conversation-key, public-key, private-key, keylogin, timestamp, credential, verifier and window.

keystone Distortion on a video monitor resulting in an image being smaller on one side than the other. *See* barrelling, blooming, bowing, convergence, flicker, persistence and pincushioning.

keystroke Process of depressing a key on a keyboard.

Khornerstone Private benchmark suite consisting of 21 tests used to test central processing unit, floating point unit and disk drive operations. Developed by Workstation Laboratories.

KHz Kilohertz. One thousand hertz or 1,000 cycles per second. *See* frequency and hertz.

kill 1. Command used by a system administrator or owner of a process to terminate the process. 2. To erase the command line before executing a command or to stop a process. One of several graphic terms used in UNIX. 3. Signal to delete a line that is sent to the kernel, or core, program which manages the elements of the UNIX operating system.

killall (*ATT*) Command used to stop all active processes. Can be initiated directly or indirectly by the superuser during the shutdown program. *See* superuser and shutdown.

kill character Traditionally, a pound sign (#) or at sign (@), but can be defined by the user. Deletes all inputs on the current command line. *See* kill and erase character.

killer app **Killer app**lication. Jargon term for a software application that is considered to be extremely successful, widely accepted and doing an outstanding job on what it is designed to do.

kill stack Term in the EMACS visual editor program for the buffer which contains as many as the last eight deletions from a text document. *See* EMACS.

kilo Prefix for 10^3 (1,000) or one thousand. Commonly abbreviated K.

kilobit 1,024 bits. Commonly abbreviated Kb or Kbit. *See* bit.

kilobits per second Abbreviated and commonly referred to as kbps. *See* kbps.

kilobyte 1,024 bytes. Commonly abbreviated KB. *See* byte.

kilo instructions per second
Commonly abbreviated and called kips. *See* kips.

kips **K**ilo **i**nstructions **p**er **s**econd. Measurement of central processing unit integer performance, interpreted as the number of instructions, in thousands, per second. *See* mips and gips.

KISS **K**eep **i**t **s**imple **s**tupid. Longstanding management philosophy that the simple approach is easy to use, understand and implement: Don't make the end product too complicated to use.

kludge Commonly spelled kluge. *See* kluge.

kluge Modification to standard software or a new application developed in a hurry with questionable design practices and without using configuration control procedures. Normally done because a system has failed and must be made operational again as quickly as possible. Generally

considered to be of lower quality than a hack. *See* hack.

kluster Group of pages related only by their location in a process' virtual address space.

kmdaemon *(ATT)* **K**ernel **m**emory **daemon**. Special program used for memory management of the operating system kernel. *See* kernel.

Korn shell Standard command interpreter and programming language. Developed by David Korn of AT&T Co.'s Bell Laboratories for System V in 1982. Contains enhancements not found in the Bourne shell. Part of the standard release for System V, Release 4, providing improved functionality, e.g. a history file, command line editing, editing, job control, etc. The default prompt for the Korn shell is the dollar sign ($). *See* Bell Laboratories.

K & R Abbreviation for Kernighan (Brian) and Ritchie (Dennis), both of whom have been instrumental in the development and evolution of UNIX. Ritchie was part of the team that originally developed UNIX, and also developed the C language. Kernighan has been credited with coining the term UNIX as a spoof of MULTICS, and with Dennis Ritchie co-authored *The C Programming Language*, which introduced the C language. *See* MULTICS, Kernighan, Brian W. and Ritchie, Dennis M.

K & R C standard First C language standard, originally documented by Brian Kernighan and Dennis Ritchie. *See* C language, K & R, Kernighan, Brian W. and Ritchie, Dennis M.

ksh 1. *(ATT)* Command used to start the Korn shell. 2. Abbreviation in UNIX which indicates a user is running the Korn shell. *See* Korn shell.

kshdb *(ATT)* **K**orn **sh**ell **d**e**b**ugger. Shell program used to locate and correct errors in other programs, released with the Korn shell. Can be used to debug both Korn and

Bourne shell scripts. *See* debugger, Korn shell and Bourne shell.

K shell Abbreviation and Jargon term for the **Korn shell**. *See* Korn shell.

KUUG **1.** Korean UNIX User Group. Formed in 1983. **2.** Kuwait UNIX Users Group. Formed in 1989 to promote UNIX systems in the Persian Gulf.

L

l *(XEN)* Command used to list the contents of a directory. *See* ls.

l10n Abbreviation for localization, where 10 letters have been removed between the letters l and n. Process of customizing computer languages to accommodate differences in characters, dates, money symbols, scientific symbols, etc. in foreign languages. *See* i18n.

label *(ATT)* Term used to describe the double-tier security classification used in secure UNIX systems. The first tier identifies the level of security, e.g. TOP SECRET or SECRET. The second tier is used to add access restrictions to secure data, e.g. identify who can access the data. *See* Orange Book and SVR4 ES.

labelit *(ATT)* **Label it**. Command used to create, update or read labels on disks or on tape. Puts the file system name and volume number in the superblock, which stores information for maintaining a file system, when creating a new file system. *See* labels, file system, volume number and superblock.

labels **1.** Created by the labelit command. Contains information required to perform backups, e.g. the type and name of the file system. *See* labelit, disk label and tape label. **2.** *(ATT)* Command used in System V/MLS to show the label of a file. *See* privilege and System V/MLS.

Laboratory for Computer Science
Commonly abbreviated and called LCS. *See* LCS.

LAD Legacy data access. Ability to access, update and manipulate data in legacy applications, or older proprietary computer programs carried over to new systems. *See* legacy application.

LADDIS **1.** Group formed by vendors of the Network File System. Name derived from letters in the names of its founders: Legato Systems Inc., Auspex Systems Inc., Data General Corp., Digital Equipment Corp., Interphase Corp. and Sun Microsystems Inc. *See* NFS. **2.** Vendor-independent benchmark for the Network File System running on heterogeneous networks developed by the LADDIS group.

LAFI Look And Feel Independent applications programming interface. Term derived from the development of toolkits to support and provide unique features in the visual appearance and operation of graphical user interfaces, e.g. OPEN LOOK and Motif. *See* API, GUI, OPEN LOOK and Motif.

L.aliases File which contains all the names by which a remote host may be known.

LAN Local area network. Combination of hardware and software components used to interconnect computers and peripherals in a relatively small area. The devices run a compatible communications protocol, e.g. Transmission Control Protocol/Internet Protocol, allowing them to share resources such as printers, mass-storage devices and data. A typical LAN transfers data at 10 megabits per second over a maximum distance of 1 kilometer. *See* TCP/IP and Mbps.

LANG Language. X/Open Portability Guide environmental variable for setting the language used for system messages. *See* XPG.

LAN Group Original name of LAN Group International. *See* LGI.

LAN Group International Commonly abbreviated and called LGI. *See* LGI.

language binding Point during the running of a software program when variables are identified and become part of the process.

LAPI Layered Applications Programming Interface. Approach developed by the IEEE P1201.1 working group. Provides an additional software layer to translate formats between an existing applications programming interface (API) of a graphical user interface (GUI), e.g. one specifically developed for a particular application, and the API of a standard GUI, e.g. the X Window System. *See* IEEE P1201.1 working group, API and GUI.

large grain parallelism Process of solving a very large problem by breaking it down into separate, unrelated problems. An extensive number of computations is required to solve each small part. But if the job was not tackled in this way, the load from the interprocess communications would drastically affect the performance of the computer system. *See* MP, CPU and IPC.

Large Installation System Administrators Commonly abbreviated and called LISA. *See* LISA.

laser disk read-only memory Commonly abbreviated and called LD-ROM. *See* LD-ROM.

laser printer Modern version of a mimeograph machine. Uses a laser beam to burn high-resolution dot-matrix images onto a print drum. The print drum is then covered with ink and the images are transferred through heat and pressure to paper. A selection of fonts allows users to vary the style and size of the type used. *See* font.

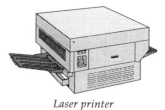
Laser printer

last Command used to display the available record of user logins and terminals used for each login.

lastcomm *(BSD)* Last command. Command used to display a list of the commands that were last executed, in reverse order.

last-in-first-out Commonly abbreviated and called LIFO. *See* LIFO.

last-in-last-out Commonly abbreviated and called LILO. *See* LILO.

last line mode Function within the vi editor program which allows a user to manipulate text or perform searches with commands from the ex line editor program or write and/or exit from the file. *See* vi, ex, command mode and input mode.

lastlogin *(ATT)* Command used to update the file containing a record of each user's last login.

LAT Local Area Transport. Proprietary protocol developed by Digital Equipment Corp. similar to the Internet TELNET protocol for terminal-to-host connection. *See* Internet and TELNET.

latency 1. Delay between when a computer receives an address to which data is to be transferred and when it actually starts the transfer. 2. Time delay in reading or writing data to a disk or diskette caused by the rotation of the device.

layer Grouping of related tasks required for data transmission. Each layer is a level in the International Organization for Standardization/Open Systems Interconnection or Internet Network model, which contain and describe the functionality related to transferring information, e.g. the first, or physical, level includes both the physical and electrical connection with the network and is responsible for setting up the communications connection. *See* ISO/OSI, Internet, OSIRM and ARM.

Layered API Commonly abbreviated and called LAPI. *See* LAPI.

Layered Management Entity
Commonly abbreviated and called LME. *See* LME.

layers 1. *(ATT)* Command used to establish windows or multiple terminal connections between a terminal and a host computer. *See* window. 2. Shell layer command used to display the shell layers. *See* shl.

LBX Low-bandwidth X. Protocol in the Massachusetts Institute of Technology X 11, Release 6 specification for the X Window System to improve the operation of X Window System terminals over lower-speed (9600 baud or less) dial-up connections. No longer includes many of the handshaking functions and information passing used in normal X Window System connectivity over a local area network. *See* X Window System and X11R6.

lc *(XEN)* Command used to list the contents of a directory in columns by file name.

LC_COLLATE Locale collate. UNIX System V, Release 4 environmental variable used to determine how collation commands, e.g. ed, pg, find, join and ls, will function. *See* locale.

LC_CTYPE Locale character type. UNIX System V, Release 4 environmental variable used to set the functions of characters and regular expressions. *See* locale, XPG and regular expression.

LC_MONETARY Locale monetary. UNIX System V, Release 4 environmental variable used to describe the text symbol for local currency, e.g. a dollar sign ($) for

the United States, Canada and Australia; and a pound sign (£) for the United Kingdom. Because currency exchange rates are very dynamic, LC_MONETARY does not provide a mechanism for converting currencies, e.g. dollars to yen. *See* locale.

LC_NUMERIC Locale numeric. UNIX System V, Release 4 environmental variable. Describes the characters and groupings used to punctuate a numeric string, e.g. European readers prefer to see the number 1,234,567.89 punctuated as 1.234.567,89 and Japanese readers prefer 123,4567.89. *See* locale.

LC_TIME Locale time. UNIX System V, Release 4 environmental variable used to set the date and time on which the computer system relies in its operations. *See* locale.

LCD Liquid crystal display. Screen display technology in which liquid crystals are sealed between two panes of glass. The screen is divided into dots that reflect light when electrified. Characters are given a specific electrical charge. LCDs use little electricity and react quickly.

L.cmds System file containing approved commands that can be run by remote systems during a UNIX-to-UNIX CoPy connection. *See* UUCP and Permissions.

LCP *(INET)* Link Control Protocol. Used with the Point-to-Point Protocol (PPP) to establish a PPP connection. Used between requesting device, routers and/or bridges and the device to which the PPP session is attempting to connect. First, determines if the device to which the connection is being made supports PPP. Second, sets connection parameters, e.g. authentication needs and packet size, with the device. Third, used to determine if a higher-level protocol, e.g. the Internet Protocol or AppleTalk, is supported by either the requesting or receiving device. *See* PPP.

LCS Laboratory for Computer Science. Massachusetts Institute of Technology organization for computer research that initially developed the X Window System, a bit-mapped display system for text and graphics. *See* X Window System.

ld Link editor. Command used to combine compiled program modules and libraries into an executable program or a new program module. *See* object library.

L-devices System configuration file which contains descriptions of the communication ports, e.g. line speed and modem description, that are used to make UNIX-to-UNIX CoPy connections. *See* UUCP, L.sys and Devices.

L-dialcodes Optional system configuration file containing defined strings used as substitutes for phone numbers of remote systems that can be called by the UNIX-to-UNIX CoPy programs. *See* string, UUCP and Dialcodes.

LD-ROM Laser disk-read-only memory. Storage medium based upon audio/video laser disks that can store computer data, full motion video and stereo audio.

leading edge Organization or product which uses or is considered to be the most advanced, or state of the art, technology in its class. Can be used to refer to hardware, software, communications media, etc. *See* bleeding edge.

leaf Lowest level of a hierarchical database or file system. *See* root and branch.

learn Simple computer-aided instruction tool for UNIX commands and concepts.

leased line Combination of a telephone and modem that provides a transmission rate of up to 19,200 baud.

least privilege Security principle whereby users or processes are granted the minimum amount of privilege, or a right not normally granted to them, only when needed to complete an action. *See* privilege.

least recently used Commonly abbreviated and called LRU. *See* LRU.

leave *(BSD)* Simple program to remind a user of tasks, meetings, etc.

LED Light emitting diode. Semiconductor device that uses electrical current to emit light. Colored caps can be placed over the optical fiber to create the desired color for specific functions. Used for optical data links and character displays in computers and calculators. *See* LED indicator.

LED indicator Small, flickering colored light used for many functions but primarily to show users that a computer or specific hardware device, e.g. tape or disk drive, is in operation. *See* LED.

left margin Blank space between the left edge of a page and the first column of print. *See* margin and right margin.

legacy application Computer program, e.g. a payroll, inventory or accounting application, that is transferred to a new system from an older, computer information system running under MVS, VMS, etc.

legacy data access Commonly abbreviated and called LAD. *See* LAD.

Legion of Doom Group of UNIX hackers whose members, located across the United States, were indicted as a result of a Secret Service investigation. Members were accused of trying to steal passwords and source code by placing subversive Trojan horse programs in systems, and of illegally obtaining and using telephone calling cards to make long-distance calls. The investigation resulted in convictions and sentences of up to 21 months in prison for one of the members, who was found guilty of breaking into the 911 emergency response network. It also led to controversy over the invasion of computer users' privacy. *See* hacker, Trojan horse, Federal Computer Fraud and Abuse Act of 1986, Operation Sun Devil and EFF.

Lempel-Ziv algorithm Commonly abbreviated and called LZ. *See* LZ.

less Command used to display the contents of a file. Allows the user to view the first screen of data in a file and then choose whether to view the remaining information a screen or a line at a time. Very similar to the more command. *See* more.

less than symbol (<) Used in the command line when a user wants to modify the standard input to include an existing file. For example:

CLP> mail user-name < file name 🗒

will create an electronic-mail message to the user named in the line. The e-mail will contain a file which has been redirected into that message. *See* standard input, command line and greater than symbol.

let Korn shell command similar to the expr command. Used to run all the basic arithmetic commands and conversions between different number bases. *See* expr and base.

letter quality Jargon term for a document output on a device other than a standard typewriter and on which the print quality is equal to or better than that of a typewriter, e.g. daisy-wheel, ink-jet and laser printers. *See* draft quality, near letter quality and dot matrix.

level Indicates who can access the system, e.g. single user level so that only the system administrator can perform functions or multi-user level where all users with accounts can access the system. *See* state and mode.

level 2 Commonly called data link layer. *See* data link layer.

level 3 Commonly called transport layer. *See* transport layer.

level A1 National Computer Security Center's Orange Book verified security level. Level A1 computer operating systems must have tested and documented security under which all code must comply with security requirements. Analysis must include tests for any known methods of gaining unauthorized access to the system. *See* NCSC, Orange Book, level B1,

level B2, level B3, level C1, level C2 and Level D.

level B1 National Computer Security Center's Orange Book labeled security protection. Level B1 computer operating systems must include individual user logins with audit trails for accountability. In addition, all files must include labels that identify security sensitivity and restrictions on use of data. *See* NCSC, Orange Book, level A1, level B2, level B3, level C1, level C2 and Level D.

level B2 National Computer Security Center's Orange Book structured protection level. Level B2 computer operating systems must include architecture specifically designed to limit unauthorized access. Very specific configuration management and system administration tools have to be present to enforce the structured architecture. *See* NCSC, Orange Book, level A1, level B1, level B3, level C1, level C2 and Level D.

level B3 National Computer Security Center's Orange Book security domains. All code in Level B3 computer operating systems must comply with security requirements. In addition, the design must prevent unauthorized access to and reduce the complexity of the operating system. *See* NCSC, Orange Book, level A1, level B1, level B2, level C1, level C2 and Level D.

level C1 National Computer Security Center's Orange Book discretionary security. Level C1 computer operating systems must provide user access limits and separation of users and data. *See* NCSC, Orange Book, level A1, level B1, level B2, level B3, level C2 and Level D.

level C2 National Computer Security Center's Orange Book controlled access security. Level C2 computer operating systems must have individual user logins that provide separate accounts with audit trails to provide individual accountability. *See* NCSC, Orange Book, level A1, level B1, level B2, level B3, level C1 and Level D.

level D   National Computer Security Center's Orange Book controlled access security. Level D computer operating systems have no internal security. *See* NCSC, Orange Book, level A1, level B1, level B2, level B3, level C1 and Level C2.

lex   *(ATT)* Command used to generate C language programs and to perform lexical analysis. *See* lexical analysis.

lexical analysis   Analysis of objects in programs or commands to find patterns of symbols.

lexicographic   Describes sorting that is done by alphabetic sequence.

lf   List files. Command that lists file names in horizontal sequence on the screen.

LGI   LAN Group International. Organization of local-area network distributors. Formed in the United States in 1985 as the LAN Group to act as a consolidated buying service, able to obtain large discounts and improved training and support. In 1987 membership was expanded to Canada, Europe and South Africa. *See* LAN.

/lib   Root directory in which program libraries are stored. *See* library.

library   Group of executable routines maintained on a system that are available for concurrent use by multiple programs, e.g. the UNIX standard I/O package (stdio) and the math library. The use of libraries saves programmers the time and effort of writing common routines repeatedly.

Library function   Alternative name for library routine. *See* library routines.

library routines   Also called library functions. Individual programs maintained in a system's library containing executable programs used to break large computing operations into smaller and more manageable tasks, e.g. the UNIX standard I/O package (stdio) and the math library. The use of libraries saves programmers the time and effort of writing common routines repeatedly. *See* system call.

life cycle   Time span of a software project, from concept development to release of the finished product. There are from eight to 14 phases in a life cycle. The eight recognized core phases are: the start or concept development, analysis, requirement definition, external specification or logical design, internal specification or physical design, development, implementation and use. Phases nine through 13 include documentation, quality assurance and quality control, which are part of the first eight phases. Phase 14 is termination.

LIFO   Last-in-first-out. Common methodology for data management in microprocessor stacks: the last item of data put in is the first to be taken out.

light emitting diode   Commonly abbreviated and called LED. *See* LED.

light pen   Optical device similar in operation to a mouse. Used with a video terminal as a light-sensitive stylus to manipulate data and make command inputs on a screen. *See* mouse.

Light pen

lights-out operation   Also called dark operation or unattended operation. Computer center operations done without constant, direct monitoring by personnel. Normally carried out in an unlit, or dark, room.

lightwave   Digital communication signals transmitted over fiber-optic cables. *See* fiber-optic.

lightweight process   Commonly called multithread process. *See* multithread.

LILO   Last-in-last-out. Common methodology for data management in microprocessor stacks: the last item of data put in is the last to be taken out.

limit *(BSD)* Command used to access the setrlimit system call. Displays system limits and values. *See* setrlimit.

LIMITS File in UNIX System V, Release 4 Basic Network Utilities used to limit the number of uucico, uusched and uuxqt processes that are executed simultaneously. *See* SVR4.x, BNU, uucico, uusched and uuxqt.

line **1.** *(ATT/XEN)* Command used to read a single line of a text file. Can be used to direct the output to the standard output (terminal) or to redirect it to an alternative device or file. *See* standard output and redirect. **2.** Single line of text, which can be as long as 256 characters in UNIX, followed by a carriage return to separate it from the next line.

line address Indicator, flag, number, etc., which specifies the number of a line in a text file during editing.

line discipline Routines used to convert data in the C-list, or character buffer list, to support input and output to a terminal or character device. *See* C-list and cooked mode.

line editing Process of creating and manipulating text one line at a time, using a line editor. *See* line editor.

line editor Program which can only create and manipulate text a single line at a time. Line editors, e.g. ed and ex, can access text by using line numbers or perform global searches for text strings or global search and replacement of text strings. *See* ed and ex.

linefeed Control sequence sent to a printer or terminal. Moves the paper or cursor forward one line, but does not return the print head or cursor to the first column. Can be sent either with a software command or by pressing a button or switch on the printer or terminal.

linefeed key Lever no longer found on many computer keyboards. Normally a user can press the down arrow key or control-j to give a linefeed command. *See* linefeed.

line kill character Commonly called kill character. *See* kill character.

line mode Commonly called cooked mode. *See* cooked mode.

LINENO *(ATT)* **Line** number (**no.**). Korn shell variable. Maintains the current line number in a script before a command is started.

line noise Garbage or spurious characters transmitted over a communications line. Caused by electrical interference, e.g. static electricity, electrical storms, loose connections or crosstalk between different lines.

line number Number assigned to each line in a text file by the editor.

line-oriented editor Commonly called line editor. *See* line editor.

line pitch Measurement in inches or centimeters of the proximity of lines to one another on a page.

line printer Very high-speed printer that is attached to a computer and dedicated to producing large volumes of printed data. Normally can only be used with programs that perform batch processing and batch printing. *See* batch.

Line Printer Spooling Utilities Set of programs included in UNIX System V, Release 4 to manage line printers and how they are used. *See* SVR4.x, classes, filters, forms, operations, printers, priorities, reports, requests, systems and lp.

line range Term used in editor programs to indicate which lines a specific function should begin and end on, e.g. 1,15 w newfile means a function should start on line 1 and end on line 15 and that the contents of those lines should be written to newfile.

line spacing Measurement of the distance between lines of print. Full-line spacing means a blank line the same height as a line of print is placed between lines of print. Most printers also offer both quarter- and half-line spacing. Line spacing can be set in the word processing program. *See* lpi.

lines per minute Commonly abbreviated LPM. *See* LPM.

line wrap Also called word wrapping. Word processing term for the process of automatically wrapping or moving input from the current input line to the next when the maximum number of characters per line is reached.

link 1. Association between a name in a directory and a group of related data blocks pointed to by a single inode. Any file can have one or more links or names. *See* hard link and soft link. 2. Process of combining the compiler output of one or more modules and libraries into a single executable program. 3. System call used to associate a name with an existing file. Ensures that the new name points to exactly the same data blocks as the old. *See* system call.

Link Control Protocol *(INET)* Commonly abbreviated and called LCP. *See* LCP.

link count Number of directory entries referring to a file. *See* link.

link editor Editing program used to combine separately compiled source programs into an executable program. *See* ld.

linked list List of pointers, or areas in computer memory which contains addresses to variables. *See* link.

link encryption Process used to encrypt data only during transmission between nodes on a network. *See* encrypt and node.

linker Program which combines multiple programs into a single unit to accomplish a task. Moves the new program as a single unit into memory to be run.

linking 1. Process of combining programs or operations to perform a task. *See* chaining. 2. Ability to share a file without creating a duplicate file for each user. *See* link.

link layer One of the layers of the International Organization for Standardization/Open Systems Interconnection. *See* data link layer and ISO/OSI.

Linpack Public domain benchmarks that measure the functions of a central processing unit, floating-point unit, memory and compiler. Uses FORTRAN, representing the functionality of mathematical and scientific software programs. *See* FPA and floating point.

lint *(ATT/XEN)* Debugger used to verify the syntax and look for errors in a C language program. *See* debugger.

Linux A UNIX-like operating system for Intel 386 and higher computers that was developed by Linus Torvalds, a University of Helsinki student. The operating system was released in 1992 and is available on bulletin boards free of charge.

liquid crystal display Commonly abbreviated and called LCD. *See* LCD.

LISA Large Installation System Administrators. Annual conference for system administrators of large UNIX systems sponsored by The USENIX Association. *See* USENIX Association, The.

lisp *(BSD)* Command used to interpret a Lisp language program. *See* Lisp language.

Lisp language List processing language. Originally used in symbolic computation, now principally associated with artificial intelligence. *See* artificial intelligence.

list 1. Command used to generate a list of C language source code from an object file. *See* object. 2. *(ATT)* Remote File Sharing and Network File System sysadm menu command used to display shared local or available remote resources. *See* RFS, NFS and sysadm. 3. Physical output or display of the contents of a file or directory. 4. Variable in the ex and vi editors which, when set, allows the user to run a list identifying the location of tab and end-of-line settings. *See* ex and vi. **4.** *(ATT)* UNIX System V, Release V command in the software installation and information management menu. Similar to the pkginfo command. Used to review the questions identified by the interact command which a software package asks during installation. *See* interact and pkginfo.

listen *(ATT)* Also called network listener. AT&T Co.'s port monitor. In UNIX System V, Release 4, its function was expanded to network device monitor as part of the Service Access Facility. Started by the Service Access Controller. Responsible for monitoring incoming connection requests from devices on a network. Devices to be monitored are listed in the netspec file. *See* SVR4.x, SAC, SAF and ttymon.

listener Program in the Networking Support Utilities that monitors a port for network communication and provides the services requested. *See* NSU.

listener address Set of elements, e.g. the port and Internet Protocol address, needed for a listener to be activated. *See* listener and listener address elements.

listener address elements Following are the components of a listener address:

Function Name	Description
Fmly	Four-digit field
Por	Four-digit number for the port the listener is assigned to.
Internet	Eight-digit hexadecimal number which indicates the Internet Protocol address of the host.
Reserved	Unused

listen request Message required for establishing communication with a socket. Initiated by an application software. Results in a listen system call, which is used to notify the system that user communica-

tion will be established and to listen for it. *See* listen system call and sockets.

listen system call System call that notifies the system that a user is attempting to initiate communications against a socket. Without a listen system call, the system would reject any request for communication. *See* sockets.

list hosts *(ATT)* **List hosts**. Remote File Sharing sysadm menu command used to display a list of other hosts in the domain. *See* RFS, sysadm and domain.

list nameserver *(ATT)* **List name server**. Remote File Sharing sysadm menu command used to display a list of name server hosts in the domain. *See* RFS, sysadm, domain and name server.

listpkg *(ATT)* UNIX System V, Release 4 sysadm command used to confirm that a software package has been installed using sysadm commands. *See* SVR4.x and sysadm.

listusers *(ATT)* List users. Command used to display a list of all user logins with a user identifier of 100 or greater in the /etc/passwd file. *See* UID and /etc/passwd.

liszt *(BSD)* Lisp language compiler. *See* Lisp language.

literal Object Management Group term used to describe entities other than objects. A value interpreted "literally" by a compiler, e.g. the number 1234. The opposite of a symbol. *See* OMG and object.

lithography Process of transferring the pattern from a master to another medium, e.g. using photolithography to transfer the pattern from a master die to a silicon wafer to form an integrated circuit. *See* IC.

little language Jargon term for tools which can function independently, e.g. the awk programming language. *See* awk.

LLC **L**ogical **L**ink **C**ontrol. Combined with Media Access Control, it forms the Institute of Electrical and Electronic Engineers Transmission Control Protocol/Internet Protocol equivalent of the Open Systems Interconnection (OSI) data link layer. LLC operates within the OSI protocol stack to connect the protocols in the data link layer to the top layers. *See* MAC, IEEE, TCP/IP, OSI, data link layer and OSIRM.

LME Layer management entity. Application used at each level of the Open Systems Interconnection protocol stack to manage information on the status and configuration of that layer. In addition, it provides information to the process agent for managing the local resource. *See* OSI, OSIRM, process agent and process manager.

ln Link. Command that links two files. Commonly used to allow two users concurrent access to a single file without using lengthy file path conventions. *See* symbolic link and file path.

lo *(INET)* Loopback. Internet interface which allows access to Internet services on the local host to permit either local transfer, testing or analysis of data. *See* Internet.

load average Measurement of the demand for central processing unit capacity. The numeric expression of the average number of jobs (commands, etc.) in the run queue over a specified time, normally 1, 5 and 15 minutes. Tells the system administrator and users how heavily the system is being used and the extent of the backlog in processing, both currently and previously. *See* job and run queue.

load balancing Spreading the work load of a computer system either over common resources or among other computer systems so they work equally hard. *See* process migration.

load device Physical device, e.g. tape or disk, that is identified for loading a program into main memory. *See* main memory.

loader 1. Bootstrapping program. *See* boot and bootstrapping. 2. Jargon term for link editor. *See* link editor.

local Jargon term for local host. *See* local host.

local account User account, or directory, that gives access to only one computer on a network. *See* global account.

local administrative domain *(INET)* Internet term for the domain beneath the second-level domain. Could be composed of one host, many hosts or a subdomain, depending on the configuration of the network. *See* Internet, NIC, domain, root-level domain, top-level domain and local administrative domain.

local area network Commonly abbreviated as LAN. *See* LAN.

Local Area Transport Commonly abbreviated as LAT. *See* LAT.

Local Bus An enhancement to the Industry Standard Architecture and Extended Industry Standard Architecture bus standards. Allows video and other data to be transferred from the central processing unit (CPU) to the video graphics card and other devices. There are two competing local bus standards. Video Electronics Standards Association local bus allows data to be transferred to two devices at the CPU's speed. The Peripheral Component Interconnect bus, supported by Intel Corp., allows the CPU to transfer data at 33 megahertz to 16 devices. *See* ISA, EISA, PCI and VL-bus.

locale Defined components that are used to customize an application for a nationality, e.g. language character set, currency, date and time.

local host Technically, the computer which a user is currently logged into, but normally refers to the computer at the user's location. *See* remote.

localization Commonly abbreviated l10n. *See* l10n.

local middleware Set of services above the operating system used to make development of application software easier. Isolates the application software from the specifics of the version of an operating system, Structured Query Language or graphical user interface. *See* SQL, GUI and network middleware.

local resource File system or directory on a local host that has been opened for access by remote hosts. *See* file system.

local server Term used in the Open Software Foundation Inc.'s Distributed Computing Environment distributed time service. The network host that synchronizes the time for other hosts on a local area network. *See* OSF, DCE, DTS, time server, global server, courier and LAN.

LocalTalk Apple Computer Inc.'s network layer protocol.

Local Technical Group Commonly abbreviated and called LTG. *See* LTG.

locate *(ATT)* Command used to identify possible applicable commands using key words. By entering the key word, all possible commands related to the key word will be identified. For example:

    CLP> locate edit↵

would provide a list of all commands related to edit or editing.

location transparency Database term for information being distributed over multiple physical locations but being accessed as if it were in a single logical location. *See* DBMS.

lock **1.** *(BSD)* Security tool which allows a user to leave a terminal unattended but remain logged on. Prevents others from gaining access to the system through that terminal. Normally terminated by entering the user password. **2.** When a disruption in normal processing has occurred, preventing a user from making further terminal inputs. **3.** System call or mechanism for obtaining exclusive access to a system resource, such as a file or device, e.g. when a user connects to a remote system via telephone line, a lock is established on the port being used. *See* system call.

lockd *(ATT)* **Lock d**aemon, or manager. The lockd of one host communicates with the lockd of another host to establish a communication link for transferring data.

locked inode Information number being used by a process. *See* inode.

lockf *(ATT)* **Lock f**ile. C language library routine that restricts access to a file while an update action is in progress. *See* library routines.

lock files File created when a communication port is in use. Prevents other processes from using the port. *See* uucico.

locking Commonly called database locking. *See* database locking.

LOGFILE System file which contains the record of UNIX-to-UNIX-CoPy activity locally and for remote sites. *See* UUCP.

log files Files used to record system transactions. Also may be generated by application software to maintain audit trails of transactions related to the use of the application.

logger **1.** *(BSD)* Command used to log system messages. **2.** *(OTH)* Shell script used to maintain an on-line system log.

logic **1.** Decision process, which takes into account such factors as assumptions and operational needs, in formulating and designing a software program. **2.** Circuits within an integrated circuit (IC), used to direct the operation of the IC. *See* IC.

logical block One or more physical blocks that appear as a contiguous data block to a file system or database. *See* physical block.

logical disk Disk drive (physical disk) that is divided into areas which the computer operating system considers to be separate and independent disk drives. *See* physical disk and partition.

logical drive partitions Divisions that create multiple logical disks on a physical disk drive. *See* logical disk.

Logical Link Control Commonly abbreviated and called LLC. *See* LLC.

logical unit Number which identifies a hardware device to the computer system. Part of a system's hardware management.

logical unit interface, version 6, release 2 Abbreviated and commonly known as LU6.2. *See* LU6.2.

logic bomb Also called bacteria or rabbits. Program that is maliciously planted in a computer system to cause damage at a certain time or when a preselected event occurs. Aimed at damaging or destroying the computer system through the operating system or breaking the system security.

log in Commonly spelled login. *See* login.

;login: Free newsletter provided to members of The USENIX Association. Contains articles on membership activity and technical papers. *See* USENIX Association, The and Computing Systems: The Journal of the USENIX Association.

.login *(BSD)* System file established in user accounts running in the C shell to establish user variables at the time of login. *See* .profile.

login 1. Command used to establish connection with a computer system by allowing the user to identify themselves to the computer. Started by the getty program. Requests and validates the user's password, and prints the message-of-the-day and the name of the shell. *See* getty, motd and shell. 2. Physical act of gaining access to a computer system or database.

login directory Commonly called home directory. *See* home directory.

login ID Login identifier. Name assigned to a user account, e.g. the login ID for the account assigned to this dictionary's co-author Rockie Morgan is rmorgan. Limited to eight characters, which can be either upper or lower case, but are normally lower case. *See* account.

login name Commonly called login ID. *See* login ID.

login profile File containing the environmental variables that the user uses. *See* .profile, .login and environment variables.

Login script Also called chat script. Field in L.sys that contains a detailed description of what the computer system is supposed to send and receive to make a UNIX-to-UNIX CoPy connection to a remote computer. *See* L.sys and UUCP.

login sequence Sequence of events which must be followed for a user to successfully log in to a system. Varies from system to system.

login shell Shell started by a user when he logs in. The specific shell is identified in the /etc/passwd file. *See* shell and /etc/passwd.

logname 1. System call used to obtain the login name of the current process. *See* system call. 2. *(ATT/XEN)* Command used to retrieve and display the login name of a user.

LOGNAME 1. Environmental variable started by the login process that applies to remote systems which connect to a local host. Contains the name of the account that can be used by the remote host for login 2. Abbreviation for LOGNAME Rule. *See* LOGNAME Rule.

LOGNAME Rule Security mechanism HoneyDanBer UNIX-to-UNIX CoPy and Basic Network Utilities which limits what can be done by the uucico daemon when started as a login. Specifies login names that are restricted for use. Restrictions also can include: sending files only to the /usr/spool/uucppublic directory; preventing access to any files; not sending files to remote systems; and starting only news or electronic-mail commands. *See* uucico, HoneyDanBer UUCP and MACHINE Rule.

Logo Interactive language developed as an offshoot of work related to artificial intelligence. Used primarily for work involving calculations, graphics and processing long lists. *See* AI.

log off To end communication with the computer system.

logoff Commonly spelled log off. *See* log off.

log on Commonly called login. *See* login.

logon Commonly spelled log on. *See* log on.

log out Commonly called log off. *See* log off.

logout Commonly called log off. *See* log off.

.logout System file established in each user account which contains user-defined final notices at time of log off and records time of log off.

long C language integer data type. In general, a long is at least the same length as an int. Most computers represent numbers as a series of bits, each bit representing a power of two, the rightmost bit representing two to the zeroeth power (or one). For example, the number 67 in decimal can be represented as the following bits:

```
1000011
6 5 4 3 2 1 0
(i.e. 1x2 + 0x2 + 0x2 + 0x2 + 0x2 + 1x2 + 1x2 =
64 + 0 + 0 + 0 + 0 + 2 + 1 = 67)
```

The number of bits used to represent a number is its length. On many computer systems, numbers come in two lengths: 16 bits and 32 bits. For simplicity, the C language refers to 16-bit numbers as "short" and 32-bit numbers as "long". On a typical 32-bit computer system, a long is the same as an int and has values ranging from -2147483648 to 2147483647. *See* int.

longitudinal recording Data-recording methodology where tracks of data are recorded along the entire length of a tape. Bits are recorded and electronically clocked, and mechanically aligned with the tape. Can result in unreliable storage

and recovery due to misalignment of heads. *See* helical scan.

long tape New .25-inch magnetic tape developed by 3M Corp. which doubles the amount of tape on a cartridge from 500 feet to 1,000 feet.

long word Unit of data storage equal to two normal words. If a word is 16 bits, a long word is 32 bits, or 32 bits to 64 bits MIPS and DEC Alpha. *See* word.

look 1. Command used to locate lines in a text file containing a specified string, for example:

    CLP> look g file name ⌨

2. Command used to look up words in an on-line dictionary.

look-alike Operating system which includes routines, programs, etc. that resemble UNIX but which did not originate from AT&T Co.'s UNIX code.

look and feel Physical appearance or design (look) and the operation (feel) of a graphical user interface. *See* GUI.

Look and Feel Independent API
Commonly abbreviated and called LAFI. *See* LAFI.

lookbib *(BSD)* Command used to locate references in a bibliography. One of the refer utility commands. *See* refer, addbib, indxbib, roffbib and sortbib.

loop Going in a circle. Used in programming to repeat steps of a program until all the related identified tasks or data elements have been processed. Once this has been accomplished, an exit is initiated and the program either is completed or goes on to the next task. If this is done incorrectly or the application software is corrupted, an endless loop may occur. *See* endless loop.

loopback Process of sending data or information back to the sender. Typically used in error detection, diagnostics and fault analysis.

loop pseudo-device Software test facility used with the ether pseudo-device for Ethernet connectivity. Due to addressing hosts can attempt to send messages (loop) to themselves. When this happens, the loop pseudo-device stops the attempted transmission over the network and sends the message to an internal process for delivery. *See* pseudo-device, Ethernet and loop.

loosely coupled processor architecture Computer hardware design in which each central processing unit (CPU) has its own local memory, making it almost self-sufficient. The CPUs only communicate with one another to get the programs and data needed and then output the results. *See* CPU.

lorder *(ATT)* Command used to display the ordering relation for an object library or archive file. *See* archive and object library.

lossless Data compression method that provides an exact reproduction of the original data.

lossy 1. Jargon term for communications in which a lot of data is lost. 2. Term related to data compression for methods that provide an approximate reproduction of the original data. *See* lossless.

lostfile *(OTH)* Shell script which enables users to obtain the necessary information for recovering a file from a backup. Once the information is gathered, it is mailed to the system administrator. *See* shell script.

/lost+found Directory found in all file systems. Repository where files are automatically placed by the fsck command when a file system has been damaged and the files cannot be restored to their original file addresses. *See* file system and fsck.

loud Describes text printed in upper case.

low-bandwidth X Commonly abbreviated and called LBX. *See* LBX.

lower case Printing term for small letters. *See* upper case.

low res Jargon term for low resolution. Describes a display monitor with a low density of pixels which provides less detailed picture quality. *See* pixel and high res.

low watermark Indicator of the minimum amount of data which can be put into a data buffer before starting an activity, e.g. input/output. Used to manage the flow of data. *See* high watermark.

lp 1. *(ATT/XEN)* Line printer. Command that directs the contents of a file to a line printer. 2. Collection of commands used to manage line printers. 3. Abbreviation for line printer.

LP Line Print. Term for the line printing function of a UNIX system.

lpadmin *(ATT/XEN)* Line printer administration. A line printer system command used to create or configure the line printer spooler system. *See* lp.

lpc *(BSD)* Line printer changes. A Berkeley Software Distribution line printer system command. Used to turn on and off the queuing of jobs and printing. *See* lpr and spooling.

lpc commands *See* Appendix D.

lpd *(BSD)* Line printer daemon. Background program used to schedule print jobs for line printers. *See* lpr.

LPDEST Korn shell environmental variable which identifies the user's default printer.

lpfilter *(ATT)* Line printer filter. Command used to add, change, delete or list the filters used to change a file to a format a printer can process.

lpforms *(ATT)* Line printer forms. Command used to add, change or delete specialized forms; obtain a descriptive list of forms; or, provide or deny access by a user to a form.

lpi Lines per inch. Measurement of the number of lines of print per vertical inch. *See* line spacing.

LPM Line(s) per minute. Measurement of the printing speed of a line printer.

lpmove *(ATT)* Line printer move. Line printer system command used to move line printer requests from one line printer to another. *See* lp.

lpq *(BSD)* Line printer queue. Command used to look at the print jobs that are lined up, awaiting access to a line printer.

lpr Line printer. Command used to direct the contents of a file to a line printer.

lprm Line printer remove. Command used to delete print jobs from a line printer queue.

lpsched *(ATT)* Line printer scheduler daemon. Background program used to manage the printer jobs for a line printer. *See* lp.

lpshut *(ATT)* Line printer shutdown. Line printer system command used to turn off the line printer request scheduler. *See* lp.

lpstart *(OTH)* Line printer start. Command used to turn on a specified line printer so print jobs can be sent to it.

lpstat *(ATT/XEN)* Line printer status. Line printer system command used to obtain the status of print jobs on the line printer(s), the status of printers and other information about the printers, e.g. printer names. *See* lp.

lpstop *(OTH)* Line printer stop. Command used to turn off a specific line printer so no print jobs can be sent to it.

lpsystem *(ATT)* Line printer system. Command used to identify remote systems that can use the line printer services on the local host.

lpusers *(ATT)* Line printer users. Command used to establish the highest priority a user can set for a print job.

LRU Least recently used. Concept used in allocating system resources: the least-used resources are those that are used first for new requirements.

ls List. Command used to output a list of the files or directories within a directory. Has many options that allow a user to obtain different information in various formats.

CLP> ls <<option(s)>> ⏎

lists the information specified by the option(s) for all files in the current working directory.

CLP> ls<<options(s)>> file name(s) ⏎

lists the information specified by the option(s) only for the file specified.

lseek *(ATT)* System call used to position a file at a specific byte (location). *See* system call.

lspriv *(ATT)* List privilege. Command in UNIX System V/MLS used to list privileges. *See* privilege and System V/MLS.

L.sys System configuration file containing a list of remote systems and processes to be followed to make a UNIX-to-UNIX CoPy (UUCP) protocol connection. Used by UUCP to get information the system needs to make connections to remote hosts. *See* UUCP and Systems.

LTG Local Technical Group. Type of organization formed by the USENIX Association to allow its members to work together on technical topics of interest at a local level. *See* USENIX Association, The, SAGE and STG.

LU6.2 Logical unit interface, version 6, release 2. IBM Corp. proprietary Systems Network Architecture protocol for peer-to-peer communication. Set of architectural rules that enables communication between two or more programs on different computers. *See* SNA and peer-to-peer network.

lxref *(BSD)* Lisp cross (x) reference. Command used to display cross references of a Lisp program. *See* Lisp language.

LZ Lempel-Ziv algorithm. Data compression algorithms developed by Abraham Lempel and Jacob Ziv in the late 1970s. Uses variable-length strings with fixed-length codes. LZ-1 and LZ-2 are two commonly used LZ algorithms. *See* LZ-1 and LZ-2.

LZ-1 Lempel-Ziv 1st algorithm. Variation of the Lempel-Ziv data compression algorithms. Uses a method of representing common sets of text by a specific symbol. *See* LZ.

LZ-2 Lempel-Ziv 2nd algorithm. Variation of the Lempel-Ziv data compression algorithms. Uses a method of recording and representing common sets of text by a number. *See* LZ.

M

m Abbreviation for **m**illi. *See* milli.

M Abbreviation for **m**ega. *See* mega.

m4 General preprocessor for source code or text files, written as a replacement for the C preprocessor (cpp). Used to manipulate software written in C language and other languages before it is sent for processing to another program, e.g. an analyzer or compiler. Provides similar functionality to cpp, but is general-purpose enough to be used as a preprocessor for almost any compiled language or text file. *See* cpp.

Mac 1. Registered trademark of Apple Computer Inc. for the Macintosh computer line. **2.** Jargon term for the Macintosh computer. **3. M**ake **a**nother **c**hart. Jargon saying based on the Mac acronym used for the Macintosh computer.

MAC 1. Mandatory **A**ccess **C**ontrol. Protocol specifications that set levels of security for all data maintained on a system and the level of security access for each user. Required in both the Portable Operating System Interface for Computer Environments (POSIX) and UNIX System V, Release 4.1. *See* POSIX and SVR4.x. **2. M**edia **A**ccess **C**ontrol. Set of protocol specifications that outline access control on a network for a specific type of medium. In the Transmission Control Protocol/Internet Protocol, it is used in combination with the Logical Link Control to form the equivalent of the data link layer for communication between two points. MAC is divided into two: one part manages the formation of packets to send data and the other disassembles the packets when the data is received. In addition, MAC manages the communication link. *See* TCP/IP, LLC and data link layer.

Mach Carnegie-Mellon University UNIX look-alike multiprocessing operating system. Originally based on the Fourth Berkeley Software Distribution, Second Release. Current version is based on 4.4BSD. Started as part of a joint project with Digital Equipment Corp. for the Defense Advanced Research Projects Agency. Chosen as the UNIX operating system for NeXT Inc. computers and the proposed UNIX standard by the Open Software Foundation Inc. *See* BSD, DARPA, OSF and MP UNIX.

machid *(ATT)* **Mach**ine **id**entifier. Command used to determine the type of central processing unit when writing a shell script to enhance portability. *See* i286, i386, pdp11, u3b, u3b2, u3b5, u3b15, u370 and vax.

machine 1. Jargon term for a computer. **2.** Key word used in building a kernel to identify the type of computer on which it is to run.

MACHINE Jargon term for MACHINE rule. *See* MACHINE rule.

machine address Also called absolute address. Address for any permanently assigned storage area as part of the system design.

machine check Process that automatically occurs when the computer hardware detects an error in its operation.

machine code Commonly called machine language. *See* machine language.

machine cycle Commonly called clock rate. *See* clock rate.

machine-dependent Commonly called hardware-dependent. *See* hardware-dependent.

machine error Data or data computational error caused by a hardware fault.

machine-independent Commonly called hardware-independent. *See* hardware-independent.

machine-independent shareable files Files that can be accessed by multiple users over a network, regardless of the type of computer each uses.

machine instruction Any instruction that a computer can recognize and process.

machine language Numerical (frequently hexadecimal) representation of bit patterns interpreted by the hardware as instructions, data and memory addresses. Since machine language is very difficult for most people to read or write efficiently, it is represented symbolically by an assembler language or higher level language, e.g. C language. *See* C language, high-level programming language and pseudo-language.

MACHINE rule HoneyDanBer UNIX-to-UNIX CoPy or Basic Network Utilities entry in /usr/lib/uucp/Permissions used to override default uucico restrictions for specified remote systems. When a system is called, the system names and restrictions that are lifted are identified by:

MACHINE=kem-eds:lrc-eds WRITE=/ READ=/

This allows both system kem-eds and lrc-eds, when called, to access and send any files that can be written to or read by others. *See* HoneyDanBer UUCP, LOGNAME, uucico and permissions.

macref *(ATT)* **Mac**ro **ref**erence. Part of the Documenter's Workbench. A command that reads either an nroff or a troff file and produces a cross-reference of the macros used and defined within the files. *See* DWB, nroff and troff.

macro Instructions used to automate repetitious tasks or to combine many operations into one instruction. Among the most common within UNIX are the macros used with the troff and nroff formatting programs. If a macro or specific set of instructions is identified when using these programs, the document will be formatted to conform to the set of instructions in the macro. *See* nroff, troff, mm macros, mp macros and ms macros.

macro call Term used to indicate the start or execution of a defined macro. *See* macro.

macrocode Complex computer instructions.

macro package Defined grouping of macros used to perform a specialized task, e.g. the mm macros, mp macros, ms macros and mv macros. *See* macro, mm macros, mp macros, ms macros and mv macros.

magic Toggled variable in the ex and vi editors. When set, all special characters are treated as special characters during a search operation. *See* ex, vi, toggle, metacharacter and nomagic.

MAGIC One of the gigabit test-bed networks developed by the U.S. government, industry and university representatives. Tests technologies and applications which are used in implementing networks and supercomputers that can transmit gigabits of data per second. Designed to test interfaces for gigabit local area networks and viewing data obtained from multiple locations. Participating in MAGIC are the Department of the Army Future Battle Laboratory and High-Performance Computing Research Center, Digital Equipment Corp., Lawrence Berkeley Laboratories, Minnesota Supercomputer Center, MITRE, Northern Tele-com, Southwestern Bell, Split Rock Tele-com, Sprint, SRI International, University of Kansas and US Geological Service. *See* HPCC, NREN, LAN, AURORA, BLANCA, CASA, NECTAR and VIS-TANet.

magic characters Special characters in the ex and vi editors which, when input, initiate a special function to or in a text file. Similar to metacharacters. *See* metachar-acter.

magic number Number maintained at the beginning of a binary executable file that provides the kernel information about the type and use of the file.

magnetic tape Specially coated tape used to store data from a computer.

magneto-optical Commonly abbreviated and called M/O. *See* M/O.

magtape Jargon term for magnetic tape. *See* magnetic tape.

mail 1. *(ATT)* Command that activates one of the standard electronic-mail pro-grams available with UNIX.

CLP> mail <<option(s)>> user IDs ⏎

is used to generate and send an electronic-mail message to users.

mail

is used to read or review incoming elec-tronic mail. *See* mail and e-mail. 2. *(BSD)* C shell variable used to specify the path-name(s) to be checked for incoming elec-tronic-mail text. *See* MAIL. 3. C shell variable used to check the user's mail file for the arrival of new electronic mail. When set, the C shell checks at a specified time interval (default, 10 minutes), and informs the user with a message, "You have new mail". Also, if set, the C shell checks the user's mail file when the user logs into a system. If electronic mail exists, the C shell informs the user with a mes-sage, "You have mail". *See* C shell and e-mail.

Mail 1. *(BSD)* Pronounced *CAP-MAIL.* The capital M was used to identify Mail as the Berkeley Software Distribution ver-sion of electronic mail. 2. Command used to activate the Berkeley Software Distri-bution electronic-mail program.

CLP> Mail <<option(s)>> user IDs ⏎

is used to generate and send an electronic-mail message to users.

CLP> Mail <<option(s)>> ⏎

is used to read or review incoming elec-tronic mail. *See* mail, e-mail and BSD.

MAIL Environmental variable used with both the Bourne and Korn shells to estab-lish the pathname for the mailbox file of a user.

mailalias *(ATT)* **Mail alias.** UNIX System V, Release 4 electronic-mail program that translates electronic-mail aliases into user electronic-mail addresses. *See* SVR4.x, e-mail, alias and Translate.

Mail Applications Programming Inter-face Abbreviated and commonly known as MAPI. *See* MAPI.

mail alias Shortened format defined by the user or system that lists the users who are to receive the same electronic-mail message. *See* e-mail and alias.

mailbox File containing a user's elec-tronic mail. *See* e-mail.

MAILCHECK Environmental variable used with the Bourne and Korn shells to set the time interval, in seconds, between checks for incoming electronic mail.

mail commands *See* Appendix E.

Mail exchanger Commonly abbreviated and called MX. *See* MX.

mail exploder Part of the mail software used to deliver mailing lists for electronic-mail messages. *See* e-mail.

mailfile UNIX System V file containing the electronic mail for system users.

mail gateway Computer used to pass electronic-mail messages between two or more mail systems on different networks.

mail message Contents of a message sent or received by electronic mail. *See* e-mail.

mailnet Method of distributing software that places a copy of the contents of a tape or diskette in an electronic mail system in the hope it will reach its destination undamaged. *See* sneakernet.

MAILPATH Environmental variable used with the Bourne and Korn shells to set the path for files which contain electronic mail.

mail prompt Separate prompt established when the user executes an electronic-mail program. Default electronic-mail prompts are the question mark (?) for AT&T Co.'s mail, and ampersand (&) for the Berkeley Software Distribution mail. Can be defined by the user. Electronic-mail commands are the only direct inputs which can be made from a mail prompt. UNIX commands can be executed from a mail prompt by generating a new shell. *See* e-mail and prompt.

mail.rc *(ATT)* File found in the /usr/lib/mailx directory that establishes the systemwide electronic-mail variables. *See* .mailrc.

.mailrc **Mail** **r**un **c**ommand. System file established by a user which contains the electronic-mail system variables. Variables established by a user in his .mailrc will override system electronic-mail variables. *See* .mailrc variables (Appendices F and G).

.mailrc variables 1. *(ATT) See* Appendix F. 2. *(BSD) See* Appendix G.

mail router *(INET)* Combination of programs in the Internet network used to deliver electronic mail messages between hosts. *See* Internet and sendmail.

mailsurr *(ATT)* **Mail** **surr**ogate. File found in the /etc/mail directory that contains data used to determine the correct location for an electronic-mail message to be sent.

mail surrogate Routines used to deliver and process electronic mail sent through UNIX-to-UNIX CoPy. *See* UUCP.

Mail Transfer Agent Commonly abbreviated and called MTA. *See* MTA.

Mail User Agent Commonly abbreviated and called MUA. *See* MUA.

mailx *(ATT)* Experimental mail. Command that activates the mailx program, one of the standard electronic-mail programs available with UNIX. mailx is a more advanced and powerful electronic-mail program than mail, based on the Berkeley Software Distribution Mail program.

    CLP> mailx <<option(s)>> (user IDs) ⏎

is used to generate and send an electronic-mail message to users.

    CLP> mailx <<options(s)>> ⏎

is used to read or review incoming electronic mail. *See* mail and e-mail.

main First routine called when a C language program is started. First line of a program that identifies exactly where a program is to start execution and may call other functions from a library to complete its task.

mainframe Large computer capable of processing extremely huge amounts of data at very high speeds. Term derived from the large frames that were once used to support the weight of the hardware associated with large computers.

main memory Also called internal storage, internal memory, primary storage or main storage. Memory location within the central processing unit where programs and data are placed when they are being run or used. *See* CPU, RAM, ROM and memory board.

main storage Also called core, internal memory, internal storage, main storage or primary storage. Area in which system activity, e.g. running of programs and data manipulation, takes place. Temporarily holds data on which the computer is to act, after which the data is either deleted or returned to secondary storage. *See* CPU, memory, memory board, RAM, ROM and secondary storage.

major device number Number that specifically identifies the type of device and device driver for each device being used, e.g. disk, tape or terminal. *See* device driver and minor device number.

major mode EMACS term for the modes used to manage the editing of various text formats such as Lisp or C language, troff, etc. *See* EMACS, minor mode, Lisp language, C language and troff.

major page fault When text or data has to be taken from disk instead of memory. *See* paging, page fault, virtual memory, dirty and minor page fault.

make 1. Command used to compile source code to create, update and maintain application programs. *See* executable and object. 2. Jargon term for the process of changing programmer's code into instructions that can be understood and executed by a computer.

makecats *(ATT)* Command used to preformat manual pages which describe the function and use of UNIX commands. *See* man and catman.

makedbm **Make** database **map**. Command used for initial development of a Yellow Pages database file. *See* YP and YP map.

makedev C language library routine used to make or replace device special files. *See* library routines, shell script and special file.

makefile Set of rules, including source files, object files and dependencies, used by the make utility. *See* make.

makekey *(ATT/XEN)* **Make key**. Command used by programs to generate the key or password for file encryption. *See* crypt.

malicious logic Macro term for harmful software, e.g. Trojan horses, worms and viruses. *See* Trojan Horse, worm and virus.

malloc Memory allocation. C language library function used to request allocation of memory for a program or process. *See* library routines and free.

Maltese Amoeba Virus activated on March 15 and November 1 each year that overwrites the first four sectors of a hard drive or disk drive.

man 1. Manual macro. Part of the Documenter's Workbench set of text formatting programs. Set of macros usually found in /usr/lib/tmac/tmac. Used to format and display manual pages. *See* DWB and manual pages. 2. Command usually found in /usr/bin/man used to display manual pages. *See* manual pages.

MAN Metropolitan area network. Expanded local area network which provides integrated real-time data, voice and image transmission at speeds greater than 1 megabit per second at a range of up to 50 kilometers. *See* LAN.

managed object Representation of a network resource containing a definition of the resource and what its responsibilities are on a network.

Management Agent Toolkit UNIX System Laboratories Inc.'s development tools. Provides developers a means to create management systems for heterogeneous local or wide area networks.

management console Commonly called management station. *See* management station.

Management Information Base
Commonly abbreviated and called MIB. *See* MIB.

management information systems
Abbreviated and commonly known as MIS. *See* MIS.

Management Request Broker
Abbreviated and commonly known as MRB. *See* MRB.

management station **1.** Also called management console, central console or console. Any console on a network with the ability to direct or control nodes on a network. **2.** Also called SNMP management station. Node on a Simple Network Management Protocol network that constantly polls agent software for information about devices on the network. *See* agent and SNMP.

Mandatory Access Control
Abbreviated and commonly known as MAC. *See* MAC

mandatory argument Argument which a command needs to function, e.g. the mkdir command must have a file name as an argument in order for it to work.

mantissa Fractional part of a logarithm, e.g.:

.2 is the mantissa of 7.2

manual pages On-line documentation for commands found on the computer. Manual pages with special commands used by a system or user can be added.

Manufacturing Automation Protocol
Commonly abbreviated and called MAP. *See* MAP.

Manufacturing Execution Systems
Commonly abbreviated and called MES. *See* MES.

many-to-one character mapping
Concept in locale development of application software where multiple characters are recognized as a single character. *See* locale.

map **1.** Command used to create a vi macro. *See* vi, macro and unmap. **2.** Network File System term for a file containing the mount points and their resources, to be used by the automounter program. *See* NFS, mount point and automounter. **3.** To relate a piece of data, e.g. a network address, to a physical site or location.

MAP **1.** **M**anufacturing **A**utomation **P**rotocol. One of the first attempts to have nonproprietary communications protocols for manufacturing applications. Developed by General Motors Corp. in the mid-1980s and has become an International Organization for Standardization/Open Systems Interconnection protocol for use of token bus local area networks. *See* ISO/OSI, token bus and LAN. **2.** **M**ainframe **A**lternative **P**rogram. Project begun in 1991 by the Hewlett-Packard Co. to provide Reduced Instruction Set Computing-based UNIX systems capable of competing with mainframe computers. *See* RISC.

MAPI **M**ail **A**pplications **P**rogramming **I**nterface. Microsoft Corp.'s application programming interface for sending electronic mail between clients and/or servers and applications running Microsoft Windows. *See* OCE, VIM, e-mail and API.

mapping **1.** Logical placement of data into memory, on a disk or terminal, in a specified fashion. *See* format. **2.** Predefined layout of logic to ensure a program or function can progress step by step and be completed accurately.

mapping translation table File containing user identifiers and permission used by the Remote File Sharing system to determine the level of access to the network by remote users. *See* RFS and idload.

maps Database files in the Network Information Service containing the data records or index file maintained by the master server on the network. *See* NIS.

margin Blank space at the top, bottom, right or left side of a page between the edge of the page and the character or graphic closest to that edge.

mark Place holder or invisible marker in a text contained in the editing buffer. Can be used to indicate where a section in a file starts, where data should be inserted or where work should be continued. In some types of goto commands, mark points show the user where to go, as well as which line to return to. *See* goto.

mark-and-sweep algorithm Algorithm used to clean up object code. Marks each known or referenced object in the code. After the marking is finished, it goes through the code again and removes those objects that have not been marked. *See* object code and algorithm.

markup Process of annotating changes or commenting on elements of a document. Originally referred to handwritten comments made on printed copies of documents. *See* specific markup and SGML.

martians Jargon term for packets that somehow end up on the wrong network. *See* packet.

mask Master pattern composed of chrome and glass used in photolithography to create the circuit of an integrated circuit. *See* IC, lithography, photolithography and reticle.

masquerading Commonly called spoofing. *See* spoofing.

Mass860 Group of companies including IBM Corp., Ing. C. Olivetti and Samsung, which support the Intel i860 Reduced Instruction Set Computing architecture. *See* RISC.

massively parallel processing
Commonly abbreviated and called MPP. *See* MPP.

Massive Open Systems Environment Standards Commonly abbreviated and called MOSES. *See* MOSES.

mass storage device Hardware device, e.g. diskettes, tapes and hard disk drives, used to store large quantities of information, e.g. software programs and data.

master Computer host on a network that manages or sets parameters for other computers on the network. *See* slave and timed.

master device Any hardware device which manages or controls other devices,

e.g. controllers manage the operation of disks and/or tape drives. *See* slave device.

master key 1. Key word used in building a kernel to identify tape controllers connected to the system bus. *See* kernel. 2. In the Data Encryption Standard, the program used to encrypt the key, or password, for gaining access to an encrypted file. *See* key and DES.

master map File containing the names and configurations of remote resources using the Network File System. Used in conjunction with automounter to identify a remote resource and what is required to make it available on the system. *See* NFS, direct map and automounter.

master VAR Value-added reseller who provides support to other VARs. Normally a national organization that supports local or regional VARs. *See* VAR.

MAU Multiple Access Unit. Mode on a Token Ring network which provides port access to the network. *See* Token Ring.

MAXCLYSYSPRI *(ATT)* UNIX System V, Release 4 kernel configuration parameter used to set the maximum global priority of system class priorities. *See* SVR4.x and system class.

Max Headroom effect Jerky movement of video combined with the audio and video not being synchronized. Results from inconsistency in delivery of audio and video frames and the gaps between the frames. Named for a 1980s television character, best known for his role in a soft drink commercial. *See* multimedia technology and isochronous.

maximum file descriptors Limit determined and set by the system administrator on the maximum number of files that can be simultaneously opened by a process. *See* file descriptor.

Maximum Transmission Unit
Commonly abbreviated and called MTU. *See* MTU.

maxproc parameter Parameter that defines the maximum number of processes a user can run simultaneously. Part of the kernel description file. *See* kernel description file.

maxusers Key word used in building a kernel to establish the maximum number of simultaneous users allowed on a computer system, maximum number of processes a single user can have running, etc.

Maxuuscheds Maximum file transfer daemon schedulers. File in the /usr/lib/uucp directory on HoneyDanBer UNIX-to-UNIX CoPy systems that sets the maximum number of schedulers that can be run at the same time. *See* uusched and HoneyDanBer UUCP.

Maxuuxqts Maximum UNIX-to-UNIX execute daemons. File in the /usr/lib/uucp directory on HoneyDanBer UNIX-to-UNIX CoPy systems that sets the maximum number of UNIX-to-UNIX execute daemon processes that can be run at the same time. *See* uuxqt, daemon and HoneyDanBer UUCP.

maze *(ATT)* Command used to build random mazes.

mazewar Advanced graphical version of the dungeon game rogue that allows multiple players. *See* rogue.

MB Megabyte. Measurement of storage or communications transmission capacity equal to 1,048,576 bytes.

MBone *(INET)* Internet Protocol Multicast Back**bone**. Network developed by the Internet Engineering Task Force for experiments with broadcasting messages. Experiments began in 1974 using packet networks to broadcast voice messages. The tests have progressed to the broadcasting of multimedia data. *See* Ethernet, broadcast and IP multicasting.

mbox Mail **box**. Default system file which contains the electronic-mail messages received from other users that have been read and saved. *See* e-mail.

Mbps Megabits per second. Abbreviation for 1 million bits per second. Measure-

ment of data or communications transmission rate.

Mb/s Commonly written Mbps. *See* Mbps.

Mbyte Megabyte. Commonly abbreviated MB. *See* MB.

MCA 1. Music Corp. of America. *See* definition 2. 2. Defunct acronym for Micro Channel Architecture. In 1990 MCA (Music Corp. of America) asked IBM Corp. to stop referring to Micro Channel Architecture as MCA. IBM agreed to do so. *See* Micro Channel Architecture.

MCAE Mechanical computer-aided engineering. Technique used in mechanical engineering that employs computers in the conceptual phase of the development process. *See* CIM.

MCAP Mission critical applications. Application software that is critical to the operation and survival of a company or other organization. Applications determined to be MCAP will vary among businesses and industries.

MCDA Micro Channel Development Association. Organization started in October 1990 to speed up the development and release of Micro Channel products by sharing technology. Original founders included 14 companies, sometimes referred to as the Gang of 14. They included IBM Corp., Intel Corp., NCR Corp., NEC Technologies Inc., Ing C. Olivetti and Siemens-Nixdorf. *See* Micro Channel Architecture.

mcs *(ATT)* Manipulate comment section. Command used to modify the comment section of an object file. *See* object.

MD5 Message Digest algorithm 5. Algorithm used in the Simple Network Management Protocol to provide authentication on each packet for system security. With a system-generated authentication, users are prevented from modifying data on the network. *See* SNMP.

MDT Motif Development Tool. Commonly called UnixWare Motif Development Tool. *See* UnixWare Motif Development Tool.

mean time between failure Commonly abbreviated and called MTBF. *See* MTBF.

mean time to failure Commonly abbreviated and called MTTF. *See* MTTF.

mean time to repair Commonly abbreviated and called MTTR. *See* MTTR.

mechanical computer-aided engineering Commonly abbreviated and called MCAE. *See* MCAE.

media Plural of medium. *See* medium.

media access unit Commonly abbreviated and called MAU. *See* MAU.

medium Any physical means used to store data from or iput data to a computer, e.g. tape, CD-ROM discs, disk drives diskettes and the now outdated computer cards and punch tape. Plural of medium is media.

meg Jargon term for megabyte, abbreviated MB. *See* MB.

mega Prefix for 10^6 (1,000,000) or one million. Commonly abbreviated M.

megabit One million (1,000,000) bits or binary digits of information. *See* bit.

megabits per second Abbreviated and commonly known as Mbps. *See* Mbps.

megabyte Commonly abbreviated MB. *See* MB.

megaflops Commonly abbreviated and called MFLOPS. *See* MFLOPS.

megahertz Commonly abbreviated MHz. *See* MHz.

me macros Macros for education. Text-formatting macro developed by Eric Allman and included in the Berkeley Software Distribution *(BSD)*. Included in the BSD utilities which are part of System V, Release 4. *See* text formatter, mm macros, BSD and SVR4.x.

memall *(ATT)* **Mem**ory **all**ocation. Routine used to allocate physical memory. *See* physical memory.

memcntl **Mem**ory **control**. System call used to control or modify virtual memory allocation. Used to mark memory pages as shared or private, and to set read/write protection for each page. *See* system call.

memfree *(ATT)* Routine used to free physical memory. *See* physical memory.

Memo Distribution Facility
Commonly abbreviated and called MMDF. *See* MMDF.

Memorandum Macros Commonly abbreviated and called mm macros. *See* mm macros.

memory Abbreviation for main memory. *See* main memory.

memory address Number identifying a specific location within memory. *See* physical memory address and virtual memory address.

memory allocation Process used by a kernel to determine how much memory is to be given to each process.

memory board Computer board that contains memory chips which store information and operating instructions.

memory fragmentation When a page or process has to be split in memory because there is insufficient available space to accommodate the size of the page. The divided parts are stored in noncontiguous memory addresses. *See* paging.

memory-free list Commonly called free list. *See* free list.

memory image Commonly called core dump. *See* core dump.

memory management system
Components of an operating system used to manage the memory of a computer. Controls the allocation of memory for process requirements.

memory management unit Component of computer hardware responsible for running the memory management system.

memory map Commonly called swap map. *See* swap map.

memory resident Any program or data currently in main memory. *See* main memory.

memory segment Grouping of addresses that are adjacent to one another.

menu Display of choices of computer commands.

menu driver Software program that displays a list of commands that are easily understood by most users and can be used to direct the computer to perform a specific function or functions.

menu tree Hierarchical set of command menus in which the commands become more specific at each lower level, e.g. the System V, Release 4 Service Access Facility menu.

merge 1. *(BSD)* Command used to combine the changes made in two separate files into a third file. 2. To combine two or more files into a single file. 3. To combine any portion of one file, from characters to lines, with any portion of another file.

MES Manufacturing Execution Systems. Automated manufacturing system used to manage the manufacturing processes required to physically produce a product. *See* CIM.

mesg 1. Command used to display or modify permission of other users to send messages using the write, talk or wall commands. Unless otherwise specified, the default permits receipt of messages. For example:

    CLP> mesg -n ⏎

The -n means no, or to turn off receipt of messages; a -y means yes, or permit receipt of messages. *See* write, talk and wall. 2. vi editing variable that, when set, de-

nies other users permission to directly communicate with the user while in the vi editor. *See* vi.

message 1. Medium used to transfer text or information from a computer or another user to a terminal. In UNIX there are numerous categories of messages. *See* motd, mesg and error message. 2. Data sent by one process to another as part of interprocess communication. *See* IPC, msgctl, msgget, msgrcv and msgsnd.

message-based middleware
Commonly called middleware. *See* middleware.

message buffer Area of memory used to store all system messages sent to a console terminal. In many UNIX systems, the console terminal must be turned on to receive these messages. If it is not, the message buffer will fill up and cause the system to crash. *See* crash.

Message Digest algorithm 5
Abbreviated and commonly known as MD5. *See* MD5.

Message Handling Service Commonly abbreviated and called MHS. *See* MHS.

Message Handling System Commonly abbreviated and called MHS. *See* MHS.

Message Handling System-Directory Services Commonly abbreviated and called MHS-DS. *See* MHS-DS.

message line Commonly called status line. *See* status line.

message of the day Commonly abbreviated and called motd. *See* motd.

message-oriented middleware
Commonly abbreviated and called MOM. *See* MOM.

Message Oriented Middleware Consortium Organization formed in May 1993 by seven companies, led by Digital Equipment Corp. and IBM Corp. Aims to provide alternatives to the Open Software Foundation Inc.'s Distributed Computing Environment for managing the interface between applications and the operating system. Specifically promotes messaging-based middleware and standards that enable applications to communicate between remote computer systems. Other members include Covia Technologies, Momentum Software Corp., PeerLogic, Inc. and Systems Strategies, Inc. *See* DAD, MOM, middleware, OSF and DCE.

message passing Term related to distributed multiprocessing operating systems for communications between tasks. *See* MP, threads and task.

message store Element of the X.400 standard. Temporary storage area for electronic-mail messages that is used when the receiver's host is not working. Developed by the International Telecommunication Union Telecommunication Standardization Sector, formerly known as the *Consultative Committee on International Telegraphy and Telephony. See* ITU-T, X.400, UA, MTA and access unit.

message transfer agent Commonly abbreviated and called MTA. *See* MTA.

metacharacter Any character that is used in a pattern search as a substitute for an unknown character. Metacharacters act as wild cards with special meaning to the UNIX operating system. They should not be part of an input or command line, unless either they are being used for a specific function, such as redirect, or great care is taken. For example:

CLP> rm * ⏎

would result in all the user's files being deleted. The meaning of a metacharacter can be overridden by placing a backslash (\) immediately before the metacharacter. For example:

CLP> find / -name more*tst ⏎

would search for any file starting with more and ending with tst, while

CLP> find / -name more*tst ⏎

would search for any file named more*tst. Metacharacters may be the same or vary

between utilities, e.g. regular expressions in ed, ex, vi, sed, grep, egrep and awk or search and replace operations in ex and sed. Examples include the dot or period used by all regular expressions to match a single character, and the plus used only in egrep and awk to match one or more of characters before the plus. *See* regular expression, quoting, command line, asterisk, dot, question mark, bracket, braces, plus, caret, dollar, backslash, parentheses, ampersand, tilde, escape and shell.regular expression, quoting, command line, asterisk, dot, question mark, bracket, braces, plus, caret, dollar, backslash, parentheses, ampersand, tilde, escape and shell.

metacomputing Forming a distributed processing system by linking hundreds or thousands of computers on a national or international network. Software on each computer in the network provides the ability to share resources with other computers when necessary. Specialized software on the network is used to identify and transfer required resources from one computer to another.

method 1. How something is done. 2. Object Management Group term for a program that responds to a request. *See* OMG and request.

metoo Electronic-mail variable that, when set, results in the user receiving a copy of any electronic-mail message sent. *See* .mailrc variables (Appendices F and G) and e-mail.

metrics 1. Established standards against which performance can be measured, e.g. "Analysts must develop reliable metrics to determine if the new program is effective". 2. Numeric measurement of an event, meaning the actual numbers.

metropolitan area network
Abbreviated and commonly known as MAN. *See* MAN.

MFLOPS Millions of floating point operations per second. Also called megaflops. Measurement of central processing unit floating-point performance. Originated from a benchmark developed by Linpack.

mh Mail Handler. Electronic-mail program developed by the Rand Corp. in the late 1970s. *See* e-mail.

MH Message Handling System. Alternative abbreviation. More commonly abbreviated and called MHS. *See* MHS.

mhrmail Restricted electronic-mail packet based on the Rand Mail Handler and developed by the Free Software Foundation. *See* rmail, mh and FSF.

MHS 1. Message Handling System. Sometimes abbreviated MH. X.400 standard developed by the International Telecommunication Union Telecommunication Standardization Sector, formerly known as the *Consultative Committee on International Telegraphy and Telephony*. Originally created in 1978 by Stockton Gaines and Norman Shapiro of Rand Corp. Enhanced by Bruce Borden and released internally in the Rand Corp. in 1979 and to the public domain in 1982. Consists of a user agent, message transfer agent, access unit and message store used to help in creating, sending, reading, filing and managing electronic-mail messages. *See* ITU-T, X.400, UA, MTA, access unit and message store. **2.** Message Handling Service. Alternative to the X.400 electronic-mail handling protocol developed by Action Technologies Inc. Used by Novell Inc.'s local area networks for electronic-mail handling. *See* e-mail, X.400 and LAN.

MHS-DS Message Handling System-Directory Service. Process used by X.400 message transfer agents to acquire information from remote directories and then route traffic to them. *See* MHS, X.400 and X.500.

MHz Megahertz. Measurement of a unit of frequency equal to 1 million hertz or 1 million cycles per second. *See* frequency and hertz.

MHZ Alternative abbreviation for megahertz. Most widely accepted abbreviation is MHz. *See* MHz.

MIB Management Information Base. Central repository, or document, describing the management or administrative function software used within the devices and network management stations that contain the definition of objects, devices and their addresses, operational parameters, etc. of a network, e.g. the Internet MIB-I is the first version of the Internet Simple Network Management Protocol management information base. MIB-I is based upon the objects and attributes in use by Transmission Control Protocol/Internet Protocols network users. The standard was agreed to in May 1990. Also, the Internet MIB-II is the second version of the Internet Simple Network Management Protocol management information base. MIB-II adds the extensions missing in MIB-I and expands the type of media and devices supported by over 150. The standard was agreed to in August 1991. In addition, vendors develop enterprise MIBs, called extended MIBs, for products they have developed in compliance with the MIBs. *See* Internet, TCP/IP, SNMP, IP and extended MIB.

Michelangelo Much-publicized virus that attacked unprotected personal computers on March 6, 1992, claimed by some to be in celebration of Michelangelo's 500th birthday. Due to the advanced warning and steps taken by U.S. computer users, damage was done on fewer than 50 computers. Among the most prominent organizations in the United States affected by Michelangelo were Southern Illinois University and the Department of Agriculture. Most of the damage was done in Egypt, South Africa, Australia, China, Japan and Great Britain. The virus is memory-resident and attacks both boot sectors and partition tables for hard disks. When it was activated on March 6, it reformatted the entire system hard drive, overwriting it with random characters from system memory. *See* virus, Stoned and Jerusalem.

micro 1. Jargon term for microcomputer. *See* PC. 2. Prefix for 10^{-6} (1/1,000,000) or one-millionth. Represented by the symbol *u*.

Micro Channel Architecture I B M Corp.'s 32-bit personal computer bus architecture which offers greater speed. *See* bus and throughput.

Micro Channel Development Association Abbreviated and commonly known as MCDA. *See* MCDA.

microcode Lowest-level computer hardware language in which a computer instruction set is written. Uses instructions such as "load x into address register, read memory from address register, compute logical and on bit 1 of register x and register y do etc."

Microcom Networking Protocol Commonly abbreviated and called MNP. *See* MNP.

microcomputer Commonly called PC (personal computer). *See* PC.

microfloppy Formal name for a 3.5-inch diskette. *See* diskette and minifloppy.

microkernel Set of hardware-specific operating system functions upon which other kernel functions are implemented. Can be broken up; portions of the kernel may be at different locations and run on different central processing units. *See* kernel.

microprocessor Central processing unit located on a single chip which can perform standard computer activities, e.g. arithmetic, logic and control functions. *See* chip.

Microprocess with Interlocking Pipeline Stages Abbreviated and commonly known as MIPS. *See* MIPS.

microprogramming Breaking down of large, complex computer instructions into smaller instruction sets that are easier to understand and use. *See* macrocode and microcode.

microsecond One millionth (1/1,000,000) of a second.

Microsoft Disk Operating System Abbreviated and commonly known as MS-DOS. *See* MS-DOS.

middleware 1. Also called message-based middleware. Set of services independent of the operating system that are used to make development of application software easier, e.g. drivers and application programming interfaces. Isolates the application development from the specifics of an operating system or networking protocol, providing the communication requirements related to distributed applications. First appeared with the release of IBM Corp.'s Systems Application Architecture and Digital Equipment Corp.'s Network Application support in the late 1980s. Current examples include Atlas, Open Network Computing, Distributed Computing Environment and Windows Opens Systems Architecture. *See* network middleware, local middleware, API, Atlas, ONC, DCE and WOSA. 2. Software located between client and server computers that can be used to retrieve data from the server and translate it to a format which can be used by an application, if required.

migration backup When one type of backup method is initially used, then changed to another type.

Migration Guide UNIX System V, Release 4 documentation that provides a historical perspective on the UNIX System V operating system and relationships with the Berkeley Software Distribution and XENIX systems. *See* SVR4.x, BSD and XENIX.

Military Network *(INET)* Abbreviated and commonly known as MILNET. *See* MILNET.

milli Prefix for 10^{-3} (1/1,000) or one-thousandth. Commonly abbreviated m.

millions of floating point operations per second Commonly abbreviated and called MFLOPS. *See* MFLOPS.

millions of integer operations per second Commonly abbreviated and called mips. *See* mips.

millisecond One-thousandth (1/1,000) of a second.

MILNET *(INET)* **Mil**itary **Net**work. Department of Defense computer hosts on the Internet. Originally, military networks were part of the Advanced Research Projects Network. In 1984 the MILNET became a separate network. *See* DOD, ARPANET and Internet.

MIL-STD-1777 *(INET)* **Mil**itary **Stand**ard **1777**. Document developed in the early 1980s by the Department of Defense that contains the definition for the Internet Protocol standard. *See* IP and Internet.

MIL-STD-1778 *(INET)* **Mil**itary **Stand**ard **1778**. Document developed in the early 1980s by the Department of Defense that contains the definition for the Transmission Control Protocol standard. *See* TCP and Internet.

MIL-STD-1780 *(INET)* **Mil**itary **Stand**ard **1780**. Document developed in the early 1980s by the Department of Defense that contains the definition for the File Transfer Protocol standard. *See* FTP and Internet.

MIL-STD-1781 *(INET)* **Mil**itary **Stand**ard **1781**. Document developed in the early 1980s by the Department of Defense that contains the definition for the Simple Mail Transfer Protocol standard. *See* SMTP and Internet.

MIL-STD-1782 *(INET)* **Mil**itary **Stand**ard **1782**. Document developed in the early 1980s by the Department of Defense that contains the definition for the TEL-NET Protocol standard. *See* TELNET and Internet.

MIMD **M**ultiple **I**nstructions, **M**ultiple **D**atamachine. Also called multiple-instruction, multiple-data. Massive parallel processing architecture in which the processors work as a team, solving large prob-lems by dividing them up. Each processor has its own memory. The number of processors in a MIMD system varies from 16 to 2,000. Each processor manipulates different data independently. *See* massively parallel processing and SIMD.

MIME *(INET)* **M**ultipurpose **I**nternet **M**ail **E**xtensions. Internet Activities Board standard to send and receive messages with audio, video, non-ASCII text, etc. for the Transmission Control Protocol/Internet Protocol. An extension to the Simple Mail Transfer Protocol. *See* Internet, IAB, TCP/IP and SMTP.

mimicking Commonly called spoofing. *See* spoofing.

mini Jargon term for a minicomputer. *See* minicomputer.

minicomputer Middle-sized computer normally used for one specialized function. A standard minicomputer has computing power equal to that of a mainframe but lacks the mainframe's high processing speed. Depending on its make, model and configuration, a minicomputer can handle from four to more than 1,000 users.

minifloppy Formal name for a 5.25-inch diskette. *See* diskette and microfloppy.

minimum color Color mode of a computer color monitor in which 4 bits are stored for each pixel. Enables 16 distinct colors to be displayed. *See* color mode, pixel, pseudo color, high color and true color.

minor device number Number which specifically identifies the device to be used to the device driver. Every special file in the /dev system directory has a unique major and minor device number combination. For disks, the major device number is the disk number and the minor device number is a disk partition. For terminal controllers, the major device number is the controller and the minor device number is the individual port on the controller. *See* device driver and major device number.

minor mode EMACS term for the modes used to set personal preference options within the emacs editor program, such as automatic save, height and width of the screen display, etc. *See* EMACS and major mode.

minor page fault A page fault occurs when a process references a page, text or data in its virtual memory that is not resident in real memory. A minor page fault occurs when that page has been marked as not recently referenced and will be flushed to disk. The page is then reclaimed. *See* paging, page fault, virtual memory, dirty and major page fault.

mips Millions of instructions per second. Sometimes referred to as the meaningless indicator of performance. Often provides a misleading measurement of central processing unit integer performance because 1 mip is usually equated with 1 clock cycle per second. However, on many hardware systems, a single instruction may take several clock cycles to complete. Mips are quoted as a means of comparing one manufacturer's computer to another's, and always quoted (and defined) in the seller's favor. *See* gips and kips.

MIPS Microprocess with Interlocking Pipeline Stages. Stanford University research project started in 1983 that lead to both the development of the Reduced Instruction Set Computing chip and the founding of MIPS Computer Systems Inc. when project members decided to sell the chip in 1984. *See* ACE.

Mips ABI Group Originally called the Apache Group and composed of eight computer companies that were members of the defunct Advanced Computing Environment. Renamed the Mips SVR4 Special Interest Group in 1992. Again renamed the Mips ABI Group in 1993, which has grown to 17 members. Formed as a result of an internal disagreement over architectural issues among ACE members, some of whom supported UNIX System V, Release 4, while others backed the Open Software Foundation

Inc.'s OSF/1 operating system. Members include AT&T Co., Computer Systems, NEC Corp., Ing. C. Olivetti, Prime, Pyramid Technology Inc., Siemens-Nixdorf, Sony Corp., Tandem Computer Inc., UNIX Internationals and UNIX System Laboratories Inc. *See* ACE, OSF, OSF/1 and SVR4.x.

Mips SVR4 Special Interest Group
Commonly abbreviated and called MSSIG. *See* MSSIG.

mirroring Commonly called disk mirroring. *See* disk mirroring.

MIS Management information systems. Recent buzz phrase for an organization's computer center. Previously called DP, or data processing. A future name could be DIPS or Decentralized Information Processing Systems. *See* FEDUP, mini, micro and PC.

mission critical applications
Commonly abbreviated and called MCAP. *See* MCAP.

MIT X Consortium Commonly called X Consortium. *See* X Consortium, The.

mixed protocol stack Using some of the layers of one networking approach with some of those of another networking approach, e.g. mixing the Internet and International Organization for Standardization/Open Systems Interconnection protocol layers. *See* OSIRM and ARM.

mkconf *(ATT)* Make configuration. Pre-System V program used to configure device code to computer hardware. *See* config.

mkdir Make directory. Command that allows users to create new directories.

mkfifo Make fifo. C language library routine used to make new FIFO special file used by multiple processes to pass information from one process to another. *See* library routines, FIFO and IPC.

mkfs Make file system. Command used by system administrators to create new file systems on a logical disk. Creates the superblock, inodes, free list and root directory. *See* file system, logical disk, superblock, inode, free list, root directory and newfs.

mkmsgs *(ATT)* **Make messages**. Command use to create a text string for messages in the local messages database.

mknod *(ATT/BSD/XEN)* **Make node**. System call used to create special files, e.g. device drivers for disks or tapes, and named pipes. *See* system call, special file, named pipe, creat, FIFO and device driver.

mkpart *(ATT)* **Make part**ition. Program used to display, update and maintain data used by disk drivers to access a disk. *See* partition.

mkpriv *(ATT)* **Make priv**ilege. Program used to establish user security for UNIX System V/MLS. *See* privilege and System V/MLS.

MKS Toolkit Commercially available software package developed by Mortice Kern Systems Inc. that provides UNIX-like features to personal computers using either the MS-DOS or OS/2 operating system. *See* PolyShell.

mkunix *(ATT)* **Make UNIX**. Program used to create and configure a UNIX kernel.

mkvtoc **Make VTOC** (volume table of contents Command used by the system administrator to create VTOC partitioning or write it to a new disk. *See* VTOC and SA.

MLisp **M**ock **Lisp** (List processing language). Lisp language interpreter built into many versions of the EMACS editor. Many EMACS editing primitives, such as cut, paste, indent, C language expression, etc., are implemented as MLisp functions. *See* Lisp language and EMACS.

mm *(ATT)* Shell script used to print or display documents formatted with the mm macros. *See* shell script and mm macros.

MMDF **M**aryland **M**emo **D**istribution Facility. More commonly called the Memo Distribution Facility. Program based on the Simple Mail Transfer Protocol and used to manage delivery of electronic-mail messages. *See* MTA, SMTP and e-mail.

MMF **M**ultimode **f**iber. One of the two types of fiber cable used with a Fiber Distributed Data Interface network. Capable of transmitting optical signals over multiple paths on the cable at 200 megabits per second over a distance of up to 10 miles. *See* FDDI and SMF.

mm macros **M**em**orandum **macros**. Part of Documenter's Workbench. Formatting or text processing macros used to create standard letter and memorandum formats. Can be used with either the nroff or troff programs to format text. Document layout is controlled by dot (.) commands, e.g. .ce to center text; these are read and acted on by either nroff or troff to produce a finished text document. *See* DWB, nroff and troff.

mmt *(ATT)* Shell script used specifically with the troff text formatting program to create a typeset document created with mm macros. Similar to the mm shell script. *See* shell script, mm, mm macros and troff.

mnemonic **1.** Code used to assist in remembering a specific instruction or operation. **2.** Assembly language instruction represented by a character string instead of its machine representation, e.g. BEQ (branch if equal) for (0xff). *See* assembly language.

MNLS **M**ulti-**N**ational **L**anguage **Sup**plement. A UNIX System V, Release 4 enhancement that allows developers to create UNIX programs in one of 18 foreign languages. *See* SVR4.x.

MNOS First UNIX look-alike developed in the former Soviet Union by the Advanced Training Institute of the Ministry of Automobile Industry in the early 1980s. Initially based on Version 6, then upgraded with the release of Version 7. *See* INMOS and DEMOS.

MNP Microcom Networking Protocol. Industry standard protocol for data compression, error detection and correction developed by Microcom Systems Inc. Offers 10 classes of features, e.g. Class 1 for error correction and detection for half-duplex, and Class 2 for full-duplex. Classes 1 through 5 are public domain, and are the same as the V.32/V.42 standards developed by the International Telecommunication Union Telecommunication Standardization Sector, formerly known as the *Consultative Committee on International Telegraphy and Telephony*. *See* ITU-T, full-duplex and half-duplex.

/mnt *(ATT)* UNIX System V, Release 4 root file system directory where file systems are temporarily mounted. *See* SVR4.x and root file system.

mnttab Commonly written as /etc/mnttab. *See* /etc/mnttab.

M/O Magneto-optical. Also spelled MO or M-O. Technology related to magnetically assisted optical data storage. M/O disks are 31/2- or 51/4-inch cartridge disks that provide high density, speed and reliability of optical recording, and are erasable. They can hold up to 650 megabytes of data, and allow access to that data in 30 to 100 milliseconds. *See* WORM.

mode 1. Attributes that identify a file's type and access permissions. *See* file type and permissions. 2. State or operating condition of an editor program. *See* editor, insert mode and command mode.

modem Modulator, demodulator. Device used for data communications over telephone lines. Converts analog (telephone) signals to digital (computer) signals and vice versa. *See* ACU, acoustic couple modem, auto answer modem, demodulation and modulation.

External modem

modem control When a computer provides the necessary signals to operate a modem for connecting terminals to the computer with asynchronous serial lines. *See* signal and modem.

modification date Date a file was changed. *See* access date and creation date.

modify *(ATT)* Command in the Network File System or Remote File Sharing sysadm menu used to modify shared local resources or to mount remote resources. *See* NFS, RFS and sysadm.

modulation Process of converting digital computer data into wave-like analog data, e.g. voice, for transmission over a telephone line. *See* modem and demodulation.

Moira Relational database developed as part of the Massachusetts Institute of Technology's Project Athena. *See* Project Athena.

MOM Message-oriented middleware. Software specifically designed to transfer data or requests for data between applications that run on distributed computer systems. *See* Message Oriented Middleware Consortium, middleware and DAD.

monacct *(ATT)* Monthly accounting. Accounting system shell script used to create the monthly accounting summary. *See* shell script.

monitor **1.** Also called VDT, VDU, teletype, tube, CRT or terminal. Commonly called terminal. *See* terminal. **2.** To watch or oversee a program or computer system.

Monitor

moo Command used to start the word game moo.

Moolit **M**otif **O**pen **L**ook **I**ntrinsics **T**oolkit. Commonly abbreviated and called OLIT. *See* OLIT.

Moore's Law Observation made by Gordon Murphy, the vice chairman of Intel Corp., that the number of transistors installed on a silicon chip has doubled every 18 months since the 1960s. *See* IC.

more Originally, a command that allowed a user to look at a file one screen (normally 26 lines) at a time. In UNIX System V, Release 4 invokes command line options, e.g. move forward a full or half-screen using d and Ctrl-d, and backwrd using b and Ctrl-b. *See* SVR4.x and less.

MORE Environmental variable that is checked by the more command, when executed, to determine the line options available to the user. *See* more.

MOS Operating system developed at the Hebrew University of Jerusalem.

mosaic *(INET)* Family of client programs used with the World Wide Web server program to distribute information on the Internet. Like a real mosaic that is made up of bits and pieces to form a whole picture, the mosaic client programs are used to access distributed information on the Internet to form and provide a complete picture. *See* WWW and Internet.

MOSES **M**assive **O**pen **S**ystems Environment **S**tandards. International organization founded in April 1992 by British Telecom, Burlington Coat Factory Warehouse, Millipore Corp., Oracle Corp., Sequent Computer Systems Inc. and US WEST NewVector Group Inc. Formed to identify and develop standards for common methods, tools, utilities, policies and procedures used in operating large UNIX data centers.

motd Message of the day. Message that appears when a user first logs into a system. Normally input by the system administrator for administrative announcements related to the system, e.g. to notify users of planned outages. Every time a user logs in, the motd is displayed, unless it has been suppressed.

Moth-Eye Surface design of write-once/read-many optical disks based on the structure of the eye of a moth. A layered honeycomb design that provides better light-absorbing properties when a laser writes data to the disk. *See* WORM.

Motif Graphical user interface definition developed by the Open Software Foundation Inc. Defines how the windows, icons, coding, etc. should look and operate. *See* GUI, OSF, icon, OPEN LOOK and VUE.

Motif window manager Commonly abbreviated and called mwm. *See* mwm.

motion parallax Appearance of objects, at different distances and fixation points. These objects appear to be moving by varying amounts when viewed from left to right along the horizontal, or x, axis.

mount **1.** System call that is used to activate a file system. *See* system call and file system. **2.** *(ATT/XEN)* Command used by the system administrator to make a file system or disk active on either a local system or remote system, as a part of the Distributed File System. Until the mount command has been run, the file system is not accessible by users. *See* file system, umount and DFS. **3.** Command in the Network File System or Remote File Sharing sysadm menu used to open remote resources for automatic and immediate access. *See* NFS, RFS and sysadm. **4.** Process of adding a separate file system to a computer. *See* file system.

mountable file system File system which can be added to the computer. *See* mount and file system.

mountall *(ATT)* **Mount all.** Program used to mount, or activate, multiple file systems at the same time on local systems or as part of the Distributed File System for remote systems. *See* DFS and file system.

mountd Mount daemon. Background program used in a Network File System (NFS) network that is started when the NFS is switched to multiuser operation. Responds to a request to mount, or activate, resources identified in the share table. *See* daemon, mount, /etc/dfs/sharetab and NFS.

mount point Any directory in which a file system is mounted, or activated. *See* mount and mountable file system.

mount table Table that contains a list of all file systems currently in use.

mouse Hand-operated input device used with personal computers, graphics terminals, workstations and X Window System terminals. Separate from but used as an extension of a keyboard to enter and manipulate data. By moving the mouse, a user can position a pointer on the screen and choose commands, select text, draw, etc.

A mouse is a pointing device that is useful in working with graphical user interfaces.

mousemgr *(ATT)* **Mouse manager.** Daemon used with X Window System terminals to monitor the motion of a mouse

over a surface, compute its new position and detect when buttons on the mouse are pressed. *See* mouse, X Window System and daemon.

move 1. *(ATT)* Command in the UNIX System V, Release 4 Framed Access Command Environment file system operations menu. Used to relocate a file from the current directory to another specified directory. *See* SVR4.x, FACE, file system and current working directory. **2.** To relocate data within a file.

move-up Process of changing either an application or an update to an application from test status to production, e.g. adding or deleting functionality or modifying programming code.

MP Multiprocessing. Distributing the work load on a system by using more than one processor chip. Provides faster throughput and greater reliability, and allows more users to simultaneously access data. *See* throughput, task, threads, parallel processing, loosely coupled processor architecture and tightly coupled architecture.

mp macros Macro developed by the Pentagon to format military documents. Normally found only on U.S. military computer systems.

MPP Massively parallel processing. Process of combining hundreds or thousands of processors, each with its own dynamic random access memory, to work on problems. Enables systems to be scaled to support hundreds or thousands of users; to store and transmit gigabytes to petabytes of data; and to support from hundreds to tens of thousands of transactions. *See* DRAM, parallel processing, MIMD and SIMD.

MPTN Multiprotocol Transport Networking. Protocol developed by IBM Corp. that provides the ability for applications written to run on one type of protocol to run on others, e.g. IBM's OS/2 server operating system and MVS mainframe operating system.

MP UNIX Multiprocessing **UNIX**. Modified UNIX operating system designed to take advantage of hardware architecture which allows the work load on a system to be distributed using more than one processor chip. *See* MP.

MRB Management Request Broker. Open Software Foundation Inc.'s Distributed Management Environment facility. Used by other applications to initiate various operations, e.g. to generate reports. *See* OSF, DME and DCE.

mrouted *(INET)* Multcast **routed**. Packet routing programs used to permit UNIX workstations to route a single message that is broadcast to multiple hosts on a network. *See* Internet and IP multicasting.

MRP Materials Requirements Planning. Forerunner to Manufacturing Resource Planning. Computerized methodology limited to automating the computation of materials requirements. *See* MRP-II.

MRP-II Manufacturing Resource Planning. Computerized methodology to automate management of factory production, from ordering raw materials to monitoring production schedules. *See* CIM.

ms Abbreviation for **milli**second, or one-thousandth (1/1,000) of a second.

MS-DOS Microsoft Disk Operating System. De facto standard for personal computer operating systems. First released in 1981, it is a single-task and single-user operating system used to control the disk, keyboard, video and program interface operations for personal computers. Originally developed as 86-DOS for Seattle Computer Products. The rights to 86-DOS were purchased by Microsoft Corp.

msgctl Message control. System call used in interprocess communication to manage the flow of messages among processes. *See* system call, message, IPC, msgget, msgrcv and msgsnd.

msgget Message get. System call used in interprocess communication to retrieve a queue of messages. *See* system call, message, IPC, msgctl, msgrcv and msgsnd.

msglist Message list. Electronic-mail message(s) that are to be manipulated by an electronic-mail command. *See* e-mail.

msgop Message operation. System call that manages the interprocess communications for message operations. *See* system call.

msgrcv Message receive. System call used in interprocess communication to read a message in a queue. *See* system call, message, IPC, msgctl, msgget and msgsnd.

msgsnd Message send. System call used in interprocess communication to send a message to a queue. *See* system call, message, IPC, msgctl, msgget and msgrcv.

ms macros First widely used text formatting macro. Provides a layout for a standard manuscript. Developed by Mike Lesk in 1974 and available in the Documenter's Workbench text formatting programs. *See* text formatter, macro, mm macros, me macros and DWB.

MSSIG Mips SVR4 Special Interest Group. Originally called the Apache Group, renamed MSSIG in 1992 and then renamed the Mips ABI Group in 1993. *See* Mips ABI Group.

mt *(BSD)* Command used to control magnetic tape devices. Functions include rewind, unload (or off-line), forward space a record or file, backspace a record or file, or write a tape (end-of-file) mark.

MTA Message Transfer Agent. Also called Mail Transfer Agent. Element of the X.400 standard. The part of the electronic-mail system which routes e-mail messages to their destinations. Developed by the International Telecommunication Union Telecommunication Standardization Sector, formerly known as the *Consultative Committee on International Telegraphy and Telephony*. See ITU-T, e-mail, UA, access unit, message store and X.400.

MTBF Mean time between failure. Measurement of the expected frequency of system failures.

MTTF Mean time to failure. Measurement of the frequency between component or system failures.

MTTR Mean time to repair. Measurement of the time it takes to repair a computer system failure.

MTU Maximum Transmission Unit. Maximum packet size that can be transmitted by a network. *See* packet.

MUA Mail user agent. Interface to the electronic-mail software which the user sees and which allows the user to call up, show, create and/or archive electronic-mail messages. Interacts with the sending or transport agent, e.g. Simple Network Transport Protocol, that delivers the mail message to its destination. *See* e-mail and SNMP.

MUD Multiple User Dungeon. Also called Multiple User Dimension, Multiple User Dialogue or multi-user dungeon. Interactive computer games available to users through the Internet, USENET and other bulletin board systems. Games available include TinyMUD, TeenyMUD, Diku and AberMUD. These vary from adventure games where users collectively or individually do battle with monsters, solve puzzles, create their own game environment or engage in combat with each other. *See* Internet and USENET.

MULTIBUS Bus architecture developed by Intel Corp. *See* bus.

multibyte characters Representation of international ideograms with a sequence of bytes instead of single bytes, e.g. Japanese and Chinese where the character set exceeds 256 characters.

multicast Commonly called broadcast. *See* broadcast.

Multicast Backbone *(INET)* Abbreviated and commonly known as Mbone. *See* Mbone.

MULTICS Multiplexed Information and Computing System. Jointly developed by the Massachusetts Institute of Technology, AT&T Co.'s Bell Laboratories and General Electric Co. in the 1960s as part of Project MAC to create a second-generation time-sharing program. Use of MULTICS lead Ken Thompson and Dennis Ritchie, then working for Bell Labs, to develop UNIX. *See* Project MAC, Thompson, Ken, Ritchie, Dennis M., UNICS, UNIX, Bell Laboratories and time-sharing.

multilevel feedback queue Process management scheme that has multiple levels of priorities. Processes are moved among the priority levels and within a priority level depending on system requirements and resources.

multimedia Jargon term for multimedia technology. *See* multimedia technology.

multimedia mail Electronic-mail system capable of including data, graphics, images and audio in an electronic-mail message. *See* e-mail and multimedia technology.

multimedia technology Combination of data, graphics and video animation with high-quality images and audio. Requires the high-storage capabilities of CD-ROM to store and manipulate the data required for "living" books. *See* CD-ROM.

multimode fiber Commonly abbreviated and called MMF. *See* MMF.

Multi-National Language Supplement Commonly abbreviated and called MNLS. *See* MNLS.

Multiple Instructions, Multiple Datamachine Commonly abbreviated and called MIMD. *See* MIMD.

Multiple User Dialogue Commonly abbreviated and called MUD. *See* MUD.

Multiple User Dimension Commonly abbreviated and called MUD. *See* MUD.

Multiple User Dungeon Commonly abbreviated and called MUD. *See* MUD.

multiplex 1. To transmit two or more signals over a single channel. 2. Ability to manage two or more communications channels at the same time.

Multiplexed Information and Computing System Abbreviated and commonly known as MULTICS. *See* MULTICS.

multiplexer Also called mux or multiplexor. Device used to divide a single line of one speed into multiple lines of a lower speed, whose sum plus overhead equals the speed of the single line. Normally used to operate multiple terminals on a single line between a host computer and terminal location.

multiplexor Commonly spelled multiplexer. *See* multiplexer.

multipoint protocol Class of transmission protocol that connects multiple senders to one or more receivers. *See* Ethernet.

multiprocessing Commonly abbreviated and called MP. *See* MP.

Multiprocessing UNIX Commonly abbreviated and called MP UNIX. *See* MP UNIX.

multiprocessor Computer with two or more central processing units capable of sharing the work load. *See* CPU, loosely coupled processor architecture and tightly coupled architecture.

multiprogramming Commonly called multitasking. *See* multitasking.

Multiprotocol Transport Networking Commonly abbreviated and called MPTN. *See* MPTN.

Multipurpose Internet Mail Extensions *(INET)* Commonly abbreviated and called MIME. *See* MIME.

multiscanning Ability of a monitor to synchronize with many different refresh rates, the speed at which a computer redraws the characters or graphics on a screen. *See* refresh rate.

multitasking Ability of an operating system to perform more than one task or run more than one program at a time.

multithread Also called lightweight process. Ability of a process to handle many different communications messages, or tasks, at the same time by sharing the memory assigned to one task with other tasks, e.g. when a peripheral device is able to receive input/output requests from multiple programs simultaneously.

multi-user Any operating system or computer system that allows more than one user to share the processing power and database of the computer.

Multi-User Computing London-based magazine that publishes articles for UNIX, Pick and OS/2 users.

multi-user dungeon Commonly abbreviated and called MUD. *See* MUD.

multi-user state Also called state 2. When the computer and operating system are operating normally with all the file systems mounted, or activated, and the multi-user process activated. *See* file system and multi-user.

multi-user system Operating system that allows more than one user to access the computer at the same time.

munge Jargon term for a damaged software program or computer.

Murphy's Law "If there are two or more ways to do something, and one of those ways can result in a catastrophe, then someone will do it." Quote attributed to Edward A. Murphy Jr. while he was working on an Air Force project in the late 1940s. Today, it is paraphrased as, "Anything that can go wrong will go wrong," and is widely considered to be an axiom about how computer systems operate.

mush Mail user's shell. Public domain electronic-mail program, the parameters of which can be set so that it can function on a line-based terminal, a screen (e.g. PC, Wyse or VT type monitor) or X Window System terminal.

mux Jargon term for multiplexer. *See* multiplexer.

mv Move. Command used to change the name of a file or directory. Even though mv is most commonly referred to as move, technically the file is not moved but renamed.

CLP> mv file newfile ⏎

renames the file and keeps it in the same working directory.

CLP> mv file name1 directory ⏎

renames the file so it appears in a new directory.

mvdir *(ATT)* Move directory. Command used only by superusers to change the name of a directory. *See* mv and superuser.

mview Part of the Documenter's Workbench set of text formatting programs. Used with the troff formatting program to typeset view graphs and slides. *See* DWB and troff.

mv macros Part of the Documenter's Workbench text formatting programs. Macros used with the troff program to typeset slides. *See* DWB and troff.

mvt *(ATT)* Shell script used to typeset view graphs and overhead slides with the troff formatting program. *See* shell script and troff.

mwm Motif window manager. Window manager developed by the Open Software Foundation Inc. *See* X Window System and window manager.

MX Mail exchanger. Data file required for the Domain Name Service which contains the information required to identify a host in the domain with the ability to deliver electronic mail. *See* DNS, domain and e-mail.

N

n Abbreviation for **n**ano. *See* nano.

NAC Network Application Consortium. Group of 23 companies and government agencies that promotes improved interoperability among network products. Among its leaders are MCI Communications Corp., Compaq Computer Corp. and Pacific Gas & Electric.

NACK 1. Negative acknowledgment. Communications signal sent by a receiving host to indicate it is not capable of communicating and cannot respond to a request for information. **2.** Response from a receiving host that indicates a transmission was unsuccessful. *See* ACK.

NADF North American Directory Forum. Group of U.S. and Canadian companies, associations and government agencies that supports electronic-mail products based upon the X.400 message handling system for electronic mail and X.500 directory services standards. Formed in 1990 of members who use either X.400 or X.500, including AT&T Co., BT North America Inc., Canada Post, GE Information Services, IBM Corp., Sprint International and the U.S. Postal Service. *See* X.400 and X.500.

nailed-up circuit Jargon term for a dedicated, point-to-point communications circuit.

NAK Negative acknowledgment. Commonly abbreviated NACK. *See* NACK.

name Object Management Group term for a general set of objects, e.g. files or programs. *See* OMG, object and handle.

named 1. Name daemon. Pronounced *NAME-D*. Background program in Berkeley Internet Name Domain used to establish a connection between, send queries to and respond to queries from hosts on a network. Maintains the Internet address and host name of all hosts on the network. *See* BIND, Internet, daemon and domain. **2.** AT&T Co.'s name for the Berkeley Internet Name Domain which is used to start and manage the Domain Name Service. *See* BIND and DNS.

NAME-D Pronunciation of named, the abbreviation for name daemon. *See* named.

named buffer In the vi editor program, a temporary storage area for text. There are 26 named buffers, identified by the letters a through z. Text is placed into the named buffers by using either the yank, change text or delete commands. *See* vi, working buffer, numbered buffer, unnamed buffer and vi commands (Appendix T).

named.ca File in the Domain Name Service which contains the names and addresses of root servers on a network. *See* DNS and named.

named.local File in the Domain Name Service which contains the name and address of a host used for local loopback, a process in which data is checked for errors. *See* DNS and loopback. *See* DNS.

named pipe AT&T Co.'s interprocess communication method that, using pipes, allows information to pass between two unrelated processes. Named and unnamed pipes are both FIFOs (first-in-first-out), file types that can be read only once before the data is removed. A named pipe has a file system representation, or name that it is given in an arbitrary directory. An unnamed pipe does not. A named pipe is created by the mknod(1) system call while an unnamed pipe is created by the pipe(2) system call. *See* IPC, named pipe, unnamed pipe, pipe, mknod, FIFO and UNIX domain sockets.

named server Commonly called named. *See* named.

namei *(ATT)* **Name** information number (inode). Routine used in creating a new process. Converts the name of an executable file created by the fork and exec system calls to an inumber, which gives the disk address of a file or position of an inode in the inode table. *See* fork, exec and inode.

namelist Commonly called symbol table. *See* symbol table.

Name Registration Service Commonly abbreviated and called NRS. *See* NRS.

NAMERT *(ATT)* UNIX System V, Release 4 parameter. Activates the real-time class, which processes data rapidly enough to enable the results to be used in response to another process that is taking place simultaneously. *See* SVR4.x and real-time class.

Name Server Commonly abbreviated and called NS. *See* NS.

nameserver Host on a Transmission Control Protocol/Internet Protocol network designated to provide network addresses to another host that wants to send traffic to a third host on the network.

name service Network service which converts symbolic host names to numeric addresses which can be used by the network.

Name Space/Directory Services Commonly abbreviated and called NS/DS. *See* NS/DS.

nano Abbreviation for 10^{-9} (1/1,000,000,000) or one-billionth. Commonly abbreviated n.

nanosecond Commonly abbreviated NS. *See* NS.

Nanotechnology Computer or communication technology capable of processing data in one-billionth of a second.

(national body) conforming POSIX application *(POS)* Any application using the Portable Operating System Interface for Computer Environments (POSIX) standard and approved International Organization for Standardization (ISO) standards, plus approved national standards of an ISO member. *See* ISO and POSIX.

National Bureau of Standards Commonly abbreviated and called NBS. *See* NBS.

National Computer Security Association Commonly abbreviated and called NCSA. *See* NCSA.

National Computer Security Center Commonly abbreviated and called NCSC. *See* NCSC.

National Information Infrastructure Commonly abbreviated and called NII. *See* NII.

National Information Infrastructure Testbed Commonly abbreviated and called NIIT. *See* NIIT.

National Institute of Standards and Technology Commonly abbreviated and called NIST. *See* NIST.

National ISDN National Integrated Services Digital Network. Commonly abbreviated and called ISDN 1. *See* ISDN 1.

National Research and Education Network Abbreviated and commonly known as NREN. *See* NREN.

National Science Foundation Commonly abbreviated and called NSF. *See* NSF.

National Science Foundation Network Commonly abbreviated and called NSFNet. *See* NSFNet.

National Software Testing Laboratories Commonly abbreviated and called NSTL. *See* NSTL.

native language Computer operating system that runs only on a single manufacturer's computer systems.

native mode When software, specifically an operating system, runs on its own, not as a process of another operating system. *See* OS.

native tool Utility program that is part of the standard UNIX operating system.

nawk *(ATT)* New **awk**. Updated version of awk, a pattern scanning and processing language. *See* awk.

NBS National Bureau of Standards. Forerunner to the National Institute of Standards and Technology. *See* NIST.

ncheck *(ATT/XEN)* Node **check**. Superuser command used to create pathnames for inumbers, 2-byte numbers in file names which give information for locating these files. Used to determine the name of a file when only the inode number is known. Checks the file system by providing the inode and file names when only the disk partition is provided as an argument. For the most part, replaced by fsck as a means of performing file system checks. *See* file system, fsck, superuser, pathname, inumber and inode.

NCR paper Carbonless paper, used in multiple-copy forms, originally developed by NCR Corp. *See* carbonless paper.

NCS Network Computing System. Software jointly developed by Apollo and the Hewlett-Packard Co. Selected by the Open Software Foundation Inc. as its standard remote procedure call for interhost connectivity over a network that allows commands or programs to function on remote systems as if they were being executed on a local system. *See* RPC, OSF and UNIX Wars.

NCSA National Computer Security Association. Washington, D.C. based organization that works on issues related to computer security. Performs research, evaluates products and provides information on viruses to users.

NCSC National Computer Security Center. Part of the National Security Agency. Publishes requirements and certifies the security levels of computer systems for the federal government. Established in 1982 and originally known as the *Department of Defense Computer Security Center*. Located in Fort Meade, Maryland. *See* Orange Book.

ndx *(ATT)* **N**roff in**dex**. Command used with the nroff and troff document formatting programs to create an index for a document. *See* nroff and troff.

near letter quality Commonly abbreviated and called NLQ. *See* NLQ.

near-line storage Data storage medium, e.g. optical disk, that provides access to data at a slower rate than fixed disk but faster than magnetic tape or other off-line storage medium. *See* online storage, offline storage and HSM.

NECTAR One of the gigabit test-bed networks developed by the U.S. government, industry and university representatives. Tests technologies and applications which are used in implementing networks and supercomputers that can transmit gigabits of data per second. Designed to test interfaces between wide area and local area networks, High Performance Parallel Interface and new computer designs. Participating in NECTAR are Bell Atlantic, BellCore and the Carnegie-Mellon University Supercomputing Center. *See* HPCC, NREN, LAN, HiPPI, WAN, AURORA, BLANCA, CASA, MAGIC and VISTANet.

negative acknowledgment Commonly abbreviated and called NACK. *See* NACK.

neqn *(ATT)* **N**roff **eqn**uation. Part of Documenter's Workbench text formatting software package, used with the nroff text formatting program to format text containing mathematical symbols and equations. *See* DWB, nroff and eqn.

netbench *(BSD)* Benchmark program used to measure the throughput between two nodes using various network protocols, e.g. Transmission Control Protocol/Internet Protocol and User Datagram Protocol. *See* TCP/IP and UDP.

NetBios **Net**work **B**asic **I**nput/**O**utput **S**ystem. Software interface originally developed by IBM Corp. for a controller on personal computer local area networks. Accepted as a de facto standard for Token Ring interface. *See* LAN and Token Ring.

nethack Newer version of hack, the dungeon game. Used on X Window System terminals. *See* hack.

net ID *(INET)* Specific number that is part of the 32-bit Internet IP address assigned by the Network Information Center. Identifies the network on which a host is located. *See* Internet, IP address, host ID and NIC.

netmasks Jargon term for /etc/netmasks. *See* /etc/netmasks.

netnews **Net**work **news**. Also called A news. First set of programs used to exchange and read articles on the USENET, an international UNIX bulletin board. Articles and programs are contained in separate news groups identified by topic. *See* USENET.

net number *(INET)* Commonly called net ID. *See* net ID.

netpath *(ATT)* Command used by a system administrator under the STREAMS input/output mechanism in UNIX System V, Release 4. Establishes environmental variables used for making connections to remote hosts. *See* STREAMS, SVR4.x and environment variables.

.netrc **Net**work **r**un **c**ommand. User file which contains the data necessary for establishing a File Transfer Protocol connection with a remote host, allowing files, directories and directory trees to be moved or copied from one computer to another. *See* FTP.

netspec File added in UNIX System V, Release 4, that contains a list of the devices on a network which listen, the network device monitor, checks for incoming connection requests. *See* SVR4.x and listen.

netstat **Net**work **stat**istics. Network administration command used to display information on the status of a network, e.g. the current status of active connections; summary information on such things as traffic and errors for each network interface; amount of memory buffer used; summary of packet traffic by protocol; and status and amount of use of routing (address) tables.

netutil *(XEN)* **Net**work **util**ity. Program used to manage hosts running the XENIX operating system on a network.

NetWare IPX Internet protocol developed by Novell Inc. *See* IP.

network Group of computers and/or terminals that are interconnected to allow the exchange of information or data. More advanced networks allow peripheral devices to be shared.

network address Number which uniquely identifies a host on a network. *See* domain.

network administration commands Set of commands and programs used by a network system administrator to manage such things as network system processes, users, security and operation of networking programs. *See* NFS, newkey, NSU, NUA, RFS, network listener, nlsadmin, nsquery and remote mapping.

network analyzer Device used to capture and segregate network traffic into separate functions for analysis.

Network Application Consortium Commonly abbreviated and called NAC. *See* NAC.

network architecture Design or composition of a network, which can vary with an implementation. Basic elements include hardware, protocols, functions performed and formats.

network aware Ability of an object, e.g. application program or hardware device, to work on a network. *See* object.

Network Basic Input/Output System Abbreviated and commonly known as NetBios. *See* NetBios.

Network Computing System Commonly abbreviated and called NCS. *See* NCS.

network file system Commonly called distributed file system. *See* distributed file system.

Network File System Commonly abbreviated and called NFS. *See* NFS.

Network Independent File Transfer Protocol Commonly called Blue Book. *See* Blue Book.

Network Information Center Commonly abbreviated and called NIC. *See* NIC.

Network Information Service Formerly called Yellow Pages. Commonly abbreviated and called NIS. *See* NIS.

networking commands Commonly called communications commands. *See* communications commands.

Networking Support Utilities Commonly abbreviated and called NSU. *See* NSU.

network interface layer Commonly called network layer. *See* network layer.

network is the system Phrase that describes the aggregate computing power of distributed multiprocessing networks.

network layer Third layer of the International Organization for Standardization/Open Systems Interconnection model or second layer of the Transmission Control Protocol and Internet Protocol. The network layer, e.g. the Internet Protocol, is responsible for routing, or determining the links necessary to get data from the sending to the receiving host. *See* ISO/OSI, ARM, OSIRM, IP and TCP/IP architecture.

network license Commonly called dynamic license. *See* dynamic license.

network listener Commonly called listener. *See* listener.

Network Lock Manager Daemon in the Network File System which manages file sharing and locking. Prevents more than one user from modifying a file at the same time but allows for synchronized access to files. *See* daemon and NFS.

network management Methods or standards for accounting, configuration, fault isolation, performance and security on a network.

Network Management Forum Commonly abbreviated and called NMF. *See* NMF.

network management protocol Common set of rules or instructions used to pass information between network management functions, e.g. Common Management Information Protocol, Simple Network Management Protocol and Systems Network Architecture. *See* CMIP, SNMP and SNA.

Network Management Station Commonly abbreviated and called NMS. *See* NMS.

network manager Either a hardware device with an application software package or a software package added to a network node that is used to control other nodes on a network.

network mask *(INET)* Network address scheme that cross-references the Internet Protocol address of a host with that host's address on a subnetwork. *See* IP.

network middleware Set of services above the operating system that helps to make development of client/server application software easier. Isolates the application software from the specifics of the version of the network protocols, e.g. establishing communications links, recovering from errors and remote procedure calls. Located between client and server computers. Used to retrieve data from the server and translate it to a format that can be used by an application, if required. *See* local middleware.

network monitor Management tool on a network used to gather and report on network statistics, e.g. total message traffic, number of re-transmissions or number of collisions.

Network News Transfer Protocol
(INET) Commonly abbreviated and called NNTP. *See* NNTP.

Network Operating System
Commonly abbreviated and called NOS. *See* NOS.

network protocol Set of standards that describes how software and hardware should interface with a network to transmit data. *See* Internet Protocol Suite.

network provider Protocol or methodology for a Transmission Control Protocol/Internet Protocol network to communicate with computers using other protocols, e.g. Ethernet, wide area network and X.25. *See* TCP/IP, Ethernet and X.25.

networks *(INET)* File in the /etc system directory which contains information, e.g. name, number and alias names, for networks that are part of the Internet network. *See* /etc and Internet.

Network Security Monitor Commonly abbreviated and called NSM. *See* NSM.

network services Functionality or service provided by one layer of a network protocol model to the next highest layer, e.g. electronic mail, file transfer and remote login. *See* OSIRM and ARM.

Network Services, Inc. Commonly abbreviated and called NSI. *See* NSI.

Network Software Utilities Commonly abbreviated and called NSU. *See* NSU.

Network Status Monitor Commonly called statd. *See* statd.

Network Support Utilities Commonly abbreviated and called NSU. *See* NSU.

network system administrator
Person(s) responsible for the daily operation and maintenance of the network. May be responsible for upgrading software, adding and deleting hosts to the network, and hardware preventative maintenance. Also may be the primary liaison with the maintenance vendor.

Network Time Protocol Commonly abbreviated and called NTP. *See* NTP.

network topology Organization of a network, specifying the connections between computer hosts on the network.

Network User's and Administrator's Guide Commonly abbreviated and called NUA. *See* NUA.

network video *(INET)* Commonly abbreviated and called nv. *See* nv.

network virtual terminal Any terminal capable of receiving and transmitting data over a network connection.

Network Voice Terminal Commonly abbreviated and called NEVOT. *See* NEVOT.

NEVOT *(INET)* **Net**work **Vo**ice **T**erminal. Interactive voice program developed by the University of Massachusetts. Used by workstations or X Window System terminals to transmit and receive voice data using the IP multicasting protocol. *See* Internet, IP multicasting and X Window System.

newaliases *(BSD)* Command used to maintain the database for the electronic-mail aliases file. *See* e-mail.

NEW-E Pronunciation of NUI, the acronym for Notebook User Interface. *See* NUI.

newform *(ATT)* **New form**at. Command used to reformat the contents of a file.

newfs **New f**ile system. Command used by a system administrator to create a file system on a disk partition. *See* SA, file system and disk partition.

newgrp *(ATT/XEN)* **New gr**oup. Command that allows a user to temporarily change from one to another group of common user accounts, in which all the users can share files and directories. But the user can only switch to a group with permissions, established in the /etc/group file, which allow group access.

newkey **New key**. Command used by a network system administrator on a secure Network File System or Remote Procedure Call system to create a new public and secret key for a user. *See* network system administrator, DES, key, NFS, RPC, public-key encryption, encrypted key and chkey.

new line Commonly spelled newline. *See* newline.

newline Jargon term for newline indicator. *See* newline indicator.

newline indicator Signal sent by software and represented as \n. Tells a computer or peripheral device to terminate the current line and start a new line. Used to separate lines within text files. Formed by combining a carriage return and linefeed command. *See* carriage return and linefeed.

newproc **New process**. Function called by the fork system call when a new process is to be generated. Creates an entry which details the data structure of the new process and is placed in the process table in main memory. *See* function, fork and process table.

news 1. *(ATT/XEN)* Command used to access a directory which contains on-line information about the system or other items of interest. The directory is similar to a bulletin board and contains files which are maintained by the system administrator or others who have permission to update the news items. **2.** Directory that users can access to obtain system and/or UNIX-related news items. The system directory contains files with messages for all users of the system. Unlike the message of the day, which normally can only be changed by the system administrator, news can be updated by all users. During the login sequence, news is checked, through setups in environ-

mental variables, to determine if the user has read all current items in the directory. If not, the user is notified that there are new items to be read. *See* motd.

newsgroup Topic of interest or grouping of like messages, e.g. all the articles posted about Corvettes, on USENET, the international UNIX bulletin board. *See* newsgroup categories.

newsgroup categories Following are the standard USENET newsgroup categories:

Category	Description
comp	*Computer*. Group of messages that has any relation to computer science.
news	*News*. Group of messages containing information on network software or general interest.
rec	*Recreation*. Group of messages related to any recreational activity
soc	*Social*. Group of messages discussing social issues.
talk	*Talk*. Group of messages around extended discussions between users on any topic.
misc	*Miscellaneous*. Group of messages that do not fit into any other category.

.newsrc **News run command**. System file established either by the system administrator or automatically in a user account to identify items of interest in the news directory which should be reviewed by the user with the news command. *See* news.

New Technology OS/2 Commonly abbreviated and called NT OS/2. *See* NT OS/2.

newtset *(OTH)* **New terminal set**. Shell script used to set terminal dependent settings whenever a user logs in to the computer. Checks the termcap file to determine the individual characteristics of the terminal being used and sets characters like the erase and kill. *See* shell script and tset.

newuser *(ATT)* Shell script used to add new user accounts to a system.

newvt *(ATT)* **New v**irtual **terminal.** Command used to start a new terminal connection to a host through a window. Allows more than one connection to be made to a host from a single terminal through separate windows. To the network, these additional connections appear to be made by actual terminals.

next-frm *(ATT)* **Next frame.** Operations menu command in the UNIX System V, Release 4 Framed Access Command Environment file system. Used to move between frames, creating a new frame. *See* SVR4.x, FACE, file system, frame and prev-frm.

NextStep UNIX-like object-oriented operating system developed by Next Computer Inc. and based on the Carnegie-Mellon University Mach operating system. *See* Mach.

NFS **N**etwork **F**ile **S**ystem. File transfer protocol for heterogeneous networks, implemented in 1984 by Sun Microsystems Inc. Similar to the Defense Advanced Research Projects Agency File Transfer Protocol, which allows files to be transferred between systems for use. NFS allows computer systems to share files with other systems; a file remains on the remote system but appears to be activated, or mounted on, and to actually belong to the local system. *See* RFS, DARPA and FTP.

nfsd 1. **N**etwork **F**ile **S**ystem **d**aemon. Background program that manages client requests over a network. 2. Network administration command used to start the Network File System daemon. *See* NFS and daemon.

N-group writing Digital data storage format that writes data to tape multiple times, as a form of backup. Data can be written as many as eight times, or up to eight copies of the same data can be made, depending on the user's selection. This ensures that if an error occurs while data is being written from the tape to a disk drive, the tape can be advanced until an uncorrupted copy of the data is found. *See* DDS and DAT.

NI Programmer's Guide: Networking Interfaces. UNIX System V, Release 4 documentation on how to develop applications for network use. *See* SVR4.x, TLI, RPC and sockets.

NIC 1. *(INET)* **N**etwork **I**nformation **C**enter. Organization responsible for the overall management and administration of the Internet, including approval of new hosts and users. Since 1991, operated by GSI of Chantilly, Virginia. Originally operated by SRI International of Menlo Park, California. *See* Internet and SRI International. 2. **N**etwork **i**nterface **c**ard. Device in a computer- or network-aware peripheral, e.g. printer or tape device, that provides connectivity allowing the device to send and receive communication on the network.

nice 1. Command used to change the scheduling of a program or command. Users can only lower the priority, but superusers can either lower or raise the priority. A positive nice value lowers the priority while a negative nice value raises the priority. 2. *(ATT)* System call used to change the scheduling priority of a program or command. *See* nice and system call.

NIFTP **N**etwork **I**ndependent **F**ile **T**ransfer **P**rotocol. Commonly called Blue Book. *See* Blue Book.

NIH Used by some as the abbreviation for not invented here. *See* not invented here.

NII **N**ational **I**nformation **I**nfrastructure. Formal name for the electronic highway. *See* electronic highway.

NIIT **N**ational **I**nformation **I**nfrastructure **T**estbed. Group of approximately 20 academic, government and corporate organizations responsible for accelerating implementation of the National Research and Education Network. Forms the forerunner of a national scientific research and development network across the United States using a combination of frame-relay, Asynchronous Transfer Mode and Fiber Distribution Data Interface. *See* NREN, frame-relay, ATM and FDDI.

nineteen dot two Commonly written 19.2. *See* 19.2.

nineteen two Commonly written 19.2. *See* 19.2.

NIS Network Information Service. Formerly called Yellow Pages or YP. Program used to centrally manage password and group files, access permissions, host address information, and data for a network running the Network File System file transfer protocol for heterogeneous networks. *See* NFS.

NIST National Institute of Standards and Technology. Formerly called the National Bureau of Standards. Responsible for security in the private sector and developing American standards for the American National Standards Institute. Prepares and publishes the Federal Information Processing Standards. Located in Gaithersburg, Maryland. *See* NCSC, ANSI and FIPS.

NIST FIPS 146 Commonly called GOSIP (Government Open Systems Interconnection Profile). *See* GOSIP.

NIST FIPS 146 v. 1 Commonly called GOSIP (Government Open Systems Interconnection Profile) 1, 2 or 3. *See* GOSIP, GOSIP 1, GOSIP 2 and GOSIP 3.

NIST FIPS 151 Federal government standard for using Portable Operating System Interface for Computer Environments (POSIX). *See* POSIX.

NIST OIW Commonly called OIW (Open Systems Interconnection Implementation Workshop). *See* OIW.

NIST Workshop Commonly called OIW (Open Systems Interconnection Implementation Workshop). *See* OIW.

nl *(ATT/XEN)* Number lines. Command similar to the wc command except it counts only the number of lines in a file.

NLQ Near letter quality. Enhanced print quality of dot matrix printer almost equivalent to the letter quality produced by a laser printer. The enhancement comes from using more print pins. *See* dot matrix and letter quality.

nlsadmin *(ATT)* Network listener **ad**ministration. Originally a command in the Remote File Sharing networking program. Part of UNIX System V, Release V, used to configure the network listener. Can be used to display the current configuration of the network, start the files needed for the listener to work with a network, add a network, install a listener, register the network address or start a listener. *See* RFS, SVR4.x and listener.

NLUUG National UNIX Systems Users Group. Dutch UNIX users group formed in 1982.

nm *(ATT/XEN)* Name list. Command used to print symbol names from executable files. Normally used by software engineers to display the names of modules and functions in object files, libraries and executables. *See* executable file.

NMF Network Management Forum. Originally known as the *OSI/Network Management Forum*, or *OSI/NM Forum*. Nonprofit international organization formed in 1988 to develop and promote the Common Management Information Protocol. In the early 1990s it changed direction, and consequently its name, to include non-Open Systems Interconnection protocols. Membership consists of more than 100 private companies and government agencies from 18 countries, including AT&T Co., IBM Corp., British Telecom, Japan Air Lines and Royal Bank of Canada. Located in Bernardsville, New Jersey. *See* OSI, CMIP, Open Management Roadmap and OMNIPoints.

NMOS N-channel Metallic Oxide Semi-conductor Specially developed integrated circuit chip that uses negative charges, resulting in higher processing speeds.

NMS *(INET)* Network Management Station. Simple Network Management Protocol term for a device on the Internet which has software to query other network devices for statistics on data transmission. Normally includes a graphic package to display devices on the network; a method of gathering and displaying statistics about devices on the network; and the ability to automatically identify and map devices on the network, monitor in real time and display network activity, and automatically log system activity. *See* SNMP and Internet.

NMS agent Network Management Station **agent**. Commonly called agent. *See* agent.

nn Network news. Visual interface with USENET news. A news reader intended to simplify finding and reading news. It is a replacement for rn and readnews. *See* USENET, rn, readnews and news.

NNTP *(INET)* Network news transfer protocol. Protocol used to move news articles over a network. Used to distribute access to news articles residing on one computer system to many clients and thus eliminate the need for each of the clients to maintain its own news directory. *See* USENET and news.

nntpd *(INET)* Network news transfer protocol **daemon**. Internet background program used to manage the movement of USENET news over a network. *See* Internet, NNTP, daemon, USENET and news.

noai No automatic indent. Toggled option in the vi editor program which turns off the autoindent variable. When it is set, a user has to depress the spacebar to move the cursor to the desired starting point on each line, creating whitespace at the start of each line. *See* vi, toggle, whitespace and ai.

noaw No automatic write. Toggled option in the vi editor program which turns off the autowrite variable. When it is set, data is not automatically written, or saved, when certain commands are invoked. *See* vi, toggle and aw.

NOC *(INET)* Network Operations Center. The central organization that monitors and controls the networks which compose the Internet. *See* Internet.

noclobber Originally a C shell toggle variable that has been incorporated in the Korn shell. Used to prevent a user from accidentally overwriting a file with another file. *See* C shell, Korn shell and toggle variables.

node Element of a communications network ranging from a single terminal to a computer that has a network connection and address.

node encryption Encryption of data passing through a node. Encryption and decryption take place at each node.

node locking license Commonly called site license. *See* site license.

nodename *(ATT)* UNIX System V, Release 4 system setup menu command similar to the setuname command. Used to set the system name or node name of a computer on a network. *See* setuname and hostname.

node name Name given to a host on a network.

nohup *(ATT/XEN)* No hang-up. Bourne shell command that allows the user to establish a background process and log off without the process being terminated by the system. Prevents hang-up or quit signals from stopping a program that is running. *See* Bourne shell, background process, ampersand (&) and signal.

noic No ignorecase. Toggled option in the vi editor program which turns off the ignorecase variable. When it is set during a search operation, the user must specify whether the characters in the search string are uppercase or lowercase. *See* vi, toggle and ic.

noise Any disturbance, e.g. static, which could interfere with the electronic or optical recording, playback or transmission of data.

nomagic No magic. Toggled option in the ex and vi editors which turns off the magic variable. When it is set, the meaning of special characters is ignored in search operations. *See* vi, toggle and magic.

non-ASCII character Any character not included in the set of 256 American Standard Code for Information Interchange characters. *See* ASCII and ASCII characters.

nonblocking I/O Nonblocking input/output. Method of managing input and output. Whenever an input or output function gives a nonstandard response, the computer sends an error message instead of either turning off the function or blocking the communication channel.

non-conductor Also called insulator. Any material that does not conduct electricity, e.g. glass, plastic and rubber. *See* conductor and semiconductor.

no news is good news Principle on which UNIX commands function. UNIX commands generally respond to user inputs only when an error is made in a command line. If no response is received, the user can assume the command was successfully completed. *See* command line.

nonfatal error 1. Error, typically detected by a compiler, from which the compiler can recover after taking some corrective action. 2. Any error from which the software or hardware may recover, e.g. trying to delete a file that does not exist. *See* fatal error.

nonimpact printer Any printer that transfers images without mechanically striking them onto the paper, e.g. laser, ink-jet and thermal printers. Originally, a printer that used specially coated paper that responded to either heat or other methods to produce images.

non-interlacing Process of scanning video images on a screen with an electron gun, line by line, in turn, as the gun moves down the monitor screen. *See* interlacing.

nonovice Environmental variable in the vi editor program that turns off the novice environmental variable, which indicates the mode the user is in. *See* vi and novice.

nonpageable When a page is marked to remain in main memory while a program is being executed. *See* page and paging.

nonprinting character Any character which is not seen, either on the screen or printed on paper depending on where the output is directed, e.g. blank space, control characters, tabs and other special characters without a graphical figure.

nonresident Object program that is kept in mass storage, e.g. on a disk drive, instead of in main memory. *See* resident.

nonstandard extensions *(POS)* Any add-on to an operating system which does not meet the Portable Operating System Interface for Computer Environments (POSIX) specifications. *See* POSIX.

NonStop-UX Tandem Computer Inc.'s UNIX operating system based upon AT&T Co.'s UNIX System V. *See* System V.

nonswitched network A network in which data does not have a predefined path to follow from the sender to the receiver, e.g. the Internet. *See* Internet and switched network.

nonu No number. Toggled variable in the vi editor program that turns off the number variable. When it is set, text lines are not numbered. *See* vi, toggle and number.

nore No redraw. Environmental variable in the vi editor program. When set, information displayed on the screen is not refreshed unless the user requests this by inputting control l while in the vi command mode. *See* vi and redraw.

NOREAD Variable for UNIX-to-UNIX CoPy used to indicate which directories cannot be included in the READ variable.

Precludes a remote host from reading directories on the local host. *See* UUCP and READ.

North American Directory Forum
Commonly abbreviated and called NADF. *See* NADF.

NOS Network operating system. Any operating system designed to operate and manage a computer network.

noshowmode Commonly abbreviated and called nosmd. *See* nosmd.

nosmd No showmode. Option in the vi editor program used to turn off the display of the phrase INPUT MODE at the lower right-hand corner of the screen when the user is in that mode. *See* vi and smd.

notebook computer Small portable personal computer. Approximately 2 inches thick, 12 inches wide and 10 inches deep, and weighs as little as 4.5 pounds. Can be a 286, 386 or 486 16- to 25-megahertz-based system. Features may include VGA graphics capable of up to 32 gray scales, support for an external color monitor, up to 64 megabytes of random access memory, 3.5-inch high density disk drives and as much as an 80-megabyte hard disk drive. *See* pen-based computer and palmtop computer.

Notebook computer

notebook entry Commonly called inode. *See* inode.

Notebook User Interface Commonly abbreviated and called NUI. *See* NUI.

noterse Environmental variable for the vi editor program that, when set, sends a user easily understood error messages. *See* vi and terse.

notify 1. *(ATT)* UNIX System V, Release 4 electronic-mail-related command used to tell a user when a new e-mail message has arrived. Turned on with the -y option and off with the -n option. *See* SVR4.x and e-mail. 2. C shell toggle variable that, when set, notifies a user when a background process has been completed. *See* C shell and toggle variables.

not invented here Sometimes abbreviated NIH. Mentality of individuals or organizations who reject ideas without studying or analyzing them. Usually, the only reason for the rejection is that another organization or individual came up with the idea first.

Novell DOS Novell Disk Operating System. Until early 1993 called Digital Research Disk Operating System (DR DOS). The 5.0 version of DR DOS was the first disk operating system that could use up to 640 kilobytes of memory for an application. *See* DOS.

novice 1. Environmental variable for the vi editor program that indicates at the bottom of the screen which mode the user is in. *See* vi, mode and nonovice. 2. Individual who has heard about the editor and is trying to find out who he or she is to get some free help reviewing documents. 3. Used rm for the first time but with an asterisk.

nowa No writeany. Default vi editor variable that stops the vi editor from saving the contents of the temporary buffer created for an open vi file to any writeable file. *See* vi and writeany.

Noyce, Robert (1928-90) Innovator whose creation helped to found California's Silicon Valley, the heartland of the computer industry. He first conceptualized the integrated circuit (IC) in 1959 and, along with Gordon Moore, invented the integrated circuit and co-founded Intel Corp. *See* IC.

NREN National Research and Education Network. Also called the information superhighway. An extension of the National Science Foundation Network and Internet that provides real-time high-speed connectivity between more than 1,000 government, commercial and research institutions nationwide. In addition, it is a fiber-optic network used as a test bed for new high-speed communication and computer technology, and provides access to large databases on supercomputers. Results applied to the efforts of commercial firms to formulate and implement the electronic highway providing users in-home services, such as video on demand, and interactive television services, such as home shopping. Originated from a 1989 President's Office of Science and Technology Policy report, and was created by the High Performance Computing Act of 1991. Sponsoring federal agencies include the Defense Advanced Research Projects Agency, Department of Energy, National Aeronautics and Space Administration, National Science Foundation and National Institute of Standards and Technology. *See* Internet, DARPA, NSF, NSFNet, NIIT, NIST, NII, NIIT, NIST, HPCC and electronic highway.

nroff New run **off**. Pronounced *N-ROFF*. Text formatting program that is part of the Documenter's Workbench package. Consists of several macros, which can display on screen and ultimately instruct the printer to output the document according to the formatting commands embedded in the text file.

    CLP>nroff <macro option> file name ⌨

will display the finished document on the terminal.

    CLP>nroff <macro option> file name > (newfile) ⌨

will format the file and redirect the output to a new file.

    CLP>nroff <macro option> file name I lp <printer name>⌨

will redirect the output to a printer device. *See* DWB, runoff, troff, ditroff and macro.

N-ROFF Pronunciation of nroff, the abbreviation for new run off. *See* nroff.

NRS Name Registration Scheme. Secured version of the Domain Name Service. *See* DNS and Coloured Book.

NS 1. Nanosecond. One-billionth of a second. **2.** Name Server. Data record which is required for the operation of the Domain Name Service and which contains the name of the host responsible for the domain. *See* DNS and domain.

NSC Hyperchannel Network Systems Corp. **Hyperchannel**. High-peed local area network that can transmit over a distance of 5,000 feet at a rate of 50 megabits per second versus the standard LAN rate of 10 megabits per second. *See* LAN and Mbps.

NS/DS Name Space/Directory Services. Applications program interface used to create the user interface to the X.500 directory services. *See* API and X.500.

NSF National Science Foundation. Government organization that promotes and sponsors scientific research. Funds a backbone network that connects supercomputers used for research and development projects. Assumed the financing role for the Internet when Department of Defense funding was cut. *See* NSFNet.

NSFNet National Science Foundation Network. National and international computer and communications network connecting the networks of universities, government research agencies and industry research facilities. Used by more than 5 million people on approximately 5,000 interconnected networks in the United States and 36 other countries. *See* NSF.

NSI *(INET)* Network Services, Inc. Organization that took over the operation of the Internet Network Information Center in October 1991 from the Stanford Research Institute International. Based in Chantilly, Virginia. *See* Internet, SRI International and NIC.

nslookup *(ATT)* Program used to obtain information about hosts on the Internet. *See* Internet, dig and whois.

NSM Network Security Monitor. Program available within the Department of Defense to perform security functions for a network. Checks network traffic for possible intruders by analyzing connection information to determine if connections by unknown hosts have been either attempted or completed.

ns pseudo-device Pseudo-device used to connect computers to Xerox Corp.'s Network System. *See* pseudo-device.

nsquery *(ATT)* **N**ame **s**erver **query**. Remote File Sharing command used to display resources that can be shared and are currently available on the network. *See* RFS.

NSTL **N**ational **S**oftware **T**esting Laboratories. Independent agency that tests and evaluates personal computer and local area network software and hardware. Established in 1983 and located in Plymouth Meeting, Pennsylvania.

NSU **N**etworking **S**upport **U**tilities. Also called the Network Software Utilities. Utility package in UNIX System V, Release 4, required to establish network interfaces for network-related software used with the Transmission Control Protocol and Internet Protocol. *See* SVR4.x, TCP/IP, EMD, RFS and NFS.

nswap **N**umber **swap**. Kernel parameter that sets the number of 512-byte blocks of disk space to be used for the swap area. *See* swap space.

NT Abbreviation for Microsoft Corp.'s Windows **N**ew **T**echnology. Also called Windows NT. Microsoft's windows-based 32-bit portable, multitasking and multithreading operating system for servers and large desktop workstations. Original name for the multiprocessing version of Operating System/2 (OS/2), version 3.0, but was changed by Microsoft. Windows NT is compatible with MS-DOS, Microsoft Windows, OS/2 and the Portable Operating System Interface for Computer Environments (POSIX). Some consider it to be a replacement for UNIX. *See* POSIX.

ntalk *(BSD)* Command that allows one user to "talk" to, or exchange interactive messages with, another user, Splits the screen on each user's computer and allows them to communicate with each other at the same time. *See* write and talk.

NT OS/2 **N**ew **T**echnology **O**perating **S**ystem/2. Original name for Microsoft Corp.'s multiprocessing version of Operating System/2. Now called Windows NT. *See* OS/2 and Windows NT.

NTP *(INET)* **N**etwork **T**ime **P**rotocol. Internet protocol which handles time-keeping for a network. Used to synchronize the clocks of multiple computers that are connected by a network. *See* Internet.

ntpd *(INET)* **N**etwork **T**ime **P**rotocol **d**aemon. Background program used in the first version of the Network Time Protocol to synchronize the clocks of multiple computers that are connected on a network. *See* NTP and Internet.

nu **Nu**mber. Toggled variable in the ex and vi editors that, when turned on, numbers each line of text. *See* ex, vi, toggle and nonu.

NUA **N**etwork **U**ser's **a**nd **A**dministrator's Guide. UNIX System V, Release 4 documentation on networking facilities and the administration of facilities such as the Remote File Sharing system, Network File System and Transmission Control Protocol and Internet Protocol. *See* SVR4.x, RFS, NFS and TCP/IP.

nucleus Downsized kernel used in the Chorus/Mix operating system. *See* Chorus/Mix and microkernel.

NUI **N**otebook **U**ser **I**nterface. Pronounced *NEW-E*. Proprietary graphical user interface developed for notebook computers. *See* notebook computer and GUI.

nuke Jargon term for deliberately deleting a file or directory.

null Special value indicating the end of a character string, end of a file or an empty pointer.

nulladm *(ATT)* Accounting system shell script used to create a system accounting file with the correct permissions for accessing it.

null character Generally a special character, e.g. ASCII character 0 or \0 in a string, used to indicate the end of a character string. Fills space and has no value, but is expected to be found there by the system.

null string Empty character string. Contains no characters and is empty (zero length). Frequently used to represent missing or meaningless data, e.g. to indicate to a C language program that entry has been completed, the user can create a null string by hitting the return key twice, first to end the last line of input and second to indicate end of input. *See* null character.

number Commonly abbreviated and called nu. *See* nu.

number cruncher Older jargon term for a computer. Initially, computers were only intended to manipulate, or crunch, large volumes of numbers for scientific, mathematical and batch processing purposes.

numbered buffer Storage area used with the vi editor to automatically store text that has been deleted from a file. In vi, nine numbered buffers are available to temporarily store deleted text. When a tenth deletion is made, that data is sent to the first buffer, which is overwritten. Either the P (put text to the left of the cursor) or p (put text on a new line below the cursor) commands can be used to recover text in a numbered buffer. *See* vi, working buffer, named buffer and unnamed buffer.

number register Process control mechanism in both the nroff and troff text formatting programs. More than 30 number registers store information about what is happening with nroff and troff processes, e.g. to determine line and page location. *See* nroff and troff.

numeric Prefix indicating that only number characters can be or have been used, e.g. as in a field or variable in a database. In contrast, only alphabetic characters may be used in an alpha field or variable while a combination of letters and numbers may be used in an alphanumeric one. *See* alpha and alphanumeric.

numeric options Editor variables or options that require a number as an argument to specify a value. *See* wm, string options and toggle options.

nusend *(ATT)* Command used to transfer files to a UNIX system on a Network Systems Corp. network.

NUUG Norsk UNIX-Bukers Forening. Norwegian UNIX Users Group.

nv *(INET)* Network video. Interactive video program developed by the Xerox Palo Alto Research Center. Used by X Window System terminals to transmit and receive video data using the IP multicasting protocol. *See* Internet, IP multicasting, Xerox PARC and X Window System.

NWRITE Variable for the UNIX-to-UNIX CoPy communications system that is read by the uucico (UNIX-to-UNIX CoPy-in copy-out) daemon. Identifies the directories that are not in the WRITE list. *See* UUCP, uucico, WRITE and /usr/spool/uucppublic.

O

OA Office automation. Buzz term for add-ing computers to the office environment, e.g. buying a low-cost personal computer with word processing software, or net-working a company's offices throughout the world with a broad range of applica-tions software.

OAM *(ATT)* Commonly written OA&M. *See* OA&M.

OA&M Operations, Administration **and** Management. Feature in UNIX System V, Release 4, that provides new menu-based facilities for backup, diagnostics, network services and printer services, and soft-ware installation tools for system admin-istrators. *See* SVR4.x.

OBIOS Open Basic Input Output Sys-tems. Set of standards that defines the interface between a real-time operating system and input/output devices. *See* RTOS and ORKID.

object **1.** Instructions or programs that a computer understands and executes. The result of compiling a source program to produce machine language commands that are loaded into memory for execution. *See* executable code. **2.** Graphical display of a computer function or task. **3.** Data to be acted on. **4.** Output or target of an operation. Each module contains both data and in-structions for the manipulation of the data. Once developed, objects can be re-used in various application programs. *See* OOP, OMG, request and client. **5.** Almost any-thing on, in or related to a computer, includ-ing bits, bytes, words, video displays, printers and network nodes. 6. Any device or application program on a network.

object code Commonly called object. *See* object.

Object Compatibility Standard Commonly abbreviated and called OCS. *See* OCS.

Object Database Management Group-1993 Commonly abbreviated and called ODMG-93. *See* ODMG-93.

Object Database Management Group, Inc. Commonly abbreviated and called ODMG. *See* ODMG.

object file Result of compiling a source program with an assembler. Contains ma-chine language commands that are loaded into memory for execution. *See* assembler.

object implementation Object Manage-ment Group term for the definitions for data composition, how programs work, and how the system selects programs and data to satisfy a request. *See* OMG and request.

object library Collection of executable in-structions or programs that are loaded into memory for execution and main-tained in a system. Can be used repeat-edly and/or by multiple users The programs in the object library have been used and tested previously. *See* object.

Object Management Architecture Commonly abbreviated and called OMA. *See* OMA.

Object Management Computing Commonly abbreviated and called OMC. *See* OMC.

Object Management Group Commonly abbreviated and called OMG. *See* OMG.

object module Commonly called object file. *See* object file.

object-orientation Commonly abbreviated and called OO. *See* OO.

Object-oriented Database Management System Commonly abbreviated and called ODBMS. *See* ODBMS.

object-oriented programming
Commonly abbreviated and called OOP. *See* OOP.

Object-oriented Structured Design
Commonly abbreviated and called OOSD. *See* OOSD.

object program Commonly called object file. *See* object file.

Object Request Broker Commonly abbreviated and called ORB. *See* ORB.

Object Services Commonly abbreviated and called OS. *See* OS.

occlusion Process of hiding objects from sight by aligning them behind other objects on the screen.

OCE Open Collaboration Environment. Apple Computer Inc.'s application programming interface for sending electronic mail between clients and/or servers and applications, released with Apple's System 7 operating system. *See* MAPI, VIM, e-mail and API.

OC-n Optical Carrier level number. United States measurement of transmission rates of data that has been converted to optical signals. OC-n levels are:

Optical Carrier level	Transmission rate (Megabits per second)
OC-1	51.84 (Mbps)
OC-3	155.52
OC-12	622.08
OC-24	1,244.16
OC-48	2,488.32

Another United States level for non-optical signals is called Synchronous Transport Signal. Synchronous Transmission Module is the equivalent transmission level developed by the International Telecommunication Union Telecommunication Standardization Sector, formerly known as the *Consultative Committee on International Telegraphy and Telephony*. *See* STS-n, STM-n and ITU-T.

OCR 1. Optical character recognition. Form of information processing that uses a scanning device and specialized software to convert the text and images in a printed document into digital format. A computer can recognize this format and store it as a file. **2.** Optical character reader. Input device, or scanner, used in converting text and images in a printed document into digital format.

OCS Object Compatibility Standard. Test and verification suite used to determine if a software compiler creates objects that meet the standards established by the 88open Consortium. *See* 88open Consortium, ACT/88, AVS/88 and ITS/88.

octal Number system with a base of 8 that uses the digits 0, 1, 2, 3, 4, 5, 6 and 7. Used in programming to represent binary numbers. *See* base.

octal dump Output of a file's contents in octal format. *See* od.

od *(ATT/XEN)* Octal dump. Command used to review files in increments of 2 bytes or 2 words. Outputs the file contents as octal, decimal or hexadecimal numbers. Very useful for examining text files with hidden, or nonprinting, characters, and non-text files, written in machine code.

ODA Office Document Architecture. Government Open System Interconnection Profile standards for the format and architecture of word processing, fax, spreadsheet and other application software. *See* GOSIP.

ODBMS Object-oriented Database Management System. Sometimes called OODBMS. Database management system developed for object-oriented programming. With an ODBMS the storage format of the data can be modified without affecting the application software programs. *See* OOP and 007.

ODMG **O**bject **D**atabase **M**anagement Group, Inc. Off shoot of the Object Management Group formed to speed up development of a standard object-oriented database interface and an object-oriented database equivalent to Structured Query Language. Formed in 1991 by O^2 Technology, Objectivity, Inc., Object Design, Inc., Ontos, Inc. and Versant Object Technology, Corp. *See* OMG, SQL and ODMG-93.

ODMG-93 **O**bject **D**atabase **M**anagement **G**roup-1993. Specification developed by the Object Database Management Group, Inc. for a Structured Query Language-like function. Provides vendors the ability to develop object-oriented applications that can access various vendor relational databases over a network. Functionality defined in the specification includes object models, query language for objects and object interfaces to both C++ and Smalltalk object-oriented languages. *See* object, OMG, ODMG and SQL.

OEM **O**riginal **e**quipment **m**anufacturer. Any company that produces computers, peripherals or software for sale to vendors rather than to end-users.

OEM maintenance **O**riginal **e**quipment **m**anufacturer **maintenance**. Maintenance and service support provided by the manufacturer of hardware, software or peripherals. *See* self-maintenance, TPM and OEM.

off Part of the init process. Initiated to kill or stop a process when switching from one level or state to another to gain access to a computer. *See* init, process, level and state.

office automation Commonly abbreviated and called OA. *See* OA.

Office Document Architecture Commonly abbreviated and called ODA. *See* ODA.

office environment Temperature and humidity levels established by a manufacturer to ensure that vendor's computer hardware operates properly in an office. Not as strict as those ranges set by such manufacturers as IBM Corp. Controls on electrical power are also recommended, e.g. through a dedicated circuit with an uninterrupted power supply, which provides surge and brownout protection, along with battery backup to shut down the system with no loss of data.

off-line **1.** State in which a computer system or component, piece of hardware or application software is not functioning and is unable to accept input or provide output. **2.** Any user not currently logged in. **3.** Any file not resident in the file system or stored on either tape or another medium that is separate from the active computer system. *See* file system.

offline storage Data storage medium, e.g. magnetic tape, used to store data outside the computer system. *See* online storage, nearline storage and HSM.

OH S*!T!! command Comment made after inputting a command which is not what was intended and creates a system lock or loss of data. This command should never be input by a system administrator. If it is, the command can cause the system to stop or crash. *See* OOPS!! command.

OIW **O**pen Systems Interconnection Implementors' **W**orkshop. Government backed organization of users and vendors originally formed to promote Opens Systems Interconnection standards and development of open systems products for computers networking. Since its inception, OWI has changed its charter to include other open operating systems and interfaces. *See* OSI, AOW and EWOS.

olam Commonly called xhost. *See* xhost.

OLDPWD *(ATT)* **Old** print working directory. Korn shell variable. Maintains the name of the previous current working directory. *See* PWD.

olfm *(ATT)* OPEN LOOK file manager. File manager program in the OPEN LOOK application software. *See* OPEN LOOK, .olinitrc, olinit and olwm.

olh *(OTH)* On-line help. Command that provides a reference of command summaries and options list.

olinit *(ATT)* OPEN LOOK init. Command that starts the OPEN LOOK application software. *See* OPEN LOOK, .olinitrc, olfm and olwm.

.olinitrc *(ATT)* OPEN LOOK init run commands. File in the OPEN LOOK application software used to start the elements of OPEN LOOK, such as the file manager and window manager. *See* OPEN LOOK, olinit, olfm and olwm.

OLIT OPEN LOOK Intrinsic Toolkit. Also called the Motif Open Look Intrinsics Toolkit (Moolit). UNIX System Laboratory's X toolkit that provides the basic framework for developing applications. *See* intrinsics library and Xt Intrinsics.

OLTP On-line transaction processing. Method of database processing capable of rapid, high-volume data entry or update. Results in a large number of users **being able** to concurrently access, query and/or update a database. Used in performing simple, repetitive tasks with predictable patterns on large volumes of data. Provides a measurable level of service in a specified period of time, approaching real time, e.g. airline reservation service and customer order processing. *See* RTOS.

olwm *(ATT)* OPEN LOOK window manager. Window manager program in the OPEN LOOK application software. *See* OPEN LOOK, .olinitrc, olinit and olfm.

OMA Object Management Architecture. Object Management Group architecture that describes the systems used to manage requests from and responses to clients. *See* OMG, request and client.

OMC Object Management Computing. Process that provides users a graphical

representation, or drawing, of an entity, e.g. a computer or communications network.

omf *(ATT)* Command used to change AT&T Co.'s Common Object File Format code to XENIX Object Module Format code format. *See* COFF and OMF.

OMF *(XEN)* XENIX version of AT&T Co.'s Common Object File Format. Revised format of C language executable and object files that provide support for dynamically linked object libraries. Used to create shrink-wrapped software programs that are easily transportable between computers using the same architecture, e.g. 386-based systems. *See* COFF.

OMG Object Management Group. Nonprofit corporation formed by vendors and users in 1989. Works with industry to establish standards for commercial products based on current 8- and 16-bit architecture. Includes more than 330 members, such as Microsoft Corp., IBM Corp., Sun Microsystems Inc., Apple Computer Inc., Digital Equipment Corp. and the Hewlett-Packard Co. *See* ORB, object, OO, OOP, CORBA and Patriot Partners.

OMNIPoints Open Management Interoperability **Points**. Information releases from the Network Management Forum, sponsored by Open Systems Interconnection. Contain specifications, testing requirements, contracting guides and a list of approved products. *See* OSI and NMF.

ONC Open Network Computing. Originally developed by Sun Microsystems Inc. as its distributed computing environment. Adopted by UNIX International as application development software to be used on networks. Applications written with ONC are modular, with each module running on a node best suited to execute that module. *See* DCE, WOSA and node.

one-to-one character mapping Concept in locale development of application software where a character of one language is recognized as a character in another language, e.g. a B in Russian is v.

one-to-two character mapping Concept in locale development of application software. A single character of one language is recognized as multiple characters in another language, e.g. an x in Russian represents kh in English and bi in Russian is y in English.

on-line 1. Computers or peripherals that are switched on and ready for operation, e.g. a printer that is ready to accept and print output from a computer. **2.** User who is currently logged in. **3.** Any file which is part of the file system and immediately accessible. *See* file system.

on-line documentation Documentation that is resident in a computer system and electronically accessible by users, e.g. help manual. *See* man and manual pages.

on-line insertion Alternative term for hot swap. *See* hot swap.

online storage Data storage medium, e.g. fixed disk, that provides users or applications immediate access to data. *See* nearline storage, offline storage and HSM.

on-line transaction processing Commonly abbreviated and called OLTP. *See* OLTP.

OO Object-orientation Program. Design in which software is broken into modules, representing a specific thing (object), e.g. printing. *See* OODBMS and OOP.

OODBMS Object-oriented Database Management System. Commonly abbreviated and called ODBMS. *See* ODBMS.

OOP Object-oriented programming. Programming methodology for developing application software. Aids programmers in writing less complicated code by handling implementation details in the background. The program in broken into modules, each representing an object. Each object is a pictorial representation of a task like a print routine. Separate objects

can be combined to form an application and the objects can be used in different applications. *See* object.

OOPS!! command Same as the OH S*!T!! command but used only by those who refrain from the use of four-letter words. *See* OH S*!T!! command.

OOSD Object-oriented Structured Design. Method used by programmers to outline a detailed design for a program before writing code. *See* CASE.

open 1. System call used to open a file for processing. *See* system call, read and write. **2.** Editing variable in the vi editor program that, when set, allows the user to switch from line editor to vi. *See* vi.

Open Basic Input Output Systems Commonly abbreviated and called OBIOS. *See* OBIOS.

Open Collaboration Environment Commonly abbreviated and called OCE. *See* OCE.

opendir *(BSD)* Open directory. UNIX library function that provides a standard method to access file system directories. *See* closedir.

open file 1. File currently in use (open for user access), as indicated by a file descriptor. *See* file descriptor. **2.** File that has been moved into memory so it is directly accessible by the user for reading and/or writing.

open file description Commonly called file description. *See* file description.

OpenGL Open Graphics Library. Set of standard applications that allows developers to create 3-D graphics programs for workstations running PHiGS (Programmer's Hierarchical Interactive Graphics System) Extension to the X Window System (PEX), a graphics extension to the X Window System. Developed by Silicon Graphics Inc. and supported by companies such as Intel Corp., IBM Corp. and Microsoft Corp. Competes with PEXlib, which is supported by members of the X

Consortium as a standard application programming interface. *See* PEX, PEXlib, 3-D data, API and X Consortium.

openi *(ATT)* Routine used in managing data input and output to provide user access to devices.

OPEN LOOK Design specification of a graphical user interface, developed by Sun Microsystems Inc. and used in UNIX System V, Release 4. *See* GUI, SVR4.x, Motif and VUE.

OPEN LOOK Intrinsic Toolkit
Commonly abbreviated and called OLIT. *See* OLIT.

OPEN LOOK window manager
Commonly abbreviated and called olwm. *See* olwm.

Open Management Interoperability Points Commonly abbreviated and called OMNIPoints. *See* OMNIPoints.

Open Management Roadmap A l s o called the Roadmap. Plan developed by the Open Systems Interconnect-sponsored Network Management Forum. Outlines requirements that vendors must address for their systems to work on a network. *See* OSI, NMF and OMNIPoints.

open mode State in which the vi editor program acts like a line editor instead of a full visual editor. Results when the terminal type either has not been identified by the user or has not been recognized by the computer. *See* termcap, terminfo, vi, line editor and visual editor.

Open Network Computing Commonly abbreviated and called ONC. *See* ONC.

Open Real Time Kernel Interface Definition Commonly abbreviated and called ORKID. *See* ORKID.

Open Shortest Path First *(INET)* Commonly abbreviated and called OSPF. *See* OSPF.

Open Software Foundation Commonly abbreviated and called OSF. *See* OSF.

open system architecture C o m m o n l y called open systems. *See* open systems.

open systems 1. Describes hardware or software components that are not dependent on any vendor's proprietary architecture. Such components, e.g. microprocessor architecture, bus, protocol and graphical user interface, utilize well-defined and documented in public specifications. The computer system can be upgraded with any hardware component or software application manufactured by any vendor without damaging or failing to work with components already in use. Provide for portability, interoperability and scalability by following published standards, e.g. from the Open Software Foundation Inc. or UNIX System Laboratories Inc. *See* portability, interoperability and scalability. 2. Ability to move between computer systems on a network that uses established protocols or standards.

open systems environment Commonly abbreviated and called OSE. *See* OSE.

Open Systems Foundation Commonly abbreviated and called OSF. *See* OSF.

Open Systems Interconnect
Commonly abbreviated and called OSI. *See* OSI.

Open Systems Interconnection
Commonly abbreviated and called OSI. *See* OSI.

Open Systems Interconnection Implementors' Workshop Commonly abbreviated and called OIW. *See* OIW.

Open Systems Interconnection Reference Model Commonly abbreviated and called OSIRM. *See* OSIRM.

Open Systems Interconnection Transaction Processing Commonly abbreviated and called OSI TP. *See* OSI TP.

Open Systems International Network
Abbreviated and commonly known as OSINet. *See* OSINet.

Open Systems Today Called UNIX Today! until March 1991. Monthly magazine published by CMP Publications Inc. that is free to qualified readers who use UNIX on the job. Features articles on UNIX and open systems products, and projected trends in the UNIX and open systems industry.

Open User Recommended Systems Commonly abbreviated and called OURS. *See* OURS.

operand Any data on which a function is being performed, e.g. a letter, line or word that is the subject of a command in the vi editor program. *See* vi.

operating system Commonly abbreviated and called OS. *See* OS.

Operating System/2 Commonly abbreviated and called OS/2. *See* OS/2.

Operating System Command and Report Language Commonly abbreviated and called OSCRI. *See* OSCRL.

operating system snob Any individual who is totally dedicated to a single operating system and refuses to recognize the merits of others. *See* shell snob and UNIX Wars.

operation Any previously identified action to be taken by a computer instruction, e.g. define ADD a,b as add contents of b to a, HCF as halt and catch fire or, WME as Why ME?

operations *(ATT)* Command in the UNIX System V, Release 4 line printer services menu. Combines the accept, reject, enable, disable, lpadmin, lpsched, lpshut and lpstat commands. Used to perform normal print management functions, from turning on and off print requests to indicating if a printer is available. *See* SVR4.x, accept, reject, enable, disable, lpadmin, lpsched, lpshut and lpstat.

Operations, Administration and Management Commonly abbreviated and called OA&M. *See* OA&M.

Operation Sun Devil Secret Service antihacker operation conducted May 8, 1990. Targeted a group of hackers from New York to California at 27 locations in 14 cities. As a result, the group was accused of theft and abuse of credit cards,

phone cards and alteration of medical records. Losses were estimated at $50 million. Following these raids, Mitch Kapor, co-founder of Lotus Development Corp., helped form the Electronic Frontier Foundation to educate and inform computer users of changes in the industry and to support perceived infringement of First Amendment rights due to investigations and arrests of hackers. *See* EFF.

operator 1. *(ATT)* Command in the UNIX System V, Release 4 restore service management menu. Used to establish those users who are authorized to run restore requests. Similar to the rsnotify command. *See* rsnotify. 2. Individual responsible for the day-to-day running of a large computer system. 3. Term in the vi editor program for a command that is to be executed, e.g. append, insert, delete or change. *See* vi and operand.

Oppose Sun Forever Commonly abbreviated and called OSF. *See* OSF.

/opt UNIX System V, Release 4 root file system directory used to hold additional application software programs. *See* SVR4.x and root file system.

opt Optimize. Editing variable in the vi editor program. When set, enhances the operation of terminals that lack addressable cursors, which can be moved anywhere on the screen. *See* vi.

OPTARG *(ATT)* Option argument. Korn shell variable. Maintains the last value of an option argument used, where the option required an argument. Supports programmers by providing a standard mechanism for parsing command arguments. *See* Korn shell and parse.

Optical Carrier level number Commonly abbreviated and called OC-n. *See* OC-n.

Optical character reader Commonly abbreviated and called OCR. *See* OCR.

Optical character recognition Commonly abbreviated and called OCR. *See* OCR.

optical disc drive Storage device that uses laser technology to write data to and read data from a disk. Provides greater access speed and storage capacity than magnetic tape media.

optical fiber Commonly called fiber-optic. *See* fiber-optic.

Optical Read-Only Memory Abbreviated and commonly known as O-ROM. *See* O-ROM.

optical scanner External light-sensing device which reads the shape of characters and images, and converts them into data or bit patterns for storage in a computer.

optical tape Tape on which laser light can imprint and store data, like data is stored on compact discs. The tape is made from the same polyester film used in magnetic tapes. Metallic layers are added that react with laser light to imprint data on the tape. *See* CD-ROM, WORM, acousto-optics and DOTS.

Optical Time-Domain Reflectometer Commonly abbreviated and called OTDR. *See* OTDR.

optimize Editing variable in the vi editor program. *See* opt.

OPTIND *(ATT)* **Opt**ion **ind**ex. Korn shell variable. Contains the index of the argument for the next option.

option Modifier that allows a user to alter a command and vary the information which the command outputs. Normally preceded by a dash (-) or sometimes a plus sign (+). Precedes the file name in the command input.

CLP>ls -l⌐

Option that indicates a user is running a long list of the contents of a file.

optional argument Command argument which is not required for a command to function but acts on the information provided by the command, e.g. in ls -la, ls does not need the la arguments to function since these only modify the format and content of the information provided by the ls command.

OPTIONAL Components Expansion of the definition of X/Open Co. Ltd.'s Common Applications Environment, presented in the X/Open Portability Guides. Composed of the BASE Profile, the minimum set of software components; PLUS Profile, the standards for COBOL, FORTRAN, Pascal, Index Sequential Access Method, relational database language, terminal interfaces, X Window System management, transport interface and personal computer interface; and standards for Ada, source code transfer and interprocess communication. *See* X/Open, CAE, XPG, BASE Profile and PLUS Profile.

options Key word used in creating a kernel. Establishes various options that are either common to UNIX or added by the computer vendor, e.g. options for establishing a quota on a user's disk space, supporting Internet protocols and system permission levels.

optoelectronics Science of combining electronics and optical technology.

Orange Book Jargon term for the security standards developed by the Department of Defense for computer systems and published in August 1983 in the Trusted Computer System Evaluation Criteria by the National Computer Security Center. Named for the orange color of its cover. These physical security levels control access to the system through either passwords or implementation of access control lists. They are defined as A through D, with levels A, B and C containing numbered sublevels. Class A1 is the highest verifiable security level; D is the lowest level and has no security requirements. *See* NCSC, level A1, level B1, level B2, level B3, level C1, level C2 and Level D.

ORB **O**bject **R**equest **B**roker. Object Management Group manager of client requests. A standard for passing objects between heterogeneous computer systems on a network. *See* OMA, client, object, request and CORBA.

ordinary account Commonly called user account. *See* user account.

ordinary file Any file containing data, programs or text. No special structure is established for the file that the system must comply with. The data in the file can be randomly accessed in a sequence of characters or symbols.

ordinary pipes Commonly called pipes. *See* pipes.

original equipment manufacture Commonly abbreviated and called OEM. *See* OEM.

ORKID Open Real Time Kernel Interface Definition. Set of standards for multitasking and multiprocessor environments for real-time operating systems. *See* RTOS and OBIOS.

O-ROM Optical Read-Only Memory. In contrast to CD-ROM which was developed for audio use and then modified for information storage. O-ROM is 3.5-inch read-only optical disk technology specifically developed for computer data storage. In contrast, compact disk read-only memory (CD-ROM) was developed for audio use and then modified for information storage.

orphan file Commonly called unreferenced file. *See* unreferenced file.

orphan process Commonly called zombie. *See* zombie.

orphan task Any task or process that is not grouped with other tasks to form a cycle. *See* cycle.

OS 1. Operating system. Set of programs used by the computer to understand and process commands, control input and output, schedule, manage data and control the operation of peripheral devices. Could be considered the brain that makes the computer work. For UNIX systems, it is UNIX System V and/or the Fourth Berkeley Software Distribution, Second or Third Release, or the commercial derivations, including IBM Corp.'s AIX and Pyramid Technology Inc.'s OSx. Personal computers use DOS and derivatives but can also use UNIX or CP/M. **2.** Programs which coordinate the functions of both the computer hardware and software. **3.** Programs which allows a computer to manage its own operation. *See* UNIX. **4.** Object Services. Object Management Group facilities that enable the user to create and maintain objects or operations. *See* OMG and object.

OS/2 Operating System/2. Operating system jointly developed by IBM Corp. and Microsoft Corp. Designed to provide multitasking, virtual memory management, etc. for personal computers. Enables personal computers using DOS and derivatives to perform multitasking. *See* multitasking.

OSCRL Operating System Command and Report Language. Project undertaken in the 1980s by the International Organization for Standardization to develop a universal input/output language for all computers. *See* ISO.

OSE Open Systems Environment. Standards for interoperability, application software portability, interaction of computer users and data.

OSF 1. Open Software Foundation Inc. Also called the Open Systems Foundation. A nonprofit organization which supports open software. Involved in research and development, providing specifications and portable software products based upon industry standards and open software technology for computers and network systems. Originally formed in 1988 to develop an operating system to compete with UNIX System V, Release 4. Founding members include IBM Corp., Digital Equipment Corp., Hewlett-Packard Co., Siemens (now Siemens-Nixdorf), Groupe Bull, Nixdorf and Apollo Computer. Located in Cambridge, Massachusetts. *See* SVR4.x and OSF/1. **2.** Oppose Sun Forever. Tongue-in-cheek motto, based on the abbreviation for Open Software Foundation (OSF) and coined during the UNIX Wars. Related to the formation of OSF, which was founded to oppose the alliance between Sun Microsystems Inc. and AT&T Co. to develop UNIX System V, Release 4. *See* UNIX Wars and UI.

OSF/1 First operating system released by the Open Software Foundation Inc. Released in 1990. Based on Carnegie-Mellon University's Mach 2.5 kernel, incorporates the Application Environment Specification interface and includes parts of IBM Corp.'s AIX, AT&T Co.'s UNIX System V and Berkeley Software Distribution operating systems. Complies with the standards of both the Portable Operating System Interface for Computer Environments (POSIX) and X/Open. *See* OSF, Mach, AES, System V, POSIX and X/Open.

OSF/1 MK Microkernel version of the Open Software Foundation Inc.'s operating system. Based on Carnegie-Mellon University's Mach 3.0 operating system, with the OSF/1 utilities running on top of the microkernel. *See* microkernel, Mach, OSF and OSF/1.

OSF/Motif Commonly called Motif. *See* Motif.

OSI Open Systems Interconnection. Sometimes called the Open Systems Interconnect. Internationally accepted protocol standards program sponsored by the International Standards Organization for open systems networks and computing. The OSI model has seven layers known as the *Open Systems Interconnection Reference Model*. *See* ISO and ISO/OSI.

OSINet Open Systems International Network. Network operated by the Corporation for Open Systems International. Used to test the interoperability of products in order to obtain approval for compliance with the Open Systems Interconnection standards. OSINet is an X.25 packet switch network that was first used by the National Institute of Standards and Technology. *See* COS, OSI, X.25, NIST and COS Mark.

OSI/Network Management Forum Commonly abbreviated and called NMF. *See* NMF.

OSI/NMF OSI/Network Management Forum. Original name of the Network Management Forum. *See* NMF.

OSI/NM Forum Commonly abbreviated and called NMF. *See* NMF.

OSI Reference Model Commonly abbreviated and called OSIRM. *See* OSIRM.

OSIRM Open Systems Interconnection Reference Model. Also called the ISO/OSI protocol suite or OSI protocol suite. A set of protocols developed by the International Organization for Standardization/Open Systems Interconnection for network functions that enable communication between products of various vendors. Composed of seven protocol layers: application layer, presentation layer, session layer, transport layer, network layer, data link layer and physical layer. *See* ISO/OSI, ITU-T, FTAM, application layer, presentation layer, session layer, transport layer, network layer, data link layer and physical layer.

OSI TP Commonly called ISO TP (International Organization for Standardization transaction processing). *See* ISO TP.

OSPF *(INET)* Open Shortest Path First. Internet protocol for sending communications between routers (intelligent bridges) on a network using the Transmission Control Protocol/Internet Protocol. Determines the most efficient communication path available on the network, and can modify traffic or reroute traffic around a network failure if necessary. *See* Internet, TCP/IP, router, RIP and IS-IS.

OSPF Interoperability Group Group founded in May, 1992 by 3Com Corp., Proteon Inc. and Wellfleet to promote acceptance, growth and interoperability of hardware and applications running the Open Shortest Path First protocol. *See* OSPF.

OSx Pyramid Technology Inc.'s UNIX dual universe operating system that includes both the Berkeley Software Distribution and AT&T Co.'s UNIX System V. *See* BSD and System V.

OTDR Optical Time-Domain Reflectometer. Device used to locate problems within fiber-optic cables. Sends a signal along the wire and watches for a response to bounce back. Based upon the nature of the response and the time lapse, can determine the type of problem and approximate location. *See* TDR.

other Term related to permissions to access files or directories of other users on a computer. A category of users that is neither the owner of files and directories nor a member of the same group as the owner of the files and directories. An other may or may not have the necessary permissions to access files and directories. This depends upon what changes a user has made to the file permissions or what default settings for file and directory permissions have been established in the umask file. *See* permissions, group and umask.

OURS Open User Recommended Systems. Group formed by Novell Inc. in 1991 to identify user needs to vendors and increase interoperability among competing networking products. Has about 30 members, including Chase Manhattan Bank, Coca-Cola, Texaco and Wells Fargo Bank. Located in New York.

outbox File or directory that holds outgoing electronic mail until it is sent. *See* e-mail.

outfolder Electronic-mail variable. *See* .mailrc variables (Appendix F).

output Information that is printed as a document or sent to a file by a computer. Usually results from a command or a program having been executed.

output redirection Changing the output of a command so the information is not sent to the standard output (normally the

input device, or terminal, that initiated the command) but to either a file or alternative device. *See* standard output and device.

outsourcing Contracting out all or part of the responsibility for a company's data processing, including training, maintenance, software development, systems and network integration. *See* smartsourcing.

overlapping windows Arrangement in which multiple windows with different contents on the screen overlap one another.

overlap seeks Process in which disk controllers and disks are capable of scheduling multiple operations at the same time.

overlay Process no longer used since the development of virtual memory. To reuse blocks of storage in memory. As one program ends, it is replaced in memory by the next program needed.

overstrike Commonly called bold. *See* bold.

overtype In text processing, to replace existing text with new text.

overwrite To replace the contents of a file with new data or, sometimes, nothing at all. Often the result of a typing error. Commonly known as an *OH S*!T!!* command. *See* OH S*!T!! command.

owner 1. Normally the user who creates a file. But the user identification of the file's owner can be changed to that of another user by the original owner or root with the chown command. *See* chown. 2. Routine used to check if a user trying to access a file or directory is the owner of the file or directory. *See* FIO.

owtmp File used to archive the contents of the wtmp file, which logs user logins and init processes, when system accounting is processed. *See* runacct and /etc/wtmp.

P

p Abbreviation for pico. *See* pico.

P Abbreviation for peta. *See* peta.

p2c Pascal-2-C. Source code translator that changes programs written in Pascal to C language. *See* Pascal, C language and ptoc.

P5 Pentium 586. Jargon term for Intel Corp.'s Pentium 80586 microprocessor. *See* Pentium.

P1003 *(POS)* Commonly called Project 1003. *See* Project 1003.

P1003.0 *(POS)* Commonly called IEEE P1003.0 working group. *See* IEEE P1003.0 working group.

P1003.1 *(POS)* Commonly called IEEE P1003.1 working group. *See* IEEE P1003.1 working group.

P1003.1a *(POS)* Commonly called IEEE P1003.1a project. *See* IEEE P1003.1a project.

P1003.1b *(POS)* Commonly called IEEE P1003.1b project. *See* IEEE P1003.1b project.

P1003.1c *(POS)* Commonly called IEEE P1003.1c project. *See* IEEE P1003.1c project.

P1003.1d *(POS)* Commonly called IEEE P1003.1d project. *See* IEEE P1003.1d project.

P1003.1e *(POS)* Commonly called IEEE P1003.1e project. *See* IEEE P1003.1e project.

P1003.1f *(POS)* Commonly called IEEE P1003.1f project. *See* IEEE P1003.1f project.

P1003.1g *(POS)* Commonly called IEEE P1003.1g project. *See* IEEE P1003.1g project.

P1003.2 *(POS)* Commonly called IEEE P1003.2 working group. *See* IEEE P1003.2 working group.

P1003.2a *(POS)* Commonly called IEEE P1003.2a project. *See* IEEE P1003.2a project.

P1003.2b *(POS)* Commonly called IEEE P1003.2b project. *See* IEEE P1003.2b project.

P1003.2c *(POS)* Commonly called IEEE P1003.2c project. *See* IEEE P1003.2c project.

P1003.2d *(POS)* Commonly called IEEE P1003.2d project. *See* IEEE P1003.2d project.

P1003.3 *(POS)* Commonly called IEEE P1003.3 working group. *See* IEEE P1003.3 working group.

P1003.4 *(POS)* Commonly called IEEE P1003.4 working group. *See* IEEE P1003.4 working group.

P1003.4a *(POS)* Commonly called IEEE P1003.4a project. *See* IEEE P1003.4a project.

P1003.4b *(POS)* Commonly called IEEE P1003.4b project. *See* IEEE P1003.4b project.

P1003.5 *(POS)* Commonly called IEEE P1003.5 working group. *See* IEEE P1003.5 working group.

P1003.6 *(POS)* Commonly called IEEE P1003.6 working group. *See* IEEE P1003.6 working group.

P1003.7 *(POS)* Commonly called IEEE P1003.7 working group. *See* IEEE P1003.7 working group.

P1003.7.1 *(POS)* Commonly called IEEE P1003.7.1 project. *See* IEEE P1003.7.1 project.

P1003.7.2 *(POS)* Commonly called IEEE P1003.7.2 project. *See* IEEE P1003.7.2 project.

P1003.7.3 *(POS)* Commonly called IEEE P1003.7.3 project. *See* IEEE P1003.7.3 project.

P1003.8 *(POS)* Commonly called IEEE P1003.8 working group. *See* IEEE P1003.8 working group.

P1003.9 *(POS)* Commonly called IEEE P1003.9 working group. *See* IEEE P1003.9 working group.

P1003.10 *(POS)* Commonly called IEEE P1003.10 working group. *See* IEEE P1003.10 working group.

P1003.11 *(POS)* Commonly called IEEE P1003.11 working group. *See* IEEE P1003.11 working group.

P1003.12 *(POS)* Commonly called IEEE P1003.12 working group. *See* IEEE P1003.12 working group.

P1003.13 *(POS)* Commonly called IEEE P1003.13 working group. *See* IEEE P1003.13 working group.

P1003.14 *(POS)* Commonly called IEEE P1003.14 working group. *See* IEEE P1003.14 working group.

P1003.15 *(POS)* Commonly called IEEE P1003.15 working group. *See* IEEE P1003.15 working group.

P1003.16 *(POS)* Commonly called IEEE P1003.16 working group. *See* IEEE P1003.16 working group.

P1003.17 *(POS)* Commonly called IEEE P1003.17 working group. *See* IEEE P1003.17 working group.

P1003.18 *(POS)* Commonly called IEEE P1003.18 working group. *See* IEEE P1003.18 working group.

P1003.19 *(POS)* Commonly called IEEE P1003.19 working group. *See* IEEE P1003.19 working group.

P1003.20 *(POS)* Commonly called IEEE P1003.20 working group. *See* IEEE P1003.20 working group.

P1003.21 *(POS)* Commonly called IEEE P1003.21 working group. *See* IEEE P1003.21 working group.

P1003.22 *(POS)* Commonly called IEEE P1003.22 working group. *See* IEEE P1003.22 working group.

P1201 *(POS)* Commonly called IEEE P1201 working group. *See* IEEE P1201 working group.

P1201.1 *(POS)* Commonly called IEEE P1201.1 working group. *See* IEEE P1201.1 working group.

P1201.2 *(POS)* Commonly called IEEE P1201.2 working group. *See* IEEE P1201.2 working group.

P1224 *(POS)* Commonly called IEEE P1224 working group. *See* IEEE P1224 working group.

P1237 *(POS)* Commonly called IEEE P1237 working group. *See* IEEE P1237 working group.

P1238 *(POS)* Commonly called IEEE P1238 working group. *See* IEEE P1238 working group.

P1238.1 *(POS)* Commonly called IEEE P1238.1 working group. *See* IEEE P1238.1 working group.

P1238.2 *(POS)* Commonly called IEEE P1238.2 working group. *See* IEEE P1238.2 working group.

P1387.1 *(POS)* Commonly called IEEE P1387.1 project. *See* IEEE P1387.1 project.

P1387.2 *(POS)* Commonly called IEEE P1387.2 project. *See* IEEE P1387.2 project.

P1387.3 *(POS)* Commonly called IEEE P1387.3 project. *See* IEEE P1387.3 project.

P1387.4 *(POS)* Commonly called IEEE P1387.4 project. *See* IEEE P1387.4 project.

pac *(BSD)* Printer accounting. Command used to display information on printer use.

pacct Commonly called /usr/adm/pacct. *See* /usr/adm/pacct.

pack *(ATT/XEN)* Command used to compress files to conserve storage area. Also used to reduce the size of a file before transmitting over a data network, thereby reducing network overhead. A packed file is normally 25 to 40 percent smaller than the original file. Following the pack, the original file is replaced with new file with a ".z" added to the name, e.g. file name becomes file name.z. *See* pcat and unpack.

package Jargon term for a software program.

packet One or more bytes of data bundled into a unit. Contains address information so it can be sent, like an envelope, to a receiving location. The size of a packet varies from vendor to vendor, according to the type of computer or network on which the transmission is taking place. Networks using packet technology can transmit information faster, more efficiently and more accurately than those using older communications protocols, which transmit data byte by byte. *See* TCP/IP.

Packet Assembler Disassembler
Commonly abbreviated and called PAD. *See* PAD.

packet filter Program used to establish a firewall to protect computer systems and networks from external hostile action. Installed in a router connected to a network and used to review all external requests for service. Establishes predefined parameters, e.g. sets rules that do not permit any external TELNET connections but do allow electronic mail to pass. Data packets considered to be dangerous may be discarded while others may be routed to computers for action. *See* firewall, TELNET and e-mail.

Packet InterNet Groper *(INET)* Commonly abbreviated and called PING. *See* PING.

Packetized Ensemble Protocol
Abbreviated and commonly known as PEP. *See* PEP.

packet switch network
Communications network based on packet switch technology, in which data is bundled and sent in packets, or envelopes, and there are multiple paths over which the data can be sent. The physical data can be switched between the various paths depending upon the availability of paths, contention on paths, or the most direct available route in operation. *See* packet.

Packet Switch Node Commonly abbreviated and called PSN. *See* PSN.

Packet Transfer Mode Abbreviated and commonly known as PTM. *See* PTM.

PAD Packet Assembler Disassembler. Protocol used to connect a terminal to a remote host on an X.25 network. *See* X.25.

page 1. Command used to display either all or part (starting at a specific line number) of a file, or to search for a specific string in a file. 2. Section of a program. To better manage memory resources, a program is divided into pages. The size of a page, measured in bytes, depends on the architecture of the vendor's hardware. Program pages can then be logically moved in to and out of main memory. *See* paging. 3. Electronic-mail variable. *See* .mailrc variables (Appendix F). 4. Terminal screen full of data. 5. To scroll through a document, one page at a time.

pagedaemon Page daemon. Background program responsible for moving pages, or sections of a program, out of main memory to support paging. *See* daemon and paging.

page-description languages
Abbreviated and commonly known as PDL. *See* PDL.

page fault A page fault occurs when an active process references a page, text or data, in its virtual memory that is not resident in real memory. *See* paging, virtual memory, dirty, minor page fault and major page fault.

page fixing Marking a page as nonpageable, leaving it in main memory while a program is executed. *See* nonpageable.

pagein Process of moving a page, or section of a program, into main memory. *See* paging.

page length Maximum length of the space in which text and graphics can be printed on a page. Measured in either the number of lines or distance (inches or centimeters).

page offset Term in the nroff text formatting program for the left margin. *See* nroff.

pageout 1. *(ATT)* Paging daemon. Background program used to manage free memory as pages, or portions of programs, are moved out of memory. *See* paging. 2. Process of moving a page, or section of a program, out of main memory. *See* paging.

page push To send pages, or sections of a program, on which errors are detected to secondary storage.

pager Program used to display a file on a terminal, one page at a time. *See* pg, more and less.

PAGER Electronic-mail variable. *See* .mailrc variables (Appendix F).

page reclaim Process of retrieving or reusing virtual memory pages that are marked as unused.

pagesize *(BSD)* Command used to display the size of the system memory page, or number of bytes of memory defined as a page for that computer. *See* page and paging.

pages per minute Commonly abbreviated and called ppm. *See* ppm.

page table entry Commonly abbreviated and called PTE. *See* PTE.

page width Maximum width of the area in which text or graphics can be printed on a page. Measured in either the number of characters or distance (inches or centimeters).

pagination Process of dividing a document into pages.

paging 1. Process originally developed for the Berkeley Software Distribution operating system. Similar to swapping in that it frees up space in memory to allow more programs to be started and run at the same time. Not all parts of a program run in memory at once. When memory is full, pages, or sections, of programs which are not in use are moved to a memory buffer, called the dirty page list. When there is no more room in the memory buffer, pages are moved to disk. When certain pages are needed, the computer first looks for them on the dirty page list, then on the disk. Since smaller segments of a program are moved, there is less impact on input/output. Paging frees memory for more processes and does not slow down the system. But, if more processes are initiated than memory can accommodate, and initiated faster than paging can handle, the computer will start swapping. *See* dirty, I/O, backing storage, secondary storage and swapping. 2. Word processing term for scrolling through a text file, one page at a time.

paging rate Measurement of the average number of pages moved into and out of main memory during a specific period of time.

paint Also called paint a screen. Process of writing characters or drawing graphic displays on a screen.

palmtop computer Small, hand-held computer that uses a combination of hardware and built-in software to provide portability. Generally, measures approximately 9 inches by 4 inches by 1 inch, and weighs from 8.5 ounces to 3 pounds. Uses a display screen of 5 inches by 2 inches, and color graphic adapter or video graphics array display. Offers 256 kilobytes to 3 megabytes of random access memory, and 4 to 40 megabytes of storage capacity. Microprocessors used in palmtop computers range from 8086 to 486. Applications are loaded in read-only memory chips with batteries that provide 3.5 to 80 hours of operation. Some use penlike devices instead of keyboards for entering data. *See* pen-based computer.

Palo Alto Research Center
Abbreviation for the Xerox Palo Alto Research Center. Commonly called Xerox PARC. *See* Xerox PARC.

panic **1.** System failure detected by the kernel that cannot be fixed. When a panic occurs, the kernel begins shutting down the system to prevent damage to the file system. *See* kernel and file system. **2.** System program started when an unrecoverable error occurs. Sends a message to users indicating there is a system failure and shuts down the system by ending all operations and writing the data in main memory to disk. *See* sync, core and crash.

PAP Password Authentication Protocol. Security protocol used in the Point-to-Point Protocol for one computer to identify itself to another. A two-way handshake containing an identifier and password is continually sent between the peer computers until either their identify is verified or the connection is broken. *See* PPP and CHAP.

paper copy Commonly called hard-copy. *See* hard-copy.

paperless society Electronic age in which all transactions would be performed with computers and communication networks, and not confirmed on paper.

paper tape Large roll of paper, approximately 1 to 2 inches wide, used in an outdated process of inputting and outputting data on a computer. Patterns of dots representing characters were punched out on the paper.

PAR *(POS)* Project Authorization Request. Documentation used by the Institute of Electrical and Electronic Engineers to request either new specifications or modifications to existing specifications of Portable Operating System Interface for Computer Environments (POSIX) standards. *See* POSIX.

paradigm Process or pattern in which a change in one factor will result in a change in all factors.

parallel interface Method of interfacing, or connecting, computers with other computers or peripherals to transfer data 1 byte at a time. Faster than a serial interface, but limited by the length of wire that can be run from the computer to the peripheral. Connections normally cannot exceed 100 feet unless devices are added to boost the transmission signal or expensive gold wire is used. *See* serial.

parallel port Type of connection on a computer or peripheral configured for a parallel interface in which data is transmitted 1 byte at a time. *See* port.

parallel processing Approach to computer processing in which a large task is broken down into smaller tasks and separate processors in the computer simultaneously work on each task. When work on the smaller tasks is completed, the results are recombined. *See* MP, threads, task and massively parallel processing.

parallel programming Writing a program so that separate elements of it are executed at the same time. Concurrent C/C++ is an example of a language written for parallel programming. *See* Concurrent C/C++ language.

parameter **1.** Set of values used to define a computer's level of tolerance, e.g. input speed, number of concurrent users or number of concurrent processes. **2.** Set of values or variables which a user enters to define, modify or limit the output of a program. *See* argument and option.

PARC Palo Alto Research Center. Commonly called Xerox PARC. *See* Xerox PARC.

parent Jargon term for parent directory and parent process. *See* parent directory and parent process.

parent directory In the UNIX hierarchical design, a directory which contains the current working directory. When a ls -l, long form listing of a directory's files is run, the current working directory is identified by . (dot) and the parent directory is identified by .. (dot dot). The names are not provided, only the permissions, ownership and date of last update. *See* current working directory.

parentheses () Metacharacter used in regular expressions in the egrep and awk programs. Used to create a subexpression to match strings in conjunction with other metacharacters, such as *, ? or +. For example, *(myil)* would match stings like kajmyilb or tnfmyilb. *See* metacharacter and regular expression.

parent PID Commonly abbreviated and called PPID. *See* PPID.

parent process First process started by a program that in turn creates separate, or child, processes that are required to execute the program. *See* fork, process and child process.

parent process ID Commonly abbreviated and called PPID. *See* PPID.

parent process identifier Commonly abbreviated and called PPID. *See* PPID.

PA-RISC Precision Architecture Reduced Instruction Set Computing. Reduced instruction set computing computer chip technology developed by the Hewlett-Packard Co. *See* RISC.

parity Method of ensuring accuracy of data transmission between computers, or computers and external devices, e.g. printers and terminals, by checking for equivalent counts of binary data. Parity is set and measured in bits at either odd, even or none to represent the number of 1s that must always be transmitted. The parity for both the sending and receiving units must be the same. *See* binary.

parity bit An additional 0 or 1 bit transferred each time a character is transmitted to match the number of bits (odd or even) used in the system. *See* parity.

parity disk Disk used to maintain parity data in Redundant Array of Inexpensive Disks technology. Parity information is maintained on a separate disk to reduce the possibility of a total loss of data. *See* RAID.

parse 1. To divide an input string into smaller sections and then study each section in order to understand the whole. For example, the expression:

a = b + 2 + c * 3

consists of nine parts: the letters a, b and c, the numbers 2 and 3 and the symbols +, + and *. Parsing is the process of breaking down the expression ('a = b + 2 + c * 3') into these component parts, determining what the parts mean, that is:

2 is the number two
+ means add
* means multiply

and determining what to do with the parts. In this example, it means: multiply c by three; add the result, two and b; and call the new result a. It also could mean: fetch the contents of the memory location referred to by b and add two to it; fetch c, multiply it by three and add it to the previous result; and store the final result in a. 2. To preprocess raw data for manipulation by subsequent programs. 3. Shell preprocess. *See* token.

parser Program that preprocesses data. *See* parse.

partial backup Complete backup of a specific file system. *See* backup, full backup, incremental backup and file system.

partition Commonly called disk partition. *See* disk partition.

partitioning Process of dividing a disk drive, or physical disk, into logical disks, or areas that the computer operating system considers to be separate and independent disk drives. Used to allocate a portion of a disk drive to a file system. *See* physical disk and logical disk.

PASC *(POS)* **P**ortable **A**pplication **S**tand-ards **C**ommittee. Called the Technical Committee on Operating Systems and Application Environments (TCOS) until 1993. The Institute of Electrical and Electronics Engineers sponsor committee for Portable Operating System Interface for Computer Environments. *See* IEEE and POSIX.

Pascal 1. Computer language developed by Nicklaus Wirth in 1971 for teaching computer science. 2. Compiler for the Pascal language.

passive open socket Transmission Control Protocol term for a socket that monitors a network for a request by an active open socket to be connected. When it receives such a request, the passive open socket establishes a connection and accepts incoming data. *See* TCP, sockets and active open socket.

passive tool UNIX security-related program. Passive tools are used for such tasks as checking the ability of user passwords to resist being compromised; overall file security; and weakness within the operating system. *See* active tool.

passwd 1. *(ATT/BSD/XEN)* Command used to change or create the login password. 2. Commonly accepted abbreviation for password. *See* password. 3. Common name given to the file /etc/passwd which contains the encrypted passwords for a system's user accounts. *See* encrypt and account.

passwdck *(OTH)* **Passw**ord **ck** check. Shell script used to review the password file for accounts without a password, root permissions, incorrect user identifier or group identifier and write permission. *See* shell script, UID and GID.

password Security measure used with a user account to help ensure only authorized persons obtain access to the system. A user enters the user account name and the system asks for the user account password, e.g. Myilb1. The characters in the password are masked so they are not visible on the screen as they are entered. The system then checks a file called passwd to match the password. If a match is found, access to the system is granted; if not, the user must begin the process again. A password has at least six but no more than eight characters, one of which should be nonalphabetic. The user should be able to easily remember the password, and should not write it down or tell anyone else what it is. *See* /etc/passwd and shawdowpassword.

password aging Security measure which requires a user's password to be changed at set intervals. The interval (a certain number of weeks) is established by the system administrator and is part of the password file. *See* /etc/passwd.

Password Authentication Protocol Commonly abbreviated and called PAP. *See* PAP.

password cracker Writer of a program, or the program itself, that is used in an attempt to obtain user passwords.

password ordering 1. Putting user identifiers in sequence as a method of keeping track of passwords being used to access a computer system. Allows the system administration program to automatically assign the next unused user identifier in the sequence. *See* UID. 2. On some older systems, putting the user sequence in the /etc/passwd file in order according to extent of use. Failed to speed up the login process for those using the system a lot since the password file was screened sequentially.

paste *(ATT/XEN)* Command used to combine characters or columns from different databases into a single line, or merge the same lines of several files or subsequent lines of one file. *See* cut.

patch 1. *(OTH)* Program used to fix program bugs in software source code. Available through the USENET international

UNIX bulletin board. *See* debugger and USENET. **2.** Quickly prepared, temporary solution to a problem in software code.

path **1.** Route to a file or document. In UNIX, all absolute paths begin with slash / or the root file system. *See* root file system, absolute path and relative pathname. **2.** Also called search path. Directories to be searched by a command that has been input by a user. **3.** *(BSD)* C shell environmental variable used to search for executable files or commands. *See* PATH.

PATH Environmental variable used with the Bourne and Korn shells that identifies all the paths to be searched for executable files or commands.

pathalias File used with the UNIX-to-UNIX CoPy (UUCP) communications system in connecting two computers for data transmission. Determines the remote host and what is needed to make connection for a UUCP session. *See* UUCP.

path name Commonly spelled pathname. *See* pathname.

pathname **1.** Also spelled path name. Address or road map which leads to or uniquely identifies a specific file and indicates where it is in a hierarchical file system. Each level of the pathname is separated by a slash (/), e.g. /usr/SHE/collier/myfile would be the pathname to a file named myfile for a user whose login ID is collier and who works for an organization named SHE. *See* file system, absolute pathname and relative pathname. **2.** Field in the file USERFILE used to identify the files that remote systems can access via the UNIX -to-UNIX CoPy communications system. *See* USERFILE and UUCP.

Pathologically Eclectic Rubbish Listener Commonly abbreviated and called Perl. *See* Perl.

Patriot Partners Organization formed by IBM Corp. and Metaphor Computer Systems Inc. to establish standards for interfaces used with 32-bit computer architecture, e.g. OS/2. *See* OS/2 and OMG.

pattern matching Process of searching for a character or string of characters.

pause *(ATT)* System call that stops the running, or call, of a process until a specified signal is received. *See* system call.

payload protocol The communications protocol of messages that have been encapsulated and carried over another protocol, known as the *carrier protocol*, between two networks. *See* encapsulation and carrier protocol.

PC Personal computer. Small, general-purpose, single-user computer which is growing larger and faster with every new release of hardware and operating systems. The central processing unit in these microcomputers is a single chip, which distinguishes them from larger computers. *See* chip.

The IBM XT was instrumental in ushering in the PC revolution.

pcat *(ATT)* Command used to look at a file that has been compressed with the pack command. Does not unpack the file. The compressed file can be redirected to another file, device or command, but will remain packed. *See* pack and unpack.

PCB Abbreviation for printed circuit board. *See* printed circuit board.

pc board Printed circuit **board**. Commonly called printed circuit board. *See* printed circuit board.

PCC Portable C Compiler. Version of the C compiler written by Stephen Johnson that allows the C compiler to be easily ported to several types of computers.

PC-DOS Personal Computer Disk Operating System. IBM Corp.'s implementation of the DOS operating system. *See* DOS and MS-DOS.

PCF Portable Compiled Font. X Window System font format released with the Massachusetts Institute of Technology X 11, Release 5 specification of the X Window System. Based upon the Server Normal Format (SNF). With PCF, fonts are architecture-independent and can be moved between different computers, unlike SNF fonts. *See* X Window System, BDF and SNF.

PCI 1. Protocol Control Information. Open Systems Interconnection term for data that is passed from one protocol layer to another for management and processing. *See* OSI and OSIRM. **2.** Peripheral Component Interconnect. Commonly abbreviated and called PCI bus. *See* PCI bus.

PCI bus Peripheral Component Interconnect **bus**. The local bus standard developed by Intel Corp. which allows the central processing unit (CPU) to transfer data to 16 devices at 33 megahertz along a 32- or 64-bit pathway. This version is a separate bus isolated from the CPU unlike the competing Video Electronics Standards Association local bus standard, which is an extension of the bus the CPU uses to access main memory. The PCI bus first appeared in hardware in 1993. Both standards are a response to the need for faster graphics display that could not be met by the slower Industry Standard Architecture and Extended Industry Standard Architecture buses operating at 16 megahertz. *See* EISA, ISA, local bus, VL-Bus and CPU.

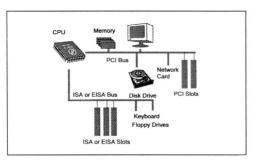

The PCI bus is characterized by its ability to use high speed 64-bit PCI devices while maintaining compatibility with older ISA or EISA peripherals.

PC-IP *(INET)* Personal Computer Internet Protocol. Developed in the early 1980s by Massachusetts Institute of Technology. Provides the same communica-

tions functionality, e.g. TELNET and Simple Network Management Protocol, as the Internet Protocol to PC users who are running MS-DOS. *See* IP, PC/TCP and MS-DOS.

PC/IX IBM Corp.'s implementation of UNIX System III for personal computers.

PCL Printer control language. Interface developed by the Hewlett-Packard Co. for LaserJet printers.

pclose Pipe **close**. Standard input/output library routine used in shell scripts to close a connection that was made to pipe, or input/output, data between two processes. *See* library routines, popen, pipe, shell script, I/O and process.

PCM Pulse-code-modulation. Data recording format used in the Digital Audio Tape digital data storage format. Writes data in 288-bit sections, of which 256 are used for data and the remainder is used for address, control, information synchronization and parity. *See* DAT and DDS.

PCMCIA Personal Computer Memory Card International Association. Formed in 1989 and has approximately 320 members composed of hardware and peripheral vendors. Develops standards for memory cards and input and output cards for small hand-held or notebook computers. Devices developed to conform with PCMCIA have to fit into a slot measuring 2.126 by 3.37 inches. The association is headquartered in Sunnyvale, California.

Personal Computer/Transmission Control Protocol *(INET)* Abbreviated and commonly known as PC/TCP. *See* PC/TCP.

PCN 1. Personal Communications Network. Wireless communication technology that can transmit voice, data and video signals. **2.** Physician Computer Network. Commercial fiber-optic network for physicians that allows them to contact pharmaceutical companies directly.

p-code Pseudocode. Description written in plain English of the functionality and use of a code. Done by developers and specifications writers in preparation for coding of software. Provides internal documentation in the code that can be used for debugging, either as the code is being written or afterward.

PC/TCP *(INET)* Personal Computer/Transmission Control Protocol. Provides personal computer users the same communications functionality, or services, as Transmission Control Protocol/Internet Protocol, e.g. Simple Mail Transfer Protocol and TELNET. *See* PC-IP, TCP/IP, SMTP and TELNET.

PCTE *(POS)* Portable Common Tools Environment. Portable Operating System Interface for Computer Environments (POSIX) standard for storage of computer aided software engineering. *See* POSIX and CASE.

PCTS *(POS)* POSIX (Portable Operating System Interface for Computer Environments) Conformance Test Suite. Developed by the National Institute of Standards and Technology to test conformance of hardware and software products developed by vendors to POSIX standards. *See* POSIX, FIPS and NIST.

PDA Personal digital assistant. Also called personal communicator or wallet personal computer. A small computer that fits into a hand and uses a pen-type instrument for input combined with built-in communications and personal organizer software. Can be used to replace pagers, cellular phones, daily planners, fax machines, laptop computers, etc. Approximately 2 to 2.5 inches wide, 3 to 4 inches long, and .5 to .75 inches high, and weighs between .9 and 4 pounds, e.g. Apple Computer Inc.'s Newton, AT&T Co.'s EO and Tandy's Zoomer.

PDI One of the public data networks. Commercial version of the Internet network that provides subscribers a Transmission Control Protocol/Internet Protocol service. Such networks provide services ranging from electronic mail to real-time applications. *See* Internet, TCP/IP and e-mail.

PDL Page-description languages. Software used in printing which allows for full graphics. Pages are sent to the printer as images which can be rotated, scaled, cut and otherwise manipulated. Unlike bit-mapped images which draw each character, point by point, PDLs store an image description of each line, curve or shape. *See* bit-mapped graphics.

PDN Public data network. Type of privately owned network service to which users can subscribe, as they would for long-distance telephone service. Each time a user logs on to connect with another computer on the network, the user is charged a fee. The amount is based on either how long the user is connected or amount of data transmitted during the connection. Examples of PDNs include those operated by AT&T Co., British and French Telecom, MCI and Telenet.

pdp11 *(ATT)* Command used to determine if a computer system is a DEC PDP 11. Returns a 0 value (TRUE) if the system is, or a non-zero value (FALSE) if it is not. *See* machid.

PDU 1. Protocol Data Units. Term in a Fiber Distribution Data Interface network for tokens, which are used to access the network, or frames, which are used to pass data. *See* FDDI. 2. Term in the Transmission Control Protocol for a Local Link Control packet which has an address and control header to direct data to the end-user. *See* TCP and LLC. 3. Simple Network Management Protocol term for the formatted messages sent between Network Management Station agents and the Network Management Station. *See* SNMP, NMS and NMS agent. 4. Open Systems Interconnection term for a packet that is being passed through the protocol layers and consists of information about the previous protocol and the data. *See* OSI and OSIRM.

P.EDI Electronic Data Interchange Approach to resolving conflicts between X.400 and Electronic Data Interchange standards taken by a study group of the International Telecommunication Union Telecommunication Standardization Sector, formerly known as the *Consultative Committee on International Telegraphy and Telephony*. *See* ITU-T, X.400 and EDI.

peer Network Time Protocol term for computers that are on the same level, or at the same distance, from a master computer with a master clock. *See* NTP, stratum, client, peer and server.

peer-to-peer network Network in which each computer is either a server or a client or both at the same time. *See* network, LAN, server, client and dedicated server network.

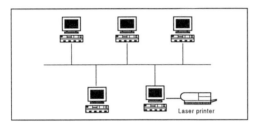

In a peer-to-peer network each workstation may be a fileserver or share its resources such as a printer or harddisk with other network members.

pels Picture **elements**. Commonly called pixels. *See* pixel.

PEM *(INET)* Privacy **E**nhanced **M**ail. Internet Engineering Task Force standard for secure mail. Based on public-key cryptography, in which a user must know both the public and private passwords to access the data. *See* IETF, Internet, public-key and private-key.

pen-based computer C o m p u t e r i z e d clipboard. Measures as little as 3 by 4 by 1.5 inches and weighing as little as 1 pound. Uses a penlike instrument for input, and learns to recognize the user's handwriting. Data can be entered either directly with the pen or by using the pen to touch a computerized form on the screen. Data can be transferred from it to another computer through a local area network or wireless network. *See* palmtop.

pending signal Period of time from when a signal is generated until it is delivered. *See* signal.

penetration When computer security is circumvented or disabled.

Pentium Also called P5. Intel Corp.'s marketing name for the 80586 microprocessor and design successor to the 80486, released in 1993. Has a 64-bit internal architecture and a 256-bit external data path with clock speeds starting at 60 megahertz. *See* PC, 64-bit computer, clock speed and microprocessor.

pentop computer Commonly called pen-based computer. *See* pen-based computer.

PEP 1. *(POS)* **P**latform **E**nvironment **P**rofile. Attempt by the Institute of Electrical and Electronic Engineers P1003.18 working group for system interface to provide a Portable Operating System Interface for Computer Environments (POSIX) specification of an environment for a standard UNIX system. *See* POSIX. 2. **P**acketized **E**nsemble **P**rotocol. Proprietary modulation and error correction protocol for modems developed by Telebit Corp. Divides a communication line into multiple channels, analyzes them and selects the best one for use. 3. **P**ersonal **E**fficiency **P**rogram. Personal computer application used for daily and/or weekly personal planning. 4. **P**hase **E**ncoded **P**art. Term used in magneto-optical disc technology for a code implanted on a CD-ROM disk indicating the disc can only be recorded on once, not many times. *See* M/O, CD-ROM and SFP.

percent sign *(%)* Default command or system prompt for users running the C shell. *See* system prompt and C shell.

performance management 1. Process used to manage and measure how well a computer system or communications network is performing. Includes monitoring to compare actual performance with ex-

Pen-based computer

pected performance, and performance tuning to make modifications needed to meet expectations. *See* performance monitoring and performance tuning. **2.** Method used to measure the use of resources and determine the resources that should be added to support growth.

performance monitoring Process of checking or measuring expected and acceptable system performance to determine if additional resources or modifications to hardware and/or an operating system are required. *See* performance management and performance tuning.

Performance Testing Alliance
Commonly abbreviated and called PTA. *See* PTA.

performance tuning Changes made to computer systems, networks, operating systems, etc. to modify performance to meet user requirements. *See* performance management, performance monitoring and performance tuning.

period *(.)* Commonly called dot. *See* dot.

peripheral Add-on or external hardware device for input to or output from a computer, e.g. disk or tape drive, modem and printer.

Peripheral Component Interconnect bus Commonly abbreviated and called PCI bus. *See* PCI bus.

Perl Practical Extraction and Report Language. Also called Pathologically Eclectic Rubbish Listener. A programming language in the public domain developed by Larry Wall to correct recognized weaknesses in the awk language. *See* awk.

permck *(OTH)* Permission check. Shell script used to check the database file created by the permsetup shell script for the permissions and security aspects. *See* shell script and permsetup.

permission bits Nine specifically identified bits used to establish file permissions. The permission bits are laid out as follows:

```
bit position:  8 7 6 5 4 3 2 1 0
meaning:       r w x r w x r w x
```

The first group of three bits describe the file owner's access permission. If set, the corresponding bit give read, write or execute permission. The next group of three bits describe members in the file's group access permission. The last group of three give the permission for everyone else. *See* group and permissions.

permissions Security measure that determines the level of access that a user has to read, write and execute commands in files or directories in a computer system. Each system automatically sets the levels of permissions on each newly created file. System permission levels can be reset by the superuser by modifying the system umask. Individual users can set permissions for their own files and directories by establishing a separate umask for their user account. Users also can modify the permission of existing files and directories with the chmod command. *See* chmod, default creation mask, umask, UID, GID, read-only file, write permission and execute permission.

Permissions System file for an operating system using the HoneyDanBer UNIX-to-UNIX CoPy (UUCP) or UNIX System V, Release 4 Basic Networking Utilities. Contains the list of files that remote systems can run during a UUCP connection and the access rights the local host has when connected to the remote host. *See* L.cmds, BNU, SVR4.x, HoneyDanBer UUCP and UUCP.

perms *(OTH)* Program which enables the superuser to either check or create permissions on a file. *See* permissions and superuser.

permsetup *(OTH)* **Perm**ission **set up**. Shell script used to maintain a database of

permissions and checksums of files established to monitor critical system files. *See* shell script and checksum.

permuted index List of commands that can be found using either the command name, part of the name or key words. Describes the commands and what they do.

perror Print error. C language library routine used to initiate standard error messages. *See* library routines.

persistence When part of a graphic image remains on a video monitor screen following its removal. *See* barrelling, blooming, bowing, convergence, flicker, keystone and pincushioning.

persistent object In object-oriented programming, a data object that continues to exist (i.e. persists) after a program finishes executing. Used to preserve state or data between executions of a program. *See* OMG, transient object and object.

persist timer Timer used in the Transmission Control Protocol to maintain connection while data is being output. *See* TCP.

Personal Addition Abbreviation for and commonly called UnixWare Personal Edition. *See* UnixWare Personal Edition.

Personal Communications Network. Commonly abbreviated and called PCN. *See* PCN.

personal communicator Commonly called PDA (personal digital assistant). *See* PDA.

personal computer Commonly abbreviated and called PC. *See* PC.

Personal Computer Disk Operating System Abbreviated and commonly known as PC-DOS. *See* PC-DOS.

Personal Computer Integration Service Function in the Open Software Foundation Inc.'s Distributed Computing Environment. Allows personal computers using the DOS or OS/2 operating systems to share files with a UNIX host and users, and to run print jobs on a network.

Personal Computer Internet Protocol (INET) Abbreviated and commonly known as PC-IP. See PC-IP.

Personal Computer Memory Card International Association Commonly abbreviated and called PCMCIA. *See* PCMCIA.

personal digital assistant Commonly abbreviated and called PDA. *See* PDA.

personal directory Commonly called login directory. *See* login directory.

Personal Efficiency Program Abbreviated and commonly known as PEP. *See* PEP.

personal information manager Commonly abbreviated and called PIM. *See* PIM.

peta Prefix for 10^{15} (1,000,000,000,000,000) or one quintillion. Commonly abbreviated P.

Peter Principle Principle taken from the book by Laurence J. Peter which states that employees will be promoted to their level of incompetence.

Petrotechnical Open Systems Corporation Commonly abbreviated and called POSC. *See* POSC.

PEX PHiGS (Programmer's Hierarchical Interactive Graphics System) Extension to the X Window System. Addition to the Massachusetts Institute of Technology (MIT) X 11, Release 5 (X11R5) specification of the X Window System, that enables X Window to map PHiGS, 2-D or 3-D graphics, to a network protocol. The PEX version numbers coincided with the release of the MIT X Window System, e.g. PEX 5 was the first release for X11R5 and PEX 6 for X11R6. *See* X Window System, X11R5, X11R6, PHiGS, 2-D data and 3-D data.

PEX Interoperability Committee PHiGS (Programmer's Hierarchical Interactive Graphics System) Extension to the X Window System **Interoperability Committee**. Group of X Window System vendors, including IBM Corp., Digital Equipment Corp. and the Hewlett-

Packard Co., that was formed to prove the PEX standard could work as an open standard. *See* PEX.

PEXlib PHiGS (Programmer's Hierarchical Interactive Graphics System) Extension to the **X** Window System **library**. Set of standard applications that allows developers to create 3-D graphics programs for workstations running PEX. Supported by members of the X Consortium. Competes with OpenGL, developed by Silicon Graphics Inc., as a standard application programming interface. *See* PEX, 3-D data, API, X Consortium and OpenGL.

pg *(ATT/XEN)* **Pager.** Command used to look at a file one screen (normally 26 lines) at a time.

phantom tty Commonly called pseudo-tty. *See* pseudo-tty.

Phase Encoded Part Commonly abbreviated and called PEP. *See* PEP.

PHiGS Programmer's Hierarchical Interactive **Graphics System.** Also spelled PHIGS. Graphic language application program interface used for developing 2-D and 3-D images. *See* PEX, API, 2-D data and 3-D data.

PHiGS Extension to the X Window System Abbreviated and commonly known as PEX. *See* PEX.

PHiGS Extension to the X Window System Interoperability Committee Abbreviated and commonly known as PEX Interoperability Committee. *See* PEX Interoperability Committee

PHiGS Extension to the X Window System library Abbreviated and commonly known as PEXlib. *See* PEXlib.

phong shading Method of producing realistic shading in graphic displays by determining the brightness of a surface pixel through linear interpolation of points on a polygon combined with the cosine of the viewing angle. *See* polygon and wire frame.

photolithography Process used to manufacture integrated circuits (IC). The pattern of the IC is transferred from the master to a silicon wafer by using light-sensitive emulsions and light. *See* IC and wafer.

phototypesetter Hardware system controlled by a computer on which high-resolution images are created on photographic paper by projecting light through a stencil. Capable of rapidly producing high-quality images on either film or paper.

PHY **Phy**sical layer protocol. Protocol layer in the Fiber Distribution Data Interface which establishes the standards for accomplishing tasks including encoding, decoding and monitoring lines. *See* FDDI.

physical block 1. Contiguous disk sectors used to form a logical block. *See* sector and logical block. 2. Data as it is actually stored or modified on a system. UNIX systems store data in groups of 512 or 1,024 bytes.

physical disk Physical storage size of a disk drive, measured in bytes.

physical layer First layer of the International Organization for Standardization/Open Systems Interconnection network model. Describes the physical and electrical connection between the network and any device, e.g. X.25 board or a router, that is connected the network, and is used in setting up the communications connection. *See* ISO/OSI and OSIRM.

Physical layer protocol Commonly abbreviated and called PHY. *See* PHY.

physical media 1. Computer term for the type of media, e.g. diskettes, disks, tapes or CD-ROMs, used to store data. 2. Communication term for physical devices used to transfer communication signals.

Physical medium-dependent Commonly abbreviated and called PMD. *See* PMD.

physical memory Physical size of the memory within a computer, measured in bytes. *See* RAM.

physical memory address Address in memory assigned to a physical location in memory.

physical security Use of restraints, such as locks, to prevent people from physically damaging a computer system.

physical unit number Number (generally, but not restricted to, hexadecimal) that identifies a specific hardware device to a computer. *See* device number.

Physician Computer Network Abbreviated and commonly known as PCN. *See* PCN.

pic *(ATT)* Picture. Preprocessor program in the troff text formatting program that is part of Documenter's Workbench. Translates a graphics language into troff commands for drawing simple pictures. Developed in 1981 at AT&T Co.'s Bell Laboratories by Brian Kernighan. *See* Bell Laboratories, DWB and troff.

pica 1. Unit of measurement in printing that equals approximately one-sixth of an inch, or 12 points, in height. 2. Unit of measurement on a typewriter that describes the number of characters, or pitch of print, and equals 10 characters per linear inch. *See* pitch, cpi and elite.

PICK Competing multi-user operating system to UNIX. Named for Richard Pick, who co-developed it with Don Nelson. Developed at TRW Inc. for the Department of Defense in the mid-1960s.

pico Prefix for 10^{-12} (1/1,000,000,000,000) or one-trillionth. Commonly abbreviated p.

picosecond Commonly abbreviated and called psec. *See* psec.

Picture Level Benchmark Commonly abbreviated and called PLB. *See* PLB.

PID Process identifier. Unique number assigned to each process which is started on a computer system. *See* process.

PII *(POS)* Protocol Independent Interface. Portable Operating System Interface for Computer Environments (POSIX) for application programming interfaces for process-to-process communication over a network. Provides the ability to communicate regardless of the protocol stack being used, e.g. Xerox Network Service, Open Systems Interconnection or Transmission Control Protocol/Internet Protocol. *See* XNX, OSI, TCP/IP and P1003.1g project.

PIM Personal information manager. Type of software program specifically developed to help manage resources and projects.

pincushioning Distortion on a video monitor which causes images at the top and/or side of the screen to appear to curve in. *See* barrelling, blooming, bowing, convergence, flicker, keystone and persistence.

ping 1. Originates from PING, or Packet Internet Groper. Command used to get a response from a remote host to determine if it is operating and connected to the network. 2. Jargon term for sending a signal to determine if a remote host is alive. *See* PING and alive.

PING *(INET)* Packet InterNet Groper. Originally implemented as an Internet program for sending a signal to a remote host to see if it is alive. Now part of the Transmission Control Protocol/Internet Protocol used on may local area networks. *See* Internet, ICMP, TCP/IP, LAN and alive.

P Internet Protocol *(INET)* Commonly abbreviated and called PIP. *See* PIP.

PIP *(INET)* P Internet Protocol. Replacement for the Internet Protocol (IP) developed by Bell Communications Research. Provides the protocol for interhost connection over a communications network. Messages are broken into packets, addressed, routed and reassembled. PIP overcomes the shortage of IP addresses in IP. *See* Internet, IP, SIP and SIP-P.

pipe 1. *(|)* UNIX feature which allows users to combine commands to perform more complex functions. Considered to be a one-way flow of interprocess communication. By putting a pipe symbol between two commands on a command line, the output of one command is sent as the input of another command. This then modifies standard input and standard output.

CLP> ps -ef | grep peters⏎

This says to run a process check and direct the output to grep, which then searches only for user name peters. If peters is currently logged on, all of that user's processes will be displayed on the screen. *See* IPC, command line, standard input and standard output. **2.** System call used to initiate an interprocess communication channel. *See* system call, IPC and pipes.

pipedev **Pipe dev**ice. Kernel parameter used to set the major and minor device numbers for temporary buffers in which the output from a pipe will be stored. *See* pipe, major device number and minor device number.

pipe fitting Input/output connection between processes made by the pipe system call. *See* pipe and pipes.

pipeline **1.** Actual interprocess communication where the standard output of one process becomes the standard input of the next process. *See* pipe. **2.** Command line input in which two or more commands are combined with a pipe symbol. For example:

CLP> ps -ef | grep tcole ⏎

This combines the ps command with options and grep to search for the process associated with the user tcole. Both the ps and grep processes run simultaneously but the information read and passed by the pipe is incorporated in the second process in the same order as it was read. *See* IPC and pipe.

pipelining Combining a series of programs using pipes so that more than one instruction can be run at the same time. Instructions are obtained from memory and processed; the results are returned to memory for storage. *See* pipe.

pipes Also called unnamed pipes and ordinary pipes. Special data file used in interprocess communications to manage the flow of data between processes on a first-in, first-out basis. Sends the standard output of one process to another process as standard input while both processes are running. Initially conceived by Doug McIlroy. *See* IPC, FIFO and pipe.

pitch Term originating with typewriters. Indicates the spacing of characters on a line of print, measured by the number of characters per inch or centimeter. The most common are: 10 pitch or pica, equivalent to 10 characters per linear inch; and 12 pitch or elite, equivalent to 12 characters per inch. *See* cpi, pica and elite.

pixel Picture (**pix**) **el**ement. Measurement of the smallest element on a picture tube that is electronically traceable and adjusted in intensity. Used to indicate the sharpness of a screen. Pixel ratings, or display resolution, are expressed as the number of dots per line by the number of lines on the screen, e.g. 640 x 480 pixels. The greater the number of pixels, the smaller the dots and, therefore, the clearer the picture, e.g. 640 x 480 pixels for video graphics array (VGA) to support graphics applications on IBM Corp.'s personal computers versus 640 x 200 pixels for color graphics adapters (CGA) which support limited graphics applications on PCs. On color monitors, the number of bits stored for each pixel determines the number of distinct colors that can be displayed, e.g. 4 bits per pixel displays 16 colors, 8 bits displays 256 colors, 15 bits displays 32,768 colors and 24 bits displays 16,777,216 colors. *See* CGA, EGA, super VGA, VGA, XGA and color mode.

pixel rating Also called display resolution. Expression of the number of dots or pixels that can be displayed on a line by the number of lines on the screen, e.g. 1024 x 768 pixels for an Extended Graphics Array monitor. *See* pixel.

pkgadd *(ATT)* **P**ac**k**a**g**e **add**. One of the commands that can be called by the UNIX System V, Release 4 sysadm command and used to install application software programs on a system. *See* SVR4.x.

pkgask *(ATT)* **Package ask**. One of the commands that can be called by the UNIX System V, Release 4 sysadm command and used to list the questions an application software package asks during installation. The questions are collected in a file for review and response preparation by the system administrator or person responsible for installing the package before installation.

pkgchk *(ATT)* **Package check**. One of the commands that can be called by the UNIX System V, Release 4 sysadm command and used to confirm that a new application software package has been installed and is functioning properly. *See* pkgmap.

pkginfo *(ATT)* **Package info**rmation. One of the commands that can be called by the UNIX System V, Release 4 sysadm command. Used to review the questions identified by the pkgask command that an application software package asks during installation. *See* pkgask.

pkgmap *(ATT)* **Package map**. File used to maintain information about the application software packages installed on a computer system. This data is used by the pkgchk command to determine if a software package is functioning properly. *See* pkgchk.

pkgparam *(ATT)* **Package param**eter. One of the commands that can be called by the UNIX System V, Release 4 sysadm command and used to display the parameters for application software packages installed on a computer system.

pkgrm *(ATT)* **Package rem**ove. One of the commands that can be called by the UNIX System V, Release 4 sysadm command and used to delete an application software package from a computer system.

pkgtrans *(ATT)* **Package trans**late. One of the commands that can be called by the UNIX System V, Release 4 sysadm command and used to convert an installed application software package from one format to another.

PLA Programmable logic array. Also called FPLA. Integrated logic chip that provides an alternative method to read-only memory for storing system instructions or programs which are used repeatedly. Can be programmed only once with the special instructions, normally when it is installed. *See* ROM.

placement policy System architecture for handling page management when there is a page fault. *See* paging and page fault.

plain old telephone service Commonly abbreviated and called POTS. *See* POTS.

plaintext Original, readable text, before it is encrypted and after it is decrypted. *See* encrypt, decrypt and ciphertext.

Plan 9 Operating system in development by Brian Kernighan, Ken Thompson, Dennis Ritchie and Rob Pike of AT&T Co.'s Bell Laboratories. Looks like UNIX but is not compatible with UNIX. Has the potential to handle 10,000 to 20,000 users, supporting terabytes of disk capacity, using only 160 kilobytes of disk storage for the operating system and running on computers ranging in size from laptops to large servers. Name derived from a 1950s science fiction camp movie, *Plan 9 from Outer Space*, considered by many as the worst movie ever made. *See* Bell Laboratories, Thompson, Ken and Ritchie, Dennis M.

plasma display panel Neon-filled panel. When electrodes are activated, the gas is ionized and light is emitted in the form of characters. Used with laptop computers.

platen Roller on a printer which supports the paper and which the printer head strikes to form an impression on the paper.

platform Jargon term for computer hardware.

Platform Environment Profile *(POS)* Abbreviated and commonly known as PEP. *See* PEP.

platter Plate in a disk drive that has been specially coated with oxide. A disk drive is composed of one or more platters to which data is written or read using recording or read/write heads. *See* track.

playpen status Jargon term for software that is ready to be used.

PLB Picture Level Benchmark. Public domain benchmark developed by the National Computer Graphics Association and released in late 1991 to measure the 2-D and 3-D graphics capability of hardware systems. *See* benchmark, 2-D data and 3-D data.

plock *(ATT)* Process lock. System call that opens and closes areas of process memory to access by a process. *See* system call.

plot Simple graphics filter used to generate and draw 2-D line graphs.

plotter External computer device, similar to a printer except it produces graphical displays, e.g. charts, maps and graphs. Can use either pens or electrostatic charges to transfer line-based graphics to paper maintained on a flatbed, drum or pinch-roller.

Plotter

plug n' play Jargon term for hardware or software that, after being installed (plug), can immediately be used (play).

plus *(+)* Metacharacter used in regular expressions to match one or more characters identified before the plus, e.g. ka+j would match kaj and kaaj but not kj since the letter a has to be in the string. Used only with the egrep and awk programs. *See* metacharacter and regular expression.

PLUS Profile Expansion of the definition of X/Open Co. Ltd.'s Common Applications Environment defined in the X/Open Portability Guides. Composed of the BASE Profile, the minimum set of software components; and standards for CO-

BOL, FORTRAN, Pascal, Index Sequential Access Method, relational database language, terminal interfaces, X Window System management, transport interface and personal computer interface. *See* X/Open, CAE, XPG, BASE Profile and OPTIONAL Components.

PM Preventive maintenance. Regularly or irregularly scheduled time when a computer is taken down for inspection and diagnostic testing.

pmadm *(ATT)* Port monitor administration. Command used in the UNIX System V, Release 4 Service Access Facility to administer a specific port monitor. Starts and runs the programs of the Service Access Facility; the action taken is determined by the argument, e.g. -a = add a port monitor, and -d = disable a service for a port monitor. *See* SVR4.x, SAF and sacadm.

PMC *(POS)* Project Management Committee. Institute of Electrical and Electronics Engineers' Portable Applications Standards Committee. It is a Portable Operating System Interface for Computer Environments (POSIX) committee formed in 1991 that oversees POSIX projects and new requests for changes to POSIX. *See* POSIX and PASC.

PMD Physical medium-dependent. Lowest layer or the Fiber Distribution Data Interface standard which specifies the transceivers, transmission media, connectors, etc. to be used. *See* FDDI.

PMX/TERM Application available from AT&T Co. for UNIX System V, Release 4. Provides a user-friendly interface to the commercially available AT&T Mail Service. *See* SVR4.x.

pointer Area in computer memory which contains the address of a variable.

Pointer record Commonly abbreviated and called PTR. *See* PTR.

point-to-point Connection of a transmission source directly to a receiving location.

point-to-point communication Class of communications protocol used to connect a single transmission point to a single receiving point. *See* PPP and SLIP.

Point-to-Point Protocol Commonly abbreviated and called PPP. *See* PPP.

Point-to-Point Protocol Consortium Commonly abbreviated and called PPP Consortium. *See* PPP Consortium.

poll *(ATT)* Program used to suspend a process while information is being sent to or received from a specific file.

Poll File in systems running HoneyDanBer UNIX-to-UNIX CoPy or UNIX System V, Release 4 Basic Network Utilities that contains the time(s) at which connection is to be made to remote systems for data transfer. *See* HoneyDanBer UUCP, BNU, SVR4.x and UUCP.

polling Process used by programs to determine if the devices attached to a computer have data to be sent to or requested from the computer.

polygon Ordered set of vertices connected by sides that can be dynamically created and textured using image data. Polygons are displayed as outlines that are either not filled in, smooth shaded or textured. *See* phong shading, gouraud and wire frame.

polymorphism Concept in object-oriented programming that permits developers to identify various objects, e.g. functions performed, that have been developed for one class of objects and to use them in another class of objects. *See* object. OOP, class, encapsulation and inheritance.

PolyShell Software package developed by Polytron which provide a UNIX command set and feel to DOS personal computers. *See* MKS Toolkit.

pop 1. Also called pull. To remove the set of data placed at the top of a data stack, or list. *See* stack, push, shift, and unshift. 2. Sudden change in an object's appearance or the appearance of an object out of nowhere on a screen.

POP Post Office Protocol. Used to send and receive electronic mail between personal computers and UNIX e-mail systems. Versions are identified with a numeric ending, e.g. POP (the original), POP2 and POP3. *See* IMAP.

popd 1. *(BSD)* **Pop d**irectory. csh or tcsh shell command used to change the current working directory (CWD) to the directory named at the top of a directory stack, or list, maintained by the shell. After the CWD is changed, the previous directory name is removed from the stack. *See* csh, tcsh, stack, current working directory, cd and pushd. 2. Post Office Protocol **d**aemon. Background program used to manage the connectivity and mail transfer between a UNIX host and a personal computer.

popen *(ATT)* Standard input/output library routine used in shell scripts to open and pipe input/output from one process to another. *See* library routines, pclose, pipe, shell script, I/O and process.

pop-up menu Master list that provides a subset of menus. Offers more choices, special functions, commands, help information, etc.

Pop-up menu in Microsoft Windows

pop-up window Temporary window created from an existing window to provide more choices, special functions, commands, help information, etc.

Pop-up window in Microsoft Windows

port **1.** Physical device on a computer or peripheral which allows data to flow in and out of the computer. **2.** To tailor, modify or recompile the programming code of an operating system or application software package to meet the specifications of a particular brand and model of computer. **3.** Term used with the Transmission Control Protocol for the second level of the address scheme. A combination of the address of the application program (process) and the address of the node. *See* TCP, process, node and sockets.

portability Ability to easily transfer an operating system and/or application software program from one vendor's hardware to another's without affecting the software's functionality.

Portable Application Standards Committee Commonly abbreviated and called PASC. *See* PASC.

Portable C Compiler Abbreviated and commonly known as PCC. *See* PCC.

Portable Common Tools Environment. Commonly abbreviated and called PCTE. *See* PCTE.

Portable Compiled Font Commonly abbreviated and called PCF. *See* PCF.

Portable Operating System Interface for Computer Environments Commonly abbreviated and called POSIX. *See* POSIX.

port driver Commonly called device driver. *See* device driver.

portmap Remote Procedure Call daemon that looks up available ports. *See* RPC.

port monitor Commonly abbreviated ttymon. A process that watches for and manages terminal connections to a system. New function in UNIX System V, Release 4. Replaced both the getty and uugetty commands to manage activity on system ports. When a connection is made, the port monitor passes the connection to the login process. *See* ttymon, SAF, SAC, pmadm, sacadm and SVR4.x.

PortSoft Group of representatives from China, Hong Kong, Japan, Singapore and Taiwan that develops documentation to help developers write software in Asian languages. *See* i18n and l10n.

POSC **P**etrotechnical **O**pen **S**ystems **C**orporation. One of the user organizations formed to defend customers from the standards organizations and the UNIX Wars. Formed by leading companies in the oil industry and their software developers to develop industry standards. Formed in late 1990, its headquarters are located in Houston, Texas. *See* UNIX Wars, User Alliance for Open Systems and IPSIT.

positional parameter Commonly called positional variable. *See* positional variable.

positional variable Used to specify tasks within a shell script to be performed by the shell script. *See* shell script.

position trigger Input device, e.g. hot spot, sensitive spot or button, that starts a computation when touched.

POSIX **P**ortable **O**perating **S**ystem **I**nterface for Computer Environments (**X**). Also called Portable Operating System, based on UNIX. POSIX is neither an operating system nor a replacement for UNIX. It is an attempt by the Institute of Electrical and Electronic Engineers to establish a set of international open systems environment standards for system interfaces, shells and tools, testing and verification, real-time processing, Ada, security, system administration, networking, FORTRAN, supercomputers, transaction processing, etc. These are referred to as the POSIX family of standards. The first portion of the standards was approved in October 1988. *See* IEEE and Project 1003.

POSIX.0 *(POS)* Abbreviation for the Institute of Electrical and Electronic Engineers Portable Operating System Interface for Computer Environments (POSIX) P1003.0 working group. Responsible for writing the *Guide to POSIX Open Systems Environment*, known as *The Guide*. The guide is an overview of the open systems concept, use, interrelationships and how to develop a specification for a system. *See* IEEE, POSIX, Project 1003 and IEEE P1003.0 working group.

POSIX.1 *(POS)* Abbreviation for the Institute of Electrical and Electronic Engineers Portable Operating System Interface for Computer Environments (POSIX) P1003.1. Also called System Interface. Used to identify both the working group and standard for the application programming interface between an application program and the operating system. *See* IEEE, POSIX, Project 1003 and IEEE P1003.1 working group.

POSIX.1a *(POS)* Abbreviation for the Institute of Electrical and Electronic Engineers Portable Operating System Interface for Computer Environments (POSIX) P1003.1a project. Originally responsible for defining system interface requirements. Following the release of the 1003.1-1990 standard, the group began working on miscellaneous additions to the standard, e.g. checkpoint/restart, interfaces for file tree walking and symbolic links. *See* IEEE, POSIX, Project 1003 and IEEE P1003.1a project.

POSIX.1b *(POS)* Abbreviation for the Institute of Electrical and Electronic Engineers Portable Operating System Interface for Computer Environments (POSIX) P1003.1b project. Responsible for defining computer language independent specifications. In 1993 the work of the

IEEE P1003.4 working group for real-time operating systems requirements were moved to POSIX.1b. *See* IEEE, POSIX, Project 1003, IEEE P1003.1b project and IEEE P1003.4 working group.

POSIX.1c *(POS)* Abbreviation for the Institute of Electrical and Electronic Engineers Portable Operating System Interface for Computer Environments (POSIX) P1003.1c project. Responsible for developing kernel standards for C language code. *See* IEEE, POSIX, Project 1003, IEEE P1003.1c project and C language.

POSIX.1d *(POS)* Abbreviation for the Institute of Electrical and Electronic Engineers Portable Operating System Interface for Computer Environments (POSIX) P1003.1d project. Responsible for developing real-time UNIX additions requested by X/Open Co. Ltd., UNIX International and the Open Software Foundation Inc. *See* IEEE, POSIX, Project 1003, POSIX, IEEE P1003.1d project, RTOS, X/Open, UI and OSF.

POSIX.1e *(POS)* Abbreviation for the Institute of Electrical and Electronic Engineers Portable Operating System Interface for Computer Environments (POSIX) P1003.1e project. Responsible for POSIX system security standards for system interface requirement. *See* IEEE, POSIX, Project 1003, IEEE P1003.1e project, DAC and MAC.

POSIX.1f *(POS)* Abbreviation for the Institute of Electrical and Electronic Engineers Portable Operating System Interface for Computer Environments (POSIX) P1003.1f project, Responsible for standards for networking of POSIX systems. *See* IEEE, POSIX, Project 1003 and IEEE P1003.1f project.

POSIX.1g *(POS)* Abbreviation for the Institute of Electrical and Electronic Engineers Portable Operating System Interface for Computer Environments (POSIX) P1003.1g project. Responsible for developing standards for application programming interfaces and protocol-independent processing. *See* IEEE, POSIX, Project 1003 and IEEE P1003.1g project.

POSIX.2 *(POS)* Abbreviation for Institute of Electrical and Electronic Engineers Portable Operating System Interface for Computer Environments (POSIX) P1003.2. Used to identify both the working group and standard for shell programming language, commands and utilities needed for portability of shell scripts. *See* IEEE, POSIX, Project 1003, IEEE P1003.2 working group and shell.

POSIX.2a *(POS)* Abbreviation for the Institute of Electrical and Electronic Engineers Portable Operating System Interface for Computer Environments (POSIX) P1003.2a project. Was responsible for developing standards for commands not found in shell scripts, such as vi. *See* IEEE, POSIX, Project 1003 and IEEE P1003.2a project.

POSIX.2b *(POS)* Abbreviation for the Institute of Electrical and Electronic Engineers Portable Operating System Interface for Computer Environments (POSIX) P1003.2b project. Was responsible for developing standards for the command line and functional interfaces to P1003.2 utilities. *See* IEEE, POSIX, Project 1003 and IEEE P1003.2b project.

POSIX.2c *(POS)* Abbreviation for the Institute of Electrical and Electronic Engineers Portable Operating System Interface for Computer Environments (POSIX) P1003.2c project. Responsible for developing standards for POSIX system security extensions for shells and utilities. *See* IEEE, POSIX, Project 1003 and IEEE P1003.2c project.

POSIX.2d *(POS)* Abbreviation for the Institute of Electrical and Electronic Engineers Portable Operating System Interface for Computer Environments (POSIX) P1003.2d project. Responsible for developing standards for batch queuing. *See* IEEE, POSIX, Project 1003 and IEEE P1003.2d project.

POSIX.2 shell language *(POS)* Based on the Bourne shell with Korn shell, C shell and Institute of Electrical and Electronic Engineers Portable Operating System Interface for Computer Environments (POSIX) P1003.2 working group additions. *See* IEEE, POSIX, Project 1003, IEEE P1003.2 working group, shell, Bourne shell, Korn shell and C shell.

POSIX.3 *(POS)* Abbreviation for Institute of Electrical and Electronic Engineers Portable Operating System Interface for Computer Environments (POSIX) P1003.3. Used to identify both the working group and standard for test and verification of the IEEE P1003.1 standard for system interface. *See* IEEE, POSIX, Project 1003, IEEE P1003.1 working group and IEEE P1003.3 working group.

POSIX.4 *(POS)* Abbreviation for Institute of Electrical and Electronic Engineers Portable Operating System Interface for Computer Environments (POSIX) P1003.4. Used to identify both the working group and standard for application environment profiles for real-time systems. *See* IEEE, POSIX, Project 1003, IEEE P1003.4 working group and RTOS.

POSIX.4a *(POS)* Abbreviation for Institute of Electrical and Electronic Engineers Portable Operating System Interface for Computer Environments (POSIX) P1003.4a project. Was responsible for developing a standard for threads, independent basic units of computation or action used to run a task involving several different processors at the same time. *See* IEEE, POSIX, Project 1003, IEEE P1003.4a project and RTOS.

POSIX.4b *(POS)* Abbreviation for Institute of Electrical and Electronic Engineers Portable Operating System Interface for Computer Environments (POSIX) P1003.4b project. Was responsible for developing standards for real-time UNIX additions requested by X/Open Co. Ltd., UNIX International and the Open Software Foundation Inc. *See* IEEE, POSIX, Project 1003, IEEE P1003.4b project and RTOS.

POSIX.5 *(POS)* Abbreviation for Institute of Electrical and Electronic Engineers Portable Operating System Interface for Computer Environments (POSIX) P1003.5. Used to identify both the working group and standard for an ADA Language interface. *See* IEEE, POSIX, Project 1003, IEEE P1003.5 working group and ADA.

POSIX.6 *(POS)* Abbreviation for Institute of Electrical and Electronic Engineers Portable Operating System Interface for Computer Environments (POSIX) P1003.6. Was used to identify both the working group and standard for security. *See* IEEE, POSIX, Project 1003 and IEEE P1003.6 working group.

POSIX.7 *(POS)* Abbreviation for Institute of Electrical and Electronic Engineers Portable Operating System Interface for Computer Environments (POSIX) P1003.7. Was used to identify both the working group and standard for POSIX system administration standards for utilities and interfaces in a distributed environment. *See* IEEE, POSIX, Project 1003 and IEEE P1003.7 working group.

POSIX.7.1 *(POS)* Abbreviation for Institute of Electrical and Electronic Engineers Portable Operating System Interface for Computer Environments (POSIX) P1003.7.1. Responsible for developing standards for printer system management. *See* IEEE, POSIX, Project 1003 and IEEE P1003.7.1 project.

POSIX.7.2 *(POS)* Abbreviation for Institute of Electrical and Electronic Engineers Portable Operating System Interface for Computer Environments (POSIX) P1003.7.2. Was responsible for developing standards for software management. *See* IEEE, POSIX, Project 1003 and IEEE P1003.7.3 project.

POSIX.7.3 *(POS)* Abbreviation for Institute of Electrical and Electronic Engineers Portable Operating System Interface for Computer Environments (POSIX) P1003.7.3. Was responsible for developing standards for user and group management. *See* IEEE, POSIX, Project 1003 and IEEE P1003.7.3 project.

POSIX.8 *(POS)* Abbreviation for Institute of Electrical and Electronic Engineers Portable Operating System Interface for Computer Environments (POSIX) P1003.8. Used to identify both the working group and standard for networking of POSIX systems. *See* IEEE, POSIX, Project 1003 and IEEE P1003.8 working group.

POSIX.9 *(POS)* Abbreviation for Institute of Electrical and Electronic Engineers Portable Operating System Interface for Computer Environments (POSIX) P1003.9 working group. Was used to identify both the working group and standard for the FORTRAN-77 Language interface. *See* IEEE, POSIX, Project 1003, FORTRAN-77 and IEEE P1003.9 working group.

POSIX.10 *(POS)* Abbreviation for Institute of Electrical and Electronic Engineers Portable Operating System Interface for Computer Environments (POSIX) P1003.10. Used to identify both the working group and standard for supercomputer application environment profile. *See* IEEE, POSIX, Project 1003 and IEEE P1003.10 working group.

POSIX.11 *(POS)* Abbreviation for Institute of Electrical and Electronic Engineers Portable Operating System Interface for Computer Environments (POSIX) P1003.11. Used to identify both the working group and standard for an on-line transaction processing application environment profile. *See* IEEE, POSIX, Project 1003 and IEEE P1003.11 working group.

POSIX.12 *(POS)* Abbreviation for Institute of Electrical and Electronic Engineers Portable Operating System Interface for Computer Environments (POSIX) P1003.12. Was used to identify both the working group and standard for network applications programming interface. *See* IEEE, POSIX, Project 1003 and IEEE P1003.12 working group.

POSIX.13 *(POS)* Abbreviation for Institute of Electrical and Electronic Engineers Portable Operating System Interface for Computer Environments (POSIX) P1003.13. Was used to identify both the working group and standard for application environment profiles for real-time system support. *See* IEEE, POSIX, Project 1003, IEEE P1003.13 working group, AEP and RTOS.

POSIX.14 *(POS)* Abbreviation for Institute of Electrical and Electronic Engineers Portable Operating System Interface for Computer Environments (POSIX) P1003.14. Used to identify both the working group and standard for multiprocessing application environment profile. *See* IEEE, POSIX, Project 1003 and IEEE P1003.14 working group.

POSIX.15 *(POS)* Abbreviation for Institute of Electrical and Electronic Engineers Portable Operating System Interface for Computer Environments (POSIX) P1003.15. Was used to identify both the working group and standard for traditional interactive multi-user system. *See* IEEE, POSIX, Project 1003 and IEEE P1003.15 working group.

POSIX.16 *(POS)* Abbreviation for Institute of Electrical and Electronic Engineers Portable Operating System Interface for Computer Environments (POSIX) P1003.16. Used to identify both the working group and standard for C language interfaces to system services. *See* IEEE, POSIX, Project 1003 and IEEE P1003.16 working group.

POSIX.17 *(POS)* Abbreviation for Institute of Electrical and Electronic Engineers Portable Operating System Interface for Computer Environments (POSIX) P1003.17. Was used to identify both the working group and standard for Name Space/Directory Services. *See* IEEE, POSIX, Project 1003 and IEEE P1003.17 working group.

POSIX.18 *(POS)* Abbreviation for Institute of Electrical and Electronic Engineers Portable Operating System Interface for Computer Environments (POSIX) P1003.18. Was used to identify both the working group and standard for Platform Environment Profile, description of the standard UNIX multi-user computer. *See* IEEE, POSIX, Project 1003 and IEEE P1003.18 working group.

POSIX.19 *(POS)* Abbreviation for Institute of Electrical and Electronic Engineers Portable Operating System Interface for Computer Environments (POSIX) P1003.19. Was used to identify both the working group and standard for FORTRAN-90 Language interface. *See* IEEE, POSIX, Project 1003 and IEEE P1003.19 working group.

POSIX.20 *(POS)* Abbreviation for Institute of Electrical and Electronic Engineers Portable Operating System Interface for Computer Environments (POSIX) P1003.20. Was used to identify both the working group and standard for Ada language interface for real-time extensions. *See* IEEE, POSIX, Project 1003 and IEEE P1003.20 working group.

POSIX.21 *(POS)* Abbreviation for Institute of Electrical and Electronic Engineers Portable Operating System Interface for Computer Environments (POSIX) P1003.21. Was used to identify both the working group and standard for real-time distributed computing systems. *See* IEEE, POSIX, Project 1003 and IEEE P1003.21 working group.

POSIX.22 *(POS)* Abbreviation for Institute of Electrical and Electronic Engineers Portable Operating System Interface for Computer Environments (POSIX) P1003.22. Was used to identify both the working group and standard for developing the Open Systems Environment Security Framework Guide. *See* IEEE, POSIX, Project 1003 and IEEE P1003.22 working group.

POSIX Conformance Test Suite
Abbreviated and commonly known as PCTS. *See* PCTS.

POSIX OSE *(POS)* Portable Operating System Interface for Computer Environments (POSIX) open systems environment. Standards for interoperability, application software portability, interaction of people and data based on International Organization for Standardization standard. Includes application software development support services, character-based user interface services, communication services, core system services, data interchange services, database services, graphic services, internationalization services, language services, system security services, systems management services, transaction processing services, user command interface services and windowing system services. *See* ISO.

POSIX Real-time Extensions and Profiles *(POS)* Originally called the IEEE POSIX.4 working group. In 1993 the work of the IEEE P1003.4 working group was moved to the IEEE P1003.1b, 1003.1c and 1003.1d projects. *See* POSIX, Project 1003, IEEE P1003.1b project, IEEE P1003.1c project and IEEE P1003.1d project.

POSIX Security Extensions *(POS)* Originally called the IEEE POSIX.4 working group. In 1993 the work of the IEEE P1003.6 working group was moved to the IEEE P1003.1e project. *See* POSIX, Project 1003 and IEEE P1003.1e project.

POSIX Transparent File Access *(POS)* Originally called the IEEE POSIX.8 working group. In 1993 the work of the IEEE P1003.8 working group was moved to the P1003.1f project. *See* IEEE P1003.1f project.

postmark Date and time stamp, including the sender's login ID, placed on the first line of an electronic-mail message. Tells the receiver when and by whom the message was sent. *See* e-mail.

postnews *(OTH)* Command used to access and send news to a bulletin board available through USENET, a worldwide UNIX bulletin board. *See* USENET.

Post Office Protocol Abbreviated and commonly known as POP. *See* POP.

postprocessing commands Electronic-mail commands used to perform close-out functions once a message has been delivered, e.g. informing the sender that it has been received and read. *See* e-mail.

PostScript Page description language developed by Adobe Systems Inc. Tells any printer or typesetter which has PostScript built in how to print a page that consists of text and/or graphics. The page has to be generated by software that includes a driver which converts the page into PostScript code; the code, in turn, is translated by the printer or typesetter. PostScript has become the de factor PDL standard for high-end desktop publishing because, among other features, it can operate across a range of platforms, is very precise and has color capabilities. *See* desktop publishing and PDL.

Post, Telephone and Telegraph Abbreviated and commonly known as PTT. *See* PTT.

POTS Plain old telephone service. Normal analog telephone service used for analog data transmission.

pound sign *(#)* **1.** Metacharacter or special character which is the default system erase character for AT&T Co.'s UNIX. *See* metacharacter and erase character. **2.** Comment sign in programs recognized by all three major shells (Bourne shell, C shell and Korn shell). A line preceded by a pound sign is recognized as explanatory text, not a command, and does not affect the operation of the shell program. *See* shell.

power conditioner Electrical device placed between a computer and source of electrical power. Provides a stable power source for the computer by monitoring power surges or fluctuations, providing the computer system a stable power source.

power down To turn off the electrical power supply to a computer or peripheral device. *See* power up.

PowerOpen Association Group formed in 1993 by Apple Computer Inc., Groupe Bull, Harris Corp., IBM Corp., Motorola Inc., Tadpole Technology Inc. and Thomson-CSF. Focuses on promoting the PowerPC 601 microprocessor developed by some of the group's founders. The association is attempting to assure competitors that there will be equal access to the technology of the PowerPC architecture and developing an application binary interface for the PowerPC. Headquartered in Burlington, Massachusetts. *See* ABI and PowerPC 601.

PowerPC 601 Reduced Instruction Set Computing 66-megahertz microprocessor architecture developed by IBM Corp., Apple Computer Inc. and Motorola Inc. The operating systems to be ported to the PowerPC 601 by the end of 1994 are Apple's System 7, IBM's AIX and OS/2, Microsoft Corp.'s Windows NT, Novell Inc.'s NetWare and an object-oriented operating system called Pink from Taligent Inc., a joint venture between IBM and Apple. *See* PowerOpen Association.

power surge Unexpected increase in power that can cause a system crash and, at worst, result in damage to a computer system. *See* UPS and crash.

power up To turn on the electrical power supply to a computer or peripheral device. *See* power down.

power-up diagnostics Tests run by a computer system when it is turned on to verify that hardware connected to the system is functioning properly. *See* diagnostic test.

power-up handshake Part of the communications process between two devices, in which their speed, parity and other variables are set to allow data to pass between them.

PP Program similar to sendmail, used to manage delivery of electronic mail with X Window System. *See* sendmail, MTA, e-mail and X Window System.

PPID 1. Parent process identifier. Unique number assigned to a process that has generated subsequent processes on a computer system. *See* PID and parent process. 2. Korn shell variable that contains the process identifier of the last process started by the shell.

ppm Pages per minute. Measurement of a printer's output.

PPP *(INET)* Point-to-Point Protocol. Replacement for the Serial Line Internet Protocol that provides serial interface over a network. First formal Request for Comment outlining standards was released in 1989. Can function over the Transmission Control Protocol and Internet Protocol, Ethernet and Novell networks. A set of protocols combined to connect and transmit packets of data over point-to-point links. Includes the Link Control Protocol used to establish a connection, Network Control Protocol used to configure the various network-layer protocols, and the Password Authentication Protocol or the Challenge-Handshake Authentication Protocol used for security. Works over modems that transmit data at 300 to 50,000 bits per second. *See* C-SLIP, SLIP, LCP, NCP, PAP, CHAP and TCP/IP.

PPP Consortium Organization composed of 10 companies in the network manufacturing industry. Formed to test and ensure interoperability of routers and associated products running the Point-to-Point Protocol. Members include 3Com Corp., Cisco Systems Inc., Novell Inc. and Telebit Corp. *See* PPP.

pr Print. Command used to format a file for printing. The output is normally displayed on the terminal screen. To obtain a hard copy, this standard output has to be redirected to a printer.

Practical Extraction and Report Language Commonly abbreviated and called Perl. *See* Perl.

prctmp *(ATT)* Print ctmp. System accounting shell script used to format and print the files containing system accounting statistics, e.g. /usr/adm and /acct/nite/ctmp, created by acctcon2. *See* acctcon2.

prdaily *(ATT)* Print daily. System accounting shell script used to format and print the system accounting reports from the previous day.

Precision Architecture Reduced Instruction Set Computing Commonly abbreviated and called PA-RISC. *See* PA-RISC.

Precision RISC Organization Commonly abbreviated and called PRO. *See* PRO.

preemptive multitasking The operating system's ability to suspend one process in order to start or resume another. UNIX has had this ability from its inception but was absent in desktop systems such as MS-DOS, the Macintosh and Windows 3.x. More advanced desktop systems such as OS/2 and Windows NT have this ability. *See* multitasking.

preferred network *(INET)* First or preferred choice of network connectivity in Transmission Control Protocol/Internet Protocol networks where multiple networks are connected to a host. *See* TCP/IP.

prefetching Method of reducing processing time by retrieving program instructions from memory before they are needed so they are available when required.

prepaging Method of reducing processing time by retrieving pages from memory before they are needed so they are available when required. *See* paging.

preprocessor Program that manipulates software written in a high-level language, such as C language, before it is sent for processing to other programs, such as an analyzer or compiler. Deletes comments, imports special files, such as headers, and tracks preprocessor macros.

presentation graphics Computer-generated, predesigned graphic displays used to enhance presentations.

presentation layer Sixth layer of the International Organization for Standardization/Open Systems Interconnection network model. Responsible for the interface with applications to format the output for display on a terminal or printing. Also is the translator which converts data into an international format, which can be read by both the sending and receiving computers. *See* ISO/OSI and OSIRM.

preventive maintenance Commonly abbreviated and called PM. *See* PM.

prev-frm *(ATT)* **Previous frame.** Previous frame. Command in the UNIX System V, Release 4 Framed Access Command Environment file system operations menu. Used to move from the current frame, an independent subregion used to display information or make inputs to the computer, operating system and/or application software, to the previous frame. *See* SVR4.x, FACE, file system, frame and next-frm.

prfdc *(ATT)* Part of the System Performance Analysis Utilities in UNIX System V, Release 4. Program used to get data from the operating system profiler and store it in a file for analysis. *See* profiler, SPAU, prfld, prfpr, prfsnap, prfstat, sadc, sadp, sag, sar, sa1, sa2, timex and OS.

prfld *(ATT)* Part of the System Performance Analysis Utilities in UNIX System V. Program used to start the operating system profiler. *See* profiler, SPAU, prfdc, prfpr, prfsnap, prfstat, sadc, sadp, sag, sar, sa1, sa2, timex and OS.

prfpr *(ATT)* Part of the System Performance Analysis Utilities in UNIX System V. Program used to format data generated by prfdc and prfsnap. *See* profiler, SPAU, prfdc, prfld, prfsnap, prfstat, sadc, sadp, sag, sar, sa1, sa2 and timex.

prfsnap *(ATT)* Part of the System Performance Analysis Utilities in UNIX System V. Program used to run and collect a snapshot of the operating system profiler. *See* profiler, SPAU, prfdc, prfpr, prfld, prfstat, sadc, sadp, sag, sar, sa1, sa2, timex and OS.

prfstat *(ATT)* Part of the System Performance Analysis Utilities in UNIX System V. Program used to start and stop the operating system profiler. *See* profiler, SPAU, prfdc, prfpr, prfsnap, prfld, sadc, sadp, sag, sar, sa1, sa2, timex and OS.

PRI Primary Rate Interface. Also called 23B + D, which stands for 23 bearer channels for voice and data and one signal channel for network management. One of two types of Integrated Services Digital Network. Provides an aigrette of 1.544

megabits per second through twenty-four 64-kilobits-per-second channels. *See* ISDN and BRI.

primary master server C o m m o n l y called primary name server. *See* primary name server.

primary memory Commonly called main memory. *See* main memory.

primary name server Host on a Domain Name Service network that is responsible for the administration of the file sharing environment for the hosts in the domain. Includes a list of available resources and addresses for the hosts with those available resources, etc. *See* DNS, NS and secondary name server.

primary prompt Default user prompt established by a shell. *See* prompt and system prompt.

primary rate interface Commonly abbreviated and called PRI. *See* PRI.

primary storage Computer's main memory. System activity, including running of programs and manipulation of data, takes place in primary storage. All data is placed in the main memory temporarily for the computer to act on it. When the computer is finished, the data in primary storage is either deleted or returned to secondary storage. *See* memory and secondary storage.

primitive Command used to perform an rdist action. Specifies what action is to be taken in modifying files on remote hosts. *See* rdist and distfile.

print 1. *(ATT)* Command in the UNIX System V, Release 4 Framed Access Command Environment file system operations menu. Used to direct the output of a file to a printer. *See* SVR4.x, FACE and file system. **2.** C shell script for printing a document that uses the pr command (for formatting a file for printing) and redirects the output to a printer. *See* pr. **3.** Korn shell command that emulates the features of the echo command. *See* Korn shell and echo. **4.** Any operation that re-

sults in data being displayed in a form that can be read by users, e.g. on a video terminal or printed on paper.

printcap *(BSD)* File in the /etc system directory which contains a description of the printers used on computer systems running the lpr command. *See* lpr.

printed circuit board Commonly abbreviated PCB. Also called circuit board, pc board or board. Computer component used for memory, communications, central processing, etc. A flat board made of non-conducting material such as fiber glass or plastic. Pre-defined electronic paths are created by printing the board with a conductive material. Holes are punched into the board to hold components such as memory modules or microprocessor chips. Components are attached to the board with conductive solder. Metal leads are placed on the edge of the board so it can be connected to a computer.

printenv *(BSD)* **Print env**ironment. Command used to display environmental variables. *See* environment.

printer Electromechanical device used to record information on paper or another physical medium.

printer command language Commonly abbreviated and called PCL. *See* PCL.

printers *(ATT)* Command in the UNIX System V, Release 4 line printer services menu similar to the lpadmin command. Used to configure a printer for use. *See* SVR4.x and lpadmin.

printf Print format. C language library routine used to convert, format and print a standard message or program output. *See* library routines, fopen, fread, getc, fgetc, gets, fgets, scanf, fscanf, fwrite, putc, fputc, puts, fputs, fclose and fprintf.

printout Printed, or hard, copy of a document.

print out To make a hard, or printed, copy of a document. *See* hard copy.

print queue List of files or documents waiting to be printed. *See* buffer.

print server Computer dedicated to managing users' printing requirements on a network. Manages the print queue, assigning print jobs to specific printers.

priocntl *(ATT)* **Priority control.** System call used to manage the scheduling parameters of an active process. Controls the allocation of computer time for running real-time or time-share class processes, and is used to display scheduling parameters of processes. Can only be run by root or while the users is in a real-time shell. *See* root, real-time class, time-sharing class, shell and tqntm.

priorities *(ATT)* Command in the UNIX System V, Release 4 line printer services menu similar to the lpadmin command. Used to assign the level of priority for a specific user requesting use of a printer. *See* SVR4.x and lpusers.

priority Ranking assigned to a process, indicating when it will be executed in relation to other processes.

priority scheduling facilities *(POS)* POSIX.4 (real-time operating system) term. Provide the ability to manage schedules with multiple priorities. *See* POSIX.4 and RTOS.

Privacy Enhanced Mail Commonly abbreviated and called PEM. *See* PEM.

private-key Data encryption methodology in which both the sender and receiver of a message know a key used to translate the message to readable text. The private-key is known only by the creator of the key and is used to encrypt messages to be sent out and to decrypt messages that are received. *See* public-key.

Private Management Domain Commonly abbreviated and called PRMD. *See* PRMD.

private MIB Private management information base. Commonly called extended MIB. *See* extended MIB.

privilege Right not normally granted to all users to perform a process or action on a computer.

privileged account Account established with special, or privileged, permissions, enabling a user to read, write and execute commands in files or directories in a computer system, e.g. root or any user account established with superuser permissions. *See* superuser and root.

privileged process Any process established with special or privileged permissions with an effective user identifier (EUID) of 0, e.g. the root or a superuser UID. Privileged processes bypasses security checks. *See* superuser and EUID.

PRM Programmer's Reference Manual. UNIX system documentation which provides a list and explanation of commands, system calls, formats, etc., needed by programmers. *See* User's Guide, URM, Programmer's Guide, SARM and System Administrator's Guide.

prmail *(BSD)* **Print mail.** Command used to format electronic mail so that it can be printed. *See* e-mail.

PRMD Private Management Domain. Term in the X.400 electronic-mail handling system, developed by the International Telecommunication Union Telecommunication Standardization Sector, formerly known as the *Consultative Committee on International Telegraphy and Telephony*. Delivers electronic-mail messages from the X.400 gateway to a user's electronic-mail file. *See* ITU-T, X.400, e-mail and ADMD.

PRO Precision RISC Organization. Formed by the Hewlett-Packard Co., Convex Computer Corp., Hitachi Ltd., Hughes Aircraft Co., Mitsubishi Electric Corp., Oki Electric Industry Co. Ltd., Prime Computer Inc., Sequoia Systems Inc. and Yokogawa Electric Corp. Promotes the use of Hewlett-Packard's Precision Architecture Reduced Instruction Set Computing (PA-RISC) technology. Also tests and certifies software compliance with PA-RISC. *See* PA-RISC and RISC.

probe routine Program that checks to see if a piece of hardware is connected to a computer and sends interrupt signals to hardware devices to stop the normal flow of a running process. *See* interrupt.

probing Process of running probe routines. *See* probe routine.

/proc *(ATT)* System directory in UNIX System V, Release 4 that contains a list of all the processes currently running on the system. *See* SVR4.x and process.

proc Abbreviation for process. *See* process.

procedural language 1. Computer- or program-readable input, e.g. an embedded command in the nroff or troff text formatting program, that results in graphs, tables and/or text being created. *See* text formatting, nroff, troff and descriptive language. 2. Any computer language in which the running of an instruction is dependent on the running of previous instructions:

```
main()
{
        printf("hello, world\n");
}
```

procedural security Commonly called administrative security. *See* administrative security.

process 1. Program or the separate elements of a program which are running. In UNIX, the same program can be run more than once, at the same time. Each running of the program is a process. The distinction between a process and a program is that a process runs in memory while a program remains on the disk. A UNIX process is composed of three elements: the text, data and bss segments. *See* parent process, child process, text segment, data segment and bss segment. 2. Transmission Control Protocol term for the first level of the addressing scheme. The process is a unique address of an application or program. *See* TCP, port and sockets.

process agent Application software used to manage local resources under direction from a remote manager. *See* process manager.

process control Processes and commands related to starting, managing and ending a process. *See* exec, fork and signal.

process group Group of related processes, e.g. all the child processes of a parent process. *See* process, process group leader, child process and parent process.

process group leader Commonly called superparent. *See* superparent.

process ID Commonly abbreviated and called PID. *See* PID.

process identifier Commonly abbreviated and called PID. *See* PID.

process image Representation of a process' memory, generally on disk. May be produced by the gcore command. *See* process and gcore.

process manager Software application used to manage network activities. *See* process agent.

process memory locking *(POS)* POSIX.4 (real-time processing) term. Prevents critical parts of a process from being paged. *See* POSIX.4, RTOS and paging.

process migration Moving a process from one computer to another to spread the workload across several computers.

process one Also called init. Daemon that is the first process started when the system is activated and is assigned the process identifier 1. *See* init.

process open file table Commonly called descriptor table. *See* descriptor table.

processor allocation Parallel processing term for dividing up the use of the central processing unit to complete programs and prevent conflicts over resources. *See* parallel processing, static allocation and dynamic allocation.

processor priority level Priority ranking determines whether an interrupt signal can be successfully sent to a central processing unit. *See* interrupt and CPU.

processor scheduling Parallel processing term for programming code elements, or instructions, into a specific processor for execution.

processor synchronization P a r a l l e l processing term for coordinating communication between tasks and the various processors. *See* parallel processing and task.

process priority Method of determining the priority of a process in obtaining system resources. Dynamically determined by the kernel based on total system requirements and resources. Can be externally modified using the nice command. *See* process scheduling and nice.

process scheduler Commonly abbreviated and called sched. *See* sched.

process scheduling Assignment or management of process priorities for access to system resources, e.g. memory allocation. *See* process priority, swapper and nice.

process state Definition of the status of a process. There are eight *process states*: running in user mode, running in kernel mode, waiting, sleeping, idle, swapping, zombie and stopped.

process synchronization Method of managing the timing of several processes. Ensures that the resulting action of each process takes place on schedule to support subsequent or related processes. *See* IPC.

process table List maintained in main memory of the data structure for all active processes. *See* proc structure.

process table entries Commonly called proc structure. *See* proc structure.

Process to Support Interpretability Commonly abbreviated and called PSI. *See* PSI.

process zero Also called swapper. Process identifier number of the system or central processing unit scheduler. *See* sched.

proc file system /dev/proc. File system that shows all the active processes in an AT&T System V, Release 4 system. Used to make debugging programs for processes. *See* process.

procs parameter Old kernel parameter in the Berkeley Software Distribution used to establish the maximum total number of processes that can be run on a system at any one time. *See* kernel description file.

proc structure Process structure. Also called process table entries. Data structure for each active process. Continually maintained in the kernel.

production environment C o m p u t i n g resources needed to provide commercial business computer system solutions to meet customer requirements. Includes computer hardware, peripherals, communication network, application software, utilities, tools, environmental facilities, and management policies and procedures. The sole purpose of a production environment is to deliver a stable computing environment for business applications. No research, development or testing is performed in a production environment.

Product Overview and Master Index UNIX System V, Release 4 system documentation that provides a brief overview of the features in UNIX System V, Release 4, and a list of UNIX-related subjects in other documents and how to such information.

prof *(ATT/XEN)* **Prof**ile. Command used to display profiling data accumulated on a program under development.

Professional Office System Commonly abbreviated and called PROFS. *See* PROFS.

profil *(ATT)* **Profile**. Process system call used to obtain information from the kernel about the execution or run-time profile. *See* system call and kernel.

profile 1. *(ATT)* Command used to create the default environment for the Bourne shell. *See* Bourne shell. **2.** Description of a user's operating environment, contained in the .profile file. *See* .profile. **3.** Also called functional standard. A description of requirements for a user group or specific industry, e.g. the software standards developed for the oil industry by the Petrotechnical Open Systems Corp. A standard in itself that also references other standards in whole or part and may require creation of an interface or relationship between two or more standards. *See* standard and base standard.

.profile *(ATT)* System file established in a user account. Located in the user's home directory and accessed whenever the user logs in. Established in System V to describe the user's operating environment, e.g. the path of the files and programs the user is authorized to use, definition of the terminal, personalized system prompt, and permissions for files and directories created by the user. *See* .login and .cshrc.

Profiler Collection of programs that provides statistical data on the amount of time the operating system spends on user and system tasks and the amount of time it is idle.

PROFS Professional Office System. IBM Corp.'s proprietary electronic-mail system.

program 1. Machine-readable instructions that give a computer step-by-step instructions on how to perform specific tasks. **2.** Link between a user and a computer. The distinction between a program and a process is that a process runs in memory and a program remains on the disk. *See* process. **3.** Jargon term for Trojan horse. *See* Trojan horse.

program development tool Commonly called tool. *See* tool.

programmable logic array Commonly abbreviated and called PLA. *See* PLA.

programmable macro logic *See* PMD.

programmable read-only memory Abbreviated and commonly known as PROM. *See* PROM.

Programmer's Guide UNIX system documentation which provides an overview of how to do UNIX programming, and a list and explanation of programming tools. *See* User's Guide, URM, PRM, SARM and System Administrator's Guide.

Programmer's Guide: ANSI C and Programming Support Tools UNIX System V, Release 4 documentation on the programming tools that can be used to include utilities, file formats and libraries in SVR4. *See* SVR4.x and ANSI C.

Programmer's Guide: Character User Interface (FMLI and ETI) Commonly abbreviated and called CHAR. *See* CHAR.

Programmer's Guide: Networking Interfaces Commonly abbreviated and called NI. *See* NI.

Programmer's Guide: OPEN LOOK Graphical User Interface UNIX System V, Release 4 system documentation for end-users developing graphical user interfaces using OPEN LOOK, e.g. window applications for networks. *See* SVR4.x, GUI and OPEN LOOK.

Programmer's Guide: POSIX Conformance UNIX System V, Release 4 documentation describing how UNIX System V, Release 4 complies with POSIX. *See* SVR4.x and POSIX.

Programmer's Guide: STREAMS Commonly abbreviated and called STRM. *See* STRM.

Programmer's Guide: System Services and Applications Packaging Tools Commonly abbreviated and called SS. *See* SS.

Programmer's Guide: X11/NeWS Graphical Windowing System NeWS UNIX System V, Release 4 documentation on how to build windows-based applications. *See* SVR4.x and X Window System.

Programmer's Guide: XWIN Graphical Windowing System Addenda: Technical Papers UNIX System V, Release 4 documentation on the implementation of the Massachusetts Institute of Technology X 11, Release 3 specification for the X Window System. *See* SVR4.x and X Window System.

Programmer's Guide: XWIN Graphical Windowing System The X toolkit UNIX System V, Release 4 documentation on the use of the X Window library, toolkit and widget set. *See* SVR4.x, X Window System, xlib, Xt and widget.

Programmer's Hierarchical Interactive Graphics System Abbreviated and commonly known as PHiGS. See PHiGS.

Programmer's Reference Manual Commonly abbreviated and called PRM. *See* PRM.

Programmer's Work Bench Commonly abbreviated and called PWB/UNIX. *See* PWB/UNIX.

programming language Symbolic representation of algorithms, instructions and data, suitable for translation into machine instructions.

Project 1003 Commonly called P1003 Committee. Formed in 1984 by the Institute of Electrical and Electronics Engineers to create standards for an open systems environment for system interface, shells and tools, testing and verification, real-time processing, Ada, security, system administration, networking, FORTRAN, supercomputers, transaction processing, etc. *See* POSIX.

Project Athena Massachusetts Institute of Technology project (1983-91) that resulted in development of the X Window System, Kerberos user authentication system and others. Jointly sponsored by MIT, IBM Corp. and Digital Equipment Corp.

to develop a networking environment common to all users regardless of the hardware used. *See* X Window System, Kerberos, Moira, Hesiod and Zephyr.

Project Authorization Request Commonly abbreviated and called PAR. *See* PAR.

Project MAC 1965 Massachusetts Institute of Technology project that included Bell Laboratories and General Electric Co. Aimed to develop an operating system capable of supporting a large number of users who would simultaneously be accessing a computer and sharing data. Resulted in the MULTICS operating system. Bell Laboratories team members included Ken Thompson and Dennis Ritchie, whose work on MULTICS helped lead to the creation of UNIX. *See* MULTICS, Thompson, Ken and Ritchie, Dennis M.

Project Management Committee *(POS)* Commonly abbreviated and called PMC. *See* PMC.

Project Pink Joint project started in 1992 by IBM Corp. and Apple Computer Inc. to develop a new personal computer operating system.

PROM Programmable read-only memory. Read only memory which holds programs that can only be read by other system programs and cannot be altered.

promiscuous mode When a controller of a device on a network is set to receive all traffic on the network.

prompt 1. Special character, symbol or message which indicates the computer system is ready for command input. 2. Identifies the point where information is input, or where a request for information input. *See* system prompt and mail prompt. 3. Variable in the ex and vi editors that, when set, establishes a prompt whenever the command mode is started. *See* ex and vi. 4. Electronic-mail variable. *See* .mailrc variables (Appendix F). 5. *(BSD)* C shell environment variable used to define the system prompt. The percent sign (%) is the default. *See* system prompt and PS1.

propagation delay Time needed for 1 bit to travel from its point of origin to its destination across a network.

proportional printing System of printing in which the width of each printed character and the horizontal space it occupies are proportional to each other, so that the letter m uses more space than an l. A proportionally spaced document looks as if it were typeset, not typewritten. In contrast, when a document is not proportionally spaced, each letter occupies the same amount of space on a line, regardless of its actual width. *See* fixed space printing.

proprietary Property of a vendor, e.g. software or type of architecture, which can be obtained only through that vendor, maintained only by that vendor and run only on that vendor's systems.

proprietary architecture *See* proprietary.

proprietary software *See* proprietary.

protected memory Memory to which only the kernel can write page tables, process lists, memory buffers, free lists, etc. Normally built into hardware as part of the microprocessor addressing architecture. *See* kernel address space.

protocol Standards or common set of rules, instructions or formats for organizing data so it can be transferred between computer systems and/or peripherals.

Protocol Control Information Commonly abbreviated and called PCI. *See* PCI.

protocol converter Network device used to convert one protocol to another, e.g. a Transmission Control Protocol/Internet Protocol (TCP/IP) to X.25 protocol converter would be required to connect a computer with a TCP/IP Ethernet board to a X.25 network. *See* TCP/IP and X.25.

Protocol Data Units Commonly abbreviated and called PDU. *See* PDU.

protocol family Commonly called protocol stack. *See* protocol stack.

Protocol Independent Interface Commonly abbreviated and called PII. *See* PII.

protocol model Documentation or description of the interrelationship of protocols. *See* ARM and OSIRM.

protocols File in the /etc system directory which contains information, e.g. name, number and alias names, of protocols used on the Internet. *See* /etc and Internet.

protocol stack Protocol layers of network. Consists of the various protocol definitions that pass data to the protocol directly above or below it, e.g. the Internet Protocol and Transmission Control Protocol. *See* Internet, TCP/IP and ISO/OSI.

protocol suite Protocols which make up the protocol model. *See* protocol model.

protocol tunneling Placing the packets of a protocol that is not supported by a network into the packets of a protocol that is supported by a network for transmission. *See* packet.

prototyping Using new hardware and/or software technology to help determine the requirements of or to learn about that technology. Can prove costly in terms of time, money and personnel.

providers Commonly called server. *See* server.

Providers Grouping of related protocols for UNIX network interfaces, e.g. X.25 and the Internet Protocol.

Proxy Agent 1. Open Systems Interconnection term for network devices which have limited capabilities, e.g. printers and modems. *See* OSI. 2. Software used to translate information between two different network management protocols.

prs *(ATT)* **Pr**int **S**ource Code Control System. One of the 13 Source Code Control System (SCCS) commands used to print information about SCCS files. If a SCCS file is specifically identified upon input, information is provided based upon a keyword input for data wanted. If a directory is identified upon input, then the user is provided a list of SCCS files in the directory. *See* SCCS, admin, cdc, comb, delta, get, help, rmdel, sact, sccsdiff, unget, val, vc and what.

prtacct *(ATT)* **Print acc**ounting. Accounting system shell script used to format and print system accounting files created by the acctcon2, acctprc2 and acctmerg accounting system programs. *See* acctcon2, acctprc2 and acctmerg.

ps Process status. Command used to determine the status of currently running processes. *See* process.

PS1 1. Prompt string 1. Primary prompt string. Environmental variable used with the Bourne and Korn shells to indicate where and when to make a command input. The default is the dollar sign ($), but can be customized by the user. 2. Power Source 1. Integrated Service Digital Network definition for power carried on transmission leads for emergency power.

PS2 1. Prompt string 2. Secondary prompt string. Environmental variable used with the Bourne and Korn shells to indicate when a shell is expecting additional input to finish a command. The default prompt is the greater than sign (>) and usually is not customized by the user. 2. Power Source 2. Integrated Service Digital Network definition for power used to transmit signals.

PS3 Prompt string 3. Tertiary or select command prompt string. Korn shell prompt used by the select command to read replies from standard input. The environmental variable needed to complete the action specified by the standard input is then set. *See* Korn shell.

PS4 Prompt string 4. Debug prompt string. Prompt in the Korn shell used for parameter substitution that indicates the line before an execution trace. The default prompt is the plus sign (+).

psec Picosecond. One-trillionth of a second (1/1,000,000,000,000).

pseudocode Commonly abbreviated and called p-code. *See* p-code.

pseudo color Color mode of a computer color monitor in which 8 bits are stored for each pixel. Enables 256 distinct colors to be displayed. *See* color mode, pixel, minimum color, high color and true color.

pseudo computer nerd Someone who physically resembles a computer nerd, and thinks he knows UNIX but in reality is only fooling himself and others who know very little about UNIX. Unlike a true computer nerd, he starts counting at 1 instead of 0. *See* computer nerd and super computer nerd.

pseudo-device Hardware function performed by options in the operating system kernel that appear to be hardware devices. *See* ether pseudo-device, imp pseudo-device, loop pseudo-device, ns pseudo-device and pty pseudo-device.

pseudo-device driver Software program used to perform hardware functions within the operating system kernel. Appears to be a hardware device but is not even backed up by any actual device. *See* ether pseudo-device, imp pseudo-device, loop pseudo-device, ns pseudo-device and pty pseudo-device.

pseudo-language Program code that must be compiled into machine language before it can be understood by a computer. *See* high-level programming language and machine language.

pseudo-login Also called pseudo-user. Login that does not relate to an actual person. Established with its own passwords, home directory and login shell to perform a special function or execute a command, e.g. uucp, bin and lp.

pseudo-run level One of three run, or access, levels which the superuser can enter without affecting the current run level of the computer. *See* state.

pseudo state Also called state a, b and/or c. Used to set up a temporary state to run commands without changing the system state.

pseudo-tty Jargon term for pty pseudo-device. *See* pty pseudo-device.

pseudo-user Commonly called pseudo-login. *See* pseudo-login.

PSI **P**rocess to **S**upport **I**nteroperability. Interoperability testing and certification program developed by the Standards Promotion and Application Group for compliance with Open Systems Interconnection protocols. Products that pass the test are awarded a PSI Mark. *See* OSI and SPAG.

PsiNet Commercial Internet Exchange company located in Reston, Virginia, that charges a fee to connect users to the Internet. *See* Internet and CIX.

PSN **1.** *(INET)* **P**acket **S**witch **N**ode. Called an IMP (Interface Message Processor) in the early days of the Internet. Handles the traffic control and packet switching of data sent over the network. *See* IMP. **2.** **P**ublic **S**witch **N**etwork. Original name for the Public Switch Telephone Network. *See* PSTN.

pstat *(BSD/XEN)* **P**rocess **stat**istics. Command used to collect a wide variety of information on the size and current usage of kernel tables, including the inode table, process table, terminals and swap space.

PSTN **P**ublic **S**witch **T**elephone **N**etwork. Originally called the Public Switch Network. A communications term for standard telephone lines.

PTA **P**erformance **T**esting **A**lliance. Consortium including users, vendors and product analysts that works with networks and network products. Formed to create a standard for testing and benchmarking local area network products. *See* LAN.

PTE **P**age **t**able **e**ntry. List of data used to map virtual memory pages to physical memory.

pti *(BSD)* **P**hototypesetter **i**nterpreter. Used to interpret phototypesetter commands.

PTM **P**acket **T**ransfer **M**ode. Use of packets to encapsulate and transmit data. PTM is used in networks such as Ethernet, ARPANET and Internet. *See* ATM and STM.

ptoc **P**ascal-**to-C**. Source code translator that changes programs written in Pascal to C language. *See* Pascal, C language and p2c.

PTR **D**omain Name **P**ointer or **P**ointer record. Data file required by the Domain Name Service which contains the cross-reference table between special address names and the actual host names for other hosts on the network. *See* DNS.

ptrace **P**rocess **trace**. System call used to trace or audit the execution of a process for debugging purposes. *See* system call and debug.

PTT **P**ost, **T**elephone and **T**elegraph. Generic name for national telephone companies in Europe.

ptx *(ATT/XEN)* Command used to generate a permuted index. *See* permuted index.

pty pseudo-device Fake tty terminal connection used in networking. Appears to a program as a tty device file, but in reality is a communication termination point used to move data on to a network. *See* tty.

PUBDIR Variable for UNIX-to-UNIX CoPy (UUCP) that is used to define the directory which holds files that are sent to or received from a remote system using the UUCP communications system. Normally this is /usr/spool/uucppublic. *See* UUCP and /usr/spool/uucppublic.

public data internet Commonly abbreviated and called PDI. *See* PDI.

public data network Abbreviated and commonly known as PDN. *See* PDN.

public domain Class of software that the developer has made available with no copyright or other restrictions on its use e.g. Massachusetts Institute of Technology's X Window System software. *See* X Window System.

public-key 1.Term related to the Data Encryption Standard and secure Remote Procedure Call. A user-generated key, or password, that is stored in a public database. Combined with a secret key by the Keyserver to form a common-key. *See* DES, RPC, client, server, encrypt, decrypt, common-key, conversation-key, private-key, keylogin, Keyserver, timestamp, credential, verifier and window. **2.** *(ATT)* File in the /etc system directory used by the secure Remote Procedure Call to store the information related to the user's public-key. Includes the user's name or hostname, user's public-key and user's secret key, or password. *See* public-key and private-key.

public-key cryptography Cipher system consisting of a public and private-key. The public-key is used by anyone with knowledge of the key to send encrypted messages to the creator of the key or decrypt messages received from the creator of the key. The private-key is known only by the creator of the key and is used to encrypt messages to be sent out and decrypt messages that are received. *See* public-key and private-key.

public-key encryption Form of data encryption developed by Whitfield Diffie and Martin Hellman in the mid-1970s. Public-key encryption uses one key that is known by anyone who can initiate and send encrypted messages to the creator of the key. A second private-key, only known by the creator of the key, is used to decrypt the data. *See* DES and private-key.

Public Switch Network Commonly abbreviated and called PSN. *See* PSN.

Public Switch Telephone Network
Commonly abbreviated and called PSTN. *See* PSTN.

pull Commonly called pop. *See* pop.

pull-down menu List of computer commands that remains hidden from view until the user selects that menu, which rolls down like a window shade.

Pull-down menu in Microsoft Windows

pulse-code-modulation Commonly abbreviated and called PCM. *See* PCM.

punch cards Commonly called computer cards. *See* computer cards.

punct Punctuation. Part of the Writer's Workbench set of text processing tools. Used to check documents for punctuation errors. *See* WWB.

pure demand paging Operating system function when as part of demand paging, only those portions of a program actively used are maintained in memory. There is no prepaging or retrieving pages from memory before they are needed. Only those parts of a program that are being actively used are moved into memory. *See* prepaging and demand paging.

purge To remove data from a computer's hard disk or memory.

push Also called put. Process of putting data sets at the top of a data stack (list). *See* stack, pop, shift and unshift.

pushd *(BSD)* **Push d**irectory. csh or tcsh shell command that puts the name of the current working directory (CWD) at the top of a stack of directory names. Changes the CWD to the directory specified on the command line. *See* csh, tcsh, stack, current working directory, cd and popd.

pushpin Pictorial representation, similar to an icon, in the OPEN LOOK graphical user interface. Used to maintain access to a window or pop-up window. *See* OPEN LOOK, GUI and pop-up window.

put 1. *(INET)* File Transfer Protocol command used to transport or move a file from the local host to a remote host over a Transmission Control Protocol/Internet Protocol network. *See* FTP, TCP/IP, remote host and take. 2. UNIX-to-UNIX CoPy command used to transport or move a file from the local host to a remote host. *See* UUCP, remote host and take. 3. *(ATT)* Command that is a part of the cu command. Used to transfer a file to a remote host from the local host. *See* cu. 4. Process commonly called push. *See* push.

putc C language standard input/output library routine used to write information to a file which has been opened with fopen, a C language library routine. *See* library routines, fopen, fread, getc, fgetc, gets, fgets, scanf, fscanf, fwrite, fclose, fputc, puts, fputs, printf and fprintf.

putpwent *(ATT)* **Put** password **ent**ry. C language library routine used to change or add an entry to the system password file. *See* library routines.

puts C language standard input/output library routine used to write information to a file which has been opened with fopen, a C language library routine. *See* library routines, fopen, fread, getc, fgetc, gets, fgets, scanf, fscanf, fwrite, putc, fputc, fclose, fputs, printf and fprintf.

PUUG **P**ortuguese **U**NIX **U**ser **G**roup formed in 1988.

pwadm *(OTH)* **P**assword **adm**inistration. Program used by the system administrator to manage password aging. Can be input by users to get information about their password, e.g. when the password will age. *See* password aging.

pwadmin *(XEN)* Program used to manage password aging. *See* password aging.

PWB **P**rogrammer's **W**ork **B**ench. Set of software development tools developed by AT&T Co. in the mid-1970s for 32V UNIX. *See* PWB/UNIX.

PWB/UNIX **P**rogrammer's **W**ork **B**ench **UNIX**. Set of software tools derived from Version 6. Designed to ease development of UNIX-based application software. It was the first commercial release of UNIX in 1977. AT&T Co. developed the original Programmer's Workbench in the mid-1970s and incorporated it with Version 7 to make System III in 1981. *See* Version 6, Version 7, System III, RJE, SCCS and tool.

pwcheck *(XEN)* **P**assword **check**. Command used to review the password file.

pwck *(ATT)* **P**assword **ck**ecker. Command used to check the validity of the password file, /etc/passwd. *See* grpck.

pwconv **P**assword **conv**ert. Command used by the system administrator to convert password management from the /etc/passwd file to shadow passwords using the /etc/shadow file to enhance password security. /etc/passwd is readable by everyone where /etc/shadow can be accessed only by root. *See* /etc/passwd and /etc/shadow.

pwd **P**rint **w**orking **d**irectory. Command used to determine the name of the current working directory and indicate a user's location in the file system. *See* current working directory and file system.

PWD **P**rint **w**orking **d**irectory. Korn shell variable. Contains the name of the current working directory. *See* Korn shell and OLDPWD.

pwexp *(OTH)* **P**assword **exp**ire. Program used to calculate and indicate the number of weeks before a password expires.

pxp *(BSD)* **P**ascal e**x**ecution **p**rofiler. Program that provides statistical data on the amount of time a Pascal program spends on user and system tasks, and is idle. *See* Pascal, profiler and gprof.

Q

Q-DOS Forerunner of MS-DOS. Also called quick and dirty DOS. *See* MS-DOS.

QIC Quarter Inch Cartridge. Standard format for .25-inch magnetic tape drives.

Typical QIC data cartridge

QNX UNIX-like operating system developed by Quantum Software Systems Ltd. that is compliant with Portable Operating System Interface for Computer Environments (POSIX). A 32-bit multitasking operating system based upon microkernel technology. Consists of 605 lines of source code in the kernel that offers interprocess communication, command language operations, limited network services, process scheduling and interrupt management. Other functions, such as device and process managers and memory management, are not in the microkernel. *See* POSIX and microkernel.

quantum Measurement of the maximum time allowed for a process to run under a real-time system. *See* RTOS.

Quarter Inch Cartridge Abbreviated and commonly known as QIC. *See* QIC.

query Request by a user or program for data formatted into usable information from a database, e.g. request for statistics on computer system uptime for a specified time to be found and displayed.

query condition Any element placing a limit on a query, e.g. specifying which database record(s) or type of database record(s) is to be accessed.

query language English-like programming language used by nonprogrammers to develop simple programs and manipulate a database.

query tools Programming applications that provide the ability for the user to access and manipulate data in a database without having to understand the functionality of a system query language or the database. *See* SQL.

question mark *(?)* Metacharacter used within regular expressions as a wild card for a single character, e.g. a command followed by ?1 will act only on files with file names that are two characters long and end in the number 1. Used in the egrep and awk programs. *See* metacharacter and regular expression.

queue Line of processes, print jobs or other items that are waiting to use the next available resource, e.g. a printer. Priorities can be attached to items in a queue to move them ahead of or behind other items.

queuing theory Study of data communications to determine the extent of delays caused by waits for shared resources.

quiet Electronic-mail variable. *See* .mailrc variables (Appendix F).

quit 1. *(ATT)* Command used to exit the shell layer. When executed, all the layers are stopped. *See* shl. 2. Commonly called exit. *See* exit. 3. Signal sent to the kernel that terminates a running process and writes a copy of the process to a core file. Sent by a program when either the user, root or hardware terminates the program, for whatever reason. *See* core.

quiz *(ATT)* Command used to start a game to that quizzes a user's knowledge.

quot **Quot**a. Command used to quickly check a user's disk usage. Shows the number of blocks and number of files utilized by all users. *See* block.

quota **1.** Command used to display disk usage and limits. **2.** Limit placed on scarce system resources, e.g. disk space and memory. *See* soft limit and hard limit.

quotacheck Command used to checks disk usage of a file system. *See* file system.

quotaoff **Quota off.** Command used to turn off the quotas on disk limits for users established for a file system. *See* quotaon and file system.

quotaon **Quota on.** Command used to activate the quotas on disk limits for users established for a file system. *See* quotaoff and file system.

QUOTE *(INET)* **Quote** of the Day Protocol. Defense Advanced Research Projects Agency Internet protocol. Allows a developer to set up a two-way communication with another host to test software that is being developed to run on the network. Sends an American Standard Code for Information Interchange message back to the originator. Used by developers and others in debugging. *See* DARPA, Internet and ASCII.

Quote of the Day Protocol *(INET)* Commonly abbreviated and called QUOTE. *See* QUOTE.

quoting **1.** Overriding or turning off the meaning of special characters. **2.** Passing the literal meaning of an input to a command. **3.** Using special characters (quotation marks) to indicate that the characters between the quotation marks are to be regarded as a string.

R

RAB RAID Advisory Board. Sponsored by the Technology Forums of Lino Lakes, Minnesota. Evaluates vendors' RAID product offerings and assigns the correct RAID level and certification to each product. *See* RAID.

rabbits Commonly called logic bomb. *See* logic bomb.

race condition When two or more processes send an interprocess communication at the same time. *See* IPC.

RAD Rapid application development. Methodology developed to enhance and speed development of new computer systems. Consists of four basic elements: a small, skilled development team; reusable tools (terminals, software and workstations); computer-aided design tools; and end-user involvement throughout the product life cycle.

radio frequency interference Commonly abbreviated and called RFI. *See* RFI.

radiogram Electronic-mail message sent and/or received by devices that are connected to a network through wireless communication modes. *See* e-mail and wireless network.

radiosity Technology applied to graphics workstations to provide photo-quality images. Compares the light reflection among different types of surfaces to determine how light from one surface affects the color of other surfaces.

radix Commonly called base. *See* base.

ragged Word processing term indicating lines of text do not end evenly at the right margin. *See* justify.

RAID Redundant Array of Inexpensive Disks. Sometimes called Redundant Array of Independent Disks. Originally defined in 1988 by the University of California, Berkeley. Method of obtaining fault tolerance and correcting errors in programming code by writing data to multiple disks so that information can be rebuilt if there is a disk failure. Except for RAID 1, all levels of RAID use disk striping to enhance performance by providing parallel access to an array of disks. The degree of fault tolerance is defined by RAID levels 0 through 5; level 6 is under development. *See* RAID-0, RAID-1, RAID-2, RAID-3, RAID-4, RAID-5, RAID-6, ECC, striping and disk mirroring.

RAID-0 Redundant Array of Inexpensive Disks, Level 0. Transfer of data by a user from one disk to an array of disks, using a method called disk striping, e.g. data is split into groups and divided, but not duplicated, among the available disks. During the transfer, the computer does not automatically check the data to ensure none has been or will be lost if there is a disk or system failure. Since the data is not duplicated, it can be lost if one of the disks fails. *See* RAID and striping.

RAID-1 Redundant Array of Inexpensive Disks, Level 1. Also called disk mirroring. Method of copying the contents of a disk onto a second disk, on a computer. Whenever data is written to a disk, the same data is automatically written to a twin disk. *See* RAID and disk mirroring.

RAID-2 Redundant Array of Inexpensive Disks, Level **2**. Method of interleaving, or disk striping, data (alternating the output of data between multiple disks). Enhanced with error detection and correction software. Stripes data a single byte or bit at a time. *See* ECC and RAID.

RAID-3 Redundant Array of Inexpensive Disks, Level **3**. RAID-2 for microcomputers. Method of saving data to a parallel set of disks, with parity data maintained on a separate disk. Data is spread across multiple disks in bytes. If a disk fails, the data from the other disks and the parity information is used to recover the missing data. *See* parity, parity disk, byte, striping and RAID.

RAID-4 Redundant Array of Inexpensive Disks, Level **4**. Method of saving data to a parallel set of disks, with parity data maintained on a separate disk. Data is spread across multiple disks in sectors. If a disk fails, the data from the other disks and the parity information is used to recover the missing data. *See* parity, parity disk, sector, striping and RAID.

RAID-5 Redundant Array of Inexpensive Disks, Level **5**. Method of saving data and parity checks to a parallel set of disks in sectors. If a disk fails, the data from the other disks and the parity information is used to recover the missing data. *See* parity, sector, striping and RAID.

RAID-6 Redundant Array of Inexpensive Disks, Level **6**. Method that provides the ability to have double error correction and duplicate disk controllers. Protects against failures in error checking and correction either while information on a failed disk is being reconstructed or if there is a multiple disk failure. RAID-6 is still under development. *See* ECC and RAID.

RAID-10 Redundant Array of Inexpensive Disks, Level **10**. Not an original RAID level. Commercially developed by ECCS of Tinto Falls, NJ. Combines RAID-1, or disk mirroring, where the computer system copies the contents of a disk onto a

second disk, and RAID-0, or disk striping, where data is transferred from one disk to an array of disks. *See* RAID.

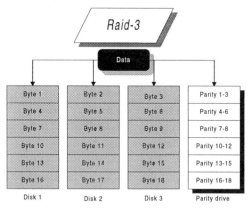

Raid-3 strips the data across the data drives one byte at a time. The information stored on the parity drive enables the system to reconstruct the data stored on a failed drive. Raid-3 is suited to transferring large blocks of data.

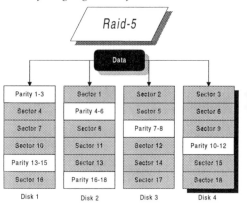

Raid-5 strips the data across all drives one sector at a time. The parity information is stored across the drives. Raid 5 is suited to transferring small blocks of data, such as the storage of word processing files.

RAID Advisory Board Commonly abbreviated and called RAB. *See* RAB.

Rainbow Series Jargon term for the set of technical books published by the National Computer Security Center. *See* Orange Book and NCSC.

RAM Random access memory. Temporary memory within a mainframe, minicomputer, personal computer or printer.

Area where programs or data are loaded, or read, when transferred from the fixed storage area, generally a disk or tape. The user can then modify the information. Once the user is finished with it, the program or data is either returned, or written, to the fixed storage area or deleted from RAM so the space can be used by other information. Information stored in RAM is lost when power to the computer is turned off. *See* buffer.

RAMDAC chip **R**andom **a**ccess **m**emory **d**igital to **a**nalog **c**onverter **chip**. Integrated circuit used in graphics boards to convert digital images to analog data representations which can be interpreted by computer monitors.

random **1.** *(XEN)* Command used to generate a random number. **2.** Lack of a specific, definable sequence.

RANDOM *(ATT)* **R**andom number generator. Korn shell variable for random generation of numbers from 0 to 32,767. Used in games, statistics, probability and data generation.

random access memory Commonly abbreviated and called RAM. *See* RAM.

random access memory digital to analog converter chip Commonly abbreviated and called RAMDAC chip. *See* RAMDAC chip.

ranlib *(BSD)* **Ran**dom **lib**raries. Command used to convert archive files, created by the ar command, into libraries that the ld link editor command can combine into compiled program modules and libraries. *See* ar and ld.

rapid application development Abbreviated and commonly known as RAD. *See* RAD.

RARE **R**eseaux **A**ssocies pour la **R**echerche **E**uropeenne. Association of European research and development networks.

RARP *(INET)* **R**everse **A**ddress **R**esolution **P**rotocol. One of the protocols in the Internet Protocol Suite developed by the Defense Advanced Research Projects Agency. Used to convert an address on an Ethernet local area network into an address on the Internet. *See* DARPA, Internet Protocol Suite, Ethernet and Internet.

rarpd *(INET)* **R**everse **A**ddress **R**esolution **P**rotocol **d**aemon. Background program used to manage responses to requests to convert an address on an Ethernet local area network into an address on the Internet network. *See* daemon and RARP.

raster Horizontal scanning lines on a screen created by a beam of light displayed in a fixed pattern. Input data is electronically converted so the correct dots (pixels) are lit up, producing the desired characters. *See* raster display, raster graphics, raster image, RIP, rasterization and pixel.

raster display Any video display, e.g. computer monitor or television, on which the image is displayed from top to bottom using horizontal scan lines. *See* raster, raster graphics, raster image, RIP, rasterization and pixel.

raster graphics Also called bitmap or raster image. Graphics generation process in which the images are stored in multiple independent pixels. The graphics are generated and displayed by manipulating rows and columns of pixels to form the desired image. *See* pixel and vector graphics.

raster image Commonly called raster graphics. *See* raster graphics.

raster image processor Commonly abbreviated and called RIP. *See* RIP.

rasterization Process of converting images, created using mathematically generated points of light, to produce a line (vector graphics), consisting of sets of dots (pixels) that are stored and used to generate images as computer bits. *See* vector graphics, raster graphics and pixel.

raster-scan display Commonly called raster display. *See* raster display.

ratfor *(ATT)* **Rat**ional **FOR**TRAN Dialect. So called because it modifies, or translates, FORTRAN language into C language or Pascal typing or control structures. *See* FORTRAN, f77 and C language.

rationalization Commonly called software rationalization. *See* software rationalization.

rat's nest Cabling found under the average raised flooring in a computer room.

raw Jargon term for files or programs which have not been through final processing to produce a finished product. A file containing dot commands from the nroff text editor program is the raw nroff version while one generated by processing those commands is the cooked, or finished, version. *See* nroff and cooked.

RAW check Read after write check. Error-checking method in Digital Audio Tape technology that is used when there are four disk drive heads, two of which are for reading and two for writing data. *See* DAT.

raw data Unprocessed data, e.g. data related to customer purchases that has not been formulated into a bill.

raw device Also called unbuffered device. Device to which input and/or output is read or written directly, without the aid of kernel buffering, e.g. disk or tape.

raw mode Terminal operation mode that bypasses the UNIX input/output system, resulting in direct input of characters without any interpretation. Faster than cooked mode but is device-dependent, which does away with the portability advantage UNIX offers. *See* cooked mode.

raw socket Interprocess communication that provides a direct link to low-level protocols. Provides the superuser direct access to network protocols and thus is used by network administration programs for controlling network software.

raytracing Method of converting a graphics object into pixels by tracing the path of light from the object to light sources.

rbash Restricted Bourne Again Shell. The Free Software Foundation's secure shell or command interpreter that provides Bourne shell syntax, command line editing, job control, and C shell command history. Limits users to read-only access to files and directories, and does not allow them to change paths or shells. *See* shell, C shell, bash and FSF.

RBOC Regional Bell Operating Companies. Sometimes called Regional Bell Operation Companies. Also known by the jargon term *Baby Bells*. The seven regional telephone companies formed when AT&T Co. was broken up in 1984. Includes Ameritech, Bell Atlantic, BellSouth, NYNEX, Pacific Telesis, Southwestern Bell and US WEST.

rc0 *(ATT)* Run command 0. Shell script used to shut down a computer system. *See* shell script.

rc2 *(ATT)* Run command 2. Shell script used to start up a computer system. *See* shell script.

.rc file Run command file. File that contains scripts used to start up and establish environmental variables for users. *See* .exrc and .mailrc.

r* commands Collection of commands used on remote systems in UNIX System V, Release 4. *See* SVR4.x.

rcp Remote copy. Command that allows a user to copy files, directories and directory trees from one computer to another, including personal computers. Offers no password protection but can authenticate the user by checking files on the remote host that indicate whether the user has permission for remote copying.

rcs *(BSD)* Command used to change Revision Control System file attributes. *See* RCS.

RCS Revision Control System. Developed at Purdue University. Used to manage program source code and text libraries. Maintains configuration control and changes to source files.

rcsdiff *(BSD)* **RCS diff**erence. Command used to compare Revision Control System revisions to determine differences between two RCS files. *See* RCS.

rcsintro *(BSD)* **RCS intro**ductions. Command used to print an introduction to Revision Control System commands. *See* RCS.

rcsmerge *(BSD)* **RCS merge**. Command used to combine Revision Control System revisions into a single file. *See* RCS.

rdate *(ATT)* **R**emote **date**. Command used to set the date and time on the local host based upon the date and time of a specified remote host.

RDBMS **R**elational **d**atabase **m**anagement **s**ystem. Collection of data files related to each other through one or more common fields. Data storage and retrieval is based upon the relationship of the data maintained in rows and columns within a table. When data is spread across multiple tables, the tables are linked, providing a path to locate, read, update and otherwise manipulate the data. *See* database and BLOB.

rdd *(BSD)* **R**emote **dd**. Network version of the dd command. Used to perform an image copy (bit-for-bit) system backup. *See* dd and image copy.

rdist **R**emote **dist**ribution. Originally developed for the Berkeley Software Distribution. A remote version of the make command used to maintain or distribute files to remote hosts. Establishes and maintains like files on remote hosts by comparing the modification date and time on the remote host with those on the master host. If the date and time on the remote host vary from those of the master, the file is changed. *See* make, distfile and primitive.

rdump *(BSD)* **R**emote **dump**. Network version of the dump command. Used to make either full or incremental backups on remote hosts. *See* dump.

rdwr **R**ead and **wr**ite. Routine called by the read or write system calls. Used to manage access to files in which a user wants to perform read and/or write operations. *See* read, write, readi and writei.

re **1.** Abbreviation in the awk program for a regular expression or text patterns, e.g. letters, numbers and/or special characters, used to match strings for search and replacement of text. *See* awk and regular expression. **2.** Variable in the vi editor program that, when set, is used to make a dumb terminal resemble an intelligent terminal. *See* vi.

read **1.** For users or processes, the ability to access a file and only look at its contents. *See* permissions. **2.** Process in which computers have access to a source file and can copy an image of the data in it to another location, e.g. from a disk to random access memory or from a diskette to a hard drive. *See* RAM. **3.** To obtain data from a file, memory or peripheral device. **4.** System call used with programs to read data in a file after the file has been accessed with the open system call. *See* system call, open and write.

READ Variable for the UNIX-to-UNIX CoPy communications system read by the uucico (UNIX-to-UNIX CoPy-in copy-out) daemon that identifies the directories that can be read by remote hosts. Normally the default is set so only the uucp-public directory can be read. *See* UUCP, uucico, NOREAD and /usr/spool/uucp-public.

read_in *(ATT)* UNIX System V, Release V command in the software installation and information management menu. Similar to a function in the pkgadd command, it is used to copy a new software package to a computer system without installing the package. *See* pkgadd.

read-ahead capability Ability of a UNIX operating system to read and process current input while simultaneously responding to earlier input.

read consistency Ensuring data is not being modified by other actions while it is being read by a process. *See* database locking.

readi Routine called by the rdwr routine to perform the actual read, or retrieval and reading getting of or looking at the data of a file. *See* read, write, rdwr and writei.

Read Me Commonly spelled README. *See* README.

Readme Commonly spelled README. *See* README.

ReadME Commonly spelled README. *See* README.

README Also spelled Readme, ReadME or Read Me. Also called README file or readme.txt. File that accompanies a newly released executable file or program. Contains instructions, documentation and other information about using the file or program, e.g. author(s), revisions, tips, known bugs and work-around solutions.

README file Commonly called README. *See* README.

readme.txt Commonly called README. *See* README.

readnews *(OTH)* **Read news**. Command used activate a program that can access and read bulletin board news available through USENET, an international UNIX bulletin board. *See* USENET.

read-only file File in which a user is allowed to read, but not write or modify, the contents. However, a copy of the file can be made and modified. *See* permissions, execute, write and write permission.

read-only memory Commonly abbreviated and called ROM. *See* ROM.

read-only permission Level of user access to a file. *See* read-only file.

read permission Level of user access to a file. *See* read-only file.

Ready for Next Message Commonly abbreviated and called RFNM. *See* RFNM.

ready-to-send Commonly abbreviated and called RTS. *See* RTS.

real estate 1. Method of activating a window by placing the mouse pointer in the window and clicking it. *See* window, click to activate and double click. 2. Jargon term for the number of pixels on the screen of a workstation or X Window System terminal. *See* pixel.

real GID **Real g**roup **id**entifier. Initially, the group identifier of the user who started a process. But, during the lifetime of a process, the group identifier may be changed as a result of switch user system calls, etc. Therefore, the real GID is whatever group identifier is recorded in the accounting system when the process ends. *See* GID and setgid.

real group ID Commonly called real GID. *See* real GID.

REAL/IX Real-time UNIX operating system developed by MODCOMP. *See* RTOS.

real memory Commonly called RAM (random access memory). *See* RAM.

real-time class Type of process that is given a higher scheduling priority than time-sharing processes by a system. Data is processed rapidly enough that the results may be used in response to another process which is taking place at the same time, e.g. transaction processing on an airline reservation point of sale system. *See* time-sharing class and system class.

Real Time Consortium Organization composed of software vendors and hardware manufacturers to promote standards for real-time operating systems and applications. *See* RTOS.

real-time database Commonly abbreviated and called RTDB. *See* RTDB.

real-time file *(POS)* POSIX.4 (real-time operating system) term. Files used to establish a standard interface between databases, transaction processing and other processes. *See* POSIX.4 and RTOS.

real-time operating system Commonly abbreviated and called RTOS. *See* RTOS.

real-time priority value Commonly abbreviated and called rtpi value. *See* rtpi value.

real-time UNIX Abbreviated and commonly known as RTU. *See* RTU.

real UID Real user identifier. Initially the user identifier of the user who starts a process. But during the lifetime of the process, the user identifier may be changed as a result of switch user system calls, etc. Therefore, the real UID is that of the individual who owns the process at the time it ends and is recorded in the accounting system at the point. *See* UID and setuid.

real user ID Commonly abbreviated and called real UID. *See* real UID.

reassembly Reformation of larger packets previously broken into smaller units for transmission over a network. *See* MTU and fragmentation.

reboot 1. Also called boot. Generally means a system has crashed and been restarted, while boot generally means a system has been started after being turned off for some time, e.g. at the start of a workday or after a planned shutdown. **2.** Berkeley Software Distribution command used by the system administrator to restart (reboot) the system to multi-user or single-user state. *See* multi-user state and single-user state.

receive window Transmission Control Protocol function which identifies the type of data a host will accept during a connection. If an attempt is made to connect for data not identified in the receive window, the connection will be canceled. *See* TCP, sliding window scheme and send window.

reclaim Commonly called page reclaim. *See* page reclaim.

reclaim from free Paging process when a segment of a program is reclaimed from the free list, or list of non-allocated elements in memory. *See* paging and free list.

record 1. Common set of information stored in a database. Just as a directory is made up of files, a database is composed of records, e.g. in a mailing list database,

the elements of an individual's address make up a record. **2.** Electronic-mail variable. *See* .mailrc variables (Appendix F).

record locking Ability of a computer system to limit access by users to a record in a file. Allows only one user at a time to edit the record, and prevents other users from making modifications, although they may be allowed to read the record. Modifications to the record, and thus who is responsible for making them, can thus be better controlled.

record separator In a database, the point that indicates the end of one record and the beginning of another, e.g. a space, comma or colon.

recover To restore data from a backup medium after a computer system crashes or the data is inadvertently erased. The data may consist of either a file, an entire database, or all or part of an operating system.

recovery Restoration of data. *See* recover.

recursion Restarting of an active program after it has been suspended. *See* sleep.

recursive program Program that calls itself to perform a function, e.g. most algorithms for calculating a factorial are recursive. The factorial of six, for example, is:

$$6! = 6 \times 5 \times 4 \times 3 \times 2 \times 1$$

which is equal to

$$6 \times 5! \text{ (i.e., } 5! = 5 \times 4 \times 3 \times 2 \times 1)$$

Since $5! = 5 \times 4!$, and $4! = 4 \times 3!$, and so forth, this leads to an algorithm for calculating a factorial:

```
if (n 1)
        fact(n) = n * fact(n - 1);
else
        fact(n) = 1;
```

Which means, if n is greater than 1, the factorial of n is equal to n times the factorial of (n-1). If n is equal to 1, the factorial is 1. Since this algorithm calls itself in calculating the result, it is called recursive.

red *(ATT)* Restricted **edi**tor. Line editor program normally used with the restricted shell to limit a user's access to the system through the editor, e.g. initiate a new shell. Functions like the ed line editor, except the user can only edit files in his current working directory and cannot invoke a shell while he is in the editor program. *See* ed, restricted shell and shell.

Red Book **1.** Communications standards of the 1984 International Telecommunication Union Telecommunication Standardization Sector, formerly known as the *Consultative Committee on International Telegraphy and Telephony.* Contains the first release of the X.400 standard. *See* Blue Book, Green Book, ITU-T and X.400. **2.** 1985 Adobe Systems Inc. PostScript printing manual. *See* Blue Book and Green Book.

redirect To change the default standard input (source) and/or standard output to another device or file. *See* standard input, standard output, output redirection and input redirection.

redirection Change in standard input or standard output. *See* redirect.

redirect symbol Also called greater than symbol or less than symbol. *See* greater than symbol and less than symbol.

redraw Variable in the vi editor program. *See* re.

Reduced Instruction Set Computing Commonly abbreviated and called RISC. *See* RISC.

Redundant Array of Inexpensive Disks Commonly abbreviated and called RAID. *See* RAID.

redundant disk Commonly called parity disk. *See* parity disk.

redundant file skipping Process of comparing files on two systems before data is transferred from one to the other. If their names, sizes, dates and times match, the transfer is canceled.

reexamine inittab state Also known as *reexamine the inittab file for the current run level,* or *state Q.* A system state or run level.

Used after making updates to inittab so the system does not have to be switched to single-user state. *See* inittab.

refer Set of commands or utility used to find and insert bibliographic references or footnotes in documents. *See* addbib, indxbib, lookbib, roffbib and sortbib.

reference bit Indicator in the paging process that shows if a process has used the required section of a program stored in memory. *See* paging, PTE and referenced.

referenced Term that indicates a page has been used, read or written to, during the running of a process. *See* paging.

reform *(ATT)* **Reform**at. Command used in UNIX systems before Pre-System V to reformat text files.

refresh rate Speed, measured in hertz (Hz), at which a computer redraws the characters or graphics on a screen, e.g. if the refresh rate is 72Hz, the picture is repainted 72 times per second. The refresh rate depends on the type of chip used in the computer, the chip's clock speed, available bandwidth between the computer and the terminal, and the resolution of the monitor. *See* clock speed, Hz and pixel.

regcmp *(ATT/XEN)* **Reg**ular expression **c**o**mp**ile. General-purpose library routine used to compile a regular expression so that it can be added to a C program. *See* library routines, regular expression and C language.

Regional Bell Operating Companies Commonly abbreviated and called RBOC. *See* RBOC.

register Central processing unit device used for temporary storage of data during paging or swapping. *See* RISC, CPU, paging and swapping.

regression test Commonly called string test. *See* string test.

regular expression **1.** Generalized pattern-matching language found in grep and commands used to perform pattern searches. *See* grep. **2.** Text patterns (letters, numbers and/or special characters) used to match strings for search and replacement of text. The special characters perform specific functions in the search and the character, numbers, etc. form the pattern for the search. Regular expression characters include:

. $ * \ ^ [ ]

In addition, single quotes (' ') are used to set off the string used in the search. *See* string, dot, dollar sign, asterisk, backslash, caret and brackets.

regular file Commonly called ordinary file. *See* ordinary file.

Regulus UNIX operating system look-alike modified for real-time computing. *See* RTOS.

rehash Command used to rebuild the hashing table. This table is used by the C shell to execute user commands. *See* hashing and hash table.

reject *(ATT)* Line printer (lp) system command. Turns off print jobs being sent to a line printer. *See* lp.

Relational database management system Commonly abbreviated and called RDBMS. *See* RDBMS.

relative pathname Shortened pathname for a file that indicates the relative location of the path to the current working directory. *See* path, pathname and absolute pathname.

relay 1. Commonly called application gateway. *See* application gateway. **2.** Term for the movement of electronic mail from one message transfer agent to another in the X.400 standard. Developed by the International Telecommunication Union Telecommunication Standardization Sector, formerly known as the *Consultative Committee on International Telegraphy and Telephony. See* ITU-T, submission, delivery and MTA.

release New software product or an update that adds new features or corrects problems in an existing software product.

Release 1 First release of UNIX System V in 1983. Commonly called System V. *See* System V.

Release 4 Commonly abbreviated and called SVR4.x. *See* SVR4.x.

release medium Commonly called distribution medium. *See* distribution medium.

reliability Characteristic of a computer system or network on which users can depend to do what is expected or required.

reliability layer Jargon term for the Open Systems Interconnection transport layer. *See* transport layer.

reliable transfer service element Commonly abbreviated and called RTSE. *See* RTSE.

reliably delivered message socket Socket that checks for errors (dropped bits) during delivery of messages. *See* sockets.

relocatable Pertaining to any data which does not have to be maintained at a specific address to ensure operation of the system.

relocation Copying or moving data from one address to another.

relogin *(ATT)* **Re**name **login**. Command that allows a user to change the current login userid without first logging off the system. Used with windows in UNIX to ensure information is passed from a host computer to the correct window on a terminal. *See* window.

remote 1. *(XEN)* Command used to run a command on remote computer systems. **2.** Physically separated from the local host. Describes either a terminal connected to a host computer or another computer that has to be accessed by a communications network. **3.** Jargon term for a terminal.

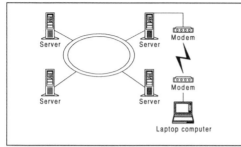

Remote computers are often attached to the host by modem.

Remote File Sharing Commonly abbreviated and called RFS. *See* RFS.

Remote File Sharing state Also called state 3 or init 3. Level of multi-user access to a computer system in which the Remote File Sharing (RFS) system can be started, users can be connected with an RFS network, resources can be mounted, or activated, for a remote session and local resources can be mounted for remote activity. *See* RFS.

Remote File Sharing Utilities Set of programs included in UNIX System V, Release 4 to facilitate sharing of files between among computer systems. *See* SVR4.x and RFS.

remote host Commonly called remote. *See* remote.

Remote Job Entry Commonly abbreviated and called RJE. *See* RJE.

remote login Signing on to, or logging into, a remote computer system to access and manipulate files as a local user would.

remote mapping Remote File Sharing security method for controlling access by remote users to shared resources. For example, can be used to set groups (collection of common users) and group permissions. *See* RFS.

Remote Monitor Commonly abbreviated and called RMON. *See* RMON.

remote monitoring MIB Commonly abbreviated and called RMON MIB. *See* RMON MIB.

Remote Operations Service Element Commonly abbreviated and called ROSE. *See* ROSE.

Remote Procedure Call Commonly abbreviated and called RPC. *See* RPC.

remote resource File system or directory located on a remote host that is available for access by remote users. *See* RFS and file system.

remote server Commonly called remote host. *See* remote host.

remote system administration Remote management and administration of computer systems from a primary location.

Remote Terminal Emulation Commonly abbreviated and called RTE. *See* RTE.

remote.unknown *(ATT)* Shell script that records attempts to log in to a computer system by unknown systems, e.g. by an authorized new host or a host whose name has changed but whose name has not been updated in the table, or a hacker.

removable disk Commonly called disk pack. *See* disk pack.

remove **1.** *(ATT)* System accounting shell script used to remove older files from the accounting summary directory. *See* shell script. **2.** To delete a file, directory or user from a computer. **3.** UNIX System V, Release V command in the software installation and information management menu. Similar to a function in the pkgrm command, it is used to delete a software package from a computer system. *See* pkgrm. **4.** *(ATT)* C language library routine used to make empty files or directories inaccessible. *See* library routines, unlink and rmdir.

remove_host *(ATT)* **Remove host**. Command in the Remote File Sharing sysadm menu used to delete a host from the password file. *See* RFS and sysadm.

remove namesvr *(ATT)* **Remove name server**. Command in the Remote File Sharing sysadm menu used to delete name server hosts. *See* RFS, NS and sysadm.

remsh *(ATT)* **Rem**ote **sh**ell. AT&T Co.'s version of the rsh command. Allows a user to execute a shell command on a remote host. *See* rsh and shell command.

rename 1. *(ATT)* Operations menu command in the UNIX System V, Release 4 Framed Access Command Environment file system. Performs the same function as the mv command, moving a file from one location to another, except the default destination is always the current working directory. *See* FACE, SVR4.x, file system, mv and CWD. 2. *(ATT)* System call used to rename a file. *See* system call.

render Process of converting a graphics object into pixels.

renice Command used to change the priority of a running command. *See* nice.

repagination Process of readjusting the page length and page numbers of an existing document. *See* pagination.

repeat control Function in the Massachusetts Institute of Technology X 11, Release 6 specification for the X Window System. Permits a physically disadvantaged user to define the length of time a key will be held down until that characters is repeated. *See* X Window System and X11R6.

repeater Hardware device used at the physical layer (layer 1) of the Open Systems Interconnection model of a network. Connects portions of the network that are separated geographically, generally from 100 feet to approximately 1 mile Passes data packets between portions of a network by copying each bit of a packet. *See* OSI, OSIRM, physical layer, router, gateway, bridge and brouter.

repetitive motion injury C o m m o n l y called repetitive strain injury. *See* RSI.

repetitive strain injury Commonly abbreviated and called RSI. *See* RSI.

replace In text or word processing, to substitute one or more characters with other characters.

replacement policy Function of the demand paging process that determines which pages are reused, or overwritten, when memory is unavailable. *See* demand paging.

replication Practice of maintaining several copies of a database to speed access to and enhance recovery of information.

report Option in the ex and vi editors used to display at the bottom of the screen the number of lines that have been changed, deleted or yanked. *See* ex and vi.

report delivery Actions that must be taken to send a report to a specific printer, e.g. initiating a print request, directing output to a specific printer, detecting printer errors, placing the print job on hold, restarting the print job, canceling a print request and setting priorities for print jobs.

reports *(ATT)* Command in the UNIX System V, Release 4 line printer services menu similar to the lpadmin command. Used to determine the status of print jobs, printers or other information about the printers, such as printer names. *See* SVR4.x and lpstat.

report writer Program that extracts data from files or a database, then creates and prints reports based upon a pre-defined format.

repquota **Rep**ort **quota**. Command used to provide information on quotas for each user's actual disk usage. *See* quot and quotacheck.

reprogrammable read-only memory Commonly abbreviated RPROM. Commonly called EPROM (Erasable Programmable Read-Only Memory). *See* EPROM.

request Term used to describe when a computer system's line printer services start printing a file. *See* LP.

REQUEST Variable for the UNIX-to-UNIX CoPy communications system used to indicate if a remote host is allowed to set up and run data transfers from the local host. *See* UUCP.

Request for Comment *(INET)* Commonly abbreviated and called RFC. *See* RFC.

Request for Information C o m m o n l y abbreviated and called RFI. *See* RFI.

Request for Proposal Commonly abbreviated and called RFP. *See* RFP.

Request for Quotation Commonly abbreviated and called RFQ. *See* RFQ.

Request for Technology Commonly abbreviated and called RFT. *See* RFT.

requests *(ATT)* Command in the UNIX System V, Release 4 line printer services menu similar to the lp, cancel and lpmove commands. Used to start and cancel print requests or redirect a print request from one printer to another. *See* SVR4.x, lp, cancel and lpsched.

Requirements Interest Group Abbreviated and commonly known as RIG. *See* RIG.

Research Parallel Processing Prototype Commonly abbreviated and called RP3. *See* RP3.

Reseaux Associes pour la Recherche Europeenne Commonly abbreviated and called RARE. *See* RARE.

Reseaux IP Europeens *(INET)* Commonly abbreviated and called RIPE. *See* RIPE.

reset 1. *(BSD)* Command used to reset the teletype bits or connection settings for a terminal. *See* stty and sane flag. 2. Process of changing the current settings on a mainframe, minicomputer, personal computer, printer or other peripheral. Can either temporarily change the default settings, return from alternative settings to the default settings or permanently change the default settings. Temporary or permanent changes must be made with software or control settings provided with the device. Temporarily changed set-

tings can be returned to their defaults by either using the control settings or turning the power off and then back on. The latter method is not recommended, although it can be used after work on the device is completed.

resh **Re**mote **sh**ell. Command used to make a connection with a remote host and run a command.

resident Object or executable program in main memory. *See* object and main memory.

resolution Measurement of the clarity of a screen, monitor or print image produced by a printer. Clarity of monitors is normally measured in the number of pixels per inch and print image in the number of dots per inch. *See* pixel.

resolv.conf First file accessed by the resolver programs to set a computer's configuration, e.g. address of the name server to be queried, name of the domain or list of addresses. Located in the /etc system directory. *See* resolver.

resolver Library of programs used with the Domain Name Service by hosts to resolve host names into Internet Protocol addresses. *See* DNS and IP.

resource 1. Any component of a computer, e.g. disk drives, memory, file system, file, directory, application software or database. A computer's resources provide a measure of its capability. 2. Any separately identifiable piece of a network. Usually means a hardware component but may also refer to an application software used to enhance or manage the network.

resource sharing When a single resource, e.g. a file, central processing unit or memory, is used by two or more processes at the same time, without causing them to interfere with one another. When there is interference, a deadly embrace occurs. *See* deadly embrace.

resources identifier Remote File Sharing name for a resource, or file system, when it is shared or opened for access to remote hosts. *See* RFS.

respawn Part of the init process used when starting an operating system and during normal operation. Restarts a process that has died, or ceased to function. *See* init, process and operating system.

respond *(ATT)* Command in the UNIX System V, Release 4 restore service management menu used to run restore jobs Similar to the rsoper command with the -t, -o and/or -m options. *See* rsoper.

response time Commonly abbreviated and called RT. *See* RT.

restor Alternative version of the restore command. *See* restore.

restore **1.** Command used by root to recover data from backups generated using the dump command. Used to recover all the data on a disk, data partition or complete file system. *See* urestore and file system. **2.** To recall data from an inactive storage medium, e.g. a tape, diskette or hard disk, to an active storage medium. The term is applied either to recalling data which may have been corrupted or inadvertently erased, or to reloading the operating system if there is a system crash. **3.** *(ATT)* Command in the UNIX System V, Release 4 restore service management menu used to restore files from backup media. Similar to the restore and urestore commands. *See* restore and urestore.

restricted accounts Accounts established with fewer permissions than normal to increase security or limit access by users. *See* restricted shell.

Restricted Bourne Again Shell Commonly abbreviated and called rbash. *See* rbash.

restricted editor Commonly abbreviated and called red. *See* red.

restricted Korn shell Commonly abbreviated and called rksh. *See* rksh.

restricted mail Commonly abbreviated and called rmail. *See* rmail.

restricted shell Shell used to provide limited access to users when a system administrator establishes accounts for guests or needs to maintain strict separation of users. Users can be restricted from changing directory, PATH or SHELL variables; from using any command with a slash /; from redirecting any output; and from starting a program.

resume **1.** *(ATT)* Command used to switch between shell layers. Used to indicate the shell layer that is to be restarted. *See* shl, unblock and toggle. **2.** Command used to restart a suspended process. *See* bg, fg and stop.

reticle Used in the photolithographic process of manufacturing integrated circuits (IC). A piece of glass on which the pattern of the IC is formed with chrome. The image is transferred from the reticle to the silicon wafers used to make the IC. *See* IC and photolithography.

retransmission timer Function in the Transmission Control Protocol that initiates attempts to retransmit a message to a remote host if the initial attempt fails. *See* TCP, keepalive packet and keepalive timer.

return Character that signals the kernel to terminate the current line and start a new line. Same as a newline indicator. All commands or inputs in the UNIX operating system at the shell prompt must be followed by a return. *See* newline.

return code Commonly called exit code. *See* exit code.

return key Originally a key on a typewriter keyboard. On computers, commonly called the Enter key. *See* Enter key.

rev *(BSD)* **Rev**erse. Command used to display the lines of a file in reverse order, e.g. starting with the last line of a file and going to the first.

Reverse Address Resolution Protocol Commonly abbreviated and called RARP. *See* RARP.

reverse video Screen attribute which reverses the normal colors of the background and characters. Normal video for a color monitor could be white letters on a blue background. With reverse video, the background would remain blue except around the characters affected. There, the background would be white and the letters would be blue.

reversi *(ATT)* Command used to start the board game Reversi.

Revision Control System Commonly abbreviated and called RCS. *See* RCS.

revolutions per minute Commonly abbreviated and called rpm. *See* rpm.

rexec *(ATT)* Remote execution. System call used when connecting to remote Internet hosts. Confirms the remote host name and continues the connection if the name is correct. If the remote host is not recognized, it returns an error message. *See* system call, Internet and rexecd.

rexecd Remote execution daemon. Background program that is started with the Internet daemon. When a request arrives from a remote computer system to execute a command, rexecd is responsible for managing the programs that check user identifiers and passwords before the commands are permitted to run. *See* daemon, rexec, inetd, UID and password.

rfadmin *(ATT)* Remote File Sharing administration. Command used to either add or delete hosts and their passwords from the domain member list, or determine if the Remote File Sharing system is operating. *See* RFS and domain member list.

RFC *(INET)* Request for Comment. Document developed by the Internet Activities Board's Internet Engineering Task Force. Defines the standards for protocols and utilities used on the Internet. These standards are distributed to anyone who is interested, including vendors and standards organizations, for comment during the review process or compliance in products being offered. The RFC begins as a proposed standard and is implemented after review, discussion and testing. *See* Internet, IAB and IETF.

RFI 1. Radio-frequency interference. Electrical or radio wave interference that can lead to operating failure of a computer system. Caused by components in the compute that are not properly grounded or shielded. 2. Request for Information. Preliminary document to a Request for Proposal (RFP). Prepared by an organization and sent to vendors to obtain information ranging from what type of technology is available to the level of support and services that can be provided. Information gathered from an RFI is used to determine the approach and specifications to be made in the RFP. Seeks a broader range of information than a Request for Technology, e.g. level of support and services available. *See* RFP and RFT.

rfmaster *(ATT)* Remote File Sharing **master**. File in the /etc system directory maintained by the primary name server in a Remote File Sharing system. Lists the primary name server and the secondary name servers. *See* /etc, RFS, primary name server, secondary name server and rfstart.

RFNM Ready for the next message. Message sent to a host by a Public Switched Network (PSN) indicating the PSN is ready to accept transmissions. *See* PSN.

rfork Remote fork. IBM Corp.'s AIX system call similar to the fork system call, except it starts new processes on remote systems. Makes a copy of an ongoing process to create an identical new process on a remote system. *See* AIX, system call and fork.

RFP Request for Proposal. Document sent to potential suppliers. Outlines the customer's specifications for the technology required, and asks suppliers to show how they could satisfy them and at what price. *See* RFI and RFT.

rfpasswd *(ATT)* Remote File Sharing **password**. Command used to change the password of a Remote File Sharing host. *See* RFS.

RFQ Request for Quotation. Similar to a Request for Proposal but less detailed. Asks suppliers to indicate how they could satisfy the general specifications for a particular technology provided and how much this would cost. *See* RFP.

RFS *(ATT)* Remote File Sharing. Networking program used to share data from files among computers. Allows part of one computer's file system to be mounted, or activated, on other computers within the network. *See* file system.

RFS daemon Commonly called rfudaemon. *See* rfudaemon.

RFS parameters *See* Appendix H.

RFS password Host password assigned by the primary name server. Used to verify a host when it attempts to access resources on a remote computer host. *See* RFS and primary name server.

rfstart *(ATT)* Remote File Sharing **start**. Command used to start a Remote File Sharing (RFS) system, in which computers on a network can share data. Contacts the primary name server and configures the computer system for using RFS on a network. *See* RFS, primary name server and rfstop.

rfstop *(ATT)* Remote File Sharing **stop**. Command used to stop the Remote File Sharing system, in which computers on a network can share data. Before running rfstop, all shared resources have to unshared, or disconnected, with the unshare command and unmounted with the rumountall command. *See* RFS, rfstart, unshare and rumountall.

RFT **1.** Request for Technology. Document sent to potential suppliers. Used to find out what technology is available. This information is used to determine an approach and develop specifications for a Request for Proposal. *See* RFI and RFP. **2.** Methodology used by the Open Software

Foundation Inc. to gain and review technology, applications, etc., for inclusion in OSF standards. *See* OSF.

rfuadmin *(ATT)* Remote File Sharing **un**expected **admin**istration. Remote File Sharing system shell script that handles unexpected events, e.g. loss of connection or loss of access to resources. The grace period for shutdowns is maintained in rfuadmin along with warning messages, which can be sent to users when unexpected events occur. *See* RFS and rfudaemon.

rfudaemon *(ATT)* Remote File Sharing unexpected **daemon**. Background program that is started when the Remote File Sharing (RFS) system is activated. Runs while RFS, which allows computers on a network to share data, is active. Looks for unexpected processes, manages disconnects and unmounts, or removes, operational resources from a computer system. *See* RFS, rfuadmin and daemon.

RGB monitor Commonly called color monitor. *See* color monitor.

.rhosts User file that contains a list of hosts that are authorized to access the user's account.

RIG Requirements Interest Group. Special organization within the Corporation for Open Systems International structure. Mandate is to further specific industry interests. *See* COS and User Alliance for Open Systems.

right justified When all lines end at the same point on the right side of a page. *See* justify and margin.

right margin Area between the right edge of a page and right edge of the text or graphics on the page. *See* margin.

rightsizing Alternative term for downsizing. Matching a computer system to the computing needs of a user. The size of the system can be either decreased or increased, e.g. using personal computers and a medium-sized UNIX computer running a financial database instead of a large proprietary system to maintain a corporate accounting system. Computer applications are placed on a computer architecture that best fits the need of the user and design of the application. *See* downsizing.

ring technology Closed loop network topology, e.g. Token Ring, in which data is passed from one node to the next until it has been received by all nodes. The last node passes it back to the originating node, which removes the data from the network. *See* Token Ring.

RIP 1. Routing Information Protocol. Originally developed as the basis of the route daemon in the Berkeley Software Distribution operating system. Incorporated into the Transmission Control Protocol/Internet Protocol networks. Used to pass information among hosts on a network to create paths for communication traffic. *See* route, routed, BSD and TCP/IP. **2.** Raster image processor. Device consisting of both hardware and software used with printers, plotters and phototypesetters to convert mathematically generated lines of vector graphics to dots (pixels) of raster graphics for printing. *See* vector graphics, raster graphics, rasterization and pixel.

RIPE *(INET)* Reseaux IP Europeens. European group formed to promote research and development of networks using the Transmission Control Protocol and Internet Protocol. *See* TCP/IP.

RISC Reduced Instructions Set Computing. Software architecture design that optimizes computer instruction streams. Minimizes the number of instructions sent to a chip. Computer speed is increased since the chip can then be quickly and easily accessed. This is done by limiting the amount of firmware, or computer instructions, that is hardcoded, or built into, the system. RISC systems are up to twice as fast as Complex Instructions Set Computing systems. *See* firmware, CISC and WISC.

Ritchie, Dennis M Part of the 1965 Bell Laboratories team that worked with the Massachusetts Institute of Technology and General Electric Co. on Project MAC, through which MULTICS was developed and became a forerunner to UNIX. Along with Ken Thompson, initiated the project in the late 1960s at the Computing Science Research Center at AT&T's Bell Laboratories to develop the UNIX operating system to improve programming support environments. Worked with Brian Kernighan to modify the B language to create the C language, in which the UNIX operating system was written. Developed the UNIX file system along with Ken Thompson and Rudd Canaday. Along with other team members who were involved with the development of UNIX, he developed the UNIX-like operating system known as *Plan 9. See* Bell Laboratories, Project MAC, MULTICS, B language, C language, Thompson, Ken, Kernighan, Brian, and Plan 9.

RJ-11 Small, modular connector containing four to six connections, originally designed as a telephone connector but adapted for use in connecting computers and/or peripherals to communication systems. *See* RJ-45 and RS-232-C.

RJ-45 Modular, eight-wire connector used for data links in computer systems. Similar in appearance to an RJ-11 connector, but larger. *See* RJ-11

RJE 1. Remote Job Entry. Collection of programs for running batch job processes. Enables users to prepare an entry on a local host, to be processed on remote IBM Corp. hosts running Job Entry Subsystem. *See* JES. **2.** Part of the Programmer's Workbench. Enables communication between UNIX and non-UNIX computer systems so programs developed on a UNIX system can be sent to non-UNIX systems. *See* PWB.

rjestat *(ATT)* Remote Job Entry status. Process that emulates an IBM Corp. remote console to obtain the status on Remote Job Entry processes. *See* RJE.

rksh Restricted Korn shell. Restricted version of the Korn shell. Used to provide limited access to users, preventing them from changing directory, PATH or SHELL variables; from using any command with a slash (/); redirecting any output; and/or starting a program. *See* Korn shell, restricted shell and rsh.

rlog *(BSD)* RCS **log**. Command used to print log messages and other information about Revision Control System files. *See* RCS.

rlogin Remote **login**. Command used to make a terminal-to-remote-host connection on a Transmission Control Protocol/Internet Protocol network. *See* TCP/IP.

rlogind Remote **login** daemon. Internet background program that is responsible for managing login requests from remote users over a network. *See* Internet and daemon.

rm Remove. Command used to erase a file. Should be used with care.

rmail Restricted **mail**. Also could be called remote **mail**. Command used to start the rmail program, used for security. Limits the activity of a remote host so that it only passes electronic mail when connected to a local system. Cannot be used to read electronic mail. Version available through the Free Software Foundation that can be used with GNU emacs. *See* e-mail, FSF and GNU emacs.

rmdel Remove **delta**. Command used to remove a change from a Source Code Control System file. *See* SCCS.

rmdir Remove **dir**ectory. Command used to delete an empty directory from a computer system. Like the rm command, it should be used with care. *See* rm.

rmntstat *(ATT)* Remote **mount status**. Remote File Sharing command used to obtain information about all resources or a specific resource available for access from a remote host. *See* RFS, mount, adv, fumount and unadv.

rmnttry *(ATT)* Remote **mount try**. Command used by the system administrator to attempt to mount, or activate, resources on a remote host identified in the remote mount table. *See* /etc/rfs/rmnttab, mount, rmount and rumount.

RMON *(INET)* Remote **Mon**itor. Internet protocol to remotely monitor networks. Used to store and monitor network activity, create alarms and analyze network traffic. The standard RMON protocol was ratified in November 1991. *See* Internet.

RMON MIB Remote **Monitor** management information base. Set of management objects describing the tools and elements used for monitoring and managing an Ethernet local area network.

rmount *(ATT)* Remote **mount**. Remote File Sharing command used to attempt to mount, or activate, a specified remote resource in the /etc/rfs/rmnttab file. If input without specifying a resource, used to provide a list of resources in /etc/rfs/rmnttab that are waiting to be mounted. *See* RFS, mount and /etc/rfs/rmnttab.

rmountall *(ATT)* Remote **mount all**. Remote File Sharing command used to mount, or activate, all remote resources identified in the file system table. *See* RFS and mount.

rmt *(BSD)* Remote **mount**. Network version of the mount command used to mount, or activate, a file system or disk. *See* mount and file system.

rmuser *(XEN)* Remove **user**. Shell script designed to automatically delete a user and all the user's files from a system. *See* shell script and adduser.

rn *(OTH)* Read **news**. Program used to access news available through USENET, an international UNIX bulletin board. Activated by inputting rn on the command line. *See* USENET and news.

rnews *(OTH)* Restricted **news**. Command that is run at the location where articles for the USENET are received. Starts to transfer the articles onto the USENET, an international UNIX bulletin board. *See* USENET.

Roadmap Jargon term for a document that provides details on the direction of an organization, its technical efforts or specifications, e.g. the document prepared by

UNIX International that outlines the future plans and requirements for the UNIX System V operating system; the document on the future of distributed computing prepared by X/Open Co. Ltd.; and the direction document prepared by the Network Management Forum. *See* UI, X/Open, Open Management Roadmap and NMF.

robustness Ability of a system to continue to operate while it handles internal errors or hardware errors.

roff First UNIX text formatting program developed in the early 1960s. Only capable of producing simple text on line printers. *See* runoff, troff, nroff and ditroff.

roffbib *(BSD)* **Run off bib**liography. One of the commands of the refer utility. Formats and prints data in a bibliographic database. *See* refer, addbib, indxbib, lookbib and sortbib.

roffs Jargon term for roff, nroff and troff, UNIX text processing programs. *See* roff, nroff and troff.

rogue Advanced dungeon game introduced in the early 1980s that provided a full-screen multilevel of play.

role Purpose or use of a computer.

roll Left-to-right angular displacement of a view along a horizontal axis. *See* yaw.

roll back Ability of an application to stop a transaction before it is placed into a database.

roll forward Ability of a database to recover from a crash or other type of disaster by reading a transaction log and re-executing the transactions that have taken place since the database was backed-up.

ROM **R**ead-**o**nly **m**emory. Memory area used to permanently store system instructions or programs that are encoded in the computer system during the manufacturing process and continually used. Cannot be written to, or modified, by users.

Roman Style of type in which the characters are upright.

root **1.** Abbreviation or common name for the root directory, which forms the basis or top of the hierarchical UNIX directory tree and contains the system administration and configuration files. Used interchangeably with superuser in referring to the individual (usually the system administrator) who has the password, or permissions, to access and modify the root files. *See* root directory. **2.** Upper level of a hierarchical database or file structure. *See* branch and leaf.

Root Bimonthly journal published by InfoPro Systems that is written for system administrators of UNIX and XENIX systems.

rootdev **Root dev**ice. Kernel variable used to set the major and minor device numbers (which identify the type of devices and device drivers used by the computer system) of the root file system. *See* root, root file system, major device number and minor device number.

root directory Top of the hierarchical UNIX directory structure.

root file system File system which contains the root directory. Identified in the kernel as the file system to be used when the computer system is booted. *See* file system, kernel and boot.

root-level domain *(INET)* Top level of the Internet. Maintained by the Network Information Center. *See* Internet, NIC and domain.

root parameter Part of the kernel description file. Identifies the location of the root file system. *See* kernel description file and root file system.

ROSE **R**emote **O**perations **S**ervice **E**lement. Open Systems Interconnection Remote Procedure Call programs which enable applications to be used interactively in a distributed computer environment. *See* OSI and RPC.

rot13 Command used to encode information which can be exchanged and read with the netnews programs on the USENET international UNIX bulletin board. Text encoded by rot13 can be decoded using the tr command. *See* netnews and tr.

rotational gap Physical difference between the actual location of data on a disk and the location of the disk head. Used to compensate for the high rotation speed of the disk to ensure the head is positioned correctly for a read or write operation.

rotational layout table Part of the file resource management system. Determines where storage space (blocks) on a disk is available for use by a file. *See* block.

ROUND ROBIN Algorithm used to manage queuing of user requests on a first-in first-out basis similar to FIFO. Varies from FIFO in that a limit is set on the run time, or amount of time needed to execute each process. Once the run time limit is exceeded, the process is returned to a queue to allow another process to run. *See* queue.

route 1. *(ATT)* Command used instead of the route daemon, by the system administrator, to manually modify data in the network routing tables. *See* routed and system administrator. 2. Path that a data transmission follows from the originating host to the destination host in packet switch networks. *See* destination host and packet switch network.

routed *(INET)* **Route d**aemon. Pronounced *ROUTE-DEE*. Internet background program used to create network routes between hosts on a Transmission Control Protocol/Internet Protocol network. *See* Internet, daemon, route, TCP/IP and RIP.

ROUTE-DEE Pronunciation of routed, the abbreviation for route daemon. *See* routed.

router Intelligent bridge between networks and computers that is limited to passing data packets between systems running the same protocol. Checks the address of each data packet and determines the most efficient way, or route, by

which to send the data. Operates at the network layer (layer 3) of the Open Systems Interconnection model. *See* OSI, OSIRM, network layer, repeater, gateway, bridge and brouter.

router-to-router protocol Networking protocol for managing communications traffic sent between network routers. *See* router, RIP and OSPF.

routine Also called subroutine, function or procedure. Programming code that can be started within a program to perform specific functions, e.g. printing, checking grammar or checking spelling.

routing Table which contains the information about a network or host needed to determine which interface to use for data transmission.

routing daemon Dynamic message routing database in the Fourth Berkeley Software Distribution, Third Release used to transmit data from one location to another. The database is continually updated as changes occur in the availability of routes. *See* route, database and BSD.

Routing Information Protocol Commonly abbreviated and called RIP. *See* RIP.

routing redirect message Data transmission management tool in gateways. Redirects the routing of messages based on the most direct route known. *See* gateway and route.

routing table Table maintained on a router that is used to determine what the router is to do with incoming and outgoing packets of information. *See* router.

row Horizontal elements of an array, e.g. horizontal components of a spreadsheet. *See* column.

RP3 Research Parallel Processing Prototype. Project sponsored by the Defense Advanced Research Projects Agency for highly parallel multiprocessing.

RPC Remote Procedure Call. Network File System interface for interhost connectivity over a network. A system network call that allows commands or programs to function on remote systems over a network as if they were being executed on a local system. *See* NFS, caller and client.

rpcbind *(ATT)* **RPC** (Remote Procedure Call) **bin d**aemon. Background program used by RPC to change an address for an RPC program to an address that a remote client can use to access the program. *See* RPC, client and daemon.

rpcgen *(BSD)* Remote Procedure Call protocol compiler found in Sun Microsystems Inc.'s Network File System. *See* RPC and NFS.

rpcinfo **RPC** (Remote Procedure Call) **in**formation. Command used to check and report the status of a host running RPC. *See* RPC.

RPD Remote **p**rint **d**elete. Utility which allows a personal computer user connected to a network to delete a request for a print job in a queue on a printer attached to a remote computer.

rpm Revolutions **p**er **m**inute. Measurement of the rotation speed of devices, e.g. disk drives.

RPR Remote **p**rint **r**equest. Utility which allows a personal computer user connected to a network to send a print job to a printer attached to a remote computer.

RPROM Reprogrammable Programmable Read-Only Memory. Commonly called EPROM (Erasable Programmable Read-Only Memory). *See* EPROM.

RPS Remote **p**rint **s**tatus. Utility which allows a personal computer user connected to a network to check the status of a print job on a printer attached to a remote computer.

rrestore *(BSD)* Remote **r**estore. Network version of the restore command used to reload files from a tape backup. *See* restore.

RS232 Commonly written as RS-232-C. *See* RS-232-C.

RS-232-C Recommend Standard **232** C (third standard in a series). Electronic Industries Association standard for cable and 25-pin electrical connection between computers and peripheral devices using a serial binary data interchange. Used for slower communications, requiring speeds of no greater than 20 kilo bits per second, with a standard limit of 75 feet. Devices up to 1,000 feet apart can be linked with an RS-232-C connection using special cable. *See* EIA and kbps.

RS232-C Commonly written as RS-232-C. *See* RS-232-C.

RS-422 Recommend Standard **422** (first standard in a series). High-speed variant of RS-232-C, an Electronic Industries Association standard for cable and 25-pin electrical connection between computers and peripheral devices. Reduces noise and provides connectivity for computers and peripherals more than 50 feet apart. *See* RS-232-C.

rsh **1.** *(ATT)* **R**estricted **sh**ell. Command used by a system administrator to initiate a restricted shell, which limits access by users to a computer system. *See* restricted shell. **2.** Abbreviation in UNIX that indicates the user is in the restricted shell. **3.** *(BSD)* **R**emote **sh**ell. Command used to start a shell on a remote host when using a Transmission Control Protocol/Internet Protocol network. *See* TCP/IP and remsh.

rshd *(INET)* **R**emote **sh**ell **d**aemon. Internet background program that manages login requests from users over a network. *See* Internet and daemon.

RSI **R**epetitive **s**train **i**njury. Also called cumulative trauma disorder or repetitive motion injury. Injury to muscle, nerves or tendons that causes inflammation. Results from repetitious activity or work that is either beyond what the body is capable of doing or is performed in an awkward or unnatural position. Common among people who sew, play musical instruments or do keyboard entry.

rsnotify *(ATT)* **R**estore **notify**. Command used to notify a designated operator that files from backup media need to be re-stored. Also can be used to identify users capable of doing a restore job. *See* restore.

rsoper *(ATT)* **R**estore **oper**ation. Command used to run restore jobs that are queued or cancel requests in a queue to restore files from backup media. *See* restore.

rsstatus *(ATT)* **R**estore **status**. Command used by a system administrator or author-ized user to obtain the status of a restore request. Also can be used to obtain a list of requests in a queue to restore files from backup media. *See* restore and ursstatus.

RT 1. **R**esponse **t**ime. Measurement of the percentage of transactions completed in a specified time, e.g. the number of transac-tions per-second. 2. Abbreviation for real-time process or class. Normally measured from the moment a user completes the input to when a response to that input is received. Also may be a measurement of the time taken for a character to be echoed following a keystroke. *See* real-time class and RTOS.

rtar *(BSD)* **R**emote **tar**. Network version of the tar command used to back up and recover files on remote systems. *See* tar.

RTDB **R**eal-**t**ime **d**ata**b**ase. Database spe-cifically designed to support real-time ap-plications. Data is processed rapidly enough that the results may be used in response to another process taking place at the same time, e.g. as in transaction processing. Provides fast, predictable per-formance with a guaranteed, fixed re-sponse time. *See* DBMS and RTOS.

rt dptbl parameter table *(ATT)* UNIX System V, Release 4 table that contains the values used to manage real-time proc-esses, e.g. priority assigned to a process and length of time a process can run per priority. *See* SVR4.x and real-time class.

RTE **R**emote **T**erminal **E**mulation. Bench-mark measurement used to simulate and interaction of a terminal with host com-puters. Can test response times from the central processing units, the operating system and application programs.

RTFM **R**ead **t**he **f**!@#&*g **m**anual. Also means read the fine manual or read the fancy manual. What to do when all else fails. First, try to locate the documenta-tion. And, second, read it.

RTOS **R**eal-**t**ime **o**perating **s**ystem. Mode of action and reaction by an operating system and application software. Allows priorities to be changed instantly and data to be processed rapidly enough that the results may be used in response to another process taking place at the same time, e.g. as in transaction processing. Paramount to a real-time operating system is the abil-ity of the computer system to immediately respond, in a predetermined and predict-able way, to external events. Features in-clude memory locking; semaphores or indicators used to identify and track spe-cial processes, and manage the order of events related to process requests and execution; contiguous disk files; and sys-tem calls that can be stopped or changed while they are running.

rtpi value **R**eal-**t**ime **p**riority **i**value. Proc-ess with a priority value between 0 and n, with n being the highest priority value assigned by the system. The process with the highest rtpi value will run before all other processes except system class proc-esses. *See* process, real-time class and sys-tem class.

RTPRI **R**eal-**t**ime **pri**ority. System pa-rameter used to establish the maximum priority level. *See* RTOS.

RTS **R**eady-**t**o-**s**end. Communications signal indicating a data device is ready to send data.

RTSE **R**eliable **T**ransfer **S**ervice **E**lement. Open Systems Interconnection protocol used to transfer data between applica-tions over a network. Can recover data lost in a failure caused by network failures during a transmission, reducing the num-ber of retransmissions. *See* OSI.

RTU **R**eal-**t**ime **U**NIX. A UNIX operating system look-alike with modifications for real-time operations, in which data is processed rapidly enough that the results may be used in response to another process taking place at the same time, e.g. as in transaction processing. *See* RTOS.

RUB Abbreviation for rubout key. *See* rubout key.

rubout Commonly called kill. *See* kill.

rubout key Key on some terminal keyboards that cancels, or kills, the input on a command line. *See* command line.

rumount *(ATT)* Remote File Sharing command used to cancel a request to mount, or activate, one or more resources in the remote mount table. *See* RFS, mount and /etc/rfs/rmnttab.

rumountall *(ATT)* Remote **unmount all**. Remote File Sharing command used to unmount or deny access to resources on all remote hosts. *See* RFS and unmount.

run To initiate and execute a program. *See* execute.

runacct *(ATT)* **Run** accounting. Accounting system shell script used to execute the daily accounting summaries and produce reports. Also transfers the current wtmp log of user logins and processes generated by the init daemon to an old or archived file (owtmp); and summarizes and then deletes the process accounting files. *See* /etc/wtmp, owtmp, /usr/adm/pacct and dodisk.

runbig *(XEN)* **Run** big. Command used to run programs which are larger than the system memory can execute.

run level Commonly called state. *See* state.

runnable process Process that has met all the requirements to be started but is waiting until the central processing unit has the capacity to process it. *See* process and CPU.

running When a computer and/or software are operating, performing its designed function.

running footer Text in the bottom margin that is repeated on two or more consecutive pages. *See* footer and margin.

running header Text in the top margin that is repeated on two or more consecutive pages. *See* header and margin.

runoff Commonly spelled run off. Commonly abbreviated and called roff. *See* roff.

run off Commonly abbreviated and called roff. *See* roff.

run queue List, or file, of jobs, or processes, waiting to be run by a computer. *See* job.

run state Commonly called state. *See* state.

runt Accidental or intentional data packet that is smaller than the minimum size for a protocol, e.g. in Ethernet, data packet smaller than 64 bytes. Accidental runts can be caused by a faulty hardware device or software program. Intentional runts can be caused by a network monitoring program, like the Simple Network Management Protocol, so packets generated by the program are ignored by devices on the network. *See* packet, Ethernet and SNMP.

run time Commonly spelled runtime. *See* runtime.

runtime Total amount of time it takes to execute, or run, a program.

runtime library Collection of standard programs resident on a computer that a programmer can easily incorporate into a new program. The programs are constantly running in the library and the new program calls the desired runtime library program to be executed as part of the new program. *See* library.

ruptime Remote **uptime**. Command used to display the host status of local computers linked via a Transmission Control Protocol/Internet Protocol Ethernet connection. *See* TCP/IP and Ethernet.

rusers Remote **users**. Command used to show who is logged on to a local host linked via a Transmission Control Protocol/Internet Protocol Ethernet connection. *See* TCP/IP and Ethernet.

rusersd Remote **users d**aemon. Continually running process used to provide a list of users on a remote host. *See* daemon.

rwall Remote write **all**. Command used to send a message to all users over a network. *See* wall.

rwalld Remote write **all d**aemon. Background program that runs the rwall program, which sends messages to all users on a network. *See* daemon.

rwho Remote **who**. Command used to display a list of all users logged on to a local computer connected by Transmission Control Protocol/Internet Protocol Ethernet network. Shows user activity, idle time, etc. *See* TCP/IP and Ethernet.

rwhod Remote **who d**aemon. Internet background program used on network hosts to send and receive data packets which identify users logged on to a host. *See* who, daemon and Internet.

S

s5 *(ATT)* Abbreviation for the type of file system found in UNIX System V, Release 4. *See* file system, SVR4.x and ufs.

sa System **a**ccounting. System accounting program used to read the data collected by the accton accounting system program. *See* accton.

SA System administrator. Person or persons responsible for the daily operation and maintenance of the operating system and hardware configuration. May be responsible for hardware preventive maintenance and be the primary liaison with the maintenance vendor. Also may be responsible for training users and resolving their technical problems and errors. Responsibilities vary according to the organization.

sa1 *(ATT)* Shell script used for automatic data collection. Included in the System Performance Analysis Utilities in UNIX System V. *See* SPAU, prfdc, prfld, prfpr, prfsnap, prfstat, sadc, sadp, sag, sar, sa2, and timex.

sa2 *(ATT)* Shell script used for creating an output of data collected by the sa1 shell script. Included in the System Performance Analysis Utilities in UNIX System V. *See* SPAU, prfdc, prfld, prfpr, prfsnap, prfstat, sadc, sadp, sag, sar, sa1 and, timex.

SAA Systems Application Architecture. Tools used in the IBM Corp. mainframe environment for system management and administration. SAA is IBM's specification on how the user interfaces with application and communication programs.

The intent is to provide the same look and feel to all applications running on a computer.

sac 1. *(ATT)* Service **a**ccess **c**ontroller. Command used to start, configure or administer the port monitoring functions of the Service Access Controller. *See* SAC. **2.** Daemon used to manage the Service Access Controller. *See* SAC.

SAC *(ATT)* Service Access Controller. Process responsible for monitoring the Service Access Facility (SAF) available in UNIX System V, Release 4. Started from the /etc/inittab file when a system is switched from single to multi-user state. When the system is in multi-user state, starts the monitoring process identified in the SAF, the process which manages external connectivity to a system through ports. *See* SAF, /etc/inittab, state and SVR4.x.

sacadm *(ATT)* Service **a**ccess **c**ontroller **ad**ministration. Command used to start and run Service Access Facility (SAF) programs, e.g. to add or delete, turn on or off, start or stop a port monitor; modify SAF configuration; and print port information. The command argument determines which process is to be accomplished, for example:

```
-s = start port monitor
-k = stop port monitor
```

See SAC, sac, port monitor and SAF.

sact *(ATT/XEN)* Source Code Control System **act**ivity. One of the 13 Source Code Control System (SCCS) commands used to display SCCS files that are being edited. *See* SCCS, admin, cdc, comb, delta, get, help, prs, rmdel, sccsdiff, unget, val, vc and what.

sadc *(ATT)* **S**ystem **a**ctivity **d**ata **c**ollection. System accounting program used to collect information about system activity, e.g. who has done what and how many times. Included in the System Performance Analysis Utilities in UNIX System V. *See* SPAU, prfdc, prfld, prfpr, prfsnap, prfstat, sadp, sag, sar, sa1, sa2 and timex.

sadp *(ATT)* System accounting program used to accumulate information on disk space usage by each user. Records information on disk locations, or addresses, and disk drive head seek distance. Included in the System Performance Analysis Utilities in UNIX System V. *See* SPAU, prfdc, prfld, prfpr, prfsnap, prfstat, sadc, sag, sar, sa1, sa2 and timex.

SAF **S**ervice **A**ccess **F**acility. Process that manages external connectivity to a system through ports. A facility, or feature, of UNIX System V, Release 4, that treats all connection requests the same, regardless of the source. *See* port, SVR4.x and feature.

SAFE **S**ecurity **A**lliance **F**or **E**nterprise Computing. Organization formed by Uni-Forum, a nonprofit association of UNIX professionals, to work on security issues related to using UNIX for client/server applications and to promote UNIX as a safe operating system and environment. *See* UniForum and client/server.

sag 1. *(ATT)* **S**ystem **a**ctivity **g**raph. Provides a graphic display of information about system use, potential problems and user changes contained in a file created by the most recent run of the sar command. Included in the System Performance Analysis Utilities in UNIX System V. *See* SPAU, prfdc, prfld, prfpr, prfsnap, prfstat, sadc, sadp, sar, sa1, sa2 and timex. 2. Electrical term for a decrease in voltage over a short period of time.

SAGE **S**ystem **A**dministrators' **G**uild. First of the UNIX special interest groups formed by the USENIX Association in mid-1993. Primarily aims to advance system administration as a profession by setting guidelines for education and requirements for excellence, and creating a process for certification of members. *See* USENIX Association, The and STG.

salt Information added to a user's password by the operating system, making it difficult for intruders to determine what the password is. *See* password.

SANE Condition flag for gettydefs, a system file containing the definitions for a port, used by the getty program. *See* /etc/gettydefs and flag.

sane flag Indicator used with the stty command to restore a terminal to its normal, or standard, operating state. *See* reset.

sane state Normal, or standard, operational state of a terminal.

SANS **S**ystem **A**dministration, **N**etworking and **S**ecurity. Conference jointly sponsored by FedUNIX, a federal council on advanced computing, the USENIX Association and the USENIX-sponsored System Administrators' Guild. Provides a medium for UNIX system administrators, network administrators and security technicians to meet and exchange information. Those in attendance exchange experiences and new concepts, and evaluate the use and operation of new tools. *See* USENIX Association, The and SAGE.

sans serif Without serif, or stroke. Style of any typeface that produces printed letters without ornate ascenders and descenders. *See* serif.

SAP **S**ervice **A**ccess **P**oint. Open Systems Interconnection term for the point were data is passed from one layer of a protocol suite to another. *See* OSI and OSIRM.

sar *(ATT)* **S**ystem **a**ctivity **r**eporter. Command used to collect and save specific system accounting information for use in analyzing system use, potential problems or user charges. Included in the System Performance Analysis Utilities in UNIX System V. *See* SPAU, prfdc, prfld, prfpr, prfsnap, prfstat, sadc, sadp, sag, sa1, sa2, timex and sar.

SAR System Activity Report. Collection of programs that provides reports, when required, on the performance of the operating system, central processing unit and hardware devices, e.g. time counters, input/output activity, context switching, system calls and file access. *See* CPU.

SARM System Administrator's Reference Manual. UNIX system documentation which provides a list and explanation of commands, formats, etc. used by system administrators. *See* SA, User's Guide, URM, Programmer's Guide, PRM and System Administrator's Guide.

sash Stand-alone shell program. Started during the bootstrap process. Used to start the UNIX operating system or to run stand-alone programs. *See* boot.

SASI Shugart Associates Standard Interface. Pronounced *SASSY*. Forerunner of small computer system interface. *See* SCSI.

sassy Pronounciation of SASI. *See* SASI.

save 1. To write to a new file or overwrite an existing file after modifications have been made to it. 2. Electronic-mail variable. *See* .mailrc variables (Appendices F and G).

savehist *(BSD)* C shell environmental variable used to set the maximum number of commands most recently run by a user to be maintained in the history file. A user can activate or re-run a previous command from the history file to save time. *See* .history.

savewtmp *(OTH)* Shell script used to save the wtmp file, which shows a list of user logins and processes generated by the init daemon. Can be used by the system administrator at any time during the day, in contrast with the runacct accounting sys-

tem shell script that is generally used at the end of each day. *See* shell script, wtmp, init and runacct.

SAW Surface acoustic wave. Technology used for touch screen terminals. *See* touch screen.

/sbin *(ATT)* UNIX System V, Release V directory that contains programs for starting the computer system and system recovery.

SBPC Software Business Practices Council. Vendor organization founded in 1990 to self-police business practices in the computer industry. SBPC was formed by companies such as Banyan Systems, Computer Associates, Digital Equipment Corp. and Lotus Development Corp. Its charter is to set standards, and monitor and correct industry problems related to advertising, marketing, public relations, product comparisons and financial reporting.

sbrk *(ATT)* System call that frees previously allocated memory. *See* system call.

scalability 1. Ability of a computer system to be optimized to perform a specific function by adjusting the size of the central processing unit and the throughput to the needs of the application software being run. *See* CPU and throughput. 2. Ability of application software to operate without modification on any type of computer, from a laptop to a supercomputer. Such software is developed to a binary standard and called binary compatible software (BCS), e.g. Lotus Development Corp.'s software, developed using BCS methodology for the Intel 386 microprocessor, can run on either a DOS or UNIX 386 computer. *See* BCS.

scalable file system Commonly called dynamic file system. *See* dynamic file system.

scalable processor Computer on which the capacity of the central processing unit can be changed to fit the size of the task to be performed.

Scalable Processor Architecture
Abbreviated and commonly known as
SPARC. *See* SPARC.

scanf Scan function. Standard input/out-
put library routine used to read information from a file that has been opened with
fopen, a C language library routine. *See*
library routines, fopen, fread, getc, fgetc,
gets, fgets, fclose, fscanf, fwrite, putc,
fputc, puts, fputs, printf and fprintf.

scat *(ATT)* Synchronous concatenate.
Command used to concatenate, or combine, multiple files into a new file and
print the output on a synchronous printer.
See cat and synchronous communication.

scatter loading Main memory allocation
and management technique. Processes are
placed in memory wherever space is available, resulting in better space management.
But also can lead to memory fragmentation
if there is not a single contiguous area available which is large enough for a process. *See*
memory fragmentation.

scc Standalone C Compiler. C compiler
used to create standalone programs. *See*
compiler and standalone program.

sccs *(ATT)* Source Code Control System.
Program which provides the command
line input to access to the Source Code
Control System revision control program.

SCCS *(ATT/XEN)* Source Code Control
System. Part of the Programmer's Workbench, a set of software development
tools for UNIX and look-alike operating
systems. One of two major software revision control programs. Used to maintain
source code libraries, control access to
source code files and document changes
made to such files. Enables users to revert
to older versions of the source code if
problems arise with the current version.
Creates a read-only version of the source
code file that cannot be modified. The
only way to modify the source code is to
use SCCS to create a new version. *See* PWB
and RCS.

sccsdiff *(ATT/XEN)* Source Code Control
System **difference**. One of the 13 Source
Code Control System (SCCS) commands

used to compare versions of a SCCS file.
See SCCS, admin, cdc, comb, delta, get, help,
prs, rmdel, sact, unget, val, vc and what.

SCCS Identification number
Commonly abbreviated and called SID.
See SID.

sched Also called swapper. System call
used to manage the programs for swapping data between main (computer) and
secondary (disk) memory. *See* system call,
primary storage and swap device.

schedule To assign allocation of system
resources, e.g. memory or central processing unit, to a process.

scheduler UNIX program which provides for the time-sharing or multi-user
capability of UNIX. Determines use of the
central processing unit by managing the
order in which processes are run, at what
time and for how long. *See* time-sharing
and multi-user.

scheduling Planning how computer resources will be used. For internally shared
resources, e.g. the central processing unit,
main memory and printers, it is done with
the cron daemon to schedule programs.
Externally, it is done with the nice command to change the priority of a process.
See cron and nice. **2.** Also called calendaring. Commonly called calendar. *See* calendar.

scheduling priority Predetermined priority within the kernel that determines
what priority a process will have in obtaining access to system resources. *See*
scheduler and scheduling.

schema Set of definitions that describes
how data is laid out in database tables.

SCI Institute of Electrical and Electronic
Engineers standards working group for
computers with speeds exceeding the current 200 million instructions per second
limit of a bus. *See* IEEE, mips and bus.

scratchpad Jargon term for cache memory. *See* cache memory.

scratch tape Tape that does not contain
any usable data, and that can be used for

backup or transferring information. Sometimes labeled as such. In many data centers, however, the standard policy is that any unlabeled tape is treated as a scratch tape. *See* tape.

screamer Jargon term for an extremely fast computer.

screen 1. Jargon term for terminal, referring to the cathode ray tube of a video display terminal. 2. Display surface of a video terminal. 3. Electronic-mail variable. *See* .mailrc variables (Appendix F).

screen editor Commonly called visual editor. *See* visual editor.

script 1. *(ATT)* Program used to make a copy of a terminal session, to a file named typescript or another specified file. Copies everything appearing on a terminal screen, including commands, text and anything else that crosses the screen and is written to the file during a specific time 2. Jargon term for shell script. *See* shell script.

scroll Editing variable in the vi editor program that, when set, establishes the number of lines moved with the use of the Ctrl-d or Ctrl-u commands. *See* vi.

scrollable cursor Cursor with the ability to move forward and backward in text or data. *See* cursor.

scrollbar Term in the window environment for the bar at the side or bottom of the screen which a user can manipulate with a mouse to move either up and down a file several lines or a full screen at a time, or from side to side on the screen.

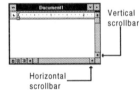

Vertical scrollbar

Horizontal scrollbar

Scrollbar in Microsoft Windows

scrolling Video terminal characteristic. A method of moving around in a file, either up or down or from side to side on the screen. In UNIX, the visual editors re-spond to keyboard input to do scrolling, e.g. Ctrl d in vi scrolls down and Ctrl u scrolls up. Can also be accomplished by using the scrollbar. *See* scrollbar.

SCSI Small computer system interface. Pronounced *SCUZZY*. In the early 1980s, NCR Corp. enhanced the Shugart Associates Standard Interface (SCSI) and offered it to the American National Standards Institute (ANSI) as a standard intelligent input/output interface. ANSI accepted the new interface as a standard intelligent interface for disks, tape controllers and other devices in 1986, formally naming it ANSI X.3.131-1986. Designed for high bandwidth over a short distance. *See* SASI, ANSI, I/O, SCSI-1, SCSI-2, SCSI-3 and IPI.

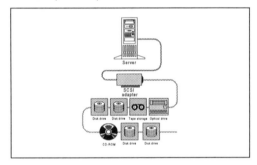

The SCSI subsystem creates a simple way to connect up to seven devices to a single adapter.

SCSI-1 Small computer system interface-1. First small computer system interface written. Designed to be flexible enough to be used with a large number of buses. Uses an 8-bit data path and can transmit up to 5 megabytes of data per second. *See* SCSI.

SCSI-2 Small computer system interface-2. Second-generation small computer system interface. Developed to overcome the shortfalls of SCSI-1 and improve communications between products from various manufacturers. Standard SCSI-2 uses an 8-bit data path and transmits 5 megabytes of data per second. Also has a protocol called Fast-Wide SCSI that uses either a 16-bit data path which can transmit 20 megabytes of data per second or a 32-bit data path which can transmit 40 megabytes of data per second. *See* SCSI.

SCSI-3 Small computer system interface-3. Generation of small computer system interfaces planned to follow SCSI-2. Will take advantage of enhanced hardware capabilities, including fiber optics and a larger number of devices (16 versus 8), and use a 32-bit data path that can transmit 100 megabytes of data per second and a longer cable run. *See* SCSI, CAM and CAM Committee.

SCU Sociedad Chilena UNIX. Chilean UNIX users group formed in 1989.

SCUZZY Pronunciation of SCSI, the abbreviation for small computer system interface. *See* SCSI.

sd *(INET)* Session directory. Application developed by Lawrence Berkeley Laboratories. Used with the IP multicasting protocol to permit X Window System terminals to identify data being broadcast and the channels on which it is being broadcast. Also can be used to identify data that is to be broadcast and when this is to take place. Allows the sender to identify the channel over which a broadcast message is to be sent. *See* Internet, IP multicasting and X Window System.

sdb *(ATT)* Symbolic debugger. Program used to debug C language and FORTRAN f77 object files, or to read core files. *See* C language, f77, object file and core.

sddate *(XEN)* Command used to set or reset the date on which the next backup should be done.

sdiff *(ATT/XEN)* Side-by-side **difference.** Command that allows the user to compare two files, line by line.

SDK Software development kit. Collection of tools and library routines provided by the developer of an operating system to programmers that are used to create applications, e.g. SDKs provided by Novell Inc. for NetWare and Microsoft Corp. for Windows NT.

SDLC 1. Synchronous data link control. Synchronous communications protocol that allows data to be transferred bit by bit, developed by IBM Corp. *See* synchro-

nous communication. 2. Software development life cycle. Method of software development using a sequence of steps, including requirement definition, system analysis, system design, software coding, system testing, implementation and maintenance.

SDU Service Data Unit. Term used in Fiber Distribution Data Interface technology for data prepared by users that is sent over a network. *See* FDDI.

seamless Integration of various hardware and software protocols into a cohesive system connected by interfaces that are invisible to users.

seamless e-mail Type of electronic-mail system that can transparently send electronic mail in a heterogeneous computer environment to a user on any computer without knowing what steps must be taken to route the message to the destination. A user can send an electronic-mail message to another user without knowing the name of the computer system used by the recipient.

search Process of locating either a specific word, set of words or characters within a document or database, or the location of a file in a file system.

search and replace Process of locating and replacing a character or set of characters with another character or set of characters. Also can be used to search for and delete a character or set of characters.

search bit Commonly called execute bit. *See* execute bit.

search path Also called path. The directories to be searched for a command.

search pattern String identified in the search commands which is to be located in a document, file in a file system or active process. *See* string.

search permission Commonly called execute permission. *See* execute permission.

secondary master server Commonly called secondary name server. *See* secondary name server.

secondary memory Commonly called swap device. *See* swap device.

secondary name server In a Domain Name Service network, a host that takes over the monitoring and maintenance of the name service environment for the network if the primary name server fails. There may be one or multiple secondary name servers on a network, or none at all. *See* DNS, RFS, primary name server.

secondary prompt Prompt given by the shell to indicate that a command has not been entered in full and more information is required. The default secondary prompt is the greater than sign (>). *See* prompt and shell.

secondary storage Disk, tape or other physical medium where data that is not being processed in a computer's main memory is kept. *See* primary storage and backing storage.

second-level domain *(INET)* Internet term for the first layer of hosts immediately below the top-level domain. Consists of hosts with a common function, e.g. when the European Distribution System's hosts were active, all 26 were included in a second-level domain known as *eds*. One host in the second-level domain is designated as the domain administrator responsible for interfacing with the Network Information Center. *See* Internet, NIC, domain, root-level domain, top-level domain and local administrative domain.

SECONDS Korn shell environmental variable. Shows how long, in seconds, a user has been logged on to a system.

secret key Commonly called private-key. *See* private-key.

sector 1. Measurement of the smallest storage capacity of a diskette or disk drive. *See* block. 2. One of the divisions of a track on a disk drive. *See* track and cylinder.

secure *(OTH)* Command used to check a computer system to determine how safe its operating system is.

security 1. *(ATT)* Command in the UNIX System V, Release 4 Framed Access Command Environment file system operation menu. Used to change the access permissions on a file. *See* SVR4.x, FACE, file system and permissions. 2. Protection of a system and its users. Consists of maintaining the availability, integrity and confidentiality of data; and ensuring that access to accounts, files, applications, etc. is properly authenticated and authorized. Basic UNIX security protects users from one another by using file and directory permissions and passwords.

security administration Management and execution of defined policies and procedures needed to protect the information assets on a computer system or network. Includes controlling access to computer or network resources, monitoring users' activities to ensure they are not abusing their privileges and deleting user accounts for individuals who no longer have access privileges. *See* privilege.

Security Administration Utilities Set of programs included in UNIX System V, Release 4 to encrypt and decrypt files, and maintain security. *See* SVR4.x, security, encrypt and decrypt.

Security Alliance for Enterprise Computing Commonly abbreviated and called SAFE. *See* SAFE.

Security Service Function within the Open Software Foundation Inc.'s Distributed Computing Environment that provides network security. Based upon Kerberos, a user-authentication method developed by the Massachusetts Institute of Technology. Provides communication security and user authentication and authorization. In addition, includes secure remote procedure call to identify corrupted messages and security for messages. *See* OSF, DCE, RPC and ACL.

sed *(ATT/XEN)* **Stream editor.** Batch editor program that uses the same syntax as the ed line editor. Can be used to make massive changes to large text files. Frequently used as a filter to edit data streams in a pipeline, a communication process in which the standard output of one process becomes the input of the next process. *See* batch, editor, filter and pipeline.

see *(BSD)* Command used to display non-printing characters of a file, e.g. formatting commands, line feed and carriage return characters.

seed Data Encryption Standard term for a random number selected by either the transmitter or receiver to start encrypting and transmitting data. *See* DES.

seek Process of moving the head on a disk drive to the correct position on the platter to read or write data. *See* head and platter.

seek time Amount of time it takes the arm of a disk drive to move the read/write head to the correct position on the platter. Normally, a short seek time means faster random access.

segment Range of continuous data, data elements or memory addresses used by a process when it is running. *See* memory segment and communications segment.

segmentation Commonly called fragmentation. *See* fragmentation.

segmentation fault Error caused by a program that is trying to use memory not allocated to it. Results in a core dump, in which a copy of the date in memory is saved. *See* core dump.

select **1.** *(BSD)* Command used to monitor input/output activity and report on those activities that are complete. **2.** *(ATT)* Korn shell command used to ask a user to select an option from a list.

select statement Database command sent to a server requesting specific data from the database. *See* server.

self-maintenance System of internal organization for maintaining an inventory of spare parts and staff who are trained to service installed hardware. *See* TPM and OEM maintenance.

Self-Teaching and Interpretive Communications Interfaces Commonly abbreviated and called STICI. *See* STICI.

self-test Method provided by computer and computer peripheral manufacturers for users to test all the functions of a device. With personal computers, the self-test is normally contained on a diskette titled User Diagnostics. With printers, the user may need to reset DIP switches or depress two of the buttons simultaneously. With terminals, the user may have to depress a specific set of characters in conjunction with either an escape or control sequence to activate the self-test. Manufactures who provide a self-test give step-by-step instructions for starting it.

semaphore Flag or indicator. Like flags used in signaling, semaphores are used to identify, track and manage the order of events related to process requests. Manages interprocess communications and conflict over devices, files, etc. Also manages multiple access to a file, preventing two or more users from modifying data at the same time. *See* IPC and deadly embrace.

semaphore service Process or function which rely on semaphores, or special flags, to manage interprocess communications. *See* IPC and semaphore.

Sematech Consortium of semiconductor manufactures formed in 1987 to improve the ability of U.S. companies to compete with Japanese firms for central processing unit business.

semctl *(ATT)* **Sem**aphore **ctl**. System call used to establish or obtain the value of semaphores, or special flags used to manage interprocess communications. *See* system call, semaphore and semval.

semget *(ATT)* **Sem**aphore **get**. System call used to start a set of semaphores, or special flags, for a specific interprocess communication. *See* system call, semaphore and IPC.

semicolon (;) **1.** Punctuation mark used as a command separator in shell scripts and C language programs. *See* shell script and C language. **2.** Special character used on the command line to separate multiple commands. *See* command line.

semiconductor **1.** Material with some of the properties of an electrical conductor, e.g. a metal like copper, gold or silver, and a non-conductor of electricity or an insulator, e.g. rubber or glass. The most commonly known semiconductor is silicon, which is used in manufacturing integrated circuits and transistors. *See* IC, conductor and non-conductor. **2.** Jargon term for any electrical component made of a semiconductor material.

semncntl *(ATT)* **Sem**aphore **n**umber **c**on**t**rol. One of the four fields that make up the structure of a semaphore, a flag used in interprocess communications. Contains the number of processes to be run but are waiting on a semaphore. *See* semaphore, sempid, semval and semzcntl.

semop *(ATT)* **Sem**aphore **op**erations. System call used to initiate semaphore operations in interprocess communications. *See* system call and semaphore.

sempid *(ATT)* **Sem**aphore **p**rocess **id**entifier. One of the four fields that make up the structure of a semaphore, a flag used in interprocess communications. Contains the process identifier of the process that last used the semaphore. *See* semaphore, semncntl, semval and semzcntl.

semval *(ATT)* **Sem**aphore **val**ue. One of the four fields that make up the structure of a semaphore, a flag used in interprocess communications. Maintains the current value of the semaphore. *See* semaphore, semncntl, sempid and semzcntl.

semzcntl *(ATT)* **Sem**aphore **z**ero **c**ontrol. One of the four fields that make up the structure of a semaphore, a flag used in interprocess communications. Maintains the processes that are waiting for the current value of the semval field to equal zero. *See* semaphore, semncntl, sempid and semval.

send *(ATT)* Command used to send a file to a batch remote job entry system for processing. *See* RJE.

SENDFILES Variable for the UNIX-to-UNIX CoPy communications system used to indicate if remote hosts are allowed to run locally queued jobs while they are connected to the local host. *See* UUCP.

sendmail **1.** Originally developed for the Berkeley Software Distribution operating system as the daemon used to monitor and manage delivery of electronic-mail messages. Converts addresses for delivery to remote systems or users on the local system, manages the electronic-mail headers, passes electronic mail to the Transmission Control Protocol/Internet Protocol for remote delivery, etc. *See* e-mail, TCP/IP and MTA. **2.** Electronic-mail variable. *See* .mailrc variables (Appendix F).

sendmail.cf Configuration file for the sendmail daemon that contains comments and definitions, and establishes the rules on managing inbound and outbound electronic mail. *See* e-mail and sendmail.

send window Grouping of sequence numbers and associated data that is to be transmitted over a network when a Transmission Control Protocol connection is made. *See* TCP and sequence number.

sentmail Electronic-mail variable which allows a user to have copies of outgoing messages put into a file specifically identified by the user. *See* e-mail.

Sequenced Pocket Exchange Abbreviated and commonly known as SPX. *See* SPX.

sequence number Number assigned to a specific set of data. Used to manage temporary storage, transmission, receipt and delivery of the data in a communications network.

sequence space Range of sequence numbers, each assigned to a specific set to data, to be transmitted during a Transmission Control Protocol connection. *See* TCP, sequence number and send window.

sequential access Method of moving up or down on a disk, one position at a time, to reach an address.

sequential operating system Computer operating system that processes one task at a time in a specific sequence.

sequential processing Processing of only one task at a time by a computer. The current task has to be completed before the computer can start work on the next.

serial Protocol which allows data to be transmitted one character at a time.

serial access Commonly called sequential access. *See* sequential access.

Serial Line Internet Protocol *(INET)* Commonly abbreviated and called SLIP. *See* SLIP.

serial printer Printer using a serial interface to transmit and print data one character at a time.

serif Font type that produces letters with ornate ascenders and descenders that generally make the typeface easier to read. Times and Gourdy are two popular serif typefaces. *See* sans serif.

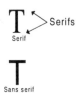

The line ornaments at the end of the character stroke differentiates serif from sans serif

server 1. Computer system which provides service, e.g. database and file storage, or owns, or controls, the devices which it makes available for use by client computers. 2. Software program or process operating within the same computer or a different computer. Provides services such as electronic-mail routing, database sharing and file transfer to local or remote users.

Server Natural Font Commonly abbreviated and called SNF. *See* SNF.

Server Normal Format Commonly abbreviated and called SNF. *See* SNF.

server process Process which provides interprocess communications services to client processes. *See* IPC, client and server.

service 1. Functionality provided by a protocol to a user or another protocol in a higher layer in a protocol model. *See* protocol model and protocol stack. 2. Abbreviation for Service Access Facility service, which is used to monitor a port or port activity. *See* SAF and SAC.

Service Access Controller Commonly abbreviated and called SAC. *See* SAC.

Service Access Facility Commonly abbreviated and called SAF. *See* SAF.

Service Access Point Commonly abbreviated and called SAP. *See* SAP.

service bureau Computer support service company that provides computer-related services to businesses which do not either own or operate certain types of computers and peripherals, e.g. fax machines and plotters.

Service Data Unit Commonly abbreviated and called SDU. *See* SDU.

Service Level Agreement Commonly abbreviated and called SLA. *See* SLA.

service requester Commonly called client. *See* client.

services 1. Methods used to transfer data over a network. 2. *(INET)* File in the /etc system directory that lists the Internet services available on the computer, e.g. TELNET and File Transfer Protocol. Gives the Internet name, port used and aliases for each service. *See* /etc and Internet.

Services Grouping of related protocols for UNIX network interfaces, e.g. electronic mail, Remote Procedure Call, UNIX-to-UNIX CoPy, TELNET and File Transfer Protocol.

service tag Port, or connecting point, for the flow of data, operating under AT&T Co.'s UNIX System V, Release 4 Service Access Facility. *See* SAF.

session Period of time a user is on, or uses, the computer, from login to logoff.

session directory *(INET)* Commonly abbreviated and called sd. *See* sd.

session key Data Encryption System (DES) term for the encryption key defined by a user and used in transmitting data using DES. *See* DES and encryption key.

session layer Fifth layer of the International Organization for Standardization/Open Systems Interconnection model. Responsible for maintaining security while establishing and ending communications between an application and data transmission. Also groups messages being sent, and tracks requests for data and responses to those requests. *See* ISO/OSI and OSIRM.

session layer 5 Commonly called session layer. *See* session layer.

session leader Commonly called superparent. *See* superparent.

Session Packet Exchange Abbreviated and commonly known as SPX. *See* SPX.

set **1.** C shell toggle variable used to display or establish variables in the user environment, electronic-mail system or other processes defined by a user in UNIX. *See* C shell, toggle variables, environment variables and unset. **2.** *(ATT)* Remote File Sharing sysadm menu command used to establish the network support, or type of communication, required for a local host, e.g. Transmission Control Protocol/Internet Protocol. *See* RFS and sysadm. **3.** Command used to establish option variables in the vi editor. *See* vi. **4.** System management message in the Simple Network Management Proto-

col. Used by a network manager to reset the value of a device on a network. *See* SNMP, get and trap.

setclk *(ATT)* **Set clock.** Command invoked as part of the boot process that loads the system clock (i.e. date and time) from the hardware clock.

setcolor *(ATT/XEN)* **Set color.** Command used to set colors on a color monitor screen, e.g. blue letters on a white background.

set domain *(ATT)* Command in the Remote File Sharing sysadm menu used to establish the domain for a local host. *See* RFS, sysadm and domain.

setenv **Set env**ironment. C shell command used to define a user's operational environment. *See* C shell.

setgid *(ATT)* **Set g**roup **id**entifier. System call used to establish the effective group identifier, which determines if a user has permission to access files. *See* system call and EGID.

set gid mappings *(ATT)* **Set g**roup **id**entifier **mappings**. Command in the Remote File Sharing sysadm menu used to establish the default group permissions for file access. *See* RFS, sysadm, GID and permissions.

setgrent *(ATT)* **Set g**roup **ent**ry. C programming language library routine used to set a system group file entry. *See* library routines, getgrnam, getgrid and endgrent.

set group ID Commonly abbreviated and called SGID. *See* SGID.

set group identifier program Program that, when run, sets its group identifier (GID) instead of using the GID it inherits from the user running the program. Generally, programs that include this feature are granted privileges that the user may not have. *See* GID.

setgrp *(ATT)* **Set group.** System call that sets the group identifier number, a 16-bit numeric indicating the permissions assigned to members of a group. *See* system call and GID.

sethostid *(BSD)***Set host id**entifier. Command used by the system administrator to establish the 32-bit Internet address for a local host. *See* gethostid, Internet, sethostname and gethostname.

sethostname *(BSD)* **Set host name**. System call used by the system administrator to establish the name for a computer host. *See* gethostname, sethostid and gethostid.

setitimer **Set** interval **timer**. C language library routine used by the system administrator to set the interval timer. The computer system maintains three interval timers: real (wall-clock), virtual (time used by a process) and profiled (like virtual time, but includes time taken by the kernel to execute instructions on behalf of the process). *See* library routines and getitimer.

setkey *(ATT)* **Set key**. Command used to create the key used in encrypting data in the Data Encryption Standard. *See* encryption key and DES.

setlocale *(OTH)* **Set locale**. C language library routine used with internationalization of another program. Used to provide the information required for setting up a program to run in a specific international environment, e.g. to set the specific characters or numerics for the language. *See* library routines and i18n.

setmnt *(ATT/XEN)* **Set m**ount table. Command used to establish the system mount table, /etc/mnttab, in which a list of all active local and remote file systems is maintained. *See* mount table.

setpwent **Set** password **ent**ry. C programming language library routine used with the getpwent library routine to maintain an entry in the system password file, /etc/passwd. getpwent returns an entry in /etc/passwd. *See* library routines, getpwent, endpwent and /etc/passwd.

setrlimit *(BSD)* **Set** restricted **limit**. System program used to set resource limits on a computer, e.g. central processing unit usage per process, maximum size of a file and core dump size.

setsockopt *(BSD)* **Set sock**et **opt**ions. System call used to set options for sockets, used for interprocess communications. *See* system call, sockets, getsockopt and IPC.

settime *(XEN)* **Set time**. Command used to reset access and modification times of files. Changes the date and time a file was last modified and thus accessed, e.g. touch foobar sets the modify and access time of the file foobar to NOW (whatever time the system clock is currently showing).

settimeofday *(BSD)* **Set time of day**. C language library routine used to set the time, in microseconds, on a computer system. *See* library routines and gettimeofday.

set UID Commonly abbreviated and called SUID. *See* SUID.

setuid *(ATT)* **Set u**ser **id**entifier. System call used to set the real and effective user identifier of a process. *See* system call, real UID and EUID.

set uid mappings *(ATT)* **Set u**ser **id**entifier **mappings**. Command in the Remote File Sharing sysadm menu used to establish the default user permissions for file access. *See* RFS, sysadm, UID and permissions.

setuname *(ATT)* System administration command used to change the system name or node name on a network. Depending on the argument, the change can be either permanent or temporary.

setup *(ATT)* Initial system administration command or login used by the first system administrator who accesses the system. Used to establish logins, date, time zone and other basic elements of the system configuration.

set user ID Commonly abbreviated and called SUID. *See* SUID.

set user identifier program Program that, when run, sets its user identifier (UID) instead of using the UID it inherits from the user running the program. Generally, programs that include this feature are granted privileges that the user may not have. *See* UID and SUID.

seven by twenty-four Commonly written 7 x 24. *See* 7 x 24.

sexadecimal Commonly called hexadecimal. *See* hexadecimal.

sex changer Commonly called gender bender. *See* gender bender.

sexist Part of the Writer's Workbench text processing tools. Used to locate sexist language in a document. *See* WWB.

SFP Standard Format Part. Term used in magneto-optical disk technology for a code implanted in a CD-ROM disc that indicates whether information can be written to the disk only once or many times. *See* M/O, CD-ROM and PEP.

SGID Set group identifier. Attribute or function of the UNIX security system that establishes group access to a file or directory at the time it is created. Indicates who can have access to a file or directory. *See* GID, UID, real GID, EGID, real UID and EUID.

SGID trap Set group identifier trap. Program used by a hacker that looks for and exploits mistakes in programs that allow others to establish group access to a file or directory. Obtains the same permissions for the hacker as the owner of the file or program. *See* SGID.

SGML Standard Generalized Markup Language. A document encoding language standard. In the early 1980s an industry graphics association and an American National Standards Institute committee independently began to develop a standard for a markup language. Their efforts were combined in 1986, resulting in an International Organization for Standardization SGML standard. Originally developed for use on UNIX systems, this standard has been adopted by major industries for preparing and maintaining large documents, such as aircraft and automotive manuals. It is currently used by the Department of Defense for the Computer-Aided Acquisition Logistics Support program to manage system documentation, contract proposals and contracts. The standard establishes a definition for formatting documents so they may be modified, viewed or output to any computer system, application and storage or viewing media. It also defines the formatting of documents, identifying each element as a separate data object. By using data objects, documents can be maintained and distributed more easily, and components can be re-used in other documents. Each SGML document has two components. The first, the Document Type Definition, defines the structure of the data objects. The second, the document instance, is the data, or text, of the document. Industry support for SGML has expanded to include Microsoft Corp., Lotus Development Corp., WordPerfect Corp., Interleaf Inc., Frame Technology Corp., Fujitsu Ltd. and Oracle Corp. *See* ANSI, ISO, markup, specific markup, DTD and document instance.

SGMP *(INET)* Simple Gateway Management Protocol. Forerunner to the Simple Network Management Protocol, used to manage devices on a network. *See* SNMP.

sh 1. *(ATT)* Shell. Command used to start the default Bourne shell. 2. Command used to start or spawn a new shell in order to perform functions not possible either with the current shell or program being used. A user can invoke sh while in an editor or electronic-mail program to obtain additional information without terminating either the e-mail or editor session. For example, a user in the vi editor can initiate the ex command line indicated by a colon (:). At the colon, the user escapes (!) and creates a new shell (sh) for command execution:

    CLP> :!sh⏎

After the information is obtained, sh must be terminated, normally using Ctrl d, so that the original function can be continued. **3.** Program used to run commands from a shell file with changes made to specified parameters. *See* shell, shl, resh, rsh, jsh, ksh and rksh. **4.** Abbreviation in UNIX which indicates the user is running the basic Bourne shell. *See* Bourne shell.

shadowed disk *See* disk mirroring.

shadowing Commonly called disk mirroring. *See* disk mirroring.

shadow password Commonly written as /etc/shadow. *See* /etc/shadow.

Shamrock Application programming interface developed by the Shamrock Document Management Coalition. Provides an improved method for intracompany communication and data sharing between document management systems. *See* Shamrock Document Management Coalition.

Shamrock Document Management Coalition Organization formed by vendors and users of document management systems. Aims to develop means to ensure accurate interchange of documents between organizations using proprietary mainframes, personal computers and/or UNIX systems. Members include Adobe Systems Inc., Aetna Life and Casualty Co., Coca Cola Co., EDS Corp., Hewlett-Packard Co., IBM Corp., Merck and Co., Microsoft Corp., Saros Corp. and Sybase Inc.

shar Shell archive. Shell script used to archive files and combine several small files into one file to be transmitted by electronic mail. *See* archive and e-mail.

share **1.** *(ATT)* Distributed File System root command that opens up system resources, e.g. disks, memory and files, to additional users on a distributed network. Used by the system administrator to specifically identify the resources available for access. *See* DFS, RFS, NFS, shareall, unshare, adv and exportfs. **2.** Command in the Network File System, sysadm menu that opens local resources for automatic and immediate access. *See* NFS and sysadm. **3.** Command in the Remote File Sharing sysadm menu used to make available shared local resources or to mount, or activate, remote resources. *See* RFS and sysadm. **4.** To make resources available for use by more than one user.

shareall *(ATT)* Distributed File System command similar to the share command except it can be used to identify multiple resources that may be accessed by other users and systems, e.g. programs using assets on other hosts, on a distributed network. *See* DFS, RFS, NFS, share, unshareall, adv and exportfs.

shared memory Type of computer memory that allows two or more separate processes to access the same area in it at the same time. This avoids delays since the information in memory does not have to be passed between the processes.

shared memory multiprocessor Computer system with multiple central processing units that share a common memory connected by a high-speed bus. *See* MP, CPU, bus, tightly coupled architecture and distributed memory multiprocessor.

shared text Text that can be shared by several processes simultaneously.

shared text segment Text segment, or code, containing machine instructions used by processes while a program used by more than one process is being loaded into memory. *See* shared text.

sharetab Commonly written as /etc/dfs/sharetab. *See* /etc/dfs/sharetab.

share table List of resources that have been made available for use by other users or systems, e.g. programs using assets on other hosts, through the Remote File Sharing system. *See* share, automatic share table, automatic mount list and RFS.

shareware Class of software that is made available for general use without charge. However, the developer may ask those who use it to pay a nominal fee, e.g. ProComm, personal computer communications software, was initially released as shareware with a requested fee of $25. Note: ProComm PLUS is not shareware.

shar file **Sh**ell **ar**chive **file**. File created using the shar shell script. Can contain several small files and be transmitted by electronic mail. *See* shar.

sharing Making local resources available to users on remote computers. *See* share, shareall and unsharing.

shelfware **1.** Software that does not survive the development and production process. When a development program is canceled, the software is "put on the shelf" in the hope it will be finished or implemented later. **2.** Software purchased because of a stated policy or because someone feels it is required when, in reality, it is not. Such software normally is put on a shelf and never used.

shell **1.** Translator of user input. Program that acts as a user's connection with the kernel and, ultimately, the whole UNIX system. Takes the user commands and changes them into terms understood and then acted on by the kernel and system utilities. The kernel starts a shell for each user or program that logs in to the system to establish and maintain the separation of user environments. Four shells currently used within UNIX are: the Bourne shell and Korn shell for AT&T Co.'s UNIX; the C shell and Tennex shell for Berkeley Software Distribution. *See* kernel, token and utility. **2.** Programming language which provides an interface to the kernel. Each shell has its own programming language that enables a user to write programs without having to resort to conventional programming languages. **3.** *(BSD)* C shell environmental variable set by the login process. Indicates which shell the user operates in. **4.** Variable in the vi editor program used to identify the shell executed by vi commands. *See* vi and vi commands (Appendix T).

SHELL **1.** *(ATT)* Shell environmental variable set by the login process indicating the path to the shell the user operates in. *See* shell. **2.** Electronic-mail variable. *See* .mailrc variables (Appendix F).

shell archive Commonly abbreviated and called shar. *See* shar.

shell command User input that, when interpreted by the kernel, initiates a program to complete a predefined process. *See* shell script.

shell escape Process of creating a new shell while the user is in a program. *See* exclamation point.

shell file Any file containing shell commands. *See* shell script.

shell function **1.** Output of information or action taken by a computer as a result of the commands given in a shell script. **2.** Separate function within a shell script, analogous to a subroutine in the C language.

shell layers Ability of users to run more than one shell at the same time. *See* shl.

shell out Jargon term for creating a new shell while a user is in an existing shell program. *See* shell and execute.

shell parameter Commonly called argument. *See* argument.

shell program Commonly called shell script. *See* shell script.

shell prompt On-screen message sent by the computer to the user to indicate which shell is being used. *See* system prompt.

shell script Commands or instructions developed in the shell programming language and maintained as ordinary files, which can be executed by a shell.

shell snob User who adamantly feels the shell they use is the only one that should be used, regardless of the merits of other shells. *See* operating system snob and UNIX Wars.

shell variable Function in a shell that has a specific value and is used by processes to set the type of shell to be used while a user is logged on. *See* environment variables.

shielded twisted pair Commonly abbreviated and called STP. *See* STP.

shift **1.** Shell command used to change the parameters of arguments in a shell program. *See* shell. **2.** To remove the first set of data at the beginning of a stack, a temporary storage list in a computer's main memory. *See* stack, push, pop and unshift.

Shift key Key found on a computer keyboard that, when depressed along with an alphabetic key, generates an uppercase letter. Depressing the Shift key and a numeric key generates a special character, e.g. the dollar sign ($) or asterisk (*). Depressing the Shift key and an alphabetic key while the caps lock key is on will generate a lowercase letter. *See* caps lock key.

shift lock key Commonly called caps lock key. *See* caps lock key.

shiftwidth Equivalent of a tabstop in the vi editor program. *See* vi and tabstop.

shl *(ATT)* **Sh**ell **l**ayer. Like the sh command, allows a user to start a new shell. Enables the user to run more than one interactive shell at the same time, and to switch back and forth between them. *See* shl commands.

shl commands Once the shl, or shell layer, has been established, the following commands can be used:

Command	Description
block	Blocks the output of the specified layer
help	Outputs the syntax of shl commands
?	Same as help
layers	Produces a list of the layer
resume	Makes the layer named the current or active layer
toggle	Restarts the previous current or active layer as the current layer
unblock	Unblocks the output of a layer
quit	Stops all running layers and processes

shlock *(OTH)* Commonly called lock. *See* lock.

shmat *(ATT)* **Sh**ared **m**emory **at**tach. System call used to link newly allocated shared memory to existing elements of shared memory. *See* system call, shared memory, shmctl, shmdt and shmget.

shmctl *(ATT)* **Sh**ared **m**emory **c**on**t**ro**l**. System call used to manage the shared memory operations by either establishing the needed shared memory segment, or retrieving the status the shared segment allocated, or deleting the shared memory segment. *See* system call, shared memory, shmat, shmdt and shmget.

shmdt *(ATT)* **Sh**ared **m**emory **d**e**t**ach. System call used to delete allocated shared memory when a process is finished. *See* system call, shared memory, shmat, shmctl and shmget.

shmget *(ATT)* **Sh**ared **m**emory **get**. System call used to allocate a portion of shared memory. Returns an identifier for that portion of memory when it is allocated. *See* system call, shared memory, shmat, shmctl and shmdt.

shmop *(ATT)* **Sh**ared **m**emory **op**erations. System call used to set up and manage interprocess communications to manage shared memory. *See* system call and shared memory.

shoelace programming Use of simple macros to form applications instead of using standard programming practices, such as using a development specification to create application code.

short C language integer data type. Most computers represent numbers as a series of bits, each bit representing a power of two, the rightmost bit representing two to the zeroeth power (or one). For example, the number 67 in decimal can be represented as the following bits:

```
1000011
6 5 4 3 2 1 0
(i.e. 1x2 + 0x2 + 0x2 + 0x2 + 0x2 + 1x2 + 1x2 =
64 + 0 + 0 + 0 + 0 + 2 + 1 = 67)
```

The number of bits used to represent a number is its length. On many computer systems, numbers come in two lengths: 16 bits long and 32 bits long. For simplicity, the C language refers to 16 bit numbers as 'short' and 32 bit numbers as 'long'. On a typical 32-bit computer system, a short is 16 bits long and has a value between -32768 and 32767. *See* int.

shortcut Way of getting around commands to reduce the number of keystrokes needed to input the command. A standard method in UNIX is to use aliases created by either the system or user, e.g. substituting the letters pe for the command ps -ef. Another shortcut is to use characters which have specific meanings to minimize the number of keystrokes, e.g. to move from one user account to another, a user would normally type:

    CLP> cd /usr/she/jacobs ⏎

But in UNIX, the user can also enter as a shortcut:

    CLP> cd ~jacobs ⏎

Shortcuts work well most of the time, but not always. *See* tilde (~). OH S*!T!! command and OOPS!! command.

short-term scheduling algorithm Set of clearly defined rules used in the scheduling management process. Selects the next process to be run, thus determining the sequence in which all the processes will be run. *See* scheduler, scheduling and scheduling priority.

shovelware Jargon term for software products that are developed by moving an existing product, e.g. a novel, dictionary or encyclopedia, to a CD-ROM disc without making any changes or additions to it. *See* CD-ROM.

showmode 1. Electronic-mail variable that allows a user to have messages displayed on the status line, located at the bottom of the screen. *See* e-mail and status line. 2. Commonly abbreviated smd. *See* smd.

showto Electronic-mail variable which allows the user to receive copies of message receipts. *See* e-mail.

shrink-wrapped Jargon term for binary compatibility standard. Describes soft-

ware that is developed for and ported to a particular type of central processing unit (CPU). Once ported to that type of unit, it does not have to be re-ported to other manufacturers' computers if they use the same type of CPU. In 1989 the 88open Consortium published the first binary compatibility standard for systems running UNIX with Motorola 88000 chips. *See* CPU and 88open Consortium.

Shugart Associates Standard Interface Abbreviated and commonly known as SASI. *See* SASI.

shutacct *(ATT)* **Shut**down **acc**ounting. Accounting system program used to turn off system accounting and to record the shutdown in wtmp, a temporary log of entries in the /etc system directory. *See* /etc/wtmp.

shutdown 1. /etc/shutdown. Script normally used by a system administrator to gracefully shut down a system. 2. Process of turning off active processes and user access to the computer. 3. Process of turning off the electrical power to the computer.

shutdown state Also called state 0. The computer is powered down, or turned off.

SID SCCS **id**entification number. Number assigned to each version of a source code file created using the Source Code Control System. *See* SCCS.

sig Jargon term for signal. *See* signal.

SIG **S**pecial **i**nterest **g**roup. Group within an organization that has common interests or goals. For example, the Massive Open System Environment Standards (MOSES) consortium sponsored the formation of the UNIX Data Center Special Interest Group to provide an interface between MOSES and others in the UNIX industry. *See* MOSES.

SIG_DFL **Sig**nal **d**efau**l**t. System macro that establishes the interpretation of signals to their default meaning. When SIG_DFL is set, the process is stopped when any signals, except SIGPWR and SIGCLD, are received. For selected signals, a core also is produced. *See* signal, signal values (Appendices I, J and K), SIG_IGN and core.

SIG_IGN **Sig**nal **ign**ore. System macro that identifies signals which are not to receive a response, or be ignored. The SIGKILL signal, which terminates a process, cannot be ignored. *See* signal, signal values (Appendices I, J and K) and SIG_DFL.

sigcont Command used to restart a sleeping, or temporarily halted, process.

SIGIO *(BSD)* **Sig**nal Input/Output. System program that tells the computer that an input/output request has been completed.

sign Electronic-mail variable. *See* Appendix F.

Sign Electronic-mail variable. *See* Appendix F.

signal 1. Part of the system's process control. A message that notifies the computer hardware, operating system, other processes or application software of an external event or condition. When it receives a signal, a process can either follow the default action of the signal, ignore the signal or execute a signal handling function defined within the process. 2. Electronic mark made on a recording medium which represents a data element. 3. System call used to specify action to be taken on receipt of a specified signal. *See* system call and signal.

signal handler Special routine contained in some processes that is started by a specific direction, e.g. a signal. If the process does not contain a signal handler, the kernel provides a default one. *See* catching a signal, process and signal.

signal mask Bit mask used in the setsig-mask operating system call. Defines signals that are blocked, or cannot be sent to a process. If a bit in the mask is set to 1, the corresponding signal is ignored; otherwise, the signal is processed. *See* signal and process.

signal quality error Commonly abbreviated and called SQE. *See* SQE.

Signal System 7 Abbreviated and commonly known as SS7. *See* SS7

signal-to-noise ratio Measurement of the clarity of a signal in data recording and playback. *See* signal and noise.

signal values 1. *(ATT) See* Appendix I for pre-UNIX System V, Release 4 operations performed by signals. 2. *(ATT) See* Appendix J for UNIX System V, Release 4 operations performed by signals: to indicate signals before and after SVR4. 3. *(BSD) See* Appendix K for Berkeley Software Distribution operations performed by signals.

signed long Integer data type whose values include positive and negative numbers. A typical signed long on a 32-bit computer system can be from -2147483648 to 2147483647. Signed data is used to represent any data that can have negative as well as positive amounts, e.g. money, duration or counters. *See* signed short, unsigned short and unsigned long.

signed short Signed data type not longer than an integer. A typical signed short on a 32-bit computer system can be from -32768 to 32767. Signed data is used to represent any data that can have negative as well as positive amounts, e.g. money, duration or counters. *See* signed long, unsigned short and unsigned long.

sign in Commonly called log in. *See* log in.

sign out Commonly called log out. *See* log out.

silent character Commonly called hidden character. *See* hidden character.

silent operation Commands that end without notifying the user.

silicon Neutral, non-metallic element found in sand and clay. Used to form layers in electrical circuits, created in the process of manufacturing integrated circuits. *See* IC.

silicon chip Commonly called IC (integrated circuit). *See* IC.

Silicon Valley Region of California surrounding San Jose that is known for its production of integrated circuits, which are etched onto silicon chips. As a result, the largest corridor of computer companies in the world has developed in this area. Hardware, software and peripherals are all manufactured there.

silly window syndrome Situation in which the window management program substitutes several small windows when there is insufficient space to allocate a larger window that has been requested. *See* window.

SIMD Single instruction, multiple data. Massively parallel processing architecture with large numbers of processors working on a single problem but sharing distributed memory. SIMD computers have between 1,000 and 16,400 processors. *See* massively parallel processing and MIMD.

SIMM Single in-line memory module. Type of random access, or temporary, computer memory made in the form of a circuit board. Approximately 3 inches wide by .25 to .5 inches high with a single row of metal connector pins (30 to 72) along one side. Holds surface-mounted memory chips, permitting more memory chips to be installed in a smaller space inside a computer. *See* RAM.

simple *(ATT)* Variation of the dumb script that can be used with slower printers and smaller printing jobs. *See* LP, dumb and fancier.

Simple Gateway Management Protocol *(INET)* Commonly abbreviated and called SGMP. *See* SGMP.

Simple Internet Protocol *(INET)* Commonly abbreviated and called SIP. *See* SIP.

Simple Internet Protocol-P Internet Protocol *(INET)* Commonly abbreviated and called SIP-P. *See* SIP-P.

Simple Mail Transfer Protocol *(INET)* Commonly abbreviated and called SMTP. *See* SMTP.

Simple Management Protocol *(INET)* Commonly abbreviated and called SMP. *See* SMP.

Simple Network Management Protocol *(INET)* Commonly abbreviated and called SNMP. *See* SNMP.

Simple Protocol-P Protocol *(INET)* Commonly abbreviated and called SIP-P. *See* SIP-P.

simplex Ability to send communications in one direction only over a single communications link. *See* duplex.

simulated storage Portion of a disk drive allocated to store programs or data not currently being used.

single in-line memory module Commonly abbreviated and called SIMM. *See* SIMM.

single in-line package Commonly abbreviated and called SIP. *See* SIP.

single instruction, multiple data Commonly abbreviated and called SIMD. *See* SIMD.

single large expensive disk Commonly abbreviated and called SLED. *See* SLED.

single-mode fiber Commonly abbreviated and called SMF. *See* SMF.

single quote (') **1.** Special character that tells the shell to ignore the normal meaning of characters placed between single quotes. Can be used to override the meaning of metacharacters, e.g. the asterisk (*), used as a wild card, is only an asterisk when enclosed by single quotes. *See* metacharacter. **2.** Special character used to make a single argument. Everything input between an opening and closing single quote becomes a single argument. *See* metacharacter and argument.

single thread Set of processes which complete all actions on a message before starting on the next message, e.g. opens a file, performs a function, waits for the function to finish, closes the file and then moves to the next message.

single-user mode Commonly called single-user state. *See* single-user state.

single-user state Also called state s or state S. Computer or system state in which only the system administrator has access to the system and only the root file system is mounted, or activated. There are no multi-user processes running and the system can only be accessed through the console, the terminal reserved for system administration. *See* root file system and console.

single-user system Computer system that can be accessed by only one person at a time.

Sinix Singapore **UNIX** Association. UNIX users group formed in 1985.

SIOCADDRT Command which is part of the ioctl system call and is used to add an entry to a network routing table. *See* ioctl and routing.

SIOCDELRT Command which is part of the ioctl system call and is used to delete an entry from a network routing table. *See* ioctl and routing.

SIOCGIFADDR Command which is part of the ioctl system call and is used to retrieve an interface address for an Internet protocol. *See* ioctl and Internet.

SIOCGIFDSTADDR Command which is part of the ioctl system call and is used to retrieve an address for a point-to-point interface. *See* ioctl and point-to-point protocol.

SIOCGIFFLAGS Command which is part of the ioctl system call and is used to retrieve an interface flag, which indicates the operational status of an Internet interface. *See* ioctl and Internet.

SIOCGIFNETMASK Command which is part of the ioctl system call and is used to retrieve a network mask. *See* ioctl and network mask.

SIOCSIFADDR Command which is part of the ioctl system call and is used to establish an interface address for an Internet protocol. *See* ioctl and Internet.

SIOCSIFDSTADDR Command which is part of the ioctl system call and is used to establish an address for a point-to-point interface. *See* ioctl and point-to-point.

SIOCSIFFLAGS Command which is part of the ioctl system call and is used to establish an interface flag, which indicates the operational status of an Internet interface. *See* ioctl and Internet.

SIOCSIFNAME Command which is part of the ioctl system call and is used to establish an Internet interface name. *See* ioctl and Internet.

SIOCSIFNETMASK Command which is part of the ioctl system call and is used to establish a network mask for the interface with the network. *See* ioctl and network mask.

SIOGIFCONF Command which is part of the ioctl system call and is used to retrieve a configuration list for the Internet interfaces. *See* ioctl and Internet.

SIP 1. Single in-line package. Plastic or ceramic housing used to hold electronic components, e.g. random access, or temporary, computer memory. Has connector pins only on one side like a single in-line memory module, but looks similar to a dual in-line package. *See* RAM, SIMM and DIP. **2.** *(INET)* Simple Internet Protocol. Proposed modification to the Internet Protocol (IP) to change fields of the IP packet header and expand it from the current 32-bit IP address to a 64-bit IP address. *See* Internet, IP and IP address.

SIP-P *(INET)* Simple Internet Protocol-P Internet Protocol. Combination of two proposed protocols, Simple Internet Protocol and P Internet Protocol, into a new protocol to overcome the shortage of Internet Protocol (IP) addresses in the current IP. In SIP-P, a new header is created, reducing the fields to permit larger address fields. *See* Internet, IP, IP address, SIP and PIP.

Site Field in the L.sys system file which contains the host names for remote systems, used by the system in making connections to remote hosts. *See* L.sys.

site license Licensing of a software package to a location or organization so it can be used by multiple users instead of to each computer, for which the organization would have to buy individual licenses. *See* dynamic license.

size *(ATT/XEN)* Command used to display the data, bss and text segment size of an object or binary file. *See* bss segment, text segment, data segment and object.

skinny FTAM **Skinny** File Transfer, Access and Management. Jargon term for the implementation of FTAM that uses FTAM Type 1 and FTAM Type 3. Open Systems Interconnection file transfer method that uses both unstructured, or American Standard Code for Information Interchange, text files and unstructured binary files. *See* FTAM, FTAM Type 1, FTAM Type 2, FTAM Type 3, OSI and ASCII.

skulker *(OTH)* Shell script run by the cron daemon. Used to search for and delete old files and potential security problems, e.g. improperly set permissions, from a file system. *See* cron and root file system.

SL Stereolithography. Technique to convert data for a solid computer model into an actual model. Data is turned into slices matching the tolerances of the machinery that will be used to make the model. The slices are passed to the tooling machinery to be built, slice by slice.

SLA Service level agreement. Terms drawn up between a service provider who operates a computer and its users. Outlines the service provider's obligations in terms of operating the computer including normal hours of operation, percentage of uptime, when backups are to be done, etc.

slash *(/)* File separator. Also called solidus. Used to distinguish individual directories and files, e.g. /usr/SHE/collier/myfile indicates that myfile is an individual file or directory of collier, which is an individual file or directory of SHE. *See* path.

slave **1.** Term used to describe the dependent relationship of a host computer on a network to a computer that manages or sets network variables. *See* master and timed. **2.** Commonly called hardwired. *See* hardwired.

slave device Hardware component that depends on another piece of hardware to function, e.g. tape drives and disk drives which need controllers to function. *See* hardwired.

slave routine Device driver for a slave device. *See* slave device.

SLED Single large expensive disk. Jargon term for standard disk drives that have not been configured with stripping found in Redundant Array of Inexpensive Disks. *See* RAID.

sleep **1.** Command entered by a user that suspends an operation or program for a specified time. **2.** C programming language library routine that suspends a process for a specified time. *See* library routines.

sleep queue Waiting line for processes that have been suspended for a specified time as a result of the sleep command. *See* sleep.

slew To move paper through a printer.

slice Commonly called disk partition. *See* disk partition.

slider Moveable bar displayed on a screen that is used to control functions within a computer, e.g. volume, color hues and location of an image in a window.

sliding window scheme Transmission Control Protocol communications control or management method. A receiving host establishes and notifies the sending host of the amount of data it will receive, using sequence numbers. As data is passed, the sequence numbers falling into the acceptable window slide forward. *See* TCP, receive window and send window.

slink *(ATT)* STREAMS **link**er. Program used to tie together modules and drivers needed for STREAMS-based Transmission Control Protocol/Internet Protocol operations. *See* STREAMS and TCP/IP.

SL/IP Commonly written as SLIP. *See* SLIP.

SLIP *(INET)* Serial Line Internet Protocol. Not a standard protocol of the Internet. Developed in 1984 and documented in 1988. Used for transmission of Internet Protocol packets over conventional voice-grade telephone lines. Uses the Transmission Control Protocol and Internet Protocol to transmit packet switch data over a serial interface, normally at speeds of 9,600 to 19,200 baud. Designed to work only with IP and lacks the ability to detect errors. *See* C-SLIP, baud, TCP/IP, serial and PPP.

slip sector Sector that replaces a bad sector, or area of a mass storage device that cannot be used due to incorrect formatting or a physical defect. *See* sector.

slip-sector forwarding Process of identifying the slip, or replacement, sector address for a bad sector, or area of a mass storage device that cannot be used due to incorrect formatting or a physical defect. *See* slip sector.

slow Editing variable in the vi editor program that, when set, slows down communication between a terminal and central processing unit. *See* vi and CPU.

smail Program similar to sendmail. Used to manage delivery of electronic-mail messages. *See* sendmail, MTA and e-mail.

Small Computer Systems Interface Commonly abbreviated and called SCSI. *See* SCSI.

Smalltalk First of the better-known object-oriented programming languages, developed by the Xerox Palo Alto Research Center in the mid-1980s. *See* Xerox PARC, OOP and C++ language.

smartsourcing Term related to outsourcing. When a company hires its computer staff through a third party but retains management control of that staff. *See* outsourcing.

smart terminal Commonly called intelligent terminal. *See* intelligent terminal.

smd **Show**mode. Option in the vi editor program used to display the current mode of the editor program, e.g. INPUT MODE when the program is in an operating mode that allows data to be entered. By knowing the program's operating mode, a user can better understand the cause of an error message. *See* vi and nosmd.

SMDS Switched Multimegabit Data Service. Data communications technology for metropolitan area and wide area networks developed by BellSouth Services and based upon fixed-length (53-byte) cell relay technology. A connectionless technology with no pre-established paths between the sending and receiving nodes for the data to follow. Proposed replacement for the Defense Advanced Research Projects Agency's X.25 packet switch system. SMDS is a high-speed packet switch service that can transmit data at 1.2 to 34 megabits per second, and may reach 600 megabits per second in the future. *See* cell relay, MAN, WAN, DARPA and X.25.

SMDS Interest Group Switched Multimegabit Data Service Interest Group. Formed in May 1991 by Ungermann-Bass, Digital Link, Verilink, Wellfleet Communications and Advanced Computer Communications to develop a standard interface to SMDS networks. *See* SMDS.

SMF Single-**m**ode fiber. One of the two types of fiber cable used with a Fiber Distributed Data Interface network. Uses a single thin core of fiber to limit data transmissions to a single path. Capable of transmitting at 2 gigabits per second over a distance of up to 50 miles. *See* FDDI and MMF.

SMI *(INET)* Structure of Management Information. Component of the Internet Simple Network Management Protocol. Defines how information is formatted for the management information base. *See* Internet, SNMP and MIB.

smount *(ATT)* Routine used to determine if the user who is attempting to mount, or activate, a file system is a superuser. *See* mount and file system.

SMP 1. Symmetric multiprocessing. A multiprocessor design where all the processors have equal status versus the master and slave relationship of asymmetric multiprocessing. The processors are identical and share common memory; each runs its own copy of the operating system kernel. With SMP, processes are not tied to a specific processor and can be run by any available processor. *See* asymmetric multiprocessing and multiprocessor. 2. *(INET)* Simple Management Protocol. Improved version of the Simple Network Management Protocol. Provides better security and data transfer between agents and management stations. Also can run on AppleTalk, Internetwork Packet Exchange and Open Systems Interconnection along with the Transmission Control Protocol/Internet Protocol. *See* SNMP, AppleTalk, IPX, OSIRM and TCP/IP.

SMS Storage Management Services. Architecture and application program interface developed by Novell Inc. that provides the ability to jointly use various storage media, e.g. disks flash cards, optical disks or tapes. The use of standard interfaces allow other vendors to develop, track and manage data storage and the medium.

SMT Station management protocol. Standard for how Fiber Distribution Data Interface connections are made, then monitored for problems. Includes procedures for diagnostics, logging and configuration management. *See* FDDI.

SMTP *(INET)* Simple Mail Transfer Protocol. Internet electronic-mail protocol. Provides the standard methodology for sending electronic mail to users on a Transmission Control Protocol/Internet Protocol network. *See* TCP/IP, DARPA and e-mail.

smtpd *(INET)* Simple Mail Transfer Protocol daemon. Background program used on hosts connected to a network using the Transport Control Protocol/Internet Protocol. Listens for incoming electronic-mail messages. *See* SMTP and TCP/IP.

SNA Systems Network Architecture. Proprietary network software, developed by IBM Corp. in 1974. Defines the rules for transmitting and receiving data between mainframe computers and dumb terminals over a network. Developed as a result of the inability of 28 proprietary applications to communicate with one another. Another of the IBM terms entering UNIX with the growth of larger UNIX production systems and interface with IBM proprietary mainframes.

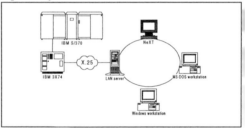

SNA provides the means for various types of networks to communicate with an IBM mainframe computer.

snafu Situation normal all fouled up. (Fouled is used here as a euphemism.) Originally a military Jargon term but used in the computer world to describe a computer, computer operation, software application or any situation that is bad and getting worse.

snailnet Commonly called sneakernet. *See* sneakernet.

sneakernet 1. Jargon term for a communications system in which data is passed by physical medium, e.g. paper being carried from point to point. 2. Use of a group of technicians who upgrade software on individual computers, one machine at a time. *See* mailnet.

SNF Server Normal Format. Also called Server Natural Font. X Window System font format, released with the Massachusetts Institute of Technology X11, Release 4 specification of the X Window System. SNF bitmap fonts are converted from Bitmap Distribution Fonts and compiled to run on a specific server. *See* X Window System, BDF and PCF.

SNMP *(INET)* Simple Network Management Protocol. Also called SNMPv2. Originally released in November 1987 by the Internet Engineering Task Force, defining reporting protocols and message formats, as a means of improving and easing the management of network protocols and devices on the Internet. The first public domain protocol capable of managing devices and networks manufactured by multiple vendors. It is a protocol layer above the Transmission Control Protocol/Internet Protocol, enabling the network manager to monitor and control the network and devices connected to it. *See* Internet, IETF, TCP/IP, NMS, agent, MIB and CMIP.

SNMP-2 *(INET)* Simple Network Management Protocol, Version 2.0. Updated version of SNMP that provides enhanced speed in data collection; ability for peer-to-peer communication between various network management domains and nodes; and improved security and expanded use beyond the Transmission Control Protocol/Internet Protocol because it can operate over different network protocols, e.g. Systems Network Architecture and Synchronous Data Link Control. *See* SNMP, TCP/IP, SNA and SDLC.

SNMP management station
Commonly called management station. *See* management station.

sno *(ATT)* Command used to start the interpreter in the SNOBOL programming language, which manipulates character strings in text editing to create indexes, bibliographies, etc. *See* SNOBOL.

SNOBOL String Oriented Symbolic Language. High-level programming language developed at the AT&T Co.'s Bell Laboratories. Used to manipulate character strings in text editing, creating indexes, bibliographies, etc. *See* Bell Laboratories.

SOA Start of Authority. Data file required for the operation of the Domain Name Service. Contains the starting point, name of the host and other information about the zone of authority, the list of computers in a network for which the name daemon manages connectivity. *See* DNS and zone.

social engineering Illegal activities by hackers in obtaining telephone card numbers. Looking or listening while a number is being dialed or given to an operator. *See* hacker and Operation Sun Devil.

socket 1. *(BSD)* System call used to create UNIX-domain sockets. *See* system call and UNIX-domain sockets. 2. Transmission Control Protocol term for the third level of the addressing scheme. A combination of the port address and the network address used to uniquely identify processes operating a specific node of a network. *See* TCP, node, process, port, active open socket and passive open socket.

socket library Implementation of interprocess communications within the Fourth Berkeley Software Distribution, Third Release. Allows a user to write an application that interfaces with the Transmission Control Protocol and Internet Protocol. *See* sockets, BSD and TCP/IP.

sockets Method of interprocess communications in the Fourth Berkeley Software Distribution, Third Release. A kernel data structure used to establish the two-way communications channel between processes which need to exchange data. Added to UNIX System V, Release 4. *See* BSD, SVR4.x and IPC.

soelim *(BSD)* Program used to delete .so (secondary input file call) commands from text files formatted by the nroff program. *See* nroff.

soft copy Copy of a document or program maintained on a magnetic medium, e.g. a diskette or hard disk drive. *See* hard copy.

soft interleave Process of leaving gaps between blocks of data when creating a file system. These gaps are used later to store information about files as the files are created. *See* file system.

soft limit Any system limit or quota that can be exceeded occasionally or for a short time without causing the computer system to crash. *See* quota and hard limit.

soft link To reference or address a file to another file by using a pathname instead of a specific inode address. Using an absolute pathname, or full address of a file starting at the root directory, soft links can cross file systems. Originally developed for the Berkeley Software Distribution operating system. *See* link, hard link, inode, absolute path and file system.

soft reset Method, controlled by software, of resetting a terminal or the connection between a terminal and host computer, e.g. repainting the screen in the vi editor by simultaneously pressing the Ctrl, Alt and Delete keys.

software Commonly called program. *See* program.

Software Business Practices Council Abbreviated and commonly known as SBPC. *See* SBPC.

Software Business Practices Council Vendor organization founded in 1990 to self-police business practices in the computer industry.

software development kit Commonly abbreviated and called SDK. *See* SDK.

software development life cycle Commonly abbreviated and called SDLC. *See* SDLC.

software house Company that specializes in the development and sale of software programs.

software interrupt Signal initiated by a software program that stops the normal flow of a running process, e.g. SIGKILL, which cannot be interrupted and in which the process is killed; SIGSTOP, which requests the process to stop; and SIGCHLD, which notifies a process that one of its children has changed status. *See* interrupt and hardware interrupt.

software library Commonly called library. *See* library.

software maintenance Defect correction, not product enhancement. *See* version.

Software Publishing Association Commonly abbreviated and called SPA. *See* SPA.

software rationalization Process of writing a software application once and then recompiling it so that it can be run on a wide variety of computers offered by different vendors. Avoids necessity of rewriting the application for each type of computer operating system or platform.

software security Use of specifically designed software programs to restrict access to a computer system by users. *See* restricted shell.

Software Standards Initiative Commonly abbreviated and called SSI. *See* SSI.

Solaris Sun Microsystems Inc.'s UNIX operating system based upon SunOS. A 32-bit operating system with symmetric multiprocessing and multithreading. Solaris 1.X is based upon the Berkeley Software Distribution; Solaris 1.0 on SunOS 4.1.2; and Solaris 2.X on System V, Release 4. *See* SunOS, SMP and multithread.

Solbourne window manager Abbreviated and commonly known as SWM. *See* SWM.

solidus Commonly called slash. *See* slash.

SONET Synchronous optical network. Optical network technology developed by Bell Communications Research to use fiber-optic cable to replace copper cabling. Can operate from approximately 52 megabits to almost 2.4 gigabits per second on a fiber-optic network. *See* BellCore.

sort 1. *(ATT/XEN)* Command used to arrange the contents of a text file into alphabetical or numerical sequence based on a specified field (column number). The following example lists files from largest to smallest:

    ls -l l sort -nr +3

The results can be either displayed on the screen or redirected to another device or file. The contents of the original file remain unaffected by the sort. 2. To put data in alphabetical or numerical sequence.

sortbib *(BSD)* **Sort bib**liography. Program used to sort a database of bibliographic information that has been inserted in a document using the refer set of commands. *See* refer, addbib, indxbib, lookbib and roffbib.

SOS **S**tandards and **O**pen **S**ystems. Organization formed in 1991 by the management information systems managers of 10 major corporations, including American Airlines, General Motors and Kodak. Like the User Alliance for Open Systems, SOS attempts to increase user input in the process of setting standards, and encourage vendors to abide by standards. *See* User Alliance for Open Systems.

source 1. Command used in the C shell to read a file one line at a time and then execute each line as if it were input on a command line. *See* dot and command line. 2. Jargon term for source code. *See* source code.

source code File, usually a text file, in which a programmer writes the instructions in high-, mid- or low-level programming language to execute a program. These instructions are then translated by a translator or compiler into terms the computer can understand and carry out. *See* compile.

Source Code Brand X/Open Co. Ltd.'s brand program for system software source code. *See* X/Open and brand program.

Source Code Control System Commonly abbreviated and called SCCS. *See* SCCS.

source-code translator Program that converts software written in one computer language to another language. *See* p2c and ptoc.

source compatibility Term referring to application software. Means software can be compiled without change on a given computer system.

source file 1. File containing an uncompiled version of a program. *See* source code. 2. File from which data is obtained to perform a function, e.g. file name1 is the source file in the following:

    CLP>cp file name1 file name2 ⏎

SPA **S**oftware **P**ublishers **A**ssociation. Based in Washington, D.C., represents software vendors. Received extensive publicity in late 1990 and early 1991 when, in conjunction with U.S. Marshals, it raided several corporations to determine if they were using legally licensed software.

spacebar Bar on a computer keyboard found immediately below the alphabetic keys. Used to insert blank space.

spacegripe *(OTH)* Shell script used by system administrators to check excessive use of a disk by users.

Space Travel One of the elements that led to the creation of the UNIX operating system. Program, written in FORTRAN by Ken Thompson, to simulate the movement of planets. When the program did not function well and was too expensive to run on a General Comprehensive Operating System computer, Thompson teamed with Dennis Ritchie to rewrite it on a Digital Equipment Corp. PDP-7 computer. The experience in rewriting Space

Travel helped lay the foundation for UNIX. *See* UNIX, Thompson, Ken, Ritchie, Dennis M. and GCOS.

SPAG **S**tandards **P**romotion and **A**pplication **G**roup. Consortium of international vendors similar to the Corporation for Open Systems International. Formed to promote connectivity and interoperability of computer and communications hardware by using Open Systems Interconnection protocols and standards. Headquarters are in Brussels, Belgium. *See* PSI, OSI and COS.

SPARC **S**calable **P**rocessor **Arc**chitecture. 32-bit reduced instruction set computing hardware and operating system developed by Sun Microsystems Inc. for use in high-end desktop workstations. *See* RISC.

SPARCalike Jargon term, believed to have originated in the SunExpert magazine, for clones of Sun Microsystems Inc.'s computers using Scalable Processor Architecture.

SPARC Compliance Definition
SPARC International Inc.'s validation suite. Used to determine if a product conforms to binary compatibility requirements of the Scalable Processor Architecture. *See* SPARC and SPARC International.

SPARC International Nonprofit organization consisting of more than 200 members that promotes the use and standardization of Scalable Processor Architecture (SPARC). To comply with SPARC, a product must pass a SPARC validation suite provided by SPARC International Inc. *See* SPARC and SPARC Compliance Definition.

SPAU *(ATT)* **S**ystem **P**erformance **A**nalysis **U**tilities. Collection of programs in UNIX System V used by a system administrator to identify potential performance problems. *See* SVR4.x, system tuning and tunefs.

spawn To create a process. *See* process, fork and exec.

SPEC **S**ystems **P**erformance **E**valuation **C**ooperative. A nonprofit organization formed in 1988 and made up of more than 20 workstation manufactures that develops industry standard benchmark tools. Among the members are AT&T Co., Digital Equipment Corp., IBM Corp., NCR Corp. and Sun Microsystems Inc. Located in Fairfax, Virginia. *See* SPEC benchmark, SPECmark, benchmark and workstation.

Spec 1170 **Spec**ification **1170**. Also called 1170 or 1170 specification. Part of the Common Open Software Environment (COSE) effort to provide a standard graphical user interface for desktop UNIX. An operating system application programming interface specification that consists of 1,170 interfaces, which provide sufficient commonality between operating systems to ensure almost total source-code compatibility between applications. Used by X/Open Co. Ltd. to determine if a product can be branded as a UNIX product. The specification was started in September 1993 by 75 vendors including the founders of COSE, Hewlett-Packard Co., IBM Corp., The Santa Cruz Operation Inc., SunSoft Inc., Univel Inc. and UNIX Systems Laboratories. Univel and UNIX Systems Laboratories are now the UNIX Systems Group. *See* COSE, API, GUI and CDE.

SPEC benchmark **S**ystems **P**erformance **E**valuation **C**ooperative **benchmark**. Suite of standard tests consisting of 10 tests to measure performance of a workstation with certain types of application software. Six of these test floating-point processor performance and four test integer performance to measure the performance of the workstation's central processing unit. *See* SPEC, SPECmark, benchmark and workstation.

SPECfp92 **SPEC** **f**loating-**p**oint **92**. Systems Performance Evaluation Cooperative floating-point benchmark test, released in 1992. SPECfp92 combined with SPECint92 replaces the SPEC benchmark, measuring the number of tasks a system can do in a period of time. The benchmark contains 12 FORTRAN floating-point and 2 C language floating-point tests. *See* SPEC, SPECmark, SPECrate_fp92, SPECrate_int92 and SPECint92.

SPECFS *(ATT)* Feature with UNIX System V, Release 4, that provides for special files, file renaming function and improved file and recording locking. A layer of the operating system that hides device semantics from the user. Implements open, close, read, write and ioctl operating system calls and translates them into the appropriate device driver calls. *See* SVR4.x, file locking and record locking.

special character Character defined either for a specific use in application software or for a special application in an operating system, e.g. the question mark which represents a wildcard for a single character. *See* metacharacter.

special file File which has a specific meaning to an operating system. Normally contains either the kernel address for programs; block or character files, called device drivers; or fifo files used in internal communications. *See* kernel, device driver, fifo, block special files and character special files.

special-interest group Commonly abbreviated and called SIG. *See* SIG.

special key Keyboard key with a specific purpose, e.g. the ESC key which can be used to send an interrupt which will stop a process.

special-purpose operating system Operating system specifically designed to run a particular type of application, e.g. the version of UNIX that AT&T uses on its communication switches, the operating system used by the AirLine reservation system and the system used by ATM machines. *See* RTOS.

Special Technical Group Commonly abbreviated and called STG. *See* STG.

specific markup Process of electronically coding and embedding comments or changes in a document. *See* markup and SGML.

SPECint92 SPEC integer 92. Systems Performance Evaluation Cooperative integer performance benchmark test, released in 1992. SPECint92 combined with SPECfp92 replaces the SPEC benchmark, measuring the number of tasks a system can do in a period of time. The benchmark contains six C language program integer tests. *See* SPEC, SPECmark, SPECrate_fp92, SPECrate_int92 and SPECfp92.

SPECmark Also called SPECmark89. Performance measurement of the Systems Performance Evaluation Cooperative workstation benchmark. The geometric mean of all the scores of the 10 tests that measure integer, floating point, cache performance and throughput. Replaced by the SPECfp92 and SPECint92 benchmarks in 1992. *See* SPEC, SPECfp92, SPECint92, SPEC benchmark, workstation and benchmark.

SPECmark89 Commonly abbreviated and called SPECmark. *See* SPECmark.

SPECrate Systems Performance Evaluation Cooperative benchmark developed to run multiple copies of the integer and floating point tests simultaneously. Determines how much work can be accomplished over a specified period of time. Uses the same SPECrate_fp92 and SPECrate_int92 as the measurement of output capacity. *See* SPEC, SPECfp92 and SPECint92.

SPECrate_fp92 SPEC rate floating process 92. Systems Performance Evaluation Cooperative output capacity measurement used with the SPECfp92 benchmark to determine the maximum throughput of a computer for any function. Can be used for both uni- and multiprocessors. *See* SPEC, SPEC benchmark, SPECmark, SPECrate_fp92, SPECint92 and SPECfp92.

SPECrate_int92 SPEC rate integer 92. Systems Performance Evaluation Cooperative output capacity measurement used with the SPECint92 benchmark to determine the maximum throughput of a computer for any function. Can be used for both uni- and multiprocessors. *See* SPEC, SPECmark, SPECint92 and SPECfp92.

spell UNIX command used to find spelling errors in a file. Also can be used to verify tense, pluralism, prefix and other grammatical points. Users can establish and maintain their own spell dictionaries. The system administrator can add and delete words from the master system spell dictionary. *See* spellin, hashcheck and hashmake.

spellhist *(ATT)* **Spell hist**ory. File used to maintain a log of misspelled words identified by the spell command. Used by the system administrator to identify additions that should be made to the system dictionary. *See* spell.

spellin Command used to create a list of words to be added to the spell dictionary from a converted list provided by the hashmake command. *See* spell, hashcheck and hashmake.

Spell Utilities Set of programs included in UNIX System V, Release 4, to check the spelling in documents. *See* SVR4.x and spell.

spellwwb Spell Writer's Workbench. Part of the Writer's Workbench set of text processing tools. Used to check for spelling errors. *See* WWB.

spike Excess voltage coming from the power system. A fluctuation of less than 300 volts. *See* surge.

spin loop State in which a software instruction causes the central processing unit to continue to process the same function over and over. *See* endless loop.

splat Jargon term for asterisk. *See* asterisk.

spline *(ATT/XEN)* Command used to create graphs from data points contained in an input file.

split *(ATT/XEN)* Command used to break a large file into smaller files of equal size. Defaults to 1,000 lines per file if the user does not indicate otherwise. *See* csplit.

splitinf Split infinitive. Part of the Writer's Workbench set of text processing tools. Used to locate split infinitives. *See* WWB.

split screen Terminal screen that can be divided into two or more separate sections to display either several different applications or several copies of a file in a single application, e.g. a word processing program in one, a spreadsheet program in a second and a desktop publishing program in a third, or three different parts of the same file. Under graphical user interfaces, e.g. the X Window System, each section is called a window. Different applications can be run in each window and information can be transferred among applications, from one window to another. *See* window.

spoof Program designed by someone who wants to try to gain passwords to a system. Tricks users into providing information. Similar to a Trojan horse. *See* Trojan horse.

spoofing Attempting to gain or gaining access to a system by gaining a user's account name and password.

spool Simultaneous peripherals operation on line. Software designed to manage the use and sharing of external devices, e.g. printers. Information is temporarily stored until the device it needs is available.

/spool System directory used for queuing, or spooling, files that are to be processed later.

spool area Directory containing output files waiting for a device, e.g. a printer or fax modem, to become available. *See* spool.

spooler Daemon which acts like a traffic cop, controlling the input and output of printing jobs to line printers. Frees the computer to perform other functions while files are being printed.

spooling In batch processing, the temporary storage of input or output data until a central processing unit is ready to run a batch job. *See* batch.

spooling directory Temporary storage area for files which are waiting to be processed, e.g. /usr/spool/UUCP and /usr/spool/mail. *See* spooling.

spray *(ATT)* **Spray** packets. Program used first to send a group of packets of data to a host computer running the Remote Procedure Call, and then to determine how many were received and how quickly they were transferred. *See* RPC and sprayd.

sprayd *(ATT)* **Spray** **d**aemon. Pronounced *SPRAY-DEE*. Background program used to record the number of packets of data sent by the spray program. *See* spray and daemon.

SPRAY-DEE Pronunciation of sprayd, the abbreviation for spray daemon. *See* sprayd.

spreadsheet Software that resembles an accounting ledger. Used to perform a wide variety of mathematical computations.

SPUT Scientific-Production Union Tsentroprogrammsystem. Soviet organization responsible for developing and porting UNIX operating system look-alikes.

SPX Sequenced Pocket Exchange. Also called Session Packet Exchange. Novell Inc. protocol used with the Internetwork Packet Exchange to guarantee reliable transmission of data between a sender, e.g. client, and receiver, e.g. NetWare server. Confirms the receipt of a packet delivery. *See* IPX.

SQE Signal quality error. Institute of Electrical and Electronic Engineers term for a collision. *See* collision.

SQL Structured Query Language. Developed by IBM Corp. SQL is the de facto industry standard of fourth-generation programming languages used for addressing, generating, obtaining, sending or querying data from a relational database. *See* 4GL and RDBMS.

square brackets *[ ]* Metacharacters used in wild card matching in file searches, file manipulations, etc. In a search, a computer looks for only those characters enclosed in square brackets, e.g. a command followed by [xyz]4 will act only on files which start with an x, y or z followed by the number 4. *See* metacharacter, character-class and regular expression.

SRAM Static random access memory. Pronounced *ESS-RAM*. Random, or temporary, computer memory similar to dynamic random access memory (DRAM). Extends read-only memory by using main memory that can be read or written to by the central processing unit or other computer hardware devices. SRAM is faster but holds less information than DRAM. Unlike DRAM, it does not have to be constantly updated since the contents do not change unless it is written to. Like DRAM, all information stored in SRAM is lost when the computer is turned off. *See* CPU and DRAM.

srchtxt *(ATT)* **Search** **text**. Command used with the message database (a database of standard error messages contained in the operating system) to search for a string of text.

SRI *(INET)* Commonly called SRI International. *See* SRI International.

SRI International *(INET)* Stanford Research Institute **International**. Not-for-profit organization located in Menlo Park, California, that operated the Internet Network Information Center until October 1991. *See* Internet and NIC.

SRI-NIC *(INET)* Jargon term for the Internet Network Information Center, run by SRI International until the center's operation was assumed in October 1991 by GSI of Chantilly, Virginia. *See* NIC.

SS Programmer's Guide: System Services and Applications Packaging Tools. UNIX System V, Release 4 documentation for the development of application software. Provides information on the tools available for development and installation. *See* SVR4.x and application software.

SS7 Signal System 7. Packet switch standard jointly developed by the American National Standards Institute and International Telecommunication Union Telecommunication Standardization Sector, formerly known as the *Consultative Committee on International Telegraphy and Telephony.* Allows Integrated Services Digital Network traffic to be transmitted separately from normal traffic on a network. *See* ISDN and ITU-T.

SSI Software Standards Initiative. Japanese international standards organization that supports development of international standards which cross the entire spectrum of system software.

st Synchronous terminal. Set of commands used to operate synchronous terminals. *See* synchronous communication, stlogin and stgetty.

stack Temporary directory in which files are stored sequentially in a disk drive. Data is not given an address in the stack, but withdrawn from the top of the stack as last-in-first-out and from the bottom of the stack as first-in-first-out. Stack memory is allocated on entry into a function and freed on exit. *See* LIFO, FIFO, pop and push.

/stand Root directory used to store standalone programs for starting, or booting, the system. *See* standalone program and /unix.

standalone device driver Program that enables a software application to connect with and send information to a peripheral device, e.g. a printer. Used when a computer system cannot interrupt processes, manage memory requirements or handle virtual memory mapping. *See* interrupt, memory management, virtual memory management and standalone.

standalone I/O library Collection of pre-written programs used to develop standalone programs. *See* library and standalone program.

standalone program Any program on a computer which can perform independently of other programs, e.g. hardware diagnostics, new system installation code and the bootstrap.

standard Definition of, or common set of rules for, an interface, operating system, communications protocol or other software or hardware component, e.g. Portable Operating System Interface for Computer Environments (POSIX). A common practice may be accepted as a standard by a business or industry, while an international standard may require formal approval by a recognized standards organization, e.g. Institute of Electrical and Electronic Engineers. Also, there are two levels of standards: forma, or de jure; and informal, or de facto. Products that adhere to these guidelines usually are compatible with one another, even if they are manufactured by different vendors, e.g. UNIX System V. *See* POSIX, IEEE, ANSI, ISO/OSI, base standard, profile, de jure and de facto.

standard error Default location to which UNIX commands send error messages. The default is the input terminal. Users can redirect error messages to another device or to a file.

standard extension *(POS)* Portable Operating System Interface for Computer Environments (POSIX) term meaning an extension, or program in POSIX, conforms to POSIX standards. *See* POSIX.

Standard Format Part Commonly abbreviated and called SFP. *See* SFP.

Standard Generalized Markup Language Commonly abbreviated and called SGML. *See* SGML.

standard in Jargon term for standard input. *See* standard input.

standard input 1. Also called standard in. Default location or device from which the computer system accepts commands from a user. Normally it is the terminal at which the user is working, but can be a file or command. 2. Default source of data input required to run and complete a process.

standard I/O Abbreviation for standard input/output. *See* standard input and standard output.

standard out Jargon term for standard output. *See* standard output.

standard output 1. Also called standard out. Default location or device to which the system sends the results of a command. Normally it is the controlling terminal at which the user is working unless it is redirected to another device. *See* redirect. 2. Euphemism for "let the system handle it".

Standards and Open Systems Abbreviated and commonly known as SOS. *See* SOS.

Standards Promotion and Application Group Commonly abbreviated and called SPAG. *See* SPAG.

Stanford Research Institute International *(INET)* Abbreviated and commonly known as SRI International. *See* SRI International.

star Commonly called asterisk. *See* asterisk.

StarLAN Local area network developed by AT&T Co. which uses twisted pair wiring. Capable of transmitting data at up to 1 million bytes per second. *See* LAN and byte.

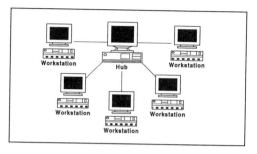

In a StarLAN system, all nodes are directly connected to a hub or server.

start 1. Command in the Network File System sysadm menu, Initial Networking File System Setup, that starts NFS operations. Also used for the same purpose in the Network File System Control menu. *See* NFS and sysadm. 2. Signal sent to the kernel that restarts a suspended operation. *See* resume.

start bit Bit of data at the beginning of a character transmission which notifies the receiving device that the transmission is starting. *See* bit and stop bit.

starter *(ATT)* On-line information to help new users understand and learn how to use the UNIX operating system. *See* learn.

Start of Authority Commonly abbreviated and called SOA. *See* SOA.

start routine Program, or device driver, which starts a device and sends output to the device.

startup 1. Account system shell script used to turn on system accounting. *See* shell script. 2. Commonly called boot. *See* boot.

stat 1. *(ATT)* **Stat**istics. Set of commands used to collect and move statistics in creating computer graphics. 2. *(ATT)* **Stat**us. System call used to determine file attributes, including the type of file, user identifier of the owner and last time the file was read. *See* system call and file attributes.

statd *(ATT)* **Status daemon.** Network Status Monitor running on all hosts in a Network File System network. Used by the Network Lock Monitor to determine the operational status of other hosts on a network. Works with the lock daemon on each host to monitor network connections and provide a log of activity that can be used to recover files if there is a failure. *See* Network Lock Manager, NFS and daemon.

state **1.** Also called system state, run level or run state. Level of access to a computer system that is granted to users. Two basic states are single user, which limits access only to the superuser; and multi-user, which provides access to multiple users. Single user and multi-user are broken into a further 10 states, which can be set by the system administrator to define the extent of use and activity of a computer. *See* shutdown state, administrative state, single-user state, multi-user state, remote file sharing state, user-defined state, firmware state, stop and reboot, pseudo state and reexamine inittab state. **2.** Condition, or priority level, of a process. *See* background process, foreground process and suspend.

state 0 Commonly called shutdown state. *See* shutdown state.

state 1 Commonly called administrative state. *See* administrative state.

state 2 Commonly called multi-user state. *See* multi-user state.

state 3 Commonly called remote file sharing state. *See* remote file sharing state.

state 4 Commonly called user-defined state. *See* user-defined state.

state 5 Commonly called firmware state. *See* firmware state.

state 6 Commonly called stop and reboot state. *See* stop and reboot state.

state a, b and/or c Commonly called pseudo state. *See* pseudo state.

stateful service Computer network on which the server monitors all resources being used by clients as well as which clients are using the resources, e.g. the Remote File Sharing system. *See* RFS, client, server and stateless service.

stateless file system Commonly called stateless service. *See* stateless service.

stateless service. Also called stateless file system. Computer network on which the server does not monitor all resources being used by clients, e.g. the Network File System. *See* NFS, client, server and stateful service.

state Q Commonly called reexamine inittab state. *See* reexamine inittab state.

state s Commonly called single-user state. *See* single-user state.

static allocation Parallel processing term for pre-allocation of processor resources to a program task. Until that task is completed, processors cannot be allocated to any other process. *See* parallel processing, task and dynamic allocation.

static binding Object Management Group term for the process of combining the program that responds to a request and the data required to respond to a request, before the request is made. *See* OMG, request, binding and dynamic binding.

static display Text formatting term for displaying portions of text exactly as they were input. When all the text cannot fit on the current page, the remainder is moved to the next page. *See* display and floating display.

static random access memory Abbreviated and commonly known as SRAM. *See* SRAM.

station management Commonly abbreviated and called SMT. *See* SMT.

station management protocol
Commonly abbreviated and called SMT. *See* SMT.

status *(ATT)* Command in the UNIX System V, Release 4 restore service management menu. Used to remove requests in the restore queue for restoring files from backup media, cancel a restore job or get the status on restore jobs in a queue. Similar to the rsoper, rsstatus and ursstatus commands. *See* rsoper.

status line In the vi editor program, the bottom line of a terminal screen. Commands in the line editing mode are entered on the status line. Messages from vi or the system on the status of commands also are displayed here, e.g. if a file is not found in a search, the program will respond with the message, "No such file or directory". *See* vi and showmode the actual message with directory in it.

status monitor Program that provides system administration information about processes currently being executed.

stderr Standard error. Also called diagnostic output. Standard operating system error messages sent in response to an error. If the message is sent to a program, its file descriptor is 2; if it is sent to a screen, it is shown as a standard message, e.g. "File not found". *See* standard error, file descriptor, stdout and stdin.

stdin Standard input. Logical path by which a command accepts input; default is a keyboard. When stdin becomes a file, it is identified with either the number 0 as a file descriptor or stdin. *See* standard input, file descriptor, stdout and stderr.

stdio Standard input/output. Set of standard input/output library routines used to manage user input and output data in temporarily memory buffers. *See* library routines.

stdout Standard output. Logical path to which command output is sent; default is the user's input terminal screen. When stdout becomes a file, it is identified with either the number 1 as a file descriptor 1 or stdout. *See* standard output, file descriptor, stdin and stderr.

stereolithography Abbreviated and also known as SL. *See* SL.

STG Special Technical Group. Organizations formed by the USENIX Association to advance technical and professional interests of its members. The first STG formed was the System Administrators' Guild to promote system administration as a profession. *See* USENIX Association, The, SAGE and LTG.

stgetty *(ATT)* Synchronous terminal get a tty. UNIX user login manager for synchronous terminals. Program that monitors ports on synchronous terminals for attempts by users to log in. *See* getty, synchronous communication and synchronous terminal.

STICI Self-Teaching and Interpretive Communicating Interfaces. Pronounced *STICKY*. Application software interface intended to replace graphical user interfaces. Uses artificial intelligence to understand how a user uses a software package and tailors the software to the user.

STICKY Pronunciation of STICI, the acronym for Self-Teaching and Interpretive Communicating Interface. *See* STICI.

sticky bit Permission setting established on a file indicating the text is to be kept, or stuck, in memory and not moved into a swap area when it is not being use. *See* swapping and sticky text.

sticky file Commonly called sticky text. *See* sticky text.

sticky keys Function in the Massachusetts Institute of Technology X 11, Release 6 specification for the X Window System for physically disadvantaged users who are unable to depress two keys at the same time, e.g. the control key and d key to send an interrupt signal. *See* X Window System and X11R6.

sticky text Text identified by a sticky bit, or permission setting, which is kept in memory and not moved into a swap area when it is not being used. Usually, applications are developed with sticky text to prevent swapping. Used to reduce system overhead. Generally rendered obsolete by modern swapping algorithms. *See* sticky bit, paging and swapping.

stime *(ATT)* Set **time**. System call used to set the time of day on a computer's internal clock. *See* system call and time.

stlogin *(ATT)* Synchronous terminal **login**. Like the login in a program, allows users to access the system, but is used for synchronous terminals, which can simultaneous send and receive data. *See* login, synchronous communication and synchronous terminal.

STM-n Synchronous Transport **M**odule level **n**umber. Measurement of transmission rates developed by the International Telecommunication Union Telecommunication Standardization Sector, formerly known as the *Consultative Committee on International Telegraphy and Telephony.* STM-n levels are:

STM level	Transmission speed
STM-1	155.52 megabits per second
STM-4	622.08 Mbps
STM-8	1,244.16 Mbps
STM-16	2,488.32 Mbps.

The United States has two transmission-level measurements, one for non-optical signals known as *Synchronous Transport Signal*, and the other for signals which are converted to optical signals, known as *Optical Carrier level number. See* ITU-T, STS-n and OC-n.

Stoned Computer virus that corrupts disk drives and prevents the creation of new system disks. Leaves a flashing message, "Legalize Marijuana", on the screen of each computer it attacks. *See* virus.

stop 1. *(ATT)* Command used to suspend a running program. The stopped program can either be restarted or killed. *See* resume, fg and bg. 2. Signal sent to the kernel that suspends terminal output. 3.

Command in the Network File System sysadm menu, the Network File System Control, used to terminate NFS operations. *See* NFS and sysadm.

stop and reboot state Also called state 6. Used to stop the operating system, e.g. for maintenance purposes, and reboot it to a state predefined in the inittab file. *See* state.

stop bit Bit of data at the end of a character transmission which notifies the receiving device that the transmission is ending. *See* bit and start bit.

storage block Partition of a file system used to hold the contents of a file. *See* block and file system.

storage capacity Measurement of the amount of data, in megabytes, gigabytes or terabytes, which can be stored on a mass storage device, e.g. a diskette or hard drive. *See* diskette and hard drive.

storage fragmentation Commonly called memory fragmentation. *See* memory fragmentation.

Storage Management System Commonly abbreviated and called SMS. *See* SMS.

Storage Module Device Commonly abbreviated and called SMD. *See* SMD.

store and forward Process of providing temporary storage for a message en route from its originating host to its destination host. Used when the destination host is already busy or the network is down.

stored procedure Program stored along with a database that enables the database to be used by a client or remote application which accesses, uses or modifies information in the database. *See* trigger.

stored program Program which is resident in the memory of a computer and is not erased when the computer is turned off. *See* external program.

STP Shielded twisted pair. Shielded coaxial cable through which data can be transmitted between 4 and 16 megabits per second. A metallic foil shielding over the twisted pair cable protects it from electromagnetic interference. *See* UTP.

str Abbreviation in the awk language for string. *See* awk and string.

strace *(ATT)* STREAMS **trace**. Command used to print trace messages from STREAMS, the interprocess communications or input/output mechanism introduced in UNIX System V, Release 3. *See* STREAMS.

strap Commonly called hardwired. *See* hardwired.

strapping Changing the functionality of a card or hardware device through physical modifications, e.g. setting dip switches to modify the baud rate and parity on a modem. *See* dip switches.

stratum Network Time Protocol term for the hierarchical relationship among computers based upon the distance of any computer on a network that has a master clock from the other computers that do not have a master clock. *See* NTP, peer, server and client.

strcf *(ATT)* STREAMS configuration. File in the /etc system directory which contains the script initiated by the slink command to configure STREAMS, the interprocess communications mechanism released in UNIX System V, Release 3. for use with the Transmission Control Protocol and Internet Protocol. *See* STREAMS, /etc and TCP/IP.

strclean *(ATT)* STREAMS **clean**. Command used to clean the error log directory of STREAMS, the interprocess communications or input/output mechanism released in UNIX System V, Release 3. *See* STREAMS.

stream cipher Method of encrypting data a single byte at a time.

stream I/O system Commonly abbreviated and called STREAMS. *See* STREAMS.

stream-oriented Describes data that flows at a constant, known rate, with user access and use being predictable. *See* bursty.

STREAMS *(ATT)* Interprocess communications or input/output mechanism release in UNIX System V, Release 3, that provides a dynamic buffer allocation. Provides a layered approach for two or more processes to pass data to each other. *See* IPC and SVR4.x.

strerr *(ATT)* STREAMS **error**. Command used to log error messages related to STREAMS interprocess communications. *See* STREAMS.

strictly conforming POSIX application *(POS)* Any application program that strictly adheres to the Portable Operating System Interface for Computer Environments (POSIX). *See* POSIX.

strictly conforming POSIX shell application *(POS)* Any shell that strictly adheres to the Portable Operating System Interface for Computer Environments (POSIX) standards, with no extensions, or enhancements, allowed. *See* extension, shell and POSIX.

string 1. Distinguishable set of characters, e.g. letters, numbers or special characters. 2. C language library routine used to perform search and data manipulation functions based upon specific set of characters. *See* library routines.

string options Options in an editor program that require a string variable, or argument, to be executed. *See* string, numeric options and toggle options.

String Oriented Symbolic Language Abbreviated and commonly known as SNOBOL. *See* SNOBOL.

strings 1. Command used to locate and print specific character strings in an object or binary file. 2. Command used to display on a screen or redirect to an alternative device or file the contents of an object file in a format that can be read by a user. *See* object.

string search Command built into line editor programs which allows a user to search for a specific set of characters within a document. Initiated while a text file is being edited.

string test Method of incrementally testing software modules that reduces the amount of programming code that has to be checked and retested. When a module is completed, it is independently tested and certified; then parts of it are tested with previously tested modules using specifically developed test data. If a failure occurs, the most recently completed module is removed and the previously certified modules are tested with the test data prepared for the module that failed. If a failure occurs in one of the certified modules, that module is fixed and retested. If there is no failure, the most recently completed module is checked, fixed and retested.

string variable Set of American Standard Code for Information Interchange characters used in a program or variable as an argument. *See* ASCII and shell.

strip *(ATT/XEN)* Command used to remove a symbol table, debugging and relocation bits, used during either the writing or debugging of software, from an object module so that the module can be used. *See* object file.

stripe pitch Also called line pitch. Measurement, in millimeters, of the distance between phosphor stripes of the same color on the screen of a vacuum tube. *See* dot pitch.

striping Disk and data management term for spreading data across several disks, transferring the same data to each disk at the same time. *See* block striping, byte striping and RAID.

STRM Programmer's Guide: **Streams.** UNIX System V, Release 4 documentation on the use of STREAMS, the interprocess communications or input/output mechanism released in UNIX System V, Release 3. *See* SVR4.x and STREAMS.

struct Program used to convert ordinary FORTRAN files into structured FORTRAN source programs. *See* FORTRAN.

structured programming Combined macro and micro approach to software programming in which major tasks are identified and then broken down into smaller tasks. These smaller tasks can be, and are. broken down into even smaller tasks until the smallest possible programming tasks are reached. Allows more people to work on one job, making the task easier.

Structured Query Language Commonly abbreviated and called SQL. *See* SQL.

structure of management information *(INET)* Commonly abbreviated and called SMI. *See* SMI.

STS-n NEW Synchronous Transport Signal level number. United States measurement of transmission rates of non-optical signal data. STS-n levels are:

STS level	Tranmission rate
STS-1	51.84 megabits per second
STS-3	155.52 Mbps
STS-12	622.08 Mbps
STS-24	1,244.16 Mbps
STS-48	2,488.32 Mbps

Another United States level for optical signals is known as *Optical Carrier level.* Synchronous Transmission Module is an equivalent transmission level developed by the International Telecommunication Union Telecommunication Standardization Sector, formerly known as the *Consultative Committee on International Telegraphy and Telephony. See* OC-n, STM-n and ITU-T.

stty Set teletype. Command used to either display or set selected terminal characteristics, e.g. baud and parity, or terminal functions, e.g. defining the erase or kill keys. *See* baud, parity, erase and kill.

sttydefs *(ATT)* Set teletype **def**initions. UNIX System V, Release 4 command used by system administrators to maintain settings for the communications ports in the ttydefs file. *See* ttydefs.

style   Part of the Writer's Workbench set of text processing tools. Used to check grammar and sentence structure in text files. Identifies poor grammar or syntax by locating unnecessary words, improper sentence structure and wordy or trite phrases. *See* WWB.

style guide   Specification for an interface between a graphical user interface and an application. *See* GUI.

su   Set **u**ser identity. Also called switch user. Command used by a user who is logged in to a system and wants to log in again, without first logging out, under another person's user identifier. To do so, the user must have the password for the second userid. On many systems the su command is turned off as a security precaution. Normally used for accessing the root account, but many organizations do not permit users who have root access to have the root password. *See* userid.

subareas   Collective term used in Digital Audio Tape technology for the Automatic Track Following and subcode area. *See* DAT, ATF and subcode area.

subcode area   Area on Digital Audio Tape where information is recorded concerning the address of data records, file markers and save set markers. *See* DAT and file marker.

subdirectory   Directory within a directory, which a user may allocate for either files or other directories, or subdirectories. *See* directory.

subj   **1.** *(ATT)* **Subj**ect. Command used to create a list of subjects found in a document. **2.** Header line for an electronic-mail message that gives a short descriptive name for the contents of the message. *See* e-mail.

submission   Term for moving the electronic-mail header (addressing elements) and body (text) of an e-mail message from the user agent to the message transfer

agent in the X.400 standard. Developed by the International Telecommunication Union Telecommunication Standardization Sector, formerly known as the *Consultative Committee on International Telegraphy and Telephony. See* ITU-T, X.400, UA, MTA, relay and delivery.

subnet   Jargon term for subnetwork. *See* subnetwork.

subnet mask   Commonly called network mask. *See* network mask.

subnetwork   Network which is part of another larger network. *See* domain.

subnotebook computer   Also   called companion PC. Small computer system weighing 3 to 4 pounds, measuring approximately 9 inches by 7 inches by 1 inch, with a 25 megahertz 386 central processing unit, 2 megabytes of memory, and at least 60 megabytes of storage on an internal hard drive and either an internal or external floppy drive. *See* notebook computer.

subshell   Control process which is started by another shell. Translates user commands so they can be executed by the kernel and system utilities, e.g. a user running the C shell must spawn a Bourne shell if they want to start a Bourne script. *See* shell.

substitute   To replace one or more characters with another character or set of characters.

subsystem   Component of a major system.

suck   Jargon term for retrieving a file or data from one computer and loading it onto another computer, e.g. transferring, or sucking down, a binary file from a network.

sudo   *(OTH)* Set **u**ser and **do**. Program that allows a user to execute selected commands like a superuser, who may access and modify the system's root files. The user must have permission from the system administrator to do this, but is not given access to the root login. Allows users to perform functions assigned to them as part of their job or to perform mundane tasks, e.g. resetting user passwords, to help lighten the system administrator's workload. *See* root and su.

SUID Set user identifier. Operating system program used to set permissions. Part of the UNIX security system that establishes a user's level of access to a file or directory at the time it is created. Indicates who can have access to the file or directory. *See* UID, GID, real UID, EUID, real GID and EGID.

suidck *(OTH)* Set user identifier check. Shell script used to compare current files with a set user identifier to those maintained in a database containing set user identifier files. *See* shell script and SUID.

SUID trap Set user identifier trap. Program used by a hacker that looks for and exploits mistakes in programs that establish user access to files and directories. Obtains the same permissions as the owner of the file or program, enabling the hacker to enter the system.

Suite X First commercial benchmark suite for X Window System, developed by AIM Technology to test the performance of X Window System terminals. *See* benchmark and X Window System.

sulog Jargon term for /usr/adm/sulog. *See* /usr/adm/sulog.

sulogck *(OTH)* sulog check. Program used by system or security administrators to screen the /usr/adm/sulog for users trying to guess the root password. *See* /usr/adm/sulog.

sum *(ATT/XEN)* Command used to verify or determine the size of a file by counting the blocks and computing the checksums. *See* block and checksum.

sumount *(ATT)* Routine called by the umount system call to unmount, or deactivate, a file system. *See* umount and file system.

SunOS Sun Operating System. Sun Microsystems Inc.'s UNIX operating system, which is an implementation of the Berkeley Software Distribution. *See* BSD.

super block Commonly spelled superblock. *See* superblock.

superblock Also spelled super block. Second region of storage space in a file system that is always retained in main memory. Contains information required to maintain a file system. This information defines the location of data in a file system, and includes fixed information, e.g. the file system size, and changing information, e.g. the location of free blocks. *See* file system and free blocks.

supercomputer Extremely large capacity computer capable of high-speed processing and extensive computations, e.g. the Cray. Processing speed is measured in millions of instructions per second. As computers become faster, the processing speed of those rated as supercomputers increases. A few years ago supercomputers were defined as those capable of doing complicated graphics, but today the advanced graphics in the film *Jurassic Park* were done on a UNIX system. Used in performing extensive scientific research and calculations by such institutions as the Lawrence Livermore National Laboratories. *See* mips.

Supercomputer

super computer nerd Same as a computer nerd except capable of speaking in assembly language. *See* assembly language and computer nerd.

super data highway Commonly called electronic highway. *See* electronic highway.

super desktop document processor Software program which combines the graphical capabilities of a desktop publisher and the text manipulation abilities of a word processor. *See* desktop publishing and word processor.

super-floppy disk
Three-and-a-half-inch floppy diskette capable of storing between 10 and 50 megabytes of data.

superparent Process that starts the majority of new, or child, processes, e.g. init for the system or login for a user. *See* process group, child process, init and login.

superpipelining Method of enhancing the performance of computers by overlapping the execution of multiple instructions. Superpipelining is a technique used in the Reduced Instruction Set Computing architecture in which many computer instructions are fetched, decoded and executed in parallel and not necessarily in the order expected by a programmer. Thus, effective use of pipelines, and especially superpipelines, requires tremendous knowledge of the architecture by the compiler. *See* pipeline, CPU, CPI, RISC and superscalar.

superscalar Method of enhancing the performance of computers by using one or more scalar (integer and/or floating point coprocessors) to perform arithmetic operations in parallel to other central processing unit (CPU) operations. Permits a CPU to run multiple instructions simultaneously, speeding operations. *See* CPU, pipeline and superpipelining.

superserver UNIX-based microcomputer used as a file server. Can range in size from personal computers to tower-sized microcomputers with up to 96 megabytes of main memory and up to 16 gigabytes of disk storage. *See* microcomputer.

superuser User who has access to an entire computer system and, unlike a regular user, is not restricted by permissions. Usually, the system administrator but can be anyone who has a userid of 0 (root permission) or logs in as root. *See* system administrator and root.

super VAR Commonly called master VAR. *See* master VAR.

super VGA **Super** **v**ideo **g**raphics **a**rray. Video graphics array, the graphics ability of which has been enhanced by increasing the resolution from 640 x 480 to at least 800 x 600 and up to 1,024 x 768 pixels. *See* VGA, CGA, EGA, XGA, 8514/A and pixel.

surface acoustic wave Commonly abbreviated and called SAW. *See* SAW.

surge Increase in voltage that can be harmful to the circuitry of a computer or peripheral devices. Can result from power line propagation (an electrical wave moving through a power line), lightning strikes or sudden increases or decreases in the load on power lines.

surge protector Device used to protect electrical circuits from sudden increases in electrical voltage. Can be placed either between the source of power and a computer or peripheral devices, or within the internal circuits. *See* surge and UPS.

Surge protector

suser Routine used by a system administrator to determine if the user who is trying to access a file or directory is a superuser. *See* FIO.

sushi **S**et **u**serid **sh**ell **i**nteractive. Similar to a Trojan horse. Program that specifically does a switch user id from root and establishes the user with full root permissions. Used by a hacker trying to access the root directory, thereby providing access to the entire system. *See* Trojan horse.

suspend To temporarily stop a process or program which can then be either restarted or killed. *See* sleep and kill.

SVID **S**ystem **V** **I**nterface **D**efinition. Set of documents initially released in January 1985 by the AT&T Co., defining System V interfaces and operating system calls. Provides developers documentation they need to develop code compatible with AT&T UNIX System V. For products to use the term UNIX, they must conform to X/Open Portability Guide, third or fourth edition, and System V Interface Definition, Version 2 or 3. *See* System V and XPG.

SVID 2 System **V** Interface Definition, Issue **2**. Second version of the SVID that documents the interfaces and operating system calls in System V, Release 3. Provides developers documentation they need to develop code compatible with AT&T UNIX System V, Release 3. *See* SVID and SVR3.x.

SVID 3 System **V** Interface Definition, Issue **3**. Third version of the SVID that documents the interfaces and operating system calls in System V, Release 4. Provides developers documentation they need to develop code compatible with AT&T UNIX System V, Release 4. *See* SVID and SVR4.x.

SVR3.x Abbreviation for AT&T Co.'s UNIX System V, Release 3. The .x represents the version, e.g. SVR3.2.

SVR4 Abbreviation for AT&T Co.'s UNIX System V, Release 4. *See* SVR4.x.

SVR4.2 ESMP System **V**, Release **4.2** Enhanced **S**ecurity and **M**ultiprocessing **P**lus. Also spelled SVR4 ES/MP. Multiprocessing release of UNIX System V, Release 4 with enhanced, B-2 level security. Capable of addressing 30 central processing units. Offers enhanced tools for development and monitoring of multiprocessing software. *See* SVR4.x, SVR4 ES, SVR4 MP, Orange Book and SMP.

SVR4 Desktop System **V**, Release **4** **Desktop**. Also called Destiny and UNIX Lite. Univel Inc.'s version of AT&T Co.'s UNIX System V, Release 4.1, for use on 386 and 486 personal computers. Designed in modules to allow users to install only those tools and utilities they need. *See* SVR4.x.

SVR4 ES System **V**, Release **4** Enhanced **S**ecurity. Version of AT&T Co.'s UNIX System V operating system. Based in part on the UNIX System V/Multi-Level Security system. it offers a B2 level, or relatively high degree, of security based on the security standards for computer systems established by the Department of Defense and published in the Orange Book. Security features include resource control, auditing and prevention of unauthorized access. *See* SVR4 and Orange Book.

SVR4 ESMP System **V**, Release **4** Enhanced **S**ecurity and **M**ultiprocessing **P**lus. Multiprocessing release of AT&T Co.'s UNIX System V, Release 4, capable of addressing 30 central processing units. Offers enhanced tools for developing and monitoring multiprocessing software. *See* SVR4.x, SVR4 ES, SVR4 MP and SMP.

SVR4 ES/MP Commonly written SVR4.2 ESMP. *See* SVR4.2 ESMP.

SVR4 MP System **V**, Release **4** Multiprocessing. AT&T Co.'s UNIX System V multiprocessing operating system capable of addressing 30 central processing units. Offers enhanced tools for developing and monitoring multiprocessing software. *See* SVR4.x, SVR4 MP and SMP.

SVR4.x System **V**, Release **4.0**. Released by AT&T Co. in November 1989. Includes enhancements from the Berkeley Software Distribution, XENIX, Portable Operating System Interface for Computer Environments (POSIX) standards, SunOS, ANSI C, UNIX File System and other AT&T functions, e.g. the Korn shell. *See* System V, BSD, XENIX, POSIX, SunOS, UFS and Korn shell.

SVVS System **V** Verification Suite. First UNIX system test suite, developed by AT&T Co. Used to determine compliance of a vendor's release of a UNIX System V operating system with the System V Interface Definition. *See* SVID.

SWAG **S**cientific **w**ild **a**ss **g**uess. Also called second wild ass guess. Basic approach taken by experienced maintenance personnel to hardware and/or software maintenance and repair, where a similar guess as to the cause of a problem has been made at least once before. In contrast, a WAG is a first guess. *See* WAG.

swap **1.** *(ATT)* Command used by a system administrators or superuser to modify or monitor swap space, a disk holding area to which processes are temporarily moved when a computer's main memory is full. *See* swap space. **2.** To temporarily move a process to a disk holding area from a computer's main memory. When space becomes available again in main memory, the process is moved back. This allows more processes to be loaded at the same time, even if there is not enough space available in main memory.

swap area Commonly called swap space. *See* swap space.

swapctl *(ATT)* **Swap** control. Set of commands and programs used to manage swap space, a temporary storage area for processes that are awaiting space in main memory, e.g. update information on resources used for swap. *See* swap.

swapdev **Swap dev**ice. Kernel parameter used to set the major and minor device numbers for a swap device, which has temporary storage area for processes awaiting space in a computer's main memory, e.g. a hard disk drive. *See* major device number, minor device number and swap device.

swap device Device which has a swap space, or temporary storage area for processes awaiting space in a computer's main memory, e.g. a hard disk drive. *See* swap space.

swapin **Swap in**. System call used to move a process from the swap space, or temporary storage area, on a device, e.g. a hard disk drive, into main memory to be run. *See* system call and swapping.

swap map Description of the amount of room available in the swap space, or temporary storage area for processes awaiting space in a computer's main memory. *See* swap space.

swapon **Swap on**. Command that allows a system administrator to add a second swap device without having to redo the kernel. *See* swap device and kernel.

swap parameter Part of the kernel description file. Identifies the swap space, disk area used to temporarily store process awaiting space in main memory. *See* kernel description file and swap space.

swap partition Commonly called swap space. *See* swap space.

swapper **1.** *(BSD)* Daemon responsible for managing swapping. *See* swapping. **2.** Central processing unit (CPU) scheduler. Schedules the tasks to be accomplished by the CPU. *See* sched and process zero.

swapping Process of moving programs between main memory and the swap space, e.g. temporary storage area on disk, to free up main memory. Noticeably slows down a computer's response time. *See* backing storage, paging and secondary storage.

swapping mechanism Operating system programs that perform the swapping process by moving processes from main memory when it is full into a temporary storage area on disk and then back into main memory when space allows. *See* swap.

swap space Area of disk space reserved for use during swapping or paging. Temporary storage area for processes that are awaiting space in main memory. *See* swapping and paging.

Swipnet European public network running the Transmission Control Protocol/Internet Protocol. Gives small to medium-sized companies and private individuals who cannot afford to use expensive private networks access to a network that can transmit data from 9.6 to 64 kilobits per second. *See* TCP/IP.

switch Command used in C shell programs to move control of a program from one location to another. Compares expression values with stated constants. If an expression value matches one of the constants, then program statements that follow the expression value are executed. *See* case, C shell, breaksw and endsw.

switched 56 Data or voice communication service that provides point-to-point leased lines with a capacity of 56 kilobits per second for multiple interconnected locations. Lines are leased into the service provider's network, allowing for temporary switching from the normal locations to alternate locations. *See* DDS.

Switched Multimegabit Data Service Commonly abbreviated and called SMDS. *See* SMDS.

Switched Multimegabit Data Service Interest Group Abbreviated and commonly known as SMDS Interest Group. *See* SMDS Interest Group.

switched network Data communications system in which data is transferred from a computer to a switch on a network, which then sends the data directly to the receiving host. *See* nonswitched network.

switcher Jargon term for swtch. *See* swtch.

SWM **S**olbourne **w**indow **m**anager. Developed by Solbourne Computer for the Massachusetts Institute of Technology X 11, Release 4 specification for the X Window System Provides the look and feel of both OPEN LOOK and Motif. *See* X Window System, X11R4, OPEN LOOK and Motif.

swplo **Sw**ap **lo**w. Kernel parameter used to specify the starting block number for the swap partition when the root partition and swap partition are mounted on the same disk device. Swplo functions are now managed by swapctl. *See* swapctl, partition, swap.

swtch Also called switcher. System call used to determine which process in the run queue to execute next. Transfers a process from run status, saves it and then starts a new running process. *See* system call, process and run queue.

symbol Representation of a value, operation, command, etc., by association or convention, e.g. the caret ($\wedge$) to signify the control character.

symbolic debugger Program used to debug other programs. Permits debugging (setting breakpoints, tracing execution and examining or changing data) using the same symbols (i.e. names) as the programmer used to create the program. A precursor to source-level debuggers. *See* debugger.

symbolic disassembler Software program used to take apart or convert an executable program image into a format resembling an assembler source program. Disassemblers are generally used to reverse-engineer a program, or retrieve lost sources.

symbolic link Commonly called soft link. *See* soft link.

symbol table 1. File containing the names of data objects and their functions. Used to compile object files to debug programs. 2. List or collection of related symbols. *See* symbol.

symlink Jargon term for symbolic or soft link. *See* soft link.

symmetric multiprocessing Commonly abbreviated and called SMP. *See* SMP.

symorder *(BSD)* **Sym**bol **order**. Command used to rearrange the symbol name list. *See* symbol, object and library.

sync 1. *(ATT/XEN)* Command that is either run automatically by a computer system or input by a system administrator while the system is being shut down. Forces input/output operations to end, updates changes that have been made in memory and writes the data in memory to disk. *See* I/O. 2. Jargon term for synchronous or matching. *See* synchronous communication. 3. *(ATT)* System call initiated by the sync command. Used while a system is being shut down or can be forced at any time by the system administrator. *See* system call and superblock.

sync character Synchronous character. Also called SYN character. Predetermined symbol used to adjust timing and recognition of elements related to the start and end blocks of character transmission between a receiving device (usually a terminal or modem) and sending device (the computer). One or two characters are sent to the recipient at set intervals throughout the data transmission to ensure the receiver and sender are in phase.

SYN character Commonly called sync character. See sync character.

synchronization Process of adjusting the timing between elements (data and control bits) of data transmission so that the timing and recognition of these elements on the sending and receiving devices match. Applicable to components within a computer system or peripheral devices, or between computers on a network. See sync character and synchronous communication.

synchronized I/O (POS) POSIX.4 (real-time operating system) term for a system that provides guaranteed communication with an output device. See POSIX.4 and RTOS.

synchronous Jargon term for synchronous communication. See synchronous communication.

synchronous communication Internal and external means of data transfer in which there is a pre-established and constant interval between the release of data characters. This allows data to be sent and received at the same time. See asynchronous communications.

synchronous data-link control
Commonly abbreviated and called SDLC. See SDLC.

synchronous optical network
Commonly abbreviated and called SONET. See SONET.

synchronous terminal Device capable of sending and receiving data at the same time by transmitting the data at pre-established and constant intervals. See synchronous communication.

Synchronous Transport Signal level number Commonly abbreviated and called STS-n. See STS-n.

synopsis Summary of a command's syntax. See syntax.

syntactic analyzer Program used in the process of converting programming code into usable application software. Syntactic analyzer.

syntax Rules that govern the order and relationship of the elements in a command or script. Similar to the grammatical rules that apply to the structure of a sentence.

syntax error Message sent by a computer, notifying a user or programmer that there is a mistake in entering a command, qualifier or parameter, e.g. the elements of a command may not have been typed in the correct order or the wrong symbol may have been used. Errors result from improper use of a language's syntax, e.g. input of an incorrect symbol or input of symbols in incorrect order.

SYS Abbreviation for system class. See system class.

/sys Berkeley Software Distribution root directory set aside that is reserved for working with the kernel. See kernel.

sysadm (ATT) System administration. System administration command used to call a menu that contains a list of commands for performing basic system administration functions. The menu includes commands to set up the system, install software, add and delete users, back up files, restore files, and manage disks and file systems. See sysadm commands (Appendices L and M) and file system.

sysadm commands 1. See Appendix L for pre-UNIX System V, Release 4 sysadm commands. 2. See Appendix M for UNIX System V, Release 4 sysadm commands.

sysadmin 1. *(XEN)* **System admin**istration. Set of commands used to backup and recover system files. 2. Common abbreviation for system administration.

sysadminsh *(XEN)* **System admin**istration **shell**. Shell developed by The Santa Cruz Operation for the XENIX operating system. *See* shell.

syscall **System call**. System call that manages. *See* system call.

sysdef *(ATT)* **System def**inition. System administration command used to create the kernel or obtain information about the operating system definitions stored in the kernel description file. The information is used to fine-tune the operating system and optimize the performance of the hardware. *See* kernel, kernel description file, swap and OS.

sysdump *(ATT)* **System dump**. Command used by the system administrator to move into alternative storage media a copy of the system core, the data in the computer's memory, when a system crashes or illegal operation is performed by an application program. *See* core.

Sysfiles /etc/uucp/**Sysfiles**. File used with UNIX System V, Release 4 Basic Network Utilities. Contains a list of files related to the services available for UNIX-to-UNIX CoPy connection, including information about systems, devices and dialers. *See* SVR4.x, BNU, UUCP, Systems, Devices and Dialers.

sysinit Part of the init process used in starting the operating system. Started before the init daemon, and directs all output or responses to the system console. *See* init, operating system and level.

sysline *(BSD)* **System line**. Command used to display system status information on the status line of a terminal with that feature.

syslog Software package written by Eric Allman to record network-generated errors.

SYSLOG File which contains a statistical record of UNIX-to-UNIX CoPy (UUCP)

activity, including the size (in bytes) of data transmissions, who initiated each one, the remote site involved, the time at which each one was started and the amount of time used to complete each UUCP transmission. *See* UUCP.

syslogd *(INET)* **System log d**aemon. Internet background program which manages error messages generated by system programs and daemons over a network. Receives and routes error messages to the recipient identified in the stderr. *See* Internet, daemon and stderr.

SYS NAME *(ATT)* Configuration parameter used to set the name of the system scheduler class, e.g. system class, time sharing or real time, in the UNIX System V, Release 4 kernel. *See* SVR4.x and system class.

systat *(BSD)* **System stat**istics. Released with the Fourth Berkeley Software Distribution, Third Release. Command that provides an interactive interface that enables a user to examine the statistics provided by the pstat system call. *See* pstat.

system *(ATT)* Standard input/output library routine used to execute or start a command. *See* library routines.

system account Type of account, similar to a user account, established to provide the means to perform specific system maintenance functions or operational access. The root user account is the primary example of a system account used for administration. System administrators can log in using the root account to make changes to the operating system. The uucp account is an example of a system account established to provide ownership of files by the UNIX-to-UNIX CoPy communication system when connection is made between two host computers to transfer of files.

system accounting Commonly called accounting. *See* accounting.

system activity Any process resulting in an entry, e.g. a system call or interrupt, to the kernel. *See* system call, hardware interrupt, hardware trap and software interrupt.

System Activity Report A b b r e v i a t e d and commonly known as SAR. *See* SAR.

System Administration *(ATT)* Set of programs in UNIX System V, Release 4, that includes screens and interactive prompts. Used to perform system administration tasks, e.g. user administration, printer management and batch processing commands. *See* sysadm and SA.

system administration commands S e t of commands and programs used by a system administrator to manage system processes, users, security and other tasks. *See* SA, nice, fsck, mkfs, kill and runacct.

System Administration, Networking and Security Commonly abbreviated and called SANS. *See* SANS.

system administrator Commonly abbreviated and called SA. *See* SA.

System Administrator's Guide U N I X system documentation which provides a list and explanation of tasks, from managing users to tuning the system, *See* SA, User's Guide, URM, Programmer's Guide, PRM, SANS and SARM.

System Administrators' Guild Commonly abbreviated and called SAGE. *See* SAGE.

System Administrator's Reference Manual Commonly abbreviated and called SARM. *See* SARM.

system banner Message which identifies a system and is sent to a user who is logging in.

system bus Primary bus, or set of circuitry, that connects the central processing unit to other devices, depending on the manufacturer's architecture. *See* bus.

system call Any command which is automatically run by the operating system in response to a command given by a process and asks the kernel to perform a specific function. The number of system calls

varies among operating systems. UNIX System V, Release 3 has fewer than 100, the Fourth Berkeley Software Distribution, Third Release, has more than 100 and the Portable Operating System Interface for Computer Environments (POSIX) standard has approximately 100. *See* kernel, SVR3.x, 4.3BSD, POSIX, internals and library routines.

system class Type of process with a set priority reserved for use in managing the computer system. System class processes have the highest priority on the system. *See* kernel, real-time class and time-sharing class.

system clock Internal device used to maintain the date and time for the system.

system command Commonly called system call. *See* system call.

system configuration file C o m m o n l y called kernel description file. *See* kernel description file.

system console Commonly called console. *See* console.

System/D Jargon term for Tuxedo System/D. *See* Tuxedo System/D.

system global area Area set aside in main memory that is shared by different functions and used to control on-line processes.

System III First major release by AT&T Co. of its UNIX operating system in 1981 before System V. It combined elements of UNIX Version 6 and the Publisher's Workbench/UNIX. It was the original basis of most UNIX implementations for microcomputers, e.g. The Santa Cruz Operation's release of XENIX. *See* PWB/UNIX, XENIX and System V.

system integration Commonly called systems integration. *See* systems integration.

system integrator Commonly called systems integrator. *See* systems integrator.

System Interface *(POS)* Name for both the Institute of Electrical and Electronic Engineers P1003.1 working group and standard. *See* POSIX.1.

System IV Version of AT&T Co.'s UNIX operating system released only for use within AT&T to avoid possible confusion in consumers' minds between it and the Fourth Berkeley Software Distribution products. *See* BSD.

system mail Commonly called e-mail. *See* e-mail.

system mailbox Commonly called mailfile. *See* mailfile.

system mode Commonly called kernel mode. *See* kernel mode.

systemname Field in the USERFILE used for the names of the remote systems which can make UNIX-to-UNIX CoPy connections. *See* USERFILE and UUCP.

system name Distinctive name for a computer host. When there is a single computer system that is not part of a network, the name is not critical but must be no longer than six characters. Computers in a network configuration need a name that individually identifies each host to avoid confusion in the exchange of electronic mail and other files.

System Network Architecture Commonly abbreviated and called SNA. *See* SNA.

system page table Table containing the available virtual address space, or simulated storage, e.g. a disk drive, which can be used as memory locations for programs and data that cannot fit in main memory. *See* virtual address space.

System Performance Analysis Utilities Commonly abbreviated and called SPAU. *See* SPAU.

system prompt Special character, symbol or message that is sent to the screen by the computer. Indicates the computer is waiting for the user to enter an instruction. The default system prompt varies with the shell used, e.g. the dollar sign ($)

for the Bourne and Korn shells and percent sign (%) for the C shell. *See* shell, dollar sign, percent sign, Bourne shell, C shell and Korn shell.

system reliability Measurement of the time, in percentages, that a computer system is operational and running properly, compared to the established time the computer system is to be operational in support of customer requirements.

system reset Rebooting a computer system using software commands instead of manually switching the power off and on. *See* reset and reboot.

systems *(ATT)* Command in UNIX System V, Release 4 line printer services menu, similar to the lpsystem command. Used to identify remote systems that can use the line printer services on the local host. *See* SVR4.x and lpsystem.

Systems File in /usr/lib/uucp on systems running HoneyDanBer UNIX-to-UNIX CoPy. Also, on UNIX System V, Release 4 Basic Network Utilities found in /etc/uucp/Systems. Provides the information on how connections to remote hosts are to be made. Contains the name of the remote host and specifies when to call, the device used for the connection, data transfer speed, phone number, and the script which outlines the steps taken to make the connection. *See* L.sys, UUCP, HoneyDanBer UUCP, SVR4.x, BNU, baud and chat script.

Systems Application Architecture Commonly abbreviated and called SAA. *See* SAA.

systems house Software company which develops application software packages and/or modifies or recompiles existing applications designed for one type of hardware system to meet the specifications of another type of system. Usually works on contract for an original equipment manufacturer.

systems integration Process of combining all elements that compose a system, e.g. one or more computers, operating system, application software and communications devices, so that they work together as advertised and/or specified. The components may or may not be from the same vendor. *See* turnkey system.

systems integrator Individual, company or organization responsible for combining various hardware and software elements into a functional computer system. *See* systems integration.

Systems Management Requirements Specification Set of requirements for networking and systems management published by UNIX International Inc. Prepared as a guideline for developing its Atlas architecture for computer and network management. *See* UI and Atlas.

system software Operating system, support software, etc. provided with the computer system.

Systems Performance Evaluation Cooperative Commonly abbreviated and called SPEC. *See* SPEC.

system state Commonly called state. *See* state.

System/T Jargon term for Tuxedo System/T. *See* Tuxedo System/T.

system test Test performed by software developers to determine if a product meets design specifications and requirements. *See* alpha test and beta test.

system, the 1. Computer system, including the hardware, operating system, application software and peripherals, on which the operator is an authorized user. 2. If a user has accounts on more than one system, refers to the specific computer that person uses most. 3. Computer to which the user is currently logged on or attempting to log on.

system throughput Commonly called throughput. *See* throughput.

system time Commonly called runtime. *See* runtime.

System/T Transaction Manager Jargon term for Tuxedo System/T. *See* Tuxedo System/T.

system tuning Maximizing system performance by modifying parameters in a computer's operating system to match the software applications running on the computer, number of users, number of processes to be run, etc. *See* tunable parameters, sysdef and tunefs.

System V Version of AT&T Co.'s UNIX operating system released in 1983. AT&T continued to refine the System V operating system with the release of System V, Release 2 in 1985, Release 3 in 1987 and Release 4 in 1989. Release 4 complies with both Portable Operating System Interface for Computer Environments (POSIX) and X/Open Co. Ltd. specifications, includes the Fourth Berkeley Software Distribution, Second and Third Releases, and XENIX extensions. AT&T externally released its first version of the UNIX operating system, Programmer's Workbench/UNIX, which was based on Version 6, in 1977. *See* SVR3.x, SVR4.x, PWB/UNIX, Version 6, POSIX, X/Open and extension.

System V Desktop Commonly abbreviated and called SVR4 Desktop. *See* SVR4 Desktop.

System V Interface Definition Commonly abbreviated and called SVID. *See* SVID.

System V/MLS UNIX **System V/Multi-Level S**ecurity. Version of UNIX System V, Release 3.1, developed to meet Department of Defense security requirements by AT&T Co. Offers a B1, or relatively high, level of security based on the security standards for computer systems established by the Department of Defense and published in the Orange Book. *See* SVR3.x, SVR4 ES and Orange Book.

System V, Release 4 Enhanced Security Commonly abbreviated and called SVR4 ES. *See* SVR4 ES.

System V, Release 4 Multiprocessing Commonly abbreviated and called SVR4 MP. *See* SVR4 MP.

System V, Release x Volume Manager
Abbreviated and commonly known as VxVM. *See* VxVM.

System V Verification Suite
Commonly abbreviated and called SVVS. *See* SVVS.

SYSV System V. Fifth version of the UNIX operating system released by AT&T Co. *See* System V.

sysviz System administration visual. System administration program which is similar to sysadm but to which access is not limited to system administrators. Provides menus that allow users to send electronic mail, execute applications, etc. *See sysadm.*

T

T Abbreviation for **tera**. *See* tera.

T-1 Digital communications link capable of transmitting both analog and digital data at 1,544,000 bits per second. *See* T-2, T-3, T-4 and fractional T-1.

T-2 Digital communications link capable of transmitting both analog and digital data at 6,312,000 bits per second. *See* T-1, T-3 and T-4.

T-3 Digital communications link capable of transmitting both analog and digital data at 44,736,000 bits per second. *See* T-1, T-2 and T-4.

T-4 Digital communications link capable of transmitting both analog and digital data at 274,176,000 bits per second. *See* T-1, T-2 and T-3.

t300 *(BSD)* Command that handles the graphic filters for the special plotting functions of DASI 300, GSI 300 or DTC 300 terminals. *See* filter.

t300s *(BSD)* Command that handles the graphic filters for the special plotting functions of DASI 300s, GSI 300s or DTC 300s terminals. *See* filter.

t450 *(BSD)* Command that handles the graphic filters for the special plotting functions of the DASI 450 terminal. *See* filter.

tab **Tab**ulation character. Nonprinting character which moves the cursor either horizontally a specified number of spaces to the next tab stop in word processing document or from point to point in a database or spreadsheet record. *See* tab stop.

tab character Commonly abbreviated and called tab. *See* tab.

Tab key Keyboard key used to insert a tabulation character. Used for indenting or creating columns in a word processing document and for moving around in a database or spreadsheet record. *See* tab.

table Horizontal and vertical array of pre-defined values used in a repetitive management process. Users input information variables which are compared to the data in the table and processed accordingly. For example, data is maintained in a table on users of cellular telephones and each user is identified by a unique number. When a user dials a number, the table is checked to determine if that user's unique number exists; if so, the user is authorized to make a cellular phone call. Information related to the phone call is updated in the table to be used later for billing, customer inquiries, etc.

table driven Comparison of variables input by a user with a list of predefined variables, e.g. used to validate a user, who can then perform processes such as sending electronic mail, login security and remote host connectivity.

table join Combining database tables by using one or more common variables to form a new table, e.g. comparing a table containing data on employees with a table of available medical benefits to create a table of medical benefits for each employee.

table lookup Process of checking a table of predefined variables to see if a variable entered by a user is recognized, e.g. during the login process when the system confirms a user password with the data recorded in the password file.

tablet computer Commonly called pen-based computer. *See* pen-based computer.

tabs *(ATT/XEN)* Command used to establish or change tab settings on a terminal.

tabstop Environmental variable in the vi editor used to set the number of spaces over which the cursor moves when the Tab key is depressed. *See* vi.

tab stop Predefined point on a line at which the cursor stops each time the Tab key is depressed, as in creating columns in a document. Defined by the user. *See* tab.

Tab Window Manager Commonly abbreviated and called twm. *See* twm.

tag Database entry used to identify a specific function and its location in the source program.

TAG Jargon term for the U.S. Technical Advisory Group. *See* U.S. TAG.

tags file File used by the ex and vi editors that contains function and data definitions from C language, Pascal, FORTRAN or Lisp source code. *See* ctags.

tail Command used to view or extract a selected number of lines from the end of a file, particularly a large file. Also may be used to monitor in real time a file which is continually being updated. Prints the last 10 lines of a file by default if the user does not specify the number of lines. Output can be displayed on the screen, moved to a file or directed to another device. *See* head.

take *(ATT)* Command within the cu command that is used to transfer a file from a remote host to a local host. *See* cu and put.

talk Command used for interactive communication with another user on the system. Splits the screen and allows both users to communicate at the same time. Similar to the write command. *See* write.

talkd *(INET)* **Talk d**aemon. Internet background program used to complete requests for the talk command between users over a network. *See* Internet, daemon and talk.

talk mode Operating condition in which users on the same computer system or on a network are able to establish real-time, interactive communication. *See* talk and write.

talk-mode jargon *See* Appendix N.

tape 1. Electronic storage medium on which magnetically encoded data is stored in thin strips of plastic coated with a metal oxide. Common tape formats are .5-inch reel or 9-track, .25-inch cartridge, 8-millimeter video cartridge and VHS cartridge. 2. Key word used in building the kernel. Identifies tape drives managed by a controller. *See* kernel.

tape backup unit Commonly abbreviated and called TBU. *See* TBU.

tapecntl *(ATT)* **Tape c**ontrol. Command used to locate or move a tape to perform a read or write function.

tape label Identification created by the labelit program at the beginning of a tape. Provides information about the format of the tape and the data it contains. *See* labelit.

tape management Utilities, policies and procedures implemented to manage tapes created as part of the backup function, archiving, system tapes, etc.

tapesave *(ATT)* Shell script used to perform weekly disk-to-tape backups. *See* shell script.

tar **T**ape **ar**chiver. Command used to either back up system files on tape or recover one or more files from backup tapes. *See* backup and archiver.

Tariff 12 AT&T Co. program to custom design long-distance communications service. Approved by the Federal Communications Commission and instituted in 1985 for the Department of Defense.

tarskip *(OTH)* Tape **ar**chiver **skip**. Command that stops when there is an input, output or read error while the tar command is being used to back up a system or recover files. Overcomes one of the problems with tar by skipping over read errors and allowing the user to continue the operation.

task 1. Any application program or individual element of an application program that is able to stand alone and/or must be performed to execute program code. For example, a print command, such as lp or lpr, can be either a separate standalone application or incorporated, or called, by an application to be executed as part of the program. 2. Elements of system resources needed to support a job when it is split up for parallel processing, e.g. a central processing unit that is dedicated to support an element of an application program. *See* parallel processing, MP and threads.

task switching Process in which a computer changes from one process to another while a command or program is running. Allows the computer to make better use of its resources. In multi-processing, if one task temporarily frees a resource or if a task with a higher priority starts, then the resource, e.g. memory or the central processing unit, is released and can run a task or process of another program. *See* MP and process.

tbl *(ATT)* **T**able. Part of the Documenter's Workbench set of text formatting programs. Developed in 1976 by Mike Lesk at AT&T Co.'s Bell Laboratories. A preprocessor for nroff and troff text formatting programs to create or update table layouts in text documents. *See* DWB, Bell Laboratories, nroff and troff.

Tbps **T**era**b**ytes **p**er **s**econd. Measurement of the transfer of data in trillions of bytes per second. *See* terabyte.

TBU **T**ape **b**ackup **u**nit. External tape drive used for system backups. Generally refers to a system using 8MM, 4MM or similar tape.

Tbyte Abbreviation for terabyte. *See* terabyte.

tc 1. *(ATT)* Command that enables Tektronix 4014 terminals to read troff documents. 2. Program that simulates the actions of a phototypesetter. Generally used to debug macros and related troff programs. *See* troff and macro.

TCAP **T**ransaction **Ca**pability **P**art. Protocol developed for the Signal System 7 packet switch standard that permits out of band signaling. Allows transmission of multimedia traffic separately from normal traffic on a network. Used in transmitting information to and requesting information from databases. *See* SS7.

Tcl **T**ool **C**ommand **L**anguage. Pronounced *TICKLE*. Developed by John Ousterhout at the University of California, Berkeley. A script used to write applications or scripts that can be included in a C language program. Runs on the UNIX, DOS, Macintosh and VMS operating systems. *See* wish, Tk and C language.

TCOS **T**echnical **C**ommittee on **O**perating **S**ystems and Applications Portability. Name was changed to the Portable Application Standards Committee in 1993. *See* PASC.

TCOS-SEC *(POS)* **T**echnical **C**ommittee on **O**perating **S**ystems-**S**ponsor **E**xecutive **C**ommittee. Operating body which monitors activities related to Portable Operating System Interface for Computer Environments (POSIX). Reviews and approves Project Authorization Requests which are used to recommend either new POSIX criteria or modifications to existing POSIX criteria. *See* POSIX and PAR.

TCP *(INET)* **T**ransmission **C**ontrol **P**rotocol. Also called Transport Control Protocol. One of the protocols of the Internet Protocol Suite developed by the Defense Advanced Research Projects Agency. Used in packet network communications systems to manage the movement of information. Guarantees delivery of uncorrupted data in the correct sequence. *See*

Internet Protocol Suite, DARPA and TCP/IP.

TCP/IP *(INET)* **Transmission Control Protocol/Internet Protocol.** The two fundamental protocols used to establish a connection for data transmission (TCP) and to define the composition of the packet of information being transmitted (IP). As a result of the fundamental nature of the two protocols, the Internet suite is normally referred to as TCP/IP. Developed by the Department of Defense in the early 1970s. *See* DARPA, TCP, IP and packet.

TCP/IP architecture *(INET)* Four layers of protocols built on a fifth, the hardware. Developed by the Department of Defense in the early 1970s. *See* DARPA, Internet, TCP/IP, application layer, transport layer, internet layer and network layer.

TCP/IP protocol suite *(INET)* Commonly called ARM (ARPANET Reference Model). *See* ARM.

TCP/UDP with Bigger Addresses Transmission Control Protocol/User Datagram Protocol with **Bigger Addresses**. More commonly abbreviated and called TUBA. *See* TUBA.

TCSEC Trusted Computer System Evaluation Criteria. Formal name for the Orange Book, published by the National Computer Security Center, which describes the security standards for computer systems. *See* Orange Book.

tcsh Abbreviation or working name indicating a user is running a C shell with Tenex shell extensions. *See* TC-shell.

TC-shell Jargon term for the Tenex shell developed for the DECsystem-10 by Bolt, Beranek and Newman, Inc. In the Berkeley Software Distribution, it was adopted as a version of the C shell with file name and command completion. This was to allow users to enter a unique abbreviation of a file name as an argument to a command or an abbreviation of a command instead of the full name of the file or command. *See* BSD and C shell.

TDM Time division multiplex. Communication protocol used to establish a multiplexed circuit between devices. Divides the range of frequencies available to transmit communication signals into time slices, minuscule amounts of time in which the processor can carry out part of each user's process in turn. When a time slice is available, a device can transmit data. The process is so fast that, like voice transmissions during a phone call, it is not noticeable to users.

TDR Time-Domain Reflectometer. Device used to locate problems within wire cables. Sends a signal along the wire and watches for a response to bounce back. Based upon the nature of the response and the time lapse, can determine the type of problem and approximate location. *See* OTDR.

tear-off menu Set of commands contained in a menu that can be separated from the original menu and repositioned on the screen.

techie Commonly called computer nerd. *See* computer nerd.

Technical and Office Protocol Commonly abbreviated and called TOP. *See* TOP.

Technical Committee on Operating Systems and Applications Portability Originally abbreviated and commonly called TCOS. Name was changed to the Portable Application Standards Committee in 1993. *See* PASC.

Technical Committee on Operating Systems-Sponsor Executive Committee Commonly abbreviated and called TCOS-SEC. *See* TCOS-SEC.

technobabble Jargon term for using confusing technical terms instead of plain English to explain or describe a situation or topic.

tee *(ATT/BSD/XEN)* Command used to view and save the output of a command. Sends the output to the standard output, normally the screen, as well as to redirect it to a file.

TEE-ROFF Pronunciation of troff, the abbreviation for typesetter run off. *See* troff.

tek *(BSD)* Program used to display plotting instructions from a plot on the Tektronix 4014 and other compatible graphics display devices. *See* graph.

telecommunications Sending or receiving of data, sound, television signals, etc.

Telecommunications Education Research Network Commonly abbreviated and called TERN. *See* TERN.

telecommute To work from a remote location using a combination of telephone lines, a remote terminal and a host terminal, e.g. as in sending work done at home to a main office. The term was first coined by Jack Nilles in 1973.

teleconference Meeting held between two or more people at different geographic locations using telephones, computers and other communications media to exchange information.

teleprocessing Commonly called telecommunications. *See* telecommunications.

teletype 1. Trademark for teletypewriter, a device used to send and receive information. 2. Device that is a combination of a keyboard and printer. 3. Any terminal device. *See* tty and terminal.

telinit *(ATT)* Command used to manage the init daemon. Sends a signal to init, telling it to either change the system from single to multi-user state or restart init. *See* init.

telnet *(INET)* Command used to initiate a TELNET connection.

TELNET *(INET)* Teletype Network. Defense Advanced Research Projects Agency protocol for remote terminal connection. *See* DARPA.

TELNET arguments *(INET) See* Appendix O.

TELNET commands *(INET) See* Appendix P.

telnetd *(INET)* TELNET daemon. Background program that supports and manages the operation of the TELNET protocol. Started by the Internet daemon when a TELNET session is started. *See* TELNET, daemon and inetd.

TELNET flags *(INET) See* Appendix Q.

TELNET variables *(INET) See* Appendix R.

template 1. Cheat sheet. Normally, a guide or card which graphically displays the combinations of keys to be pressed to activate different functions of a software package. 2. Predesigned set of formulas or forms used for repetitive actions in spreadsheets or flowcharts.

temporary directories Collection of UNIX root directories used to retain temporary data or files, e.g. /tmp, /lost+found and /usr/spool/uucppublic.

temporary storage Area in main memory set aside for holding the results of intermediate processing until the primary process has finished with the data.

tera Prefix for 10^{12} (1,000,000,000,000) or one trillion. Commonly abbreviated T.

terabyte Measurement of the data storage capacity of a computer's memory or disk drive. Commonly accepted as equal to 1 trillion bytes, but actually equals 1,009,511,627,776 bytes. Abbreviated TB.

tera floating point operations per second Abbreviated and commonly known as TFLOPS. *See* TFLOPS.

term 1. *(BSD)* C shell variable which contains the terminal type names. 2. ex editor variable that, when set, allows vi to be used with a specific type of terminal. *See* vi and TERM.

TERM Environmental variable used to identify the type of terminal being used, as required by the vi editor and other screen-oriented programs. *See* environment variables and vi.

termcap *(BSD)* File containing descriptions of various types of terminals recognized by the computer system. Maintains data on each terminal, e.g. screen-mapping information needed for screen-oriented programs to correctly place text and graphic characters on the screen. *See* terminfo.

terminal **1.** Also called CRT, VDU, VDT, teletype, monitor or tube. Device, e.g. keyboard and monitor, used to access data and programs stored on a multiuser computer system, usually a mainframe or minicomputer system. Relies on the central processing unit of the mainframe or minicomputer system to execute programs and process information. **2.** *(POS)* Portable Operating System Interface for Computer Environments (POSIX) term for the special file for the device driver. *See* POSIX, special file and device driver.

Terminal

Terminal Control Utilities Set of programs included in System V, Release 4 to create software application programs that will run on any type of terminal. *See* SVR4.x.

terminal device file Also called control terminal. File that is opened when a user logs into a system. Used for the standard input, output and error output.

terminal emulation Ability of a terminal to emulate the characteristics of other types of terminals. *See* emulator and termcap.

terminal emulator Software program that allows a personal computer to operate as a terminal on a multi-user system. On some PC systems, allows users greater flexibility by enabling them to switch between the multi-user and PC systems. *See* terminal emulation.

terminal modes There are six groups of terminal modes used: control modes, to set and/or control communication with a computer; input modes, to enter information and commands for processing; output modes, to output information that has been processed; local modes, for miscellaneous terminal input and output; combination modes, to modify the other modes; and control assignments, for recognizing special characters that have been input.

terminal multiplexer Commonly called multiplexer. *See* multiplexer.

terminal server Hardware device that provides an interface, or connection, between an asynchronous American National Standard Code for Information Interchange terminal and an Ethernet local area network. *See* asynchronous communications, ASCII terminal, Ethernet and LAN.

terminate Set of signals sent to a computer or peripheral device which halts a running process.

terminate-and-stay-resident program
Commonly abbreviated and called TSR. *See* TSR.

terminfo *(ATT)* First introduced in Release 2 of UNIX System V in 1984. A collection of files, each of which describes a terminal. Contains the screen mapping information needed for screen-oriented programs to correctly place text and graphic characters on the screen. *See* termcap.

termio *(ATT)* Terminal interface definition based on the ioctl system call, which is used to establish, control and manage input and output to devices. *See* ioctl.

TERN Telecommunications Education Research Network. Educational network formed in June 1991 by the International Communications Association and the University of Pittsburgh. Provides a nationwide communications backbone for educational research.

terse Variable in the ex and vi editors that, when set, results in error messages in fairly plain English. *See* ex, vi and noterse.

tertiary prompt Commonly called PS3. *See* PS3.

test *(ATT/XEN)* Command used to determine if a file exists. Also, depending on the option input by the user, determines conditional information about the file, e.g. file type (directory, character special file or block special file) and permissions.

testing Methodical examination of system software, hardware, etc. to prove it works as it was designed to before it is released commercially. *See* system test, acceptance testing, alpha test, beta test and string test.

TeX Text formatter developed by Donald E. Knuth. Similar to the nroff and troff formatting programs. Can be used to typeset mathematical functions. *See* text formatter, nroff and troff.

texi2roff TeX input to troff. Program used to convert a document from a TeX program format to a troff program format. *See* TeX and troff.

text Characters (letters, numbers and punctuation marks) that, when combined, convey information, e.g. computer text files may contain lists, shell scripts, business letters or other types of documents.

text editor Commonly called editor. *See* editor.

text formatter Utility that provides standard formats for preparing documents. *See* me macros, mm macros, mp macros, ms macros and TeX.

text formatting Creating documents, normally with the use of a formatting tool such as the nroff or troff text formatting programs. Addresses issues related to the appearance of a document and its style, e.g. margin settings, indentations, etc. *See* text formatting tool, nroff and troff.

text formatting tool Program used with preprocessors (eqn, tbl, etc.) to produce a finished document. The user inputs embedded commands into a document to indicate the formatting desired. The text formatting tool reads these commands and produces a document formatted as specified. *See* nroff, troff, eqn, neqn, tbl, pic and grap.

text mode Commonly called insert mode. *See* insert mode.

text processing commands Commonly called editing commands. *See* editing commands.

text segment Code portion of an executable file in a.out format. The other segments are data, for initialized data, and bss, for uninitialized data. *See* a.out, bss segment and data segment.

TFA Transparent File Access. Term in distributed file systems for a type of file access where users are able to access data without remote logins or remote command execution.

tfadmin *(ATT)* Trusted facility **admini**stration. Program within the UNIX System V, Release 4.1 Enhanced Security used to define access privileges based upon roles, or jobs, performed, versus the user's account. Limits the extent of privileges granted.

TFLOPS Tera floating point operations per second. Measurement in 1 trillion increments of floating point operations per second. *See* tera and FPA.

TFT Thin-film transfer. Electronic movement of data from memory, disk drive, diskette, etc. to a computer storage device made of an insulated base with a thin film of magnetic material on top.

tftp *(INET)* Command used to start the Trivial File Transfer Protocol, used to connect with a remote host and transfer data and files. *See* TFTP.

TFTP *(INET)* Trivial File Transfer Protocol. Set of Internet standards similar to the File Transfer Protocol (FTP), used mainly with personal computers and smaller client computers to connect with a remote host and transfer data and files, e.g. allows users of personal computers to copy single files over a network from or to a remote host. There are two significant differences between TFTP and FTP: first, TFTP connections are not interactive; second, no password protection is used other than confirming that the user has a password entry on the remote host. TFTP also is less expensive, less sophisticated and written with much less code than FTP. *See* FTP.

TFTP commands *(INET)* There are fewer TFTP commands than File Transfer Protocol (FTP) commands: ?, ASCII, binary, connect, get, mode, put, quit, rexmt, status, timeout, trace and verbose. The definitions are the same, except for rexmt, which establishes the timeout, in seconds, on the retransmission of packets. *See* FTP commands (Appendix C).

tftpd *(INET)* Trivial File Transfer Protocol daemon. Background program started by the Internet daemon to support and manage TFTP connections. *See* TFTP, daemon and inetd.

TFTPD *(INET)* Trivial File Transfer Protocol, Dedicated. Set of standards that allow a user to set up a personal computer as a dedicated file server so that other users on a network can access files and directories on the PC.

tgrind Command used to make neatly formatted listings of source programs. Creates TeX or text formatted documents of C language source code programs. *See* C language.

TGS Ticket-granting service. Function within Kerberos used to manage printing or file storage over a network. *See* Kerberos and ticket.

then Shell command used in conjunction with the if command in shell scripts. After the command started by the if command

is completed, then begins the execution of subsequent commands. For example:

```
if condition1 then
statement1
else
statement2
fi
```

See if, else, elif and fi.

thermal transfer Print technology where a printhead is heated to transfer a wax based ink to form the characters.

thick binding *(POS)* Term used in Portable Operating System Interface for Computer Environments (POSIX) standards for definitions that provide both the interface to POSIX definition and functionality. *See* POSIX, binding and thin binding.

thicknet Jargon term for 10Base5. Institute of Electrical and Electronic Engineers standard for the physical layer of an Ethernet network that uses half-inch-thick double-jacketed (coaxial) cable laid in conduit. Transmits data at a rate of 10 megabits per second over a maximum distance of 1000 meters. Makes the network more expensive to install, but enables transmission over a greater distance (1000 meters versus 300 meters for thinnet) and offers more reliability due to the shielded cable used. *See* IEEE, Ethernet, 1Base5, 10Base2, 10Base5, 10Base-T, thinnet and twisted pair.

thin binding *(POS)* Term used in Portable Operating System Interface for Computer Environments (POSIX) standards for definitions that provide the interface to POSIX definition. *See* POSIX, binding and thick binding.

thin-film transfer Commonly abbreviated and called TFT. *See* TFT.

thinnet Jargon term for 10Base2. Also called cheapnet. Institute of Electrical and Electronic Engineers standard for the physical layers of an Ethernet network that use thinner, single shielded, flexible coaxial cable resembling that used for cable television installation. Transmits data at a rate of 10 megabits per second over a maximum distance of 300 meters. Makes the network cheaper to install, but decreases its size and reliability because it does not use thick shielded cable. *See* IEEE, Ethernet, thinnet, 1Base5, 10Base2, 10Base5, 10Base-T, thicknet and twisted pair.

third-party maintenance C o m m o n l y abbreviated and called TPM. *See* TPM.

Thompson, Ken Part of the 1965 Bell Laboratories team that worked with the Massachusetts Institute of Technology and General Electric Co. on Project MAC, through which MULTICS was developed and became a forerunner to UNIX. Along with Dennis Ritchie, initiated the project in the late 1960s at the Computing Science Research Center at AT&T's Bell Laboratories to develop the UNIX operating system to improve programming support environments. Developed the B language in the late 1960s, which was modified by Ritchie to create the C language and used to write the UNIX operating system. Along with Dennis Ritchie and Rudd Canaday, created the UNIX file system. With other team members who were involved in the development of UNIX, he developed the UNIX-like operating system known as *Plan 9. See* Bell Laboratories, Project MAC, MULTICS, Ritchie, Dennis M., B language, C language and Plan 9.

thrashing Almost constant movement of programs or data into and out of memory, to the point where little else can be done. The result of not having enough memory to meet demand. *See* paging and swapping.

thread Also called lightweight process. Term in multiprocessing or parallel processing for independent basic units of computation or action. Provides the ability to run a task using several different processors at the same time. *See* MP, parallel processing and task.

Threads library Also called DCE Threads or Threads Service. Based upon the Portable Operating System Interface for Computer Environments (POSIX)

working group real-time UNIX additions standard. Facility in the Open Software Foundation Inc.'s Distributed Computing Environment that provides multiple threads, or the ability to concurrently run multiple tasks on different processors at the same time within an application. *See* OSF, DCE, POSIX, IEEE P1003.4a project and threads.

Threads Service Commonly   called Threads library. *See* Threads library.

THREE HUNDRED S Pronunciation of 300S. *See* 300S.

throughput Measurement of a computer's productivity in the amount of data that is usefully processed in a set period of time.

tic *(ATT)* terminfo compiler. Command used to compile terminfo data and move it to the correct directories. *See* terminfo.

ticket Controlling packet of the ticket granting service within Kerberos used to manage and control user access and use of the network for printing and file storage. A ticket is an information packet that contains the user's name and address, the service requested (print, access to a file, etc.), time allocated to run the service, security information and authorization to use the service. *See* Kerberos and TGS.

ticket-granting service Commonly abbreviated and called TGS. *See* TGS.

tickle Pronunciation of Tcl, the abbreviation for Tool Command Language. *See* Tcl.

tightly coupled architecture Computer design in which the central processing units share memory through a bus. *See* CPU and bus.

TIH The Information Highway. Alternative name for the electronic highway. *See* electronic highway.

tilde *(~)* Control character used as a shortcut. Can reduce the number of key strokes when moving from one working directory to another. When used alone, takes a user to that person's home directory. Used with a login ID, places a user in that user's account. Used with a plus sign, gives a user the absolute path of the current working directory. *See* metacharacter and regular expression.

tilde commands Also called tilde escapes. Set of special commands used with mailx that allows users to edit messages, execute shell commands, and turn on and off special features in electronic mail. The commands must begin with a tilde (~) for mailx to recognize and execute them. *See* Appendix S (tilde commands), tilde, mailx and e-mail.

tilde escape Commonly called tilde command. *See* tilde commands (Appendix P).

tiled windows Set of windows lined up side by side without overlapping, so that the contents of all the windows can be seen.

time 1. *(ATT/XEN)* Command used to report how many seconds it takes for a specified command to be executed. Included in the UNIX System V, Release 4 Framed Access Command Environment file system operation command menu. *See* SVR4.x, FACE and file system. 2. *(BSD)* C shell environmental variable used to display timing statistics for running commands. 3. System call that displays the number of seconds that have elapsed since 00:00 a.m. Greenwich Mean Time, January 1, 1970. Provides a universal date from which clock time can be measured. *See* Epoch.

TIME *(INET)* Time Server Protocol. Defense Advanced Research Projects Agency Internet protocol. TIME sends the time in the form of a number of seconds from a specified time reference. *See* DARPA and Internet.

timed *(INET)* **Time d**aemon. Internet background program originally developed in the Berkeley Software Distribution to support the Transmission Control Protocol. Used to synchronize time between hosts on a network, e.g. to ensure that computerized record-keeping is ac-

curate. One host is selected as the master and time is checked and reset, if necessary, based on the master host's time. *See* Internet, daemon, TCP and adjtime.

time division multiplex Abbreviated and commonly referred to as TDM. *See* TDM.

Time-Domain Reflectometer Commonly abbreviated and called TDR. *See* TDR.

time-of-day register Commonly abbreviated and called TODR. *See* TODR.

timeout 1. Termination of an attempt to connect to a remote host when a predetermined deadline has been reached and no response has been received from the host. 2. Protocol used to retransmit data after a specified period of time has elapsed and there has been no acknowledgment that the previous transmission was received. 3. Utility that automatically logs off users if they have not made an input in a specified period of time. 4. Specified period of nonactivity, after which a program or process is stopped, e.g. if a user finishes with a program but does not exit from it and there is no further activity after a specified period, the program will be stopped. Prevents programs or processes from remaining resident in memory when there is no activity related to them.

time quantum Commonly abbreviated and called tqntm. *See* tqntm.

timer *(POS)* POSIX.4 (real-time operating system) term. Provides multiple timing facilities that operate in nanoseconds to support real-time operations. Provide the ability to generate an interrupt or schedule an operation based on time-of-day or elapsed time, e.g. a timer can be used to cause a program to read an input device every 5 milliseconds. *See* POSIX.4 and RTOS.

times *(ATT)* System call used to determine how long a process has been running. Used by system accounting to collect processing time of programs.

Times Field in L.sys which indicates the time of day that one or more connections are to be made to specified remote hosts. *See* L.sys.

time server Term used in the Open Software Foundation Inc. Distributed Computing Environment distributed time service. A network host that synchronizes the time for other hosts on the network. *See* OSF, DCE, DTS, local server, global server and courier.

Time Server Protocol *(INET)* Commonly abbreviated and called TIME. *See* TIME.

time-sharing Function of the UNIX operating system that allows more than one user to use the system at the same time and permits more than one user to access the same program simultaneously. *See* multi-user and multitasking.

timesharing Commonly spelled time-sharing. *See* time-sharing.

time-sharing class Type of process with a lower priority than either a real-time process or system class process in scheduling access to a system's resources. Time-sharing class processes take turns running by sharing system resources. They are scheduled based upon such factors as availability of the resources needed and time planned for the process to run. Any process can be designated as a time-sharing class process. Normally, less critical processes, such as those related to electronic mail, are classified as time-sharing. *See* real-time class and system class.

Time-Sharing Operation Commonly abbreviated and called TSO. *See* TSO.

time-sharing user priority value Commonly abbreviated and called tsupri. *See* tsupri value.

time slice Minuscule amount of time during which a central processing unit executes part of each user's process, in turn. Used in time-sharing environments. *See* CPU.

timestamp Term related to the Data Encryption Standard and secure Remote Procedure Call. Used to compare the system time between a client and server as part of the authentication process. An encrypted time is sent from one to the other; the timestamp shows the receiver what the sender's time should be and if the encrypted time does not match this within a specified period, the connection is refused. *See* DES, RPC, client, server, encrypt, decrypt, conversation-key, common-key, public-key, private-key, keylogin, Keyserver, credential, verifier and window.

timex *(ATT/XEN)* Command used when another command is running to report how many seconds the execution of the other command takes and what the system is doing while that command is being executed. Included in the System Performance Analysis Utilities in UNIX System V. *See* SPAU, prfdc, prfld, prfpr, prfsnap, prfstat, sadc, sadp, sag, sar, and sa2.

timezone 1. Command used to display or set the correct time zone in which a computer is located. 2. Key word used in creating the kernel that establishes the time zone in which the computer is located. *See* kernel and TZ.

tip *(BSD)* Command used to establish a connection to a remote system by calling out through terminal ports and/or modems.

TI-RPC **T**ransport **I**ndependent **R**emote **P**rocedure **C**alls. Sun Microsystems Inc.'s release of Remote Procedure Calls capable of running on protocols other than the Transport Control Protocol/Internet Protocol. The original release of RPC ran only on the Transport Control Protocol/Internet Protocol. *See* RPC and TCP/IP.

TIS **T**ool **I**nterface **S**tandards committee. Group formed by Borland International Inc., IBM Corp., Intel Corp., Lotus Development Corp., Microsoft Corp., The Santa Cruz Operation Inc., MetaWare Inc., and Watcom in early 1993. Aims to establish standards for interoperability and portability of application development tools used with 32-bit operating systems, such as Microsoft's Windows New Technology, IBM's Operating System/2 or UNIX. *See* 32-bit computer, Windows NT and OS/2.

Tk Toolkit. X Window System applications development kit for the Tool Command Language, developed at the University of California, Berkeley, by John Ousterhout. Provides users the ability to develop graphical applications that have the look and feel of Motif programs. *See* Tcl, Tk and Motif.

TLI *(ATT)* Transport Layer Interface. Programmable interface program, used to develop applications independent of network protocols.

tlock *(OTH)* Terminal **lock**. Shell script that allows users to lock their terminals and deny access to others. Users can remain logged in while leaving their terminals unattended yet relatively secure. The users must enter their passwords to break the lock.

TM Transaction **m**anager. Commonly abbreviated and called TP. *See* TP.

TMOUT **T**ime**out**. Korn shell variable set to indicate how many seconds a terminal may remain inactive before it automatically logs off its user.

/tmp Root directory used to store temporary files. For example, whenever a file is edited, modifications are actually made on a mirror image of the original file that is maintained in /tmp during the editing process.

tmpfile *(ATT)* **T**e**mp**orary **file**. C language library routine used to create a unique temporary file name. *See* library routines.

tn3270 *(INET)* Subelement of the Internet TELNET protocol that allows a user to connect to IBM Corp. computers using the 3270 protocol. *See* Internet and Telnet.

tnamed *(INET)* **T**rivial **name** **d**aemon. Background program started by the Internet daemon. Used to support and manage the ports used by different Internet protocols. *See* daemon, inetd and Internet.

toall *(OTH)* **To all**. Public domain command used to broadcast information to users on a computer system. If a getty process is identified to support a terminal, toall sends a message to the terminal, whether or not a user is logged in. *See* wall.

toc *(ATT)* **T**able **o**f **c**ontents. Set of graphics routines, including dtoc, ttoc and vtoc, which generates tables of contents for directories and subdirectories. *See* dtoc, ttoc and vtoc.

TODR **T**ime-**o**f-**d**ay **r**egister. Hardware clock, with a separate battery used to inform the computer of the correct time, e.g. used to reset system time following a power failure.

toggle 1. *(ATT)* Shell layer command used to switch between shell layers. Moves the user from the current shell to the previous shell, or vice versa.-*See* shl and resume. **2.** Option in a software program which allows a user to start or stop a function. Derived from toggle switch, which can be flicked from the on to the off position.

toggle options Editor options that can be turned on and off by the user, e.g. error-bells, which is used to send an audible sound with each error message; ignore-case, which allows for string searches that are not case specific; and list, which is used to display hidden control characters. *See* numeric options and string options.

toggle variables C or Korn shell variables that can be turned on and off using the set and unset commands. Allow users to customize their environment, e.g. set the editor, prompt or shell to be used. *See* C shell, Korn shell, filec, notify, set and unset.

token 1. Short electronic message, or signal, passed in a specific order from host to host on a Token Ring or Fiber Distribution

Interface network. Allows each host, in turn, to transmit data over the network and ensures that all the hosts do not transmit data at the same time. *See* Token Ring and FDDI. **2.** Subdivided section of a string of characters. Monatomic unit of data that cannot be further subdivided into meaningful units. Studied by itself as a step toward understanding the meaning of the whole string, e.g. components of a shell command that are analyzed to determine what action should be executed. *See* parse.

token bus Network topology consisting of nodes connected by a single transmission line. Access to the network is managed by a token, or signal, used to determine which node has the right to send traffic. The token is passed in a circular motion from node to node on the network; but it is passed logically, so that the next node in the priority may or may not be the next physical node. When a node receives the token, it transmits queued messages. If there are no messages or the transmission is completed, the token is passed to the next node on the network. *See* Token Ring.

token passing Method of transmitting data on a Token Ring or Fiber Distributed Data Interface network in an orderly fashion. A short electronic message, or token, is passed in a specific order from host to host. If a host needs to transmit data, it attaches its message

to the token and sends it on. Once the transmission is completed, the token continues its circuit until another host is ready to communicate. The traffic pattern can be altered so that the token stops more often at those hosts that most frequently transmit data. On networks on which all the hosts are extremely busy, token passing actually increases the system's efficiency because less time is spent passing the token to idle hosts and there are no data collisions.

Token Ring Local area data communications network that uses a ring topology and was developed by IBM Corp. The name is derived from the process of passing a short electronic message, called a token, in sequential order. A host on the network cannot access the network until it receives the token. Once the host has completed transmission, it releases the token. A Token Ring network transfers data at 4 megabits per second or 16 megabits per second. Depending on the type of wiring used, up to 270 devices, including mainframe, mini- and microcomputers, can be connected to this kind of network.

Token Rotation Timer Process in a Fiber Distribution Data Interface network used to determine how long a host can retain a token before releasing it. *See* FDDI and token.

Tom's Window Manager Commonly abbreviated and called twm. *See* twm.

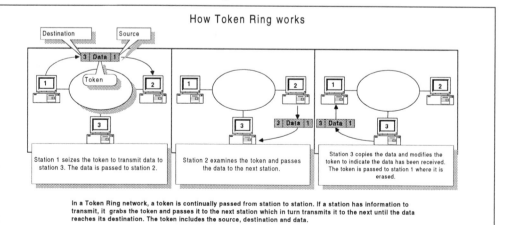

How Token Ring works

Station 1 seizes the token to transmit data to station 3. The data is passed to station 2.

Station 2 examines the token and passes the data to the next station.

Station 3 copies the data and modifies the token to indicate the data has been received. The token is passed to station 1 where it is erased.

In a Token Ring network, a token is continually passed from station to station. If a station has information to transmit, it grabs the token and passes it to the next station which in turn transmits it to the next until the data reaches its destination. The token includes the source, destination and data.

tool Also known as *program development tool*. Application program, e.g. compiler, assembler and debugger, that helps users write and maintain their own programs. Not necessary for the basic operation of a system. *See* compiler, assembler and debugger.

Tool Command Language Commonly abbreviated and called Tcl. *See* Tcl.

Tool Interface Standards committee Abbreviated and commonly known as TIS. *See* TIS.

toolkit 1. Collection of programs and/or routines used by programmers as a shortcut to develop common elements of application software, e.g. menus, forms and scrollbars. *See* widget. 2. Abbreviated Tk. *See* TK.

tool palette Set of icons used to represent tools available for creating graphical images or documents, e.g. if a telephone number program is created it can be represented by an image of a telephone. *See* icon.

TOP Technical and Office Protocol. Originally developed by Boeing Computer Services and based on Open Systems Interconnection standards. Used in an office or engineering environment to move and control design and production data. *See* ISO/OSI.

top half Programs in an operating system that are started as a result of a system call or trap. *See* bottom half, system call and trap.

top-level domain *(INET)* Second level of the Internet. Divided into several primary categories to which all hosts are assigned by the Network Information Center, based on the primary use of the host, e.g. ARPA for the ARPANET, GOV for government other than military and MIL for military. *See* Internet, NIC, domain, root-level domain, second-level domain and local administrative domain.

toplines Electronic-mail variable. *See* .mailrc variables (Appendix F).

touch 1. *(ATT/BSD/XEN)* Command used to create an empty file. Can be used to update the access and modification dates of a file. This prevents files from being automatically deleted if a system program is used to look for and automatically delete files created before a specific date 2. Jargon term meaning to modify a file.

touchpad Computer interface that uses a pad which emulates screen display. A user manipulates data on the pad with a pen.

touch screen Monitor on which a user can enter data and commands, select options and move a cursor by simply touching the surface. Acts as a replacement for a keyboard or a mouse. *See* keyboard and mouse.

tout *(OTH)* Timeout. Program that allows users to set the maximum amount of time their terminals can remain idle before they are automatically logged off by the system. A terminal is idle when a user is logged in but not making any input, or when a process is running in the background and no other activity is taking place. *See* idle and idle time.

Towers of Hanoi Mathematical sequence used to determine how extensive a backup should be and when it should be done. The sequence is usually used with the dump command and represents dump levels, or how extensive the backup will be, e.g. a complete dump, level 0, to any portion of a file system as indicated by a numeric between 1 and 9. Allows files to be backed up every two days, using a minimum number of tapes. The name is derived from an ancient Buddhist game.

tp *(BSD)* Preprocessor for the tar backup utility. Used to maintain tape file archives. *See* preprocessor and tar.

TP Transaction processing monitor. Also called a transaction manager, transaction monitor, TPM, TP monitor or TM. Provides the ability to optimize response time and throughput, real-time database access and manage multiple concurrent updates of data. It is the element of an on-line transaction processing system which manages the sequence of multiple transactions, routing, load balancing, scalability, fault resistance and recovery from failures. Used in AT&T Co.'s Tuxedo System which routes a client request to the correct server. *See* OLTP, Tuxedo, Tuxedo System/T, CICS and client/server.

TP0 Transport Protocol Class **0**. Basic transport layer protocol of the International Organization for Standardization/Open Systems Interconnection which breaks up packets of data that are to be sent over a network and then reassembles them when they are received. *See* ISO/OSI, fragmentation and transport layer.

TP1 Transport Protocol Class 1. Provides reliability enhancements to the International Organization for Standardization/Open Systems Interconnection TP0 protocol. *See* ISO/OSI, TP0 and transport layer.

TP2 Transport Protocol Class 2. Transport layer protocol used in multiplexing, when a single data stream is split into several streams. An International Organization for Standardization/Open Systems Interconnection protocol. *See* ISO/OSI and transport layer.

TP3 Transport Protocol Class 3. Enhanced version of the International Organization for Standardization/Open Systems Interconnection TP2 protocol that offers the greater reliability of TP1 and the multiplexing capability of TP2. *See* ISO/OSI, TP1, TP2 and transport layer.

TP4 Transport Protocol Class 4. International Organization for Standardization/Open System Interconnection transport protocol similar to Transport Control Protocol. *See* ISO/OSI and TCP.

TPC Transaction Processing Performance Council. Nonprofit organization started in 1988, with more than 40 members drawn from leading hardware and software companies. Develops industry standard benchmarks for transaction processing systems. Members include

AT&T Co., Digital Equipment Corp., IBM Corp. and NCR Corp. *See* TPC-A, TPC-B and TPC-C.

TPC-A TPC (Transaction Processing Performance Council) Benchmark **A**. Benchmark specification developed by the Transaction Processing Performance Council to measure the performance of a central processing unit, memory, input and output sub-systems, terminal interface and database activity. Specifically designed for minicomputers and servers operating in the distributed network processing environment. Measures performance, in transactions per second, of software and hardware to include input terminals related to on-line transaction processing for client/server environments. TPC-A was released in November 1989. *See* benchmark, TPC, TPC-B, TPC-C and OLTP.

TPC-B TPC (Transaction Processing Performance Council) Benchmark **B**. Benchmark specification developed to measure database performance for batch processing on a single system. Also can be used to measure throughput by different numbers of users and by the amount each user is inputting. Does not simulate user processes like TPC-A. Released in August 1990. *See* benchmark, TPC, TPC-A, TPC-C and DBMS.

TPC Benchmark A Commonly abbreviated and called TPC-A. *See* TPC-A.

TPC Benchmark B Commonly abbreviated and called TPC-B. *See* TPC-B.

TPC Benchmark C Commonly abbreviated and called TPC-C. *See* TPC-C.

TPC-C TPC (Transaction Processing Performance Council) Benchmark **C**. Benchmark specification developed by Transaction Processing Performance Council to measure the performance of central processing unit, memory, input and output subsystems, terminal interface, database activity and forms processing. TPC-C specifically measures on-line transaction processing across networks with hundreds of users for multiple and varying types of processes, e.g. inventory control (input and output) orders and payments made or received; multiple on-line terminal connections; high disk input and output operations; and running multiple transactions simultaneously. Released in early 1992. *See* benchmark, OLTP, TPC, TPC-A, TPC-B and DBMS.

tplot *(ATT)* Terminal **plot**. Graphics filter (300, 300S, 450, 4014 and ver) capable of handling special graphics plotting instructions for a specified terminal. *See* 300, 300S, 450, 4014 and ver.

TPM 1. Transaction processing monitor. Commonly abbreviated and called TP. *See* TP. **2.** Third-party maintenance. Service provided by a company that specializes in computer hardware maintenance, independent of the equipment's manufacturers. Providers are able to offer maintenance support for products from multiple vendors. Service is usually available for a wide variety of brands, independent of the equipments' manufacturers. *See* OEM maintenance and self-maintenance.

TP monitor Transaction processing **monitor**. Commonly abbreviated and called TP. *See* TP.

t protocol *(BSD)* TCP/IP **protocol**. Data protocol supported by the UNIX-to-UNIX CoPy communications system to pass data between networks. The t protocol was designed to deliver files over Transmission Control Protocol/Internet Protocol (TCP/IP) networks. Since TCP/IP is designed to guarantee delivery of error-free messages, it assumes data is being transferred error free and performs neither error checking nor flow control functions. *See* UUCP, X.25, e protocol, f protocol, g protocol, G protocol and x protocol.

TPS 1. Transactions per second. Measurement of throughput for a computer. **2.** Performance measurement of an on-line transaction processing system in a specified environment. *See* OLTP.

tput *(ATT)* Command initiated automatically by a program or by a user, with arguments, to start or reset the type of terminal or clear the screen of the terminal being used. *See* stty, clear, terminfo and TERM.

tqntm Time **quantum**. Maximum amount of central processing unit time which can be used by a process. *See* CPU.

tr Translate. Filter used to manipulate text files, e.g. to replace one string of characters with another, or to change all lowercase characters to uppercase characters.

tr2tex Translate **to TeX**. Program used to translate documents from a text format created by the troff program to a format created by the TeX text formatter. *See* troff and TeX.

track Sectors of a tape or disk that can be written to or read by a head in a single position. The number of tracks varies with the storage capacity of the tape or disk. Tracks on tape are like parallel lines running along the edge of the tape. On a disk, a track is a circle slightly larger than the read/write head of the disk drive. *See* sector.

trackball Also spelled track ball. Palm-size, hand-operated input device used with personal computers, graphics terminals, workstations and X Window System terminals. Similar to a mouse. Consists of a movable ball set in a case, connected to the terminal by a cable. Used as an extension of a keyboard to enter and manipulate data, commands, graphics, etc. By rotating the ball and depressing a button to activate commands, a user can move the cursor, enter text, draw, etc. Very useful in tasks which require precision, such as drawing. Requires far less work space than a mouse.

Trackball

---

tractor feed System that feeds paper into a printer using studded sprockets. Paper with small, regularly spaced holes along both sides can be continuously pulled through the printer by the sprockets. *See* fanfold paper and friction feed.

trade journal Technical news magazine or paper published about hardware, software, communications and other computer-related topics. A vast number of them can be subscribed to at no cost.

trade rag Jargon term for trade journal. *See* trade journal.

traffic 1. Jargon term for data transmitted over a network. 2. Program that monitors and gathers statistics about how an Ethernet network is being used. Developed by Sun Microsystems Inc. Provides a graphical display of load, packet sizes, traffic by protocol, traffic source and traffic destination. *See* Ethernet.

traffic cop Jargon term for the kernel. *See* kernel.

trailer Data added to the end of a packet. Used to identify the packet so it can be reassembled into a complete data message at the receiving end. *See* header and packet.

trailer protocol Protocol used to encapsulate Internet Protocol packets and transmit them over Ethernet or other local area networks.

transaction Database operations that result in a change in the information stored in the database.

Transaction Capability Part Commonly abbreviated and called TCAP. *See* TCAP.

transaction logging Maintaining a detailed account of all inputs related to a database transaction. If there is corruption or loss of data, the log can be used to reconstruct the database.

transaction manager Commonly called TP (transaction processing monitor). *See* TP.

transaction monitor Commonly called TP (transaction processing monitor). *See* TP.

transaction processing Interactive updating of files as a result of data entry. A prime example of a transaction processing system is an airline ticketing and seat assignment system.

Transaction Processing Performance Council Commonly abbreviated and called TPC. *See* TPC.

transactions per second Commonly abbreviated TPS. *See* TPS.

transceiver Device capable of transmitting and receiving signals.

transfer protocols Software used to move large amounts of data between computers. Transfer protocols are differentiated by the way they check for errors, and store, handle, bundle, send and receive data. *See* X.25.

transfer rate Measurement of the speed at which data moves from one medium to another, e.g. from memory to disk, from disk to disk, from disk to tape and from memory to terminal. Normally expressed in the number of characters per second.

transient object Object Management Group term for any program or operation that is not saved after a process is completed. *See* OMG, object and persistent object.

transients Commonly called electrical noise. *See* electrical noise.

Translate *(ATT)* System V, Release 4 electronic-mail command used to identify how electronic-mail addresses are to be converted. *See* SVR4.x, e-mail, mail alias and mailalias.

Transmission Control Protocol *(INET)* Commonly abbreviated and called TCP. *See* TCP.

Transmission Control Protocol/Internet Protocol *(INET)* Commonly abbreviated and called TCP/IP. *See* TCP/IP.

Transmission Control Protocol Utilities
Set of programs included in System V, Release 4. Used to manage Transmission Control Protocol and Internet Protocol connectivity. *See* SVR4.x and TCP/IP.

transmission medium Physical medium over which communications are carried, e.g. fiber-optic cable and copper wire.

transparent Term used to describe a software package that can be transferred from one type of computer to another without change.

transparent access When a user is able to obtain data without the knowledge of the source database or file.

Transparent File Access Commonly abbreviated and called TFA. *See* TFA.

transport Generic term for all the elements used to send data across a network, e.g. the protocol, cable, etc.

TRANSPORT Commonly called transport provider. *See* transport provider.

transportation layer Commonly called transport layer. *See* transport layer.

Transport Control Protocol Commonly abbreviated and called TCP. *See* TCP.

Transport Control Protocol/Internet Protocol *(INET)* Commonly abbreviated and called TCP/IP. *See* TCP/IP.

Transport Independent Remote Procedure Call Commonly abbreviated and called TI-RPC. *See* TI-RPC.

transport layer Also called reliability layer. Fourth layer of the Internet Transmission Control Protocol and Internet Protocol, and International Organization for Standardization/Open Systems Interconnection network model. Responsible for maintaining data flow and the integrity of communications between applications between the sending host and the correct destination. *See* DARPA, Internet, TCP, IP, TCP/IP architecture, ARM, ISO/OSI and OSIRM.

Transport Layer Interface Commonly abbreviated and called TLI. *See* TLI.

Transport Protocol 0 Commonly abbreviated and called TP0. *See* TP0.

Transport Protocol 1 Commonly abbreviated and called TP1. *See* TP1.

Transport Protocol 2 Commonly abbreviated and called TP2. *See* TP2.

Transport Protocol 3 Commonly abbreviated and called TP3. *See* TP3.

Transport Protocol 4 Commonly abbreviated and called TP4. *See* TP4.

transport provider Physical network used to connect hosts on a network, e.g. Ethernet and Token Ring.

Transport Service Bridge Commonly abbreviated and called TSB. *See* TSB.

Transport Service Convergence Protocol Commonly abbreviated and called TSCP. *See* TSCP.

trap 1. Signal sent to the kernel to initiate a specific action that is to be taken, e.g. a system call. The action depends upon the signal sent and conditions leading to the signal. A trap may be sent to ensure that an interrupted process has been stopped correctly and necessary functions have been completed, e.g. deleting files created in /tmp by a process that are normally deleted when the process is complete. 2. Simple Network Management Protocol system management message. Used by network agents to report status changes to the network manager. *See* SNMP, get, set and agent.

trapdoor Commonly called back door. *See* back door.

trapdoor algorithm Formula that forms the basis for the password system of UNIX. Ciphers are created from plain text to protect the true identity of a password. The ciphers cannot be reverse engineered to reveal the password.

tree structure Organization of the UNIX file system, which looks like an upside-down tree with a root and branches. *See* hierarchical file system and file system.

triad Arrangement of phosphorescent dots in groups of three (green, blue and red) on color monitors or picture tubes.

trigger Specific procedure stored with a database that is executed when a pre-identified event takes place.

Triple-X X.25 network protocol used to log in from remote terminals.

Trivial File Transfer Protocol *(INET)* Commonly abbreviated and called TFTP. *See* TFTP.

Trivial File Transfer Protocol, Dedicated *(INET)* Commonly abbreviated and called TFTPD. *See* TFTPD.

TRIXI Tri-Partite International X.25 Interconnection. X.25 network used to support research and development in the United Kingdom, Germany and France. Transmits data at 2 megabits per second.

trman *(BSD)* Translate **man**ual macros. Translates UNIX version 6 manual macros to UNIX version 7 macros. *See* macro.

trn Threaded news reader. Also abbreviation for tree read news. A public domain utility that groups USENET electronic news articles based on common subject matter into "threads". A derivative of the widely used rn news reader. Graphically displays the pedigree, or hierarchy, of related articles. *See* rn, news and USENET.

troff 1. Typesetter run off. Part of Documenter's Workbench set of text formatting programs. Pronounced *TEE ROFF*. Originally written by Joseph Osanna and rewritten by Brian Kernighan. A direct descendant of roff, the original runoff, troff is a document or text formatting program that allows scaleable fonts to be used. Used to typeset text for graphic devices or phototypesetters. Commands embedded in the text are read by one of the standard UNIX formatting macros, e.g. ms and mm. The macro in turn sends commands to the printer, which produces a finished document formatted in the

specified style. *See* phototypesetter and dvi troff. 2. Command used to run the troff text formatter. *See* DWB, runoff, nroff and macro.

troff preprocessor Collection of programs run before the troff text formatting program that manipulate data in specific ways, e.g. create tables using tbl. *See* troff, eqn, grap, pic and tbl.

Trojan horse Subversive program. Any program that, while appearing to perform a known or obvious function, is actually performing other functions that are harmful to the system. May gather information that can be used for illegal purposes or to damage a system, e.g. collecting user passwords to gain access to a system. Name derived from the Greek legend in which a huge wooden horse, with Greek soldiers hidden inside, was left at the gates of the enemy city of Troy. After the Trojans wheeled the horse inside, the Greek soldiers climbed out and opened the gates for their waiting army, which destroyed Troy. *See* virus and worm.

trpt *(ATT)* Transliterate protocol trace. Command used to review error records when problems arise with Transmission Control Protocol communications. *See* TCP and netstat.

true 1. Shell command used in programs to test whether a task or tasks have been completed successfully. 2. Command that can be used to set up and run a loop. As long as a successful response is returned, indicated by a value of 0 (zero), the loop continues to run. If anything other than a zero is returned, the loop is terminated.

true color Color mode of a computer color monitor in which 24 bits are stored for each pixel. Enables 16,777,216 distinct colors to be displayed. *See* color mode, pixel, minimum color, pseudo color and high color.

true color monitor Color monitor capable of displaying 16,777,216 colors. *See* CRT and color mode.

truncate 1. C language library routine used to set a file to a specific length. *See* library routines. **2.** To remove characters from either the beginning to a specified location or from a specified location to the end of a file. Normally done to reduce the size of a file.

Truscott UUCP UNIX-to-UNIX CoPy program released in the Fourth Berkeley Software Distribution, Second Release. Named after the lead developer, Tom Truscott. *See* UUCP.

TRUSIX Trusted UNIX Working Group. Formed by the National Computer Security Center in 1987 to support vendors in developing UNIX systems that meet the Department of Defense's B3-level security standards. *See* Orange Book and NCSC.

truss *(ATT)* Command used to monitor the system calls executed by a command. truss executes the command, then maintains a record of system calls that were run, and reports on any machine faults or signal calls. Often used to help identify a problem or perceived problem in running a program or programs. *See* system call.

trusted Synonym for secure or security. *See* security.

Trusted Computer System Evaluation Criteria Commonly abbreviated and called TCSEC. *See* TCSEC and NCSC.

Trusted Path Security feature that requires a user to input a specified sequence of characters on a keyboard to gain access to a system. *See* feature.

Trusted UNIX Working Group
Commonly abbreviated and called TRUSIX. *See* TRUSIX.

trusted user Any user who can modify the sendmail address in the UNIX electronic-mail system. *See* e-mail and sendmail.

TS Abbreviation for time-sharing class. *See* time-sharing class.

TSB Transport Service Bridge. Bridge between two networks at the Open Systems

Interconnection transportation layer. Created by running OSI applications on the Transport Control Protocol/Internet Protocol. *See* OSI, transportation layer and TCP/IP.

TSCP Transport Service Convergence Protocol. Open Systems Interconnection (OSI) protocol used to transmit messages between an OSI and Transmission Control/Internet Protocol network. TSCP runs with the Internet Transmission Control Protocol to make it appear to another OSI transport service as an OSI transport service.

ts dptbl parameter table *(ATT)* Time-sharing class parameter in UNIX System V, Release 4 which contains a table of values used to manage time-sharing processes. *See* SVR4.x.

tset *(BSD)* Terminal set. Command used to set terminal-dependent settings whenever a user logs in to the computer. tset checks the termcap file to determine the individual characteristics of the terminal being used and sets characters like the erase and kill. *See* termcap.

ts kmdpris parameter table *(ATT)* Time-sharing class parameter in UNIX System V, Release 4 which contains a table of values used to manage time-sharing processes that are sleeping, or suspended. *See* SVR4.x and sleep.

TSMAXUPRI *(ATT)* Time-sharing class parameter in UNIX System V, Release 4 used to set the priority level at which user processes can be run. The range is -20 to +20. *See* SVR4.x, priocntl, tsupri value and time-sharing class.

TSO Time-Sharing Operation. IBM Corp.'s interactive shell replacement for the Job Control Language. *See* JCL.

tsort *(ATT/XEN)* Topological **sort**. Command used with the lorder command to make an object library. *See* lorder.

TSR Terminate-and-stay-resident program. Any program operating under DOS that stays loaded in computer memory even when it is not active and can be called on to perform a task while other applications are running. *See* DOS.

tsupri value Time-sharing user priority value. Used as part of a system for setting scheduling priorities of time-sharing processes, using values between -n and n. The tsupri value, however, is only one factor in scheduling processes, and increasing the value of a process will not ensure that it will be run before other time-sharing class processes. *See* process and time-sharing class.

ttoc *(ATT)* Table table of contents. One of the toc graphical table of contents routines. Used with the nroff mm macros to generate a table of contents. *See* toc, nroff and mm macros.

ttt Command used to start a tic-tac-toe game.

tty 1. *(ATT/XEN)* Teletypewriter. Command used to determine to which tty number a terminal is connected. 2. Device handler used to manage terminal transmissions in an asynchronous mode emulating a TTY device. 3. Communications port on a computer for terminals and printers.

TTY Teletypewriter. A low-speed asynchronous communication device composed of a keyboard and printer.

ttyadm *(ATT)* tty administration. Command used to configure new ports under the System V, Release 4 Service Access Facility. *See* SVR4.x, SAF and SAC.

ttydefs *(ATT)* Teletypewriter definitions. File that contains information such as line speed, set up hang up character and erase character, under System V, Release 4. *See* ttymon and SVR4.x.

tty driver Teletypewriter driver. Device driver for terminals. Program that provides the interface between the operating system and a peripheral device. Software within a computer that translates commands into terms understood and acted upon by a terminal. *See* device driver.

tty file System file found in the /dev system directory that identifies which user is using a specific port on the system. *See* port.

ttymon Teletypewriter monitor. Port monitor that replaces the older getty and uugetty commands. Released in UNIX System V, Release 4 to monitor ports and permit login request. A single ttymon can monitor several ports. Each ttymon process is separately identified with a numeric suffix, e.g. ttymon1 and ttymon2. *See* SVR4.x, getty, uugetty, listen and SVR4.x.

ttyname Teletypewriter name. C language library routine used to identify a terminal with a specific set of file descriptors, established whenever a file is opened and containing the file's disk address, file size, creation date and time, last access date and time, last modified date and time, link information and permissions. *See* library routines and file descriptor.

TUBA Transmission Control Protocol/User Datagram Protocol with Bigger Addresses. Open Systems Interconnection alternative to the Internet Transmission Control Protocol/Internet Protocol. Provides more host and node addresses. *See* OSI, Internet, TCP/IP, IP address, PIP, SIP and SIP-P.

tube Jargon term for a terminal. *See* terminal.

tunable parameters System parameters, e.g. the amount of swap space, devices and processes per user, that place limits on the use of system resources and can be modified if necessary. *See* sysdef and tunefs.

tunefs *(BSD)* Tune file system. Normally used to modify the number of blocks of data the system can process at a time, thereby enhancing speed. *See* block and file system.

tuning Commonly called system tuning. *See* system tuning.

tunneling Encapsulation of a protocol into another protocol for transmission.

---

over a single network rather than several networks, e.g. encapsulating X.25 to run over TCP/IP.

turnacct *(ATT)* **Turn** on **acct**ounting. Shell script used to turn on the accounting system by directing accounting information to the /usr/adm/pacct log. *See* shell script and /usr/adm/pacct.

turnkey system Complete computer system that is customized to meet the needs of a particular user or a type of user, e.g. the computer, terminals, communications network, software and services used to manage a distribution warehousing system. Includes both the components (hardware, operating system, application software, peripheral devices) and support services (delivery, installation, training). May also include communications support and maintenance.

Tuxedo UNIX System Laboratories Inc.'s transaction monitor for on-line transaction processing software. Originally developed in 1974 by the AT&T Co. Includes a transaction and resource manager. *See* OLTP, SVR4.x, Tuxedo System/D, Tuxedo System/H, Tuxedo System/T, Tuxedo System/WS and two-phase commit.

Tuxedo System/D Element of UNIX System Laboratories Inc.'s Tuxedo System. A transaction-oriented database manager with an interactive Structured Query Language interpreter (SQL), SQL for C language and library. *See* SQL, Tuxedo, Tuxedo System/H, Tuxedo System/T and Tuxedo System/WS.

Tuxedo System/H Element of UNIX System Laboratories Inc.'s Tuxedo System. Provides the ability to integrate Tuxedo with proprietary transaction monitors, e.g. Customer Information Control System developed by IBM Corp. *See* CICS, Tuxedo, Tuxedo System/D, Tuxedo System/T and Tuxedo System/WS.

Tuxedo System/T Manager for Tuxedo System, UNIX System Laboratories Inc.'s on-line transaction processing software. The core transaction monitor in Tuxedo. Allows multiple users point-to-point ac-

cess. Also allows transactions to be sent between heterogeneous servers running dissimilar databases. *See* OLTP, Tuxedo, BB, Tuxedo System/D, Tuxedo System/H, Tuxedo System/T and Tuxedo System/WS.

Tuxedo System/WS Element of UNIX System Laboratories Inc.'s Tuxedo System. Provides a front-end module with the ability to distribute output to workstations. *See* Tuxedo and Tuxedo System/D, Tuxedo System/H and Tuxedo System/T.

tweak To slightly modify a software program or make adjustments to hardware, either to make it run or to improve its current performance.

twin tail Computer system where multiple central processing units share (access, read, write, etc.) a common set of peripheral devices, e.g. disk or tape drives.

twisted pair 1. Cable composed of two separate insulated wire strands twisted together. One strand of wire is used to carry a signal and the second is used as a ground. 2. Jargon term for an Ethernet system that uses telephone lines as the transport medium. It is easier and cheaper to lay this type of cable. *See* Ethernet, thicknet and thinnet.

twm **T**ab **W**indow **M**anager. Originally called Tom's Window Manager, after its developer, Tom LaStrange. Window manager in X 11, Release 4 of the X Window System. Also called awm in the X 11, Release 3 version. *See* X Window System, window manager, X11R3 and X11R4.

two-phase commit Distributed process protocol under which transactions must be accepted or rejected by all the hosts on a network. A resource manager for load balancing, in which the system's work load is spread out equally among its resources. In the first phase, the protocol checks the network to determine if a message may be sent. In the second phase, the receiving system indicates if it can receive the message. Used to ensure an all-or-nothing guarantee of the completion of a database transaction. *See* atomicity and load balancing.

type   Characteristic of variables within a specific programming language, e.g. size and bit pattern.

typeahead   1. Input that is entered before the system prompts the user to do so from the system. *See* prompt. **2.** Condition in which there is a delay between when a user enters characters on a keyboard and when those characters appear on the monitor. Can be caused by delays on the data network due to heavy traffic loads.

typeahead buffer Temporary   storage area for input being entered faster than it can be displayed. Used when a system is writing data to disk or is simply overloaded. When resources are available, the input is moved from the buffer and is displayed on the screen. Users may notice this feature if they type in a few words but nothing appears on the screen instantly.

type-scaling   Technology developed by Bitstream and donated for inclusion in the Massachusetts Institute of Technology X 11, Release 5 specification of the X Window System. Enables a system to produce scalable, typeset-quality fonts. *See* X11R5 and X Window System.

typescript   File created when a user starts the command script, which is used store all the inputs or outputs for a terminal. *See* script.

typeset   *(ATT)* Korn shell command used to create or display local or user variables to specify timing and formatting instructions which the programmer or user wants the shell to follow.

typo 1. *(ATT)* Command used to locate misspelled words. **2.** Commonly called fat finger. *See* fat finger.

TZ   *(ATT)* Timezone. Environmental variable used to set the timezone of where the computer is located.

U

u Symbol for 10^{-6} (1/1,000,000) or micro. *See* micro.

u *(BSD)* Command used to display a compact list of users on the system. *See* who.

u370 *(ATT)* Command used to test if a computer system is an IBM Corp. System/370. Returns a 0 (TRUE) value if it is, or a non-zero (FALSE) value if it is not. *See* machid.

u3b *(ATT)* Command used to test if a computer system is an AT&T 3B. Returns a 0 (TRUE) value if it is, or a non-zero (FALSE) value if it is not. *See* machid.

u3b2 *(ATT)* Command used to test if a computer system is an AT&T 3B2. Returns a 0 (TRUE) value if it is, or a non-zero (FALSE) value if it is not. *See* machid.

u3b5 *(ATT)* Command used to test if a computer system is an AT&T 3B5. Returns a 0 (TRUE) value if it is, or a non-zero (FALSE) value if it is not. *See* machid.

u3b15 *(ATT)* Command used to test if a computer system is an AT&T 3B15. Returns a 0 (TRUE) value if it is, or a non-zero (FALSE) value if it is not. *See* machid.

UA **U**ser **A**gent. Element of the X.400 standard. Handles the receipt and sending of electronic mail messages. Developed by the International Telecommunication Union Telecommunication Standardization Sector, formerly called the Consultative Committee on International Telegraphy and Telephony. *See* CCITT, X.400, MTA, access unit, message store and e-mail.

UART **U**niversal **A**synchronous **R**eceiver **T**ransmitter. Integrated circuit in personal computers responsible for serial communication within a computer. Collects single bits of data and packages them into 1-byte (or 8-bit) packages to be transferred to the central processing unit (CPU). Also takes bytes of data from the CPU and converts them into single bits for transmission. *See* bit and byte.

UCA **U**tility **C**ommunications **A**rchitecture. Model based upon Open Systems Interconnection protocols developed by the Electrical Power Research Institute. Used to connect similar and dissimilar computer systems and networks. *See* OSI.

UDF **U**nshielded **T**wisted **P**air **D**evelopment **F**orum. Consortium composed of Apple Computer Inc., AT&T Co., British Telecommunications, PLC, Crescendo Communications Inc., Fibronics International Inc., Ungermann-Bass Inc. and Hewlett-Packard Co. Sponsors development of standards related to transmitting Fiber Distributed Data Interface communications using standard telephone wire. Located in Sunnyvale, California. *See* UTP, DIW-24 and FDDI.

UDP *(INET)* **U**ser **D**atagram **P**rotocol. Protocol added above the Internet Protocol Suite used for packet transmission. Developed by the Defense Advanced Research Projects Agency. Sends packets, called datagrams, from an application program on a local host to an application program on a remote host, but does not guarantee delivery. *See* Internet Protocol Suite, DARPA, packet and IP.

UDP/IP User Datagram Protocol/Internet Protocol. Transport protocol based upon the Transport Control Protocol/Internet Protocol. Version of the Internet Protocol modified by the International Organization for Standardization to provide, for example, a larger address size and the ability to work with protocols that allow for either connection or connectionless protocols. *See* TCP/IP.

ufs *(ATT)* Abbreviation for a Berkeley Software Distribution type of file system in System V, Release 4. *See* BSD, file system, SVR4.x and s5.

UFS UNIX File System. AT&T Co.'s name for the Berkeley Software Distribution Fast File System, which was incorporated in System V, Release 4. *See* BSD and Fast File System.

UI **1.** UNIX International Inc. Also called UII. Organization similar to the Corporation for Open Systems International. Formed in 1988 by AT&T Co., Amdahl Corp., Control Data Corp., Motorola Inc., NCR Corp., Sun Microsystems Inc. and others, and closed in November 1993. An association of approximately 250 companies that promotes System V and was responsible for defining releases of System V. Was headquartered in Parsippany, New Jersey. *See* USG and COS. **2.** User Interface. Tool used in developing X Window System applications. Used to combine the control codes, screen layout, application interface, run-time component and application software into a finished product. *See* X Window System, D language, widget and X toolkit.

UI-ATLAS Commonly called Atlas. *See* Atlas.

UID User identifier. Positive numeric identifier in the /etc/passwd file that uniquely identifies an individual and, along with the group identifier, that user's access permissions to the system. *See* GID and permissions.

UID 0 User identifier 0. Numeric identifier for the superuser, or root, the individual who has the password or permissions to access and modify all files in the system. *See* root.

.uid.rules *(ATT)* User identifier rules. File used in the Remote File Sharing system by the idload command to establish user access permissions in the mapping translation tables. The full file path is /etc/rfs/auth.info/.uid.rules. *See* RFS, idload, permissions, UID and mapping translation table.

UII UNIX International Inc. Commonly abbreviated UI. *See* UI.

UIL User Interface Language. Open Software Foundation/Motif language used to provide an interface between a development toolkit and an application being developed. *See* OSF/Motif.

UIMS User interface management system. Also called graphical user interface builder. A set of tools used to help developers more easily create and test interfaces between the X Window System and an application. *See* GUI and X Window System.

uio User input/output. Kernel data structure representing the input and/or output started in the user mode. Contains descriptive information required to manage a system's input and/or output. *See* I/O.

UKUUG United Kingdom UNIX System User Group.

ul *(BSD)* Underline. Command used to read the underline commands in documents formatted by the nroff program so the underlining can be displayed by the terminal. *See* nroff.

UL approved Underwriters Laboratories **approved**. Safety verification and seal of approval based upon tests performed on hardware for fire and electrical safety. Some fire departments will not allow installation of equipment that is not UL approved.

ulimit *(ATT)* System program used to set limits on a process based on command parameters, e.g. limits can be placed on usage of the central processing unit by a process and maximum size of a file. Limits can only be modified by the superuser. Normal users can use ulimit to display the system limits. *See* system call.

Ultra-Hyper VGA Ultra-Hyper video graphics array. VGA monitor with a resolution of 3300 x 2560 pixels. *See* VGA, 8514/A, CGA, EGA, super VGA, XGA and pixel.

Ultra VGA Ultra video graphics array. VGA monitor with a resolution of 1280 x 1024 pixels. *See* VGA, 8514/A, CGA, EGA, super VGA, XGA and pixel.

Ultrix-32 Berkeley Software Distribution operating system look-alike, developed by a Digital Equipment Corp. team headed by Armando Stettner. *See* BSD.

Ultrix Window Manager C o m m o n l y abbreviated and called uwm. *See* uwm.

umask 1. User **mask**. Command used to display, create or change the default creation mask for file and directory permission settings. **2.** File created for either systemwide or individual use. Contains default octal values indicating the access permissions for files. *See* cmask and permissions.

umount 1. *(ATT)* **Unmount**. Command used by a system administrator to unmount, or disable, a file system or disk. Makes a file system inaccessible to users on a local system or on a remote system that is part of the Distributed File System. *See* system call, unmount, file system, mount and DFS. **2.** *(ATT)* System call initiated by the umount command to disable a file system.

umountall *(ATT)* **Unmount all** file systems. Distributed File System command used by a system administrator to unmount, or disable, all file systems. When the umountall command is run, it makes all the file systems inaccessible to users. Can be used on local systems or as part of the Distributed File System for remote systems. *See* file system, mount and DFS.

unadv Unadvertise. Remote File Sharing command used to turn off the notice that indicates a network resource is available for access by users on client computers. *See* RFS, adv and share.

unalias *(ATT)* **Unalias**. Command used to delete an alias created for a command. *See* alias.

uname *(ATT/XEN)* Command used to provide the name of the system to which a user is logged in. Using various options, the user can obtain additional information about the system, e.g. which node the system is connected to, if on a network; which version of an operating system is being used; and the brand of hardware being used.

unattended operation Commonly called lights-out operation. *See* lights-out operation.

unblock *(ATT)* Shell layer command used to permit output from one layer to appear on the screen while a user is working in another layer. *See* shl and block.

unbuffered device Commonly called raw device. *See* raw device.

unbuffered disk device Disk to which input and/or output is read or written directly, without the aid of kernel buffering. *See* raw device.

unbundle To sell services, programs, software and hardware separately.

uncompact *(ATT)* Command used to decompress files that have been reduced in size, using the compact command, so they occupy less space on either a disk when stored or on a channel when transmitted. *See* compact.

uncompress 1. Command used to decompress files reduced in size with the compress command so they occupy less space on either a disk when stored or a channel when transmitted. *See* compress. **2.** To return a file that has been compressed to its normal state, that is, size and format.

uncompressdir *(BSD)* Shell script used to decompress all files in a directory.

undo Command used to reverse the previous command or action.

unget *(ATT/XEN)* **Un**do **get**. One of the thirteen Source Code Control System (SCCS) commands used to cancel a SCCS get command before the delta command making changes to a file. *See* SCCS, admin, cdc, comb, delta, get, help, prs, rmdel, sact, sccsdiff, val, vc and what.

UNIBUS Digital Equipment Corp. input/output bus hardware design specifically designed to connect medium- to low-speed peripheral devices to a computer. *See* I/O and bus.

UNICES Plural of UNIX.

UNICS **Uni**plexed **I**nformation **C**omputing **S**ystem. Original name for the UNIX operating system. *See* MULTICS and UNIX.

unifdef *(BSD)* Command used to remove a #ifdefed line (C language conditional source code) from a file.

UniForum Formerly called /usr/group. Nonprofit association formed in 1980 to improve the UNIX operating system through the open exchange of information among and mutual cooperation of members, outside groups and businesses. Has more than 60,000 members and headquarters in Santa Clara, California. *See* Forum, The.

UniForum Canada Canadian UNIX users group formed in 1986.

UniForum NZ Formerly NZUSUGI or New Zealand UNIX Systems User Group Inc. UNIX users group formed in 1985.

UniForum SA UNIX users group formed in 1987 for users in southern African countries.

UniForum UK United Kingdom UNIX users group, formerly known as /usr/group/UK and formed in 1983.

UNIGS Swiss UNIX users group.

UniNews Formerly called /usr/digest. Biweekly newsletter for UniForum members. Provides information on UNIX conferences and shows, and product announcements. *See* UniForum.

uninterruptible power supply Commonly abbreviated and called UPS. *See* UPS.

Uninterruptible Uptime Users Group Commonly abbreviated and called UUUG. *See* UUUG.

Uniplexed Information Computing System Abbreviate and commonly known as UNICS. *See* UNICS.

uniprocessor Computer system with a single processor which performs all computations. *See* MP.

uniq *(ATT/XEN)* Command used when there are two or more identical lines in a file to delete all but one of the lines.

UNIQUE Quarterly magazine released on videotape, published by InfoPro Systems. Provides information for nontechnical users of all types of computers, with emphasis on personal computers.

units *(ATT/XEN)* Software program for converting one type of unit of measurement to another, e.g. miles to kilometers.

unit start routine Device driver or program that provides the interface between the operating system and a peripheral device. Performs the preliminary work before either establishing an interface, or connection, or transferring data between a computer and a peripheral. *See* device driver and special file.

Univel **UNIX No**vell. Company formed in late 1991 by UNIX Systems Laboratories Inc. and Novell Inc. to integrate personal computer local area networks with UNIX. Released a desktop UNIX product called UnixWare. Dissolved by Novell, along with USL, in July 1993 following Novell's purchase of USL from AT&T Co. Univel's operations were incorporated into those of the UNIX Systems Group. *See* USL, USG and Destiny.

Universal Asynchronous Receiver Transmitter Commonly abbreviated and called UART. *See* UART.

Universal Code Set Combination of all character, symbol and code sets, e.g. English, Japanese, German, French, Spanish and Latin, to provide every possible character in a single code set.

Universal Product Code Commonly abbreviated and called UPC. *See* UPC.

universe 1. *(OTH)* Command used to display the operating system in which a user is currently working. 2. Any operating system, e.g. System V or the Berkeley Software Distribution.

unix File in the /stand directory that contains the version of the kernel used to boot or activate the computer. *See* /unix and /stand.

UNIX Registered trademark of X/Open Co. Ltd. Computer operating system developed in 1969 by programmers (Ken Thompson and Dennis Ritchie) at the AT&T Co.'s Bell Laboratories to provide an environment in which program development would be made easier. UNIX was first developed on Digital Equipment Corp.'s PDP-7 computers. Until the mid- to late 1980s UNIX was primarily used in number manipulation and scientific applications. In the early 1980s the Department of Defense took the lead in using UNIX for administrative and operational purposes, e.g. the Defense Data Network combined UNIX with X.25 communications protocol. In addition, the European Distribution System's Logistics Command and Control system combined UNIX with a database management system to manage the flow of spare parts. In the mid- to late 1980s UNIX became more widely accepted and used in business. As an operating system, UNIX controls or directs the computer. As an interface with the user, UNIX interprets commands into signals the computer understands. In addition, UNIX provides tools or software packages specially designed to perform communication, text processing and other functions. As a data manager, UNIX provides the user with a logical file system to collect, store and retrieve data. The UNIX name is derived from UNICS (UNiplexed Information Computing System), a pun on the name MULTICS, an operating system of the 1960s. MULTICS was developed by some of the same programmers who went on to work on UNIX. MULTICS was a multiplexing system, which could do many things and handle many users at once. In contrast, UNIX, as the prefix uni suggests, was developed to do one thing at a time and, initially, to serve only one user. For vendors to use the term UNIX on their products, the product must conform to either the X/Open Portability Guide, third or fourth edition, and the System V Interface Definition, Version 2 or 3. *See* X/Open, XPG, SVID, file system, MULTICS and UNICS.

/unix Root directory which contains the kernel, the most crucial element of the operating system. On some computer systems, the kernel is found in a directory called /stand, in a file called unix. *See* OS and kernel.

unix2dos *(ATT)* **UNIX to DOS**. Command used to convert UNIX files to DOS formatted files. Specifically, adds a return to every line of a file. *See* dos2unix.

UNIX domain UNIX interprocess communications domain. UNIX domain commands use the interprocess communications facilities to accomplish a task on a single computer system without necessarily using a network, e.g. exec, login, print spoolers and the shell.

UNIX-domain sockets Berkeley Software Distribution files used to provide fast and reliable interprocess communication. *See* BSD, IPC and named pipe.

UNIX editor Program used to create and modify text files. There are several UNIX editors, the best known of which are the ed and ex line editors and the vi screen editor. *See* bfs, ed, edit, EMACS, ex, red, sed, vi, view, EDIX and INed.

UNIX file system Commonly called hierarchical file system. *See* hierarchical file system.

UNIX File System Abbreviated and commonly known as UFS. *See* UFS.

UNIX Group Argentina A r g e n t i n e UNIX users group formed in 1987.

UNIX International Inc. Commonly abbreviated and called UI. *See* UI.

UNIX in the Office Monthly newsletter published by Patricia Seybold's Office Computing Group. Includes articles on new products and trends in UNIX in the office environment.

UNIX Lite Commonly called SVR4 Desktop. *See* SVR4 Desktop.

UNIX look-alike Commonly called look-alike. *See* look-alike.

UNIX Magazine Monthly UNIX magazine published for users in Japan.

UNIX Novell Abbreviated and commonly known as Univel. *See* Univel.

UNIX Programmer's Manual Commonly abbreviated and called UPM. *See* UPM.

UNIX Review Monthly magazine published by the Miller Freeman Publishing Co. Contains articles on new UNIX products and hints for programming. Free to qualified readers who work with UNIX.

UNIX Software Operation Commonly abbreviated and called USO. *See* USO.

UNIX Specification for ACE Technical Workgroup Group formed by the board of directors of the Advanced Computing Environment. Its charter was to develop a binary standard that would allow software to run on multiple platforms without being modified. *See* ACE.

UNIX System III Commonly abbreviated and called System III. *See* System III.

UNIX Systems London-based monthly UNIX publication on open systems computing.

UNIX Systems Group Commonly abbreviated and called USG. *See* USG.

UNIX Systems Laboratories Inc. Commonly abbreviated and called USL. *See* USL.

UNIX System V/386, Release 3.2 System V release for personal computers that use a 386 microprocessor chip. *See* System V and 386.

UNIX System V/Multi-Level Security Commonly abbreviated and called System V/MLS. *See* System V/MLS.

UNIX System V, Release 1 Commonly abbreviated and called System V. *See* System V.

UNIX System V, Release 3 Commonly abbreviated and called SVR3.x. *See* SVR3.x.

UNIX System V, Release 4 Commonly abbreviated and called SVR4.x. *See* SVR4.x and System V.

UNIX System V, Release 4 Enhanced Security Commonly abbreviated and called SVR4 ES. *See* SVR4 ES.

UNIX System V, Release 4 Multiprocessing Commonly abbreviated and called SVR4 MP. SVR4 MP.

UNIX System V, Release 4 SM. Commonly abbreviated and called SVR4 MP. *See* SVR4 MP.

UNIX timeshare System Commonly abbreviated and called UTS. *See* UTS.

UNIX Today! Former name of Open Systems Today. *See* Open Systems Today.

unix-to-dos *(ATT)* Operation menu command in UNIX System V, Release 4 Framed Access Command Environment file system. Converts UNIX programs for use on DOS-based computers. *See* SVR4.x, FACE and file system.

UNIX-to-DOS command comparison *See* DOS-to-UNIX command comparison.

UNIX-to-UNIX communications program Referred to by some as the meaning of UUCP. *See* UUCP.

UNIX-to-UNIX CoPy Commonly abbreviated and called UUCP. *See* UUCP.

UNIX-to-UNIX copy protocol Referred to by some as the meaning of UUCP. *See* UUCP.

UNIX-to-UNIX system copy
Commonly abbreviated and called uucp. *See* uucp.

UNIX Version 4 Commonly called Version 4. *See* Version 4.

UNIX Version 5 Commonly called Version 5. *See* Version 5.

UNIX Version 6 Commonly called Version 6. *See* Version 6.

UNIX Version 7 Commonly called Version 7. *See* Version 7.

UnixWare UNIX operating system developed through a joint venture between Novell Inc. and UNIX System Laboratories Inc. Based upon UNIX System V. Release 4.2 with Novell Inc.'s Internetwork Packet eXchange protocol used to establish, maintain and terminate connections on a local area network; Novell Inc.'s Sequenced Pocket eXchange protocol used to guarantee reliable end-to-end transmission: and X Window System support. Complies with both Portable Operating System Interface for Computer Environments (POSIX) and X/Open Portability Guide, fourth edition. In addition, supports MS-DOS programs, Intel 386 UNIX software from the Santa Cruz Operation, Ethernet, Token Ring and a wide range of bus architecture including Industry Standard Architecture, Enhanced Industry Standard Architecture and Micro Channel. *See* SVR4, POSIX, XPG, IPX, SPX, ISA, EISA, X Window System and Micro Channel.

UnixWare Application Server A l s o called Application Server. The unlimited user version of Novell Inc.'s UnixWare for large servers. In comparison to the Personal Edition, the Application Server offers expanded features such as the Transmission Control Protocol/Internet Protocol and Network File System. *See* UnixWare, UnixWare Personal Edition, TCP/IP and NSF.

UnixWare Motif Development Tool
Also called MDT. Novell Inc.'s add-on product used to develop Motif applications for UnixWare. Provides developers with a large selection of Motif applications as an alternative to converting to the OPEN LOOK Intrinsic Toolkit. *See* UnixWare, Motif and OLIT.

UnixWare Personal Edition Also called Personal Edition. Novell Inc.'s version of UnixWare for desktop computers. Limited to two users and lacks the full features of UnixWare, such as the Transmission Control Protocol/Internet Protocol and Network File System. *See* UnixWare, UnixWare Application Server, TCP/IP and NSF.

UnixWare Software Development Kit
Novell Inc.'s software development tools and documentation for the UnixWare desktop and server UNIX operating system. Includes UNIX System V. Release 4 development tools, ANSI C compiler, Motif and OPEN LOOK programming tools, X Window System development tools, a graphical user interface development tool and a graphical program debugger. *See* UnixWare, Motif, OPEN LOOK and X Window System.

UnixWare Technology Group
Commonly abbreviated and called UTG. *See* UTG.

UNIX Wars Generic term for disagreements among members of the UNIX community over either which version of the operating system or which shell is the best. These disputes have been rooted in technical and personal preferences, as well as in the competition among vendors for market share. The protagonists and topics of dispute have varied. Recently, "war" has broken out between Novell Inc.'s UNIX System Laboratories and

UNIX International, which back the System V, Release 4 operating system, and IBM Corp., leader of the Open Software Foundation Inc., which supports the OSF/1 operating system. In the early years, disagreement flared between the users of AT&T Co.'s version of UNIX and those of the Berkeley Software Distribution version of UNIX. Throughout this, disagreements have continued between the various UNIX shell advocates: Bourne versus C, and Bourne or C versus Korn. *See* USL, UI, SVR4.x, OSF, OSF/1. 2, operating system snob, shell, Bourne shell, C shell, Korn shell and shell snob.

UnixWorld Name changed in January 1994 to UnixWorld's Open Computing. *See* UnixWorld's Open Computing.

UnixWorld's Open Computing
Originally called UnixWorld. The name was changed in January 1994. Monthly magazine published by Tech Valley Publishing Co. UnixWorld's Open Computing contains articles on a wide range of topics related to UNIX: open systems, hardware, operating systems, application software, book reviews and how-to tips on such things as shell scripts and C language programs for both novice and advanced users.

unlink **1.** System call used to delete a file by removing the path, or address, for the file's location. *See* system call. **2.** *(ATT)* Superuser command used to delete or move files that need to be recovered from the /lost + found directory. *See* /lost + found. **3.** To delete a file or directory as a result of breaking the link between the text and the inode, which contains the vital statistics that the system needs to manage file. *See* inode.

unmap Command used to undo a vi visual editor macro created with the map command. *See* vi, macro and map.

unmount To remove a mounted, or operational, file system from the computer system.

unnamed buffer Temporary buffer established by the vi editor and used to automatically save the last copies of text which a user has modified, deleted or yanked. Numbered from one to nine. *See* vi, working buffer, named buffer, numbered buffer and vi commands (Appendix T).

unnamed pipe Special file used to pass data between two processes, turning the standard output of one process into the standard input of another process. Unnamed pipes are used only with processes that have the same parent process. The pipe system call is used to create an unnamed pipe. *See* pipe and named pipe.

unpack *(ATT)* Command used to decompress a file that has been compressed with the pack command. Returns the file to its original state, that is, size and format. *See* pack.

unreferenced file Group of disk blocks allocated by an inode and for which no directory entry exists.

unset *(ATT)* C and Korn shell toggle command. Used to turn off variables that were established with the set command and defined a user environment, an electronic-mail system or other user-defined options. *See* environment variables, toggle variables and set.

unsetenv *(ATT)* Command used to turn off C shell environmental variables. *See* C shell and environment variables.

unshare **1.** *(ATT)* Command in the Distribute File System, Network File System sysadm menu and Remote File Sharing sysadm menu that is used to deny users access to network resources previously made available through the share command. *See* DFS, NFS, RFS, sysadm and share. **2.** To deny users on remote hosts access to local files. *See* unshareall and sharing.

unshareall Distribute File System command used to deny users access to all resources previously made available through the share command. *See* DFS, share and shareall.

unsharing Denying users on remote hosts access to local files. *See* unshare, unshareall and sharing.

unshielded twisted pair Commonly abbreviated and called UTP. *See* UTP.

Unshielded Twisted Pair Development Forum Commonly abbreviated and called UDF. *See* UDF.

unshift To add data to the beginning of a stack, or list. *See* stack, push, pop, and shift.

unsigned int Unsigned integer. An integer data type whose value ranges from 0 to a maximum that depends on the hardware used. All computers represent numeric data as a string of bits. The number of bits in the string depends on the size of the computer's word. Some older computers had a 16-bit word; most current computer systems use a 32-bit word. Thus, the length of the computer's word determines the length of integer data. Almost all computer systems use the uppermost bit to represent the sign (+ or -) of the remaining bits. If the uppermost bit is on, the remaining bits represent a negative number. If the uppermost bit is off, the remainder of the word is positive. Thus, on 16-bit systems, an int can represent a number between -32768 and 32767; and on 32-bit systems, an int can represent a number between - 2147483648 and 2147483647. Since it is often useful to have numbers that range from 0 to some maximum value, almost all modern computers implement an "unsigned" integer data type. In unsigned integers, the uppermost bit is NOT used to represent the sign, but rather extends the precision of the data. Thus, an unsigned 16-bit integer represents values from 0 through 65535, and an unsigned 32-bit integer represents values from 0 through 4294967295. Used to represent data that can only be zero or positive, e.g. array subscripts and memory addresses. *See* int.

unsigned long Integer data type whose values range from 0 to a maximum that depends on the hardware used. A typical unsigned long on a 32-bit computer system can be from 0 to 4294967295. Used to represent data that can only be zero or positive, e.g. array subscripts and memory addresses. *See* long.

unsigned short Unsigned data type not longer than an integer. The minimum value of an unsigned short is 0. The maximum value depends on the computer system. A typical unsigned short on a 32-bit computer system can be from 0 to 4294967295. Used to represent data that can only be zero or positive, e.g. array subscripts and memory addresses. *See* short.

until Shell command used to set up a loop to test and execute a list of activities. The loop continues as long as the results are false (returns a non-zero value). When a true (0) value is returned, the loop is terminated. For example, an until command could state: "until two sets of conditions match continue to modify one of the two conditions". As long as they do not match (or a false value is returned), processing continues. When they do match (or a true value is returned), processing is terminated. *See* if, then, for, while and done.

upas *(ATT)* Program similar to sendmail, used to manage delivery of electronic-mail messages. *See* sendmail, MTA and e-mail.

UPC Universal Product Codes. Bar code application for point-of-sale input of inventory and sales information, e.g. price and stock on hand. UPC markings are a series of perpendicular bars of uniform length but varying width and shading, located on product packaging. These markings have specific meaning to computer systems coded to read them and can be used by any industry that computerizes inventory control and management. *See* bar code.

update *(BSD)* Daemon that starts the sync system call every 30 seconds to write the contents of a superblock to disk. *See* daemon and sync.

updatehosts *(OTH)* Program used to maintain current lists of hosts and their addresses on a network.

UPE *(POS)* User Portability Extension. Name given to the Portable Operating System Interface for Computer Environments (POSIX) 1003.2a committee's work in defining interactive utilities. *See* POSIX and IEEE P1003.2a project.

upload To transfer data or software packages from a smaller computer or client to a larger computer or server, or from one storage medium to another, e.g. to upload data from a tape to a disk drive, or to transfer a text file created on a personal computer to a minicomputer running UNIX. Usually used in the context of moving software or data from a client to a host computer. *See* download.

UPM UNIX Programmer's Manual. Detailed on-line and/or printed explanations of UNIX commands and utilities. *See* man and manual pages.

upper case Printing term for large, or capital, letters. *See* lower case.

UPS Uninterruptible Power Supply. Electrical device placed between a computer and its source of power to provide protection from electrical outages or sudden variations in voltage. Not intended to be a generator but can provide as much backup emergency power as the user wants, providing it has a sufficient supply of batteries. Enables the system either to remain operational during a short power outage, as when it is switched from the normal power source to a generator, or to be shut down in a routine manner if a very long power outage is expected.

upsizing Adding a larger server to a personal computer network. Such servers provide a repository for data as well as services normally not available on a PC network, e.g. connection to remote hosts or networks. *See* downsizing.

uptime Command used to display the current time, amount of time the system has been up, number of users currently logged on, and the load average for the last 1, 5 and 15 minutes. *See* load average.

urestore *(ATT)* User **restore**. Version of the restore command which allows users to restore files they own or obtain status on restore requests. *See* restore.

urgent data Transmission Control Protocol data communications messages specifically marked by the sender for special handling and delivery to the receiver. *See* TCP.

URM User's Reference Manual. Documentation provided with the UNIX operating system that describes the basic user commands which make up the operating system. *See* User's Guide, Programmer's Guide, PRM, System Administrator's Guide and SARM.

ursstatus *(ATT)* User **restore status**. Command used to obtain the status on one of a user's restore requests. Also can be used to obtain a list of restore requests for a user in the restore queue. *See* urestore and rsstatus.

usability Buzzword of the 1990s that describes how easily a new user can learn to use a software application or computer system.

usage *(ATT)* Help program which allows the user to obtain information on UNIX commands.

USENET User's Network. A worldwide UNIX bulletin board started in the late 1970s at Duke University by Tom Truscott and James Ellis. Originally included only Duke University and the University of North Carolina, but today is a loose confederation of educational, business, government and private computer systems that share information using specified formats, e.g. USENET News and UNIX electronic mail. Provides a method of sending and reading UNIX-related articles and programs. The articles and programs, known as *netnews*, are contained in separate news groups identified by the interest or topic. Computers on USENET can be connected through the Internet network, direct dial access or UNIX-to-UNIX CoPy communications system. Computers using USENET do not have to be UNIX-based but must understand common UNIX communication protocols and electronic-mail addressing. *See* UUNET, netnews, e-mail, UUCP and B news.

USENIX Association, The
Not-for-profit association for UNIX system developers formed to promote and support research and development of UNIX and UNIX-like operating systems. *See* ;login:.

user 1. *(BSD)* Command used to display the login name of the user. 2. Any person making use of the system. Sometimes abbreviated usr.

user a Jargon term for user area, a pocket in computer memory that contains the information the kernel needs to manage user processes. *See* user area.

user account Directory that allows access to a computer system operating under UNIX and is available for personal use by an authorized user. *See* account and system account.

useradd *(ATT)* **User add**. System administration command used to display user parameters, add users to the computer system or modify user accounts.

User Agent Commonly abbreviated and called UA. *See* UA.

user agent Process used in Kerberos, a user-authentication method, that contains the user password and attempts to automatically open a packet for access to the network. *See* Kerberos.

User Alliance for Open Systems U s e r organization formed to defend customers against standards organizations and the UNIX Wars. Originally called the Atlanta 17, then the Houston 30. Formed by manufacturing companies to communicate to the standards groups their desire for open systems. Among its more than 50 members are The Boeing Co. and General Motors Corp. The alliance is a member of the Corporation for Open Systems International and has become a COS Requirements Interest Group. *See* UNIX Wars, IPSIT, COS, RIG and POSC.

user area Also called user a. Pocket in computer memory that contains the information the kernel needs to manage user processes, including user identifier, group identifier and open file descriptors for each. *See* process, UID, GID and file descriptor.

User Bill of Rights Set of seven rights for users of X.500, a directory of users or resources on a network, developed by the North American Directory Forum. Includes the right to not be listed in a directory, to be notified when added to a directory, to review an entry in a directory, to correct an entry in a directory, to remove information from an entry in a directory, to compliance by a directory with U.S. and Canadian privacy laws, and to timely compliance of the rights by the directory. *See* X.500 and NADF.

User Datagram Protocol Commonly abbreviated and called UDP. *See* UDP.

User Datagram Protocol/Internet Protocol Abbreviated and commonly known as UDP/IP. *See* UDP/IP.

user-defined field Field in an application software program or database for which a user is allowed to set the meaning.

user-defined state Also called state 4. System state that can be defined by a user, not by the system.

userdel *(ATT)* **User del**ete. System administration command used to delete a user from the system.

User Environment Utilities Set of programs included in UNIX System V, Release 4, to manage user commands, e.g. how and when commands are used. *See* SVR4.x.

USERFILE File which sets the security for UNIX-to-UNIX CoPy (UUCP) transmissions. Checked by the uucico daemon (the UUCP manager) to determine which files can be accessed by remote systems during a UUCP connection. *See* UUCP and uucico.

user friendly Phrase used to describe ease of use of a software program, computer, peripheral or other device. Includes all aspects, such as installation, training, use and upgrades.

/user/group Standards Developed by the /usr/group, now known as *Uni-Forum*, in the early 1980s to reduce machine-specific requirements. Started in 1981 and completed in 1984. These standards became the basis of future standards development by other organizations, e.g. X/Open Co. Ltd. and Institute of Electrical and Electronic Engineers' Portable Operating System Interface for Computer Environments. *See* X/Open and POSIX.

user.h File that contains the description of the user area. *See* user area.

userid Commonly abbreviated and called UID. *See* UID.

userID Commonly abbreviated and called UID. *See* UID.

user-ID Commonly abbreviated and called UID. *See* UID.

userID 0 Commonly abbreviated and called UID 0. *See* UID 0.

user interface Program available to users to communicate with the computer.

User Interface Language Commonly abbreviated and called UIL. *See* UIL.

user interface management system Commonly abbreviated and called UIMS. *See* UIMS.

user-level benchmark Specified standard against which computer hardware can be tested and compared under actual working conditions. Tests how many users can try to execute the same command before it fails to respond. *See* benchmark and kernel-level benchmark.

usermod *(ATT)* **User** mo**d**ify. System administration command used to modify

user accounts, e.g. new user identifier number, the group the user is part of, the new home directory and the date when the account can no longer be used.

user mode Hardware state in which a process can access only those instructions related to the process, not any kernel instructions or data. *See* kernel mode.

username Field in the file USERFILE which identifies the accounts used by remote systems to log in for UNIX-to-UNIX CoPy access. *See* USERFILE and UUCP.

user name Commonly called login ID. *See* login ID.

User Portability Extension Commonly abbreviated and called UPE. *See* UPE.

user program Program that is written and installed by a user.

user-request routine *(BSD)* Protocol layer in the interprocess communications (sockets) which provides the interface between interprocess communications implementation software and the communications protocol. *See* IPC and sockets.

users *(BSD)* Command used to display a list of users logged on the system. Displays the list horizontally, on a single line, versus vertically, one user per line. *See* who.

USERS *(INET)* Active **Users** Protocol. Defense Advanced Research Projects Agency Internet protocol. Protocol used to obtain a list of currently active users on a computer on the Internet. *See* DARPA and Internet.

User's Guide UNIX system documentation which provides a system overview and instructions on how to use editors, automate jobs and communicate with others on the system. *See* URM, Programmer's Guide, PRM, System Administrator's Guide and SARM.

user space Area in memory dedicated to running processes initiated by a user, from the vi editor to electronic mail.

User's Reference Manual Commonly abbreviated and called URM. *See* URM.

user structure Commonly called user area. *See* user area.

USG UNIX Systems Group. Headquartered in San Jose, California. Organization formed by Novell Inc. in July 1993 to consolidate and operate the efforts of Novell's UNIX System Laboratories, Univel Inc. and other UNIX operations. Both USL and Univel were dissolved when USG was created. *See* USL and Univel.

USL UNIX System Laboratories Inc. Formerly called the UNIX Software Operation (USO), headquartered in Summit, New Jersey. Was dissolved in July 1993 after being purchased by Novell Inc. and its operations were incorporated into the UNIX Systems Group. Originally formed as an organization within AT&T Co. to develop and market ideas generated by UNIX International Inc. USL then became an independent company with 77% of its stock owned by AT&T. In June 1990, AT&T transferred all trademark rights for UNIX and UNIX products developed by AT&T to USL. Negotiations to sell USL to Novell were announced in December 1992 and finalized in July 1993. In October 1993 the rights to the UNIX trademarks were transferred from USL to X/Open Co. Ltd. by Novell. *See* UI and USG.

USO UNIX Software Operation. Former name of UNIX System Laboratories Inc. *See* USL.

/usr **1.** User file system. **2.** Root directory which contains the files and commands required for the system to be fully functional after it has been started. *See* file system.

/usr/adm/cronlog Cron log. Records use of the cron daemon, which starts other programs identified in /usr/lib/crontab at a pre-established time. *See* cron.

/usr/adm/pacct Process account log. Records the number of times a process is run by the kernel.

/usr/adm/sulog Switch user log. Records use of the su command. *See* su.

/usr/bin System directory that contains commands available to users when the computer is in multi-user mode.

/usr/digest Former name of UniNews. *See* UniNews.

/usr/group Former name of UniForum. *See* UniForum.

/usr/group/UK Former name of the United Kingdom UNIX users group. *See* UniForum UK.

/usr/include System directory that contains header (.h) files used by the C language to describe data structures and function prototypes for various library and operating system facilities.

/usr/lib Directory that contains the libraries and files required for the UNIX commands and programs.

/usr/lib/crontab System directory used in AT&T Co. UNIX releases before System V, Release 2, XENIX and the Berkeley Software Distribution *(BSD)*. Contains the list of commands and programs to be executed by the cron daemon. In the Fourth Berkeley Software Distribution, Third Release a new file was added, /usr/lib/crontab.local, to maintain the programs to be executed by cron. *See* cron, /usr/lib/crontab.local and /usr/spool/cron/crontabs.

/usr/lib/crontab.local File in the Fourth Berkeley Software Distribution, Third Release that lists all the programs run by the cron daemon. *See* cron and crontab.

/usr/lib/uucp Directory that contains UNIX-to-UNIX CoPy maintenance and configuration files. *See* UUCP.

USRNIX Hong Kong UNIX users group formed in 1988.

/usr/sadm/skel Directory included in UNIX System V, Release 4, that contains the files automatically added to a user's account when a new user is added to the system with the -m option of the useradd command. *See* SVR4.x and useradd.

/usr/spool/cron/crontabs System directory used in AT&T Co.'s UNIX releases after System V, Release 2. Contains the list of commands and programs to be executed by the cron daemon. *See* cron and /usr/lib/crontabs.

/usr/spool/locks Directory containing files indicating the dedication of a port to UNIX-to-UNIX CoPy (UUCP) connection on systems using HoneyDanBer UUCP. *See* lock files, UUCP and HoneyDanBer UUCP.

/usr/spool/uucp Directory containing UNIX-to-UNIX CoPy requests and log files. *See* UUCP.

/usr/spool/uucppublic UNIX-to-UNIX CoPy **public**. Directory used to hold files transferred to and from a remote system. Permissions are set to allow access by all users. *See* UUCP and permissions.

/usr/ucb Directory containing most of the commands added to UNIX by developers of the Berkeley Software Distribution. *See* BSD.

U.S. TAG U.S. Technical Advisory Group. National organization composed of customers and vendors with a special interest in a technical application. A U.S. TAG is responsible for developing and recommending national standards to international organizations.

ustat *(ATT)* Command used to provide information on the current size of the file system. *See* file system.

U.S. Technical Advisory Group
Commonly abbreviated and called U.S. TAG. *See* U.S. TAG.

UTF File System Safe Universal Character Set Transformation Format. X-Open 8-bit character set.

UTG UnixWare Technology Group. Organization formed by Novell Inc. in February 1994 to provide a means of input to the evolution of the UnixWare operating system by hardware and software vendors. Acts only in an advisory role to Novell Inc. in setting direction for Unix-Ware. Along with Novell, initial members include AT&T Co., Fujitsu Ltd., ICL Inc., NEC Corp., Olivetti Co., Sony Corp., UniSoft Corp. and Unisys Corp.

utility 1. Helper software. Package provided by a software developer or vendor to aid the user in performing tasks that are either repetitive or would require specific knowledge of a programming language. **2.** Application software specifically developed for the UNIX operating system which performs user support functions, e.g. text processing or electronic mail.

Utility Communications Architecture
Commonly abbreviated and called UCA. *See* UCA.

utime *(ATT)* System call used to set and examine the amount of time it takes to find and open a file. *See* system call.

UTP Unshielded twisted pair. Lightweight, inexpensive twisted pair cable composed of two separate insulated wire strands that have been twisted together, e.g. household telephone cable. One strand of wire is used to carry a signal and the other is used as a ground. Uses no shielding other than minimal insulation. *See* 10Base-T, Ethernet, LAN, DIW-24, STP and UDF.

UTS UNIX TimeShare System. UNIX operating system developed by Amdahl Corp. for real-time applications.

uucheck *(ATT)* UNIX-to-UNIX **check**. HoneyDanBer UNIX-to-UNIX CoPy (UUCP) program used to examine the accuracy of the permissions on UUCP files and directories. *See* HoneyDanBer UUCP and UUCP.

uucico *(ATT)* UNIX-to-UNIX copy-in copy-out. Daemon that manages the intersystem UNIX-to-UNIX CoPy (UUCP) communication, e.g. transfers UUCP files, and moves a copy of a UUCP file from one computer to another. *See* UUCP.

uuclean UNIX-to-UNIX **clean**. Command used to delete unwanted files from the UNIX-to-UNIX CoPy spool directory. *See* UUCP and spool.

uucleanup *(ATT)* UNIX-to-UNIX **cleanup**. Improved HoneyDanBer UNIX-to-UNIX CoPy (UUCP) version of the uuclean command for cleaning up the UUCP spool directory. *See* HoneyDanBer UUCP and uuclean.

uucp *(ATT)* UNIX-to-UNIX **copy**. Command used to access the UNIX-to-UNIX CoPy communications system. Used with other related commands to copy or move data from one computer to another. Connection is usually made by dial up, e.g. by modem.

UUCP UNIX-to-UNIX **CoPy**. Sometimes called UNIX-to-UNIX communications program or UNIX-to-UNIX protocol. Interactive UNIX communication system for connecting two computers to send or receive data. Developed at AT&T Co.'s Bell Laboratories by Mike Lesk in 1976. *See* uucp and Bell Laboratories.

uucpd *(BSD)* UNIX-to-UNIX **copy daemon**. Uses the Transmission Control Protocol/Internet Protocol instead of a modem to facilitate UNIX-to-UNIX CoPy connections. *See* UUCP and TCP/IP.

UUCPNET UNIX-to-UNIX **CoPy Network**. Worldwide network originally developed by the AT&T Co.'s Bell Laboratories to connect UNIX computers using the UNIX-to-UNIX CoPy communications system. Used to transfer electronic mail and software between systems. *See* UUCP and Bell Laboratories.

uucppublic UNIX-to-UNIX CoPy **public**. *See* /usr/spool/uucppublic.

uudecode *(BSD)* UNIX-to-UNIX **decode**. Command used to decode data from American Standard Code for Information Interchange format to binary format for transmission by electronic mail. *See* UUCP, binary file, ASCII, e-mail and uuencode.

uudemon.admin *(ATT)* UNIX-to-UNIX **daemon admin**istration. Shell script that tries to complete UNIX-to-UNIX CoPy (UUCP) jobs that have not been delivered and runs the uustat command which sends a status report on the UUCP communications system to the system administrator. *See* UUCP and uustat.

uudemon.cleanup *(ATT)* UNIX-to-UNIX **daemon cleanup**. Shell script that is run daily to clean up the UNIX-to-UNIX CoPy (UUCP) communications system by combining log files used by UUCP into a single log. Combines the daily UUCP log files into a weekly log file. Runs the uucleanup program to remove work and data files from the spool directories that are seven days or more old and execute files that are over two days old. In addition, it returns undelivered electronic mail. *See* UUCP and uucleanup.

uudemon.day *(ATT)* UNIX-to-UNIX **daemon day**. Shell script that runs the uuclean program daily to clean up disks used by the UNIX-to-UNIX CoPy (UUCP) communications system. In addition, combines the daily UUCP log files into a weekly log file. *See* UUCP and uuclean.

uudemon.hour *(ATT)* UNIX-to-UNIX **daemon hour**. Shell script that starts the uusched daemon scheduler to process UNIX-to-UNIX CoPy (UUCP) requests and schedule them for delivery to remote systems. In addition, starts the uuxqt daemon to look for execution requests from remote systems that have not been run. Can be run every hour or more depending upon the amount of UUCP activity. *See* UUCP, uusched and uuxqt.

uudemon.hr *(ATT)* UNIX-to-UNIX **daemon hour**. Shell script run at various intervals during the day to complete UNIX-to-UNIX CoPy jobs in the queue. *See* UUCP.

uudemon.poll *(ATT)* UNIX-to-UNIX **daemon poll**. Shell script used to make a connection request to known UNIX-to-UNIX CoPy sites and check for data that is to be transmitted. *See* UUCP.

uudemon.wk *(ATT)* UNIX-to-UNIX **daemon week**. Shell script run weekly to clean up disks used by the UNIX-to-UNIX CoPy communications system. *See* UUCP.

uuencode *(BSD)* UNIX-to-UNIX **encode**. Command used to encode data from binary format to American Standard Code for Information Interchange format preceding transmission by electronic mail. *See* UUCP, binary file, ASCII, e-mail and uudecode.

UUGA UNIX Users Group Austria. UNIX users group formed in 1985.

uugetty *(ATT)* UNIX-to-UNIX **get tty**. The HoneyDanBer UNIX-to-UNIX CoPy getty, or mechanism to establish a bidirectional connection for moving files between computers using UNIX-to-UNIX CoPy in copy out. Still available in UNIX System V, Release V, but has been replaced by the Service Access Facility. *See* HoneyDanBer UUCP, UUCP, getty, uucico, SVR4.x and SAF.

uuglist UNIX-to-UNIX **grade list**. Command used to print a list of the grades or priorities of UNIX-to-UNIX CoPy service available on a system. *See* UUCP and Grades.

uuhosts *(INET)* UNIX-to-UNIX **hosts**. Utility in the Internet network used to maintain information about remote UNIX-to-UNIX CoPy hosts. *See* Internet and UUCP.

uulog *(ATT)* UNIX-to-UNIX **log**. Command used to monitor or provide a report on the activity related to UNIX-to-UNIX CoPy transmissions and use of the uux command for a system. *See* UUCP and uux.

uumail *(BSD)* UNIX-to-UNIX **mail**. A smart mailer that takes into account the best possible routes, based on their speed and/or efficiency, for transmitting electronic mail between two points. Especially effective if the UNIX-to-UNIX CoPy communications system has to send the electronic mail through another host to

get it to its final destination. *See* UUCP and e-mail.

uuname *(ATT)* UNIX-to-UNIX **name**. Command used to list known host names to which a UNIX-to-UNIX CoPy connection can be made for directly accessing and transferring data. *See* UUCP.

UUNET **UUNET** Communication Services, originally called SEISMO. Nonprofit organization started in 1987 by USENIX, which created USENET. Provides connection service to USENET and the Internet for a fee. UUNET was the first backbone network to provide news and bulletin board access to businesses. *See* USENET, Internet, netnews and UUCP.

UUPC UNIX-to-UNIX Personal Computer. Rewritten version of UNIX-to-UNIX CoPy for use with DOS and Macintosh computers. *See* UUCP.

uupick *(ATT)* UNIX-to-UNIX **pick**. Command used to scan a system's public directory, which is located in /usr/spool under a name such as uucppublic, for files sent to the user from remote systems using uuto. If any such files exist, a list of them is electronically mailed to the user. *See* UUCP and uuto.

uupoll *(BSD)* UNIX-to-UNIX **poll**. Command used to force a connection to a remote host. Bypasses the systematic polling done by the uucico daemon and attempts to force a connection with a remote host to perform a UNIX-to-UNIX CoPy transaction. *See* UUCP and uucico.

uuq *(BSD)* UNIX-to-UNIX queue. Command used to examine or manipulate the UNIX-to-UNIX CoPy queues. *See* UUCP.

uusched *(ATT)* UNIX-to-UNIX **sched**ule. HoneyDanBer UNIX-to-UNIX CoPy scheduler normally started by the uudemon.hour daemon to schedule the spooled files to be transferred to other computer hosts. *See* HoneyDanBer UUCP, spool and uudemon.hour.

uusend *(BSD)* UNIX-to-UNIX **send**. Command used to send a file to a remote host using UNIX-to-UNIX CoPy. *See* UUCP.

uusnap *(BSD)* UNIX-to-UNIX **snap**shot. Command used to display the status of active UNIX-to-UNIX CoPy transactions. *See* UUCP.

uustat *(ATT/XEN)* UNIX-to-UNIX **stat**us. Command used to determine the availability of systems, and the status of UNIX-to-UNIX CoPy (UUCP) requests and control jobs on remote systems. Also can be used to cancel a UUCP request that is still in the queue on a remote system. *See* UUCP.

uusub *(ATT)* Command used to manage and monitor a UNIX-to-UNIX CoPy network, e.g. add or delete a remote system to a network and obtain statistics on its use. *See* UUCP.

uuto *(ATT/XEN)* UNIX-to-UNIX **to**. Command used to send a file or a group of files to a user on a remote system. Cannot be used to get files from a remote system. *See* UUCP.

Uutry *(ATT)* UNIX-to-UNIX **try**. Honey-DanBer UNIX-to-UNIX CoPy (UUCP) shell script used to make a UUCP connection to another computer, with the debug-ger turned on to find the cause of errors. *See* HoneyDanBer UUCP and debugger.

UUUG **U**ninterruptible **U**ptime **U**sers **G**roup. User group composed of 150 Fortune 1000 companies. Formed in 1989 to exchange information on maintaining system uptime, environmental conditioning. and avoiding and recovering from disasters Among the members are American Power Conversion, Computersite Engineering, Exide Electronics. Headquartered in New York City.

uux *(ATT/XEN)* UNIX-to-UNIX execution. Command used to run commands or manipulate data on remote systems. The commands and data files on the remote systems can be executed and manipulated in conjunction with commands and data on the local system. *See* UUCP.

uuxqt *(ATT)* UNIX-to-UNIX **exe**cute daemon. UNIX-to-UNIX CoPy (UUCP) program, started by the uucico daemon or the uudemon.hour shell script, to run UUCP requests from remote computers. *See* UUCP, uucico and uudemon.hour.

uwm **U**ltrix **W**indow **M**anager. Developed by Digital Equipment Corp. The window manager for X 11, Release 3. *See* X Window System, window manager, X11R3 and twm.

V

V.21 Standard for 300-baud duplex modems. Developed by the International Telecommunication Union Telecommunication Standardization Sector, formerly called the Consultative Committee on International Telegraphy and Telephony. *See* ITU-T, duplex and baud.

V.22 European standard for 1,200-baud duplex modems. Developed by the International Telecommunication Union Telecommunication Standardization Sector, formerly called the Consultative Committee on International Telegraphy and Telephony. *See* ITU-T, duplex and baud.

V.22bis U.S. and European standard for 2,400-baud duplex modems. Developed by the International Telecommunication Union Telecommunication Standardization Sector, formerly called the Consultative Committee on International Telegraphy and Telephony. *See* ITU-T, duplex and baud.

V.32 U.S. and European standard for 9,600-baud duplex modems. Developed by the International Telecommunication Union Telecommunication Standardization Sector, formerly called the Consultative Committee on International Telegraphy and Telephony. *See* ITU-T, duplex and baud.

V.32bis U.S. and European standard for 14,400-baud modems. Developed by the International Telecommunication Union Telecommunication Standardization Sector, formerly called the Consultative Committee on International Telegraphy and Telephony. *See* ITU-T and baud.

V.33 European standard for 9,600-baud modems used on leased lines. Developed by the International Telecommunication Union Telecommunication Standardization Sector, formerly called the Consultative Committee on International Telegraphy and Telephony. *See* ITU-T, baud and leased line.

V.42 U.S. and European standard for error correction. Developed by the International Telecommunication Union Telecommunication Standardization Sector, formerly called the Consultative Committee on International Telegraphy and Telephony. *See* ITU-T.

V.42bis U.S. and European standard for data compression. Developed by the International Telecommunication Union Telecommunication Standardization Sector, formerly called the Consultative Committee on International Telegraphy and Telephony. *See* ITU-T.

vacation *(ATT)* UNIX System V, Release 4 electronic-mail-related command used to save incoming electronic-mail messages and send a pre-written interim response to the sender while the user is absent. *See* SVR4.x and e-mail.

val *(ATT/XEN)* **Val**idate. One of the thirteen Source Code Control System (SCCS) commands used to confirm the accuracy of a SCCS file. *See* SCCS, admin, cdc, comb, delta, get, help, prs, rmdel, sact, sccsdiff, unget, vc and what.

validate To confirm the accuracy of a program or database by running it under controlled conditions. *See* acceptance testing.

value-added network Commonly abbreviated and called VAN. *See* VAN.

value-added reseller Commonly abbreviated and called VAR. *See* VAR.

vampire Ethernet transceiver which derives its name from pins that are used to cut into the cable to connect with the network. *See* transceiver and Ethernet.

VAN Value-added network. Also called Public Data Network. *See* PDN.

vanilla Jargon term for a standard, or plain, release of a software package that does not contain a lot of additional features.

vaporware Jargon term for software that exists only in the minds of developers or software vendors, with release dates announced long before the software is ready, if ever.

vaporware factor Software that does not meet the hype, expectations or claims of the vendor.

var Abbreviation for variable. *See* variable.

VAR Value-added reseller. Company or individual that designs and installs a turnkey, or integrated, package of computer products and/or services, using several suppliers, for business customers. A recent addition to the UNIX language, its origin is attributed to IBM Corp., which used VAR to describe third-party organizations that sold IBM Series 1 minicomputers. Most VARs specialize in a specific market. *See* turnkey system and master VAR.

/var *(ATT)* Directory in UNIX System V, Release 4 root file system. Used to hold system files, the contents of which are unique to one computer system and will vary between computer systems, e.g. accounting, electronic mail and temporary files. *See* SVR4.x and root file system.

/var/adm *(ATT)* Directory in UNIX System V, Release 4 root file system used to hold the system login and accounting files. *See* SVR4.x and root file system.

/var/cron *(ATT)* File in the UNIX System V, Release 4 root file system. Used to log all activity related to the cron daemon used to start programs at a specified time. *See* SVR4.x and root file system.

variable Symbol or function within a program whose value can change during the operation of the program, e.g. if a program were created to determine the cost per mile of a road trip, a variable would be the different costs per gallon for gasoline.

variable-length record Any record that contains any number of characters. *See* fixed length record.

/var/lp *(ATT)* File in UNIX System V, Release 4 root file system used to hold the system printing log file. *See* SVR4.x and root file system.

/var/mail *(ATT)* Directory in UNIX System V, Release 4 root file system used to hold the electronic-mail files of each user. *See* e-mail, SVR4.x and root file system.

/var/news *(ATT)* Directory in UNIX System V, Release 4 root file system used to hold news files generated locally. *See* SVR4.x and root file system.

/var/options *(ATT)* Directory in UNIX System V, Release 4 root file system used to hold files that identify each utility software package loaded on the system. *See* SVR4.x and root file system.

/var/preserve *(ATT)* Directory in UNIX System V, Release 4 root file system used to hold backup files for every text file when opened with the vi or ex text editors. *See* SVR4.x and root file system.

/var/sadm *(ATT)* Directory of UNIX System V, Release 4 root file system used to hold the files needed to back up and restore system files. *See* SVR4.x and root file system.

/var/saf *(ATT)* Directory in UNIX System V, Release 4 root file system used to hold the log files for the Service Access Facility. *See* SVR4.x, root file system and SAF.

/var/spool *(ATT)* Directory in UNIX System V, Release 4 root file system used to hold the temporary spooling files for cron, lp, electronic mail and UNIX-to-UNIX CoPy requests. *See* SVR4.x, root file system, spool, cron, lp, e-mail and UUCP.

/var/tmp *(ATT)* Directory in UNIX System V, Release 4 root file system used to hold temporary files. *See* SVR4.x and root file system.

/var/uucp *(ATT)* Directory in UNIX System V, Release 4 root file system used to hold the UNIX-to-UNIX CoPy log and security files. *See* SVR4.x, UUCP and root file system.

vat *(INET)* **V**isual **a**udio **t**ool. Interactive voice program developed by the Lawrence Berkeley Laboratories. Used by workstations and X Window System terminals to transmit and receive voice data using the IP multicasting protocol. *See* Internet and IP multicasting.

vax *(ATT)* Command used to test if a computer system is a Digital Equipment Corp. VAX minicomputer. Returns either a 0 (TRUE) value if it is or a non-zero (FALSE) value if it is not. *See* machid.

VAX **V**irtual **A**ddress E**x**tension. A line of Digital Equipment Corp. minicomputers.

VAX MIPS Measurement of processor speed invented by Digital Equipment Corp., manufacturer of VAX computers. Based on the assumption that a VAX-11/780 minicomputer executes at about 1/2 mips, or 500,000 instructions per second. *See* vup and mips.

VAX units of performance Commonly abbreviated and called vups. *See* vup.

vc *(ATT)* **V**ersion **c**ontrol. One of the 13 Source Code Control System (SCCS) commands used to maintain version numbers. *See* SCCS, admin, cdc, comb, delta, get, help, prs, rmdel, sact, sccsdiff, unget, val and what.

VDT **V**ideo **D**isplay **T**erminal. Also called VDU, teletype, tube, monitor, CRT or terminal. Commonly called terminal. *See* terminal.

VDU **V**ideo **D**isplay **U**nit. Also called VDT, teletype, tube, monitor, CRT or terminal. Commonly called terminal. *See* terminal.

vectored interrupt Central processing unit interrupt that sends a specific signal which is cross-referenced to a table providing the specific interrupt and handler. *See* CPU, signal and interrupt.

vector graphics Display images created by mathematically describing the relationship between lines and angles of an image. *See* raster graphics.

VEE-EYE Pronunciation of visual interface or visual editor. *See* vi.

VEE-TAM Pronunciation of VTAM, the abbreviation for Virtual Telecommunications Access Method. *See* VTAM.

Vendor Independent Messaging Commonly abbreviated and called VIM. *See* VIM.

VENIX Real-time UNIX operating system developed by VenturCom Inc. *See* RTOS.

ver *(ATT)* One of the tplot graphic filters that handles the special plotting functions of the Versatec D1200A terminal. *See* tplot and filter.

verifier Term related to the system security for the Remote Procedure Call. Message that is sent by the server to the client in response to a credential authentication message that requests user access to the client. *See* RPC, server and credential.

Versabus Module Europe bus Abbreviated and commonly known as VMEbus. *See* VMEbus.

version Term used interchangeably with release and also called a version release, for new software, whether it be a new product or an update to add new features or correct problems in an existing product. The industry average is two version releases per product per year.

Version 4 AT&T Co.'s release of UNIX in 1974. Was used mostly by colleges and universities and replaced in 1977 by Version 6. *See* Version 6.

Version 5 AT&T Co.'s time-sharing version of UNIX. Released in 1977 to colleges and research organizations only.

Version 6 First official release of UNIX by the AT&T Co. in 1977. Used mostly by colleges and universities. A derivative of Version 6, the Programmer's Workbench/UNIX, became the first commercially available version of UNIX in 1977. *See* PWB/UNIX.

Version 7 Second official release by AT&T Co. of UNIX in 1979. First release to contain the Bourne shell. Developed for Digital Equipment Corp.'s DEC PDP-11 computers, with a similar version called 32V released for the DEC VAX computers. Like Version 6, it was mainly used by colleges and universities. *See* Version 6 and Bourne shell.

versioning Relational database term for the process of granting or guaranteeing exclusive access by a process to read or write information in a database without database locking. A separate version of the data is created for each process. Once all the processes are completed, the entries are reconciled and written to the database. *See* database locking and read consistency.

version number Number assigned to a specific version of a software package. Normally consists of a whole number and a decimal number. A totally new version normally is identified by the whole number, e.g. Version 1.0. Major changes are normally identified with a decimal number to the tenth, e.g. Version 2.1. Minor changes or bug fixes are normally identified with a decimal number to the hundredth or an alpha, e.g. Version 4.01 or 4.1a.

version release Commonly called version. *See* version.

vertical application Software developed for a very specific purpose or industry, e.g. software developed for retail point-of-sale applications. *See* horizontal application.

vertical bar | Metacharacter used in regular expressions of egrep and awk. Separates two regular expression to match either or both strings in a line, e.g. tnf | kaj would identify each incident of the string tnf and/kaj in a line. *See* metacharacter and regular expression.

very large-scale integration Commonly abbreviated and called VLSI. *See* VLSI.

very low frequency Abbreviated and commonly known as VLF. *See* VLF.

VEX Video Extension to **X**. Set of standards for an interface between video signals and computer graphics. Provides specifications for the management and transfer of video signals to the X Window System for graphical display. *See* X Window System.

vfork *(BSD)* Version of the fork system call found within the Berkeley Software Distribution. Attempts to reduce overhead, combining the functions of both the fork and exec system calls, by copying entries in the page table for parent address space instead of copying the entire address. *See* system call, fork, exec and address space.

VFS Virtual File System. Included in Sun Microsystems Inc.'s Network File System and AT&T Co.'s UNIX System V, Release 4. Allows an operating system kernel to access and map data between various dissimilar types of file systems, e.g. data can be loaded, used and moved between DOS, VMS, MVS and NFS file systems. Client computers are able to access and use VFS file systems on remote hosts as if they were loaded locally on the client computer. *See* NFS and SVR4.x.

vfstab Commonly written as /etc/vfstab. *See* /etc/vfstab.

VGA Video graphics array. IBM Corp. color video monitor with 640 x 480 pixel resolution and capable of displaying 256 colors. Also can provide black-on-white grayscale. Provides excellent resolution for use with graphics packages. *See* super VGA, 8514/A, CGA, EGA, XGA, pixel and grayscale.

vgrind *(BSD)* Command used to make neatly formatted listings of programs.

VHS tape storage Also called inch tape, half-inch tape or 19MM tape. Tape storage medium that uses half-inch-wide VHS-type magnetic tape. Can store up to 19 gigabytes of data with a sustained transfer rate of 2 megabytes per second and a burst rate of 4 megabytes per second.

vi 1. Visual interface or visual editor. Pronounced *VEE-EYE* or *VYE*. Powerful full-screen editor program written by Bill Joy. Based on the ex and ed line editors, and originally released in the Berkeley Software Distribution. Does not offer on-screen help or menus, so the user must memorize all the commands or have a cheat sheet handy. Can only be used with a video terminal.

    CLP>vi ⏎

will start a vi session but the input will be lost unless the write command is used, specifying a file name.

    CLP>vi <option(s)> file name(s)⏎

either creates a new file for editing or opens the specified file name, if it is in the current working directory. *See* ex, EMACS and current working directory. **2.** Command used to start the vi editor.

vi commands *See* Appendix T.

video display terminal Commonly abbreviated and called VDT. Also called VDU, teletype, tube, monitor, CRT or terminal. Commonly called terminal. *See* terminal.

video display unit Commonly abbreviated and called VDU. Also called VDT, teletype, tube, monitor, CRT or terminal. Commonly called terminal. *See* terminal.

Video Electronics Standards Association local bus Commonly abbreviated and called VL-Bus. *See* VL-Bus.

Video Extension to X Commonly abbreviated and called VEX. *See* VEX.

video graphics display Commonly abbreviated and called VGA. *See* VGA.

video mail Combination of audio and video provided by multimedia technology enables users to send messages. *See* multimedia technology.

Video Random Access Memory Commonly abbreviated and called VRAM. *See* VRAM.

view Full-screen document review program based on the vi screen editor program. Contains all the vi command functions except those used to modify documents. Can be considered a vi version of the less or more commands used to page through a document. *See* vi, less and more.

Viking Reduced Instruction Set Computing chip developed by Texas Instruments Inc. that runs at a clock speed of 40 megahertz and is capable of multiprocessing. *See* RISC, clock speed and MP.

VIM Vendor Independent Messaging. De facto standard by Lotus Development Corp., Novell Inc., IBM Corp., Borland International and Apple Computer Inc. Application programming interface for sending electronic mail between clients and/or servers and applications capable of running on DOS, OS/2, Microsoft Windows and UNIX. *See* OCE, MAPI, e-mail and API.

vimotd vi message of the day. Command used by the system administrator to update the message of the day (motd), a message that appears when a user first logs into a system. Invokes, or calls, the vi editor so the system administrator can create a new or update an existing motd. *See* vi and motd.

vipw **vi** password. Special editor used to edit the password file and is available to users who have access to the root directory. Makes a copy of the password file, creating a temporary file in which modifications to the password can be made without any risk of corrupting the original file. For security purposes, the temporary file is created in /etc instead of /tmp, the normal vi directory for such files. When the necessary changes have been made, the modified copy of the password file replaces the active password file. *See* /etc/passwd, password and vi.

virtual Anything that appears to be other than what it actually is, e.g. virtual memory is the apparent expansion of the computer's memory by using disk space to store programs and data.

virtual address Location in virtual memory for temporary storage of a program or data. When a program or data has to be stored on disk because there is insufficient room within main memory, it is given a virtual address by the system. When the program or data is needed, its virtual address is translated into the physical address on the disk so the system can retrieve it. *See* virtual memory.

virtual address area Area in simulated storage, such as a disk drive, which can be used as memory locations for programs and data that cannot fit in main memory.

virtual address space Use of disk drives to expand memory when there is insufficient room within main memory for the continued operation of a program or data manipulation. Additional capacity is allocated to a running program, user, system function, etc. by using disk space.

virtual address structure Definition of memory addressing.

virtual circuit Reliable connection between hosts using the Transmission Control Protocol which allows application software to communicate as if there was a physical connection. *See* TCP and hard-wired.

virtual console Feature within limited releases of System V, Release 3, and System V, Release 4. Allows the use of function keys for switching between different sessions running on a computer. Thus, a user does not have to use multiple terminals or terminate one session to start another.

virtual disk drive Combination of two or more disk drives, using software, so they appear to users as a single, large disk drive.

Virtual File System Commonly abbreviated and called VFS. *See* VFS.

virtual memory Means of expanding the memory capacity of a system by using disk space. Appears to users or programs as real memory space; thus, instructions and data can be addressed to an actual memory location. *See* paging, physical memory and swapping.

virtual memory address Commonly called virtual address. *See* virtual address.

Virtual Memory System Commonly abbreviated and called VMS. *See* VMS.

virtual office Describes technology that eliminates the need for a worker to have a fixed place of work. Enables workers to be almost anywhere and still accomplish all their normal functions by using laptop, notebook, pen-based and other computers; modems; wireless networks, cellular phones and other technologies.

Virtual Protocol Machine Commonly abbreviated and called VPM. *See* VPM.

virtual reality First developed by Ivan Southerland in the late 1960s. Creates an illusion of being immersed in an environment, allowing the user to travel through and interact with the images created by the computer. Virtual environments are based on computational mathematical models that can be represented in graphical, aural or tactile form. These imaginary environments are currently being generated by virtual interface computer technology, e.g. the holodeck depicted on the starship Enterprise in the television series *Star Trek: The Next Generation*. This technology includes the use of real-time three-dimensional graphics, sound, tactile feedback, stereoscopic displays, three- and six-dimensional sensors, and interactive user interfaces. *See* 3-D data.

virtual storage Commonly called virtual memory. *See* virtual memory.

Virtual Telecommunications Access Method Commonly abbreviated and called VTAM. *See* VTAM.

Virtual Terminal **1.** Commonly abbreviated and called VT. *See* VT. **2.** Intelligent terminal, like a personal computer, that appears to a host computer to be only a dumb terminal.

virus Program that copies itself onto other software programs. Infects a computer system by destroying data and files or reformatting disk drives, eventually causing a partial or total system failure. A UNIX virus is introduced through either common user networks or hackers or software packages taken from bulletin boards. Can be used to transport a Trojan horse. Viruses are more prevalent in personal computers, where they can be transferred from system to system on floppy diskettes. *See* Michelangelo, Trojan horse, transport, worm and diskette.

visible language Use of symbols in graphical user interfaces to communicate a message or intention. Includes such characteristics as a symbol's color, texture, animation, etc., e.g. a symbol of a telephone for a phone list or a pair of scissors to represent a cut and paste feature. *See* GUI.

VISTANet One of the gigabit test-bed networks developed by the U.S. government, industry and university representatives. Tests technologies and applications used in implementing networks and supercomputers that can transmit gigabits of data per second. Designed to test and develop applications, network technology and standards used to support public support emergency systems, e.g. disaster support and emergency medical care. Participating in VISTANet are Bell Atlantic, BellCore and the Carnegie-Mellon University Supercomputing Center. *See* HPCC, NREN, LAN, HiPPI, WAN, AURORA, BLANCA, CASA, MAGIC and NECTAR.

VISUAL **1.** Environmental shell variable in the Korn shell that sets the visual editor, e.g. vi or EMACS. Overrides the editor set by the EDITOR shell variable to the visual editor designated. **2.** Electronic-mail variable. *See* .mailrc variables (Appendix F).

visual audio tool Commonly abbreviated and called vat. *See* vat.

visual editor Commonly abbreviated and called vi. *See* vi.

visualization Use of computer graphics to convert numeric or other quantifiable relationships into a visible display, e.g. graph.

Visual User Environment Commonly abbreviated and called VUE. *See* VUE.

Visual User Environment window manager Abbreviated and commonly known as vuewm. *See* vuewm.

VL-bus Video Electronics Standards Association local **bus**. Computer bus standard that allows the central processor unit (CPU) to transfer data to two devices along a 32-bit pathway at the CPU's speed. The standard, which appeared in hardware in 1992, was designed to allow video information to be transferred between the CPU and graphics card at a faster rate than the older 16-megahertz Industry Standard Architecture standard. The VL-bus competes with the Peripheral Component Interconnect local bus standard. *See* EISA, ISA local bus, PCI bus and CPU.

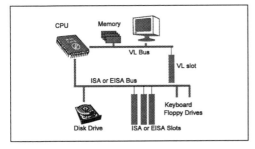

The VL-bus allows high speed peripherals to coexist with slower ISA or EISA devices.

VLF Very low frequency. Electromagnetic radiation, between 2 and 400 kilohertz, from computer screens that is suspected to have negative genetic effects on users. *See* ELF.

VLSI Very-large-scale integration. Placing thousands of transistors or other components into an integrated circuit. *See* IC.

VMEbus Versabus Module Europe **bus**. Specification for a public domain, asynchronous communications bus developed in the late 1970s by Motorola Inc., Mostek and Signetics Corp. Designed to provide a high-speed interface between processors and memory, and peripheral controllers. *See* asynchronous communications and bus.

VMS Virtual Memory System. Proprietary operating system for Digital Equipment Corp.'s VAX computer systems.

vmstat *(BSD)* Virtual memory statistics. Command used to display virtual memory statistics. Provides a broad range of information, from the number of kernel interrupts to the amount of paging activity. *See* sar.

vn *(OTH)* Visual news. Program interface used to access and read news on bulletin boards available through USENET. *See* USENET.

vnews *(OTH)* Visual news. Earlier version of a program interface used to access and read news on bulletin boards available through USENET. *See* USENET.

voice recognition User and computer interface designed to enable users to enter information, commands and other instructions into a computer system by speaking instead of by using a keyboard or mouse.

volcopy *(ATT)* Volume copy. Fast method of writing an exact copy of an entire file system to tape. Cannot be used to either back up a single file or recover a single file from a volcopy backup. *See* file system.

volt Measurement of electromotive force equal to the potential energy created by 1 ampere of current flowing against 1 ohm of resistance.

volume name Identifies the fixed disk partition. *See* partition.

volume number 1. Physical disk section on which an unmounted file system is to be mounted. 2. Tape to which a file system is written. *See* labelit.

volume table of contents Commonly abbreviated and called VTOC. *See* VTOC.

VP/ix Operating system released in 1987 by Interactive Systems Corp. and Phoenix Technologies Ltd. to allow 80386 computers to run DOS programs under UNIX. *See* DOS.

VPM Virtual Protocol Machine. Set of programs provided in UNIX System V for programmers to develop International Organization for Standardization/Open Systems Interconnection data link layer protocols. These control transmission of data between contiguous nodes on a network and the delivery of messages within a single network. *See* ISO/OSI and node.

vpr *(BSD)* Versatec printer/plotter spooler. Spooling program used to manage print jobs for Versatec raster printers or plotters. *See* spooler.

vprint *(BSD)* Versatec print. Shell script that sends the jobs in the queue to a raster printer or plotter to be printed. A raster plotter equivalent of the print queue lp command. *See* lp.

vprm *(BSD)* Versatec printer/plotter remove. Command used to delete print jobs from the raster plotter queue. Same as the lprm command for the print queue. *See* lprm.

VRAM Video random access memory. Also called dual-ported random access memory. Specially integrated circuit used in video cards. Designed for dual connectivity and data transfer between the VRAM chip and memory and the random access memory digital to analog convert chip. Introduced in 1983. *See* IC and RAM-DAC chip.

vspell *(OTH)* Visual spell. Public domain spelling utility. Performs a spelling check. Places the cursor over each word for which there is no match in the system or user's dictionary, identifies suggested changes and allows the user to correct the spelling, bypass the word or add the word to the user's dictionary. *See* spell and public domain.

V standards Set of standards for modem operation and telephone network interface. Developed by International Telecommunication Union Telecommunication Standardization Sector, formerly known as the *Consultative Committee on International Telegraphy and Telephony*. *See* ITU-T.

V-system Operating system developed at Stanford University in the early 1980s for research and development. A UNIX-like operating system, not based on any version of UNIX. Used at Stanford for the development of the W window project, the forerunner to the Massachusetts Institute of Technology X Window System. *See* X Window System and W.

VT Virtual Terminal. Open Systems Interconnection network service which allows terminals manufactured by different vendors to access a common host computer. *See* OSI.

VTAM Virtual Telecommunications Access Method. Pronounced *VEE TAM*. Another of the IBM Corp. terms entering UNIX with the growth of larger UNIX production systems and interfaces with IBM proprietary mainframes. VTAM is an IBM proprietary network communications software, developed in the mid-1970s. Defines the rules that applications must follow to get network services without having to be aware of specific information about the network, e.g. line speed and buffer size.

vtlmgr *(ATT)* Virtual terminal layer manager. Command used to start the virtual console feature which allows a user to access multiple terminal sessions. *See* virtual console.

vtoc *(ATT)* One of the toc graphical table of contents routines which produces a box diagram hierarchy chart. *See* toc.

VTOC Volume table of contents. Area reserved at the beginning of a disk on some UNIX implementations to describe the disk's partitioning. The use of a VTOC is vendor dependent. Developed at the University of California, Berkeley. *See* partition.

vtroff *(BSD)* Veratec troff. Version of the troff text formatting program that allows proportional fonts to be used. Developed for the Veratec or Benson-Varian raster plotter. *See* troff.

VUE Visual User Environment. Hewlett-Packard Co.'s graphical user interface for UNIX. *See* GUI, Motif and OPEN LOOK.

vuewm Visual User Environment window manager. Hewlett-Packard Co.'s Motif-based window manager for the X Window System. *See* mwm, Motif and X Window System.

vup VAX units of performance. Measurement of system performance invented by Digital Equipment Corp., manufacturer of VAX computers. Expressed as a multiple of VAX-11/780 performance. A VAX-

11/780 runs at approximately 1/2 mips, or 500,000 instructions per second. Therefore, a rating of 2 vups means a system operates at twice the speed of a VAX-11/780. *See* VAX MIPS and mips.

VxVM   System **V**, Release **x** Volume Manager. Provides greater system reliability by writing data across multiple disks and through disk mirroring, or simultaneously writing data to two or more disks, to protect data if there is a disk failure. *See* disk mirroring.

VYE   Pronunciation of visual interface or visual editor. *See* vi.

W

w *(BSD)* Command used to display a list of users currently logged on to the system, like the who command. Also provides information on what the users are doing and any idle time during which users are not making any input to the system. *See* who.

W Stanford University network window protocol. Stanford University network window protocol. Designed by Paul Asente and Brian Reid to run under the Stanford University research and development UNIX-like V operating system developed in the early 1980s. W provided multiple windows for dumb terminals. *See* X Window System and V-system.

W3 *(INET)* Also called World Wide Web. Commonly called WWW. *See* WWW.

WABI Windows Application Binary Interface. Pronounced *WA-BEE*. Application Binary Interface or specification that defines how application interfaces should run on various hardware architectures. Developed by Sun Microsystems Inc. to run DOS and Microsoft Windows programs on UNIX-based workstations. Microsoft applications, e.g. Word and Excel, can be run on a UNIX computer by using WABI to translate the application's system calls to UNIX system calls. *See* ABI and system call.

WA-BEE Pronunciation of WABI, the acronym for Windows Application Binary Interface. *See* WABI.

wafer Single thin silicon slice on which many integrated circuits are imprinted, then cut, to make individual dies (the non-conducting portion) of a chip. *See* IC, silicon and die.

waffle Rewritten version of the UNIX-to-UNIX CoPy communications system. Used with DOS and Macintosh computers. *See* UUCP.

WAG Wild ass guess. First guess at the cause of a hardware and/or software problem. Basic approach used by inexperienced maintenance and repair personnel. In contrast, a SWAG indicates at least one guess has already been made and usually indicates experienced maintenance personnel are at work. *See* SWAG.

WAIS *(INET)* Wide Area Information Server. Pronounced *WAYS* or *WAYZ*. Public domain protocol used to set up a client/server interface search for and retrieval of information stored in databases of documents on the Internet. The WAIS client programs can interface with multiple types of terminals, including dumb terminals, Macintoshes and X Window System terminals. *See* Archie, Gopher, WWW and Internet.

wait 1. *(ATT/XEN)* Command called by the shell when the fork system call is used to start a child process. Stops operations related to the process that initiated fork until the child process ends. Also used when a background process is running; forces other related processes to wait for completion of the background process and then reports when the process has finished. In addition, can be used in a shell script to provide some scheduling by making a process that is dependent upon other processes wait until the other processes are finished. **2.** System call that controls interprocess communication by suspending calls from the parent process until child processes that are currently running have been completed or stopped. *See* system call and wait3.

wait3 Enhanced version of the wait system call. Informs a process of child processes that have been completed and those that are about to be completed. *See* system call and wait.

wait action In UNIX System V, a process contained in programs located in the init table. Causes the init daemon to stop and wait for completion of the programs before going to the next instruction contained in the init table. *See* inittab.

wait channel Address of the data related to a process for which a wait system call has been initiated. *See* process and wait.

wait state When a central processing unit is idle, awaiting the next processing instruction. *See* CPU.

wall *(ATT)* Write all. Command that sends a message to all users currently logged on to a system, e.g. notification by the superuser that the system will be going down.

wallet personal computer Commonly abbreviated and called PDA. *See* PDA.

WAN Wide area network. Computer systems networked over a large geographic area, e.g. NSFNet and ARPANET. *See* NSFNet and ARPANET.

waning edge Jargon term for industries or technology that are either outdated or gradually being replaced by newer technology, e.g. vacuum tubes that were replaced by transistors, and 16-bit microprocessors that were replaced by 32-bit microprocessors. *See* leading edge and bleeding edge.

WARM Write and read many. Technology that allows data to be written, read and erased repeatedly on optical disks. Operates at high speed and offers greater storage capacity. *See* WORM.

warm boot Also called boot or reboot. To restart a system while the power is on, in contrast to cold boot, where the power has been off. *See* boot and cold boot.

warn Variable in the ex and vi editors. When set, sends a warning message, e.g. "No write since last change," to a user if a file has not been saved. Does so whenever the user suspends the editor and starts a shell command from the editor's command line. *See* ex and vi.

watt Measurement of electrical power equal to the dissipation of 1 Joule of energy per second (or 1 volt x 1 ampere).

WAUG Western Australian UNIX System Group. UNIX users group formed in 1985 to promote the use of UNIX-like operating systems.

WAYS *(INET)* One of the pronunciations of WAIS, the acronym for Wide Area Information Server. *See* WAIS.

WAYZ *(INET)* One of the pronunciations of WAIS, the acronym for Wide Area Information Server. *See* WAIS.

wc Word count. Command used to obtain information about a file. Includes options which allow the user to get different types of information, e.g. the number of words, lines or characters in a file.

Web *(INET)* Also called World Wide Web. Commonly called WWW. *See* WWW.

weight Printing term for the thickness of a line in a type font. *See* bold.

Well Known Services Commonly abbreviated and called WKS. *See* WKS.

what *(ATT/BSD/XEN)* One of the 13 Source Code Control System commands used to display SCCS information about executable files. *See* executable, SCCS, admin, cdc, comb, delta, get, help, prs, rmdel, sact, sccsdiff, unget, val and vc.

whatis *(BSD)* Command used to determine what a command does. Returns the first line of the manual page of a command, showing the name of the file and a curt definition, e.g. "wait - wait for child process to stop or terminate". Similar to the man command with the f option. *See* man.

what you see is what you get
Abbreviated and commonly known as WYSIWYG. *See* WYSIWYG.

whence *(ATT)* Korn shell command. When used without the -v option, provides the absolute path for a specified file. When used with the -v option, identifies what the understood meaning of the word or file is, e.g. alias, program, not found, etc. *See* absolute path, find and whereis.

whereis *(BSD)* Command used to locate the path for source, binary and/or manual files for a program. *See* find and whence.

Whetstone Public-domain synthetic benchmark written in FORTRAN for measuring floating point performance and how well compilers operate. *See* benchmark and floating point.

which *(BSD)* Command used to locate a program file in the current path.

while Shell command used to set up a loop to test and execute a list of activities. The loop continues as long as the results are true, or a zero (0) value is returned. When a false, or non-zero value, is returned, the loop is terminated. In the example "until two sets of conditions no longer match, continue to modify one of the two conditions," processing continues as long as the conditions match (return of a true). When they do not match (return of a false), processing is terminated. For instance, the trivial shell command executes the echo command 10 times (that is, as long as the variable a is less than 10):

```
a=0
while [ $a -lt 10 ]
do
        echo $a
        a='expr $a + 1'
done
```

See if, then, for, until and done.

whitespace Any area on a page that does not contain print, including the margins. *See* margin.

whitespace character Character, e.g. a space or tab, that can be used to form whitespace. *See* blank character and whitespace.

who *(ATT/XEN)* Command used to display a list of users currently logged on to the system.

who am i *(ATT)* Who command with the argument am i. Displays the user identifier of the person using a specific terminal, the device or channel on the computer used for access, and the current date and time recorded in the computer. *See* argument, userid and who.

whoami *(BSD)* Command used to display the effective user identifier of the user. *See* EUID.

whodo *(ATT/XEN)* Command used to see what users are doing on the system.

whois *(INET)* Command used to obtain directory information about a user or users on the Internet. In addition, information can be obtained about hosts, domains, networks, etc. *See* Internet, dig and nslookup.

Wide Area Information Server
Commonly abbreviated and called WAIS. *See* WAIS.

wide area network Commonly abbreviated and called WAN. *See* WAN.

widget 1. High-level programming elements, standard to the X Window System, used by programmers to create windows, menus, scrollbars, etc. that compose the physical user interface. New widgets can be designed to provide an individual look and feel to an application. *See* X Window System, X toolkit, gadgets and Xt Intrinsics. 2. Graphical displays, e.g. buttons and scrollbars, available to programmers of a graphical user interface. *See* GUI. 3. Hypothetical gadget or device universally used as an example of a product that

---

a computer and/or software application is developed to support.

widget library Set of abstract data objects developed through use of the Intrinsics library and xlib to form the X Window System toolkit of buttons, scrollbars, etc. *See* X Window System, widget and toolkit.

widget set Commonly called widget library. *See* widget library.

widget tree Outline of a completed widget, containing all the components making up the physical interface. *See* widget.

wild card Commonly spelled wildcard. *See* wildcard.

wildcard Also spelled wild card. A character understood to represent any other character. Metacharacters, the question mark and the asterisk are wildcards. The question mark can represent only a single character, while the asterisk can represent one or more characters. *See* metacharacter, asterisk and question mark.

WIMPs Windows, Icons, Mice and Pointers. Jargon term used by command line purists to refer to graphical user interface environments such as the X Window System, Microsoft Corp.'s Windows NT or Apple Computer Inc.'s Macintosh interface. *See* command line, X Window System, Windows NT and Mac.

WIN Wireless Inbuilding Network. Radio-based local area network developed by Motorola Inc. Initial WIN networks operate in the 18 to 19 gigahertz range, with transmission stations required every 120 feet. The first implementations transmit at a speed of 15 megabits per second, which is expected to be increased to 100 megabits per second. *See* LAN, Hz, G and Mbps.

Winchester drive Sealed disk drive unit which provides higher speed and greater reliability than a disk pack. The Winchester nickname has historical roots. The model number of the first sealed drive was 30-30, like the caliber of the Winchester model 70 rifle of the Old West. *See* disk and disk pack.

window 1. Division of a terminal screen into separate segments, each capable of supporting different connections, sessions or applications. 2. Term related to the Data Encryption Standard and secure Remote Procedure Call for the specified period of time by which the timestamp can vary between the client and server. As part of the authentication process, an encrypted time is sent from the client to the server or the server to the client, and must match within a specified time. *See* DES, RPC, client, server, encrypt, decrypt, conversation-key, common-key, public-key, private-key, keylogin, Keyserver, credential, verifier and timestamp. 3. Variable in the vi editor that, when set, establishes the number of lines of text that appear of the screen. *See* vi.

windowed shell Commonly abbreviated and called wish. *See* wish.

windowing Commonly called window. *See* window.

windowing model Element of the graphical user interface which contains programming tools and specifications for the movement and retrieval of data on a screen. *See* GUI.

Windowing Standards Committee Committee formed in January 1991 by companies that develop and sell X Window System products, to develop a text standard for window terminals. *See* X Window System.

window manager Software that allows a user to control elements of windows on the screen, such as placement, size, icon display and normal display. *See* X Window System.

Windows Application Binary Interface Commonly abbreviated and called WABI. *See* WABI.

Windows, Icons, Mice and Pointers Abbreviated and commonly known as WIMPs. *See* WIMPs.

Windows New Technology Commonly abbreviated and called NT. *See* NT.

Windows NT Commonly abbreviated and called NT. *See* NT.

Windows Open Services Architecture Commonly abbreviated and called WOSA. *See* WOSA.

Wind/U Windows/UNIX. Software product introduced by Bristol Technology Inc. in 1992 that can convert Microsoft Corp.'s Windows 3.0 applications to UNIX.

wired nation Term used in the 1970s for the electronic highway. *See* electronic highway.

wire frame Display of polygons, a set of vertices, in outline form and are not filled in. *See* 3-D graphics, polygon and phong shading.

Wireless Inbuilding Network Commonly abbreviated and called WIN. *See* WIN.

Wireless network System that uses infrared light to link computers for data transmission.

WISC Writeable Instruction Set Computing. Software architecture design that allows a programmer to modify the microcode in a chip in order to customize the operation of the central processing unit to the application software. *See* CICS and RISC.

WIS-EE-WIG Pronunciation of WYSIWYG, the abbreviation for what you see is what you get. *See* WYSIWYG.

wish Windowed shell. Shell developed for the Tool Command Language at the University of California, Berkeley, by John Ousterhout. *See* Tcl and Tk.

wizard **1.** User with all the answers (right or wrong) to all the questions. Has a large personal library of UNIX books, most of which look like they have been opened. Aware of the existence of the Bourne shell, C shell, Korn shell and their respective restricted versions. Member of a users group and, in some cases, it may even be an UNIX users group. **2.** Jargon term for any set of standard macros which come

with a computer system and which automate tasks, e.g. document formats for memoranda and letters.

WKS Well Known Services. Data file required to operate the Domain Name Service. Contains a list of the services, e.g. TELNET and File Transfer Protocol, that are available on the host. *See* DNS, TELNET and FTP.

wksh *(ATT)* Windowing Korn Shell. Variation of the Korn shell that includes X Window System extension. Used to provide an X Window System interface for programs developed to run under the Korn shell. Released as part of UNIX System V, Release 4.2. *See* Korn shell, SVR4.x and X Window System.

wm Wrap margin. An option in the vi editor that, when set, establishes the number of spaces from the right margin at which lines will automatically break, or wrap, to the next line. *See* vi, margin and line wrap.

wnewmail *(BSD)* Daemon used to notify a user of the arrival of electronic mail. *See* e-mail.

word Unit of storage that consists of either characters, bits or bytes. The unit of memory which the central processing unit architecture can best handle. Generally, its size varies with the processing ability of the central processing unit: 1 byte for an 8-bit CPU, 2 bytes for a 16-bit CPU, 4 bytes for a 32-bit CPU, etc.

word-erase character Character which is recognized by the terminal and deletes the last word of text that was input. Varies with the editing program used, e.g. in vi, it is Control w. *See* kill and erase character.

WORDIX Text formatter similar to nroff used with the EDIX screen editor. *See* nroff and EDIX.

word processing Preparation, manipulation, storage and processing of data to produce letters, reports, etc. A typical word processing software package can, among other things, check spelling; conduct searches for words, phrases and sentences; search for and replace specific words; and format documents.

word processor **1.** Originally a specialized computer designed and used only for manipulating words, numbers and characters to form text documents. All current computers are capable of word processing with the use of specialized software. **2.** Software package that enables a user to write and edit documents, such as letters and reports.

workflow Form of groupware used to automate daily routine operations of a group within a corporation.

work group Any set of people, in one or more organizations, that share common needs or interests.

working buffer Temporary buffer established by the vi editor when a user yanks, deletes or changes text. *See* vi, named buffer, unnamed buffer, numbered buffer and vi commands (Appendix T).

working directory Jargon term for current working directory. *See* current working directory.

working environment Environmental variables that can be changed by users. *See* environment variables.

working set Sections of a program that are located in a computer's main memory and have either been read or written to disk. *See* page, process, virtual address space and referenced.

workstation Single-user microcomputer which is normally part of a network that is capable of high performance and high resolution sophisticated graphics.

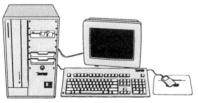
Workstation

World Forum of Open Systems Users Commonly called The Forum. *See* Forum, The.

World Wide Web *(INET)* Commonly abbreviated and called WWW. *See* WWW.

worm Standalone program that can reproduce itself. Generally, damages a computer by consuming all the machine's memory, causing it to crash. Can be sent from one system to another either via communications networks or on diskettes hidden in software packages. The term was originally attributed to the science fiction novel Shockwave Rider by John Brunner. It gained notoriety in November 1988 when a former Cornell University graduate student, Robert Tappan Morris Jr., released a program on the Internet and ARPANET that shut down more than 6,000 computers worldwide. *See* Internet Worm.

WORM Write-once/read-many. Type of optical storage medium, e.g. compact disk, that allows the data stored on it to be read many times but not changed. Used to permanently store massive amounts of data. More files can be stored and quickly retrieved on this smaller medium than on other hard media, such as microfiche. Ideal for storing data that does not change but must be maintained for a long time, e.g. history checks on customers which, under federal requirements, must be kept for seven years. In WORM technology, a laser burns the information to be stored into metal film. WORM disks come in 5.25-, 12- and 14-inch formats, and can hold from 650 megabytes to almost 7 gigabytes of data. *See* CD-ROM, M/O, MB and GB.

wormware Jargon term for the software used to support and provide an interface between the computer and write-once/read-many optical storage device. *See* WORM, CD-ROM and M/O.

WOSA Windows Open Services Architecture. Application programming interface developed by Microsoft Corp. to support the use of Windows New Technology in accessing services over a network. *See* Windows NT, DCE and ONC.

WP Word processing. *See* word processing.

wrap Commonly called line wrap. *See* line wrap.

wraparound 1. Ability within UNIX to start a search in the middle of a text file, go to the end and then return to the beginning of the file to continue the search to the starting point. 2. Commonly called line wrap. *See* line wrap.

wrapmargin Commonly abbreviated wm. *See* wm.

wrapper technology Application interface to an operating system in which the application software is added to a computer's operating system. By using hooks, or connections, the application is wrapped around the operating system.

wrapscan Variable in the ex and vi editors. Commonly abbreviated ws. *See* ws.

write 1. *(ATT)* UNIX command that allows real-time interactive communication between two users concurrently logged on to a computer. A conversation by keyboard and screen. *See* talk. 2. To modify a file. *See* permissions. 3. System call used with programs to write information to a file that has been accessed by the open command. *See* system call, open and read.

WRITE Variable for UNIX-to-UNIX CoPy read by the uucico (UNIX-to-UNIX CoPy-in copy-out) daemon. Identifies the directories that can be written to by remote hosts. Normally the default is set so only the uucppublic (UNIX-to-UNIX CoPy public) directory can be written to. *See* UUCP, uucico, NWRITE and /usr/spool/uucppublic.

Writeable Instruction Set Computing Commonly abbreviated and called WISC. *See* WISC.

write and read many Abbreviated and commonly known as WARM. *See* WARM.

writeany Variable in the ex and vi editors that permits the programs to save the contents of a temporary buffer created for an open vi or ex file to any writeable file. *See* ex, vi and nowa.

write-enable ring Small ring attached to the underside of a 9-track tape that allows data to be written to the tape. Backups and attempts to write data to a tape most often fail because a write-enable ring has not been installed.

writei Routine called by the rdwr routine to perform the actual writing of a file. *See* read, write, rdwr and readi.

write message Notification received from the system when the writing of text to disk has been completed.

write-once/read-many Abbreviated and commonly known as WORM. *See* WORM.

write permission File with permission established for creating, writing or modifying the contents of the file. *See* permissions, execute permission, read, read-only file.

Writer's Workbench Commonly abbreviated and called WWB. *See* WWB.

ws 1. Wrapscan. Variable in the ex and vi editors that, when set, automatically ends text on a line at a specified column and restarts it on the next line. *See* ex and vi. 2. Word spell. AT&T Co. script used to interactively check the spelling of one or more words.

W-TEMP Pronunciation of /etc/wtmp. *See* /etc/wtmp.

WTFO!? What the f*@! over!? A comment made to a terminal by a user after receiving an unexpected response to an input or anytime the user feels it is appropriate. Or, by a student to an instructor when learning about new software or computers. Also used by supervisors or managers when a system goes down. But, more often used by supervisors after getting a report or data they had asked for, but which does not contain what they wanted.

wtinit *(ATT)* Command used to download an object file to a windows terminal. *See* object file and window.

wtmp Commonly written as /etc/wtmp. *See* /etc/wtmp.

wtmpfix *(ATT)* System accounting program that tests the /etc/wtmp file, which contains system accounting records, for correctness or errors caused by a hardware error. *See* file consistency check and /etc/wtmp.

wump *(ATT)* Command used to start the game wumpus.

wwb Command used to run the complete set of Writer's Workbench programs at the same time. *See* WWB, diction, double, punct, sexist, spellwwb, splitinf and style.

WWB Writer's Workbench. AT&T Co.'s Bell Laboratories text processing tools capable of reviewing documents and suggesting possible grammar, syntax, spelling, sentence and word structure, etc. Written by Lorinda Cherry. *See* Bell Laboratories, diction, double, punct, sexist, spellwwb, splitinf, style and wwb.

WWW *(INET)* World Wide Web. Also spelled WorldWide Web, World-Wide Web or World-Wide-Web. Also called Web or W3. Developed in 1989 by Tim Berners-Lee with sponsorship by the European Particle Physics Laboratory, known as *CERN*. The server program used with the client program, called mosaic, to form a web, which is used to distribute information on the Internet. For example, an electronic paper about the history of UNIX found on one host may have hypertext references to an electronic paper about MULTICS found on another host half-way around the world. All of this information is linked together to form an intricate web of information. *See* hypertext, mosaic, Archie, Gohper, WAIS and Internet.

WYSIWYG **1.** What you see is what you get. Pronounced *WIS-EE-WIG*. Jargon term for a word processing program that shows on the screen how a document will appear when printed. Among the WYSIWYG word processors for UNIX are vi and WordPerfect. **2.** To reproduce on paper, as closely as possible, what is shown on the screen.

X

X Abbreviation for X Window System. *See* X Window System.

X3.129 Commonly called ANSI X3.129-1986. *See* ANSI X3.129-1986.

X3.130 Commonly called ANSI X3.130-1986. *See* ANSI X3.130-1986.

X3.131 Commonly called ANSI X3.131-1986. *See* ANSI X3.131-1986.

X3.159-1989 Commonly called ANSI X3.131-1986. *See* ANSI X3.159-1989.

X3B11.1 Commonly called ANSI X3B11.1. *See* ANSI X3B11.1.

X3H3.6 Commonly called ANSI X3H3.6. *See* ANSI X3H3.6.

X3J3 Commonly called ANSI X3J3. *See* ANSI X3J3.

X3J11 Commonly called ANSI X3J11. *See* ANSI X3J11.

X3J16 Commonly called ANSI X3J16. *See* ANSI X3J16.

X3S3.3 Commonly called ANSI X3S3.3. *See* ANSI X3S3.3.

X3T5.4 Commonly called ANSI X3T5.4. *See* ANSI X3T5.4.

X3T9.2 Commonly called ANSI X3T9.2. *See* ANSI X3T9.2.

X3T9.3 Commonly called ANSI X3T9.3. *See* ANSI X3T9.3.

X3T9.5 Commonly called ANSI X3T9.5. *See* ANSI X3T9.5.

X11perf X Window System server benchmark that contains 200 to 300 two-dimensional measurement tests for general graphics, terminal emulation, window management and X Window System-related applications. Developed by the X Consortium while it was part of the Massachusetts Institute of Technology, and is available on the UUNET network. *See* 2-D data, 3-D data, xbench, X Window System, X Consortium and UUNET.

X11R3 Jargon term for the Massachusetts Institute of Technology X 11, Release 3 specification for the X Window System. *See* X Window System.

X11R4 Jargon term for the Massachusetts Institute of Technology X 11, Release 4 specification for the X Window System. *See* X Window System.

X11R5 Jargon term for the Massachusetts Institute of Technology X 11, Release 5 specification for the X Window System. Released in September 1991, it provides X Windows the ability to support scalable fonts, international symbols, security, and 2-D and 3-D graphics. *See* X Window System, 2-D data and 3-D data.

X11R6 Jargon term for the Massachusetts Institute of Technology X 11, Release 6 specification for the X Window System. Expected to be released in early 1994 with features including enhanced imaging, object-oriented interface, improved 3-D graphics, improved ability for X Window System to run a dial-up modem, screen saver images (e.g. fish and stars), servers capable of performing multiple tasks and enhanced security. *See* X Window System, XIE, DIS, Fresco and PEX.

X12 Commonly called ANSI X12. *See* ANSI X12.

X.25 International Telecommunication Union Telecommunication Standardization Sector, formerly called the Consultative Committee on International Telegraphy and Telephony, protocol. Developed by the Defense Advanced Research Projects Agency for packet switch networks. X.25 networks operate at a transmission rate of up to 56 kilobits per second. Data is broken into packets, each containing the address information about the receiving and sending locations along with the number and sequence of packets. The packets are released on an X.25 network and may take different paths, based upon network contention, to get to the receiving location. The packets are stored at the receiving location until all are received, then reformed into the original format and delivered. If all packets do not arrive, the receiving site will request retransmission. *See* ITU-T and packet switch network.

X.75 Protocol for linking together two networks running the X.25 protocol. X.75 creates and releases virtual circuits used to connect the two networks. Developed by the International Telecommunication Union Telecommunication Standardization Sector, formerly called the Consultative Committee on International Telegraphy and Telephony. *See* X.25.

X.400 Standard for a message handling system for electronic mail. Developed by the International Telecommunication Union Telecommunication Standardization Sector, formerly called the Consultative Committee on International Telegraphy and Telephony. Adopted by the International Organization for Standardization/Open Systems Interconnection. X.400 provides the non-technical description of international standards for the exchange of electronic-mail messages. It was the first documented standard for electronic mail. The

first version of X.400 was released in 1984. The second release in 1988 included security features, e.g. encryption. *See* ITU-T, ISO/OSI and e-mail.

X.400 address elements Elements of the address field used to move a message to a remote address within the X.400 electronic message handling system. Developed by the International Telecommunication Union Telecommunication Standardization Sector, formerly called the Consultative Committee on International Telegraphy and Telephony.

Element	Description
C	Country code used to identify which country the message is to be sent to.
ADMD	Administrative domain name
PRMD	Private management domain name
ORG	Organization name.
OU	Organizational unit; identifies a sub-unit of the major organization.
DDA	Domain-defined attribute
SU	Surname
GI	Given name

X.400 APIA Commonly abbreviated and called XAPIA. *See* XAPIA.

X.400 Application Programming Interface Association Commonly abbreviated and called XAPIA. *See* XAPIA.

X.400 attributes Descriptors used in addresses in the X.400 message handling system to specify an address. Ten X.400 attributes are identified, ranging from a country code, to the type of domain the user is in, to the user's name. *See* X.400 and domain.

X.400 Recommendations Protocol standards that describe various functions within the X.400 electronic message handling system, e.g. the X.420 protocol that provides the specification for the type of information that can be included in an electronic-mail message. Developed by the International Telecommunication Union Telecommunication Standardization Sector, formerly called the Consultative Committee on International Telegraphy and Telephony. *See* X.400, ITU-T, X.402, X.403, X.407, X.408, X.411, X.413, X.419 and X.420.

X.402 Specification that provides the technical data (architecture) for the X.400 message handling system. Developed by the International Telecommunication Union Telecommunication Standardization Sector, formerly called the Consultative Committee on International Telegraphy and Telephony. *See* X.400 and ITU-T.

X.403 Specification for testing electronic-mail packages for compliance with the X.400 specification. Developed by the International Telecommunication Union Telecommunication Standardization Sector, formerly called the Consultative Committee on International Telegraphy and Telephony. *See* X.400, ITU-T and e-mail.

X.407 Specification for X.400 distributed processing. Developed by the International Telecommunication Union Telecommunication Standardization Sector, formerly called the Consultative Committee on International Telegraphy and Telephony. *See* X.400 and ITU-T.

X.408 X.400 specification for converting data from one protocol to another, e.g. text to fax. Developed by the International Telecommunication Union Telecommunication Standardization Sector, formerly called the Consultative Committee on International Telegraphy and Telephony. *See* X.400, ITU-T and fax.

X.411 X.400 specification for the movement of electronic mail between systems, including how to send electronic mail to multiple users and security procedures. Developed by the International Telecommunication Union Telecommunication Standardization Sector, formerly called the Consultative Committee on Interna-

tional Telegraphy and Telephony. *See* X.400, ITU-T and e-mail.

X.413 X.400 specification. Defines the mechanism that stores incoming electronic-mail messages for users. Developed by the International Telecommunication Union Telecommunication Standardization Sector, formerly called the Consultative Committee on International Telegraphy and Telephony. *See* X.400 and ITU-T.

X.419 X.400 specification. Defines the protocols used for message transfer agents that route electronic-mail messages to their destination; user agents responsible for handling the receiving and sending of electronic-mail messages; and message store, the temporary storage area used for electronic-mail messages when the receiver's host is not working. Developed by the International Telecommunication Union Telecommunication Standardization Sector, formerly called the Consultative Committee on International Telegraphy and Telephony. *See* MTA, ITU-T, UA and message store.

X.420 X.400 specification. Describes the type of information that can be included in an electronic-mail message and the process of transferring personal and business mail. Developed by the International Telecommunication Union Telecommunication Standardization Sector, formerly called the Consultative Committee on International Telegraphy and Telephony. *See* X.400, ITU-T and e-mail.

X.435 Protocol standard for the transmission of Electronic Data Interchange documents over an electronic-mail network based upon the X.400 standard. Developed by the International Telecommunication Union Telecommunication Standardization Sector, formerly called the Consultative Committee on International Telegraphy and Telephony. Approved in 1991. *See* EDI, ITU-T and X.400.

X.500 Standard for a network services system. Acts like a telephone directory, providing a hierarchical tree directory, or database, of users or resources on a network, wherever they are in both diverse organizational and geographic locations. The database can be located on any node on the network. Jointly developed by the International Organization for Standardization/Open Systems Interconnection and International Telecommunication Union Telecommunication Standardization Sector, formerly called the Consultative Committee on International Telegraphy and Telephony. The original standard was released in 1988 and updated in 1992. *See* ITU-T and ISO/OSI.

X.700 Standard for the Common Management Information Protocol, an international network management and monitoring protocol. Jointly developed by the International Organization for Standardization/Open Systems Interconnection and International Telecommunication Union Telecommunication Standardization Sector, formerly called the Consultative Committee on International Telegraphy and Telephony. *See* CMIP, ITU-T and ISO/OSI.

XA + X/Open transaction **plus**. Enhancement to the X/Open Co. Ltd.'s XA standard interface language that allows dissimilar transaction managers to communicate with each other. *See* XA.

XA X/Open transaction. X/Open Co. Ltd.'s transaction manager based upon Tuxedo System/T (transaction manager) to provide distributed transaction processing between dissimilar database management systems. *See* Tuxedo and Tuxedo System/T.

XAPIA X.400 Applications Program Interface Association. Group of computer and communications corporations formed in 1989 to develop standard application program interfaces for X.400. Members include AT&T Co., Lotus Development Corp., Microsoft Corp., Novell Inc. and Sun Microsystems Inc. *See* API and X.400.

xargs *(ATT/XEN)* Programming shortcut. Program that repeatedly invokes another program using data read from standard input as command line arguments. *See* argument and execute.

XA-SMDS Exchange Access-Switched Multimegabit Data Service. Specification developed by BellCore to pass data from one SMDS network to another. *See* SMDS and BellCore.

xbench X Window System public domain benchmark suite that tests 40 components of an X Window System terminal. Results of the test are expressed in a common measurement value known as an *Xstone*. *See* Xstone and X Window System.

xcalc **X** calculator. Interactive program for X Window System terminals. Acts like a programmable desk calculator but is operated with a mouse. *See* dc.

X client X Window System application, e.g. a spreadsheet that communicates with an X server. *See* X Window System and X server.

X client-server model Implementation model for the X Window System. Allows application software to run independent of the X Window hardware specifications. *See* X Window System.

XCOFF **X** Common Object Format File. Open Software Foundation Inc.'s version of the Common Object Format File. Used to create shrink-wrapped software programs that are easily transportable between computers using the same architecture, e.g. UNIX programs for 386-based systems. *See* COFF and OSF.

X Consortium, The Group of vendors which develops and maintains products based on the original X Window System specification. Formed in January 1988, sponsored by the Massachusetts Institute of Technology and funded by membership fees. Spun off by MIT in mid-1993 as a non-profit organization. *See* X Window System.

xcrypt *(OTH)* Execute **crypt**. Shell script that prompts for the password for a file to be encrypted and thereby prevents the password from remaining in the program's environment. *See* crypt and environment.

xdb **X** debugger. C language source program debugger. *See* debugger, C language and dbx.

X display management control protocol Commonly abbreviated and called XDMCP. *See* XDMCP.

X Display Manager Commonly abbreviated and called xdm. *See* xdm.

X display station Commonly called X station. *See* X station.

xdm **X** Display Manager. X Window System version of the init daemon, getty program, login command and shell used to manage user sessions. First implemented in Release 3 of the X Window System. *See* init, getty, login and shell.

XDMCP **X** **d**isplay **m**anagement **c**ontrol **p**rotocol. Developed by the X Consortium and introduced with the Massachusetts Institute of Technology X 11, Release 4 specification for the X Window System. Designed to provide services similar to the init daemon, getty program and login command. Used to validate a login and password on an X display station, and start an X session in much the same way as login does on a character terminal. *See* X Consortium, X11R4, xdm, init, getty and login.

XDOS Operating system developed by Hunter Systems Inc. to run DOS application programs on UNIX.

XDR **E**xternal **d**ata **r**epresentation. De facto industry standard, developed by Sun Microsystems Inc., for encoding data that is to be transferred between dissimilar networks. Used by Open Network Computing, the Sun Microsystems architecture for developing programs to run over a network; Remote Procedure Call, which allows commands or programs to function on remote systems over a network as if they were on the local system; and Network File System, Sun Microsystems Inc.'s file transfer protocol for heterogeneous networks. *See* ONC, RPC and NFS.

XDS **X**/Open **D**irectory **S**ervice. One of the four elements of the Open Software Foundation Inc.'s Distributed Computing Environment. X/Open Co. Ltd.'s application program interface based upon the X.500 standard. Enables a user to search for the names of other users or resources available on a network, regardless of where the database containing this information is located on the system. *See* OSF, DCE, X/Open, X.500, CDS, GDA and GDS.

XENIX Registered trademark of Microsoft Corp. Operating system developed by Microsoft to provide a user-friendly version of UNIX for microcomputers. Derived from AT&T Co.'s UNIX Version 7. Some seldom-used UNIX utilities were deleted from XENIX, while new utilities were created and selected Berkeley Software Distribution utilities were added. First released in late 1980.

Xerox Network Service Commonly abbreviated and called XNS. *See* XNS.

Xerox Palo Alto Research Center Commonly abbreviated and called Xerox PARC. *See* Xerox PARC.

Xerox PARC **Xerox** **P**alo **A**lto **R**esearch **C**enter. Xerox Corp.'s research center responsible for developing numerous breakthroughs in computer technology. One is the dynabook, a forerunner to the personal computer, that was developed 10 years before the release of the Apple Macintosh. The dynabook provided windows, icon displays with mouse control and pulldown windows. A second is Ethernet, developed in 1973 with Intel Corp. and Digital Equipment Corp. A third is Smalltalk, the first of the better-known object-oriented programming languages, developed in the mid-1980s. *See* dynabook, Ethernet, Smalltalk, OOP and C++ language.

xfd **X** font **d**isplay. Command used to display the specifics of a font.

XGA Extended Graphics Array. IBM Corp.'s graphics protocol released in late 1990. Supports a resolution on a computer screen of up to 1024 x 768 pixels. Using 640 x 480 pixels, it can support 65,536 simultaneous colors from a palette of over 24 million colors. *See* pixel, CGA and VGA.

xhost X Window System network security mechanism that controls access by remote X Window System terminals to a local host. *See* X Window System.

XIE **X** **I**maging **E**xtension. X Consortium protocol for compressing, encoding, arranging and processing image data, e.g. faxes. *See* X Window System and fax.

X Imaging Extension Commonly abbreviated and called XIE. *See* XIE.

xlib **X** **lib**rary. Also called X toolkit. File containing the library of C language programs designed for the devices (terminals) to run X Window System protocols. Contains more than 300 functions used by an X client to map the C language programs to interface with the X server. *See* X Window System, X client and X server.

xload Also called xload image. Program used to provide a graphical display of performance statistics of X Window System terminals. *See* X Window System.

xload image Commonly called xload. *See* xload.

xmh **X** **M**ail **H**andler. X Window System electronic-mail interface to the Rand Mail Handler, the Rand Corp.'s e-mail program. Developed by the X Consortium. *See* X Window System, e-mail, mh and X Consortium.

Xmodem Public domain file transfer protocol written by Ward Christensen. Sends or receives only one file at a time in packets of 128 bytes, followed by a checksum, an error detection procedure that deter-

mines is any of the data has been corrupted. *See* Xmodem-G, Ymodem, Ymodem-G, Zmodem, Kermit and checksum.

Xmodem-G Improved version of the Xmodem public domain file transfer protocol, similar to Ymodem-G. Treats each file as a single block of data and is used with faster modems operating at 9600 baud and up. Unlike Ymodem-G, it is unable to send multiple files with a single command. *See* Xmodem, Ymodem-G, Zmodem and Kermit.

XNS **X**erox **N**etwork **S**ervice. Proprietary communication protocol similar to the Transmission Control Protocol/Internet Protocol, developed by Xerox Corp. Connects networks using different communications protocols. *See* TCP/IP.

xntad *(ATT)* **X** **n**etwork **a**ccess **d**aemon. Used with X Window System terminals to manage access to the network. *See* X Window System and daemon.

XNX BSD/XENIX Compatibility Guide - Part 2. UNIX System V, Release 4 documentation on commands that were not included in UNIX System V, Release 4, but originated in the compatibility package for either the Berkeley Software Distribution or XENIX. *See* SVR4.x, XENIX and BSD.

Xol Toolkit AT&T Co.'s X Window System toolkit. Set of programs for programmers developing applications compliant with the OPEN LOOK graphical user interface. *See* X toolkit, OPEN LOOK and GUI.

X/Open X/Open Co. Ltd. Organization formed by a group of European UNIX computer manufacturers (Bull, ICL, Siemens-Nixdorf and Ing. C. Olivetti) in 1984 to develop specifications that conform to existing standards. Aims to develop a common multivendor application environment based on international standards. Has grown to more than 45 members, including U.S. and Japanese computer companies. Funding for the operation of X/Open is provided by its members. Headquarters are in London, with North American operations based in Menlo Park, California. Novell transferred ownership of the UNIX trademarks to X/Open in October 1993. *See* BISON, CAE, UNIX, USG and XPG.

X/Open Directory Service Abbreviated and commonly known as XDS. *See* XDS.

X/Open Portability Guide Commonly abbreviated and called XPG. *See* XPG.

X/Open Transaction Processing Committee Commonly abbreviated and called XTP. *See* XTP.

X/Open Transport Interface Commonly abbreviated and called XTI. *See* XTI.

Xperf Commonly called X11perf. *See* X11perf.

XPG X/Open Portability Guide(s). Documents written by X/Open Co. Ltd. that define the X/Open Common Applications Environment. Set of application interface portability standards based upon the draft ANSI C standard. Developed by X/Open, an organization composed of international computer vendors. Tells programmers how to write code that is portable between X/Open compliant systems. A numeric added to XPG indicates the edition, e.g. XPG3 for the third edition. In order for products to use the term UNIX, they must conform to either XPG3 or XPG4 and System V Interface Definition, Version 2 or 3. *See* X/Open, CAE and brand program.

xproof X proof. Command used with X Window terminals to preview or proofread a document formatted by the troff program. *See* X Window System and troff.

xprotocol *(ATT)* X.25 protocol. Data protocol supported by the UNIX-to-UNIX CoPy communications system available in early versions of AT&T's UNIX to pass data between networks. Designed to deliver files over both X.25 and Transmission Control Protocol/Internet Protocol networks. *See* UUCP, X.25, e protocol, f protocol, g protocol, G protocol and t protocol.

Xprotocol Protocol developed by the Massachusetts Institute of Technology for the X Window System. *See* X Window System.

xrn X read news. X Window System version of the rn command used to read network news. *See* X Window System, rn and news.

xsched System call used to move running programs from main memory to the swap area. Calls the sched system call to return the programs to main memory. *See* system call, primary storage and sched.

X server Program that responds to X client requests in the X Window System. Provides separate windows and communicates with the X Window terminals. *See* X client and X Window System.

X station Terminal specifically designed to run the X Window System. *See* X Window System.

Xstone Number or measurement value found in xbench, the X Window System public domain benchmark suite. Expresses the results of performance tests conducted on 40 components of an X Window System terminal. *See* X Window System.

XT + Original name for the UNIX System Laboratory's OPEN LOOK Intrinsics Toolkit. *See* OLIT and OPEN LOOK.

xterm X Window terminal emulator system for a VT 100 terminal. Like terminfo and termcap, identifies the window mapping needed for screen-oriented programs to correctly place text and graphic characters on the screen of an X Window System terminal device. *See* terminfo, termcap and X Window System.

X terminal Commonly called X station. *See* X station.

XTI X/Open Transport Interface. Programmer's interface used to develop applications independent of network protocols.

Xt Intrinsics Modified version of the original Massachusetts Institute of Technology's intrinsics library. Xt Intrinsics is a subset of the X toolkit that provides the basic framework for the development of X Window System applications. Both UNIX System Laboratories Inc. and OSF/Motif have their own commercial versions, namely OPEN LOOK Intrinsic Toolkit and OSF/Motif Toolkit. *See* X Window System, intrinsics library, X toolkit and widget.

xtk Toolkit containing a collection of programs and/or routines used by programmers as a short used to develop common elements of application software, such as menus, forms and scrollbars provided with the X Window System. *See* toolkit and X Window System.

X toolkit Also called xlib. Set of programs available to application software developers that runs under the X Window System. *See* toolkit, X Window System, Xt Intrinsics and widget.

XTP X/Open Transaction Processing committee. Formed in 1987 by X/Open Co. Ltd. to address transaction processing and networking issues. Includes two groups: one to develop the definition for an interface with the Logical Unit Interface, Version 6, Release 2, IBM Corp.'s proprietary Systems Network Architecture protocol for peer-to-peer communication; and the other to define a UNIX distributed transaction processing system. *See* X/Open and LU6.2.

xts *(ATT)* Command used to display window driver statistics.

xtt *(ATT)* Command used to display window packet traces.

Xview Toolkit Sun Microsystems Inc.'s version of the X Window System toolkit that is compliant with the OPEN LOOK graphical user interface. *See* X toolkit, OPEN LOOK and GUI.

X Window System Bit-mapped display system for both text and graphics. Designed and developed in 1984 at the Massachusetts Institute of Technology by Jim Gettys and Bob Scheifler to allow graphics applications to run over networks. Incorrectly referred to by some as an operating system, the X Window System is a communications protocol that provides users the ability to communicate with graphical-based software. Provides multiple simultaneous connections to one or more computer systems with a screen display (window) that enables a user to observe and make inputs to the processes or applications that are running. *See* V-system, W and AlphaWindow.

XXX Commonly called Triple-X. *See* Triple-X.

Y

yacc Yet another compiler-compiler. Program used to create a parser (or program that compiles text files into something else) from a simple set of rules. Used for generating C language compilers, simple programs that parse (decode) date strings, and is even used to create itself. *See* compiler and parse.

YAPS Yet another POSIX (Portable Operating System Interface for Computer Environments) subcommittee. Jargon term that facetiously describes the rapid growth of POSIX committees. *See* POSIX.

YAUB Yet Another UNIX Book. Jargon term similar to YAPS. Facetiously describes the rapid growth in the number of UNIX books in the market place. *See* YAPS.

yaw Up-and-down angular displacement of a view of the vertical, or y, axis. *See* roll.

Yellow Book Book containing the specifications for the transport layer protocol of JANET, the British national research and development network. *See* JANET and transport layer.

Yellow Pages Former name of the Network Information Service (NIS). *See* NIS.

yes *(BSD/XEN)* Command used to continuously print the same set of characters or words.

Yet Another UNIX Book Commonly abbreviated and called YAUB. *See* YAUB.

Ymodem Improved version of Xmodem, the public domain file transfer protocol. Supports the transmission of large blocks (of up to 1,024 bytes) and the transfer of multiple files at once. Uses the cyclic redundancy check method to detect and eliminate errors introduced during data transmission. *See* Ymodem-G, Xmodem, Xmodem-G, Zmodem, Kermit and CRC.

Ymodem-G Improved version of Ymodem. Treats each file as a single block of data and is used with faster modems operating at 9600 baud and up. Can send multiple files with a single command. *See* Ymodem, Xmodem, Xmodem-G, Zmodem and Kermit.

YP Yellow Pages. Former name of Network Information Service. *See* NIS.

YP map Network Information Service (formerly Yellow Pages) file.

YP server Network Information Service (formerly Yellow Pages) server. Central system in a Network File System network that runs the NIS. *See* NFS and NIS.

YP Service Yellow Pages Service. Now called NIS. *See* NIS.

ypbind Yellow Pages **bind**. Network Information Service (formerly Yellow Pages) address book. Daemon required to operate the NIS system. Maintains the address of the host on the network. *See* NIS.

ypcat Yellow Pages **cat**. Command used to output the contents in a Network Information Service (formerly Yellow Pages) database, e.g. password, group or host address information. *See* NIS.

ypclnt Yellow Pages C library **network**. Interface to the lookup service on the Network Information Service (formerly Yellow Pages) network. *See* NIS and name service.

ypinit Yellow Pages **init**. Network Information Service (formerly Yellow Pages) program that starts, or initializes, a NIS name service database on a NIS server. *See* name service and NIS.

ypmake Yellow Pages **make**. Network Information Service (formerly Yellow Pages) program used to rebuild a database after it has been updated. *See* NIS.

ypmatch Yellow Pages **match**. Network Information Service (formerly Yellow Pages) program used to display database values for a specific key, or index. *See* NIS.

yppasswd Yellow Pages **password**. Network Information Service (formerly Yellow Pages) program used to change the password for user accounts on the host on an NIS network. *See* NIS and passwd.

yppoll Yellow Pages **poll**. Network Information Service (formerly Yellow Pages) program used to obtain information about a NIX file and the server on which it is located. *See* NIS.

yppush Yellow Pages **push**. Network Information Service (formerly Yellow Pages) program used to update a NIS file on the network. *See* NIS.

ypserv Yellow Pages **server**. Daemon used to start and run a Network Information Service (formerly Yellow Pages) server. *See* NIS and server.

ypset Yellow Pages **set**. Network Information Service (formerly Yellow Pages) utility used to force NIS to bind a specific service to a named server. Useful for debugging or binding to a client that does not run NIS. *See* NIS.

ypupdated Yellow Pages **updated**. Network Information Service (formerly Yellow Pages) utility used to update information in the NIS name service. *See* name service and NIS.

ypwhich Yellow Pages **which**. Network Information Service (formerly Yellow Pages) program used to identify a NIS hostname. *See* NIS.

ypxfr Yellow Pages **transfer**. Command used to move Network Information Service (formerly Yellow Pages) files between domains or networks. *See* NIS and domain.

YUUG Yugoslavian UNIX User Group. UNIX users group formed in 1989.

Z

Z Jargon term for zulu time. *See* zulu time.

zap Jargon term for deleting a file, user, etc., normally by mistake.

zcat **Z** concatenate. Command used to uncompress a file, sending the uncompressed data to standard output for viewing. The compressed file is left unchanged. *See* compress and cat.

zcmp *(BSD)* Command used to compare the contents of compressed files. *See* compress.

zdiff *(BSD)* Command used to report the differences between the contents of compressed files. *See* compress and diff.

Zephyr Real-time electronic-mail system developed as part of the Massachusetts Institute of Technology's Project Athena. *See* Project Athena.

zeroeth argument Another name for a command input on a command line. Referred to as the zeroeth argument because the command is the first word input in a string of arguments that are to be used in accomplishing a specific function.

zero-length file File created that has no contents. Normally created as part of a program, to be used at later for a wide variety of purposes, e.g. as a lock, a make target, a place holder or a reminder to go home. *See* touch.

zero width Output with no horizontal spacing.

Zeus Zilog computer implementation of UNIX System V.

Zigzag in-line package Commonly abbreviated and called ZIP. *See* ZIP.

ZIP Zigzag in-line package. Electronic component housing similar to a dual in-line package that is used to enclose components normally installed in specialty devices, e.g. video cards. A rectangular ceramic or plastic case, approximately .33 inch wide and 1.5 inches long with two rows of off set metal connector pins (that have a zigzag appearance) on both sides of the case. *See* DIP.

Zmodem File transfer protocol. A faster version of Xmodem that produces fewer errors. Zmodem continues to transmit data until it receives a negative acknowledgment, or NACK. When this happens, it restarts the transmission from the point at which it was interrupted. Can also restart a file transfer from the point at which it was interrupted if a connection is broken. Transfers data in either 256 or 1,024 byte packets. *See* Xmodem, Xmodem-G, Ymodem, Ymodem-G, Kermit, NACK, checkpointing and redundant file skipping.

zmore *(BSD)* Command used to view the contents of compressed files. *See* compress.

zombie Child process without a parent process. When a parent process dies or has been ended, the child process (the remaining process started by the parent) becomes a zombie process. In most cases, the init daemon takes over as the parent and allows the child to complete its function. *See* process and init.

zombie process Commonly called zombie. *See* zombie.

zone *(INET)* Domain Name Service term for a collection of hosts within a domain administered by another host, e.g. the Network Information Center's zone includes all hosts on the Internet. *See* DNS, NIC, Internet, zone of authority and root-level domain.

zone of authority Berkeley Internet Name Domain term for the list of computers in a network for which the name daemon manages connectivity. *See* BIND and zone.

z time Jargon term for Zulu time. *See* Zulu time.

Zulu time Jargon term for Greenwich Mean Time.

Appendix A

Basic EMACS commands

Command	Description
Ctrl-a	Moves cursor to the beginning of the current line.
Ctrl-b	Moves cursor to the left (back) one character.
Ctrl-d	Deletes next (right) character.
Ctrl-f	Moves cursor to the right (forward) one character.
Ctrl-h	Deletes previous (left) character.
Ctrl-k	Deletes all characters from cursor to the end of the line.
Ctrl-n	Moves cursor down to the next line.
Ctrl-p	Moves cursor up to the previous line.
Ctrl-r	Searches backward (reverse) for a string.
Ctrl-s	Searches forward for a string.
Ctrl-v	Moves cursor ahead one full screen.
Ctrl-x Ctrl-c	Exits EMACS with writing the buffer contents to a file.
Ctrl-x Ctrl-f	Exits EMACS and writes buffer contents to a file.
Esc-a	Moves cursor back to the beginning of the last sentence.
Esc-b	Moves cursor back to the start of the previous word.
Esc-d	Deletes next (right) word.
Esc-e	Moves cursor to the beginning of the next sentence.
Esc-f	Moves cursor to end of the current word.
Esc-h	Delete previous (left) word.
Esc-v	Moves cursor back one screen of text.
Esc-x	Used to start the more detailed EMACS help facility.
Esc-?	Used to start the basic help facility.
Esc-)	Moves cursor to the end of the current paragraph.

Command	Description
Esc-(	Moves cursor to the beginning of the current paragraph.
Esc-!	Moves current line to the top of screen and repaints screen with new text.
Esc-.	Moves cursor to first character of the next screen of text.
Esc->	Moves cursor to the end of the file.
Esc-<	Moves cursor to the beginning of the file.

Appendix B

ex commands

1. Basic enter text mode commands:

Command	Description
a	Append. Start new text following the current or specified line.
i	Insert. Start new text before the current or specified line.
c	Change. Change or overwrite text starting on the current or specified line.

2. ex commands to manipulate lines of text:

Command	Description
co	Copy. Used to copy one or more lines of text to a specified line in the text.
d	Delete. Used to delete one or more specified lines of text.
j	Join. Used to join two lines of text into a new line of text.
m	Move. Used to move one or more specified lines of text from one location to another within the same file.
pu	Put. Used in conjunction with yank to transfer text to a new location.
y	Yank. Used to copy one or more lines from one location in a file to another.

3. Other ex commands:

Command	Description
q	Quit. Exit file without writing any modifications.
u	Undo. Reverse action of the previous editing action.
w	Write. Write modifications to file.
sh	Shell. Invoke a shell to temporarily escape from the editor and perform other functions.
vi	Visual editor. Invoke the visual editor.

Appendix C

FTP commands

Basic FTP commands for communicating with a local or remote host:

Command	Description
!	Used to create an interactive shell. This allows the user to keep the FTP session active while escaping to a shell to perform other functions.
! <Command>	Used to execute a command outside of FTP while keeping the session active.
$ <macro>	Used to execute a predefined macro.
?	Same as the help command.
account <password>	Used to provide a password required to obtain access to an account on a remote host. If no password is provided with the command the user will be prompted for one.
append <local file remote>	Used to add a local file to the end of a file on a remote host. If no file name is provided for the remote host.
ascii	Used to identify the network as being ASCII.
bell	Used to have a bell sounded after a computer has completed a command.
binary	Used to specify the file transfer type to support binary image transfer.
bye	Used to end the FTP session and exit to the user prompt.
case	Used to turn on or off transmission of uppercase characters to and from a remote host.
cd <directory name>	Used to change to a new current working directory on the remote host.
cdup	Used to move up one directory in the relative path on the remote host.
close	Used to end an FTP connection without exiting FTP.

Command	Description
cr	Used to turn on and off automatic carriage returns during file transfers.
delete <filename>	Used to delete a file on a remote host.
debug	Used to turn on and off debugging of a command sent to a remote host.
dir <remote directory>	Used to list the contents of a directory on a remote host. The output is sent to either a specified local directory or current working directory or the screen depending on the option selected.
disconnect	Same as the close command.
form	Used to set the format of the carriage control. Only one format "nonprint." is available.
get	Used to transfer a single file from a remote computer to a local computer.
glob	Used to turn on and off file name expansion.
hash	Used to turn on and off printing of the hash sign (#) for each data block transferred.
help <command>	Used to provide information on a specific command. Or if no command is identified, list commands for which help information is available.
lcd <directory name>	Permits user to do a local change directory to a specific directory. If no directory is given, returns user to the home directory.
ls <remote directory>	Provides a list of file names in a directory on a remote host. If no remote directory name is given, provides a list of the contents of the local current working directory.
macdef <macro name>	Used to define a macro developed to perform a specific function.
mdelete <remote file name>	Used to delete multiple files on a remote host.
mdir <remote directory local directory>	Used to list the contents of multiple directories on a remote host. The output is sent to a specified local directory, current working directory or the screen, depending on the option selected.
mget <file names>	Used to transfer multiple files from a remote computer to a local computer.
mkdir <directory name>	Used to make a directory on a remote host.
mls <remote directory>	Provides a list of file names of multiple directories on a remote host.
mode	Used to identify the mode to be used for a data transfer.
mput	Used to transfer multiple files from a local computer to a remote computer.

Command	Description
nmap	Used to establish or delete the mapping (locating) files when they are transferred between hosts with the put, mput, get or mget commands.
ntrans	Used to establish or delete file name character translation mechanism.
open <host name>	Used to establish a FTP connection with a remote host.
prompt	Used to turn on and off a question asking if a file is "really" to be transferred when requested by the user with the mget or mput command or if a file is "really" to be deleted when the mdelete command is used.
proxy <command>	Allows user to simultaneously connect to and transfer data with two remote hosts.
put	Used to transfer a single file from a local computer to a remote computer.
pwd	Used to display the current working directory on a remote host.
quit	Same as bye.
quote <arg, arg1, etc.>	Used to send one or more arguments, exactly as input, to a remote printer.
recv	Same as get.
remotehelp <command>	Used to send a request for help to a remote host.
rename	Used to change the name of a file on a remote host.
reset	Used to delete queues of commands or responses on a remote host.
rmdir <directory>	Used to delete a directory on a remote host.
runique	Used to turn on and turn off the creation of unique file names when transferring files.
send	Same as put.
sendport	Used to turn on and off the use of PORT commands when making a FTP connection.
status	Used to display the current status of FTP.
struct	Used to set the file structure. The only recognized structure is file.
sunique	Used to turn off and on the storage of unique files on a remote host if a file that has been transferred has the same name as an existing file on the remote host. Similar to the runique command.
tenex	Used to identify the network to which the host is connected as a TENEX machine that requires a byte size of 8.
trace	Used to turn on and off the tracking of the route that a packet follows.
type	Used to identify the type of network (ASCII, binary, image or TENEX) to which the host is connected.

Command	Description
user <user account>	Used to identify the user account to be accessed on the remote host. If no account or password is identified it prompts the user for one.
verbose	Used to turn on and off the display of all statistics related to the transfer of a file between systems.

Appendix D

lpc commands

Command	Description
abort	Kills a print job on a specific printer.
clean	Flushes out all jobs in the printer's print queue, including active jobs.
disable	Turns off queuing for a particular printer. Jobs already in the print queue will be completed.
down	Message sent to indicate the printer is not operating.
enable	Turns a printer on again.
help or ?	If run with a command name, a description of the command is provided. When run without a command name, a summary of the lpc commands is provided.
restart	Starts printing jobs in the print queue.
start	Starts queuing and printing of jobs in a print queue.
status	Displays the status of spooling, printing, number of jobs in the queue and the status of the printer daemon.
stop	Turns off a printer. If there is a job in process, it will be completed.
topq (job number)	Moves the specified job to the top of the print queue.
topq (user name)	Moves all print jobs for a specified user to the top of the print queue.

Appendix E

mail commands

mail commands executed at the mail prompt (*see* tilde commands, Appendix S):

Command	Description
?	Help command which displays the mail commands and descriptions.
*	Same as the "?".
!	Spawn or create a shell for input of commands.
! (command)	Spawn a shell and then execute the specified command.
#	Ignore the rest of the line.
=	Print current message number.
	Carriage return or enter will display the next mail message if there is one.
d	Delete a message.
dp	Delete message and print the next message.
dt	Delete message and print the next message.
e	Edit text of an electronic-mail message.
exit	Exit mail. Leaves the mail file exactly as it was when the user opened the file.
f	Display header of an incoming message.
h	Display current header.
m	Send (mail) a message to specified user(s).
n	Display next message.
p	Print specified message(s).
q	Quit mail and make updates to the mail file, including the removal of mail messages marked for deletion.
r	Answer (reply to) a message. Reply goes to the originator and users who received the message.
R	Answer (reply to) a message. Response only goes to the originator.

Command	Description
s (filename)	Save the mail message to a file or t the default mbox if no file is specified.
S	Automatically save the message in a file named for the originator of the message.
t	Display a message on the screen.
to (n)	Used to display the top number of lines of a message header.
u	Undelete a mail message. Can be used to restore a deleted file until the user quits the mail session. Once the user quits the message is gone.
v	Start the vi editor.
version	Display current version of mailx.
w	Save mail message without the header.
x	Exit mail; no updates are made.
z+	Display a full screen of previous message headers.
z-	Show a full screen of previous message headers.

Appendix F

.mailrc variables (ATT)

Standard AT&T (ATT) electronic-mail options that can be set by users:

Command	Description
append	Allows user to save mail messages to the end of the mbox instead of the beginning.
askcc	Prompts user for a list of users who should receive a carbon copy of outgoing messages.
asksub	Prompts user for the subject of messages being sent.
autoprint	Automatically prints the next message when action is completed on the current message.
cmd <Shell command>	Defines the default for the pipe command.
crt <number>	Sets the number of lines to be displayed.
DEAD <Filename>	Establishes the dead letter file.
dot	Recognizes a dot on a line, followed by a carriage return, as a signal for end of message.
EDITOR <program>	Establishes the editor to be used.
escape <character>	Defines the escape character.
folder <directory>	Defines the directory where mail is to be saved.
header	Turns on and off the automatic display of message headers.
hold	Stores undeleted message in system file instead of the mbox file.
ignore	Turns on and off the recognition of interrupts from a terminal.
ignoreeof	Turns on and off the recognition of end-of-file character (Ctrl d).
keep	Turns on and off the automatic retention of the user's mail file when empty.
Keepsave	Turns on and off the automatic deletion from the mail file when the message is saved.

Command	Description
metoo	Turns on and off the automatic sending of a copy of outgoing messages to the senders sentmail file, if the message is going to users in the same group.
outfolder	Allows the user to store outgoing mail messages in a file established in the mail storage directory.
page	Turns on and off the automatic addition of a form feed (Ctrl-l) after each message.
PAGER <program>	Sets the pager (less, more or pg) program.
prompt <character(s)>	Defines the mail prompt.
quiet	Turns on and off the introductory message when mail is started.
record <filename>	Turns on and off the automatic sending of a copy of out going messages to the sender's sentmail file.
save	Tells the system to automatically save a copy of mail message being prepared, if an interrupt is received.
screen <number>	Sets the number of header to be displayed.
sendmail <program>	Sets the mailer to be used with mailx to deliver the messages.
SHELL <program>	Sets the shell to be used when ! is invoked.
sign <string>	Sets the standard string to be inserted with the ~a command.
Sign <string>	Sets the standard string to be inserted with the ~A command.
toplines	Sets the number of lines displayed when the to (top) command is invoked.
VISUAL <program>	Specifies the visual editor to be used with the v command.

Appendix G

.mailrc variables (BSD)

Standard Berkeley Software Distribution (BSD) electronic-mail options that can be set by users:

Command	Description
append	Allows user to save mail messages to the end of the mbox file instead of the beginning.
ask	Prompts user for the subject of messages being sent.
askcc	Prompts user for a list of users who should receive a carbon copy of outgoing messages.
autoprint	Automatically prints the next message when action is completed on the current message.
crt	Displays mail messages a screen at a time, using a display program such as less or more.
dot	Recognizes a dot on a line followed by a carriage return as a signal for end of message.
hold	Stores undeleted message in system file instead of the mbox file.
metoo	Automatically sends a copy of outgoing messages to the sender's sentmail file.
save	Tells the system to automatically save a copy of mail message being prepared if an interrupt is received.

Appendix H

RFS parameters

RFS parameters used to tune a host running the Remote File Sharing system:

Parameter	Description
MAXGDP	Used to set the maximum number of virtual circuits that a computer can have open to remote hosts and that remote hosts can establish with the local hosts at any one time.
MAXSERVE	Used to set the maximum number of new processes that can be created if the number of MINSERVE processes is exceeded.
MINSERVE	Used to set the maximum number of remote processes requesting access to resources that can be run simultaneously.
NRCVD	Used to set the maximum number of local files or directories that can be simultaneously opened by remote users.
NRDUSER	Used to set the maximum number of remote users that can access a file or directory simultaneously.
NSNDD	Used to set the maximum number of files or directories that can be simultaneously opened on remote hosts.
NSRMOUNT	Used to set the maximum number of new local resources that can be opened for use by remote users.
RCACHETIME	Used to protect file integrity by preventing the use of memory for temporary data storage or establishing a delay between the times when the use of memory for temporary data storage is allowed.
RF_MAXKMEM	Used to limit the amount of kernel memory devoted to use by RFS.

Appendix I

Signal values (Pre-SVR4)

Pre-System V, Release 4 operations performed by signals:

Signal	Description
SIGABRT	Sends an abort or stop signal when a program sends an abort() function call.
SIGALRM	Sends an alarm when a program sends an alarm() function call.
SIGBUS	Indicates a bus (hardware) error.
SIGCLD	Sends notice of the end or death of a child process.
SIGEMT	Issued when an EMT or emulation trap occurs indicating a hardware-independent action.
SIGFPE	Issued when a floating point exception occurs. The arguments passed to the signal handler are hardware-dependent.
SIGHUP	Tells the system to hang up or disconnect when transmission is complete.
SIGILL	Indicates an illegal instruction that has been received. Some hardware, including VAX, produces more specific information about the type of error.
SIGINT	Sends an interrupt. Interrupt sent to a foreground process as a result of depressing the interrupt key.
SIGIO	Sent when input/output is possible on a STREAMS file descriptor.
SIGIOT	Same as a SIGABRT. Sends an abort instruction.
SIGKILL	A kill sent by a process is transmitted to other processes owned by the same user causing them to terminate. A kill signal cannot be caught or ignored.
SIGPIPE	Sends notice of a broken pipe; a program writes to a pipe where there is not another program to read it.
SIGPOLL	Issued when a file descriptor corresponding to a STREAMS file has a "selectable" event pending.
SIGPROF	Issued when profiling timer alarm occurs.
SIGPW	Sends notice of a power failure.

Signal	Description
SIGQUIT	Sends a quit signal to a foreground process. Used when the process does not recognize SIGINT.
SIGSEGV	Sends notice of a segmentation violation, including writing into protected memory.
SIGSYS	Sends notice that a bad argument was sent with a system call.
SIGTERM	Software termination request sent by a process to processes owned by the same user.
SIGTRAP	Signal trap, issued when trace traps are used to implement debuggers.
SIGUSR1	Reserved for software writers as the first user-defined signal.
SIGUSR2	Reserved for software writers as the second user-defined signal.
SSIGVTALRM	Issued when a virtual time alarm occurs.
SIGXCPU	Issued when central processing unit time limit is exceeded.
SIGXFSZ	Issued when file size limit is exceeded.

Appendix J

Signal values (SVR4)

System V, Release 4 operations performed by signals:

Command	Description
SIGABRT	Sends notice of a process abort.
SIGALRM	Sends an alarm when a system alarm is issued.
SIGBUS	Indicates a bus (hardware) error.
SIGCHLD	Sends notice of the end or death of a child process.
SIGCONT	Sends notice of the restart of a process.
SIGEMT	Issued when an EMT or emulation trap occurs indicating a hardware-independent action.
SIGFPE	Issued when a floating point exception occurs. The arguments passed to the signal handler are hardware-dependent.
SIGHUP	Sends a command to the computer to hang up or disconnect when transmission is complete.
SIGILL	Sends notice that an illegal instruction has been received. Some hardware systems, including VAX provide more specific information.
SIGINT	Sends an interrupt. Interrupt sent to a foreground process as a result of depressing the interrupt key.
SIGIO	Sends notice that socket input/output is possible.
SIGKILL	A kill sent by a process is transmitted to other processes owned by the same user causing them to terminate. A kill signal cannot be caught or ignored.
SIGPIPE	Sends notice of a broken pipe, including when a program writes to a pipe and there is not another program to read the pipe.
SIGPOLL	Issued when a file descriptor corresponding to a STREAMS file has a "selectable" event pending.
SIGPROF	Sends a notice that the profiling time has expired.
SIGPWR	Indicates a power failure.

Command	Description
SIGQUIT	Sends a quit signal to a foreground process. Used when the process does not recognize an interrupt. Normally a core dump will be generated.
SIGSEGV	Sends a notice of a segmentation violation, including writing to protected memory.
SIGSTOP	Issued when a sendable stop signal is received but not from tty.
SIGSYS	Sends notice that a bad argument has been sent with a system call.
SIGTRAP	Issued when a trace trap is started by a debugger.
SIGTSTP	Sends notice of a stopped user.
SIGTTIN	Indicates a terminal input has stopped.
SIGTTOU	Indicates a terminal output has stopped.
SIGURG	Sends notice of an urgent socket condition.
SIGUSR1	Reserved for software writers as the first user-defined signal.
SIGUSR2	Reserved for software writers as the second user-defined signal.
SIGVTALRM	Indicates a virtual timer has expired.
SIGWINCH	Indicates a change in window size or location.
SIGXCPU	Sends notice that the central processing unit time for a process has been exceeded.
SIGXFSZ	Sends notice that the file size limit has been exceeded.

Appendix K

Signal values (BSD)

Berkeley Software Distribution (BSD) UNIX signal values:

Command	Description
SIGALRM	Sends an alarm when a program issues an abort() function call.
SIGBUS	Indicates a bus (hardware) error.
SIGCHLD	Sends notice of the end or death of a child process.
SIGCONT	Tells a process to continue after it has stopped.
SIGEMT	Issued when an EMT or emulation trap occurs indicating a hardware-independent action.
SIGFPE	Issued when a floating point exception occurs. The arguments passed to the signal handler are hardware-dependent.
SIGHUP	Sends a command to the computer to hang up or disconnect when transmission is complete.
SIGILL	Sends notice that an illegal instruction has been received. Some hardware systems, including VAX, provide more specific information about the type of error.
SIGINT	Sends an interrupt. Interrupt sent to a foreground process as a result of depressing the interrupt key.
SIGIO	Issued when input/output is possible on a STREAMS file descriptor.
SIGIOT	Same as SIGABRT. Sends an abort instruction.
SIGKILL	Sent by a process to other processes owned by the same user.
SIGLOST	Indicates loss of a resource.
SIGPIPE	Sends an indication of a broken pipe.
SIGPROF	Sends an indication of a profiling timer alarm.
SIGQUIT	Sends a quit signal to a foreground process. Used when the process does not recognize SIGINT. A core dump is normally produced.
SIGSEGV	Sends notice of a segmentation violation, e.g. writing to protected memory.

Command	Description
SIGSTOP	Sends a stop to a process. The process will restart when it receives a SIGCONT.
SIGSYS	Sends notice that a bad argument was sent with a system call.
SIGTERM	Software termination request sent by a process to processes owned by the same user.
SIGTRAP	Issued when a trace trap is started by a debugger.
SIGTSTP	Keyboard stop. Suspends a foreground process with a signal initiated from a terminal keyboard, normally a Ctrl z.
SIGTTIN	tty input. Signal sent to a background process when the process attempts to read from the control or input terminal.
SIGTTOU	Indicates a stopped output from a terminal.
SIGURG	Indicates a socket problem.
SIGUSR1	Reserved for software writers as the first user-defined signal.
SIGUSR2	Reserved for software writers as the second user-defined signal.
SIGVTALRM	Indicates a virtual timer has expired.
SIGWINCH	Sends indication of a change in window size or location.
SIGXCPU	Sent when central processing unit timeout is exceeded.
SIGXFSZ	Sent when file size limit is exceeded.

Appendix L

sysadm commands (Pre-SVR4)

Pre-UNIX System V, Release 4 sysadm commands:

Command	Description
diskmgmt	Menu of commands which can be used with removable and hard disks. The commands include ways to check for errors, copy and delete data, format the disk and create file systems.
filemgmt	Menu of commands used for file management. The commands include backup and restore routines, backup scheduling, file information and usage and active user information.
packagemgmt	Menu of commands used for managing add-on software and hardware. The commands include establishing system environment and password assignment.
ttymgmt	Menu of commands used to manage terminal access environment. The commands include those to view and modify terminal connectivity.
usermgmt	Menu of commands to manage user access to the system. The commands include viewing, adding, modifying and deleting user accounts and user groups.

Appendix M

sysadm commands (SVR4)

System V, Release 4 sysadm commands:

Command	Description
backup_services	Menu of commands used to schedule, set up and control system backups.
diagnostics	Menu of commands used to diagnose system errors.
file_systems	Menu of commands for creating, checking and mounting file systems.
machine	Menu of commands used to display hardware configuration and shut down the system.
network_services	Menu of commands used to perform network administration.
ports	Menu of commands used to monitor and maintain port access.
printers	Menu of commands used to monitor and maintain printer configuration.
restore_service	Menu of commands used to restore data from backup tapes.
software	Menu of commands used to install and remove software.
storage_devices	Menu of commands used to define and manage storage devices.
system_setup	Menu of commands used to manage the system name, date, time and initial password system set-up.
users	Menu of commands used to manage user accounts and user group administration. Allows the system administrator to add, modify and delete both users and groups.

Appendix N

Talk-mode jargon

Abbreviated messages used in the talk mode to save time:

Jargon	Description
BCNU	Be seeing you.
BTW	By the way.
BYE?	Are you ready to terminate?
CUL	See you later.
ENQ?	Are you busy?
FOO?	Are you there?
FYI	For your information.
FYA	For your amusement.
GA	Go ahead.
GRMBL	Grumble (disagree).
HELLOP	Hello?
JAM	Just a minute.
MIN	Same as JAM.
NIL	No.
O	Over.
OO	Over and out.
/	Another form for Over.
OBTW	Oh.
R U THERE?	Are you there?
SEC	Just a second.
TNX	Thanks.
TNX 1.0E6	Thanks a million.

TNXE6	Thanks a million.
WRT	With regard or respect to.
WTF	What the f@&!
WHT?	What the hell?

Appendix O

TELNET arguments

Arguments that can be used to send special characters resulting in actions by the remote host during an interactive TELNET session. (*See* the send command in TELNET commands, Appendix P):

Argument	Description
?	Help. Provides help information about the send command.
ao	Sends the TELNET AO (abort output) sequence which requests the remote system to flush all output from the remote system to the user's terminal.
ayt	Sends the TELNET AYT (are you there) sequence to determine if the remote host is up. The remote system may or may not choose to respond.
brk	Break. Sends the TELNET BRK (break) or termination sequence, which may (but is not guaranteed to) have significance to the remote system.
ec	Sends the TELNET EC (erase character) sequence, which requests the remote system to erase the last character entered.
escape	Sends an escape sequence to the remote host.
el	Sends the TELNET EL (erase line) sequence, which requests the remote system to erase the line currently being entered.
ga	Sends the TELNET GA (go ahead) sequence, which likely has no significance to the remote system.
ip	Sends the TELNET IP (interrupt process) sequence, which requests the remote system to abort the current running process.
nop	Sends the TELNET NOP (no operation) sequence.
synch	Asks the remote system to discard all previously typed (but not yet read) input.

Appendix P

TELNET commands

Commands that can be used during an interactive TELNET session:

Command	Description
? <command>	Provides help information on a specified command. If no command is specified, a list of commands which have help information available is displayed.
close	Used to end and exit a TELNET session.
display <argument>	Provides a list of the currently established TELNET values.
mode <type>	Sets the mode, either line or character response, on the remote host.
open <host> or <port>	Starts a connection with a host, port or the TELNET server, if no host or port is specified.
quit	Used to end and exit a TELNET session. Same as the close command.
send <arguments>	Used to send an argument that performs a specific function to a remote host. See TELNET arguments (Appendix O).
set <variables>	Used to set TELNET variables for communicating actions to the remote host. See TELNET variables (Appendix R) and TELNET arguments (Appendix O).
status	Used to obtain the current status of the TELNET connection.
toggle <argument>	Used to turn on and off settings which specify how TELNET reacts to events. See TELNET flags (Appendix Q).
z	Suspend TELNET. Used to temporarily stop the TELNET session and generate a shell on the local host.

Appendix Q

TELNET flags

Toggle (on or off) flags that can be used to establish how TELNET will respond to events during an interactive TELNET session. (*See* the toggle command in TELNET commands, Appendix P.):

Flag	Description
?	Help. Provides help information on the toggle commands.
autoflush	Automatic flush. Used in conjunction with localchars to respond to terminations. Does not respond to the user's inputs until the data waiting to be processed is deleted.
autosynch	Auto synchronization. Used in conjunction with localchars to respond to terminations by deleting data waiting to be processed.
crmod	Carriage return mode. Turns on and off the recognition and input of a carriage return in data sent by a remote host.
debug	Debugger. Used only by system administrators to debug programs sent over TELNET.
localchars	Local characters. Turns on and off the local response to termination commands. When it is turned on, the correct argument is generated to the host as a result of an action on the local host. *See* the send command in TELNET commands (Appendix P).
netdata	Network data. Turns on and off the display of network data.
options	Turns on and off the display of internal data related to the TELNET protocol.

Appendix R

TELNET variables

Variables that can be used during an interactive TELNET session to generate commands to be sent to either the local or remote host:

Variable	Description
echo	When in the line mode, turns on and off the local echo of characters.
erase	Used in conjunction with localchars and the character mode to send an erase character signal to a remote host.
escape	Used to temporarily suspend operations on the remote host and enter the TELNET command mode.
eof	End-of-file. When used in the line mode, it indicates the last character of the line and sends the line to the remote host.
flushoutput	Used to direct a remote host to abort its output.
interrupt	Also called an intr. Sends an interrupt process to a remote host.
kill	Sends an erase line to a remote host.
quit	Sends a break signal to a remote host to break the connection.

Appendix S

tilde commands

Electronic-mail tilde commands:

Command	Description
~! <command>	Escape from mail, run command and return to mail.
~?	Help. Displays a list of tilde commands.
~ < <filename>	Import a specified file into the text of the message.
~<! <command>	Run a command and import the result into the text of the message.
~~	Ignore the tilde as an initiator of a command and put a tilde in the text of the message.
~.	Stop text input.
~a	Add mailx variable sign to the text of the message.
~A	Add alternate strings to the text of the message.
~b <user ID(s)>	Automatically add users to "Bcc:" (blind carbon copy).
~c <ID(s)>	Automatically add users to "Cc:" (carbon copy).
~d	Take a message from the dead letter file and put it into the text of an electronic-mail message.
~e	Start a predesignated text editor.
~f <msglist>	Add specified messages to the text of a message that is to be forwarded to users.
~h	Initiate a prompt for the subject to carbon copy (Cc) and blind carbon copy (Bcc).
~m <messages>	Add specified messages to the text of a message.
~p	Print message without header.
~q	Cancel message.
~r <filename>	Read, or import a file into the text of a message.
~s <string>	Make the string the subject of the message.

Command	Description
~t <ID(s)>	Automatically add names of users to a list of the people who are to receive the message.
~v	Start a predefined visual editor.
~w <filename>	Write or save a message to a specified file.
~x	Exit without saving the message to the dead letter file.
~ | <command>	Pipe a message through the specified command, making the result the text of the message.

Appendix T

Basic vi commands

Command	Description
a	Append text. Allows the user to add new text following the current location of the cursor. End by depressing Esc key.
b	Move the cursor one word back.
e	Move the cursor to the last character in a word.
h	Move the cursor one column to the left.
i	Insert. Allows the user to add new text one column ahead of the current cursor location. End by depressing Esc key.
j	Move the cursor one line down.
k	Move the cursor one line up.
n	Repeat last string search.
o	Open. Allows the user to add new text after the current line. End by depressing the Esc key.
p	Put. Used with the yank command to locate text within a document.
r	Replace only the character which the cursor is on.
u	Undo last command.
w	Move the cursor one word to the right.
x	Delete the character which the cursor is on.
y	Yank. Copy one or more lines from one location to another. Used with the put command.
A	Append at the end of the current line. End by depressing the Esc key.
D	Delete from current cursor location to the end of the line.
G	Go to the last line of the file. Or nG moves the cursor to a specified line.

Command	Description
H	Home. Move cursor to the first character of the first line on the screen. nH moves the cursor the specified number of lines from the first line on the screen.
I	Insert text at the start of the current line. End by depressing the Esc key.
J	Join current and following lines to form a single new line.
L	Last. Move the cursor to the first character on the last line on the screen. nL moves the cursor the specified number of lines up from the last line on the screen.
M	Middle. Move the cursor to the first character of the middle line on the screen.
N	Repeat search for a string in the reverse direction.
O	Open new line above current line. End by depressing the Esc key.
R	Replace characters starting from where the cursor is located. End by depressing the Esc key.
U	Undo line.
cw	Change word.
db	Delete previous word.
dd	Delete line.
dw	Delete word.
ZZ	Preceded by Esc. Writes the file and exits vi.
Ctrl b	Move text back one full screen.
Ctrl d	Move text down one half-screen.
Ctrl f	Move text forward one full screen.
Ctrl l	Repaint the screen.
Ctrl g	Show file name and current line number.
Ctrl u	Move text up one half-screen.
:q	Preceded by depressing Esc key. Quits vi without making modifications to the file.
:w	Preceded by depressing Esc key. Writes modifications; leaves user in vi.
:wq	Same as ZZ. Preceded by depressing the Esc key. Writes modifications and exits vi.
)	Move the cursor to first character in the next sentence.
)	Move the cursor back to the first character in the previous sentence.
}	Move the cursor to the start of the next paragraph.
{	Move the cursor to the start of the previous paragraph.
/	Repeat the forward search for a specified string.
?	Repeat the backward search for a specified string.
/string	Initiate a forward search for the identified string.

Command	Description
?string	Initiate a backward search for the identified string.
:	Initiate command mode for updating or exiting vi. And executing ex commands.

Bibliography

Back, Maurice J. *The Design of the UNIX Operating System*. Englewood Cliffs, New Jersey: Prentice-Hall Inc., 1986.

Coffin, Stephen. *UNIX System V Release 4: The Complete Reference*. Berkeley, California: Osborne McGraw-Hill.

Fiedler, David and Bruce H. Hunter. *UNIX System Administration*. Hasbrouck Heights, New Jersey: Hayden Book Company, 1986.

Hansen, August. *vi-The UNIX Screen Editor*. New York, New York: Prentice Hall Press, 1986.

Kochan, Stephen G. and Patrick H. Wood. *Exploring the UNIX System*, second edition. Indianapolis, Indiana: Hayden Books, A division of Howard W. Sams and Company, 1989.

McGilton, Henry and Rachel Morgan. *Introducing the UNIX System*. New York, New York: McGraw-Hill Book Company, 1983.

Nemeth, Evi, Garth Snyder and Scott Seebass. *UNIX System Administration Handbook*. Englewood Cliffs, New Jersey: Prentice-Hall Inc., 1989.

Prata, Stephen and Donald Martin. *UNIX System V Bible*. Indianapolis, Indiana: Howard W. Sams and Company, 1988.

Rosen, Kenneth H., Richard R. Rosinski and James M. Farber. *UNIX System V, Release 4: An Introduction* For New and Experienced Users. Berkeley, California: Osborne McGraw-Hill, 1990.

Sage, Russell G. *Tricks of the UNIX Masters*. Indianapolis, Indiana: Hayden Books, A division of Howard W. Sams and Company, 1987.

Stoll, Clifford. *The Cuckoo's Egg*. New York, New York: Doubleday, A division of Bantam Doubleday Dell Publishing Group, Inc.

Thomas, Rebecca, and Jean Yates. *A User Guide to the UNIX System*, second edition. Berkeley, California: OSBORNE/McGraw-Hill, 1985.

Thomas, Rebecca and Rik Farrow. *UNIX Administration Guide for System V*. Englewood Cliffs, New Jersey: Prentice Hall, 1989.

Waite, Mitchell, Donald Martin and Stephen Prata. *UNIX System V Primer Plus*. Indianapolis, Indiana: Howard W. Sams and Company, 1983.

Waite, Mitchell, Donald Martin and Stephen Prata. *UNIX System V Primer*. Indianapolis, Indiana: Howard W. Sams and Company, 1984.

Wood, Patrick H. and Stephen G. Kochan. *UNIX System Security*. Hasbrouck Heights, New Jersey and Berkeley, California: Hayden Book Company, 1985.

Also from Resolution Business Press

The Comprehensive Internet Dictionary

William H. Holt and Rockie J. Morgan

From the authors of *UNIX: An Open Systems Dictionary*. Clear, concise definitions and illustrations of more than 3,000 technical and colloquial terms and concepts that have proliferated on the Information Highway.

160 pages. ISBN 0-945264-16-X. $12.95 U.S. Coming in September 1994.

Internet: A Parent's Guide

Karen Strudwick and John Spilker

Cuts through the computerese to explain how you and your kids can use the Internet at school and at play. A handy resource to quickly finding your way around the vast knowledge banks of this international network of networks.

160 pages. ISBN 0-945264-17-8. $12.95 U.S. Coming in September 1994.

Northwest High Tech

John Spilker and Karen Strudwick

Fast facts on the $7 billion computer industry of Washington, Oregon, Idaho, British Columbia and Alberta. Detailed profiles of more than 1,800 software, hardware, computer sales and service companies.

464 pages. ISBN 0-945264-15-1. $34.95 U.S. Now in bookstores.

Northwest High Tech Database

All the data and more from the Northwest High Tech directory on diskette. Comes with a free copy of the directory.

$149.95 U.S. Only available from Resolution Business Press.

Resolution Business Press, Inc.
11101 N.E. 8th St., Suite 208, Bellevue, WA 98004
206-455-4611 / Fax: 206-455-9143
Internet address: rbpress@aol.com

IT DOESN'T MATTER HOW YOU DO IT

Love the Lord your God with all your heart and with all your soul and with all your mind. Matthew 22:37

ach Sunday, the Livingstone family went to church. Cliff taught a Sunday school class. His wife, Ruby, sang in the choir. Nuggie went to the Tiny Pebbles class to play games and hear a Bible story. And Chip . . . well, Chip just sat there.

When Chip got into his family's car after church one Sunday, Nuggie asked, "Wasn't church great?"

"Yeah, I guess," he said.

"What's wrong, Chip?" his mom asked.

"Sometimes," Chip said, "I feel like church is for old rocks, like you and Dad, not young, sparkin' rocks like me."

"Why do you think that, Chip?" his dad asked.

"The sermons, for one thing," Chip said. "They talk about marriage and raising kids."

"I didn't know you could pay so much attention to what Pastor Jasper said while you wrote notes to friends," Cliff commented.

Chip ignored this. "But most of all, it's the music. How can I worship God when there's just an old organ up there playing?"

Chip and his friends Gem, Carb, and Splinter had a praise band called The God Rocks! They made music to God with drums and guitars. It was hard for Chip to see how anybody could worship God with just an organ.

"Chip, why don't you think up some ways church could be better for sparkin' young rocks like yourself? When you have figured it out, we'll talk," his dad said.

Chip spent the next week thinking about what to tell his dad. If organ music wasn't *real* worship, then what was?

He hopped on his skateboard and buzzed over to see Big B, the local radio DJ. "What do you think *real* worship is, Big B?" Chip asked.

"Rock, that's a tough one," Big B said. "For me, *real* worship is when I put on my rockman, crank up some praise tunes, and feel the music."

Chip took notes. "Rockman. Tunes. This is great stuff, Big B! Thanks!"

Gem said *real* worship was when she sang to God with other rocks. Splinter said it was when he played his bass guitar. Carb said he worshiped God when he played his drums. And Mrs. Crag

said it's when she showed her love for God by helping others.

"You haven't asked me," Nuggie said. "What do you know about it?"

"I may be just a little rock," Nuggie said, "but I know some things about worship."

"OK, let's hear it," Chip said. He even took out his note pad and pencil to make Nuggie feel important.

"Well, my Tiny Pebbles class leader says that worship is telling God how great he is. And that it doesn't matter what kind of music you use. You don't always have to worship God out loud even."

"I don't know, Nuggie," said Chip. "I think God likes music with a good beat."

Cliff walked into the room. "Are you ready to give me a full report on worship, son?" he asked.

"I decided to ask around," Chip said, "and I got lots of different answers. Some rocks worship God quietly. Some rocks shout and jump. And some rocks worship God with what they do for others. But I learned the most about worship from somebody that surprised me."

"Who, Chip?" Nuggie asked.

"You, Nuggie. Dad, Nuggie told me that worship isn't about *how,* it's about *who.*"

"I didn't say that!" said Nuggie. "I don't even know what you mean."

"You didn't use those words exactly," Chip said. "But that's what you meant. God doesn't care if I worship with an organ, or drums, or a guitar. He just wants me to worship *him.*"

"Chip, I think you and Nuggie have figured it out," Cliff said. "Rocks were created to cry out our praises to God. There's nothing

wrong with using what you like to praise him."

"Dad, this Sunday I'll think more about what my heart is feeling than what my ears are hearing," Chip said. "And my heart will say, 'Praise God!'"

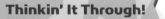

! Thinkin' It Through!

* Why did Chip complain to his parents about church?

* What did he learn that worship was really about?

* What is your favorite way to worship?

BUCK TALKS CHANGE

★ **LOVE GOD:** Worship him!

If you go to church, there is usually a "worship time," right? Usually everyone stands up and sings songs together about God. You may sing songs that someone wrote hundreds of years ago, or you may sing a song someone wrote last night. Ever since God created people, people have been worshiping him with songs. Psalm 66:1, 2 says, "Shout with joy to God, all the earth! Sing the glory of his name." Everyone on earth should sing praises to God because he made us and he loves us. The number one way we love God with all our heart and soul and mind is to worship him.

Singing in church isn't the only way to worship God, though. You can sing at home, by yourself. You can write a poem or paint a picture that shows your praise for God. You can also worship God by obeying him and loving others. When you follow God, everything you do that pleases him is an act of worship.

Telling God how great he is can be an exciting thing to do. When you are in worship time at church, think about the words you are singing, and what those words say *about* God and *to* God. He's really amazing! And each day, even when you're not in church, you can spend time telling God how great he is, and help other people to know about God's love by showing love to them.

SET IN STONE: Buck's Memory Verse

Shout for joy to the Lord, all the earth. Worship the Lord with gladness; come before him with joyful songs.

Psalm 100:1, 2

GET ROCKIN'
WANT TO BE A BETTER WORSHIPER? HERE'S HOW!

✶ Sing a song of praise to God—right now!

✶ Psalm 59:16 says, "But I will sing of your strength, in the morning I will sing of your love." Put a note next to your bed that reminds you to worship God as soon as you wake up!

✶ Draw a picture, write a poem, or make a collage that expresses your worship of God.

CHAPTER 2

WHAT ON EARTH?

Love the Lord your God with all your heart and with all your soul and with all your mind. Matthew 22:37

"**D**on't forget the recycling drive ends tomorrow," Mrs. Crag said. "The team that brings in the most cans, bottles, and papers wins a trip to Rock Coaster World!"

"Our team has *got* to win that prize," Chip whispered to Gem. "I can't wait to ride Granite Mountain!"

After school, Chip, Gem, and Splinter met to begin collecting. "Remember, Chip," Gem said, "the cans should be *empty.*"

"Oh, they'll be empty . . . once I finish all the soda rock inside!"

Carb walked past, tossing a candy wrapper on the ground. "Are you coming, Carb?" Gem asked.

"Nah, all this recycling stuff is silly," Carb said. "Besides, I've gotta buy more notebook paper."

"You just got some yesterday!" Splinter said. "What do use it for, wallpaper?"

"Sometimes," said Carb. "Mostly I use it to play waste-basket ball."

"Is that the right way to use those poor, dead trees?" Splinter asked.

The most popular sci-fi series to hit the airwaves in Rocky Ridge is **ROCKS IN SPACE.** Splinter's a huge fan!

"Never mind," said Chip. "Let's go!"

The three of them filled bags with things to recycle, then met at Chip's house.

"How much did you get?" Chip asked.

"A ton!" Gem replied. "I'm worn out. And hungry!"

"Why don't you both stay for dinner?"

"Great!" Gem said. "I'll call my dad."

"Um . . . OK," Splinter agreed.

Everyone ate like they hadn't had a meal in a week, except Splinter.

"Splinter, are you sure you're feeling OK?" Ruby asked for the third time, watching Splinter pick at his rock roast.

"I'm fine Mrs. Livingstone. It's just that I've decided not to eat meat anymore. I want to respect animal life."

"You're a *vegetarian?!*" squealed Gem.

"It's OK," said Ruby. "I'd be happy to fix you a salad, or—"

"Please don't bother, Mrs. Livingstone," said Splinter. "I don't eat vegetables, either."

"You're a—what do you even call that?" Chip asked.

"I'm a nonatarian," said Splinter. "I don't eat meat, vegetables, dairy products, grains, eggs, or candy."

"How long have you been a, um, what did you call it?" asked Cliff.

"A nonatarian. Just started today. I was inspired by Mrs. Crag's lecture on taking care of the environment."

"Mrs. Crag told you to stop eating?" Ruby asked.

"No!" said Chip. "She didn't tell us to be nothing-a-tarians. She just asked us to pick up some old cans to recycle!"

"Chip obviously didn't understand the true spirit of what Mrs. Crag had to say," said Splinter.

At school the next day, Mrs. Crag counted the bags of recycle. "The winner is . . . Kitney Stoon's team!"

"No way!" said Chip.

"Mr. Livingstone, that outburst was unnecessary. I didn't find a single bag from your team."

"What?" Chip asked.

"I can explain, Chip," said Splinter. "Those poor cans were too confined in those dark, plastic bags. So I stacked them in my room in the shape of the earth."

"What?!" asked Chip and Mrs. Crag in unison.

"I don't see what the big deal is," said Carb. "All this recycling stuff is stupid, anyway."

"What?" asked the entire class.

"You see," said Gem, "Splinter has become a nonatarian to show respect for every part of the earth, and Carb is an everything-atarian—he wastes it all!"

"I understand now," said Mrs. Crag. "It's easy to get confused. God certainly wants us to take care of the earth, Carb, and not use it wastefully. On the other hand, God gave us the earth to use and enjoy. Splinter, what precisely did you plan to eat?"

"I hadn't gotten that far in my study of nonatarianism," Splinter replied. "Maybe I don't need to worry about it anymore."

Mrs. Crag smiled and said, "No, Splinter, I don't think you do."

Thinkin' It Through!

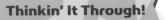

* Why did Splinter become a "nonatarian"?

* Do you agree with Carb, Splinter, or Mrs. Crag?

* How do you think God wants us to treat the earth?

BUCK TALKS CHANGE

★ **LOVE GOD:** Appreciate his gifts!

As a traveling salesrock, I've traveled the universe. The earth is the prettiest planet I've ever seen. One way God has shown his love for us is by giving us this beautiful world to live in. The air is perfect for breathing, the water great for drinking. The trees, mountains, lakes, streams, and canyons are so beautiful! The world has coal, wood, and oil to burn for heat, and rich soil to grow plants. God put everything on this earth that we need to be healthy, safe, and strong. And he put us in charge of it! He told Adam, "Fill the earth and subdue it" (Genesis 1:28). God gave humans the job of taking care of the earth, but also the privilege of eating what the earth provided.

You probably know people who mistreat the world God made. They waste the resources God gave us. God asked people to take good care of his gifts, but not everyone does.

Others forget that the world is a *gift* to us. They think that animals and plants are more important than the needs of people. This turns God's plan upside down.

So, what should you do? It's great to recycle, use resources like paper and electricity wisely, to plant trees, and to do lots of other things that keep the world God made in good shape.

But don't be scared into thinking that the earth has been ruined forever. Remember, this world isn't our final home, anyway. God knows that the earth isn't perfect. He's said that he is going to make a *new* heaven and a *new* earth (2 Peter 3:13). And *that* world will be more beautiful than we can even imagine!

SET IN STONE: Buck's Memory Verse

The earth is the Lord's, and everything in it.

Psalm 24:1

GET ROCKIN'
WANT TO HELP KEEP THE WORLD BEAUTIFUL? HERE ARE SOME IDEAS!

✶ Turn off the light when you leave a room. Most electricity comes from non-renewable resources such as coal or oil. The less you use, the longer those resources will last (and the lower your parents' bills will be)!

✶ Get special recycling containers for your home and church. Call your local recycler to find out what they take and how they take it.

✶ Thank God for the beautiful things you see in the world he's made! When you remember *who* all of this comes from, it will be easier to want to take care of the earth.

CHAPTER 3

FACE TO FACE

Love the Lord your God with all your heart and with all your soul and with all your mind. Matthew 22:37

"**T**he first meeting of the God Rocks Society for Biblical Studies will now come to order!" Chip banged on the table at the Rocky Road Ice Cream Cave.

"Society for *what?*" asked Carb.

"Oh, forget it. I just wanted a serious-sounding name for our new Bible study group," Chip said.

Chip, Gem, Carb, and Splinter took out their Bibles, notebooks, pens, highlighters, and study guides. "Are you sure we need all this stuff?" Splinter asked.

"Listen," Chip said. "Reading the Bible is really important. Turn to Genesis, chapter 1."

For the next hour, the four friends read the story of the creation of the world. They read about the serpent and about Adam and Eve's sin.

"God is so amazing!" said Gem. "He created the whole world, and then put people in it so he could love them."

"Yeah," said Splinter, "but don't you think he was a little hard on them? Kicking them out of the garden just because they ate some fruit?"

"I think God was sad when Adam and Eve disobeyed him," Gem replied. "He wanted them to spend time with him, face to face.

When they messed up, that wasn't possible anymore."

Chip was getting frustrated. "This Bible study isn't for talking. It's for learning! And we still have 15 chapters to go through this afternoon!"

The friends groaned. "Don't you think we've done enough for one day?"

Chip agreed to let them go, but only if they read those chapters at home. Everyone agreed.

The next afternoon, Chip handed each of them a piece of paper. "What's this?" Carb asked.

"Your pop quiz," Chip said. "I want to see if you *really* did the reading last night."

After Chip got the quizzes back, he shook his head. "You all failed. Don't you know how important this is?"

"I tried, Chip," Carb said. "I really did. But I got lost at the place that said so-and-so had a kid and then his kid had a kid."

"I enjoyed the Noah story so much," Gem said, "that I read it over and over."

"You're not supposed to be *enjoying* this, Gem. You're supposed to be *studying,*" Chip said. "Now, let's get cracking."

Every afternoon they met, ordered milkshakes, and studied. Chip had quizzes, charts, timelines, maps, and flashcards. On Friday, he waited for his friends as usual. Finally, Gem came through the door.

"Where have you been?" Chip asked. "And where are Splinter and Carb?"

"Splinter's home sick. He's had too many milkshakes. And Carb has a headache from studying flashcards until 3:00 A.M."

"At least you're here. Let's get started."

"Chip," Gem said, "I know that reading the Bible is important. But do you think this is really the best way?"

"Pastor J says we have to study the Bible if we want to know God," said Chip.

Pastor Jasper appeared with an ice cream cone in his hand. "Did I hear my name?"

Chip told Pastor Jasper about the maps and charts and flash-cards. "I don't think everyone understands how important this is!" Chip said.

"Hmm," said Pastor Jasper. "Reading the Bible *is* important, but it's not about how much you read or how fast you memorize. It's about learning who God is and who he wants you to be."

Chip thought for a minute. "I guess I was trying to feel important and boss my friends around. I wasn't really thinking about getting to know God better. I guess I should quit our Bible study."

"Well, Boss," said Gem, "I think we should keep on meeting. But instead of pop quizzes, maybe we could help each other understand what God wants us to know."

"Will you help us out, Pastor Jasper?" Chip asked.

"Sure will," said Pastor Jasper. "My first suggestion is to not let Splinter have any more milkshakes!"

Thinkin' It Through!

* Do you ever feel confused when you read the Bible?

* What is your favorite Bible story? Why?

* Why do you think God gave the Bible to us?

BUCK TALKS CHANGE

★ **LOVE GOD:** Get to know him!

Studying the Bible can be a little confusing. Did you know that the Bible has 66 different books in it? Some of those books are close to 3500 years old. The people have long, funny-sounding names and live in places you've never heard of. Is it really still important to read the Bible today?

The answer is a huge YES. The Bible is God's Word—his message to us. It's one of the big ways that we can get to know him. We don't get to see God "face to face," but we can still get to know him through the stories about him in the Bible. The Bible has two major sections: the Old Testament and the New Testament. The Old Testament is the story of God's relationship with the people of Israel. The New Testament is the story of God's Son, Jesus, and how he came to save us from our sins.

Not only does the Bible show us who God is, it shows us who God wants us to be. Ever heard of the Ten Commandments, God's rules for right living? They're in the Bible. "Love your neighbor"? In the Bible. "Turn the other cheek"? That's in the Bible, too! It's exciting to discover God's plans and you can do that by reading his Word. God's Word gives direction to our lives.

Sure, there are confusing parts of the Bible. There are some parts that even really smart adults don't agree about. But there is a lot to learn, and God has given you your whole life to get to know him better. So why not start today?

SET IN STONE: Buck's Memory Verse

Your word is a lamp to my feet and a light for my path.

Psalm 119:105

GET ROCKIN'
GET TO KNOW GOD BY GETTING INTO HIS WORD!

✸ If you don't have a Bible, or if the Bible you have is too hard to read, talk to an adult about getting you an easy-to-read version.

✸ Go to church—and listen! You can learn a lot about the Bible from Sunday school teachers, and even your friends. Go home and check out the stories and verses for yourself.

✸ Use the Bible to find out more about God. Read Genesis, chapters 1 and 2 to learn how God created the world. Or read about God's love in 1 John 4:7, 8.

CHAPTER 4

SECRET PAL

Love the Lord your God with all your heart and with all your soul and with all your mind. Matthew 22:37

Chip and Splinter were sitting in their favorite booth at the Rocky Ridge Café eating flint fries when Carb showed up. Carb took a seat and some flint fries. "Where's Gem?" he asked.

"She's not coming," said Chip. "She has to meet her friend."

"I thought *we* were her friends," Carb said.

"It's the third time this week Gem has blown us off," said Chip. "Do you think she's OK?"

Since she started hanging out with this friend, Gem seemed *different*. Last week when Chip was telling a joke he'd heard at school, Gem said, "I'm not sure that's a joke you should be telling."

Chip was irritated. "Wouldn't your new pal think it was funny?"

"Probably not!" Gem replied.

Chip decided that something had to be done. "We've got to find out who this new friend is, rocks. Let's follow her and get clues."

"Like Sherock Holmes!" Carb yelled. "I love that guy! I'll go get my spy glass."

"Wait a second, Watson," Splinter said. "I don't think you'll need the heavy-duty equipment. Besides, do you really think it's OK for us to sneak around on Gem?"

"Maybe she's in trouble!" said Chip.

The next day after school, the guys followed Gem home. They got there just in time to see her climb up into her tree house. They snuck underneath so they could listen.

"Thank you for all the gifts you've given me," they heard Gem say.

"Gifts!" squealed Chip.

"Shhhhh!" hushed Splinter.

"I want to find out all I can about you," she said. "I want to obey everything you tell me to do."

"This is ridiculous," Chip moaned.

"What was that?" Gem asked. Splinter, Carb, and Chip ran off before she could come down and find them there.

"So this rock is giving her gifts?" Chip asked when they were a safe distance away.

"And she's gonna do everything he tells her to," Carb added.

"This sounds even worse than we thought," said Splinter.

"You're right, rock," Chip said. "We've *got* to do something!"

They marched back to the tree house. "Gem!" Chip called. "Are you up there?"

"Yes," Gem said.

Did You Know

GEM first met Chip when her dad, Deacon Dug, heard Chip's guitar and thought it was a screaming cat!

"Can you come down?" Chip asked. "Alone?"

"Umm, OK," she said, and climbed down from the tree. "What's going on?"

"We know all about your *friend*."

"You do?" Gem asked.

Chip told her, "Just because some rock gives you gifts doesn't mean you have to do everything he says."

"And who is so much more interesting than us that you want to find out everything about him?" Splinter asked.

"Just because he's up there and you two have all these special talks doesn't mean you can't still be our friend, too," said Carb.

"What are you rocks talking about?" Gem asked.

"Your new friend! Your secret pal! The rock you've been hanging out with instead of us! Your *boyfriend*."

Gem smiled. Then giggled. Then started to laugh. She laughed so hard she fell down. "You (giggle, giggle) thought (chuckle) I (gasp) was talking (head shake) to a *boyfriend?*"

Judging by her reaction, Carb, Splinter, and Chip thought that maybe they had gotten it a little wrong. "Uh, maybe," Chip said. "If not, who were you talking to up there?"

"God!" Gem replied.

"WHAT?"

"Remember how Pastor J said that God not only created us, but he wants to be our friend? He said that praying is just talking and listening to God. So I thought I should spend time talking to him just like I do talking to you rocks."

"Your secret pal is God?" Carb asked.

"Yes, I guess. But I never meant for it to be a secret. I thought you might think it was weird. But it's been really great!"

"Gem," Chip said. "I think we should all get to know your secret pal."

"Thanks, Chip," said Gem. "I think so, too."

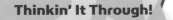

Thinkin' It Through!

* Why do you think Gem kept her "friend" a secret?

* What do you talk to God about?

* Do you think of God as your "friend"?

BUCK TALKS CHANGE

★ **LOVE GOD:** Talk to him!

When you were young, you probably learned to pray things like, "Now I lay me down to sleep." But as you get older, you may be asking, "Can God really hear me? What am I supposed to say when I pray?"

Remember what Pastor Jasper told Gem? Prayer is just talking and listening to God. You get to know your friends better by talking and listening to them. It's the same with God. God wants to hear what you're thinking and feeling. Tell him what's going on in your life—your dreams and fears. He's a really good listener.

Thank God for all the good gifts he has given you! Especially when you're sad or lonely, remembering all the ways God has taken care of you and thanking him for them can remind you how much he loves you.

Tell God when you do things that are wrong. He wants you to be honest with him when you mess up, when you sin. Sure, he already knows what you've done. He knows everything about you. But he wants to hear it from YOU.

If somebody is sick, or you have a problem at school, or if you have a friend who doesn't know God and you want to tell her about him, talk to God. He will help you. He has the power to make sick people well and to open the hearts of people who don't know him. He can also help you know what to do and give you comfort when things are hard.

SET IN STONE: Buck's Memory Verse

Pray continually; give thanks in all circumstances, for this is God's will for you in Christ Jesus.

1 Thessalonians 5:17, 18

GET ROCKIN'
THREE WAYS TO KICK START YOUR PRAYER TIME!

✱ Keep a prayer journal—a fancy book or just a list. Write down what you talk to God about. Then look back over it later to see how God has answered your prayers!

✱ Read prayers other people have prayed. You'll get ideas of things you want to talk to God about. There are lots of prayers in the Bible. Try reading 2 Samuel 7:18–29 and Matthew 6:9–13.

✱ Pick a time every day to talk to God, so it becomes part of your daily routine. But be sure to talk to God anytime you want to!

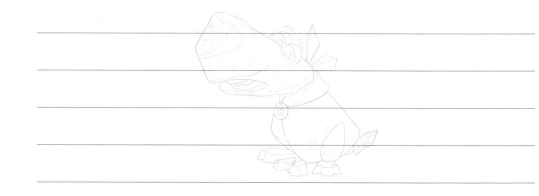

CHAPTER 5

WHO CAN YOU TRUST?

Love the Lord your God with all your heart and with all your soul and with all your mind. Matthew 22:37

"What's wrong, Gem?" asked her dad, Deacon Dug, as they rode home from passing out free sodas at the stadium. "Usually you can't stop talking after an outreach event!"

"I just don't feel like talking right now, Dad. OK?"

"Sure, sugar rock. But if you ever need to talk—"

Gem cut him off. "I *said* I don't want to talk right now!"

Dug knew something was bothering Gem. She'd been spending most of her time in her room with her door closed. But he couldn't get her to tell him *why*.

That night, Gem's dad called to her. "It's time for family devotions."

"Some kind of family this is," Gem muttered. Her dad let the comment slide.

"Would you like to pray tonight, Gem, or do you want me to?"

"You pray. I don't really know if I can trust God anymore." Gem started to cry and ran out of the room.

Deacon Dug stayed up most of that night. He thought, and prayed, and read the Bible, and cried. He didn't know how to help his daughter—he didn't even know what was *wrong* with his daughter—but he knew she was hurting. The next morning, he had an idea.

After school that day, Gem went to her favorite all-by-herself spot. She walked down to the creek that ran along Rocky Ridge and sat under her favorite tree. But she wasn't alone. She heard footsteps! "Who's there?" Gem asked.

"Oh, hello, Gem!" Ruby said. "It's me, Mrs. Livingstone. I didn't mean to scare you."

"I don't mean to be rude, but why are you here? Did my father send you?" Gem asked.

"Your father is concerned about you, but he didn't send me," Ruby replied.

"Then how did you know where I was?" asked Gem.

Ruby replied, "When I was your age, this is where I came whenever I got upset."

They sat quietly. After awhile Gem said, "Mrs. Livingstone, do you believe in God?"

"Yes, Gem, with all my heart. Do you?"

"Yeeeees," Gem said. "I *believe* in him. I'm just not sure I *trust* him."

"Gem, why haven't you talked to your father about this?"

"I don't want to hurt him. But I really miss my mom. When I was little, I didn't notice so much that I didn't have a mom like other

Did You Know

RUBY has a gentle spirit, but her "wild side" comes out at sporting events. Once her siren-like cheers at a croquet tournament sent everyone scrambling!

rocks. But now I get sad about it all the time. I know God tells us that he loves us, but how can I believe he loves me when he let my mom die?"

Ruby put her arm around Gem. "I don't know why your mom died, Gem. But I do know that God loves you. He wants you to trust him even when it seems really hard. Sometimes we can't see the whole picture, or understand his plan. But God's love is clearly all around us."

"Where?" Gem asked.

"Look at this stream. God shows his love in the beautiful world he made and by bringing special people into our lives. He's given you a dad who loves you very much. He's given you good friends like Chip and Carb and Splinter."

"And you, Mrs. Livingstone. You're a good friend, too," Gem said, wiping away a tear. "I guess I'd never thought about all the ways I *can* trust God. But I've really been praying for something that just hasn't happened."

"What is it?" asked Ruby.

"Every year at church they have that mother/daughter lunch and I always feel so left out. This year, I prayed to God that I would get to go."

"That's one of the reasons I came to look for you," Ruby said. "I got three tickets to the lunch: one for me, one for Nuggie, and one for . . . you!"

"Really, Mrs. Livingstone!" Gem said. "That's rocktastic! Thank you!"

"I'd be really proud to have a daughter like you, and I know Nuggie thinks of you like a sister."

"I've got to go talk to my dad," Gem said. "We never finished our devotions!"

Thinkin' It Through!

* Why didn't Gem feel like she could trust God?

* Are there times that you wonder if you can trust God?

* What do you think about Ruby's answer to Gem?

BUCK TALKS CHANGE

★ **LOVE GOD:** Trust in him!

Some people think that when they believe in God and love Jesus, bad things won't happen to them. The problem is, it isn't true. Bad things happen to people who follow God—and to people who don't. Sometimes bad things happen to us because we make wrong choices. Sometimes bad things happen to us because *other* people make wrong choices that hurt us. But, sometimes, bad things just . . . happen. Why would a God who loves us let us get hurt? How can we trust a God who doesn't protect us from everything?

No one but God can totally answer those questions. But the Bible does give us some ideas. Paul writes that we can rejoice when we suffer, because "we know that suffering produces perseverance; perseverance, character; and character, hope" (Romans 5:3, 4). When bad things happen to us, they help us grow up. When we're hurting, we also see pretty clearly that we can't just rely on ourselves; we need God to take care of us. We can have hope because he says that in all things he works for the good of people who love and follow him (Romans 8:28). We can trust God to take care of us because in the end, we know he is in control.

These aren't easy answers. God doesn't like to see you hurting. But instead of running away from him when something bad happens, run *to* him. Let his love make you feel better. What you're going through might even some day help you make someone else feel better, too!

SET IN STONE: Buck's Memory Verse

Trust in the Lord with all your heart and lean not on your own understanding.

Proverbs 3:5

GET ROCKIN'
NEED TO TRUST GOD MORE?
START HERE!

✸ The next time something or someone hurts you, tell God about it. Ask him for advice on what to do.

✸ Do you have questions for God? Things you wonder about? Ask a Christian adult to help you look in your Bible for answers to your questions.

✸ Make a list of all the ways God has shown you he is trustworthy (he's kept the promises he made in the Bible, he has given you many good gifts). Look at that list every time you start doubting God.

CHAPTER 6

THE IMPORTANT STUFF

Love your neighbor as yourself. Matthew 22:39

C hip was heading out the door for school when his mother stopped him. "Wait!" she said, looking out the window.

"For what?" Chip asked.

"The new neighbors are moving in today!" she explained. "Their truck just arrived."

"What are their names, again?" Chip asked.

"The Rockbridges," Ruby answered. "Sounds like a nice, important name, don't you think?"

Chip joined his mother at the window. Soon Nuggie came in, heading for the door.

"Wait!" Chip and Ruby both said.

"What's going on?" Nuggie asked.

Chip explained to her, "We just saw the movers carry in a brand new giant screen TV with rock-around sound!"

Just then, Cliff walked in. "I was looking out back," he said. "They have a Rock Griller 4000. I've wanted one of those for years!"

"Oooooooh!" squealed Nuggie. "A trampoline, a trampoline!"

"I think I'll make dinner for the Rockbridges," Ruby said, "just to make them feel welcomed to the neighborhood."

"I'll rake their leaves," said Chip, "you know, just to be nice."

"And I'll make a card!" Nuggie said.

At school, all Chip and Nuggie could think about was the Rockbridges. "I think Mrs. Rockbridge owns an airplane," Chip told Carb and Splinter.

"Their kids don't have to hang up their clothes," said Nuggie, "because they only wear each outfit one time, then throw it away."

That evening, the Livingstones went to meet the Rockbridges. "Maybe they'll take us on their plane!" Chip whispered to Nuggie. Nuggie nodded, but all she could think about was the trampoline!

Mr. and Mrs. Rockbridge answered the door. "You must be our neighbors!" Mrs. Rockbridge said. "How nice of you to come over."

"Believe me, Mrs. Rockbridge," Cliff said. "The pleasure is ours."

Mr. Rockbridge invited them inside. The Livingstones were a little surprised. The furniture wasn't nearly as nice as they had expected it to be, and the only TV was small and dented.

"Maybe they put all their money into the trampoline and plane," Chip whispered.

"Thank you so much for dinner," Mrs. Rockbridge said.

"Who made this beautiful card?" asked Mr. Rockbridge.

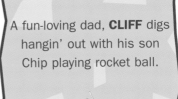

Did You Know

A fun-loving dad, **CLIFF** digs hangin' out with his son Chip playing rocket ball.

"I did, sir," Nuggie answered.

"And you must be the young rock who raked our yard this afternoon!" Mrs. Rockbridge said to Chip.

Cliff looked pleased. "Just let us know if there is *anything* we can do for you."

"Thank you," said Mr. Rockbridge. "Usually I wouldn't ask for any favors, but since you've been so nice . . . could you stay and help us load up the truck?"

"Load *up* the truck?" asked Ruby. "Didn't your things just arrive this morning?"

"Oh, goodness!" said Mrs. Rockbridge. "Most of those things weren't *ours.* The delivery truck made a mistake. One of the big movie-stones across town is moving, and we got his stuff, too."

"You mean," said Chip, "the giant TV, the trampoline, none of it is yours?"

"No!" said Mr. Rockbridge. "We couldn't afford all those things. But who needs that stuff when we've got neighbors like you?"

The Livingstones helped load every last one of those wonderful things back on to the delivery truck.

When they got home, Cliff called a family meeting. "I'm disappointed about what happened."

"Me too," said Chip. "No airplane after all."

"That's not what I mean," Cliff said. "We were nice to the Rockbridges because of all the stuff we thought they had. We weren't nice to them because we wanted to help. And that's wrong."

"Cliff, you're right," Ruby said. "God tells us that we shouldn't treat others better or worse because of the things they have."

"I think the Rockbridges are really nice," said Nuggie. "Nicer than even a trampoline!"

Thinkin' It Through!

* Why were the Livingstones so excited about their new neighbors?

* Did the Rockbridges seem like new neighbors you'd want moving in next to you?

* Have you ever met anyone who really impressed you because he was famous or rich?

BUCK TALKS CHANGE

★ **LOVE OTHERS:** Look at their hearts!

It's really exciting to meet rich or famous people, isn't it? Most people can remember the time they saw a famous athlete at the grocery store or rode an elevator with a movie star. But what about the "ordinary" people you meet each day? What do you think about them?

When God sent the prophet Samuel to pick a new king for Israel, God told Samuel to go see Jesse's sons. Samuel looked at all those young men, trying to decide who was the next king. At first he thought it was the oldest, or the smartest, or the handsomest. But when he looked at them all, he knew not one of them was the right one. "Do you have any more sons?" he asked Jesse. "Only one, but he's out in the field." Jesse didn't think his youngest son was important enough to come and see the prophet. Do you know who that son was? It was David! You see, we judge people from the outside, but God looks at the heart. He knows that who we are inside is much more important than what we wear or what our house looks like or what kind of car we drive.

We should try to look at other people through God's eyes. Instead of valuing what they have, we should value who they are— and who God wants them to become. Don't just give special attention to people with nice things. Show God's love and respect to everyone!

SET IN STONE: Buck's Memory Verse

Man looks at the outward appearance, but the Lord looks at the heart.

1 Samuel 16:7

GET ROCKIN'
TAKE GOD'S WORDS TO HEART!

✳ Make a list of the kinds of things you usually value in other people. Do you think this is God's list, too? If not, what should you change?

✳ Look around for someone who seems lonely or "unimportant." Say hello, and try to get to know that person. Pray for him, too.

✳ Think about the kind of person you want to be. How do you try to get others to like you? Is it through things on the outside, or things in your heart?

CHAPTER 7

IT'S AN EPIDEMIC!

Love your neighbor as yourself. Matthew 22:39

As Chip's sister, Nuggie, looked out the kitchen window, she asked, "Chip, why is Ruff burying all his bones and toys?"

"He doesn't want to share them with Magma, the dog down the street, so he's hiding them in the yard," Chip replied.

"Seems pretty selfish," Nuggie said.

"Sometimes you've gotta watch out for Number One," Chip said. "I'm going to practice."

Nuggie decided to go watch The God Rocks! rehearse for their next concert. She especially liked Gem who always seemed so nice. But when Nuggie got there . . .

"Chip!" Gem yelled. "Give me that microphone!"

"No!" Chip argued. "You hogged it last time."

"Can't you just share it?" Nuggie asked.

"Who asked you?" said Gem. "Chip, why is she here, anyway?"

Nuggie left with tears in her eyes. *What's wrong with everybody?* she thought.

When she got home, she heard yelling there, too. "Cliff," Nuggie's mom said, "I'm tired of watching only what *you* want to watch on TV."

"Ruby," Cliff said, "I'm not going to watch *One Rock to Live* when the stone's throw semifinals are on."

"Give me the remote, Cliff," said Ruby.

I'd better go talk to Pastor Jasper, thought Nuggie. When she got to the church, Deacon Dug went running by. He knocked on the office door. "Pastor, come out here right now!"

"What's wrong?" Pastor Jasper asked as he came outside.

"We agreed that the new church carpet would be green, didn't we?" asked Deacon Dug.

"Yes," said Pastor Jasper.

"Then why is it blue?" said Dug. Nuggie didn't stay around to hear the rest of the argument. She had to do something to stop this epidemic . . . of selfishness!

The next morning, Magma woke up to discover a tasty new bone outside her doghouse. "Rank roo, romebody!" she barked.

When Gem opened her locker at school, she found a picture of her with Chip from their last concert. It was in a frame that said, "Friends are a gift from God." *What a nice surprise,* Gem thought. When she saw Chip in the hallway later, she told him he could use the microphone as much as he wanted.

"Thanks, Gem," said Chip. "But don't worry about it. Somebody talked Mrs. Crag into loaning us one of the school's microphones so we can each have one until we get a new one."

"Who did that?" Gem asked.

"I don't know," Chip said, "but I have an idea."

At lunch, Gem split her favorite sandwich with Kitney Stoon, who had forgotten her lunch. Chip stayed after school to help Mrs. Crag carry boxes to her car. When Ruby discovered that someone had videotaped her favorite TV show for her, she told Cliff he could watch the stone's throw finals that night. Then Cliff took out the garbage without being asked.

Deacon Dug got a note that asked him to come to the church office again. When he got there, Pastor Jasper was waiting. "What do you want to say, Deacon?" Pastor Jasper asked.

"Me?" said Dug. "I thought you called this meeting!"

"Actually," said Nuggie, stepping out from behind a bush, "I called this meeting. I heard you fighting and I wanted to find a way for you to make up. I think green and blue are both pretty colors, myself."

"I guess I did get a little too upset," Deacon Dug said.

"Me, too," said Pastor Jasper. Nuggie left as they smiled and shook hands.

When she got home, Chip was waiting for her. "Nuggie," he said. "What's going on?"

"What do you mean, Chip?"

"All these things that have been happening—the dog bone, the picture, the microphone, the videotape—someone is behind them, and I think it's you!"

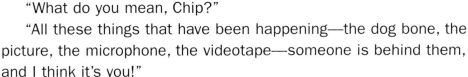

Thinkin' It Through!

* What was Nuggie's plan?

* Why did it work?

* What would you have done if you were Nuggie?

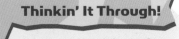

"Oh, Chip, don't be mad!" she said. "I just got tired of everybody fighting and being selfish. I thought if I did some nice things, the epidemic would turn around."

"I'm not mad at all," Chip said. "You are a genius!"

BUCK TALKS CHANGE

★ LOVE OTHERS: Put them before yourself!

It's sooo easy to be selfish, isn't it? After all, it's more fun to get what you want—right? Lots of people agree with what Chip said: it's important to look out for Number One. But who really is Number One? When people use that phrase, they mean themselves. They're saying that they are the most important people in the world. Who do you think is *really* Number One? That's right! God is Number One. He wants us to take care of what is important to him, not just what is important to us. And since God loves everyone, we should show his love to everyone, too. We can do that by not always doing things just to please ourselves. We can take time to think about what might make other people happy and do nice things for them. So if your friend wants to play his favorite video game instead of yours, you can let him—or at least work out a compromise! Sharing is one way to not be selfish.

Another way to be kind is to not say mean things when you're grumpy. Have you ever yelled at your mom when you were in a bad mood, even though she didn't do anything wrong? That's selfish. Thinking about other people's feelings and not just your own is another way to be unselfish.

So really, the saying "Look out for Number One" is true, if you've made God Number One in your life!

SET IN STONE: Buck's Memory Verse

Each of you should look not only to your own interests, but also to the interests of others.

Philippians 2:4

GET ROCKIN'
TRYING TO AVOID AN EPIDEMIC OF SELFISHNESS? TRY THESE THINGS!

✱ Every time you get the chance to share, do it!

✱ Think of ways you can do "secret acts of kindness" for your family and friends. Take out the garbage, rake the yard, or give someone a flower, and try not to let anyone catch you!

✱ The next time you're in a bad mood and someone talks to you, try counting to ten before you respond. Be kind in what you say and do!

CHAPTER 8

THE BIG STINK

Love your neighbor as yourself. Matthew 22:39

The Tenth Annual God Rocks Hall of Fame Exhibit Contest was just around the corner. Each year students from Rocky Ridge Academy competed to have their own displays showcased in the Hall of Fame. This year, Splinter was determined to win. He thought his theme—The Smallest Rocks of All: Salt and Sand in the Bible—was sure to be a crowd favorite. He worked for weeks. He made a salt sculpture of Lot's wife. He created a Shores of Galilee display with all the famous New Testament scenes—Jesus calling Peter and Andrew and Jesus cooking fish were his favorites. He even built little fishing boats with nets stretched out to dry.

The day the project was due, Splinter's dad drove him to school. No way was he taking the bus *this* morning. He carefully carried his display down the hall toward Mrs. Crag's classroom. He was almost to the door when—

CRASH! Chip threw open the door and slammed right into Splinter's project. Sand and salt went everywhere! Tiny fishermen flew in the air and their boats smashed to pieces on the ground.

"Oops," Chip said. "I didn't see you there. What is this mess, anyway?"

"This *mess*," Splinter yelled, "was my Hall of Fame winning project! You just ruined it. I will never forgive you, Chip Livingstone!"

Splinter started cleaning up the mess. When Chip tried to help, Splinter told him to go away.

Splinter didn't say a word to Chip that day or the next. When Chip tried to say "sorry" or even "hello," Splinter would say, to whatever rock was nearby, "Do you hear something? I don't hear any-thing except something that sounds like someone who *used* to be my friend." Then Splinter would walk away.

One afternoon, Mrs. Crag made Splinter and Chip partners in science lab. Chip, who was tired of the way Splinter was treating him, mixed the chemicals together to set off a stinky smoke cloud in Splinter's face.

When the smell began to fill the whole room, Mrs. Crag came over. "What seems to be the problem?" she asked.

"*He* made the smoke go off in my face!" Splinter said.

"Well *he* won't speak to me," Chip yelled.

Did You Know

SPLINTER has collected every piece of *Rocks in Space* gear that's come out since the show's been on the air!

"*He* ruined my God Rocks Hall of Fame display!" Splinter yelled back.

"Enough!" Mrs. Crag said. "I think I know what's going on here. What you need is forgiveness."

"Yeah, I guess Splinter does need forgiveness for the way he's acted," said Chip.

"I need forgiveness?" Splinter asked. "Chip's the one who keeps messing up! But I'm not forgiving him for destroying my project."

"And I'm not forgiving him for treating me like gravel!" Chip said.

"You have two choices," Mrs. Crag said. "Forgive each other, or forget your friendship. I'd like to know your decision in the morning."

That night, Splinter went to see Chip. "Chip," Splinter said. "I know what you did to my project was an accident. I forgive you."

"Splinter," Chip said. "I know how important that project was to you. I'm sorry I was careless."

"What about the stink bomb?" Splinter asked with a grin.

"That was pretty awful, wasn't it?" Chip laughed.

"I deserved it," said Splinter, "for the way I was treating you."

"I know what *really* stinks," Chip said.

"What's that?" asked Splinter.

"The idea of not having you as a friend anymore," Chip answered. "When Mrs. Crag said that, it really got me thinking. If one little fight could ruin our friendship, we wouldn't have had much of a friendship in the first place."

"I'd hate to not be your friend anymore," said Splinter.

"Me too," said Chip. "Hey, let's call Mrs. Crag!"

"Umm . . . don't you think we should wait to tell her our decision at school in the morning?" Splinter asked. "Mrs. Crag is probably home chillin' with a rockuccino and some good reading— my prize-winning English essay!"

"Sparkin!" Chip responded enthusiastically. "But let's go together!" And they did.

! Thinkin' It Through!

* Why was Splinter so mad at Chip?

* How did Splinter act when he was mad?

* What could Splinter have done differently?

BUCK TALKS CHANGE

★ **LOVE OTHERS:** Forgive them!

What's the big deal about forgiveness, anyway? Don't you have the right to be angry when someone hurts you or does bad things to you? Actually, you do. In the same way, God has the *right* to be angry with you every time you mess up, or "sin." When you sin, you break God's law, and that hurts him. He can't just ignore it. That's why he sent Jesus to die: so that he could pay the price for your sin.

So what does that have to do with whether or not you forgive other people? When Jesus was teaching his followers how to pray, he told them to say, "God, forgive us just as we forgive others." God has forgiven you of so much—of being selfish, or saying mean things, or being greedy—and he wants you to show that same forgiveness to people who hurt you. If you thought about your sin as money you owe, then you would owe God a billion dollars or more.

But he has said you don't have to pay him back! What do you think he feels when he sees you getting mad at someone who can't pay you for a ten-dollar kind of sin? When we don't forgive other people for their ten-dollar sins, we show God that we don't really understand much about his love.

Forgiving doesn't mean that you will always forget bad things that happen. It might not even mean that you totally trust someone again. Forgiveness means that you don't keep anger in your heart or try to do mean things to get back at someone who has hurt you. Instead, you keep on wanting what is best for them.

SET IN STONE: Buck's Memory Verse

Forgive as the Lord forgave you.

Colossians 3:13

GET ROCKIN'
NEED HELP WITH FORGIVENESS?
GIVE THESE TIPS A TRY!

✱ Is there anyone you need to forgive? Consider writing that person a note or talking to him to offer forgiveness.

✱ Have you done something wrong to someone else? Does that person need to forgive you? Go and ask for forgiveness—and mean it.

✱ Make a note or poster that says the memory verse for this chapter and put it on your door or mirror.

CHAPTER 9

NOBODY'S NOBODY

Love your neighbor as yourself. Matthew 22:39

arb sat in his usual seat at church—five rows back and one row over. He loved listening to Pastor Jasper's sermons. *Wow,* he thought, *Pastor Jasper must be really important to God.*

At the end of the service, Deacon Dug got up to pray. *I think God really listens to what* he *has to say,* Carb thought.

As church let out, Carb saw Chip's dad, Cliff, helping little old rocks to their cars. *I'll never be as good as Mr. Livingstone,* Carb thought.

When Chip stopped by to see Carb that afternoon, Carb had hit rock bottom. "What's wrong, Carb?" Chip asked.

"Nothing," Carb said.

Chip looked at him. "It sure seems like it's something," Chip said.

"No," said Carb, "that's the problem. I'm nothing. Nobody. I'm not good at preaching like Pastor Jasper or good at praying like Deacon Dug or even good at helping like your dad."

"Yeah, maybe," said Chip, "but you're still young. And you're good at drumming to praise God!"

Carb didn't look any happier. "That's not an important job. I don't think God even notices. Like I said, I'm nothing."

Chip told his dad about Carb's problem, and Cliff decided to have a talk with him. "Carb," Cliff said, "sometimes it's easy to look at other rock's gifts and talents and think God likes those rocks more."

"Yeah, Mr. Livingstone," Carb said. "That's just how I feel."

"God says that each of us has an important part to play. Just like in your band. Each of you needs to play a part for the music to sound just right."

Carb still looked unsure.

"Not one of you is any more important than the other in The God Rocks!, right?" Cliff asked.

"Yeah," Carb said.

"It's the same way in church. Each of us has a part to play—and God thinks we're all very important," Cliff said. "Even young rocks like you."

Carb's talk with Mr. Livingstone made him feel a lot better. He decided to ask God what part God wanted him to play. "God, please

show me what you want me to do. I really, really want to serve you!" Carb prayed.

The next night Pastor Jasper called Carb on the phone. "Carb, my young rock, I have a job for you to do," he said.

"This is it!" Carb thought. "This must be God's plan for me!"

"There is a new young rock at church. He is feeling a little lonely. I think he feels like he isn't important. But he told me that he'd really love to learn to play the drums. Do you think you could teach him?"

"Could I?" said Carb. "That would be sparkin'."

"Does that mean yes, Carb?" asked Pastor Jasper. "Sometimes I can't understand a word you young rocks say."

"Yes, sir," Carb said. "That's a yes!"

Carb met Flint the next day. Before they started the drum lesson, they went to Rocky Roads for ice cream.

"I'm really glad you said you'd teach me to play drums," said Flint. "I don't know why someone like you would say yes, though."

"What do you mean, someone like me?" Carb asked.

"Someone important. Someone special," Flint said. "I'm just a nobody."

"I used to feel the same way," Carb said. "I thought God didn't think I was important."

"But you're in The God Rocks!" Flint said, "the greatest praise band around!"

"I'm not important because I'm in a band," Carb said. "I'm important because God loves me and has a special job for me to do, just like he has a job for you!"

"What's your job?" Flint asked.

"Right now, it's to teach you to play the drums!" Carb said. And off they went.

Thinkin' It Through!

* Why didn't Carb think he was important?

* What made him feel better?

* How can you be sure you're important to God?

BUCK TALKS CHANGE

★ **LOVE OTHERS:** Be a part of the body!

Do you ever feel like you're not important to God? Sometimes even adults don't feel important. But that's not how God feels at all. In the Bible, Paul's younger friend Timothy was concerned that people wouldn't listen to him because he was young. Paul told Timothy, "Don't let anyone look down on you because you are young, but set an example for the believers in speech, in life, in love, in faith and in purity" (1 Timothy 4:12). Even young people can make a difference when they live the way God wants them to.

What's so bad about not thinking you're important? You might ask, "Aren't we supposed to be humble?" We are supposed to be humble. That means we don't think that we are *more* important than anyone else. But if you think you are nobody, that you don't matter to God, it's like you're telling God that he made a mistake. The Bible says that the church is like a body, and we are each like body parts. The eye can't say, "I'm more important than the rest of you, so I'll just go off on my own." Our bodies need our eyes, but our eyes need the rest of our bodies, too! We need to work together, each of us doing the job that God gave us, so that we can do what God wants us to do! Then we can be *somebody* and be humble, too!

SET IN STONE: Buck's Memory Verse

Now you are the body of Christ, and each one of you is a part of it.

1 Corinthians 12:27

GET ROCKIN'
**HERE'S HOW TO FIND OUT WHAT
GOD WANTS YOU TO DO!**

✴ Ask a trusted adult who knows you well to help you think of
ways you can be a part of the body of God's church.

✴ Talk to an adult you admire. Ask how God prepared her for
what she's doing now.

✴ Make a list of all the things you love to do or are good at doing.
Ask God to show you ways that you can glorify him when you do
those things.

CHAPTER 10

YOU CAN DO IT!

Love your neighbor as yourself. Matthew 22:39

Chip, Gem, Splinter, and Carb were rehearsing a new song for their concert. "OK," Chip said. "Let's try that one more time."

"But we've rehearsed this song twelve times tonight!" Carb said. "My drumsticks have turned to toothpicks!"

"We will stop," Chip said, "when you get it *right,* Carb."

Carb looked really down. He just couldn't get his part right on this song. "Forget it," he said. "I give up."

Gem looked at Carb. "You're a great drummer," she said gently. "I think if you try it one more time, you will get it right."

"Enough talking," Chip said. "Let's just get going!" Chip gave the signal to start the song. They played through it, and everything was perfect.

"Great job, Carb!" Gem said.

"See," Chip said. "I told you we just needed to keep practicing. You rocks would be such quitters if it weren't for me."

The next afternoon Gem stopped by to see Chip. He was trying to teach Nuggie how to ride a bike.

"No, Nuggie," he said when she fell off. "Not like *that.*"

"I'm trying, Chip," she said through her tears. "I really am!"

"Oh, forget it," Chip said. "You will never learn."

Nuggie started to walk away, but Gem whispered to her, "I had a hard time learning to ride a bike, too. Why don't you try one more time? You may get to be the best biker Rocky Ridge has ever seen."

Nuggie closed her eyes and kicked off. "Look at me!" she yelled. "I'm riding my bike!" She rode all the way down to the corner and back.

"Great job, Nuggie!" cheered Gem.

"It's about time you figured that out," Chip said.

"Gem," Nuggie asked, "would you come eat dinner at our house to celebrate me learning how to ride my bike?"

"I'd love to," said Gem. "Just let me call my dad."

When Chip, Nuggie, and Gem walked through the front door, Ruff came bounding in to meet them. As they patted him Gem said,

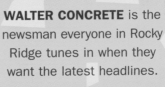

Did You Know ?

WALTER CONCRETE is the newsman everyone in Rocky Ridge tunes in when they want the latest headlines.

The rock used as a model for Chip is called **LAPIS LAZULI.** It is sought after for its deep blue color and is often used to make jewelry.

"What a sweet, smart rock hound you are, Ruff!" Ruff held out his paw for her to shake.

"I've been trying to teach him to shake hands for a month!" Chip said. "I guess I just can't teach anybody how to do anything."

"Yes, you can, Chip," Gem said. "You give really good instructions. You told Carb just the right way to play his drum and you gave Nuggie good advice on riding her bike."

"Then why doesn't anyone learn anything from me?" Chip asked.

"Because there is one thing you don't do," Gem said.

"What's that?" Chip asked.

"You don't give *encouragement,*" said Gem. "Rocks—and rock hounds—don't just need someone to teach them *how* to do something. They need someone to believe they *can* do it!"

"That's not something I'm very good at, Gem," Chip said. "I get upset when rocks don't listen to me. I always think if they would try a little harder, they would get it. Do you think I could ever learn to be encouraging?"

"Yes," Gem said. "I do."

At dinner that night, Chip saw Nuggie trying to twirl her spaghetti around her fork. Usually Ruby cut it up for her. Tonight Nuggie wanted to do it by herself, but she was having a little trouble getting any of the spaghetti to stay on her fork.

"Nuggie," said Chip, "watch how I do it. It's really easy. I know a smart rock like you can learn in no time!"

Nuggie twirled her spaghetti and took a big bite. "Great job, Nuggie!" Chip said.

"Thanks," she said, with a big smile on her face and a noodle on her chin.

"Great job to you, too, Chip," Gem said. "Thanks," said Chip.

Thinkin' It Through!

* What did Gem teach Chip about encouragement?

* Why is encouragement so important?

* How do you feel when someone encourages you?

BUCK TALKS CHANGE

★ LOVE OTHERS: Be an encourager!

Did you ever think about the word *encourage?* What word is inside it? That's right—the word *courage.* When you encourage people, you give them the courage and confidence to do what they need to do.

God thinks encouragement is really important. When God told Moses that Joshua, Moses' helper, would lead God's people to the Promised Land, God told Moses to encourage Joshua. (You remember, the guy who led the army against Jericho!) Even Joshua needed to be encouraged. There are many places in the Bible when God tells us to encourage one another.

What does it mean to be encouraging? You don't have to exaggerate or tell lies to be encouraging (like telling your little brother he could beat Michael Jordan playing basketball). Be kind and patient, look for things people are good at and tell them.

"Build up" other people with your loving words and actions. Then you'll be an encourager!

It's great to encourage your sister when she's learning to tie her shoes, or your mom when you're teaching her to play a video game. But the most important kind of encouragement is to remind one another of God's promises. Sometimes, no matter how hard we try, or how much encouragement we get, we still can't do what we want to do (like climb the tallest mountain in the world). But we can always depend on God to do what HE says HE will do: love us, forgive our sins, and make a place for us in heaven. That's pretty encouraging, don't you think?

SET IN STONE: Buck's Memory Verse

Encourage one another and build each other up.

1 Thessalonians 5:11

GET ROCKIN'
WANT TO BE AN ENCOURAGER?
HERE'S HOW!

★ Know anyone who seems a little sad? Make a card for that person and tell him that God loves him!

★ Who encourages you? Are there people in your life who believe in you and patiently teach you? Go to a teacher, your mom or dad, aunt, uncle, sibling, or friend—whoever it is—and thank that person for encouraging you!

★ Read these encouraging Bible verses whenever you feel discouraged: Deuteronomy 31:6, Psalm 28:7, and John 3:16.

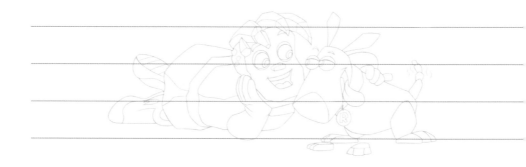

GET ROCKIN'

STORIES FEATURING YOUR FAVORITE GOD ROCKS! CHARACTERS WITH NUGGETS OF WISDOM JUST FOR YOU FROM GOD ROCKS! HEROES.

★ ROCKIN' WITH THE RULES
Understanding the Ten Commandments

Who needs rules? We all do! Follow Chip and his friends as they learn to use God's rules to help them make good decisions in tough situations.

24241 *ISBN 0-7847-1127-5*

★ BEYOND A BLAST FROM THE PAST
Discovering why God made you

Are you ready for a cosmic discovery? God made all of creation with a purpose—including you! Join *The God Rocks!* as they find out what God's plan is all about.

24242 *ISBN 0-7847-1355-3*

★ MORE THAN A SPLATBALL GAME
Squaring off with the giants in your life

Have you ever stood nose-to-knee with trouble? We all have! Chip, Gem, Carb, and Splinter experience their share of giants and wind up victorious—and so can you!

24243 *ISBN 0-7847-1457-6*

THE HIPPEST NEW ANIMATED VIDEO SERIES ON THE BLOCK WITH LIFE LESSONS AND BIBLE TRUTHS!

IF ROCKS FROM BIBLE TIMES COULD TALK, WOULD THEY KEEP SILENT ABOUT THE AMAZING EVENTS THEY WITNESSED? NO WAY! THAT'S WHY EVERY GOD ROCKS! HERO HAS SOMETHING IMPORTANT TO SAY!

★ **TEN ROCKIN' RULES** *or . . . Wakin' up is hard to do*
Chip and his friends learn from the Ten Commandment Twins that God gives us rules because he loves us. Join Chip, Gem, Carb, and Splinter on this wild ride full of twists and turns, and you'll wake up to discover Ten Rockin' Rules!
DVD includes an avalanche of extras: *Blooper gems, interviews with the creators and the band, God Rocks! desktop wallpaper, widescreen option and MORE!*

★ **A BLAST FROM THE PAST** *or . . . Anybody got change for a Buck?*
Has Rocky Ridge been invaded by mutant vegetables from outer space? Join The God Rocks! as they unearth the solution to the alien mystery. Along the way, you'll hear from Buck, a traveling sales rock, who blasts onto the scene and realizes that God created the universe and everything in it with a purpose.
DVD includes a meteor shower of extras: *"This Is the Day" music video featuring The God Rocks!, "You've Been Searching" music video featuring Sheryl Stacey, samples from the debut music CD, widescreen option and MORE!*

★ **SPLATBALL SQUARE-OFF** *or . . . Nose to knee with a defiant giant*
As the annual splatball championship begins, the Rocky Ridge Rangers are shaking in their shoes! But Bullseye (Mickey Rooney), their coach, is a God Rocks hero who has been face to face with Goliath, a very defiant giant. In the end, The God Rocks! find out that when we look to God, our giants are never as big as they seem.
DVD includes a ballpark full of extras: *The God Rocks! Cry Out tour highlights, interviews, games, and MORE!*

VHS 24214 UPC 7-07529-24214-9
DVD 24227 UPC 7-07529-24227-9

VHS 24215 UPC 7-07529-24215-6
DVD 24228 UPC 7-07529-24228-6

VHS 24216 UPC 7-07529-24216-3
DVD 24229 UPC 7-07529-24229-3

Cry Out

**SPARKIN' MUSIC THAT'S ENERGIZING, POP-DRIVEN AND CREATED
ESPECIALLY FOR KIDS WHO AREN'T AFRAID TO SHOUT "GOD ROCKS!"**

✷ CRY OUT

One great new kids' video series, four talented musicians and 14 hot-as-lava
songs combine to introduce The God Rocks! in their debut music release, *Cry
Out*. The CD features original 10-karat songs of praise and encouragement from
the first three episodes of God Rocks! and MORE! Kids will want to sing along
with this sparkin' new band as they praise God and give honor to him.

1. This Is the Day
2. God Rules
3. Be Yourself
4. Wonderful Kingdom
5. The Word
6. When God Talks, Creation Rocks
7. You've Been Searching
8. Rocks Cry Out
9. Giant
10. Such a Love
11. Wake Up!
12. Freckle
13. There Is a Place
14. God Rocks!® Theme Song

24261 *UPC 7-07529-24261-3*